Lecture Notes in Computer Science 16087

Founding Editors

Gerhard Goos
Juris Hartmanis

Editorial Board Members

Elisa Bertino, USA
Wen Gao, China

Bernhard Steffen ⓘ, Germany
Moti Yung ⓘ, USA

Formal Methods
Subline of Lecture Notes in Computer Science

Subline Series Editors

Ana Cavalcanti, *University of York, UK*
Marie-Claude Gaudel, *Université de Paris-Sud, France*

Subline Advisory Board

Manfred Broy, *TU Munich, Germany*
Annabelle McIver, *Macquarie University, Sydney, NSW, Australia*
Peter Müller, *ETH Zurich, Switzerland*
Erik de Vink, *Eindhoven University of Technology, The Netherlands*
Pamela Zave, *AT&T Laboratories Research, Bedminster, NJ, USA*

More information about this series at https://link.springer.com/bookseries/558

Bettina Könighofer · Hazem Torfah
Editors

Runtime Verification

25th International Conference, RV 2025
Graz, Austria, September 15–19, 2025
Proceedings

 Springer

Editors
Bettina Könighofer
Graz University of Technology
Graz, Austria

Hazem Torfah
Chalmers University of Technology
Göteborg, Sweden

ISSN 0302-9743 ISSN 1611-3349 (electronic)
Lecture Notes in Computer Science
ISBN 978-3-032-05434-0 ISBN 978-3-032-05435-7 (eBook)
https://doi.org/10.1007/978-3-032-05435-7

© The Editor(s) (if applicable) and The Author(s), under exclusive license to Springer Nature Switzerland AG 2026

This work is subject to copyright. All rights are solely and exclusively licensed by the Publisher, whether the whole or part of the material is concerned, specifically the rights of translation, reprinting, reuse of illustrations, recitation, broadcasting, reproduction on microfilms or in any other physical way, and transmission or information storage and retrieval, electronic adaptation, computer software, or by similar or dissimilar methodology now known or hereafter developed.
The use of general descriptive names, registered names, trademarks, service marks, etc. in this publication does not imply, even in the absence of a specific statement, that such names are exempt from the relevant protective laws and regulations and therefore free for general use.
The publisher, the authors and the editors are safe to assume that the advice and information in this book are believed to be true and accurate at the date of publication. Neither the publisher nor the authors or the editors give a warranty, expressed or implied, with respect to the material contained herein or for any errors or omissions that may have been made. The publisher remains neutral with regard to jurisdictional claims in published maps and institutional affiliations.

This Springer imprint is published by the registered company Springer Nature Switzerland AG
The registered company address is: Gewerbestrasse 11, 6330 Cham, Switzerland

If disposing of this product, please recycle the paper.

Preface

This volume contains the papers presented at RV 2025: the 25th International Conference on Runtime Verification, held on September 15–19, 2025 in Graz, Austria.

The RV series is a sequence of annual meetings that bring together scientists from both academia and industry interested in investigating novel principled methods for the runtime verification of software and hardware systems. Runtime verification techniques are crucial for system correctness, reliability, and robustness; they provide an additional level of rigor and effectiveness compared to conventional testing and are generally more practical than exhaustive formal verification. Runtime verification can be used prior to deployment, for testing, verification, and debugging purposes, and after deployment for ensuring reliability, safety, and security, for providing fault containment and recovery, and for online system repair. This year, the RV conference also broadened its scope to new topics on synergies between runtime verification and principled approaches to safe reinforcement learning and out-of-distribution detection.

RV started in 2001 as an annual workshop and turned into a conference in 2010. The workshops were organized as satellite events of established forums, including the Conference on Computer-Aided Verification and ETAPS. The proceedings of RV from 2001 to 2005 were published in Electronic Notes in Theoretical Computer Science. Since 2006, the RV proceedings have been published in Springer's Lecture Notes in Computer Science. Previous RV conferences took place in St. Julian's, Malta (2010); San Francisco, USA (2011); Istanbul, Turkey (2012); Rennes, France (2013); Toronto, Canada (2014); Vienna, Austria (2015); Madrid, Spain (2016); Seattle, USA (2017); Limassol, Cyprus (2018); and Porto, Portugal (2019). The conferences in 2020 and 2021 were held virtually due to COVID-19, whereas in 2022 RV took place in Tbilisi, Georgia, in 2023 in Thessaloniki, Greece, and in 2024 in Istanbul, Turkey.

This year, we received 62 papers and 2 tutorial proposals. Each submission underwent a rigorous single-blind review process, with an average of three reviews per paper. The evaluation and selection process involved thorough discussions among the Program Committee members and external reviewers via the EasyChair conference management system, ultimately leading to a consensus on the final decisions. The Program Committee selected 26 contributions for presentation at the conference and inclusion in these proceedings. These comprise 22 regular papers, 1 short paper, 2 tool papers, and 1 tutorial paper.

At the conference, we had four inspiring keynote talks delivered by renowned members of the community: Thomas Henzinger (IST Austria, Austria), Nils Jansen (Ruhr University Bochum, Germany), Ankush Desai (Amazon Web Services, USA), and Daniela Micucci (University of Milano-Bicocca, Italy).

RV 2025 was the result of the combined efforts of many individuals to whom we are deeply grateful. In particular, we thank the Program Committee members and sub-reviewers for their thorough and timely reviewing, all authors for their submissions, and all attendees of the conference for their participation. We are grateful for the generous sponsorship by Springer, supporting this year's Best Paper Award and Test of Time Award. The conference would not have been possible without the support and dedication of our General Chair Ezio Bartocci, our Local Chair Roderick Bloem, our Publicity Chair Martin Tappler, and the support of the Graz University of Technology. We also thank the RV Steering Committee for their support. For the work of the Program Committee and the compilation of the proceedings, the EasyChair system was employed; it freed us from many technical matters and allowed us to focus on the program, for which we are grateful.

July 2025

Bettina Könighofer
Hazem Torfah

Organisation

General Chair

Ezio Bartocci　　　　　　　　　Technische Universität Wien, Austria

Program Chairs

Bettina Könighofer　　　　　　　Graz University of Technology, Austria
Hazem Torfah　　　　　　　　　Chalmers University of Technology, Sweden

Local Chair

Roderick Bloem　　　　　　　　Graz University of Technology, Austria

Publicity Chair

Martin Tappler　　　　　　　　　Technische Universität Wien, Austria

Steering Committee

Houssam Abbas　　　　　　　　Oregon State University, USA
Erika Abraham　　　　　　　　　RWTH Aachen University, Germany
Ezio Bartocci　　　　　　　　　 Technische Universität Wien, Austria
Yliès Falcone　　　　　　　　　 Université Grenoble Alpes and Inria, France
Klaus Havelund　　　　　　　　 California Institute of Technology, USA
Martin Leucker　　　　　　　　　University of Lübeck, Germany
Oleg Sokolsky　　　　　　　　　 University of Pennsylvania, USA

Program Committee

Houssam Abbas　　　　　　　　Oregon State University, USA
Erika Abraham　　　　　　　　　RWTH Aachen University, Germany
Roderick Bloem　　　　　　　　 Graz University of Technology, Austria

Borzoo Bonakdarpour	Michigan State University, USA
Francesca Cairoli	University of Trieste, Italy
Marek Chalupa	Institute of Science and Technology Austria, Austria
Chih-Hong Cheng	Chalmers University of Technology, Sweden
Michele Chiari	Technische Universität Wien, Austria
Thao Dang	CNRS/VERIMAG, France
Jyotirmoy Deshmukh	University of Southern California, USA
Luca Di Stefano	Technische Universität Wien, Austria
Yliès Falcone	Université Grenoble Alpes and Inria, France
Chuchu Fan	Massachusetts Institute of Technology, USA
Marie Farrell	University of Manchester, UK
Bernd Finkbeiner	CISPA Helmholtz Center for Information Security, Germany
Daniel J. Fremont	University of California Santa Cruz, USA
Klaus Havelund	California Institute of Technology, USA
Bardh Hoxha	Toyota Research Institute North America, USA
Sebastian Junges	Radboud University Nijmegen, Netherlands
Michaela Klauck	Bosch Corporate Research, Germany
Jan Kretinsky	Masaryk University, Czech Republic
Bettina Könighofer	Graz University of Technology, Austria
Kim Guldstrand Larsen	Aalborg University, Denmark
Martin Leucker	University of Lübeck, Germany
Konstantinos Mamouras	Rice University, USA
Anastasia Mavridou	KBR/NASA Ames Research Center, USA
Stefan Mitsch	DePaul University, USA
Laura Nenzi	University of Trieste, Italy
Dejan Nickovic	Austrian Institute of Technology AIT, Austria
Gordon Pace	University of Malta, Malta
Nicola Paoletti	King's College London, UK
Corina Pasareanu	Carnegie Mellon University, NASA, and KBR, USA
Doron Peled	Bar-Ilan University, Israel
Violet Ka I Pun	Western Norway University of Applied Sciences, Norway
Cesar Sanchez	IMDEA Software Institute, Spain
Gerardo Schneider	Chalmers University of Technology and University of Gothenburg, Sweden
Sanjit A. Seshia	University of California, Berkeley, USA
Oleg Sokolsky	University of Pennsylvania, USA
Martin Tappler	Technische Universität Wien, Austria
Hazem Torfah	Chalmers University of Technology, Sweden

Dmitriy Traytel   University of Copenhagen, Denmark
Masaki Waga   Kyoto University, Japan
Changshun Wu   Université Grenoble Alpes, France
Teng Zhang   Aptos Labs, USA

Additional Reviewers

Balakrishnan, Anand
Basset, Nicolas
Biktairov, Yuriy
Brorholt, Asger Horn
Chakraborty, Debraj
Chen, Fei
Dankworth, Raik
Dong, Yi
Essbai, Wasim
Gorostiaga, Felipe
Grover, Kush
Hsu, Tzu-Han
Hublet, François
Kruger, Loes
Li, Yingke
Lidell, David
Luque Cerpa, Alejandro
Paul, Sheryl
Prokop, Maximilian

Rabizadeh, Milad
Rafieioskouei, Arshia
Reese, Lennard
Rieder, Sabine
Rodriguez, Andoni
Seferis, Emmanouil
Silvetti, Simone
Soueidi, Chukri
Steffen, Martin
Stolz, Volker
Stünkel, Patrick
Thoma, Daniel
Vahs, Matti
van der Vegt, Marck
Walther, Christopher
Xia, Yuan
Yalcinkaya, Beyazit
Zhang, Songyuan

Contents

Algorithmic Fairness: A Runtime Perspective 1
    Filip Cano, Thomas A. Henzinger, and Konstantin Kueffner

DSLs for Runtime Verification 22
    Klaus Havelund, Moran Omer, and Doron Peled

Execution and Monitoring of HOA Automata with HOAX 44
    Luca Di Stefano

Formal Verification of Neural Certificates Done Dynamically 54
    Thomas A. Henzinger, Konstantin Kueffner, and Emily Yu

Runtime Monitoring and Enforcement of Conditional Fairness
in Generative AIs 73
    *Chih-Hong Cheng, Changshun Wu, Xingyu Zhao, Saddek Bensalem,
    and Harald Ruess*

A ROS Adapter for RTLOLA 92
    *Jan Baumeister, Bernd Finkbeiner, Franz Jünger, Florian Kohn,
    Sebastian Schirmer, and Christoph Torens*

DynSRV: Dynamically Updated Properties for Stream Runtime Verification ... 101
    *Morten Haahr Kristensen, Thomas Wright, Cláudio Gomes,
    Lukas Esterle, and Peter Gorm Larsen*

Modular and Online Monitoring of Temporal Logic Specification
with Integral and Filter 120
    Simone Silvetti, Michele Loreti, and Laura Nenzi

Alignment Monitoring 140
    Thomas A. Henzinger, Konstantin Kueffner, Vasu Singh, and I. Sun

Instrumenting Runtime Enforcement 160
    *François Hublet, David Basin, Linda Hu, Srđan Krstić,
    and Lennard Reese*

Active Monitoring with RTLola: A Specification-Guided Scheduling
Approach 181
    Jan Baumeister, Bernd Finkbeiner, and Frederik Scheerer

The Power of Reframing: Using LLMs in Synthesizing RV Monitors 202
Itay Cohen, Klaus Havelund, Doron Peled, and Yoav Goldberg

Conformal Safety Shielding for Imperfect-Perception Agents 213
William Scarbro, Calum Imrie, Sinem Getir Yaman, Kavan Fatehi, Corina Păsăreanu, Radu Calinescu, and Ravi Mangal

Extended Timed Regular Expressions 233
Marco Muñiz, Marius Mikučionis, and Kim G. Larsen

Monitoring Distributed Systems Based on Partial Order Executions with Global States 252
Moran Omer, Doron Peled, Ely Porat, and Vijay K. Garg

Hidden-Layer Monitoring for Out-of-Distribution Localization in Image Segmentation 274
Jan Křetínský, Sabine Rieder, Gesina Schwalbe, and Youssef Shoeb

CoCAI: Copula-Based Conformal Anomaly Identification for Multivariate Time-Series 296
Nicholas Andrea Pearson, Francesca Zanello, Davide Russo, Luca Bortolussi, and Francesca Cairoli

Monitoring Progress and Failure in Autonomous Robot Navigation: A Case Study 317
Vladislav Nenchev and Prodromos Sotiriadis

Conformal Predictive Monitoring for Multi-modal Scenarios 336
Francesca Cairoli, Luca Bortolussi, Jyotirmoy V. Deshmukh, Lars Lindemann, and Nicola Paoletti

Runtime Verification for LTL in Stochastic Systems 357
Javier Esparza and Vincent Fischer

A Practical Approach to Runtime Verification 377
Raik Hipler, Hannes Kallwies, Martin Leucker, Kevin Gillian van Dommele, and Jannis Wien

Hyper Pattern Matching 397
Masaki Waga and Étienne André

Monitoring Hypernode Logic Over Infinite Domains 417
Marek Chalupa, Thomas A. Henzinger, and Ana Oliveira da Costa

A Compositional Approach to Diagnosing Faults in Cyber-Physical Systems 438
   Josefine B. Graebener, Inigo Incer, and Richard M. Murray

Statistical Runtime Verification for LLMs via Robustness Estimation 457
   Natan Levy, Adiel Ashrov, and Guy Katz

ISL: Monitoring Image Segmentation Logic in Medical Imaging Analysis 477
   Ziyan An, Daniel Moyer, Ipek Oguz, Taylor T. Johnson, and Meiyi Ma

Runtime Consultants 497
   Dana Fisman and Elina Sudit

Author Index 519

Algorithmic Fairness: A Runtime Perspective

Filip Cano, Thomas A. Henzinger, and Konstantin Kueffner(✉)

Institute of Science and Technology Austria, Klosterneuburg, Austria
{filip.cano,tah,konstantin.kueffner}@ist.ac.at

Abstract. Fairness in AI is traditionally studied as a static property evaluated once, over a fixed dataset. However, real-world AI systems operate sequentially, with outcomes and environments evolving over time. This paper proposes a framework for analysing fairness as a runtime property. Using a minimal yet expressive model based on sequences of coin tosses with possibly evolving biases, we study the problems of monitoring and enforcing fairness expressed in either toss outcomes or coin biases. Since there is no one-size-fits-all solution for either problem, we provide a summary of monitoring and enforcement strategies, parametrised by environment dynamics, prediction horizon, and confidence thresholds. For both problems, we present general results under simple or minimal assumptions. We survey existing solutions for the monitoring problem for Markovian and additive dynamics, and existing solutions for the enforcement problem in static settings with known dynamics.

Keywords: Fairness · Runtime monitoring · Runtime enforcement

1 Introduction

Fairness is essential for the responsible deployment of AI in numerous domains such as hiring, credit scoring, and criminal justice [10,17,37,41,42]. When AI influences decisions affecting human lives, equitable treatment is crucial to prevent the reinforcement of societal biases. Traditionally, fairness has been considered a *static* property of AI systems, meaning that fairness is evaluated under the assumption of having access to a fixed snapshot of the world [18,23]. This approach assumes that the environment, user behaviour, and data distribution are observable and stable over time. These assumptions often fail in dynamic, real-world applications where AI systems interact with people and adapt to new inputs.

Recognising fairness as a *sequential* property introduces a more nuanced and realistic understanding of the interaction of AI systems with the world. In runtime settings, input-output pairs can only be accessed sequentially, so fairness analysis is restricted to the evidence obtained by single traces. Furthermore, the distribution of future inputs may change, either from exogenous processes or affected by the system's own past decisions.

In this paper, we focus on sequences of biased coin tosses, where each coin may have a different, potentially evolving bias. This minimal yet expressive setting allows us to explore fundamental questions about group fairness at runtime, abstracting away the complexities of real-world domains. The aim of this paper is to serve as a roadmap for the research of fairness from a runtime perspective, unifying existing results into a coherent framework and motivating future research on the topic.

In the coin flip setting, fairness can refer to the average outcome of the coin tosses, to the average bias, or to the bias of the most recent coin. We show how these measures can be extended from finite to infinite sequences and how they can be interpreted over stochastic processes via conditional expectations, giving rise to a notion of fairness at runtime.

We then study two core problems: (1) the monitoring problem, in which the system passively observes outcomes and must estimate fairness within a confidence interval; and (2) the enforcement problem, in which the system can actively intervene to ensure fairness remains within a target range. For both problems, we survey recent work that approaches them under certain assumptions and also provide some novel results.

In this paper we provide an overview of the different concepts of fairness at runtime, the different variants of both the monitoring and the enforcement problem, and the existing approaches to both problems under concrete assumptions. We parametrise both problems by the environment dynamics, the fairness property under study, the prediction horizon, i.e., how many steps in the future we are interested in, and the confidence value, which indicates the probability of obtaining a correct solution. For the enforcement problem, we add a set of target intervals where the fairness property should lie, as an extra parameter. In both the monitoring and enforcement problems, certain assumptions about the problem's parameters lead to tailored efficient solutions, showing that there is no one-size-fits-all solution.

We connect our theoretical framework with several recent results in runtime fairness. For the monitoring problem, we show that under no assumptions on the environment dynamics, finite outcome fairness can be easily monitored, but infinite outcome cannot. We then show how to monitor any fairness property with a finite horizon under the assumption that there is a single (unknown) coin. We outline the work of Henzinger et al. [25,27] on monitoring systems whose dynamics are governed by a Markov chain, as well as their work on monitoring systems that follow additive environmental dynamics [26].

For the enforcement problem, we show that any fairness property can be enforced with high confidence, disregarding cost, under mild assumptions on the target intervals. We then study the enforcement of outcome fairness in depth in the simplest setting: a single coin of known bias. We survey work from Cano et al. [14] on synthesising enforcers with different guarantees on cost-optimality and confidence value. We also propose a new enforcer with less restrictive assumptions than those from Cano et al. and outline an extension of their work to systems where the bias of the coin changes according to known dynamics.

Taken together, the surveyed results and the unifying framework we introduce provide a comprehensive foundation for reasoning about fairness in sequential decision-making systems at runtime.

An extended version of this paper with detailed proofs is available in [13].

2 Fairness Definitions

2.1 Preliminaries

We denote the set of all natural numbers as $\mathbb{N}$, the set of all positive natural numbers as $\mathbb{N}^+$, and the set of all real numbers as $\mathbb{R}$. Let $\mathcal{A}$ be any set. We denote the set of all length $n \in \mathbb{N}$ sequences over $\mathcal{A}^n$. Moreover, we denote the set of all sequences up to length n as $\mathcal{A}^{\leq n}$, the set of all finite sequences as $\mathcal{A}^*$, and the set of all infinite sequences as $\mathcal{A}^\omega$. Let $m, n \in \mathbb{N} \cup \{\infty\}$ such that $m \leq n$ and let $u \in \mathcal{A}^* \cup \mathcal{A}^\omega$ be a sequence of length n, we denote the prefix of length m as $u_{1:m} = a_1, \ldots, a_m$, where for $m = \infty$ we have $u_{1:m} = u$.

2.2 Fairness Over Sequences

We limit our investigation of quantitative fairness measures to a simple coin flip setting. We consider fairness on finite and infinite sequences. We define two fairness measures over finite sequences. One measure quantifies fairness based on the coin tosses, the other does so over their biases. We generalise each of them by taking the limit.

Setting. We investigate fairness in a sequence of coins and coin toss outcomes, denoted by $w = (p_t, x_t)_{t \in \mathbb{N}}$. At each step $t \in \mathbb{N}^+$, the value $p_t \in [0, 1]$ represents the bias of the coin and the value $x_t \in \{0, 1\}$ represents the outcome of the coin toss, where 0 indicates tail and 1 indicates head. We denote the set of bias-outcome pairs as $\mathcal{W} = \mathcal{P} \times \mathcal{X}$ where $\mathcal{P} \subseteq [0, 1]$ is a subset set of all coins and $\mathcal{X} = \{0, 1\}$. Note that we will use the terms "bias of a coin" and "coin" interchangeably.

Outcome Fairness. In the outcome measure, we evaluate fairness only on the outcomes of the coin tosses. The measure compares the average number of heads and tails. It ranges from 0 (tails-biased) to 1 (heads-biased), with 1/2 indicating fairness. Formally, for a sequence $w \in \mathcal{W}^\omega$ and $t \in \mathbb{N}^+$ the *outcome fairness* of the prefix $w_{1:t} = w_1, \ldots, w_t$ is defined as

$$\varphi_O(w_{1:t}) = \frac{1}{t} \sum_{i=1}^{t} x_i. \qquad (1)$$

Bias Fairness. In the bias measure, we evaluate fairness on the average biases of the coins in the sequence, instead of the toss outcomes. As before, a value close to 1/2 indicates a fair sequence. Formally, for a sequence $w \in \mathcal{W}^\omega$ and $t \in \mathbb{N}^+$ the *bias fairness* of the prefix $w_{1:t} = w_1, \ldots, w_t$ is defined as

$$\varphi_B(w_{1:t}) = \frac{1}{t} \sum_{i=1}^{t} p_i. \qquad (2)$$

Current Fairness. In the current measure, we evaluate fairness on the bias of the current coin in the sequence. As before, a value close to 1/2 indicates a fair coin. Formally, for a sequence $w \in \mathcal{W}^\omega$ and $t \in \mathbb{N}^+$ the *current fairness* of the prefix $w_{1:t} = w_1, \ldots, w_t$ is defined as

$$\varphi_C(w_{1:t}) = p_t. \tag{3}$$

Infinite Outcome and Bias. We lift the fairness properties to infinite traces by taking the limit, i.e., for $\varphi \in \{\varphi_O, \varphi_B, \varphi_C\}$, whenever it exists,

$$\varphi(w) = \lim_{t \to \infty} \varphi(w_{1:t}). \tag{4}$$

2.3 Fairness over Stochastic Processes

In this section, we enrich our setting by considering the sequence of coins as a stochastic process. With this additional structure, we can study the average and outcome fairness not only on concrete sequences, but also in expectation with respect to the dynamic evolution of the stochastic process, and conditioning on a prefix of the process.

Setting. We assume the sequence of bias-outcome pairs $w = (w_t)_{t \in \mathbb{N}^+} \in \mathcal{W}^\omega$ is a realization of a stochastic process $W = (P_t, X_t)_{t \in \mathbb{N}^+}$ with support $\mathcal{W}^\omega$. The stochastic process is characterised by a dynamics function $\theta \colon \mathcal{W}^* \to \Delta(\mathcal{P})$ mapping the past sequence into a probability distribution over the following coin. The process is defined by the following dynamics. At each time step $t \in \mathbb{N}^+$ and the history $w_1, \ldots, w_{t-1} \in \mathcal{W}^{t-1}$ we define

$$P_t \sim \theta(w_1, \ldots, w_{t-1}) \quad \text{and} \quad X_t \sim \text{Bernoulli}(p_t) \tag{5}$$

where p_t is a realization of P_t. Intuitively, the next coin's bias p_t is sampled from the process dynamics θ according to the history $w_{1:t-1}$, and the toss outcome is then drawn according to this bias.

Runtime Fairness. Runtime fairness captures how the expected value of a fairness property evolves over time as the stochastic process unfolds. This requires the use of the conditional expectation. Formally, given a fairness property $\varphi \in \{\varphi_O, \varphi_B, \varphi_C\}$, the stochastic process W, a prediction horizon $h \in \mathbb{N} \cup \{\infty\}$, and the realized prefix $w_{1:t} = w_1, \ldots, w_t \in \mathcal{W}^t$ at the current point in time $t \in \mathbb{N}^+$, we evaluate the *runtime fairness* of the stochastic process for the measure φ and prediction horizon h as

$$\rho_t^h(W; \varphi) = \mathbb{E}_\theta(\varphi(W_{1:t+h}) \mid w_{1:t}), \tag{6}$$

Static vs. Dynamic. Defining fairness at runtime using the conditional expectation provides more insight into the actual fairness of the process, as compared to computing the expectation of the fairness measure directly. This is because with the conditional expectation, the property value adapts to the information accumulated as the process evolves.

3 Fairness at Runtime

3.1 The Monitoring Problem

Monitor. A monitor for a fairness measure φ is a function that reads a sequence of outcomes and estimates the value of the fairness property by providing an interval where the fairness property lies with high confidence. Formally, a monitor is a function $\mathfrak{M}\colon \mathcal{X}^* \to \mathcal{I}([0,1])$ maps a finite sequence of outcomes into an interval over $[0,1]$.

Problem Instance. A problem instance consists of a set of dynamics functions Θ, a fairness property $\varphi \in \{\varphi_O, \varphi_B, \varphi_C\}$, a prediction horizon $h \in \mathbb{N}$, and an error probability threshold $\delta \in [0,1]$. The set Θ encodes the assumption imposed onto the dynamics function used to create the stochastic process W. We want a monitor that provides a correct verdict irrespective of the actual dynamics function θ, as long as it is in Θ.

Soundness. Let $\mathfrak{M}\colon \mathcal{X}^* \to \mathcal{I}([0,1])$ be a monitor. Given a problem instance $(\Theta, \varphi, h, \delta)$ we call the monitor *pointwise sound*, if

$$\forall \theta \in \Theta \colon \forall t \in \mathbb{N}^+ \colon \mathbb{P}_\theta\big(\rho_t^h(W;\varphi) \in \mathfrak{M}(U_{1:t})\big) \geq 1 - \delta, \tag{7}$$

and *uniformly sound*, if

$$\forall \theta \in \Theta \colon \mathbb{P}_\theta\big(\forall t \in \mathbb{N}^+ \colon \rho_t^h(W;\varphi) \in \mathfrak{M}(U_{1:t})\big) \geq 1 - \delta. \tag{8}$$

Intuitively, we want the monitor to output the tightest interval possible while remaining sound. We discuss this in Sect. 7.

Problem 1. Given a problem instance $(\Theta, \varphi, h, \delta)$, synthesise a pointwise sound or uniformly sound monitor.

Pointwise vs. Uniform Soundness. We distinguish between pointwise and uniform soundness. A pointwise sound monitor has a small error probability at every point in time. This implies that it almost surely will make a mistake, i.e., the computed or target interval will fail to capture the actual fairness measure at least once on an infinite run. By contrast, a uniformly sound monitor guarantees that the invariant: "the actual fairness measure is contained within the computed or target interval at all times", holds with high probability. Note that for both monitors, uniform soundness implies pointwise soundness, but the converse does not hold. The same discussion carries through for enforcers, which are introduced next.

3.2 The Enforcement Problem

Enforcer. An enforcer (often also called *shield*) for a fairness property monitors the evolution of the fairness property at runtime and can overwrite some of the coin biases or outcomes with the goal of keeping the property inside a target interval. Formally, an enforcer is a function $\mathfrak{E} \colon \mathcal{W}^* \to \Delta(\mathcal{W})$. Intuitively, we want an enforcer that intervenes as little as possible.

Enforced Process. The presence of an enforcer modifies the distribution of bias-outcome pairs as follows. For each time step $t \in \mathbb{N}^+$ and bias-outcome sequence $w_1, \ldots, w_{t-1} \in \mathcal{W}^{t-1}$ we define $P'_t \sim \theta(w_1, \ldots, w_{t-1})$ and $X'_t \sim \text{Bernoulli}(p'_t)$. The actual bias-observation pair (p_t, x_t) is a realization of the distribution defined by the enforcer w.r.t. the history and the realized bias-observation pair of the process (p'_t, x'_t), i.e.,

$$(P_t, X_t) \sim \mathfrak{E}(w_1, \ldots, w_{t-1}, (p'_t, x'_t)). \tag{9}$$

The resulting stochastic process is now characterised by the dynamics function θ and the enforcer $\mathfrak{E}$.

Problem Instance. A problem instance consists of a set of dynamics functions Θ, a fairness property $\varphi \in \{\varphi_O, \varphi_B, \varphi_C\}$, a prediction horizon $h \in \mathbb{N}$, an error probability threshold $\delta \in (0, 1)$, and a sequence of intervals $I = (I_t)_{t \in \mathbb{N}} \subseteq \mathcal{I}([0, 1])$, where the fairness property should lie in at each step.

Soundness. Let $\mathfrak{E} \colon \mathcal{W}^* \to \Delta(\mathcal{W})$ be an enforcer. Given a problem instance $(\Theta, \varphi, h, \delta, I)$ we call the enforcer *pointwise sound*, if

$$\forall \theta \in \Theta \colon \forall t \in \mathbb{N}^+ \colon \mathbb{P}_{(\theta, \mathfrak{E})}\left(\rho^h_t(W; \varphi) \in I_t\right) \geq 1 - \delta, \tag{10}$$

and *uniformly sound*, if

$$\forall \theta \in \Theta \colon \mathbb{P}_{(\theta, \mathfrak{E})}\left(\forall t \in \mathbb{N}^+ \colon \rho^h_t(W; \varphi) \in I_t\right) \geq 1 - \delta. \tag{11}$$

Intuitively, we want an enforcer that intervenes as little as possible. We discuss this in Sect. 7.

Problem 2. Given a problem instance $(\Theta, \varphi, h, \delta, I)$, synthesise a pointwise sound or uniformly sound enforcer.

Enforcement of Bias or Outcome. With our definition of enforcer as a function $\mathfrak{E} \colon \mathcal{W}^* \to \Delta(\mathcal{W})$, we allow enforcement over both bias and outcome. However, enforcing both bias and outcome at the same time may not make sense. We can think of enforcement as changing the bias of the coin before it is tossed or as changing the outcome of the coin toss. In the first case, we are overwriting the bias p_t of the coin by another value p'_t, so it only makes sense that the outcome follows a Bernoulli of parameter p'_t. In the second case, we are tossing the coin with bias p_t, and overwriting the outcome, so this outcome is no longer correlated with the bias of any coin. In this paper, we only consider enforcers that overwrite bias our outcome, but not both.

3.3 Warm-Up Examples

3.3.1 Outcome Fairness Monitor.
We construct a pointwise sound or uniformly sound monitor for the set of all dynamics functions Θ and the outcome fairness measure with prediction horizon of 0.

Assumption 1 (Outcome fairness with null horizon) *We assume the problem to be $(\Theta, \varphi_O, 0, \delta)$, where Θ is the set of all dynamics functions.*

Monitor Construction. We construct a monitor solving Problem 1 under Assumption 1 using a single register R. This monitor incrementally updates the register to store the current value of φ_O. The register is initialised with the value 0. At time $t \in \mathbb{N}^+$ the value of this register is R_{t-1}. The monitor observes a new outcome x_t and updates the register value as follows:

$$\mathsf{R}_t \leftarrow (x + (t-1) \cdot \mathsf{R}_{t-1})/t.$$

Because the outcomes are observed, the register value at time t is guaranteed to be equal to the outcome fairness measure. This constitutes a general solution for the problem of monitoring outcome fairness with a null prediction horizon, so we will not discuss it further.

3.3.2 Limit Outcome Fairness Monitor.
It is impossible to construct a pointwise sound or uniformly sound monitor for the set of all dynamics functions Θ and the outcome fairness measure with infinite prediction horizon.

Assumption 2 (Outcome fairness with infinite horizon) *We assume the problem to be $(\Theta, \varphi_O, \infty, \delta)$, where Θ is the set of all dynamics functions.*

Counterexample. Because Θ contains all possible dynamics functions, it also contains the following set of dynamics functions $\Theta_A = \{\theta_k^A \mid k \in \mathbb{N} \cup \{\infty\}\}$, defined as follows. For each $k \in \mathbb{N} \cup \{\infty\}$, the dynamics function θ^A chooses the coin with bias 0 for all $t \leq k$, otherwise it chooses the coin with bias 1. In any concrete realisation $w \in \mathcal{W}^\omega$ generated by θ_∞^A, it is impossible for the monitor to know whether the limit of the sequence is 0 or 1.

3.3.3 Process-Agnostic Fairness Enforcement.
Fairness enforcement is not always feasible. Whether enforcement is feasible depends on both the type of fairness property and the dynamics of the desired fairness intervals. Specifically, the properties of outcome fairness and bias fairness are defined as averages over time, meaning that their values evolve slowly and cannot be arbitrarily changed in a single step. If the sequence of target intervals shifts too quickly, no sequence of decisions by the enforcer can keep the fairness measure within the desired bounds at all times. We illustrate this phenomenon with the following result.

Lemma 1. *Let $w = (p_t, x_t)_{t \in \mathbb{N}}$ be a sequence of coins and outcomes, and let $\varphi \in \{\varphi_O, \varphi_B\}$. For all $t \geq 2$ we have $|\varphi(w_{1:t}) - \varphi(w_{1:(t-1)})| \leq 1/t$.*

A reasonable restriction is to assume that the intersection of the target intervals is non-empty, i.e., there is a value of the fairness property that is considered "fair" at all times.

Assumption 3 (Enforceable bias fairness) *We assume the enforcement problem to be $(\Theta, \varphi_B, h, \delta, I)$, where $\cap_{t \in \mathbb{N}} I_t \neq \emptyset$.*

This is enough to enforce bias fairness, as we can find $p_\cap \in \cap_t I_t$ and build the enforcer $\mathfrak{E} \colon \mathcal{W}^* \to \mathcal{W}$ for all $w \in \mathcal{W}^*$ as $\mathfrak{E}(w) = (p_\cap, 0)$.

Theorem 1. *The previous enforcer solves Problem 2 under Assumption 3.*

For outcome fairness, we need a stronger condition.

Assumption 4 (Enforceable outcome fairness) *We assume the enforcement problem to be $(\Theta, \varphi_O, h, \delta, I)$, where $I = (I_t)_{t \in \mathbb{N}}$ is such that there exists $p \in [0,1]$ satisfying for all $t \in \mathbb{N}$ the condition $[\max(0, p - 1/t), \min(1, p + 1/t)] \subseteq I_t$.*

With this condition, we can build the following enforcer for outcome fairness:

$$\mathfrak{E}(w_{1:t}) = \begin{cases} 1 & \text{if } \varphi_O(w_{1:t}) \leq p, \\ 0 & \text{otherwise.} \end{cases} \quad (12)$$

Theorem 2. *The enforcer in Eq. (12) solves Problem 2 under Assumption 4.*

While these enforcers always exist, they bear no consideration on minimising interventions, and Assumptions 3 and 4 are so weak that reasoning about that is challenging.

4 Fairness Monitoring with Unknown Dynamics

There does not exist a monitor capable of solving Problem 1 in full generality. The difficulty of the problem arises from the structure of the set of dynamics functions and the choice of the fairness measure.

4.1 Static Coins

If the dynamics are restricted to the set of fixed coins, we can construct a pointwise sound or uniformly sound monitor for all fairness measures and all prediction horizons. We define θ_p to be the constant dynamics function, mapping every history into the point measure on $p \in [0,1]$, i.e., into a coin with bias $p \in [0,1]$. This problem was first studied in [3]. We present their solution to pointwise monitoring and propose an improved solution for uniformly sound monitoring.

Assumption 5 (Constant dynamics) *We assume the problem to be $(\Theta, \varphi, h, \delta)$, where Θ is the set of all constant dynamics function, $\varphi \in \{\varphi_O, \varphi_B, \varphi_C\}$, and $h \in \mathbb{N} \cup \{\infty\}$.*

Monitor Construction. For this class of processes, all properties can be monitored. As in Sect. 3.3.1, the monitor maintains the register R, which provides a point estimate of the fairness value. An error bound is then added to this estimate to form the monitoring interval. The computation of the error depends on whether a pointwise or uniformly sound monitor is required; that is, the error is computed differently in each case. They are, respectively,

$$\varepsilon_t^p = \sqrt{\frac{\log(2/\delta)}{2t}} \quad \text{and} \quad \varepsilon_t^u = \sqrt{\frac{1.1\left(2\log\left(\pi \log(t)/\sqrt{6}\right) + \log(2/\delta)\right)}{t}}.$$

The output of the monitor at time t is the interval $[R_t-\varepsilon_t, R_t+\varepsilon_t]$ for $\varepsilon_t \in \{\varepsilon_t^p, \varepsilon_t^u\}$. The soundness of the intervals is a direct consequence of known concentration inequalities [29,30]. It generalises to other properties because in this setting, all properties, except outcome fairness, coincide. Moreover, this monitor can trivially be extended to outcome fairness with horizon $h \in \mathbb{N}$ by taking the current value of the register R_t, which equals outcome fairness with horizon 0, and extrapolating the values of the interval to the given horizon, i.e.,

$$[(t \cdot R_t + h \cdot (R_t - \varepsilon_t))/(t+h), (t \cdot R_t + h \cdot (R_t + \varepsilon_t))/(t+h)].$$

Theorem 3. *The monitor described above solves Prob. 1 under Ass. 5.*

4.2 Observed Markovian Dynamics

In this section, we discuss the result presented in Henzinger et al. [25] investigating fairness on observable Markov chains. To match our setting to the assumption made in [25], we assume $\mathcal{P} = \{p^{(1)}, \ldots, p^{(n)}\}$ to be finite and we restrict our attention to the set of all dynamics functions with type $\theta \colon \mathcal{W} \to \Delta(\mathcal{P})$, such that the induced Markov chain over $\mathcal{W}$ is irreducible, i.e., every coin is visited infinitely often.

Assumption 6 (Observed Markov chain) *We assume the problem to be $(\Theta, \varphi, h, \delta)$, where $\varphi \in \{\varphi_O, \varphi_B, \varphi_C\}$ and $h \in \mathbb{N}$. We assume Θ is the set of all dynamics functions that induce a finite, irreducible Markov chain. Additionally, we assume that the monitor observes the labels of the coins, i.e., if the bias at time $t \in \mathbb{N}$ is $p_t = p^{(k)} \in \mathcal{P}$, the monitor observes $k \in [n]$.*

Properties. The monitor is designed for a specification language consisting of arithmetic expressions over single-step transition probabilities in a Markov chain.

Example 1. Let $\mathcal{P} = \{p^{(1)}, p^{(2)}\}$, the monitor can estimate the expected bias of the next coin, i.e., current fairness with horizon 1 conditioned on a fixed current bias-outcome pair. For every for every $w = (p, x) \in \mathcal{W}$ this property corresponds to the expression $\psi = p^{(1)}\theta(p,x)(p^{(1)}) + p^{(2)}\theta(p,x)(p^{(1)})$. To obtain the current fairness with horizon 1 for the state observed at time t, we can deploy one monitor for each $w \in \mathcal{W}$ and select the appropriate verdict at every time step.

As in the above example, we can construct the appropriate expressions for both the current and the biased fairness with finite prediction horizon. Because the monitor is a general purpose monitor, designed for a much richer class of time invariant properties, it is not optimised for the specific and adapting fairness properties considered here. Hence, while sound, it is not an efficient approach.

Monitor Construction. For a given expression, e.g., the one in the example above, the monitor aggregates the observed sequence of coin labels and outcomes into a sequence of independent random variables with the same expected value as the expression. This conversion is done memory-less, utilising only a few counters. The monitor estimates the expected value of this sequence and constructs the pointwise and uniform error bounds, similar to the monitor for a static coin sketched in Sect. 4.1.

Theorem 4 ([25]). *The monitor described above solves Prob. 1 under Ass. 6.*

4.3 Hidden Markovian Dynamics

In this section we discuss the result presented in Henzinger et al. [27]. In their paper, they investigate the fairness of hidden Markov chains. In Sect. 4.2 we assume that the monitor observes, in addition to the outcome, the label of the current coin. This assumption makes the setting fully observable. We now drop this assumption, i.e., the induced Markov chain is partially-observed. To compensate, we assume that the induced Markov chain is irreducible and aperiodic with its stationary distribution as its initial distribution. Moreover, we assume knowledge of a bound on its mixing time, i.e., the time required to converge to the stationary distribution [27].

Assumption 7 (Hidden Markov chain) *We assume the problem to be $(\Theta, \varphi, h, \delta)$, where $\varphi \in \{\varphi_O, \varphi_B, \varphi_C\}$ and $h = \infty$. We assume Θ is the set of all dynamics functions that induce an irreducible, aperiodic, finite Markov chain with a mixing time bounded by τ_{mix}, and starting in its stationary distribution $\eta \in \Delta(\mathcal{W})$.*

Properties. The monitor is designed for a specification language consisting of arithmetic expressions over expected values $\mathbb{E}_\eta(f(x_1, \ldots, x_n))$ of a given bounded function with arity $n \in \mathbb{N}$ evaluated over outcomes, i.e., $f: \mathcal{X}^n \to [a, b]$. The expectation is taken w.r.t. the stationary distribution $\eta \in \Delta(\mathcal{W})$ of a partially observed Markov chain. Intuitively, the stationary distribution equals the proportion of time spent in each state in $\mathcal{W}$. We give a small example below.

Example 2. Let $\mathcal{P} = \{p^{(A)}, p^{(B)}\}$, the monitor can estimate the limit average bias of the process W, i.e., bias fairness with horizon ∞, by estimating

$$\psi = \mathbb{E}_\eta(\mathbf{1}[X_1 = 1])$$

The above expressions equals the proportion of heads observed over an infinite run, i.e., the limit of bias fairness.

For stationary Markov chains the properties φ_O, φ_B, and φ_C have the same value as ψ, if the prediction horizon is ∞. Unfortunately, this monitor is not suited for finite horizon properties.

Monitor Construction. The monitor maintains a single register R to incrementally estimate the value of the given function $f\colon \mathcal{X}^n \to [a,b]$ at runtime. To evaluate the function, the monitor must maintain a fixed memory of n. The register is initialised with 0. After the monitor observes the first n elements, it updates the register at every time t as follows,

$$\mathtt{R}_t \leftarrow (\mathtt{R}_{t-1} \cdot (t-n) + f(x_{t-n}, \dots, x_t))/(t-n+1).$$

As in Sect. 4.1, it constructs an interval around R using error bounds that depend on the mixing time. The error bound is

$$\sqrt{\frac{9tn^2(b-a)^2 \tau_{mix}}{2(t-(n-1))^2}} \cdot K,$$

where $K = \log(2/\delta)$ for the pointwise sound monitor, and $K = \log(\pi^2 t^2/3\delta)$ for the uniformly sound monitor. The bound has to account for the mixing time of the Markov chain to avoid premature verdicts, as in the example below.

Example 3 (Ex. 2 cont.). Let $p^{(A)} = 0.9$ and $p^{(B)} = 0.1$. Assume the dynamics function is defined for every $x \in \mathcal{X}$ and $g \in \{A, B\}$ such that $P \sim \theta(p^{(g)}, x)$ is $p^{(g)}$ with a probability $1 - \varepsilon$ for a small $\varepsilon > 0$. Although we remain a long time with one coin, we can expect an equal number of heads and tails in the limit. However, if we were to deploy the monitor described in Sect. 4.1, we would unduly, yet confidently, declare the limit to be biased.

Theorem 5 ([27]). *The monitor described above solves Prob. 1 under Ass. 7.*

4.4 Additive Dynamics

In this section, we discuss the result presented in Henzinger et al. [26] on systems with additive dynamics. We match our setting to these assumptions by restricting our attention to dynamics functions where the bias changes additively as a function of the past outcomes. Given an additive change function $\beta\colon \mathcal{X} \to \mathbb{R}$ mapping a history of outcomes into a numeric value, we define the dynamics function θ for every $w \in \mathcal{W}^\omega$ and every $t \in \mathbb{N}^+$ such that

$$p_{t+1} = \theta(w_{1:t}) = p_t + \beta(x_t) \quad \text{and} \quad p_1 \in \mathcal{P}. \tag{13}$$

Remark 1. Note that in the original paper, the "bias", i.e., the parameter subject to change, cannot exit its bounds. For simplicity of exposition, we assume this to be true as well. Moreover, the change functions can trivially be extended to the entire sequence of outcomes, i.e., $\beta\colon \mathcal{X}^* \to \mathbb{R}$. Moreover, an extension to fully linear dynamics is also possible.

Assumption 8 (Additive dynamics) *We assume the problem to be $(\Theta, \varphi, h, \delta)$, where $\varphi \in \{\varphi_B, \varphi_C\}$ and $h = 0$. We assume Θ is the set of all additive dynamics functions defined in Eq. (13), and that the monitor has access to the change function β, but is unaware of p_1.*

Properties. The monitor is designed to track the time conditional expectation $\mathbb{E}_{t-1}(f(Z_t))$ of a bounded monotonic function $f : \mathcal{Z} \to [a,b]$ evaluated over a random variable with additive shifting conditional expectation, i.e., $\mathbb{E}_{t-1}(Z_t)$ shifts as in Eq. (13). In our setting, this equates to monitoring the current fairness with predictive horizon 0.

Monitor Construction. The monitor maintains two registers, one for the accumulated change C and one for the bias estimate R of the first coin, both are initialised with 0. At every point in time $t \in \mathbb{N}^+$, the monitor observes the next outcome x_t and updates the registers as follows

$$R_t \leftarrow (R_{t-1} \cdot (t-1) + (x_t - C_{t-1})) \quad \text{and} \quad C_t \leftarrow C_{t-1} + \beta(x_t).$$

The output of the monitor is an interval constructed around the current bias, i.e., $R_t + C_t$, using error bounds similar to the ones in Sect. 4.1. Because the monitor estimates the initial value, we can easily extend this result to cover bias fairness with horizon 0.

Theorem 6 ([26]). *The monitor described above solves Prob. 1 under Ass. 8.*

5 Fairness Enforcement with Known Dynamics

Knowing the dynamics function of the stochastic process amounts to the set Θ being a singleton, i.e., $\Theta = \{\theta\}$. We formalise it with the following assumption.

Assumption 9 (Known dynamics) *We assume the problem to be* $(\Theta, \varphi_O, h, \delta, I)$, *where* $\Theta = \{\theta\}$ *is a singleton with a known dynamics function* θ.

This problem has been studied for static systems (Assumption 5), where it reduces to a single coin of known bias. Although the monitoring problem is trivial, the enforcement problem is not, especially if we want to reason about cost-optimality. To reason about cost, we assume that we are given a cost function $\ell : \mathcal{W}^* \to \mathcal{W}$ and that we enforce over finite or periodic time windows.

Finite and Periodic Time Windows. We say that an enforcement problem is of finite window T when the only non-trivial enforcement interval is I_T. Similarly, we say that an enforcement problem is of periodic window T when the only non-trivial enforcement intervals are the same and occur every T time steps.

Assumption 10 (Finite time window) *We assume the enforcement problem to be* $(\Theta, \varphi, 0, \delta, I)$, *where* $I_T \subsetneq [0,1]$, *and* $I_t = [0,1]$ *for all* $t \neq T$.

Assumption 11 (Periodic time window) *We assume the enforcement problem to be* $(\Theta, \varphi, 0, \delta, I)$, *where* $I_{n \cdot T} = I_T \subsetneq [0,1]$, *and* $I_t = [0,1]$ *for all* $t \neq nT$ *and all* $n \in \mathbb{N}$.

Since the enforcer acts only up to time T in finite time window settings, the associated cost is necessarily finite. A sound enforcer is cost-optimal if no other sound enforcer yields a lower expected cost at the beginning of the time window.

In this section we present different approaches to the enforcement problem in finite and periodic time windows under Assumptions 5 and 9 and, at the end of the section, we sketch how the presented methods can be extended to a dynamic system, i.e., dropping Assumption 5.

5.1 Finite Time Window

5.1.1 Probabilistic Guarantees.
We propose an enforcement method for finite time windows with probabilistic guarantees by intervening only when the probability of the unenforced process reaching the target fairness interval falls below the confidence value.

Enforcer Construction. The enforcer checks for each sequence the probability that the unenforced process reaches the target interval at time T, and intervenes only when it falls below $1 - \delta$. Formally, for $w_{1:t} = (p_1, x_1), \ldots, (p_t, x_t) \in \mathcal{W}^t$:

$$\mathfrak{E}(w_{1:t}) = \begin{cases} (p_t, x_t) & \text{if } \mathbb{P}_{\theta_p}(\varphi_O(W_{1:T}) \in I_T \mid w_{1:t}) \geq 1 - \delta, \\ (p_t, 1 - x_t) & \text{otherwise.} \end{cases} \quad (14)$$

Theorem 7. *The enforcer described in Eq. (14) solves Problem 2 under Assumptions 5, 9, and 10.*

5.1.2 Deterministic Guarantees.
When restricting to problem instances with almost sure guarantees, Cano et al. [14] describe a solution to the enforcement problem that produces optimal-cost enforcers. We encode deterministic guarantees with the following assumption.

Assumption 12 (Almost-sure enforcement) *We assume the problem to be $(\Theta, \varphi, h, \delta, I)$ with $\delta = 0$.*

Enforcer Construction. The enforcer pre-computes, for each outcome sequence $x_{1:t}$, an auxiliary value function $v \colon \mathcal{X}^{\leq T} \to \mathbb{R}$ encoding the expected cost of the optimal enforcer that guarantees that outcome fairness sits in the target interval I_T after time T, conditioned on the first t outcomes being $x_{1:t}$. When computing $v(x_{1:t})$, we assign an infinite cost to those traces where no enforcer can guarantee fairness. The enforcer then chooses to flip the last outcome of a sequence whenever the resulting outcome yields a lower cost. Formally, for a given $w_{1:t} = (p_1, x_1), \ldots, (p_t, x_t) \in \mathcal{W}^t$:

$$\mathfrak{E}(w_{1:t}) = \begin{cases} (p_t, x_t) & \text{if } v(x_{1:t}) \leq v(x_{1:t-1}, 1 - x_t) \\ (p_t, 1 - x_t) & \text{otherwise.} \end{cases} \quad (15)$$

Theorem 8 ([14]). *The enforcer described in Eq. (15) solves Problem 2 cost-optimally under Assumptions 5, 9, 10, and 12.*

While not explored in [14], one could, in principle, precompute a value function v_δ representing the expected minimal cost of enforcing outcome fairness with probability $1 - \delta$, and use it to synthesize sound, cost-optimal enforcers for $\delta \in (0, 1)$, i.e., dropping Assumption 12. However, the recursive method proposed in [14, Sec. 3] for computing the value function v does not suffice for computing v_δ. A naïve extension would render the synthesis procedure exponential in the time window. Thus, a direct generalisation of the presented enforcer to arbitrary $\delta \in (0, 1)$ is computationally infeasible, and different techniques will be needed to obtain optimal enforcers at general confidence levels.

5.2 Periodic Time Window

Cano et al. [14] also propose extensions of their finite window enforcers to periodic window enforcers by repeatedly reusing or recomputing the shield every T steps. By extending the use of enforcers computed as sound and cost-optimal for a finite window, we can synthesise sound enforcers for the periodic window.

Enforcer Construction. To synthesise this enforcer, we build an auxiliary value function $v': \mathcal{X}^* \to \mathbb{R}$, which extends the value function used for finite window shields. We define the value function on time windows of size T, i.e., we restart the expected cost each time the outcome sequence reaches a length $n \cdot T$, for $n \in \mathbb{N}$. Let $k = n \cdot T$, we define the value function for an outcome sequence $x_{1:(k+t)}$, with $t \leq T$, as the minimal cost of enforcement from an outcome trace $x_{1:k}$ until step $k+T$, conditioned on the prefix $x_{1:k}$. To emphasize this conditional dependence, we denote it as $v(x_{(k+1):(k+t)} \mid x_{1:k})$. As in the finite window case, the enforcer compares $v(x_{(k+1):(k+t)} \mid x_{1:k})$ with $v((x_{(k+1):(k+t-1)}, 1-x_{k+t} \mid x_{1:k})$ to decide whether to interfere or not. Formally, for a given sequence $w_{1:(k+t)} = (p_1, x_1), \ldots, (p_{k+t}, x_{k+t}) \in \mathcal{W}^{k+t}$ with $1 \leq t \leq T$:

$$\mathfrak{E}(w_{1:k+t}) = \begin{cases} (p_{k+t}, x_{k+t}) & \text{if } v(x_{1:(k+t)} \mid x_{1:k}) \leq v\big((x_{1:(k+t-1)}, 1 - x_t) \mid x_{1:k}\big) \\ (p_{k+t}, 1 - x_{k+t}) & \text{otherwise.} \end{cases}$$
(16)

This expected cost cannot be computed offline for all $n \in \mathbb{N}$, but it can be computed at runtime every T steps.

Theorem 9 ([14]). *The enforcer described in Eq. (16) solves Problem 2 under Assumptions 5, 9, 11, and 12.*

Theorem 9 is a direct consequence of [14, Thm. 5]. Note that the original result is stated in terms of more general group fairness properties, and as a result, the produced enforcers are not sound for $\delta = 0$, but they are pointwise sound for a confidence value $\delta > 0$ dependent on the input distribution.

5.3 Enforcement on Dynamic Systems

In dynamic systems with known dynamics, the set of possible dynamics is a singleton $\Theta = \{\theta\}$, where θ can be any dynamics function. As far as we know, the enforcement problem has not been studied in this setting. The approach presented in [14] can be extended to synthesise sound enforcers for both finite and periodic windows for outcome fairness and confidence $\delta = 0$, with cost-optimal guarantees for the finite window case. To do so, we need to extend the auxiliary value function to capture the evolution of the biases. It has to be, therefore, a function $v \colon \mathcal{W}^* \to \mathbb{R}$, encoding the expected minimal cost of enforcement for any sequence $w \in \mathcal{W}^*$, accounting for the dynamics of the stochastic process. Such value functions can be efficiently computed for any dynamics function θ that can be encoded as a counter automaton [12]. This extension works both for finite and periodic time windows.

6 Related Work

Fairness in machine learning generally involves classification or regression problems where there is a feature of the input that needs to be protected, in the sense that the model should not discriminate decisions based on the value of this feature. Typical examples of protected features include age, race, and gender [6]. While our paper is written in terms of a simple coin toss setting, it captures the main complexities arising from the study of fairness in ML settings. Apart from the work we survey in this paper, fairness has been extensively studied from the perspective of machine learning [9,11,19,23,31,34–36,39,43,46,47]. From the standard ML point of view, fairness is a static property, and fairness enforcement is undertaken at design time, be it in debiasing the training data (pre-processing methods), adding fairness-inducing regularisation terms to the loss function (in-processing) or adjusting the outputs of the model after training (post-processing). Recently, formal methods-inspired techniques have been used to guarantee algorithmic fairness through the verification of a learned model [2,8,22,40,45], and enforcement of robustness [5,21,32]. All of these works verify or enforce algorithmic fairness statically on all runs of the system with high probability. A critical drawback in all this body of work is that fairness is often not a static property [15,24,37], and often fairness is satisfied too far away in the future to be practical [1], which justifies the need for a runtime perspective on it. In contrast, the monitoring and enforcement techniques covered in this paper are implemented at runtime on a system that is already deployed, allowing for the flexibility to adapt fairness verdicts or enforcement on the go, as the system execution progresses. Most monitors described in this paper are designed to check statistical properties, which is beyond the limit of what automata-based monitors for temporal properties can accomplish [4,7,16,20,33,38,44].

7 Discussion

7.1 Quality of Monitors and Enforcers

In Sect. 3, we formally defined soundness for fairness monitors and enforcers. To make the synthesis problems non-trivial, we must also consider performance. Yet, we have only informally discussed what constitutes a well-performing monitor or enforcer. This was deliberate, as existing work does not address performance in general settings, and defining such measures is far from straightforward. We highlight key challenges below.

Monitor Quality. We suggested that narrower intervals imply better performance. Fixing an error probability, the ideal monitor would produce confidence bounds that converge to the target property. Such a monitor may not always exist. At the other extreme lies the trivial monitor outputting $[0, 1]$, which always exists. All others potentially useful monitors fall in between. Hence, convergence may be too restrictive of a property. For finite samples, one might seek a monitor outputting the tightest possible interval at each point in time. While it may be possible to find a pointwise sound monitor satisfying this criteria, uniform soundness introduces a tradeoff between the interval width at different points in time, i.e., tightening the interval at time n may require widening it elsewhere. In this case, it is not clear, how performance should be measured.

Enforcer Quality. We loosely argued that good enforcers minimize interventions, but not all interventions are equal. Altering a strongly biased outcome may be costlier than one under near-fair conditions, i.e., small bias changes are less severe than drastic ones. This can be captured by a cost function $\ell: \mathcal{W}^* \times \mathcal{W} \to \mathbb{R}_{\geq 0}$, satisfying $\ell((w, (p, x)), (p, x)) = 0$ for all $w \in \mathcal{W}^*$ and $(p, x) \in \mathcal{W}$. Once a cost is defined and a error threshold is fixed, the challenge lies in aggregating the cost over time. Here none of the "classical" options seem satisfactory. For example, total cost diverges over infinite horizons; average cost overlooks short-term effects; discounted cost requires a reference time. Because of this, it is possible to define cost-optimal enforcers in special cases (e.g., [14]), but finding a general notion remains open.

7.2 Beyond Coins: Group Fairness Properties

The term *group fairness* refers to a broad class of properties formalizing the principle of treating different demographic groups equally. In this paper, we abstract group fairness using a single coin toss process to highlight core concepts. However, most of the literature we survey focuses on settings with two demographic groups, while our abstraction generalizes naturally to multiple groups. Specifically, group fairness with N demographic groups can be modeled using N coin toss processes running in parallel, one for each group.

Example 4 (Loan approval). A classical example in the fairness literature is loan approval [15], where a bank uses a classifier to predict whether a customer will repay a loan and decides accordingly. The ground truth outcome (repayment or default) is assumed to be revealed later. Formally, an individual at time $t \in \mathbb{N}$ is described by a feature vector (g_t, y_t, z_t), consisting of a protected attribute $g_t \in \mathcal{G} = \{g_1, \ldots, g_m\}$ (group membership), a hidden ground truth $y_t \in \{0,1\}$ (loan repayment), and other features $z_t \in \mathcal{Z}$. The population is modeled by some distribution $\mathcal{D}_t \in \Delta(\mathcal{G} \times \mathcal{Y} \times \mathcal{Z})$, and the classifier $f_t \colon \mathcal{G} \times \mathcal{Z} \to \{0,1\}$ maps observable features to a binary decision (accept or reject).

Commonly Studied Group Fairness Properties. Although Example 4 concerns loan repayment, the same formalism applies to any classification task with protected attributes. Fairness requires treating demographic groups, defined by their protected attribute, equally. The notion of "equal treatment" is imprecise, as various group fairness properties exist, each tied to a specific welfare metric (see Sec. 4.1 in [39]). We illustrate two widely studied properties—*demographic parity* and *equal opportunity*—within our coin-toss abstraction. Demographic parity compares the classifiers acceptance probabilities between the groups, i.e.,

$$\mathbb{P}_{\mathcal{D}_t}(f_t(Z_t, G_t) = 1 \mid G_t = g), \quad \text{for } g \in \mathcal{G}.$$

Equal opportunity compares the classifiers acceptance probabilities among those members of the groups that do repay the loan, i.e.,

$$\mathbb{P}_{\mathcal{D}_t}(f_t(Z_t, G_t) = 1 \mid G_t = g, Y_t = 1), \quad \text{for } g \in \mathcal{G}.$$

In both cases, the acceptance probability for group g at time t can be modeled by the bias p_t^g of a coin. Fairness over infinite horizons corresponds to convergence of all p_t^g to a common value; in finite horizons, it corresponds to a small deviation from a reference value. Our coin model can capture changes due to retraining or shifts in population distribution via appropriate dynamics functions.

Monitoring and Enforcement. The monitoring and enforcement problems naturally generalize to the N-coin setting by having N monitors or enforcers, one for each group. In some cases, monitoring or enforcing an aggregate property (e.g., the difference in acceptance rates between two groups) may be more efficient than tracking each group individually. While such optimizations are often used in two-group settings, we do not explore them in this paper, as they are problem-specific optimizations.

7.3 Summary

Monitoring algorithmic fairness has been explored for static distributions [3], observable [25] and hidden Markov chains [27,28], and for additive and linear dynamical systems [26]. The enforcement problem has received less attention and often assumes stronger restrictions. We examined enforcement under very mild assumptions and thoroughly covered enforcement in static systems with known dynamics, where the main technical challenge is constructing outcome fairness enforcers that are cost-optimal or nearly so [14].

Tables 1 and 2 summarise the monitoring and enforcement results discussed in this paper. Each super-column represents a fairness property, i.e., outcome fairness φ_O, bias fairness φ_B, and current fairness φ_C. Each sub-column represents the predictive horizon, i.e., $h \in \{0, n, \infty\}$. Each row represents a particular assumption on the system. The cells indicate the section where we addressed the induced monitoring or enforcing problem. We also indicate which cases are trivial to solve and which are unfeasible (✗); entries are left blank when a detailed treatment was not included.

Table 1. Summary of all surveyed monitoring results.

$\rho_t^h(\cdot;\varphi)$	φ_O			φ_B			φ_C		
	0	n	∞	0	n	∞	0	n	∞
no assumptions (1&2)	S. 3.3.1		✗			✗			✗
known static (5&9)	Trivial			Trivial			Trivial		
unknown static (5)	— S. 4.1 —			— S. 4.1 —			— S. 4.1 —		
observed Markov (6)	S. 3.3.1	S. 4.2		— S. 4.2 —			— S. 4.2 —		
hidden Markov (7)	S. 3.3.1		S. 4.3			S. 4.3			S. 4.3
additive dynamics (8)	S. 3.3.1			S. 4.4			S. 4.4		

Table 2. Summary of all surveyed enforcement results.

$\tilde{\rho}_t^h(\cdot;\varphi)$				φ_O			φ_B			φ_C		
				0	n	∞	0	n	∞	0	n	∞
no assumptions (1&2)				✗	✗	✗	✗	✗	✗			S. 3.3.3
feasible intervals (3&4)							— S. 3.3.3 —			— S. 3.3.3 —		S. 3.3.3
known dynamics (9)	static system (5)	finite (10)		S. 5.1.1			Trivial			Trivial		
		finite a.s. (10&12)		S. 5.1.2			Trivial			Trivial		
		periodic (11)		S. 5.2			Trivial			Trivial		
	Dynamic			S. 5.3								

8 Conclusion

We presented a unified perspective on runtime fairness through the lens of a simplified coin-toss setting. Within this abstraction, we formulated general problem statements for fairness monitoring and enforcement. For each surveyed work, we clarified its assumptions and results, and explained how its methods address the proposed problems.

Future Work. We discussed fairness notions such as current and bias fairness, which represent two extremes: the former considers only the most recent outcome, while the latter averages over the entire history. A promising direction is to introduce discounted fairness measures that interpolate between these extremes. Another avenue for future research is the integration of monitoring and enforcement, thus allowing the enforcement of systems with unknown dynamics.

Acknowledgments. This work is supported by the European Research Council under Grant No.: ERC-2020-AdG 101020093.

Disclosure of Interests. The authors have no competing interests to declare that are relevant to the content of this article.

References

1. Alamdari, P.A., Klassen, T.Q., Creager, E., Mcilraith, S.A.: Remembering to be fair: non-Markovian fairness in sequential decision making. In: Proceedings of the International Conference on Machine Learning (ICML), vol. 235, pp. 906–920. PMLR (2024)
2. Albarghouthi, A., D'Antoni, L., Drews, S., Nori, A.V.: Fairsquare: probabilistic verification of program fairness. Proc. ACM Program. Lang. **1**(OOPSLA), 1–30 (2017)
3. Albarghouthi, A., Vinitsky, S.: Fairness-aware programming. In: Proceedings of the Conference on Fairness, Accountability, and Transparency, pp. 211–219 (2019)
4. Baier, C., Haverkort, B., Hermanns, H., Katoen, J.P.: Model-checking algorithms for continuous-time Markov chains. IEEE Trans. Softw. Eng. **29**(6), 524–541 (2003). https://doi.org/10.1109/TSE.2003.1205180
5. Balunovic, M., Ruoss, A., Vechev, M.: Fair normalizing flows. In: International Conference on Learning Representations (2021)
6. Barocas, S., Hardt, M., Narayanan, A.: Fairness and Machine Learning Limitations and Opportunities. MIT Press (2023)
7. Bartocci, E., et al.: Specification-based monitoring of cyber-physical systems: a survey on theory, tools and applications. In: Lectures on Runtime Verification, pp. 135–175. Springer (2018)
8. Bastani, O., Zhang, X., Solar-Lezama, A.: Probabilistic verification of fairness properties via concentration. Proc. ACM Program. Lang. **3**(OOPSLA), 1–27 (2019)
9. Bellamy, R.K., et al.: Ai fairness 360: an extensible toolkit for detecting and mitigating algorithmic bias. IBM J. Res. Dev. **63**(4/5), 4:1-4:15 (2019)
10. Berk, R., Heidari, H., Jabbari, S., Kearns, M., Roth, A.: Fairness in criminal justice risk assessments: the state of the art. Sociol. Methods Res. **50**(1), 3–44 (2021)
11. Bird, S., et al.: FairLearn: a toolkit for assessing and improving fairness in AI. Microsoft, Technical Report, MSR-TR-2020-32 (2020)
12. Cano, F., Henzinger, T.A., Königshofer, B., Kueffner, K., Mallik, K.: Abstraction-based decision making for statistical properties. In: International Conference on Formal Structures for Computation and Deduction (FSCD). LIPIcs, vol. 299, pp. 2:1–2:17. Schloss Dagstuhl - Leibniz-Zentrum für Informatik (2024)
13. Cano, F., Henzinger, T.A., Kueffner, K.: Algorithmic fairness: a runtime perspective. arXiv preprint arXiv:2507.20711 (2025)

14. Cano, F., Henzinger, T.A., Könighofer, B., Kueffner, K., Mallik, K.: Fairness shields: safeguarding against biased decision makers. Proc. AAAI Conf. Artif. Intell. **39**(15), 15659–15668 (2025)
15. D'Amour, A., Srinivasan, H., Atwood, J., Baljekar, P., Sculley, D., Halpern, Y.: Fairness is not static: deeper understanding of long term fairness via simulation studies. In: Proceedings of the Conference on Fairness, Accountability, and Transparency (FAccT), pp. 525–534 (2020)
16. Donzé, A., Maler, O.: Robust satisfaction of temporal logic over real-valued signals. In: International Conference on Formal Modeling and Analysis of Timed Systems, pp. 92–106. Springer (2010)
17. Dressel, J., Farid, H.: The accuracy, fairness, and limits of predicting recidivism. Sci. Adv. **4**(1), eaao5580 (2018)
18. Dwork, C., Hardt, M., Pitassi, T., Reingold, O., Zemel, R.: Fairness through awareness. In: Proceedings of the 3rd Innovations in Theoretical Computer Science Conference (ITCS), pp. 214–226. ACM, New York, NY, USA (2012)
19. Dwork, C., Hardt, M., Pitassi, T., Reingold, O., Zemel, R.: Fairness through awareness. In: Proceedings of the 3rd Innovations in Theoretical Computer Science Conference, pp. 214–226 (2012)
20. Faymonville, P., Finkbeiner, B., Schwenger, M., Torfah, H.: Real-time stream-based monitoring. arXiv preprint arXiv:1711.03829 (2017)
21. Ghosh, B., Basu, D., Meel, K.S.: Algorithmic fairness verification with graphical models. arXiv preprint arXiv:2109.09447 (2021)
22. Ghosh, B., Basu, D., Meel, K.S.: Justicia: a stochastic sat approach to formally verify fairness. In: Proceedings of the AAAI Conference on Artificial Intelligence (AAAI), vol. 35, pp. 7554–7563 (2021)
23. Hardt, M., Price, E., Srebro, N.: Equality of opportunity in supervised learning. In: Advances in Neural Information Processing Systems (NeurIPS), pp. 3315–3323 (2016)
24. Heidari, H., Nanda, V., Gummadi, K.P.: On the long-term impact of algorithmic decision policies: effort unfairness and feature segregation through social learning. arXiv preprint arXiv:1903.01209 (2019)
25. Henzinger, T.A., Karimi, M., Kueffner, K., Mallik, K.: Monitoring algorithmic fairness. In: Proceedings of the International Computer Aided Verification (CAV), pp. 358–382. Springer, Verlag (2023)
26. Henzinger, T.A., Karimi, M., Kueffner, K., Mallik, K.: Runtime monitoring of dynamic fairness properties. In: Proceedings of the ACM Conference on Fairness, Accountability, and Transparency (FAccT), pp. 604–614. ACM (2023). https://doi.org/10.1145/3593013.3594028
27. Henzinger, T.A., Kueffner, K., Mallik, K.: Monitoring algorithmic fairness under partial observations. In: International Conference on Runtime Verification (RV), pp. 291–311. Springer (2023)
28. Henzinger, T.A., Kueffner, K., Mallik, K.: Monitoring static fairness. arXiv preprint arXiv:2507.03048 (2025)
29. Hoeffding, W.: Probability inequalities for sums of bounded random variables. J. Am. Stat. Assoc. **58**(301), 13–30 (1963)
30. Howard, S.R., Ramdas, A., McAuliffe, J., Sekhon, J.: Time-uniform, nonparametric, nonasymptotic confidence sequences. Ann. Stat. **49**(2), 1055–1080 (2021)
31. Jagielski, M., et al.: Differentially private fair learning. In: International Conference on Machine Learning, pp. 3000–3008. PMLR (2019)

32. John, P.G., Vijaykeerthy, D., Saha, D.: Verifying individual fairness in machine learning models. In: Conference on Uncertainty in Artificial Intelligence, pp. 749–758. PMLR (2020)
33. Junges, S., Torfah, H., Seshia, S.A.: Runtime monitors for Markov decision processes. In: International Conference on Computer Aided Verification, pp. 553–576. Springer (2021)
34. Kearns, M., Neel, S., Roth, A., Wu, Z.S.: Preventing fairness gerrymandering: auditing and learning for subgroup fairness. In: International Conference on Machine Learning, pp. 2564–2572. PMLR (2018)
35. Konstantinov, N.H., Lampert, C.: Fairness-aware PAC learning from corrupted data. JMLR **23** (2022)
36. Kusner, M.J., Loftus, J., Russell, C., Silva, R.: Counterfactual fairness. Adv. Neural Inf. Process. Syst. **30** (2017)
37. Liu, L.T., Dean, S., Rolf, E., Simchowitz, M., Hardt, M.: Delayed impact of fair machine learning. In: International Conference on Machine Learning, pp. 3150–3158. PMLR (2018)
38. Maler, O., Nickovic, D.: Monitoring temporal properties of continuous signals. In: International Symposium on Formal Techniques in Real-Time and Fault-Tolerant Systems, pp. 152–166. Springer (2004)
39. Mehrabi, N., Morstatter, F., Saxena, N., Lerman, K., Galstyan, A.: A survey on bias and fairness in machine learning. ACM CSUR **54**(6), 1–35 (2021)
40. Meyer, A., Albarghouthi, A., D'Antoni, L.: Certifying robustness to programmable data bias in decision trees. Adv. Neural Inf. Process. Syst. (NeurIPS) **34**, 26276–26288 (2021)
41. Obermeyer, Z., Powers, B., Vogeli, C., Mullainathan, S.: Dissecting racial bias in an algorithm used to manage the health of populations. Science **366**(6464), 447–453 (2019)
42. Scheuerman, M.K., Paul, J.M., Brubaker, J.R.: How computers see gender: an evaluation of gender classification in commercial facial analysis services. Proc. ACM Hum.-Comput. Interact. **3**(CSCW), 1–33 (2019)
43. Sharifi-Malvajerdi, S., Kearns, M., Roth, A.: Average individual fairness: algorithms, generalization and experiments. Adv. Neural Inf. Process. Syst. **32** (2019)
44. Stoller, S.D., et al.: Runtime verification with state estimation. In: International Conference on Runtime Verification, pp. 193–207. Springer (2011)
45. Sun, B., Sun, J., Dai, T., Zhang, L.: Probabilistic verification of neural networks against group fairness. In: International Symposium on Formal Methods, pp. 83–102. Springer (2021)
46. Wexler, J., Pushkarna, M., Bolukbasi, T., Wattenberg, M., Viégas, F., Wilson, J.: The what-if tool: interactive probing of machine learning models. IEEE Trans. Visual Comput. Graph. **26**(1), 56–65 (2019)
47. Zemel, R., Wu, Y., Swersky, K., Pitassi, T., Dwork, C.: Learning fair representations. In: International Conference on Machine Learning, pp. 325–333. PMLR (2013)

DSLs for Runtime Verification

Klaus Havelund[1], Moran Omer[2], and Doron Peled[2(✉)]

[1] Jet Propulsion Laboratory, California Institute of Technology, Pasadena, USA
[2] Bar Ilan University, Ramat Gan, Israel
doron.peled@gmail.com

Abstract. Runtime verification (RV) allows monitoring executions of systems against formal specifications. A major challenge in increasing the capabilities and scope of formal methods stems from the tradeoff in increasing the expressiveness of the specification formalism used, while taming down the complexity of the involved algorithms and preserving the succinctness of the specifications. The focus of RV on a single execution at a time allows great flexibility in the way RV is implemented and towards achieving these goals. We focus here on the possibilities for implementing RV logics as external DSLs (Domain-Specific Languages), internal DSLs, and hybrid DSLs - a mix of the two. We also address the use of AI to generate monitors from natural language requirements. We survey the possibilities and focus in particular on the effect it has on achieving a desired level of expressiveness. A concrete challenge on which we focus here is allowing the use of arithmetic operations and relations on data that appear in the monitored events.

1 Introduction

Runtime Verification (RV) includes the monitoring of system executions, checking them against formal specifications. Three key parameters in applying RV are Expressiveness of the formalism that is used for writing specifications, Elegance (including succinctness) of the formalism, and the Efficiency of the verification process, which we refer to as *the three E's*. Among formal methods, RV is one of the most open-ended in that it allows for writing monitors in a spectrum of languages, ranging from dedicated domain-specific languages (logics) to general-purpose programming languages. It involves instrumenting the code to emit a sequence of events that can be analyzed and compared against a (potentially formal) specification. Focusing on a single trace provides flexibility in choosing the specification formalism. The selection of the formalism needs to accord with the possibility of maintaining efficiency, in particular when RV is applied online and needs to keep track with the pace of the intercepted events. There is also

---

K. Havelund—The research performed by the first author was carried out at Jet Propulsion Laboratory, California Institute of Technology, under a contract with the National Aeronautics and Space Administration. The research performed by the second and third authors was partially funded by Israeli Science Foundation grant 2454/23: "Validating and controlling software and hardware systems assisted by machine learning".

an advantage in employing "standard" specification formalisms, used broadly and interpreted uniformly and being able to express the specification property succinctly. There is often a tradeoff between the three E's. A classical example of such a tradeoff is between using propositional LTL and monadic first order logic [36]; both have the same expressiveness, only that the complexity of deciding the latter is nonelementary higher than the former, but can allow specifications that are nonelementary shorter than the former.

It is not surprising then to witness that there is a large spectrum of RV tools. We survey here alternatives for implementing RV logics as Domain-Specific Languages (DSLs), namely *external, internal* and *hybrid* DSLs. In brief, an external DSL is a, usually "tiny", language with its own grammar and parser, existing independently from the programming language it is implemented in. In contrast, an internal DSL is embedded in a programming language, e.g., as a library. A hybrid DSL is a mix of the two. One tradeoff in selecting the specification formalism for RV is between the use of a "programming language" style formalism versus a "logic-based" formalism. The use of a programming language as a formalism allows a high degree of flexibility in describing the desired property. It permits using programming tricks to implement the runtime verification checks. On the other hand, a formal logic specification is usually succinct, and can benefit from an efficient implementation. It also makes it easier to convince oneself that the specification conforms to what was intended.

We provide examples of RV tools that fit the corresponding DSL categories, and outline advantages and disadvantages. We specifically compare the fitness of different approaches for implementing RV tools w.r.t. the ability to support specifications that include the following ingredients:

– Reasoning about traces with events that contain data.
– Comparing between data items that appear in different events with respect to first-order quantification (*exists, forall*).
– Using functions and relations from signatures such as the natural numbers, reals, strings, etc. in the specification.

In general, obtaining the three ingredients (E's) together, in their full optima, might not easily be an achievable goal. One can observe a progress from using propositional specification, as in, e.g., [25] into first-order specification [5,24] and then adding a restricted ability of using objects interpreted over integers or strings [21]. As a forward-looking perspective, the emergence of Large Language Models (LLMs) may bring us closer to achieving the three E's by allowing the generation of efficient monitors from expressive abstract high level natural language specifications. This will also be discussed.

The paper is organized as follows. Section 2 provides some comments on moving from propositional to first-order specification in the fields of formal verification and runtime verification. Section 3 provides an overview of the various flavors of DSLs. Section 4 describes a file system and its requirements, which will be used as a running example to illustrate the different approaches. Section 5 discusses external DSLs. Section 6 discusses internal DSLs. Section 7 discusses hybrid DSLs. Section 8 discusses the relevance and application of LLMs to RV synthesis. Finally, Sect. 9 concludes the paper.

Related Work

Several RV tools have been developed over time, and giving a complete overview would be a daunting task. In this section, we only mention a few which are not otherwise discussed in this paper. Some early tools supported data comparison and computations as part of the logic, including, e.g. RULER [4] (external DSL). The version of the tool MONPOLY (external DSL) in [5] supports comparisons and aggregate operations such as sum and maximum/minimum within a first-order LTL formalism. It uses a database-oriented implementation. Other tools that support limited first-order capabilities based on automata include MARQ [35] (external DSL) and LARVASTAT [7] (hybrid DSL). In [10] a framework is described that elevates the monitor synthesis for a propositional temporal logic to a temporal logic TDL (external DSL) over a first-order theory, using an SMT solver, and implemented in the $Junit^{RV}$ tool. Several internal DSLs for RV have been developed that offer the full power of the host programming language for writing monitors and, therefore, allow for arbitrary comparisons and computations on data to be performed. These include TRACECONTRACT [3], DAUT [18], LOGFIRE [19], and BEEPBEEP [17]. Stream processing systems such as LOLA [9] and TESSLA [28] (external DSLs), and HSTRIVER [16] (hybrid DSL) offer expressive DSLs, and support the concept of communicating monitors. Another related work on increasing the expressive power of temporal logic is the extension of DEJAVU with rules (external DSL) described in [23].

2 From Propositional to First-Order Specification

In this section we relate RV to the field of formal verification w.r.t. the expressiveness of the specification. In both fields we can observe a transition from propositional specifications to first-order specifications over data. In formal verification this quickly leads to undecidability, whereas in RV the concern is usually related to efficiency.

Verifying the correctness of systems is, in general, undecidable. Even the basic problem of proving that a given sequential algorithm terminates on a particular input is undecidable. In the early 80s it was observed that limiting the focus of verification to finite state systems, with a careful selection of a specification formalism, in particular based on propositional temporal logics or finite automata, allows applying effective decision procedures [14,34], which are now referred to as *model checking*. Restricting the verification to a finite model is a nontrivial limitation; it prohibits verifying algorithms that are based on data structures such as trees or queues, where the size of the data structure is not restricted. This also applies to algorithms that operate on unrestricted numerical values or strings. Nevertheless, model checking has gained a huge success and it is often sufficient to use a finite state abstraction, or to, at least, find errors by checking an implementation of the software with concrete restrictions on the size of the memory or the number of bits that is used to store numerical values.

One way to extend model checking beyond the Boolean based temporal logic and state representation is based on Bounded Model Checking (BMC). For finite state spaces and propositional based specification, BMC can use a SAT solver. Extending the scope beyond finite state systems calls for using SMT (Satisfiability Modulo Theory) solvers [2]. Still, inherent undecidability of the satisfiability for common domains (based on Gödel incompleteness for the naturals), forces limitations on this approach: either by using decidable domains, or by allowing the occasional failures of the SMT solvers (e.g., in the sense that the operation may time out).

In runtime verification, one concentrates on a single execution at a time. This is a more modest target than model checking, which addresses the entire set of executions of a system. This raises the hopes for additional capabilities of RV, especially w.r.t. expressiveness and efficiency. Indeed, progressing from propositional based specification and events encoded as Boolean minterms into first-order specification and events with data is achievable with quite efficient tools and algorithms. For example, MONPOLY [5] and DEJAVU [24] are based on first-order (past) linear temporal logic and allows events with data[1].

Adding the ability to use functions and relations from a signature that includes e.g., the natural numbers or strings is another leap in expressiveness that needs to be dealt with carefully. This capability can entail undecidability in RV. For example, it is undecidable, in general, to calculate a verdict for Diophantine equations [30], e.g., written in the form $\forall y\,(p(y) \rightarrow \exists x\, \exists z\, (x^2+z^2+y = 0))$, where $p(y)$ refers to an event with some value set to the variable y ($p(y)$ is used to make the decision depend on the input trace). In fact, this is undecidable with a single event of the form $p(y)$. However, such undecidable specifications are very unlikely to be the focus of RV in practice. Instead, going from propositional to first-order specification in RV can make the calculation of the verdict complex to compute. Consider for example: $\forall x\,(p(x) \rightarrow \exists y \exists z (\diamondsuit\, q(y) \wedge \diamondsuit\, q(z) \wedge y \neq z \wedge x = (y+z)/2))$, where $\diamondsuit$ means *previously in the past*. Verifying such a property is hard to implement efficiently, since the property requires that a new p event has a value that is the average of two distinct values observed in previous q events. This means remembering and comparing the new value of all p events against all the previous values that appeared in previously observed q events, which is growing unboundedly. This defies optimizations that are typical to RV tools with a rigid syntax (implemented as an external DSL). But it can be expressed within a tool that is open for "programming" the way we would express this property in an internal DSL or a hybrid DSL.

3 Classification of Domain-Specific Languages

In this section, we provide an overview of the various types of DSLs, highlighting their advantages and disadvantages. DSLs are specialized languages designed

---

[1] MonPoly supports assertions about a fixed number of future steps.

to simplify the expression of domain-specific tasks by providing constructs that closely align with particular domain concepts. This focus allows DSLs to enhance productivity and reduce errors compared to general-purpose programming languages.

DSLs play a significant role in runtime verification by offering tailored constructs that make it easier to specify and monitor system behaviors. They can be categorized into three main types based on their interaction with a host language. A host language refers to a general-purpose programming language, such as Python, Java, or Scala, that provides the underlying environment in which a DSL operates. The three types of DSLs are: external DSLs, which are completely separate from the host language they are implemented in (i.e., no host-language code is written by a user); internal DSLs, which are embedded directly within the host language (the specification language is the host language); and hybrid DSLs, which combine elements of both, offering a balance between domain specificity and flexibility. Figure 1 provides a visual overview of this classification.

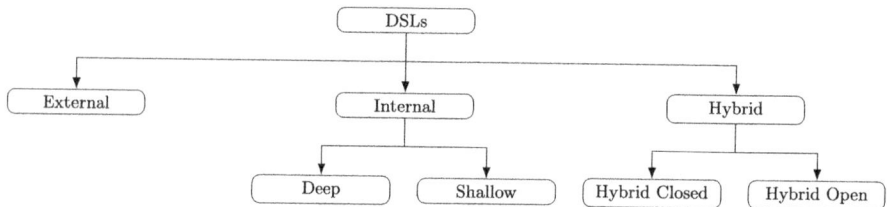

Fig. 1. DSL categorization.

3.1 External DSLs

External DSLs are stand alone languages with dedicated grammars, parsers, and interpreters or compilers, designed to address specific domain requirements independently of any host language. These languages provide users with a concise, domain-focused syntax that simplifies analysis, optimization, and transformations. They enhance reliability by making specifications more formal and analyzable. However, external DSLs come with increased implementation complexity due to the need for dedicated parsing and interpretation machinery. Additionally, their rigid structure makes it challenging to adapt to evolving requirements, a phenomenon known as "requirement creep", where new or unforeseen needs necessitate extending the language's capabilities. As discussed in [22], this can e.g. involve adding support for complex operations like arithmetic comparisons or timing constraints, features without which the language may become too limited for practical use. We illustrate some of the advantages and difficulties in using external DSLs based on the systems DEJAVU [11,24] and TP-DEJAVU [21,37].

3.2 Internal DSLs

Internal DSLs leverage the existing infrastructure of a host programming language. Unlike external DSLs that require dedicated parsers and interpreters, internal DSLs are implemented as libraries within the host language, making them more accessible and maintainable. These DSLs come in two distinct varieties.

Deep internal DSLs represent specifications or programs as data structures within the host language. This design choice means that a formula by the user is specified as an object of a data type. An external DSL is usually parsed from text into an abstract syntax tree, which is then processed further. In a deep internal DSL, we skip the parsing of text, and the specification writer manually creates the abstract syntax tree, potentially using various auxiliary functions. The implementation in [19] demonstrates this approach, presenting a runtime verification DSL that is mostly deep in nature but extends the paradigm by allowing code as part of the specification. BEEPBEEP [17] is another example. Such deep DSLs share most of the qualities of external DSLs in that they are easier to analyze, optimize, and transform, though they provide less succinct notation than external DSLs for users and are limited in expressiveness (as external DSLs). We do not present an example of a deep internal DSL in this paper.

Shallow internal DSLs, in contrast, embrace the full expressiveness of the host programming language. Deep DSLs offer better analytical properties and optimization potential but sacrifice expressiveness. Shallow DSLs provide full computational power but make static analysis and optimization more challenging, often requiring sophisticated meta-programming techniques to reason about the code. From an implementation perspective, internal DSLs typically reduce development overhead by eliminating the need for separate parsing and interpretation infrastructure. However, this comes at the cost of syntax flexibility, the DSL must conform to the host language's syntactic constraints. This limitation often leads to less concise specifications compared to purpose-built external DSLs. The success of internal DSLs in practice can be highly dependent on the programming language chosen. E.g., an internal DSL in Python is more likely to be adopted than an internal DSL in Cobol. Their integration into existing development environments and toolchains makes them particularly attractive for scenarios where seamless interoperability with existing code is prioritized over domain-specific syntactic optimization. Internal DSLs can be well suited for more general data analysis, where the result of monitoring are data of arbitrary data types, rather than just Boolean yes/no/don't know verdicts [12]. We illustrate this category with the PYCONTRACT [8,32] Python RV library.

3.3 Hybrid DSL

Hybrid DSLs represent a language design approach that combines features of both external and internal DSLs to leverage their respective strengths while mitigating their limitations. We categorize them into two distinct types: Hybrid Closed DSLs and Hybrid Open DSLs.

Hybrid Closed DSLs are external DSLs that are used/called from within a programming language. An illustrative example is Python's MySQL library [13], which allows a Python program to execute MySQL statements provided as text strings. This is a hybrid solution since the DSL is invoked from a programming language, and closed since from within the DSL there is no reference back to the programming language. One may refer to such DSLs as *programming language first* DSLs. We illustrate this category with the PyDeJaVu [22,33] DSL.

Hybrid Open DSLs go in the opposite direction by allowing an external DSL to contain statements in a programming language, typically within special brackets. One may refer to such DSLs as *programming language second* DSLs. The UNIX yacc parser generator [27] exemplifies this approach, where the grammar is specified in an external DSL while semantic actions are implemented in C within curly brackets. This is a hybrid solution since the programming language is invoked from the DSL, and open since from within the DSL there is reference back to the programming language. The aspect-oriented AspectJ language [29] is another example of a hybrid open DSL, since aspects (external DSL) can contain Java code. We do not present an example of a hybrid open DSL in this paper. RV examples include LarvaStat [7] and HStriver [16].

4 The File System Example

In this section we introduce an example that will be used to demonstrate the different approaches. The example is in particular meant to illustrate the need for different levels of expressiveness of the DSLs, and to illustrate the difference w.r.t. elegance of expression. Consider a simple UNIX-like file system, where a user can create and delete folders, open and close files in folders, and write to and read from files. The concrete events that we can monitor are the following.

create(F)	Create a folder F.
delete(F)	Delete a folder F.
open(F,f,m,s)	Open file f in folder F, with access mode m, and if write mode, a maximum writable size s in bytes.
close(f)	Close file f.
write(f,d)	Write data d (a string) to file f.
read(f)	Read from file f.

Access modes are read or write. If the mode is write, the size parameter s indicates how many bytes are maximally allowed to be written to the file. In the case of read mode it is irrelevant.

We can now formulate the requirements that we want to monitor using the different DSLs.

R_{folder} A file must be opened in a folder that has been created and not deleted since.

R_{write} If data is written to a file, the file must have been opened in write mode, not closed since, and must reside in a folder that has been created and not deleted since.

R_{total} The total number of bytes written to all files must not exceed a specified `max` value.

R_{size} The number of bytes written to a file must not exceed the `size` parameter of the open event.

R_{close} A file that is opened must eventually be closed.

The properties R_{folder} and R_{write} are past time properties. Property R_{close} is a future time property. These properties only require knowledge of identity of data observed in events. Properties R_{total} and R_{size} require storing and comparing data values. Property R_{total} only needs one summary value. Property R_{size} is slightly more complicated as it requires storing and comparison of data values per file.

5 External DSLs

In this section we present two external DSLs, namely DEJAVU, a pure temporal logic, and TP-DEJAVU which adds operational features expanding expressiveness.

5.1 The DEJAVU Temporal Logic

The tool DEJAVU [11,24] is an external DSL. Its specification language is QTL, which is first-order past linear temporal logic. A DEJAVU specification uses relation symbols to represent events. The relation symbols are uninterpreted, and the only real relation is equivalence. In fact, equivalence is intrinsic to the specification by the multiple use of a variable name within the same scope of quantification rather than explicit, e.g., by using the standard = notation.

QTL **Syntax.** The formulas of the QTL logic are defined using the following grammar, where p stands for a *predicate* symbol, a is a *constant* and x is a *variable*. For simplicity of the presentation, we define here the QTL logic with unary predicates, but this is not due to a principal restriction, and in fact DEJAVU supports predicates over multiple arguments, including zero arguments, corresponding to propositions.

$$\varphi ::= true \mid p(a) \mid p(x) \mid (\varphi \wedge \varphi) \mid \neg\varphi \mid (\varphi \, \mathcal{S} \, \varphi) \mid \ominus\varphi \mid \exists x \, \varphi$$

A formula can be interpreted over multiple types (domains), e.g., natural numbers or strings. Accordingly, each variable, constant and parameter of a predicate is defined over a specific type. Type matching is enforced, e.g., between $p(a)$

and $p(x)$, where the types of the parameter of p and of a must be the same. We denote the type of a variable x by $type(x)$. *Propositional* past time linear temporal logic is obtained by restricting the predicates to be parameterless, essentially Boolean propositions. In this case no variables, constants and quantification are needed either.

QTL subformulas have the following informal meaning: $p(a)$ is true if the last event in the trace is $p(a)$. The formula $p(x)$, for some variable x, holds if x is bound to a constant a such that $p(a)$ is the last event in the trace. The formula $(\varphi \, S \, \psi)$, which reads as φ *since* ψ, means that ψ occurred in the past (including now) and since then (beyond that state) φ has been true. (The *since* operator is the past dual of the future time *until* modality in the commonly used future time temporal logic.) The property $\ominus \varphi$ means that φ is true in the trace that is obtained from the current one by omitting the last event. The formula $\exists x \, \varphi$ is *true* if there exists a value a such that φ is true with x bound to a. We can also define the following additional derived operators: $\mathit{false} = \neg \mathit{true}$, $(\varphi \lor \psi) = \neg(\neg\varphi \land \neg\psi)$, $(\varphi \to \psi) = (\neg\varphi \lor \psi)$, $\blacklozenge \varphi = (\mathit{true} \, S \, \varphi)$ ("previously"), $\blacksquare \varphi = \neg \blacklozenge \neg \varphi$ ("always in the past" or "historically"), and $\forall x \, \varphi = \neg \exists x \, \neg \varphi$.

QTL **Formal semantics.** A QTL formula is interpreted over a *trace*, which is a finite sequence of *events*, with positions numbered $1, 2, \ldots$. Each event consists of a predicate symbol and parameters (no variables), e.g., $p(a)$, $q(7)$. Let $\mathit{free}(\varphi)$ be the set of free (i.e., unquantified) variables of φ. The bookkeeping of which variables are mapped to what values is recorded in *assignments*, which map variables to values. Let ϵ be the empty assignment. Let γ be an assignment to the variables $\mathit{free}(\varphi)$. We write $[v \mapsto a]$ to denote the assignment that consists of a single variable v mapped to value a. We denote by $\gamma[v \mapsto a]$ the assignment that differs from γ only by associating the value a to v. Let σ be a trace of events of length $|\sigma|$ and i a natural number, where $1 \leq i \leq |\sigma|$. Then $(\gamma, \sigma, i) \models \varphi$ denotes that φ holds for the prefix of length i of σ with the assignment γ. We denote by $\gamma|_{\mathit{free}(\varphi)}$ the restriction (projection) of an assignment γ to the free variables appearing in φ. The formal semantics of QTL is defined as follows, where $(\gamma, \sigma, i) \models \varphi$ is defined when γ is an assignment over $\mathit{free}(\varphi)$, and $1 \leq i \leq |\sigma|$.

- $(\epsilon, \sigma, i) \models \mathit{true}$.
- $(\epsilon, \sigma, i) \models p(a)$ if $\sigma[i] = p(a)$.
- $([x \mapsto a], \sigma, i) \models p(x)$ if $\sigma[i] = p(a)$.
- $(\gamma, \sigma, i) \models (\varphi \land \psi)$ if $(\gamma|_{\mathit{free}(\varphi)}, \sigma, i) \models \varphi$ and $(\gamma|_{\mathit{free}(\psi)}, \sigma, i) \models \psi$.
- $(\gamma, \sigma, i) \models \neg \varphi$ if not $(\gamma, \sigma, i) \models \varphi$.
- $(\gamma, \sigma, i) \models (\varphi \, S \, \psi)$ if for some $1 \leq j \leq i$, $(\gamma|_{\mathit{free}(\psi)}, \sigma, j) \models \psi$ and for all $j < k \leq i$, $(\gamma|_{\mathit{free}(\varphi)}, \sigma, k) \models \varphi$.
- $(\gamma, \sigma, i) \models \ominus \varphi$ if $i > 1$ and $(\gamma, \sigma, i-1) \models \varphi$.
- $(\gamma, \sigma, i) \models \exists x \, \varphi$ if there exists $a \in type(x)$ such that $(\gamma[x \mapsto a], \sigma, i) \models \varphi$.

As a representative DEJAVU specification, consider the property R_{write} (property R_{folder} is easily expressible as well and simpler). Informally, R_{write} asserts that if data is written to a file, the file must have been opened in write mode, not closed since, and must reside in a folder that has been created and not deleted since. The property is formalised below in a QTL-style mathematical notation and in Fig. 2 using DEJAVU syntax.

$$\forall f \, \forall d \, \text{write}(f, d) \rightarrow \begin{pmatrix} \exists F \, \exists s \\ \big((\neg \text{close}(f) \, \mathcal{S} \, \text{open}(F, f, "w", s)) \\ \wedge \, (\neg \text{delete}(F) \, \mathcal{S} \, \text{create}(F)) \big) \end{pmatrix}$$

```
prop Rwrite:
  forall f . forall d .
    write(f, d) ->
      (exists F . exists s .
        ((! close(f) S open(F, f, "w", s)) & (! delete(F) S create(F))))
```

Fig. 2. DEJAVU - an external declarative DSL.

The tool DEJAVU allows applying several optimizations on the implementation, which facilitates efficient monitoring. RV over propositional logic, where there is a finite number of events that can be encoded as Boolean combinations, requires only a finite amount of memory summarizing the observed trace, which is independent of the length of the inspected trace. Progressing into first-order temporal logic over events with data, such a summary cannot be bounded in length, as is obvious from the fact that in the above simple specification we must keep the growing set of values (e.g. file names, in this case) that appeared along the trace. However, the rigidity of DEJAVU permits optimizations that tame the size of the summary and the incremental complexity needed to update it each time a new event appears. This is done based on the following principles:

1. The values that appear in events are mapped into short bitstrings. This can be done, e.g., by enumerating the values by natural numbers as they appear, and then map these into their binary representation (note that the original values need to be stored so that subsequent occurrences of the same value are mapped to the same bitstring).
2. Subformulas in the summary of the inspected trace correspond to relations over values, where the number of arguments equals the number of free variables in the subformula. These are encoded as BDDs over the bitstring representation.
3. Updating summaries can be performed by applying BDD operations.

These implementation steps, together with other tricks used (e.g., applying some garbage collection to the utilized bit vectors) tame down the amount of memory required to process very long traces of events, where one can easily process traces with hundreds of thousands of events. It also permits, in many cases, efficient processing that facilitates online runtime processing.

However, expanding the expressiveness of the specification language to include data type operator signatures, such as integer and string operators (e.g. $\leq, +, \ldots$), while maintaining the efficiency of the algorithm, is a challenge.

5.2 The TP-DEJAVU Extension of DEJAVU

A solution that goes well with an external DSL RV tool is to select a small set of constructs that extend the expressiveness of the used formalism, while maintaining the efficiency. Such an extension is implemented in the tool TP-DEJAVU [21,37]. Extending DEJAVU is limited to the use of a small number of relations over the selected signatures of integers and strings. Moreover, the use of these relations, when comparing values from different events, is limited to a fixed (small) distance from the current intercepted event. This allows implementing the extension by keeping a limited amount of additional information about the previous events. Although the allowed additional relations are fixed, there is a great flexibility in combining them. In fact, this is done by writing a small procedure in a syntax that resembles a simple programming language, that is executed in between intercepting the event and calling DEJAVU. This code can alter the event. In particular, it can use its finite memory and calculations to perform aggregation, e.g., calculating sums or maxima.

Specifically, TP-DEJAVU consists of two components, operating in a pipeline: a new *operational* component, and DEJAVU, which is referred to as a *declarative* component. The operational component has capabilities of using relations and functions from the given signatures (e.g., integers, strings, etc.). Upon interception of an event, the operational component makes some calculations that can involve applying comparisons with events from a fixed distance (e.g., previous event, two events before, etc.), which involve some storage whose size is fixed, i.e., independent of the size of the observed trace. The code depends on the relation that appears in the input event, e.g., the procedure for processing the input event `open(F, f, m, s)` is different from the procedure for processing the event `close(f)`. As a result of the calculation, a modified event is generated and sent to the declarative component. The latter just processes the new event according to the DEJAVU logic and correspondingly updates the verdict. The code for writing the operational procedures is implemented in its own external DSL, extending the first-order temporal specification of the declarative component.

The following example shows how TP-DEJAVU enforces the requirements R_{write} and R_{total}. As in the pure DEJAVU setting, we must guarantee that every write operation satisfies the file- and folder-integrity conditions. The added operational stage lets us maintain a running counter of the bytes written across all files and flag a violation once the cumulative total exceeds a user-defined limit max. Figure 3 contains the complete TP-DEJAVU specification, combining the counting logic in the operational phase with the declarative property checked by DEJAVU.

```
initiate
   total_size : int := 0
   max: int := 1000000

on open(F: str, f: str, m: str, s: int)
   output open(F, f, m)

on write(f: str, d: str)
   total_size : int := total_size + d.length
   ok: bool := total_size <= max
   output write(f, ok)
```

Operational Phase

```
prop Rwrite_total :
   forall f .
     ! write(f, "false") &
     (write(f, "true") ->
       ( exists F . (
         (! close(f) S open(F, f, "w")) &
         (! delete(F) S create(F)))))
```

Declarative Phase

Fig. 3. TP-DEJAVU - an external operational + declarative DSL.

In this specification, the variable total_size keeps track of the total number of bytes written so far. When an open event is intercepted, it is forwarded to DEJAVU without its size argument, because that value is irrelevant to the safety conditions. On each write event, total_size is incremented by the length of the payload; the event is then resubmitted to DEJAVU with a Boolean flag ok that is *true* iff total_size has not yet exceeded the threshold max. The DEJAVU formula requires that this value must never be *false*.

Adding the operational layer to DEJAVU allows a *controlled* addition of relations and functions from domains associated with rich signatures without extending the temporal logic to permit undecidability of providing a verdict. While gaining expressiveness, the elegance of the formalism, now injecting "programming" as part of the specification, is reduced. As a consequence, it is possible to write properties that less obviously represent the intension of the specification. Furthermore, the constructs that are allowed by this DSL are rather limited, and some further features are not permitted, e.g., the flexibility to use expandable vectors so that multiple maxima can be accumulated and used over the process of monitoring.

6 Internal DSLs

An internal DSL is a library in a general-purpose programming language, referred to as the host language. We distinguished in Sect. 3 between deep internal DSLs and shallow internal DSLs. In this section we shall write a monitor for all the properties presented in Sect. 4 using the shallow internal DSL PYCONTRACT [8,32], which is a Python library for writing monitors. PYCONTRACT is inspired by the DAUT [18,20] and TRACECONTRACT [3] Scala libraries based on similar ideas. All of these are again inspired by rule-based programming as introduced in the RULER system [4] in that the memory of a monitor is a set of facts, where a fact in its basic form is a named data record. However, unlike traditional rule systems seen e.g. in expert systems, facts in PYCONTRACT, like states in state machines, can have transitions which, upon triggering, can generate other facts, while removing the fact whose transition is taken. The important idea is that a state can be parameterized with data, which is not the case in traditional automata theory.

The Library. The library provides a class Monitor, which any monitor must subclass. This class has the following structure from an outside usage point of view:

```
class Monitor:
  def eval(self, event: object): ...   # contents omitted
  def end(self): ...                   # contents omitted
  def verify(self, trace: list[object]):
    for event in trace:
      self.eval(event)
    self.end()
  ...
```

Conceptually a monitor stores a set of active states. As we shall see (Fig. 5), a user can create an instance m of a monitor, call m.eval(e) for each observed event e, and finally optionally call m.end(). Each such call of m.eval(e) will cause the monitor to call an s.eval(e) method on each active state s, which can either result in a new set of states, or an unchanged state. The m.end() method checks if there are any so-called *hot* states (see below) in the memory, and produces error messages if so. These represent bounded future time properties, things that should have happened but did not at the end of the trace in case the trace is finite. An alternative, if a whole finite trace t is available, is to just call m.verify(t).

The Events. Monitors can monitor events of any legal Python type (all types subclass type object). We will in this case program the monitor to process dictionaries as events, specifically dictionaries representing the six file operations:

```
{'name': 'Create', 'folder': str}
{'name': 'Delete', 'folder': str}
{'name': 'Open'  , 'folder': str, 'filename': str,
                   'mode'  : str, 'size': int}
{'name': 'Close' , 'filename': str}
{'name': 'Write' , 'filename': str, 'data': str}
{'name': 'Read'  , 'filename': str}
```

As we shall see, we can perform pattern matching over such dictionaries. Another common style is to alternatively define each event type as a data class, which also allows to perform pattern matching over such event objects.

The Monitor. Our monitor class FileMon in Fig. 4 inherits from the class Monitor. We deliberately program the monitor as a mixture of traditional programming and temporal programming to show that the two paradigms can live together. Some monitoring problems are just easier to just program. In a traditional manner, to handle properties R_{folder} and R_{write}, we introduce two monitor local variables: max (Line 6), storing initially the maximal number of bytes that can be written to all files, a parameter to the monitor, and folders (Line 7), storing what folders are open at any time.

```
1   from pycontract import *
2
3   class FileMon(Monitor):
4       def __init__(self, max: int):
5           super().__init__()
6           self.max = max
7           self.folders: set[str] = set()
8
9       def transition(self, event):
10          match event:
11              case {'name': 'Create', 'folder': folder}:
12                  self.folders.add(folder)
13              case {'name': 'Delete', 'folder': folder}:
14                  self.folders.discard(folder)
15              case {'name': 'Open', 'folder': folder, 'filename': filename, 'mode': mode, 'size': size}:
16                  self.check(folder in self.folders, f'Folder {folder} not created')
17                  return FileMon.File(folder, filename, mode, size)
18              case {'name': 'Write', 'filename': filename, 'data': data}:
19                  if not self.exists(FileMon.File, name=filename):
20                      return error(f' file {filename} not opened')
21
22      @data
23      class File(HotState):
24          folder: str
25          name: str
26          mode: str
27          size: int
28
29          def transition(self, event):
30              match event:
31                  case {'name': 'Delete', 'folder': self.folder}:
32                      return error('folder deleted')
33                  case {'name': 'Close', 'filename': self.name}:
34                      return ok
35                  case {'name': 'Write', 'filename': self.name, 'data': data}:
36                      self.check(self.mode == 'write', f'File {self.name} not opened in write mode')
37                      self.check(len(data) <= self.size, f'File {self.name} size exceeded')
38                      self.check(len(data) <= self.monitor.max, f'Total bytes written exceeded max value')
39                      self.monitor.max -= len(data)
40                      return FileMon.File(self.folder, self.name, self.mode, self.size - len(data))
```

Fig. 4. PYCONTRACT - a shallow Python DSL.

The monitor defines a transition function (Line 9), which is applied to every event that is submitted to the monitor with the eval method, and which can be overridden by the user as shown here. The actual type of the transition method is:

```
def transition(self, event: object) ->
        Optional[State | List[State]]
```

The function returns either None (corresponding to no match, in which case the monitor remains unchanged), a state, or a list of states. Conceptually the result of monitoring an event is a list of new states, that all become active, and all of which must lead to success corresponding to a conjunction. A single returned state s is transformed to a singular list $[s]$.

The outermost transition function pattern matches on the incoming event. In the case of folder creation and deletion it just updates the folder variable. In the case of a file opening, it checks that the folder exists, and then returns a new state (Line 17), an object of the class File, representing the fact that this file has been opened. This class (state) is defined as an inner class of the monitor (Line 23). Note that if multiple files are open at the same time, multiple such states will exist. In the case of a write event, we check that there indeed exists such a File state for that file (Line 19), and if not an error state is returned. Note that we can, in this way, query the monitor memory for the existence of a state.

The File state itself (Line 23) is defined as a HotState, meaning that it is recorded as an error if such a state exists when the end() method is called. It is parameterized with the folder the file is created in, the file name, the access mode, and the maximal number of bytes that can be written to the file. The transition function (Line 29) returns an error if the folder is deleted while the File state exists. On the other hand, the state is peacefully removed (represented by ok) if the file is closed. Finally, in the case of a write event, it is checked that it was opened in write mode and that the total size as well as the file sizes are respected. A new File state is then returned (Line 40) with the remaining size allowed.

Using the Monitor. Figure 5 illustrates how the monitor can be applied to analyze a trace of events. Events can be fed, one by one, using the eval(event: object) method. In the case of a finite sequence of observations, for example when examining a log file, a call of the end() method tells the monitor that the sequence has ended. Note that end() may not be called when monitoring is online, but if it is called, any outstanding obligations that have not been satisfied (expected events that did not occur) will be reported as errors.

```
1   m = FileMon(1000000)
2   trace = [
3     {'name': 'Create', 'folder': 'folder1'},
4     {'name': 'Open', 'folder': 'folder1', 'filename': 'file1', 'mode': 'write', 'size': 1000},
5     {'name': 'Write', 'filename': 'file1', 'data': 'data1'},
6     {'name': 'Write', 'filename': 'file1', 'data': 'data2'},
7     {'name': 'Close', 'filename': 'file1'},
8     {'name': 'Delete', 'folder': 'folder1'}
9   ]
10  m.verify(trace)
```

Fig. 5. Using the monitor.

Other Features. PYCONTRACT offers many other features, such as always-states (always active), or-states (representing disjunction), not-states (representing negation), sequence-states (representing sequencing), next-states (failing if no transition cases match an event), grouping of monitors, and user-defined indexing (slicing) to optimize monitoring, similar to what is supported in RV systems such as MOP [31] and QEA [35]. Finally, monitors can be visualized using PlantUML.

7 Hybrid DSLs

PYDEJAVU [22,33] is a Python library that refactors TP-DEJAVU's external operational DSL into standard Python while retaining the original two-phase architecture. In the operational phase, every intercepted event is routed to a user-defined function marked with the decorator @event. Because these handlers are written in unrestricted Python, they can exploit the full Python language ecosystem such as loops, rich data structures such as lists, dictionaries, and sets, comprehensions over such, higher-order functions, and external libraries, before emitting a transformed event. The declarative phase remains the unmodified DEJAVU monitor, implemented in Scala and supporting the QTL temporal logic [11,24], as described in Sect. 5.1. Although DEJAVU is implemented in Scala, Python was chosen as the front-end language due to its widespread use[2].

Communication between the two phases is mediated by PyJNIus, a JNI bridge that allows the Python runtime to instantiate the JVM-hosted DEJAVU engine, push events, adjust configuration parameters on the fly, and retrieve verdicts or result files. Compared with TP-DEJAVU, this design greatly enlarges the space of computable pre-processing tasks (e.g., complex aggregation, pattern matching, or vector manipulation) while preserving the proven efficiency of DEJAVU's temporal reasoning core.

Figure 6 demonstrates the additional expressiveness that PYDEJAVU offers over both the plain DEJAVU and TP-DEJAVU examples. Besides enforcing R_{write}, the specification now incorporates R_{size}, which limits the number of bytes that can be written to each file individually. This per-file accounting is realized in the Python layer by a global dictionary available_space that maps every open file to its remaining quota, information that TP-DEJAVU cannot represent, and which would require an extension of the framework to capture.

The monitor is created with monitor = Monitor(specification), where the argument is a QTL specification given as a string. During execution, each incoming event triggers a handler function whose name is bound to the event by the @event annotation[3]. The handler may read or update available_space, perform

---
[2] Python is by several sources evaluated to be the most popular programming language at the time of writing [26].

[3] In Python, one can define a function D that takes a decoratable object (such as a function, method, class, ...) as an argument and returns a new object, we call D a decorator. If a function g is decorated with D using the @-sign (i.e., @D), then g is effectively replaced by $D(g)$. In the case of @event("open"), the call event("open") returns a decorator that modifies the function defined below it.

```
from pydejavu.core.monitor import Monitor, event

specification = """
  prop Rwrite_size :
    forall f .
      !write(f, "false") &
      (write(f, "true") ->
        (exists F . ((!close(f) S open(F, f, "w")) & (!delete(F) S create(F)))))
"""

monitor = Monitor(specification)
available_space : dict[str, int] = {}

@event("open")
def open(F: str, f: str, m: str, s: int):
    global available_space
    if m == "w":
        available_space[f] = s
    return ["open", F, f, m]

@event("close")
def close(f: str):
    global available_space
    del available_space[f]
    return ["close", f]

@event("write")
def write(f: str, d: str):
    global available_space
    if f not in available_space:
        available_space[f] = 0
    data_len = len(d)
    ok = available_space[f] >= data_len
    if ok:
        available_space[f] -= data_len
    return ["write", f, ok]

# ----------------------------
# Applying monitor to an example trace:
# ----------------------------

events = [
    {"name":"create", "args": ["tmp"]},
    {"name":"open", "args": ["tmp", "f1", "w", "10"]},
    {"name":"write", "args": ["f1", "some text"]},
]

for e in events:
    monitor.verify(e)
monitor.end()
```

Fig. 6. PyDejaVu - a hybrid closed DSL.

arbitrary computations, and then return either a list such as ["write", f, ok], which is forwarded to the declarative DejaVu core, or None, which suppresses forwarding. For events that need no preprocessing, like create or delete, no handler is required; those events flow directly to DejaVu, preserving the default behaviour.

8 Generating Monitors with LLMs

It is always possible to program a monitor in a general-purpose programming language without the use of a DSL (internal or external). However, such monitors may be laborious to program and it may be harder to convince oneself that they are correct. However, with the emergence of Large Language Models (LLMs) the situation may be changing. In this section we shall illustrate how a file system monitor can be generated in Python from a natural language specification, using no specific monitoring library. We used the Windsurf LLM-enhanced Visual Studio IDE [38], using the Gemini 2.5 Pro LLM [15]. Specifically, we provided a version of Sect. 4 as a prompt. In addition, we described the dictionary event types. Finally we asked it to use pattern matching over the events.

It responded with a long version, which was too large to fit a figure in the paper. We therefore asked it to refactor common code patterns into an abstract Monitor class, which can be seen in Fig. 7. We also asked it to shorten error messages to fit the paper width. However, the logic of the monitor stayed the exact same during these refactorings. The FileSystemMonitor can be seen in Fig. 8.

```
class Monitor(abc.ABC):
    @staticmethod
    def require(condition: bool, message: str):
        if not condition:
            raise Exception(message)

    def process_events(self, events: list[dict]):
        for i, event in enumerate(events):
            try:
                self.process_event(event)
            except Exception as e:
                raise Exception(f"Event {i+1} failed: {e}") from e
        self.finalize()
        print("OK")

    @abc.abstractmethod
    def process_event(self, event: dict):
        pass

    @abc.abstractmethod
    def finalize(self):
        pass
```

Fig. 7. Abstract Monitor class generated by the Gemini 2.5 LLM.

We notice that the FileSystemMonitor checks for more requirements than we originally requested, all of which, however, make perfect sense (we left these out originally in Sect. 4 to keep the problem small). The monitored requirements in addition to those in Sect. 4 are (Fig. 8):

- A folder cannot be created if it is already created and not deleted (Line 11)
- A folder must exists in order to be deleted (Line 15).

```
 1  class FileSystemMonitor(Monitor):
 2      def __init__ (self, max_total_bytes: int):
 3          self . max_total_bytes = max_total_bytes
 4          self . total_bytes_written = 0
 5          self . created_folders = set()
 6          self . open_files = {}
 7
 8      def process_event(self, event: dict):
 9          match event:
10              case {'name': 'Create', 'folder': folder}:
11                  self . require(folder not in self . created_folders, "folder exists")
12                  self . created_folders .add(folder)
13
14              case {'name': 'Delete', 'folder': folder}:
15                  self . require(folder in self . created_folders, "folder missing")
16                  self . created_folders .remove(folder)
17
18              case {'name': 'Open', 'folder': folder, 'filename': filename,
19                    'mode': mode, 'size': size}:
20                  self . require(folder in self . created_folders, "folder missing")
21                  self . require(filename not in self . open_files, "file open")
22                  self . open_files [filename] = {'mode': mode, 'max_size': size, 'bytes_written': 0}
23
24              case {'name': 'Write', 'filename': filename, 'data': data}:
25                  self . require(filename in self . open_files, "file closed")
26                  file_info = self . open_files [filename]
27                  self . require( file_info ['mode'] == 'write', "write mode")
28                  data_size = len(data)
29                  self . require( file_info [' bytes_written '] + data_size <= file_info ['max_size'],
30                                "size limit")
31                  self . require( self . total_bytes_written + data_size <= self. max_total_bytes,
32                                "total limit")
33                  file_info [' bytes_written '] += data_size
34                  self . total_bytes_written += data_size
35
36              case {'name': 'Close', 'filename': filename}:
37                  self . require(filename in self . open_files, "file closed")
38                  del self . open_files [filename]
39
40              case {'name': 'Read', 'filename': filename}:
41                  self . require(filename in self . open_files, "file closed")
42
43              case _:
44                  raise ValueError("bad event")
45
46      def finalize (self):
47          self . require(not self . open_files, "file not closed")
```

Fig. 8. FileSystemMonitor class generated by the Gemini 2.5 LLM.

- A file cannot be opened if it is already open (Line 21).
- A file cannot be closed if it is not open (Line 37).
- A file cannot be read unless it is open (Line 41).

There are several ways in which LLMs can be used for generating monitors. In [1] an experiment is described where two LLM generated versions of a program are checked against each other using differential testing. In [6] an approach is described where an LLM is used to generate a monitoring framework for a user defined logic, and subsequently used to generate monitors in that framework for user provided properties in that logic.

9 Conclusion

We have discussed different formalisms for formulating monitors, ranging from external DSLs, requiring their own grammar and parser, over internal DSLs which are libraries in a general-purpose programming language, and hybrid DSLs, which combine external and internal DSLs, to using a general-purpose programming language without the use of any special RV libraries. We have shown five solutions covering this spectrum. We have discussed the advantages and disadvantages of each approach. External DSLs allow succinct specifications and are easy to analyze but usually are less expressive. Internal (shallow) DSLs are very expressive (Turing complete). They e.g. allow performing data analysis, producing data results beyond just Boolean verdicts. However, specifications are usually more verbose, and they are harder to analyze and optimize. Hybrid DSLs attempt to achieve the advantages of both while minimizing the disadvantages. One can also "just" program monitors in a general-purpose programming language. This is probably how many monitors are currently developed in industry. This approach is less attractive if there are many, or evolving, requirements to be monitored. We illustrated how LLMs can perhaps address this issue by generating monitors from natural language requirements.

References

1. Aichernig, B., Havelund, K.: Correct-ish by design: from upfront verification to continuous monitoring of LLM generated code. In: Steffen, B. (ed.) AISoLA 2024: Bridging the Gap Between AI and Reality. Springer, Heidelberg (2025)
2. Armando, A., Mantovani, J., Platania, L.: Bounded model checking of software using SMT solvers instead of SAT solvers. In: Valmari, A. (ed.) SPIN 2006. LNCS, vol. 3925, pp. 146–162. Springer, Heidelberg (2006). https://doi.org/10.1007/11691617_9
3. Barringer, H., Havelund, K.: TraceContract: a scala DSL for trace analysis. In: Butler, M., Schulte, W. (eds.) FM 2011. LNCS, vol. 6664, pp. 57–72. Springer, Heidelberg (2011). https://doi.org/10.1007/978-3-642-21437-0_7
4. Barringer, H., Rydeheard, D., Havelund, K.: Rule systems for run-time monitoring: from Eagle to RuleR. In: Sokolsky, O., Taşıran, S. (eds.) RV 2007. LNCS, vol. 4839, pp. 111–125. Springer, Heidelberg (2007). https://doi.org/10.1007/978-3-540-77395-5_10
5. Basin, D., Klaedtke, F., Marinovic, S., Zălinescu, E.: Monitoring of temporal first-order properties with aggregations. Formal Methods Syst. Des. **46**(3), 262–285 (2015). https://doi.org/10.1007/s10703-015-0222-7
6. Cohen, I., Havelund, K., Peled, D., Goldberg, Y.: The power of reframing: using LLMs in synthesizing RV monitors. In: Könighofer, B., Torfah, H. (eds.) 25th International Conference on Runtime Verification (RV). LNCS. Springer, Heidelberg (2025)
7. Colombo, C., Gauci, A., Pace, G.J.: LarvaStat: monitoring of statistical properties. In: Barringer, H., et al. (eds.) RV 2010. LNCS, vol. 6418, pp. 480–484. Springer, Heidelberg (2010). https://doi.org/10.1007/978-3-642-16612-9_38

8. Dams, D., Havelund, K., Kauffman, S.: A Python library for trace analysis. In: Dang, T., Stolz, V. (eds.) 22nd International Conference on Runtime Verification (RV), vol. 13498 of LNCS, pp. 264–273. Springer, Heidelberg (2022). https://doi.org/10.1007/978-3-031-17196-3_15
9. D'Angelo, B., et al.: Lola: runtime monitoring of synchronous systems. In: 12th International Symposium on Temporal Representation and Reasoning (TIME'05), pp. 166–174(2005)
10. Decker, N., Leucker, M., Thoma, D.: Monitoring modulo theories. Int. J. Softw. Tools Technol. Transf. **18**(2), 205–225 (2016)
11. DejaVu tool source code. https://github.com/havelund/dejavu
12. Duckett, B., Havelund, K., Stewart, L.: Space telemetry analysis with PyContract. In: Haxthausen, A.E., Huang, W., Roggenbach, M. (eds.) Applicable Formal Methods for Safe Industrial Products - Essays Dedicated to Jan Peleska on the Occasion of His 65th Birthday, vol. 14165 of LNCS. Springer, Heidelberg (2023)
13. Andy Dustman. Python MySQL (2024). https://pypi.org/project/MySQL-python/
14. Emerson, E.A., Clarke, E.M.: Characterizing correctness properties of parallel programs using fixpoints. In: de Bakker, J., van Leeuwen, J. (eds.) ICALP 1980. LNCS, vol. 85, pp. 169–181. Springer, Heidelberg (1980). https://doi.org/10.1007/3-540-10003-2_69
15. Gemini large language model. https://gemini.google.com
16. Gorostiaga, F., Sánchez, C.: HStriver: a very functional extensible tool for the runtime verification of real-time event streams. In: Huisman, M., Păsăreanu, C., Zhan, N. (eds.) FM 2021. LNCS, vol. 13047, pp. 563–580. Springer, Cham (2021). https://doi.org/10.1007/978-3-030-90870-6_30
17. Halle, S., Villemaire, R.: Runtime enforcement of web service message contracts with data. IEEE Trans. Serv. Comput. **5**, 192–206 (2012)
18. Havelund, K.: Data automata in Scala. In: 2014 Theoretical Aspects of Software Engineering Conference, TASE 2014, Changsha, China, 1–3 September 2014, pp. 1–9. IEEE Computer Society (2014)
19. Havelund, K.: Rule-based runtime verification revisited. Softw. Tools Technol. Transf. (STTT) **17**(2), 143–170 (2015)
20. Havelund, K.: Daut - Monitoring Data Streams with Data Automata (2024). https://github.com/havelund/daut
21. Havelund, K., Katsaros, P., Omer, M., Peled, D., Temperekidis, A.: TP-DejaVu: combining operational and declarative runtime verification. In: Dimitrova, R., Lahav, O., Wolff, S. (eds.) Verification, Model Checking, and Abstract Interpretation, pp. 249–263. Springer, Cham (2024). https://doi.org/10.1007/978-3-031-50521-8_12
22. Havelund, K., Omer, M., Peled, D.: Operational and declarative runtime verification (keynote). In: Proceedings of the 7th ACM International Workshop on Verification and Monitoring at Runtime Execution, VORTEX 2024, pp. 3–12. Association for Computing Machinery, New York (2024)
23. Havelund, K., Peled, D.: An extension of first-order LTL with rules with application to runtime verification. Int. J. Softw. Tools Technol. Transf. **23**(4), 547–563 (2021). https://doi.org/10.1007/s10009-021-00626-y
24. Havelund, K., Peled, D., Ulus, D.: First-order temporal logic monitoring with BDDs. Formal Methods Syst. Des. **56**(1–3), 1–21 (2020)
25. Havelund, K., Roşu, G.: Synthesizing monitors for safety properties. In: Katoen, J.-P., Stevens, P. (eds.) TACAS 2002. LNCS, vol. 2280, pp. 342–356. Springer, Heidelberg (2002). https://doi.org/10.1007/3-540-46002-0_24

26. Top programming languages (2024). https://spectrum.ieee.org/top-programming-languages-2024
27. Johnson, S.C.: Yacc: yet another compiler-compiler. https://en.wikipedia.org/wiki/Yacc
28. Kallwies, H., Leucker, M., Schmitz, M., Schulz, A., Thoma, D., Weiss, A.: Tessla – an ecosystem for runtime verification. In: Dang, T., Stolz, V. (eds.) Runtime Verification, pp. 314–324. Springer, Cham (2022). https://doi.org/10.1007/978-3-031-17196-3_20
29. Kiczales, G., Hilsdale, E., Hugunin, J., Kersten, M., Palm, J., Griswold, W.G.: An overview of AspectJ. In: Knudsen, J.L. (ed.) ECOOP 2001. LNCS, vol. 2072, pp. 327–354. Springer, Heidelberg (2001). https://doi.org/10.1007/3-540-45337-7_18
30. Matiyasevich, Y.: Hilbert's 10th Problem. MIT Press, Cambridge (1993)
31. Meredith, P.O.N., Jin, D., Griffith, D., Chen, F., Roşu, G.: An overview of the MOP runtime verification framework. Int. J. Softw. Techn. Technol. Transf. 14, 249–289 (2011)
32. PyContract. https://github.com/pyrv/pycontract
33. PyDejaVu tool source code. https://github.com/moraneus/pydejavu
34. Queille, J.P., Sifakis, J.: Iterative methods for the analysis of petri nets. In: Girault, C., Reisig, W. (eds.) Application and Theory of Petri Nets, Selected Papers from the First and the Second European Workshop on Application and Theory of Petri Nets, Strasbourg, France, 23–26 September 1980, Bad Honnef, Germany, 28–30 September 1981, vol. 52 of Informatik-Fachberichte, pp. 161–167. Springer, Heidelberg (1981). https://doi.org/10.1007/978-3-642-68353-4_27
35. Reger, G., Cruz, H.C., Rydeheard, D.: MarQ: monitoring at runtime with QEA. In: Baier, C., Tinelli, C. (eds.) TACAS 2015. LNCS, vol. 9035, pp. 596–610. Springer, Heidelberg (2015). https://doi.org/10.1007/978-3-662-46681-0_55
36. Thomas, W.: Automata on infinite objects. In: van Leeuwen, J. (ed.) Handbook of Theoretical Computer Science, Volume B: Formal Models and Semantics, pp. 133–191. Elsevier and MIT Press (1990)
37. TP-DejaVu tool source code. https://github.com/moraneus/TP-DejaVu
38. Windsurf editor. https://windsurf.com

Execution and Monitoring of HOA Automata with HOAX

Luca Di Stefano

Institute of Computer Engineering, TU Wien, Treitlstraße 3, 1040 Vienna, Austria
luca.di.stefano@tuwien.ac.at

Abstract. We present a tool called HOAX for the execution of ω-automata expressed in the popular HOA format. The tool leverages the notion of trap sets to enable runtime monitoring of any (non-parity) acceptance condition supported by the format. When the automaton is not monitorable, the tool may still be able to recognise so-called ugly prefixes, and determine that no further observation will ever lead to a conclusive verdict. The tool is open-source and highly configurable. We present its formal foundations, its design, and compare it against the trace analyser PyContract on a lock acquisition scenario.

1 Introduction

The Hanoi Omega-Automata (HOA) format is a well-established language to describe and exchange ω-automata [1], featuring a rich grammar for acceptance conditions that generalises (co-)Büchi, Strett, Rabin, and other classical families of automata. HOA is supported by mature toolboxes, including Spot [10], PRISM [18], and Owl [16], which provide valuable tools to construct and analyse automata. However, there are no tools to *execute* an automaton, i.e., to display how it evolves through its state space under a sequence of inputs.

In this work, we present an open-source utility to fill this gap, called HOAX.[1] It receives as input one or more HOA files, and executes the automata described therein, by reading input valuations from a configurable set of sources. It also allows customized behaviour when, for instance, nondeterminism or deadlock are detected in the automaton, or when user-defined conditions are met.

Runtime verification represents a natural application of this tool. To enable this, we implement within HOAX a reasoning mechanism based on the notion of *trap sets* [15], i.e., subsets of the state space that the automaton cannot leave once entered. This reasoning lets the tool monitor deterministic complete automata with any of the (non-parity) arbitrary acceptance conditions expressible in HOA. If a finite sequence of inputs is enough to deduce that the condition will be fulfilled or not, the tool reports a conclusive verdict. Although this is not guaranteed to happen in finite time, if the automaton is not monitorable HOAX can also try to detect ugly prefixes [2], to decide whether further monitoring is useful.

---
[1] Short for HOA executor.

This paper is structured as follows. Section 2 contains definitions that will be used throughout the paper. Section 3 discusses how trap sets may be computed and used for monitoring.[2]

In Sect. 4 we describe the workflow and features of HOAX, and compare it with PyContract [5], a Python library for building trace analysers. Lastly, we make our concluding remarks in Sect. 5.

Related Work. Several formats for graphs and automata support, unlike HOA, some form of execution or simulation. For instance, the CADP suite [13] contains tools for the (random or interactive) execution of transition systems expressed either explicitly or through a process calculus such as LNT [14]. mCLR2 [4] and the TLC toolbox for TLA+ [21] provide similar utilities for their respective formalisms. Since these formalism target transition systems, rather than automata, they do not usually incorporate acceptance conditions. Similarly, the aigsim tool can simulate a circuit expressed in the AIGER format [3]. Inputs may be either random or read from a stimulus file, whereas HOAX can mix different sources of input. In turn, AIGER partitions the alphabet of the circuit into *inputs* and *outputs*, making the format amenable to describe SAT and model checking queries, as well as reactive synthesis problems. PyContract [5] is a Python library by which monitors can be explicitly programmed in a shallow domain-specific language (DSL). These monitors are symbolic, as they observe data-carrying messages rather than plain Boolean signals; this, in turn, enables advanced techniques, such as slicing, to further improve performance. While the library is oriented towards trace analysis, its API may be leveraged to also implement online monitoring. Spot lets one build a HOA automaton that monitors a property φ from the safety fragment of Linear Temporal Logic (LTL [19]). The resulting automaton may deadlock on specific inputs, and finding a deadlock corresponds to detecting a violation of φ.[3] Our tool may be instrumented to support these automata, and its reasoning extends to full LTL, although with no guarantees that a conclusive verdict will be reached.

2 Background

Definition 1 (Words, prefixes, suffixes). *Given a finite set Σ (also called an* alphabet*), we denote by Σ^ω the set of (infinite) words over Σ.*

For any word $w = w_0 w_1 w_2 \ldots$ and any $i \geq 0$, we can always split w into a prefix $w_{\leq i} = w_0 w_1 w_2 \ldots w_i$ of finite length $i+1$, and an infinite suffix $w_{>i} = w_{i+1} w_{i+2} \ldots$; we denote by Σ^* the set of all word prefixes, or finite words.

Definition 2 (Automata). *An automaton is a tuple $\mathcal{A} = \langle Q, \Sigma, \rightarrow, Q_0, \varphi \rangle$ where Q is a finite set of* states*, Σ a finite* alphabet*, $\rightarrow \;\subseteq Q \times \Sigma \times Q$ a labelled transition relation, $Q_0 \subseteq Q$ a non-empty set of* initial *states, and φ an acceptance condition from acc_Q, defined as:*

---

[2] Proofs for the lemmas and theorems in this section are reported in an extended version of this paper [7].
[3] See https://spot.lre.epita.fr/tut11.html.

$$acc_Q := \top \mid \bot \mid \text{Fin}(S) \mid \text{Inf}(S) \mid acc_Q \wedge acc_Q \mid acc_Q \vee acc_Q,$$

where S denotes non-empty subsets of Q. We write $q \xrightarrow{a} q'$ iff $(q, a, q') \in \rightarrow$, and $q \rightarrow q'$ iff $(q, a, q') \in \rightarrow$ for some a.

Definition 3 (Deterministic and complete automata). *An automaton $\mathcal{A} = \langle Q, \Sigma, \rightarrow, Q_0, \varphi \rangle$ is deterministic iff i) $|Q_0| = 1$, and ii) for every pair $(q, a) \in Q \times \Sigma$ there is at most one $q' \in Q$ such that $q \xrightarrow{a} q'$. An automaton is complete if for every pair $(q, a) \in Q \times \Sigma$ there is at least one q' such that $q \xrightarrow{a} q'$.*

Note that the alphabet of a HOA automaton [1] is the set of Boolean formulas over a finite set of *atomic propositions* AP, denoted by $\mathbb{B}(AP)$.[4] Two formulas in $\mathbb{B}(AP)$ are *disjoint* iff there is no valuation of AP that satisfies both. A HOA automaton is deterministic iff it has one initial state and, in every state, outgoing transitions are labelled by pairwise disjoint formulas; and it is complete iff, in every state, the disjunction of all labels on outgoing transitions is a valid formula.

Definition 4 (Runs). *A sequence of states $\rho = \rho_0 \rho_1 \rho_2 \ldots$ is a run in $\mathcal{A}$ for a word $w = w_0 w_1 w_2 \ldots$ if $\rho_0 \in Q_0$ and, for every $i \geq 0$, $\rho_i \xrightarrow{w_i} \rho_{i+1}$. Similarly to what we did with words, we denote by $\rho_{\leq i}$ and $\rho_{>i}$ the prefix and suffix of a run. We write $w_\mathcal{A}(\rho)$ to denote the word for which ρ is a run in $\mathcal{A}$.*

Definition 5 (Accepting runs, languages). *A run ρ models a condition φ, denoted by $\rho \models \varphi$, according to the following interpretation:*

$\rho \models \top \quad \rho \models \text{Fin}(S) \Leftrightarrow \exists i. \forall j. j > i \Rightarrow \rho_j \notin S \quad \rho \models \varphi_1 \wedge \varphi_2 \Leftrightarrow \rho \models \varphi_1 \text{ and } \rho \models \varphi_2$

$\rho \not\models \bot \quad \rho \models \text{Inf}(S) \Leftrightarrow \rho \not\models \text{Fin}(S) \quad \rho \models \varphi_1 \vee \varphi_2 \Leftrightarrow \rho \models \varphi_1 \text{ or } \rho \models \varphi_2$

A run that models φ is also called an *accepting* run *for it*. The language $\mathcal{L}(\mathcal{A})$ of an automaton $\mathcal{A}$ with acceptance condition φ is the set of words $w \in \Sigma^\omega$ for which there exists an accepting run for φ in $\mathcal{A}$.

Intuitively, a run ρ is accepting for $\text{Fin}(S)$ (and not accepting for $\text{Inf}(S)$) iff it only visits S a finite number of times. For instance, a run of an automaton with a transition relation like the one in Fig. 1a starts in q_0, immediately leaves it, and can never visit q_0 again. Therefore, the run models $\text{Fin}(\{q_0\})$.

Furthermore, we will call a *transient* any set of states S of an automaton $\mathcal{A}$ such that every run of $\mathcal{A}$ models $\text{Inf}(Q \setminus S)$. Notice that a transient may still be visited infinitely often during a run: the only requirement is that every run also *leaves* it infinitely often. To determine whether S is a transient, it suffices to check that the transitions $\{q \rightarrow q' \mid q, q' \in S\}$ are acyclic, which can be done in $\mathcal{O}(|S| + |\rightarrow|)$ time in the worst case.

---

[4] This set is infinite, but its quotient modulo equivalence of truth tables is finite with size $2^{2^{|AP|}}$, and thus we may treat it as an alphabet.

Definition 6 (Strongly connected components; Bottom SCCs). *A strongly connected component (SCC) of a directed graph is any maximal set of pairwise-reachable vertices in the graph. A bottom SCC (BSCC) is an SCC that is closed under the edge relation of the graph.*

We will extend these graph-theoretical definitions to an automaton with states Q and transition relation $\rightarrow$ by considering the directed graph that has vertices Q and has an edge (q, q') if and only if $q \rightarrow q'$.

Definition 7 (Good, bad, ugly prefixes; monitorability [2,17].). *Let $\mathcal{A}$ an automaton over alphabet Σ, and $u \in \Sigma^*$ a finite word. We say that u is*

- *a good prefix iff, for all $w \in \Sigma^\omega$, $uw \in \mathcal{L}(\mathcal{A})$;*
- *a bad prefix iff, for all $w \in \Sigma^\omega$, $uw \notin \mathcal{L}(\mathcal{A})$;*
- *an ugly prefix iff, for all $v \in \Sigma^*$, uv is neither good nor bad.*

We say that $\rho_{\leq i}$ is a *good, bad, or ugly run prefix* if $(w_\mathcal{A}(\rho))_{\leq i}$ is a good, bad, or ugly prefix, respectively. An automaton is *monitorable* if it has no ugly prefixes.

Definition 8 (Trap sets [15]). *Let $\mathcal{A} = \langle Q, \Sigma, \rightarrow, Q_0, \varphi \rangle$ an automaton. Then, a non-empty set $T \subseteq Q$ is a trap set of $\mathcal{A}$ if, for every $q \in T$, $q \rightarrow q'$ implies $q' \in T$. A trap set T is minimal iff there exists no subset $T' \subset T$ that is also a trap set. Q is always a trivial trap set for $\mathcal{A}$.*

Lemma 1. *T is a trap set of a complete automaton $\mathcal{A}$ iff for every run ρ of $\mathcal{A}$, if $\rho_i \in T$ for some $i \geq 0$, then $\rho_j \in T$ $\forall j \geq i$.*

Proof. ($\Rightarrow$) By induction. If $j = i$, we already know that $\rho_i \in T$. If $j > i$, assume that $\rho_k \in T$ for $k = i, i+1, \ldots, j-1$. By definition of a run, $\rho_{j-1} \rightarrow \rho_j$. Then, by definition of T, ρ_j also belongs to T. ($\Leftarrow$) If every run ρ entering T stays within T forever, this means that there cannot exist any $q \notin T$ such that $q \rightarrow q'$. This means that T is closed under $\rightarrow$ and thus a trap set. □

3 Runtime Monitoring with Trap Sets

In this section, we describe how to compute the trap sets of an automaton (technically, of its underlying state-transition graph); then, we exploit them to monitor an acceptance condition as defined in (Def. 5) on a complete deterministic automaton. When appropriate, we can use the same technique on an incomplete automaton that we make complete by adding adequate stuttering transitions.

Computing Trap Sets. The trap sets of an automaton have a nuanced relation with its strongly connected components. For instance, Fig. 1a shows a graph with trap sets $\{q_1, q_2\}$ and $\{q_2\}$ (which is minimal), where the former is not an SCC. At the same time, in Fig. 1b, sets $\{s_0, s_1\}$ is an SCC but not a trap set, since it is not closed under $\rightarrow$. By contrast, $\{s_2\}$ is both an SCC and a trap set. We now characterise how trap sets and SCCs relate to one another:

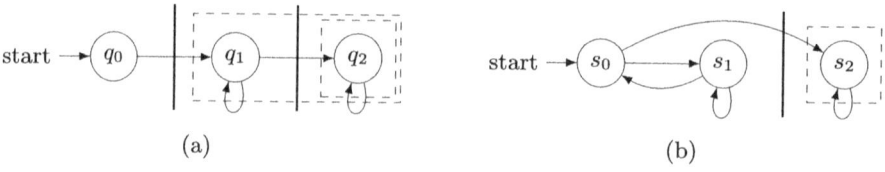

Fig. 1. Examples of graphs with their trap sets (enclosed in dashed boxes) and SCCs (separated by solid lines).

Lemma 1. *Let $\mathcal{A}$ a complete automaton and let T a subset of its states. T is a BSCC of $\mathcal{A}$ iff it is a minimal trap set of $\mathcal{A}$.*

Lemma 2. *Let K an SCC of $\mathcal{A}$ that is not a bottom SCC. Denote by $N(K)$ the set of states $n \notin K$ such that $q \to n$ for some $q \in K$. If every such state belongs to a trap set T_n, then the set $T' = K \cup \bigcup_{n \in N(K)} T_n$ is also a trap set.*

These lemmas give us a straightforward procedure (Algorithm 1) to retrieve the smallest trap set containing a given state q of an automaton $\mathcal{A}$. At initialisation time (line 1–5), we build a directed graph G out of $\mathcal{A}$, and compute its SCCs $\mathbb{S}$ as well as its condensation $\mathcal{G}$, i.e., its quotient modulo $\mathbb{S}$. Lastly, we build a map $k : Q \to \mathbb{S}$ that associates each state of $\mathcal{A}$ to the SCC to which it belongs. Then, whenever we need to obtain the smallest trap set that contains state q, we use procedure MINTRAPSETOF(q) (lines 6–7) which essentially amounts to a depth-first search (DFS) on the condensation graph, rooted in $k(q)$. Assuming that this procedure returns a list of components $K_1, \ldots, K_n$, then q belongs to the trap set $\bigcup_{i=1}^{n} K_i$. If this trap set contains the initial state of $\mathcal{A}$, then it is trivial. Notice that q may also belong to larger trap sets, which one may find by visiting the predecessors of $k(q)$ in the condensation; however, these are not useful to our monitoring approach. Both procedures in Algorithm 1 have linear time complexity in the worst case.

Monitoring for Acceptance. We now describe how we can exploit the trap sets of a complete automaton $\mathcal{A}$ to give verdicts on the satisfaction of elementary acceptance conditions based on a finite prefix of a run, or at least to detect that further monitoring is hopeless.

Theorem 1. *Let T a trap set of $\mathcal{A}$. Let ρ a run of $\mathcal{A}$ such that $\rho_i \in T$. Then, i) $\rho \models \text{Inf}(S)$ for every $S \supseteq T$; and ii) if T is minimal, then $\rho \models \text{Inf}(S)$ for every S such that $S \cap T \neq \emptyset$ and $T \setminus S$ is a transient.*

Theorem 2. *Let T a trap set of $\mathcal{A}$. Let ρ a run of $\mathcal{A}$ such that $\rho_i \in T$. Then, $\rho \not\models \text{Inf}(S)$ for every S such that $S \cap T = \emptyset$.*

Theorem 3. *Let T, S two sets of states of $\mathcal{A}$ such that T is a minimal trap set, $S \cap T \neq \emptyset$, and such that $T \setminus S$ is not empty nor a transient. Then every $\rho_{\leq i}$ such that $\rho_i \in T$ is an ugly run prefix for both $\text{Fin}(S)$ and $\text{Inf}(S)$.*

Algorithm 1: Trap sets of an automaton $\mathcal{A}$.

1 **procedure** INIT($\mathcal{A}$):
2     $G = (Q, E) \leftarrow$ directed graph of $\mathcal{A}$
3     $\mathbb{S} \leftarrow \text{SCC}(G)$ # strongly connected components of G
4     $\mathcal{G} = (\mathbb{S}, E') \leftarrow G/\mathbb{S}$ # condensation graph of G
5     $k \leftarrow \{(q, K) \in Q \times \mathbb{S} \mid q \in K\}$
6 **procedure** MINTRAPSETOF(q):
7   **return** DFS($\mathcal{G}, k(q)$)   # Depth-first search on $\mathcal{G}$ rooted in $k(q)$

Algorithm 2: One-step monitor for acceptance condition $\text{Inf}(S)$.

Input : A deterministic complete automaton $\mathcal{A}$ and its current state q
Output: good, bad, ugly, or $\bot$.

1 $Comps \leftarrow \text{MINTRAPSETOF}(q)$ # $O(|Q|)$ (Algorithm 1)
2 $q_0 \leftarrow$ initial state of $\mathcal{A}$
3 $T \leftarrow \bigcup Comps$ # $O(|Q|)$ (components are disjoint)
4 **if** $T \subseteq S$ **then return** good   # $O(|S|)$ (Theorem 1)
5 **if** $T \cap S = \emptyset$ **then return** bad   # $O(|S|)$ (Theorem 2)
6 **if** $|Comps| = 1$ **then**   # if T is minimal (Theorems 1 and 3)
7   **if** $T \setminus S$ *is transient* **then return** good **else return** ugly   # $O(|S| + |E|)$
8 **return** $\bot$

Then, we can write a procedure (Algorithm 2) that retrieves the trap set currently inhabited by an automaton, and tries to determine if the execution observed so far is a good, bad, or ugly run prefix for a condition $\text{Inf}(S)$.[5] If no verdict may be reached, the procedure returns $\bot$. This algorithm is linear-time in the size of $\mathcal{A}$: we annotate its lines with their worst-case complexity to make this evident. Then, a monitor repeatedly invokes this procedure after every transition of the automaton, until a conclusive verdict is reached. By memoization, the execution time may be amortised to sublinear time.

Lastly, we generalise to compound acceptance conditions. It is straightforward to use the following theorems as a basis to build composite monitors.

Theorem 4. *Let $\phi = \varphi_1 \wedge \varphi_2$ an acceptance condition. If $\rho_{\leq i}$ is a bad or ugly run prefix for at least one of $\varphi_{1,2}$, then $\rho_{\leq i}$ is a bad or ugly run prefix for ϕ. If $\rho_{\leq i}$ is a good prefix for both φ_1 and φ_2, then it is a good run prefix for ϕ.*

Theorem 5. *Let $\phi = \varphi_1 \vee \varphi_2$ an acceptance condition. If $\rho_{\leq i}$ is a good run prefix for φ_1 or φ_2, then $\rho_{\leq i}$ is a good run prefix for ϕ. If $\rho_{\leq i}$ is a bad run prefix for both $\varphi_{1,2}$, then it is a bad run prefix for ϕ. If $\rho_{\leq i}$ is an ugly run prefix for one of $\varphi_{1,2}$, and bad or ugly for the other, then it is an ugly run prefix for ϕ.*

---

[5] We omit the obvious, near-identical procedure for $\text{Fin}(S)$.

4 A Tool for Executing HOA ω-Automata

In this section we introduce and evaluate our tool, HOAX. The tool is implemented in Python, it is open-source and available online.[6]
Usage and Architecture. The tool accepts as input one or more HOA automata and a configuration file. The HOA files are used to construct one or more *runners* that will keep track of each automaton's state. The configuration file, in turn, describes how inputs to the automata should be retrieved or generated. Each way of providing inputs to automata is reified by means of *driver* objects. At the moment, HOAX provides drivers that implement an interactive user prompt, a text file reader, or pseudo-random Boolean generators with user-defined biases. Different atomic propositions may be mapped to different drivers, and the user may declare a default driver for propositions that remain unmapped.

In the main execution loop, HOAX collects a valuation of AP by interrogating the drivers, and feeds it to the runners which choose a suitable next state for their respective automata. Runners may also be equipped with reactive *hooks*. A hook is a combination of a *trigger* object that monitors whether the automaton has met a certain condition, and an *action* that is invoked whenever this happens. For instance, the user may use hooks to specify how the runner should resolve nondeterminism, or how it should behave on deadlock. Possible actions for these triggers include choosing a random option, prompting the user, resetting the automaton, or forcing it into a specific state. In fact, we have implemented the monitoring approach described in this work as a family of triggers that activate a reset action whenever Algorithm 2 gives a conclusive verdict.[7]
Experimental Evaluation. We consider a lock acquisition scenario from [5], where N threads compete to acquire N locks. We observe finite traces of events in the form $a_{i\ell}$ and $r_{i\ell}$, indicating that thread i has acquired or released lock ℓ. An additional event end denotes the end of a trace. We want to monitor that no lock acquired by i is then acquired by $j \neq i$ before being released (1); and that, by the end of the trace, all acquired locks have been released (2). Acquisition events that occur at the end of the trace are ignored.

$$\text{NoDoubleAcq}_{i\ell} \triangleq G(\neg end \land a_{i\ell} \implies r_{i\ell} \, R \bigwedge_{j \neq i} \neg a_{j\ell}) \quad (1)$$

$$\text{ReleaseByEnd}_{i\ell} \triangleq G(\neg end \land a_{i\ell} \implies \neg end \, W \, r_{j\ell}) \quad (2)$$

We compare how PyContract and HOAX deal with this scenario. For PyContract, we reuse monitor M1 from [5]. For HOAX, we use Spot to generate automata from the negation of the above properties for each pair (i, ℓ). We consider three systems, respectively with $N = 2, 4, 8$, and generate traces of length $L = 5 \times 10^4, 1 \times 10^5, 2 \times 10^5$ for each system. Notice that, to encode events $a_{i\ell}$ and $r_{i\ell}$ in HOAX traces, we use a single proposition a to denote whether

---
[6] https://github.com/lou1306/hoax. A persistent snapshot is also available [8].
[7] The assumption here is that, whenever a violation is detected, some external mechanism brings the environment back to a safe state.

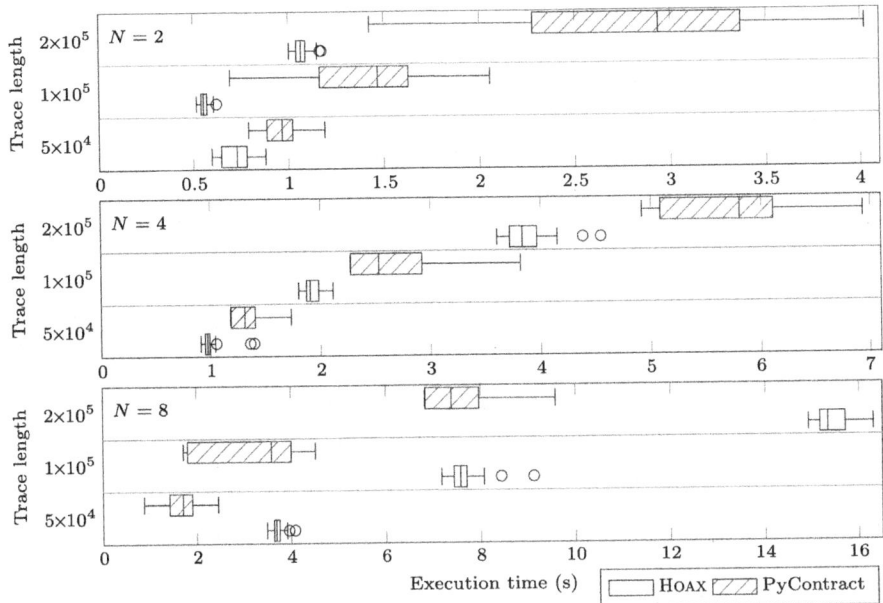

Fig. 2. Running times of HOAX and PyContract on the lock acquisition systems.

the event is an acquisition (when asserted) or a release (when negated), and an additional $2\log_2 N$ variables that binary-encode the values of i and ℓ. We ran each tool 50 times on each pair (N, L). Experiments were performed on an Apple MacBook Pro laptop with an M3 Pro CPU and 18 GiB of RAM, running macOS 14.7.3.[8]

Figure 2 reports box plots for all running times on the three systems. We only track the time that the tools spend analysing the trace and reporting violations, and ignore all setup operations (instantiating the M1 class for PyContract, and parsing the automata files for HOAX). On smaller systems ($N = 2, 4$), HOAX shows faster execution times, with a smaller variance and a lower sensitivity to the length of the trace. However, PyContract is faster in the larger setting, $N = 8$. Note that properties (1–2) correspond to $2N^2$ (deterministic and complete) automata on a system of size N. The automata all have the same size, i.e., 3 states and 6 transitions, but their set of APs grows as N increases ($2 + 2\log_2 N$). Therefore, when $N = 8$, HOAX deals with 128 automata over 8 atomic propositions, while PyContract's use of one symbolic monitor starts to pay off.

---

[8] We provide a repository at https://github.com/lou1306/hoax-experiments/ containing the code used for these experiments, to facilitate replication. A persistent snapshot is also available [9]. We used this repository to replicate our experiments on an Intel i7-5820K workstation with 32 GiB of RAM, running Ubuntu 22.04.

5 Conclusions

We have introduced HOAX, an open-source execution tool for HOA automata that supports monitoring of arbitrary acceptance conditions. We have remarked that runs of a nonmonitorable automaton may not be recognized up to any finite prefix, and shown that our tool may at least be able to recognize ugly prefixes and give up hopes of recognizing the current run. The tool is highly configurable, and its modular architecture should facilitate future extensions. Although HOAX was not designed to compete with symbolic trace analysis, our experimental comparison with PyContract looks promising. At the moment, automata are executed sequentially, and parallelisation might substantially improve performance. The main advantages of our tool, in any case, are its configurability and interoperability with the rich collection of existing utilities for HOA generation and analysis, allowing to directly create monitors from LTL specifications rather than having to program them manually.

Support for nondeterminism would be an attractive direction for future work, allowing for smaller automata than their deterministic counterparts (when they exist). After a run prefix, these automata may be in one of multiple states, possibly across disjoint trap sets, and we would need to consider all these sets before reaching a conclusion on the quality of the prefix. Likely, this would entail tracking them symbolically, to palliate state space explosion. Automata formats that can embed more general logics, such as LTL modulo theories [20], may partially overcome the scalability limitations we have observed in our experimental evaluation by enabling monitors with richer inputs, such as integers. To fully match the power of symbolic approaches such as PyContract, one would need richer, data-aware logics, such as Constraint LTL [6] or TSL [11,12].

References

1. Babiak, T., et al.: The Hanoi Omega-automata Format. In: Kroening, D., Păsăreanu, C.S. (eds.) CAV 2015. LNCS, vol. 9206, pp. 479–486. Springer, Cham (2015). https://doi.org/10.1007/978-3-319-21690-4_31
2. Bauer, A., Leucker, M., Schallhart, C.: Runtime Verification for LTL and TLTL. ACM Trans. Softw. Eng. Methodol. **20**(4), 14:1-14:64 (2011). https://doi.org/10.1145/2000799.2000800
3. Biere, A.: The AIGER and-inverter graph (AIG) format version 20071012, Technical Report, Johannes Kepler University (2007). https://doi.org/10.35011/fmvtr.2007-1
4. Bunte, O., et al.: The MCRL2 Toolset for Analysing Concurrent Systems. In: Vojnar, T., Zhang, L. (eds.) TACAS 2019. LNCS, vol. 11428, pp. 21–39. Springer, Cham (2019). https://doi.org/10.1007/978-3-030-17465-1_2
5. Dams, D., Havelund, K., Kauffman, S.: A Python library for trace analysis. In: 22nd International Conference on Runtime Verification (RV). LNCS, vol. 13498, pp. 264–273. Springer (2022).https://doi.org/10.1007/978-3-031-17196-3_15
6. Demri, S., D'Souza, D.: An Automata-theoretic Approach to Constraint LTL. Inf. Comput. **205**(3), 380–415 (2007). https://doi.org/10.1016/j.ic.2006.09.006

7. Di Stefano, L.: Execution and monitoring of HOA automata with HOAX (extended version). arXiv preprint arXiv:2507.11126 (2025)
8. Di Stefano, L.: Lou1306/hoax: V0.1.1. Zenodo (2025). https://doi.org/10.5281/zenodo.15909339
9. Stefano, L.: Software artifact for Execution and monitoring of HOA automata with HOAX. Zenodo (2025). https://doi.org/10.5281/zenodo.15908703
10. Duret-Lutz, A., Lewkowicz, A., Fauchille, A., Michaud, T., Renault, E., Xu, L.: Spot 2.0 - a framework for LTL and ω-Automata manipulation. In: 14th International Symposium on Automated Technology for Verification and Analysis (ATVA). LNCS, vol. 9938, pp. 122–129 (2016).https://doi.org/10.1007/978-3-319-46520-3_8
11. Finkbeiner, B., Heim, P., Passing, N.: Temporal stream logic modulo theories. In: 25th International Conference on Foundations of Software Science and Computation Structures (FOSSACS). LNCS, vol. 13242, pp. 325–346. Springer (2022). https://doi.org/10.1007/978-3-030-99253-8_17
12. Finkbeiner, B., Klein, F., Piskac, R., Santolucito, M.: Temporal Stream Logic: Synthesis Beyond the Bools. In: Dillig, I., Tasiran, S. (eds.) CAV 2019. LNCS, vol. 11561, pp. 609–629. Springer, Cham (2019). https://doi.org/10.1007/978-3-030-25540-4_35
13. Garavel, H., Lang, F., Mateescu, R., Serwe, W.: CADP 2011: a Toolbox for the Construction and Analysis of Distributed Processes. Softw. Tools Technol. Transf. **15**(2), 89–107 (2013). https://doi.org/10.1007/s10009-012-0244-z
14. Garavel, H., Lang, F., Serwe, W.: From LOTOS to LNT. In: Katoen, J.-P., Langerak, R., Rensink, A. (eds.) ModelEd, TestEd, TrustEd. LNCS, vol. 10500, pp. 3–26. Springer, Cham (2017). https://doi.org/10.1007/978-3-319-68270-9_1
15. Klarner, H., Bockmayr, A., Siebert, H.: Computing Maximal and Minimal Trap Spaces of Boolean Networks. Nat. Comput. **14**(4), 535–544 (2015). https://doi.org/10.1007/s11047-015-9520-7
16. Kretínský, J., Meggendorfer, T., Sickert, S.: Owl: a library for ω-words, automata, and LTL. In: 16th International Symposium on Automated Technology for Verification and Analysis (ATVA). LNCS, vol. 11138, pp. 543–550. Springer (2018). https://doi.org/10.1007/978-3-030-01090-4_34
17. Kupferman, O., Vardi, M.Y.: Model Checking of Safety Properties. Formal Methods Syst. Des. **19**(3), 291–314 (2001). https://doi.org/10.1023/A:1011254632723
18. Kwiatkowska, M., Norman, G., Parker, D.: PRISM 4.0: verification of probabilistic real-time systems. In: Gopalakrishnan, G., Qadeer, S. (eds.) CAV 2011. LNCS, vol. 6806, pp. 585–591. Springer, Heidelberg (2011). https://doi.org/10.1007/978-3-642-22110-1_47
19. Pnueli, A.: The temporal logic of programs. In: 18th Annual Symposium on Foundations of Computer Science (FOCS), pp. 46–57. IEEE (1977). https://doi.org/10.1109/SFCS.1977.32
20. Rodríguez, A., Sánchez, C.: Boolean abstractions for realizability modulo theories. In: 35th International Conference on Computer Aided Verification (CAV). LNCS, vol. 13966, pp. 305–328. Springer (2023). https://doi.org/10.1007/978-3-031-37709-9_15
21. Yu, Y., Manolios, P., Lamport, L.: Model checking TLA+ specifications. In: 10th Advanced Research Working Conference on Correct Hardware Design and Verification Methods (CHARME). LNCS, vol. 1703, pp. 54–66. Springer (1999). https://doi.org/10.1007/3-540-48153-2_6

Formal Verification of Neural Certificates Done Dynamically

Thomas A. Henzinger🆔, Konstantin Kueffner🆔, and Emily Yu(✉)🆔

Institute of Science and Technology Austria, Klosterneuburg, Austria
{tah,kkueffner,zyu}@ist.ac.at

Abstract. Neural certificates have emerged as a powerful tool in cyber-physical systems control, providing witnesses of correctness. These certificates, such as barrier functions, often learned alongside control policies, once verified, serve as mathematical proofs of system safety. However, traditional formal verification of their defining conditions typically faces scalability challenges due to exhaustive state-space exploration. To address this challenge, we propose a lightweight runtime monitoring framework that integrates real-time verification and does not require access to the underlying control policy. Our monitor observes the system during deployment and performs on-the-fly verification of the certificate over a lookahead region to ensure safety within a finite prediction horizon. We instantiate this framework for ReLU-based control barrier functions and demonstrate its practical effectiveness in a case study. Our approach enables timely detection of safety violations and incorrect certificates with minimal overhead, providing an effective but lightweight alternative to the static verification of the certificates.

Keywords: Runtime Monitoring · Neural Control · Neural Certificates

1 Introduction

Forthcoming intelligent systems are increasingly integrated into industries and numerous application domains, including autonomous driving and medical image processing [2,4]. For example, deep reinforcement learning enables the automated synthesis of neural network controllers to address complex control tasks [16]. However, in these safety-critical domains, ensuring the safety and correctness of machine-learned components presents significant challenges. Neural networks often lack transparency and explainability, undermining their trustworthiness. Without formal safety guarantees, the reliability and operation of cyber-physical systems remain constrained, thereby affecting their deployment in practice.

Certificate functions serve as mathematical proofs to establish the correctness of controllers. A certificate function [9] is a mathematical mapping from system states to real values, where the satisfaction of its defining conditions guarantees that a desired system property holds. Notable examples include Lyapunov functions [28], used to prove stability with respect to a fixed point, and

© The Author(s), under exclusive license to Springer Nature Switzerland AG 2026
B. Königshofer and H. Torfah (Eds.): RV 2025, LNCS 16087, pp. 54–72, 2026.
https://doi.org/10.1007/978-3-032-05435-7_4

barrier functions [22], which are employed to certify safety by characterizing forward-invariant sets. While the theory of Lyapunov functions has been extensively studied over the past several decades, recent advances leverage reinforcement learning to synthesize such certificates in the form of neural networks. A growing body of work in learning-based control explores the joint synthesis of both the certificate function and the control policy. We refer to [9] for a more comprehensive overview of learning-based control using certificates.

Since certificate functions are often represented as neural networks, formal verification is typically employed to ensure their correctness. This gave rise to the learner-verifier framework [6,7,20], which is a synthesis framework to obtain valid neural certificates. This framework follows the style of Counterexample-Guided Inductive Synthesis (CEGIS). It consists of two main components: *the learner*, which synthesizes both the control policy and the certificate function, and *the verifier*, which checks whether the certificate satisfies its formal defining conditions. If the verifier identifies a counterexample, it is incorporated into the training set to refine the neural networks. This iterative loop continues until the certificate is successfully verified or a predefined termination criterion, such as a timeout, is met.

While formal verification offers correctness guarantees, it often suffers from scalability limitations due to its computational complexity, restricting its use in more complex control tasks. To overcome this challenge, *runtime monitoring* has emerged as a promising complementary approach. A runtime monitor is a lightweight software module that operates in parallel to the controlled system, issuing warnings upon detecting violations of specified properties or certificate defining conditions. The Simplex architecture [8,27], for instance, employs a verified backup controller to override unsafe actions. Recent work has proposed a learner-monitor framework [32], analogous to the learner-verifier paradigm, in which the monitor continuously collects counterexamples during execution and incorporates them into the training data to refine the learned models.

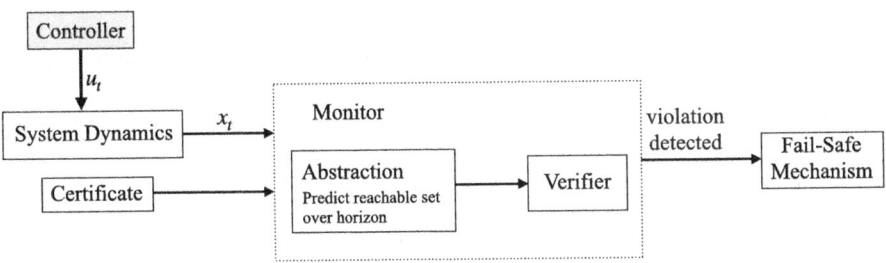

Fig. 1. Overview of our monitoring framework. At runtime, the monitor observes system states and computes an overapproximation of the reachable region using a local abstraction function. We do not assume access to the controller. A verifier checks whether the certificate remains valid in the lookahead region. If a violation is detected, a warning is issued and a fail-safe mechanism can be triggered.

In this paper, we propose a general runtime monitoring framework that integrates partial static verification over a lookahead horizon to ensure the safety of the controlled systems, as illustrated in Fig. 1. The framework is agnostic to the underlying controller and does not require access to future control inputs. At each time step, a monitor observes the system trajectory and uses a local abstraction function to over-approximate reachable states within the lookahead horizon. A certificate verifier then checks whether the safety certificate remains valid over this predicted region. If a violation is detected, the monitor issues a warning and can trigger a fail-safe response. Because our monitor detects violations ahead of time, the fail-safe mechanism is activated *before* leaving the certified region.

We instantiate this general framework using a specific verifier for ReLU-based control barrier functions (CBFs), leveraging the piecewise linear structure of ReLU networks for efficient localized verification. Our case study on a satellite rendezvous task demonstrate that the monitor can detect certificate violations as well as ensuring runtime safety with minimal overhead.

Overall, our contributions are as follows.

1. We introduce a general framework for online verification of certificates, which leverages a local abstraction function and a verifier as a sub-routine to enable local verification over a finite lookahead horizon.
2. We instantiate the framework for ReLU-based control barrier functions, and present a novel online verification algorithm that operates over neuron activation patterns. The algorithm adaptively constructs and verifies regions of the state space encountered at runtime, enabling fast detection of violations of safety as well as certificate defining conditions.

To the best of our knowledge, this is the first runtime monitoring approach that performs formal, on-the-fly certificate verification for neural-based control.

2 Preliminaries

We denote the set of natural number as $\mathbb{N}$ and the set of real numbers as $\mathbb{R}$. Their positive counterparts are denoted as $\mathbb{N}_+$ and $\mathbb{R}_+$ respectively.

Given a state space $\mathcal{X} \subseteq \mathbb{R}^m$ and an action space $\mathcal{U} \subseteq \mathbb{R}^n$, we consider continuous-time, control-affine dynamical systems of the form

$$\dot{x} = f(x) + g(x)u,$$

where $x \in \mathcal{X}, u \in \mathcal{U}, f : \mathbb{R}^m \to \mathbb{R}^m$ and $g : \mathbb{R}^m \to \mathbb{R}^{m \times n}$. A control policy $\pi : \mathcal{X} \to \mathcal{U}$ defines a closed-loop system $\mathcal{F} : \mathcal{X} \to \mathcal{X}$ with dynamics

$$\mathcal{F}(x) = f(x) + g(x)\pi(x). \tag{1}$$

The safe control problem requires that, under a given control policy, the system must never enter an unsafe state along any execution trace originating from an initial state. To prove that the process $\mathcal{F}$ satisfies properties such as safety or reachability, we rely on certificates. A certificate is a function $B : \mathcal{X} \to \mathbb{R}$ assigning a numerical value to each state. To be a valid certificate, this function B must satisfy some property dependent conditions over the state space. To prove safety, a barrier function is needed.

Definition 1 (Control Barrier Function). *Let $\mathcal{X}_0 \subseteq \mathcal{X}$ be the set of initial states, and let $\mathcal{X}_u \subseteq \mathcal{X}$ be the unsafe states. A continuously differentiable function $B : \mathcal{X} \to \mathbb{R}$ is called a* control barrier function *if the following conditions hold:*

1. $B(x) \geq 0$ *for all* $x \in \mathcal{X}_0$;
2. $B(x) < 0$ *for all* $x \in \mathcal{X}_u$;
3. $\nabla B(x)(f(x) + g(x)u)) + \alpha(B(x)) \geq 0$ *for all* $x \in \{x \in \mathcal{X} \mid B(x) \geq 0\}$.

Here, $\alpha : \mathbb{R} \to \mathbb{R}$ is a class $\mathcal{K}$ function that is strictly increasing and $\alpha(0) = 0$ [3].

The set $\mathcal{C} = \{x \in \mathcal{X} \mid B(x) \geq 0\}$ is referred to as the forward invariant set. The expression $\nabla B(x)(f(x) + g(x)u)$ denotes the Lie derivative of the barrier function B along the system dynamics. If a valid barrier function exists for a given control policy π, then the system is guaranteed to be safe. A formal proof of this result is provided in [3].

In this paper, we also consider ReLU-based barrier functions, where the barrier function is implemented as a feed-forward neural network with L layers. Each layer i has dimension size M_i, and the activation function used is the Rectified Linear Unit (ReLU), defined as $\sigma : \mathbb{R}^a \to \mathbb{R}^a$ with

$$\sigma(x) = \begin{cases} x & \text{if } x \geq 0, \\ 0 & \text{otherwise.} \end{cases}$$

Each neuron in the network is indexed by its layer and position within the layer, denoted by the pair (i, j). Given an input x, let z_i^j denote the pre-activation value at neuron (i, j). A neuron is said to be *active* if $z_i^j > 0$, *unstable* if $z_i^j = 0$, and *inactive* otherwise. We denote by $\mathcal{A} = (A_1, \ldots, A_L)$ an activation pattern, where each A_i represents the set of active neurons in layer i. Similarly, let $\mathcal{T} = (T_1, \ldots, T_L)$ represent the unstable neurons.

For a given activation pattern, evaluating the neural network becomes significantly simpler, as the weights and biases reduce to fixed linear terms. We define masked weights and biases with respect to $\mathcal{A}$. For the first layer:

$$\overline{W}_{1j}(\mathcal{A}) = \begin{cases} W_{1j} & \text{if } j \in A_1, \\ 0 & \text{otherwise,} \end{cases} \quad \overline{r}_{1j}(\mathcal{A}) = \begin{cases} r_{1j} & \text{if } j \in A_1, \\ 0 & \text{otherwise.} \end{cases}$$

This implies that the output of the j-th neuron in the first layer is simply $\overline{W}_{1j}(\mathcal{A})^\top x + \overline{r}_{1j}(\mathcal{A})$. For deeper layers $i > 1$, we recursively define:

$$\overline{W}_{ij}(\mathcal{A}) = \begin{cases} W_{ij}^\top \overline{W}_{i-1}(\mathcal{A}) & \text{if } j \in A_i, \\ 0 & \text{otherwise,} \end{cases} \quad \overline{r}_{ij}(\mathcal{A}) = \begin{cases} W_{ij}^\top \overline{r}_{i-1}(\mathcal{A}) + r_{ij} & \text{if } j \in A_i, \\ 0 & \text{otherwise.} \end{cases}$$

We write $\overline{W}(\mathcal{A})$ to denote the effective linear transformation of the final layer under the activation pattern $\mathcal{A}$. This linearized structure captures the piecewise-linear behavior of the ReLU network within the region defined by $\mathcal{A}$.

Definition 2 (ReLU-based CBF). *Let $\mathcal{X}(\mathcal{A})$ denote the region of the input space induced by activation pattern $\mathcal{A}$. A function B is a ReLU-based control barrier function if, for every activation pattern $\mathcal{A}$, the region $\mathcal{X}(\mathcal{A}) \cap \mathcal{C}$ does not intersect the unsafe set:*

$$\mathcal{X}(\mathcal{A}) \cap \mathcal{C} \cap \mathcal{X}_{\text{unsafe}} = \emptyset.$$

Moreover, there exists an activation pattern $\mathcal{A}$ such that for all x on the boundary where $B(x) = 0$, the following hold:

1. $(\overline{W}_{i-1}(\mathcal{A})W_{ij})^\top (f(x) + g(x)\pi(x)) \geq 0$ *for all* $(i,j) \in \mathcal{T}(x) \cap \mathcal{A}$;
2. $(\overline{W}_{i-1}(\mathcal{A})W_{ij})^\top (f(x) + g(x)\pi(x)) \leq 0$ *for all* $(i,j) \in \mathcal{T}(x) \setminus \mathcal{A}$;
3. $\overline{W}(\mathcal{A})^\top (f(x) + g(x)\pi(x)) \geq 0$.

This definition encodes the requirement that the barrier function B does not decrease along the system dynamics at the certificate boundary where $B(x) = 0$ [34]. This definition guarantees that B serves as a valid control barrier function over the region defined by the activation pattern S, and that the system remains within the forward invariant set $\mathcal{C}$ if it starts there.

3 Monitoring Framework

Classically the validity of a certificate function, e.g., the barrier certificate in Definition 1, is verified on the entire state space. This is expensive and wasteful, especially in high-dimensions. As the dimension of the state space increases, both, finding and validating a certificate becomes exponentially more expensive. At the same time the volume of all states visited by the process on an infinite run becomes negligible compared to the volume of the entire domain, implying that most of the work done during verification is unnecessary.

Certificates at Runtime. We use φ to denote an arbitrary certificate condition, e.g., the conditions in Definition 1. The binary value of a certificate condition is determined by the closed-loop system $\mathcal{F}$, the certificate B, and a subset of the state space $\mathcal{Y} \subseteq \mathcal{X}$, i.e., $\varphi(\mathcal{F}, B, \mathcal{Y}) \in \{0, 1\}$. In static verification we check the certificate condition over the entire state space $\mathcal{X}$. This ensures that φ is satisfied on the infinite trace $w := (x_t)_{t \in \mathbb{R}_+}$ generated by $\mathcal{F}$. Intuitively, we would expect that validating the certificate condition for a single trace, i.e., $\varphi(\mathcal{F}, B, w)$, should be significantly simpler than validating it for the entire state space $\varphi(\mathcal{F}, B, \mathcal{X})$. The reason why static verification focuses on the entire state space is because it may be impossible to obtain the trace w at development time due to uncertainty. However, for short time horizons this uncertainty remains manageable. This is where static verification done dynamically shines.

Example 1. Consider $\mathcal{X} := [0,1]^d$ for $d \in \mathbb{N}_+$ and let $w := (x_t)_{t \in \mathbb{R}_+}$. If we know that the certificate B and the system $\mathcal{F}$ are Lipschitz with a constant L, a naive approach to validating the certificate condition on $\mathcal{X}$ up to a precision $c > 0$ is to construct a c/L-grid [7]. The number of vertices in the grid increases exponentially in the dimension, i.e., for $\mathcal{X}$ we require approximately $(L/c)^d$ vertices. By contrast, a c/L-grid over w requires only L/c vertices. Hence, verifying the trace is exponentially faster than verifying the entire domain.

Certificate Monitor. Our objective is to construct a certificate monitor which detects certificate condition violations before they occur. Let $w := (x_t)_{t \in \mathbb{R}_+}$ be the trace generated by $\mathcal{F}$. The trace up to time $t \in \mathbb{R}_+$ is defined as $w_{[0,t)} := (x_t)_{t \in [0,t)}$. The monitor can only observe a finite subset of this trace as given by its observation frequency parameter $\varepsilon > 0$, which we consider as given, e.g., the parameter may be a function of the monitor's hardware constraints. For every interval $[a,b) \subseteq \mathbb{R}$ we denote $[a,b)_\varepsilon := \{a + k \cdot \varepsilon \mid k \in \mathbb{N} \land a + k \cdot \varepsilon < b\}$ as the finite discretization of $[a,b)$ w.r.t. ε. We denote the observable trace by the monitor as $w^\varepsilon_{[0,t)} := (x_t)_{t \in [0,t)_\varepsilon}$. For a given safety horizon $h \in \mathbb{R}_+$, e.g., the time required to stop a vehicle, we want a monitor $\mathbf{M} : \mathcal{X}^* \to \{0,1\}$ that maps the trace $w^\varepsilon_{[0,t)}$ into a verdict in $\{0,1\}$. We call the monitor $\mathbf{M}$ sound, iff a positive verdict guarantees that the certificate is satisfied on the trace $w_{[0,t+h)}$, i.e.,

$$\mathbf{M}\left(w^\varepsilon_{[0,t)}\right) = 1 \implies \varphi\left(\mathcal{F}, B, w_{[0,t+h)}\right) = 1. \tag{2}$$

Problem 1. For a given closed-loop system $\mathcal{F}$ as defined in Eq. 1, a certificate function B, a certificate condition φ, and a safety horizon h with epsilon ϵ, construct a sound certificate monitor $\mathbf{M}$.

3.1 Monitor Construction

We show how to construct a sound certificate monitor using a local abstraction function and a certificate verifier as subroutines. The local abstraction function provides a sound overapproximation of how the process behaves within a given time horizon. This overapproximation is a bounded region, e.g., a cone, within the state space. The verifier checks whether the certificate condition is satisfied for every state within a given region of the state space. Our monitor simply invokes the verifier on the uncertainty region computed by the local abstraction function. We chose this modular construction because there exists a plethora of predictive monitoring tools which can be utilized as a local abstraction function [14]. Similarly, there exists a variety of certificate verification tools that can assess the validity of a certificate for a given region [7,35,36]. Each tool has its own assumptions on the system, as a consequence our certificate monitor can adapt and improve depending on the available subroutines.

Abstraction and Verification. We assume access to a local abstraction function $\mathbf{A}: \mathcal{X}^* \times \mathbb{R}_+ \to \mathcal{P}(\mathcal{X})$ and a verifier $\mathbf{V}: \mathcal{P}(\mathcal{X}) \to \{0,1\}$ where $\mathcal{P}(\mathcal{X}) := \{\mathcal{Y} \mid \mathcal{Y} \subseteq \mathcal{X}\}$ is the set of all subsets of $\mathcal{X}$. First, the abstraction function maps the trace $w^{\varepsilon}_{[0,t)} \in \mathcal{X}^*$ up to time $t \in \mathbb{R}_+$ and a time horizon $h \in \mathbb{R}_+$ into a subset of the domain, i.e., $\mathbf{A}(w^{\varepsilon}_{[0,t)}, h) \subseteq \mathcal{X}$. We are guaranteed that the process is contained within the output region for the specified time horizon, i.e.,

$$\forall t \in [t, t+h].\ x_t \in \mathbf{A}(w^{\varepsilon}_{[0,t)}, h). \tag{3}$$

Second, the verifier checks whether the certificate B satisfies condition φ w.r.t. the process $\mathcal{F}$ for a given region $\mathcal{Y} \subseteq \mathcal{X}$, i.e.,

$$\forall \mathcal{Y} \subseteq \mathcal{X}.\ \mathbf{V}(\mathcal{Y}) = 1 \iff \varphi(\mathcal{F}, B, \mathcal{Y}) = 1 \tag{4}$$

In Sect. 4 we provide a concrete examples for both the abstraction function and the verifier. For now we treat both of them as black-boxes.

Local Verification. By combining the abstraction function and the verifier we construct a simple subroutine ensuring that the certificate condition is satisfied locally, i.e., the certificate remains valid within the immediate time horizon. Assume we are at time $t \in \mathbb{R}_+$, have observed the trace $w^{\varepsilon}_{[0,t)}$ derived from the actual trace $w_{[0,t)}$, and decided for a time horizon $h_t \in \mathbb{R}_+$. We invoke the abstraction function $\mathbf{A}$ with the observed trace $w^{\varepsilon}_{[0,t)}$ and time horizon h_t, and verify the generated region using $\mathbf{V}$ to guarantee the validity of the certificate up until time $t + h_t$, i.e., we compute

$$\mathbf{V}(\mathbf{A}(w^{\varepsilon}_{[0,t)}, h_t)). \tag{5}$$

If the verifier outputs 1 the validity for certificate is assured up until $t+h$, if the verifier outputs 0 the certificate condition is violated for a state in the predicted region. Hence, it may violated on $w_{[t,t+h)} \subseteq \mathbf{A}(w^{\varepsilon}_{[0,t)}, h_t)$. This gives a local overapproximation of the certificate condition value.

Lemma 1. *If the abstraction function satisfies Condition 3 and the verifier satisfies Condition 4, we are guaranteed that*

$$\mathbf{V}(\mathbf{A}(w^{\varepsilon}_{[0,t)}, h_t)) = 1 \implies \varphi(\mathcal{F}, B, w_{[t,t+h_t)}) = 1.$$

Proof. Condition 3 ensures that the over-approximation computed by the abstraction function contains the trace up to time $t + h_t$, i.e., $w_{[t,t+h_t)}) \subseteq \mathcal{Z} := \mathbf{A}(w^{\varepsilon}_{[0,t)}, h_t)$. Condition 4 ensures that $\mathbf{V}(\mathcal{Y}) = 1 \implies \varphi(\mathcal{F}, B, w_{[t,t+h_t)}) = 1$.

Soundness. The subroutine described above guarantees that the certificate condition remains satisfied within the specified time horizon. However, verifying on the fly requires time and cannot be done continuously. Therefore, constructing a sound monitor requires us to get the timing right. Assume we can start the verification procedure after having observed the current state. If we are able to compute the local guarantee, i.e., $\mathbf{V}(\mathbf{A}(w^{\varepsilon}_{[0,t)}, h_t))$, for a time horizon of

$h_t := 2 \cdot \varepsilon + h$ in less than ε-time, then we can obtain a sound monitor defined in Algorithm 1. This guarantees that the monitor raises a warning *before* the system enters a region where the certificate is invalid, allowing the system to activate the fail-safe mechanism in time.

Theorem 1. *Given a state space $\mathcal{X}$, a system $\mathcal{F}$, and a certificate B. Let* $\mathbf{A} : \mathcal{X}^* \times \mathbb{R}_+ \to \mathcal{P}(\mathcal{X})$ *be an abstraction function (satisfying Eq. 3),* $\mathbf{V} : \mathcal{P}(\mathcal{X}) \to \{0,1\}$ *be a verifier (satisfying Eq. 4), $h \in \mathbb{R}_+$ be a time horizon, $\varepsilon \in \mathbb{R}_+$ be a observation frequency parameter. If the the sub-routine* NEXT *can be computed in less than ε-time, the monitor defined by Algorithm 1 is sound, i.e.,*

$$\mathbf{M}_h(w_{[0,t)}^\varepsilon) = 1 \implies \varphi(\mathcal{F}, B, w_{[0,t+h)}) = 1.$$

Proof. The sequence of observation points is $(k \cdot \varepsilon)_{k \in \mathbb{N}}$ we prove this claim by induction over the observation points. Let $k = 0$. We assume we have already verified the first $\varepsilon + h$ time interval, if the verdict $v = 0$ we have found a potential violation and we are done. Otherwise, we know from Lemma 1 that this implies that $\varphi(\mathcal{F}, B, w_{[0,\varepsilon+h)})) = 1$. This implies that every point $s \in [0, \varepsilon)$ is covered. The induction hypothesis is that at the beginning of every observation point $k \in \mathbb{N}_+$, $v_{k-1} = 1$ implies that $\varphi(\mathcal{F}, B, w_{[0, \varepsilon \cdot k + h)})) = 1$. Assume we are at observation point $k+1$. If $v_k = 0$ we are done. If $v_k = 1$, then by the induction hypothesis we know that $\varphi(\mathcal{F}, B, w_{[0, \varepsilon \cdot (k+1) + h)})) = 1$. We start computing NEXT for the time horizon $2\varepsilon + h$, i.e. upon termination we know whether there exists a potential certificate violation on $[(k+1) \cdot \varepsilon, (k+3) \cdot \varepsilon + h]$ or not. By assumption we know that executing NEXT requires less than ε time. Hence, before time step $k+2$ we have finished computing v_{k+1}, which if $v_{k+1=1}$ guarantees that $\varphi(\mathcal{F}, B, w_{[0, \varepsilon \cdot (k+2) + h)})) = 1$.

Implementation. Algorithm 1 describes the schematic dynamic verification routine. We initialize the monitor with INIT, which creates the initial empty trace w_0 and sets the initial verdict v_0 to 1. During runtime the monitor executes NEXT whenever a new input state $x \in \mathcal{X}$ is observed. At execution $k \in \mathbb{N}_+$, it appends the observed state x to the past trace creating w_k, which is used to perform the verification step over the uncertainty region provided by the abstraction function; checking whether there is a certificate violation in the future. The verdict of this step is stored in v_{buffer}. If the previous verdict v_{k-1} is 1, i.e., no certificate violation was detected in some previous iteration, the verdict at iteration v_k is set to v_{buffer}. Otherwise, the verdict remains 0, because once a violation is detected, the monitor will consider the certificate condition violated.

Remark 1. If the execution of NEXT requires more time, parallelization can be exploited to avoid this problem, i.e., we simply execute NEXT while accounting for the additional computation time on a new thread at the end of every control interval. If the computation time remains constant, we can obtain a similar guarantee. Moreover, the number of threads can be bounded based on that time.

Algorithm 1. Schematic Monitor $\mathbf{M}_h$

1: **Given:** time horizon $h \in \mathbb{R}_+$, observation frequency parameter ε, abstraction function $\mathbf{A} : \mathcal{X}^* \times \mathbb{R}_+ \to \mathcal{P}(\mathcal{X})$, a verifier $\mathbf{V} : \mathcal{P}(\mathcal{X}) \to \{0,1\}$.
2: **function** INIT( )
3:      $w_0 \leftarrow x;\ v_0 \leftarrow 1$
4: **function** NEXT(x)
5:      $w_k \leftarrow w_{k-1} \cdot x$
6:      $v_{\text{buffer}} \leftarrow \mathbf{V}(\mathbf{A}(w_k, 2 \cdot \varepsilon + h))$
7:      $v_k \leftarrow v_{\text{buffer}}$ **if** $v_{k-1} = 1$ **else** $v_k \leftarrow 0$
8:      **return** v_k

4 Online Verification of ReLU-Based Control Barrier Functions (CBFs)

Our monitoring approach is designed to ensure runtime safety and verify the correctness of a neural certificate, without requiring full state space verification or access to future control inputs. In this section, we instantiate the general monitoring framework for ReLU-based control barrier functions.

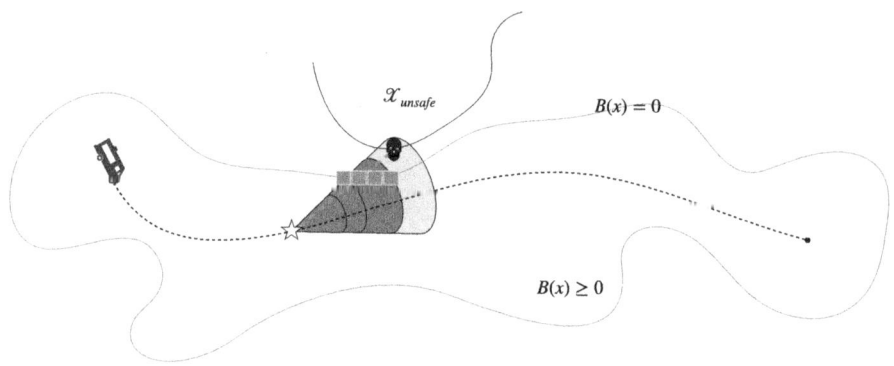

Fig. 2. Illustration of online verification with lookahead. At each time step, the monitor maintains a cone that over-approximates the reachable states within a fixed horizon. If this cone intersects the unsafe region, the monitor searches for a cube on the barrier boundary where $B(x) = 0$. The cone is then shrunk to contain this boundary, and the identified cube along with its neighbors are verified to assess certificate validity.

As illustrated in Fig. 2, the monitor continuously observes the system's trajectory and incrementally builds a conservative over-approximation of reachable states within a fixed lookahead horizon. If no violations are detected within this cone region, the system is deemed safe for the near future. If a *safety violation* is detected, e.g., the cone intersects the unsafe region, the monitor performs a refinement step. It searches for a state on the certificate boundary ($B(x) = 0$) and identifies the corresponding *activation region* (called a *cube*) in which this state lies. Because ReLU networks induce a partition of the state space into finitely many such cubes, and each cube corresponds to a fixed neuron activation pattern, the CBF condition from Def. 1 becomes a set of linear constraints within each cube. The monitor then verifies these conditions locally by checking whether the barrier certificate holds in the identified cube and its neighbors. If a violation is detected, the system triggers a fail-safe response (e.g., controller override). If all cubes are verified to be safe, the monitor continues observing and updating the cone over time.

Our approach operates over two state spaces: (1) the continuous, real-valued state space defined by the underlying dynamical system, and (2) the discrete space of activation patterns, induced by the architecture of the neural CBF. In the following, we refer to an element of (1) simply as a *state*, and to the subset of states corresponding to a particular activation pattern as a *cube*. Two states belong to the same cube if they produce identical neuron activation patterns in the CBF. We present the main monitoring loop in Algorithm 2.

Initialization. Our approach begins with a pre-trained neural CBF and an associated control policy. The control policy is treated as a black-box, meaning its internal structure is not accessible. However, we assume access to a set of known constraints that bound the range of control inputs generated by the policy, e.g., minimum and maximum allowable acceleration values. In addition, we define a fixed horizon h parameter, which determines how far into the future the monitor evaluates the system's evolution to assess safety.

Algorithm 2. Main Monitor Loop for ReLU-based CBFs

1: **Given:** forward invariant set $\mathcal{C}$, unsafe set $\mathcal{X}_u$, lookahead horizon h
2: **function** INIT( )
3: $\quad v_0 \leftarrow 1;\ \mathcal{X}_{\text{safe}} \leftarrow \mathcal{X} \setminus \mathcal{X}_u$
4: **function** NEXT(x)
5: $\quad (cone, x_{\text{unsafe}}, i) \leftarrow$ CONSTRUCTCONE($\mathcal{X}_u, x, h$) // Abstraction function call
6: $\quad$ **if** x_{unsafe} is found **then**
7: $\qquad v_{\text{buffer}} \leftarrow$ VERIFYCUBESONBOUNDARY($x, x_{\text{unsafe}}, cone, i, h$) // Verifier call
8: $\quad v_k \leftarrow v_{\text{buffer}}$ **if** $v_{k-1} = 1$ **else** $v_k \leftarrow 0$
9: $\quad$ **return** v_k

During monitoring, the cone is constructed using an abstraction function. To detect potential safety violations, the monitor expands the cone using the CONSTRUCTCONE procedure (Algorithm 3). If no intersection with the unsafe set $\mathcal{X}_u$ is found within the horizon, the system continues unimpeded. However, if an unsafe state is detected, the monitor performs a binary search between the current state and the unsafe state to locate a cube on the barrier boundary (line 2, Algorithm 4). The online verification procedure begins by adding the identified cube to a queue, referred to as the *boundary*. Each cube in this queue is then iteratively verified. Cubes that do not intersect with the current lookahead

Algorithm 3. ConstructCone (The Abstraction Function)

1: **function** CONSTRUCTCONE($\mathcal{X}_u$, x, h)
2:     $cone \leftarrow \{x\}$, $i \leftarrow 0$ // Initialize cone
3:     **while** $i < h$ **do**
4:         $slice \leftarrow$ EXPAND($cone$) $\setminus cone$
5:         $cone \leftarrow cone \cup slice$
6:         **if** $slice \cap \mathcal{X}_u \neq \emptyset$ **then**
7:             **return** ($cone$, PICK($slice \cap \mathcal{X}_u$), i)
8:         $i \leftarrow i + 1$
9:     **return** ($cone$, $\bot$, h)

---

cone are discarded, as they cannot influence the set of reachable states. If verification fails for any cube, this indicates a violation of the certificate conditions, prompting the system to enter a fail-safe mode or switch to a backup controller. Successfully verified cubes are marked accordingly and added to a queue for neighborhood expansion.

With this initial queue, we start a breadth-first search by examining the 1-bit Hamming neighbors of each verified cube, i.e., those whose ReLU activation patterns differ by exactly one neuron. A neighboring cube is discarded if it has already been verified, or does not intersect any state in $\mathcal{X}$. If it lies outside the current cone, we may verify it after expanding the cone at the next iteration. All intersection checks as well as VERIFYLINEAR in Algorithm 4 operate on a single cube, thus they can be solved efficiently as a simple set of linear inequalities.

5 Experiments

In this section, we evaluate the effectiveness of our monitoring method via a case study and compare it with static verification.

The benchmark we used is a satellite rendezvous example, adapted from [10, 15]. In this scenario, a chaser satellite attempts to approach a target satellite while remaining within a designated safe region, corresponding to its line of sight. Both satellites are assumed to be in orbit around the Earth. The system state is represented by the 6-dimensional vector $[x, y, z, v_x, v_y, v_z]$, where $[x, y, z]$ denotes the relative position of the chaser with respect to the target, and $[v_x, v_y, v_z]$ its relative velocity. The control input is given by $u = [u_x, u_y, u_z]$, representing thrust applied along each axis. The control interval is fixed to be 0.1 second.

We evaluate both static formal verification and online monitoring across different neural CBF architectures. Static verification is performed using SEEV [33], a recent tool tailored for verifying ReLU-based certificates. For online monitoring, we employ a local abstraction function that is fixed-step unrolling with known input bounds and a verifier operating on the ReLU activation patterns as described in Sect. 5.

Table 1 presents the results of static formal verification for neural CBFs of varying sizes. Notably, the verification of CBF with 8 layers and 16 neurons per

Algorithm 4. VerifyCubesOnBoundary (The Verifier)

1: **function** VERIFYCUBESONBOUNDARY(x, x_{unsafe}, $cone$, i, h)
2:     $cube \leftarrow$ BINARYSEARCH(x, x_{unsafe})
3:     $boundary \leftarrow \{cube\}$
4:     **while** $boundary \neq \emptyset$ **do**
5:         $queue \leftarrow \emptyset$
6:         **for all** $c \in boundary$ **do**
7:             **if** $c \cap \mathcal{X} \cap cone = \emptyset$ **then continue**
8:             **else if** $\neg$VERIFYLINEAR(c) **then** // Check conditions in Def. 2
9:                 FAIL-SAFE()
10:             **else**
11:                 $queue$.PUSH(c)
12:         $boundary \leftarrow \emptyset$
13:         **while** $queue \neq \emptyset$ **do**
14:             **for all** $c' \in$ NEIGHBORHOOD($queue$.pop()) **do**
15:                 **if** VERIFIED(c') or $c' \cap \mathcal{X} = \emptyset$ **then continue**
16:                 **else if** $c' \cap \mathcal{X} \cap cone = \emptyset$ **then**
17:                     $boundary$.PUSH(c')
18:                 **else if** $\neg$VERIFYLINEAR(c') **then**
19:                     FAIL-SAFE()
20:                 **else**
21:                     $queue$.PUSH(c')
22:     $cone \leftarrow cone \cup$ EXPAND($cone$)
23:     $i \leftarrow i + 1$
24:     **if** $i > h$ **then break**

Table 1. Verification results with corresponding full verification times using SEEV [33].

No. Hidden Layers	No. Neurons per Layer	Verification Result	Full Time (s)
2	8	safe	50.21
4	8	safe	253.20
8	16	-	>2 h
16	16	unsafe	6.03

layer timed out after two hours using the SEEV method. In contrast, our online monitoring approach was able to detect violations much faster (see Fig. 4).

We now evaluate how our monitoring framework performs. As shown in Fig. 4, the monitor was able to detect violations with minimal overhead with a longer lookahead horizon (¿ 70 steps). With shorter horizons, no violations were detected, as the future cones remained relatively small. This also give an insight: even incorrect certificates may suffice to ensure safety over limited parts of the system's state space. As the lookahead horizon increases, the monitor explores a broader region and is more likely to encounter violations where the certificate conditions fail. We also observe an increase in monitoring overhead around 70

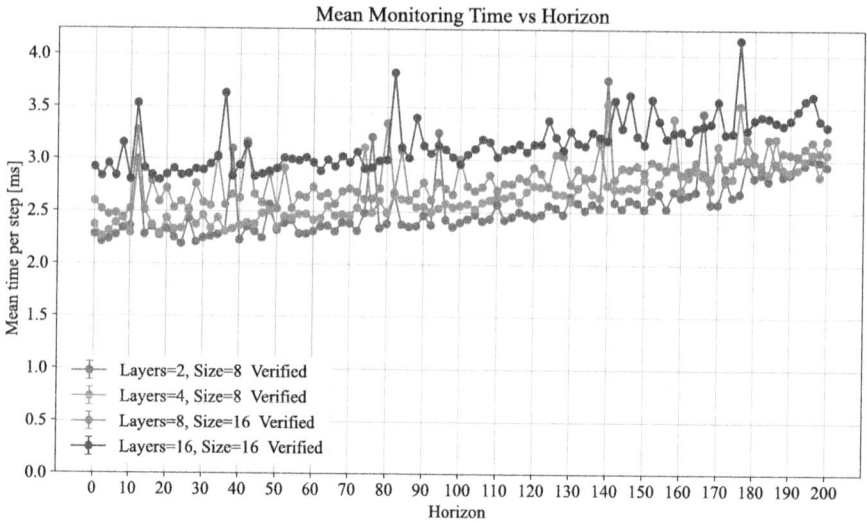

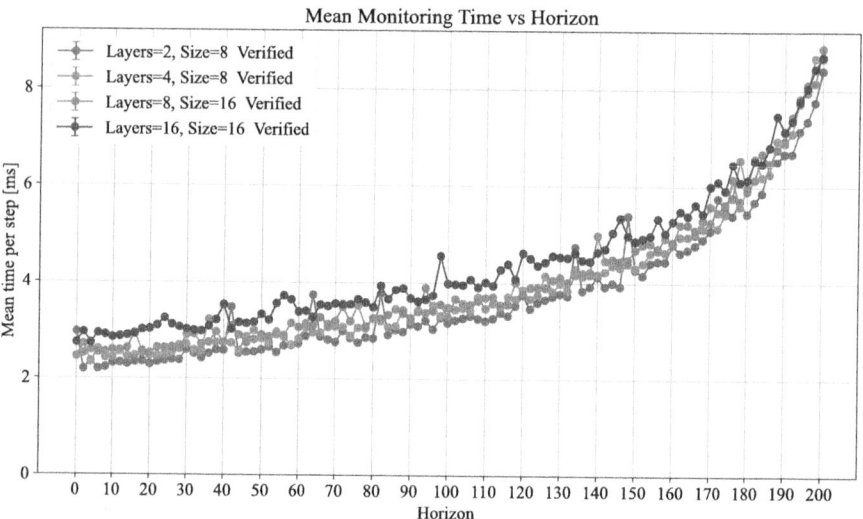

Fig. 3. Monitoring overhead measured for lookahead horizons up to 200 steps, across four network configurations with varying depth and width. All configurations were successfully verified through static analysis (see Table 1). The two plots correspond to different initial states. The monitor did not raise warnings during these runs.

steps. This is because, as the horizon increases, the over-approximation increases in size, thus intersects more barrier cubes which need to be verified.

There is a trade-off between monitoring overhead and lookahead horizon, which is as expected. However, we observe that the overhead remains well within practical limits. Figures 3 and 4 report average monitoring overheads for looka-

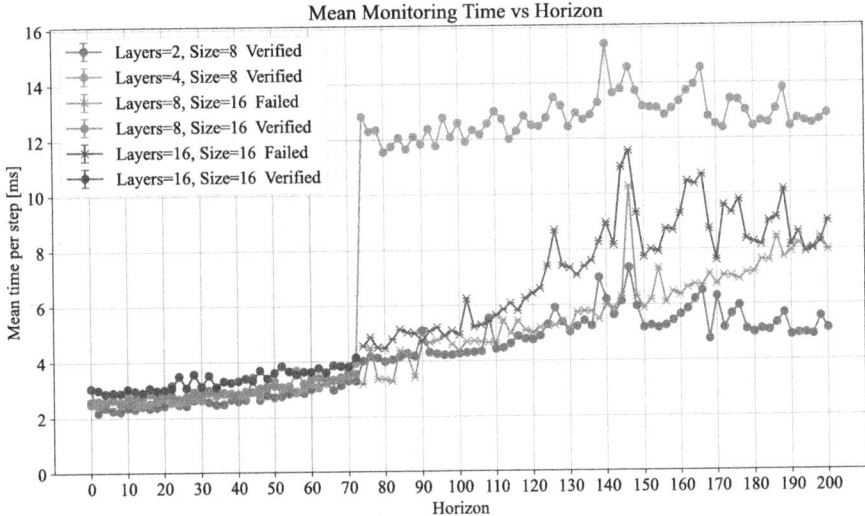

Fig. 4. Monitoring overhead measured for lookahead horizons up to 200 steps, across four network configurations with varying depth and width. Two CBFs failed static verification (one of them timed out), and our monitor successfully detected violations online in both cases, with a higher horizon.

head horizons up to 200 steps (20 s). Across all six network configurations, the average overhead remains below 16ms per step, which is substantially lower than the 0.1 s control interval. This demonstrates the practicality of our approach for real-time safety monitoring.

In Table 2, we report the results of online monitoring across different network architectures with lookahead horizons. For each configuration, we summarize the number of traces evaluated and the average runtime per monitoring step. Each configuration was tested on a total of 323 traces, generated by random initial states. As the lookahead horizon increases, our monitor successfully detects more violations in networks that failed verification, confirming the effectiveness of lookahead in revealing unsafe behaviors. The per-step verification overhead remains low across all configurations, even for larger networks.

In addition to deployment-time use, our monitor is also well-suited for identifying counterexamples *during testing*. This makes it a valuable tool for diagnosing safety and certificate violations early in the development cycle. Moreover, it can be integrated into a learnermonitor loop for iteratively repairing certificates, as proposed in [32]. This can be achieved by detecting violations online and adding counterexamples to the training data.

Discussion and Limitations. We consider our online monitoring framework to be complementary to static verification for both testing and deployment settings. This can also be particularly valuable in the presence of environmental uncertainties or model inaccuracies, where exhaustive offline verification may not capture

Table 2. Online verification results for various lookahead horizons. The outcome column indicates whether verification failed or succeeded. We also display the number of traces evaluated (#traces), with a total number of 323 traces.

				Lookahead Horizon [steps]				
Layers	Size	Outcome	Metric	40	80	120	160	200
2	8	✓	#traces	323	323	323	323	323
			time [ms]	2.52	2.85	3.27	3.82	4.06
4	8	✓	#traces	323	323	323	323	323
			time [ms]	2.72	3.64	4.90	6.69	8.21
8	16	✓	#traces	318	292	255	199	142
			time [ms]	2.76	3.01	3.35	3.75	4.01
8	16	✗	#traces	5	26	63	113	164
			time [ms]	6.18	5.09	5.18	8.64	7.84
16	16	✓	#traces	318	292	255	199	142
			time [ms]	3.09	3.33	3.70	4.07	4.39
16	16	✗	#traces	5	31	68	124	181
			time [ms]	6.49	5.70	6.47	10.37	8.93

all relevant behaviors. While in our case, the monitor still uses the system model for prediction, it performs verification adaptively along the concrete execution path, avoiding exhaustive offline analysis over the entire state space. A potential limitation arises when the system operates near the boundary of the certificate region. In such cases, verifying large numbers of cubes may introduce additional computational overhead, which can affect real-time performance. Moreover, if the system is already close to exiting the forward-invariant set, a fail-safe mechanism may not always react in time to prevent a safety violation. This is a fundamental challenge of runtime monitoring in general, where monitors are expected to signal warnings timely while minimizing false alarms. Finally, while our case study focuses on a linearized orbital rendezvous model and a corresponding verification procedure, the proposed framework is general. It applies to nonlinear control-affine systems, provided that suitable local abstractions and verifiers are available. The frameworks capabilities scale with the performance of either component.

6 Related Work

Black-Box Simplex Architecture. The Simplex architecture is a runtime assurance method that has been widely adopted in control applications [11,21,23]. It consists of an active controller responsible for primary decision-making and a backup controller that can override the active controller when necessary to ensure runtime safety. Recent research has extended this framework to black-box settings, where the internal architecture of the controllers is assumed to be unknown [17,19]. This is a similar setting to our work where we perform on-the-fly verification, however, they do not consider certificates.

Runtime Enforcement Using Certificates. Shielding is a widely adopted runtime enforcement technique [5] where the shield overrides control inputs to ensure safety. Certificate functions, such as barrier functions, have been integrated with shielding, as demonstrated in [31], where the barrier functions are given in advance. However, in that setting the certificates are not formally verified thus there is no correctness guarantee. More recently, Corsi et al. [18] propose verification-guided shielding, which uses pre-computed verification to identify specific regions for shielding. Unlike these approaches, our method performs real-time verification over a lookahead horizon without requiring preprocessing.

Concolic Testing. Related to our work is also concolic testing [24–26], which combines concrete and symbolic execution to explore the local state space of software programs more effectively. Our work draws a parallel to this idea by applying a similar concolic approach in the context of certificate-based control.

Formal Verification of Certificates. To verify a neural certificate, we need to check whether the network satisfies certificate conditions w.r.t. the controlled system. Broadly speaking there are two approaches, a symbolic approach and a search approach. In the symbolic approach the system, the network, and the certificate condition are encoded as a logical formula and solved using a SMT solver [1,12,35], or they are encoded as a mixed integer linear program and solved with a solver such as Gurobi [13,36]. In the search approach the Lipschitz constant of a neural network is exploited to systematically search the state space, e.g., grid search, to detect potential certificate violations [7,30].

7 Conclusion

In this work, we proposed a general framework for online verification of neural certificates that integrates partial static verification over a finite lookahead horizon. Our method is lightweight, does not require access to future control inputs, and supports modular integration of local abstraction function and certificate verifiers. This enables runtime safety assurance even in settings where static verification is infeasible. We instantiated our framework with a verifier tailored to ReLU-based control barrier functions and demonstrated its practicality on a satellite rendezvous example. The monitor was able to effectively detect certificate violations as well as ensuring runtime safety with minimal overhead.

Our framework is general and readily applies to other types of certificate functions, such as Lyapunov functions and contraction metrics [29], and opens the door to further integration with runtime enforcement mechanisms such as shielding. As future work, we plan to investigate how this monitoring framework can be embedded into training loops to iteratively repair unsafe certificates. We also plan to extend our approach to probabilistic settings to account for environmental uncertainties.

Acknowledgement. This work is supported by the European Research Council under Grant No.: ERC-2020-AdG 101020093.

References

1. Abate, A., Ahmed, D., Edwards, A., Giacobbe, M., Peruffo, A.: Fossil: a software tool for the formal synthesis of Lyapunov functions and barrier certificates using neural networks. In: Proceedings of the 24th International Conference on Hybrid Systems: Computation and Control, pp. 1–11 (2021)
2. Abiodun, O.I., Jantan, A., Omolara, A.E., Dada, K.V., Mohamed, N.A., Arshad, H.: State-of-the-art in artificial neural network applications: a survey. Heliyon **4**(11) (2018)
3. Ames, A.D., Grizzle, J.W., Tabuada, P.: Control barrier function based quadratic programs with application to adaptive cruise control. In: 53rd IEEE Conference on Decision and Control, pp. 6271–6278. IEEE (2014)
4. Anwar, S.M., Majid, M., Qayyum, A., Awais, M., Alnowami, M., Khan, M.K.: Medical image analysis using convolutional neural networks: a review. J. Med. Syst. **42**, 1–13 (2018)
5. Bloem, R., Könighofer, B., Könighofer, R., Wang, C.: Shield synthesis: runtime enforcement for reactive systems. In: International Conference on Tools and Algorithms for the Construction and Analysis of Systems, pp. 533–548. Springer (2015)
6. Chang, Y.C., Roohi, N., Gao, S.: Neural Lyapunov control. Adv. Neural Inf. Process. Syst. **32** (2019)
7. Chatterjee, K., Henzinger, T.A., Lechner, M., Zikelic, D.: A learner-verifier framework for neural network controllers and certificates of stochastic systems. In: TACAS (1). LNCS, vol. 13993, pp. 3–25. Springer (2023)
8. Crenshaw, T.L., Gunter, E., Robinson, C.L., Sha, L., Kumar, P.: The simplex reference model: limiting fault-propagation due to unreliable components in cyber-physical system architectures. In: 28th IEEE International Real-Time Systems Symposium (RTSS 2007), pp. 400–412. IEEE (2007)
9. Dawson, C., Gao, S., Fan, C.: Safe control with learned certificates: a survey of neural Lyapunov, barrier, and contraction methods for robotics and control. IEEE Trans. Robot. **39**(3), 1749–1767 (2023)
10. Dawson, C., Qin, Z., Gao, S., Fan, C.: Safe nonlinear control using robust neural Lyapunov-barrier functions. In: Conference on Robot Learning, pp. 1724–1735. PMLR (2022)
11. Desai, A., Ghosh, S., Seshia, S.A., Shankar, N., Tiwari, A.: SOTER: a runtime assurance framework for programming safe robotics systems. In: 2019 49th Annual IEEE/IFIP International Conference on Dependable Systems and Networks (DSN), pp. 138–150. IEEE (2019)
12. Giacobbe, M., Kroening, D., Pal, A., Tautschnig, M.: Neural model checking. In: The Thirty-eighth Annual Conference on Neural Information Processing Systems (2024)
13. Gurobi Optimization, LLC: Gurobi Optimizer Reference Manual (2024). https://www.gurobi.com
14. Henzinger, T.A., Kresse, F., Mallik, K., Yu, E., Zikelic, D.: Predictive monitoring of black-box dynamical systems. In: L4DC. Proceedings of Machine Learning Research, PMLR (2025)

15. Jewison, C., Erwin, R.S.: A spacecraft benchmark problem for hybrid control and estimation. In: 2016 IEEE 55th Conference on Decision and Control (CDC), pp. 3300–3305. IEEE (2016)
16. Kiumarsi, B., Vamvoudakis, K.G., Modares, H., Lewis, F.L.: Optimal and autonomous control using reinforcement learning: a survey. IEEE Trans. Neural Netw. Learn. Syst. **29**(6), 2042–2062 (2017)
17. Maderbacher, B., Schupp, S., Bartocci, E., Bloem, R., Ničković, D., Könighofer, B.: Provable correct and adaptive simplex architecture for bounded-liveness properties. In: International Symposium on Model Checking Software, pp. 141–160. Springer (2023)
18. Mandal, U., et al.: Formally verifying deep reinforcement learning controllers with Lyapunov barrier certificates. In: #PLACEHOLDER_PARENT_METADATA_VALUE#, pp. 95–106. TU Wien Academic Press (2024)
19. Mehmood, U., Sheikhi, S., Bak, S., Smolka, S.A., Stoller, S.D.: The black-box simplex architecture for runtime assurance of autonomous CPS. In: NASA Formal Methods Symposium, pp. 231–250. Springer (2022)
20. Peruffo, A., Ahmed, D., Abate, A.: Automated and formal synthesis of neural barrier certificates for dynamical models. In: International Conference on Tools and Algorithms for the Construction and Analysis of Systems, pp. 370–388. Springer (2021)
21. Phan, D., Yang, J., Grosu, R., Smolka, S.A., Stoller, S.D.: Collision avoidance for mobile robots with limited sensing and limited information about moving obstacles. Formal Methods Syst. Des. **51**(1), 62–86 (2017). https://doi.org/10.1007/s10703-016-0265-4
22. Prajna, S., Jadbabaie, A., Pappas, G.J.: A framework for worst-case and stochastic safety verification using barrier certificates. IEEE Trans. Autom. Control **52**(8), 1415–1428 (2007)
23. Schierman, J.D., et al.: Runtime assurance framework development for highly adaptive flight control systems, Technical report, Barron Associates Inc., Charlottesville (2015)
24. Sen, K.: Concolic testing. In: Proceedings of the 22nd IEEE/ACM International Conference on Automated Software Engineering, pp. 571–572 (2007)
25. Sen, K.: DART: directed automated random testing. In: Haifa Verification Conference. LNCS, vol. 6405, p. 4. Springer (2009)
26. Sen, K., Marinov, D., Agha, G.: CUTE: a concolic unit testing engine for C. In: ESEC/SIGSOFT FSE, pp. 263–272. ACM (2005)
27. Seto, D., Krogh, B., Sha, L., Chutinan, A.: The simplex architecture for safe online control system upgrades. In: Proceedings of the 1998 American Control Conference. ACC (IEEE Cat. No. 98CH36207), vol. 6, pp. 3504–3508. IEEE (1998)
28. Smith, M.C.: The general problem of the stability of motion : translated and edited by A. T. Fuller. Taylor and Francis (1992). Automatica **31**(2), 353–354 (1995)
29. Sun, D., Jha, S., Fan, C.: Learning certified control using contraction metric. In: Conference on Robot Learning, pp. 1519–1539. PMLR (2021)
30. Tayal, M., Zhang, H., Jagtap, P., Clark, A., Kolathaya, S.: Learning a formally verified control barrier function in stochastic environment. arXiv preprint arXiv:2403.19332 (2024)
31. Yin, J., Dawson, C., Fan, C., Tsiotras, P.: Shield model predictive path integral: a computationally efficient robust MPC method using control barrier functions. IEEE Robot. Autom. Lett. **8**(11), 7106–7113 (2023)

32. Yu, E., Žikelić, Đ., Henzinger, T.A.: Neural control and certificate repair via runtime monitoring. In: Proceedings of the AAAI Conference on Artificial Intelligence, vol. 39, pp. 26409–26417 (2025)
33. Zhang, H., Qin, Z., Gao, S., Clark, A.: SEEV: synthesis with efficient exact verification for Relu neural barrier functions. In: NeurIPS (2024)
34. Zhang, H., Wu, J., Vorobeychik, Y., Clark, A.: Exact verification of Relu neural control barrier functions. Adv. Neural. Inf. Process. Syst. **36**, 5685–5705 (2023)
35. Zhao, H., Zeng, X., Chen, T., Liu, Z.: Synthesizing barrier certificates using neural networks. In: Proceedings of the 23rd International Conference on Hybrid Systems: Computation and Control, pp. 1–11 (2020)
36. Zhao, Q., Chen, X., Zhao, Z., Zhang, Y., Tang, E., Li, X.: Verifying neural network controlled systems using neural networks. In: Proceedings of the 25th ACM International Conference on Hybrid Systems: Computation and Control, pp. 1–11 (2022)

Runtime Monitoring and Enforcement of Conditional Fairness in Generative AIs

Chih-Hong Cheng[1,2](✉) ⓘ, Changshun Wu[3](✉) ⓘ, Xingyu Zhao[4] ⓘ,
Saddek Bensalem[5] ⓘ, and Harald Ruess[6] ⓘ

[1] Chalmers University of Technology, Gothenburg, Sweden
chihhong@chalmers.se
[2] Carl von Ossietzky Universität Oldenburg, Oldenburg, Germany
[3] Université Grenoble Alpes, Grenoble, France
changshun.wu@univ-grenoble-alpes.fr
[4] University of Warwick, Coventry, UK
[5] CSX-AI, Saint-Didier-au-Mont-d'Or, France
[6] SRI International, Menlo Park, CA, USA

Abstract. The deployment of generative AI (GenAI) models raises significant fairness concerns, addressed in this paper through novel characterization and enforcement techniques specific to GenAI. Unlike standard AI performing specific tasks, GenAI's broad functionality requires "conditional fairness" tailored to the context being generated, such as demographic fairness in generating images of poor people versus successful business leaders. We define two fairness levels: the first evaluates fairness in generated outputs, independent of prompts and models; the second assesses inherent fairness with neutral prompts. Given the complexity of GenAI and challenges in fairness specifications, we focus on bounding the worst case, considering a GenAI system unfair if the distance between appearances of a specific group exceeds preset thresholds. We also explore combinatorial testing for assessing relative completeness in intersectional fairness. By bounding the worst case, we develop a prompt injection scheme within an agent-based framework to enforce conditional fairness with minimal intervention, validated on state-of-the-art GenAI systems.

Keywords: generative AI · conditional fairness · monitoring and enforcement

1 Introduction

Generative AI (GenAI) inherits and reinforces societal stereotypes and biases through the content it generates, and through the virtually open-ended ways in which it is used in everyday life [4, 10]. But established design-time techniques for improving the fairness of machine-learned models are not applicable to black-box GenAI systems. In addition, any notion of fairness for GenAI must be flexible in relation to its social context. We address these challenges by a new notion of relative fairness specifications for GenAI, which we call *conditional fairness*.

For the purposes of this paper, we consider GenAI to be a web service (similar to ChatGPT) that can be called sequentially by a potentially infinite number of clients. The underlying interaction model between the GenAI model and its clients, therefore, is an infinite sequence of pairs of input prompts and corresponding GenAI-generated content. Now, given a set of sensitive concept groups such as *gender* or *demographics*, fairness specifications constrain the eventual or repeated appearance of sensitive concept groups. These temporal fairness specifications are clearly inspired by *linear temporal logic* (LTL) [22] and its bounded *metric interval temporal logic* (MITL) [2] variant. We also link this rather logic-centric view to the prevailing frequency-centric view of fairness.

Due to the virtually open-ended ability of GenAI to generate content of different categories, we propose a notion of fairness that is *conditional* on individual sensitive concepts such as "economically disadvantaged people" or "successful business leaders". These conditions serve as an Archimedean point in the definition of relative notions of fairness for virtually open-ended GenAI. We further distinguish between the fairness that is manifested in the generated sequence and the *inherent fairness* of the GenAI, where the latter term refers to conditions where the input prompt does not influence the GenAI to bias the output toward a particular concept value (e.g., a particular gender).

Considering fairness along single dimensions, such as gender or race in isolation, is clearly not sufficient to ensure fairness at their intersections, such as groups of dark-skinned women [3,6]. However, the main challenge of *intersectional fairness* lies in the impracticality of directly ensuring fairness across all combinations of subgroups, as this approach leads to an exponential proliferation of subgroups with each additional axis of discrimination [4,16,25]. To address this *combinatorial explosion*, we develop a technique that is inspired by k-way combinatorial testing [21] to provide a less stringent version of intersectional fairness whose evidence can be manifested by an image sequence of polynomially-bounded size.

To avoid worst-case scenarios where repeated image manifestations of the same concept group value exceed given fairness thresholds, we develop an agent-based *fairness enforcement* algorithm that proactively monitors the generative AI model and prevents fairness violations over individual sensitive concepts. For each value in the group of sensitive features, the enforcement algorithm (as an agent) uses counters to track potential violations of deadlines as derived from the given fairness constraints. Whenever the GenAI comes close to violating such a fairness constraint, a special *prompt* is generated and injected into the user prompt to the neural model (as another agent), with the purpose of steering the GenAI away from a possible fairness violation.

We have implemented a software prototype for evaluating fairness for GenAI systems, and used it for some initial fairness assessments of OpenAI's ChatGPT 4.0 connected with DALL·E3, and of ZHIPU AI's GLM-4.[1] Some qualitative results are highlighted in Fig. 1. These evaluations strongly support the view that the notion of fairness for generative AI is indeed conditional on con-

---
[1] GLM-4 is available at https://open.bigmodel.cn/.

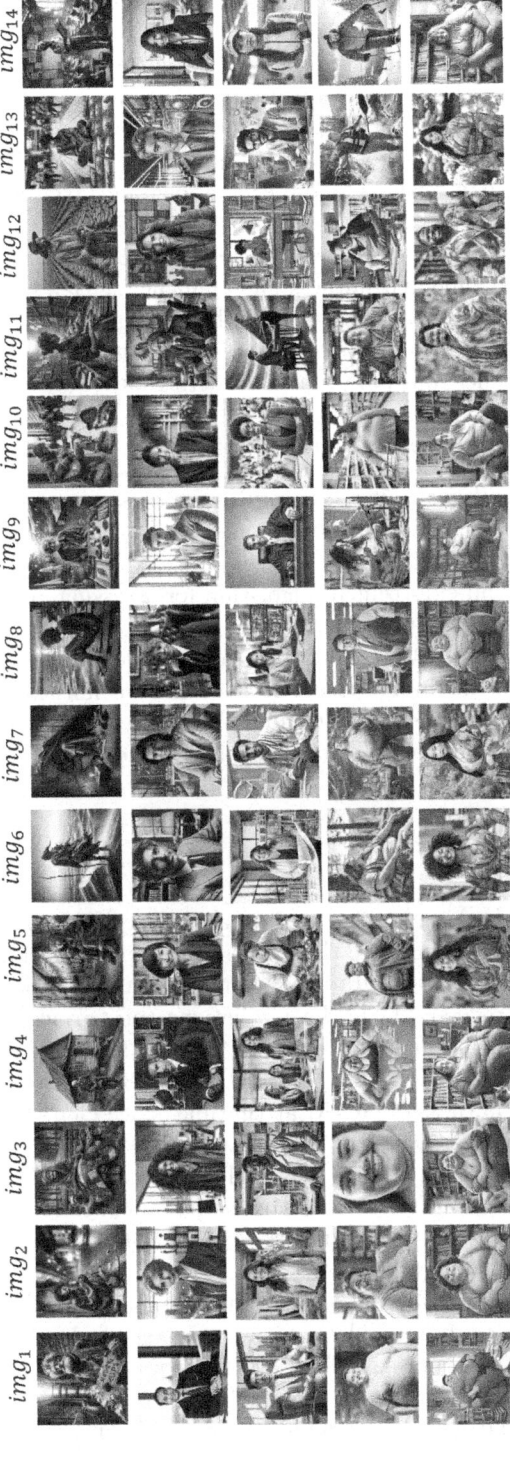

Fig. 1. Image sequences of an economically disadvantaged person (1st row) and successful business leaders (2nd row) created by Chat-GPT 4.0 connected with DALL.E3, image sequences of the successful person of any occupation (3rd row) and overweight person (4th row) created by the ZHIPU GLM-4 tool, as well as an image sequence of overweight people created by GLM-4 with demographic fairness enforcement using Algorithm 1 (5th row).

cepts. For example, while fairness is strongly manifested when image sequences are conditioned to the idea of "successful person" (row 2 and 3 of Fig. 1), fairness against gender or demographic groups is weak when image sequences are conditioned to the idea of "poor/economically disadvantaged person" or "overweight person" (row 1 and 4 of Fig. 1), where for GLM-4 on generating images for overweight people, it is strongly biased towards white/Caucasus. We also observe that even for all-pair fairness by eventual appearance (the simplest form of approximate intersectional fairness), models such as GLM-4 fail to achieve a fairness coverage of 35%, and thus have considerable room for improvement. Finally, we have also implemented fairness enforcement for GenAI, where as a qualitative example, for the same GLM-4 tool, the demographic fairness manifested in the image sequence for row 5 of Fig. 1 is substantially superior to the non-enforced image sequence in row 4 (almost all with white/Caucasian looking) of Fig. 1.

The main contributions of this work are as follows:

- A novel notion of *conditional fairness* to capture fairness constraints of open-ended GenAI, which can be flexibly conditioned on use-case specific sensitive features.
- Runtime monitoring and enforcement algorithm for assessing and guaranteeing conditional fairness constraints for GenAI.
- Experimental fairness evaluations demonstrating the flexibility and scalability of our approach to monitor and enforce conditional fairness constraints for some popular GenAI systems at runtime. A prototype implementation is available at https://github.com/SEMTA-Group/FairGenAI

2 Related Work

In order to mitigate bias by learning fair models, a number of design phase techniques have been proposed to improve the fairness of machine learning models. These techniques are typically applied to the training data (pre-processing), the learning algorithm (in-processing), or the predictions (post-processing). Main focus areas of research include dataset bias [9,13,19,26,30,31] as well as bias measurement and mitigation of models [8,15,20,23,24,28,32]. In contrast, we monitor and enforce the fairness of GenAI at runtime, since GenAI usually is a black-box system (e.g., neither access to training data nor realistic possibility of retraining for fairness purposes). Another key difference from mitigating unfairness in the design phase of uni-functional machine learning systems is that the fairness of multi-functional GenAI must be explicitly specified depending on the specific applications and their context.

Recent work on estimating fairness using runtime monitoring techniques is based on the assumption that the underlying system is a Markov chain [1,14]. Nevertheless, these developments have focused exclusively on estimating average individual fairness, whereas in our approach, we consider the worst case of conditional fairness and go beyond merely monitoring it by incorporating proactive fairness enforcement. We argue that conditional fairness is essential for GenAI, a concept not addressed in [14]. For example, we observe that gender fairness is only manifested in images of "successful business leader" but not in images of "poor person". Another relevant approach is Fairness Shields [5], which enforces fairness over sequences of structured decisions via runtime monitoring and optimal control. Unlike decision models with discrete actions and fixed horizons, generative AI systems produce unstructured, open-ended outputs where conditional fairness must be ensured across a wide range of semantic contexts, resulting in a setting not addressed by prior runtime fairness methods.

Another relevant direction in the literature on fairness is intersectional fairness [12,16–18,25,27], which addresses biases that emerge at the intersection of multiple attributes such as gender, race, or ethnicity. Ensuring fairness across these intersections presents a significant challenge due to the exponential increase in subgroup combinations [16]. Our approach addresses this by focusing on *pairwise intersectional conditional fairness*, inspired by k-way combinatorial testing [21]. We prioritize pairwise interactions here because our experiments suggest that existing GenAI models already face severe fairness problems at these rather coarse abstractions. However, this basic approach can be generalized to more refined approximations by also considering higher-order (i.e., ternary and beyond) interactions between concept groups.

3 Formulation

For simplicity, we assume that the GenAI takes input prompts as a string and produces output as an image. However, the formulation can be easily adjusted to other types of modality (e.g., output as texts).

Definition 1 (Stochastic Generator). *Let $\mathcal{G} : \Sigma^* \to \mathcal{D}(\mathcal{I})$ be the generator that maps an input string (prompt) $p \in \Sigma^*$ to a probability distribution over images $\mathcal{I}$. For the distribution returned by $\mathcal{G}$ on input p, we use $\mathcal{G}^s(p)$ to denote an image sampled from this distribution.*

- Σ *is the set of possible tokens in a textual language.*
- $\mathcal{I} \stackrel{\text{def}}{=} \{0, \ldots, 255\}^{H \times W \times 3}$, *where $H, W \in \mathbb{N}_+$ are the height and width of an image, and 3 represents that an image has three (RGB) channels. $\mathcal{D}(\mathcal{I})$ denotes the set of all probability distributions over the image space $\mathcal{I}$.*

Consider different users using $\mathcal{G}$ at different times by offering different input prompts $p_1, p_2, \ldots$ respectively. One can view the generated result as an *infinite image sequence* $\langle img_i \rangle \stackrel{\text{def}}{=} img_1 \cdot img_2 \cdot img_3 \cdots \in \mathcal{I}^\omega$, with $img_i = \mathcal{G}^s(p_i)$, ordered based on the request/result being produced.

Example 1 (Generating images for a poor person). As a motivating example, we take ChatGPT 4.0 with DALL·E3 as the generator $\mathcal{G}$ to synthesize images of economically disadvantaged people. Let Σ be the set of tokens for ChatGPT. One user may provide an input prompt:

$$p_1 \stackrel{\text{def}}{=} \text{``Please generate an image of a poor person''}.$$

Then one can use $\mathcal{G}$ to generate an image $img_1 \stackrel{\text{def}}{=} \mathcal{G}^s(p_i)$ as illustrated in the top left of Fig. 1.

Subsequently, we define concept groups, which serve as the basis for characterizing the *group fairness* of an infinite image sequence as well as the fairness of the generator. Throughout the paper, we use $[a \cdots b]$ to represent the set of integers ranging from a to b.

Definition 2. *Let* $\text{cgf}_i : \mathcal{I} \to [0 \cdots \text{CG}_i]$ *be the* **concept grouping function** *that returns the index (concept group value) that an image belongs, where* CG_i *is a non-negative integer, with value 0 being reserved for "unrelated".*

Example 2. Throughout the paper, we define three concept grouping functions and apply them in images within the top row of Fig. 1.

- Let $\text{cgf}_{poor} : \mathcal{I} \to \{0, 1, 2\}$ return a simplified categorization based on the character of an image is considered economically disadvantaged, with the value having the following semantics: 0 for "unrelated" (i.e., not a person), 1 for "no", and 2 for "yes". Then $\text{cgf}_{poor}(img_1) = \text{cgf}_{poor}(img_2) = 2$.
- Let $\text{cgf}_{gender} : \mathcal{I} \to \{0, 1, 2\}$ return a simplified categorization based on the gender of an image character, with the value having the following semantics: 0 for "unrelated" (i.e., not a person or unrecognizable), 1 for "female", and 2 for "male". Then $\text{cgf}_{gender}(img_1) = 2$.
- Let $\text{cgf}_{age} : \mathcal{I} \to \{0, 1, 2, 3\}$ return a simplified categorization based on the seniority of the character within the image, with the value having the following semantics: 0 for "unrelated" (i.e., not a person), 1 for "child", 2 for "adult", and 3 for "elderly". Then $\text{cgf}_{age}(img_1) = 3$.

Finally, we define the concept of *removal*, which enables us to focus on a subsequence with elements sharing the same concept group values.

Definition 3 (Removal). *Let* cgf *be a concept grouping function, and let* $\langle img_i \rangle \stackrel{\text{def}}{=} img_1 \cdot img_2 \cdots \in \mathcal{I}^\omega$ *be the infinite sequence of images. Let* $\text{rm}(\langle img_i \rangle, \text{cgf}, S)$ *return a subsequence of* $\langle img_i \rangle$ *by removing every element* img_i *from* $\langle img_i \rangle$ *where* $\text{cgf}(img_i) \in S$.

Example 3. $\text{rm}(\cdot, \text{cgf}_{gender}, \{0\})$ removes all images from a sequence that do not contain a person or a person whose gender can not be recognized.

Example 4. $\text{rm}(\cdot, \text{cgf}_{poor}, [0 \cdots 2] \setminus \{2\})$ only keeps images of economically disadvantaged people (i.e., keeps only images with value $\text{cgf}_{poor}(\cdot) = 2$).

4 The Different Facets of Fairness

4.1 Sequence-Level Fairness

We establish the theoretical framework for defining conditional fairness on an infinite sequence of images. As stated earlier, we propose the following three types of specification to characterize the worst-case acceptable behavior, namely *eventual appearance* (analogous to $\Diamond$ in LTL) of every concept group value, *repeated appearance* ($\Box\Diamond$), and repeated appearance with bounded distance ($\Box\Diamond_{\leq\beta}$).

Definition 4 (Sequence fairness with eventual appearance). *Let* cgf_1 *and* cgf_2 *be two concept grouping functions, and let* $\langle img_i\rangle \stackrel{\text{def}}{=} img_1\cdot img_2\cdots \in \mathcal{I}^\omega$ *be the infinite sequence of images. Then* $\langle img_i\rangle$ *is* **fair with eventual appearance** *for concept group 2* **conditional to** cgf_1 *evaluated to* cg, *abbreviated as* $\langle\frac{\text{cgf}_2}{\text{cgf}_1\Leftarrow cg}\rangle$ $\Diamond$-*fair, if given* $\langle img'_i\rangle$ *defined by Eq.* (1),

$$\langle img'_i\rangle \stackrel{\text{def}}{=} \text{rm}(\text{rm}(\langle img_i\rangle, \text{cgf}_1, [0\ldots CG_1]\setminus\{cg\}), \text{cgf}_2, \{0\}) \quad (1)$$

then the following condition holds.

$$\forall k \in [1\ldots CG_2] : \exists m \geq 1 : \text{cgf}_2(img'_m) = k \quad (2)$$

Essentially, Eq. (1) considers a subsequence from $\langle img_i\rangle$ that is relevant when evaluated to cg under $cgf_1(\cdot)$, and fairness needs to ensure that all related grouping values (apart from 0 being reserved for unrelated) evaluated under $cgf_2(\cdot)$ are covered.

Example 5. Let $\langle img_i\rangle \in \mathcal{I}^\omega$ be an infinite image sequence, where the first row of Fig. 1 shows the first 14 images. Therefore, $\forall i \in \mathbb{N} : \text{cgf}_{poor}(img_i) = 2$ (all for depicting different economically disadvantaged characters), implying that applying function $\text{rm}(\cdot, \text{cgf}_{poor}, \{0,1\})$ does not remove any images. However, applying function $\text{rm}(\cdot, \text{cgf}_{gender}, \{0\})$ shall remove img_6 due to the gender of the character being unrecognizable (image showing only the back of the person). We can conclude that $\langle img_i\rangle$ is $\langle\frac{\text{cgf}_{age}}{\text{cgf}_{poor}\Leftarrow 1}\rangle$ $\Diamond$-fair, as we can find child, adult, and elderly images. Similarly, $\langle img_i\rangle$ is $\langle\frac{\text{cgf}_{gender}}{\text{cgf}_{poor}\Leftarrow 1}\rangle$ $\Diamond$-fair.

As the definition utilizes infinite image sequences, one can go beyond fairness with eventual appearance by considering the *average*, *minimum*, or *maximum* distance of *repeated occurrence* of every concept group value. For instance, the following definition characterizes fairness by ensuring that the minimum distance of repeated occurrence is bounded by β_i for every possible concept group value i.

Definition 5. (Sequence fairness by β-bounded repeated appearance) *Let* cgf_1 *and* cgf_2 *be two concept grouping functions, and let* $\langle img_i\rangle \stackrel{\text{def}}{=} img_1\cdot img_2\cdots \in \mathcal{I}^\omega$ *be an infinite sequence of images. Let* $\boldsymbol{\beta} \stackrel{\text{def}}{=} (\beta_1,\ldots,\beta_{CG_2})$ *where*

$\forall j \in [1 \cdots CG_2] : \beta_j \in \mathbb{N}$. Then $\langle img_i \rangle$ is **fair with β-bounded repetition** for concept group 2 **conditional to** cgf_1 evaluated to cg, abbreviated as $\langle \frac{\text{cgf}_2}{\text{cgf}_1 \Leftarrow cg} \rangle$ $\Box \Diamond_{\leq \beta}$-fair, if given $\langle img'_i \rangle$ defined by Eq. (1), the following condition holds.

$$\forall k \in [1 \cdots CG_2] : \exists m : 1 \leq m \leq \beta_k \wedge \text{cgf}_2(img'_m) = k \\ \wedge \\ \forall m_1 \geq 1 : (\text{cgf}_2(img'_{m_1}) = k \rightarrow \\ \exists m_2 : m_1 < m_2 \leq m_1 + \beta_k : \text{cgf}_2(img'_{m_2}) = k) \qquad (3)$$

In Definition 5, the distance estimation for repeated appearance is based on first removing unrelated images via $\text{rm}(\cdot)$, following Eq. (1). The formulation is needed, as in the deployment of GenAI, users can provide different prompts and thus generate images (e.g., a motorcycle) that are unrelated to the condition where fairness shall be enforced (e.g., gender fairness for successful business leaders). Calculating the distance between two occurrences, as formulated in Eq. (3), shall not consider these unrelated images.

The following lemma considers a special case where all elements in β are equal and provides a sound upper bound on the *frequency* difference under β-bounded repeated appearance fairness. The extension to the general case is straightforward.

Lemma 1. *Let* $\text{cgf}_2 : \mathcal{I} \to [0 \cdots CG_2]$ *be the concept grouping function, and* $\langle img_i \rangle \in \mathcal{I}^\omega$ *be an infinite sequence of images. Given* $cg \in [1 \cdots CG_2]$*, let* $\langle img'_i \rangle$ *be defined using Eq. (1), and define* $\mathcal{F}(cg, \langle img'_i \rangle)$ *using Eq. (4).*

$$\mathcal{F}(cg, \langle img'_i \rangle) \stackrel{\text{def}}{:=} \lim_{n \to \infty} \frac{|\{m \leq n : \text{cgf}_i(img'_m) = cg\}|}{n} \qquad (4)$$

Assume that $\langle img_i \rangle$ *is* $\langle \frac{\text{cgf}_2}{\text{cgf}_1 \Leftarrow cg} \rangle$ $\Box \Diamond_{\leq \beta}$*-fair where* $\forall j \in [1 \cdots CG_2] : \beta_j = \beta$, *then following condition holds.*

$$\forall cg_x, cg_y \in [0 \cdots CG_2] : \\ |\mathcal{F}(cg_x, \langle img'_i \rangle) - \mathcal{F}(cg_y, \langle img'_i \rangle)| \leq 1 - \frac{CG_2}{\beta} \qquad (5)$$

Proof. The extreme case occurs when the concept group value 1 has the highest frequency of occurrence (i.e., $cg_x = 1$) while the rest of concept group values $2, \ldots, CG_2$ have the lowest occurrence frequency (we do not need to consider group value 0 due to removal). For each concept group value $cg_y \in [2 \cdots CG_2]$ having the lowest frequency, it implies that in Eq. (3), $m_2 = m_1 + \beta$, i.e., $\mathcal{F}(cg_y, \langle img'_i \rangle)$ has the smallest value of $\frac{1}{\beta}$. Consequently, the frequency of $\mathcal{F}(cg_x, \langle img'_i \rangle)$ can at most be $1 - (CG_2 - 1)\mathcal{F}(cg_y, \langle img'_i \rangle) = 1 - \frac{CG_2 - 1}{\beta}$. Therefore, the frequency difference (if the limit exists) is bounded by $(1 - \frac{CG_2 - 1}{\beta}) - \frac{1}{\beta} = 1 - \frac{CG_2}{\beta}$.

Lemma 2. *Let* $\langle img_i \rangle \in \mathcal{I}^\omega$ *be* $\langle \frac{\text{cgf}_2}{\text{cgf}_1 \Leftarrow cg} \rangle$ $\Box \Diamond_{\leq \beta}$*-fair where* $\text{cgf}_2 : \mathcal{I} \to [0 \cdots CG_2]$. *If* $\forall j \in [1 \cdots CG_2] : \beta_j = \beta$, *then* $\beta \geq CG_2$.

Proof. The smallest possible β_{min} occurs when concept group values occur in $\langle img'_i \rangle$ in a strictly round-robin fashion, implying that $\beta_{min} = \text{size}([1 \cdots CG_2]) = CG_2$.

4.2 Generator-Level Fairness

Observe that an image sequence $\langle img_i \rangle$ can be *fair due to the explicit control of the input prompts* given (i.e., $p_1, p_2, \ldots$); it thus can not fully reflect the inherent limitation of the generator $\mathcal{G}$. Therefore, we aim to consider the fairness of a generator, under the consideration that the input prompts $p_1, p_2, \ldots$ provide *no hints* on the concept group in which fairness should be manifested. Before precisely characterizing the meaning of "hints", we offer some examples to assist in understanding the idea.

Example 6. The first prompt provides no hint on the gender (cgf_{gender}) and age (cgf_{age}) information, while the second prompt does.

- "Generate an image of a poor person."
- "Generate an image of an economically disadvantaged young lady."

Definition 6 (Biased prompts). *A prompt $p \in \Sigma^*$ is biased/non-neutral subject to concept group $\text{cgf}_i(\cdot)$, iff the following condition holds:*

$$\exists cg \in [1 \cdots CG_i] \quad \forall img \in \text{supp}(\mathcal{G}(p)) : \text{cgf}_i(img) = cg$$

where $\text{supp}(\mathcal{G}(p)) \stackrel{\text{def}}{=} \{img \in \mathcal{I} \mid \mathbb{P}_{\mathcal{G}(p)}(img) > 0\}$ *is the support of the distribution $\mathcal{G}(p)$.*

Intuitively, the definition of a biased prompt implies that by using prompt p in the generation process, one guarantees that the immediately generated image, when evaluated on the concept group cgf_i, always[2] leads to manifesting concept group value cg. In implementation, whether a prompt is biased or not can also be checked via querying an LLM.

Altogether, by clearly defining the meaning of a biased prompt, we can now define the *inherent fairness* of a generator, which requires that *when all input prompts used to generate images of a group are neutral, fairness remains ensured.* Definition 7 characterizes eventual fairness, while it is a straightforward extension to characterize repeated fairness.

Definition 7 (Inherent fairness of the generator). *Let cgf_1 and cgf_2 be two concept grouping functions, and let $\mathcal{G}$ be the generator function. Let $\langle img_i \rangle \stackrel{\text{def}}{=} img_1 \cdot img_2 \cdots \in \mathcal{I}^\omega$ be any infinite sequence of images, generated by $\mathcal{G}$ using prompt sequence $\langle p_i \rangle$. Given $\langle img'_i \rangle$ defined by Eq. (1), let $\langle p'_i \rangle$*

---

[2] Here we omit technical details, but one can also have relaxations such as having a probabilistic guarantee.

be the corresponding prompt sequence. Then $\mathcal{G}$ **is inherently fair with eventual appearance** for concept group 2 under cgf_1 evaluated to cg, abbreviated as $\langle \frac{\text{cgf}_2}{\text{cgf}_1 \Leftarrow cg} \rangle$ $\Diamond$-fair, if the following condition holds:

$$\forall i > 0 : p'_i \text{ is not biased subject to } \text{cgf}_2(\cdot) \\ \rightarrow (\forall k \in [1 \cdots \text{CG}_2] : \exists m \geq 1 : \text{cgf}_2(img'_m) = k) \quad (6)$$

In Eq. (6), it demands that if the prompt is not biased (utilizing Definition 6), then fairness of eventual occurrence should hold in the generated image sequence, resembling the formulation in Definition 4.

4.3 Assessing Fairness on Finite Sequence

While the previously stated theoretical framework is based on infinite sequences of images, in practice, assessing fairness is commonly done on image sequences of finite length. In this situation, it is natural to change in Definition 4 from $\mathcal{I}^\omega$ (infinite word) to $\mathcal{I}^*$ (finite word) so that eventual appearance should be manifested in the finite image sequence.

Defining fairness with β-bounded repeated appearance requires an assumption on extrapolating what happens if the finite image sequence is further extended, where we borrow the idea of *weak-next* $\bigcirc_w$ operator as defined in LTL over finite traces [11] which assumes the repetition trend will hold. Further details on the formulation can be found in the appendix (as supplementary material).

4.4 Approximating Intersectional Fairness

So far, the $\langle \frac{\text{cgf}_2}{\text{cgf}_1 \Leftarrow cg} \rangle$ $\Diamond$-fairness has been used to ensure the presence of all concept group values when considering a single categorization with cgf_2. We can extend the concept to build fairness of manifesting *fairness in criterion pairs* $\langle \frac{\text{cgf}_x, \text{cgf}_y}{\text{cgf}_w \Leftarrow cg} \rangle$ and in *criterion triplets* $\langle \frac{\text{cgf}_x, \text{cgf}_y, \text{cgf}_z}{\text{cgf}_w \Leftarrow cg} \rangle$, where the definition immediately follows (e.g., Definition 8). As an example, consider the gender and age as two category groups, the extension on fairness in criterion pairs $\langle \frac{\text{cgf}_{gender}, \text{cgf}_{age}}{\text{cgf}_w \Leftarrow cg} \rangle$ then demands fairness to be observed in image sequences with all combinations defined by the following set $\{(cg_x, cg_y)\}$ with $cg_x \in \{1/\text{female}, 2/\text{male}\}$ and $cg_y \in \{1/\text{child}, 2/\text{adult}, 3/\text{elderly}\}$.

Definition 8 (Sequence paired fairness with eventual appearance). Let cgf_w, cgf_x and cgf_y be three concept grouping functions, and let $\langle img_i \rangle \stackrel{\text{def}}{:=} img_1 \cdot img_2 \cdots \in \mathcal{I}^\omega$ be the finite sequence of images. Then $\langle img_i \rangle$ is **paired-fair with eventual appearance** for concept group x and y under cgf_w evaluated to cg, abbreviated as $\langle \frac{\text{cgf}_x, \text{cgf}_y}{\text{cgf}_w \Leftarrow cg} \rangle$ $\Diamond$-fair, if given $\langle img'_i \rangle$ defined by Eq. (1), the following condition holds.

$$\forall k_1 \in [1 \cdots \text{CG}_x], k_2 \in [1 \cdots \text{CG}_y] : \\ \exists m \geq 1 : \text{cgf}_x(img'_m) = k_1 \wedge \text{cgf}_y(img'_m) = k_2 \quad (7)$$

Given cgf_w and additional K concept grouping functions $\text{cgf}_1, \ldots, \text{cgf}_K$, one can extend Definition 8 and analogously define $\langle \frac{\text{cgf}_1, \ldots, \text{cgf}_K}{\text{cgf}_w \Leftarrow cg} \rangle$ $\Diamond$-fairness, which demands that all combinations of concept group values should eventually appear. This leads to a concept similar to avoiding intersectional biases defined in the literature [3,4,18]. However, given K concept grouping functions with each having a binary assignment $\{1, 2\}$ (e.g., female and male), it is well known that *combinatorial explosion* exists, meaning that there is a need to manifest 2^K assignments (thereby enforcing the sequence to be at least 2^K in length) to achieve intersectional fairness.

Encountering this, we thus borrow the technique from k-way combinatorial testing [21] to provide a weaker form of intersectional fairness (*approximate intersectional fairness*) whose satisfaction requires only a polynomially bounded number of images. Definition 9 ensures that for every pair (2-way combinations) of concept group functions, all concept group value combinations are eventually manifested. The universal quantifier $x, y \in [1 \cdots K], x \neq y$ in Definition 9 only selects pairs of concept group functions as the conditions to be satisfied.

Definition 9 (Sequence all-paired fairness with eventual appearance).
*Given cgf_w and additional K concept grouping functions $\text{cgf}_1, \ldots, \text{cgf}_K$, let $\langle img_i \rangle \in \mathcal{I}^*$ be the finite sequence of images. Then $\langle img_i \rangle$ is **all-paired-fair with eventual appearance** for concept groups $[1 \cdots K]$ under cgf_w evaluated to cg, abbreviated as $\langle \frac{\forall x, y \in [1 \cdots K] \text{cgf}_x, \text{cgf}_y}{\text{cgf}_w \Leftarrow cg} \rangle$ $\Diamond$-fair, if given $\langle img'_i \rangle$ defined by Eq. (1), the following condition holds.*

$$\forall x, y \in [1 \cdots K], x \neq y:$$
$$\forall k_1 \in [1 \cdots CG_x], k_2 \in [1 \cdots CG_y]: \qquad (8)$$
$$\exists m \geq 1 : \text{cgf}_x(img'_m) = k_1 \wedge \text{cgf}_y(img'_m) = k_2$$

5 Enforcing Fairness of GenAI

Finally, while previously stated definitions assume the prompts to be not biased (cf. Definition 6), one can also explicitly *inject* prompts biased towards a specific concept group value to *enforce* fairness, where we focus on enforcing $\langle \frac{\text{cgf}_2}{\text{cgf}_1 \Leftarrow cg} \rangle$ $\Box\Diamond_{\leq \beta}$-fairness as characterized in Definition 5.

Note that when all elements in $\boldsymbol{\beta}$ are the same ($\forall j \in [1 \cdots CG_2] : \beta_j = \beta$), one trivial way is to explicitly control every prompt to manifest round-robin behavior. An example for cgf_2 being $\text{cgf}_{age}(\cdot)$ would be to enforce the generator to create the images strictly using the following ordering of values: "child", "adult", "elderly". Our interest, however, is to aim for *minimum interference*. We aim to inject biased (enforcing) prompts when necessary. Algorithm 1 presents our fairness enforcement method via prompt injection.

Initially (line 1), define an array c ranging from 1 to CG_2, with initial value of $c[i]$ set to β_i. $c[i]$ tracks the deadline before the concept group value i shall manifest. The algorithm continues by using an infinite loop to continuously fetch prompts from users sending image synthesis requests (lines 2, 3). If the received

Algorithm 1. Enforcing $\langle \frac{\text{cgf}_2}{\text{cgf}_1 \Leftarrow cg} \rangle \square \lozenge_{\leq \beta}$-fairness

1: let $c[i] \leftarrow \beta_i$ (for all $i \in [1 \cdots CG_2]$)
2: **while true do**
3:     $p \leftarrow$ Get prompt from the user for image generation
4:     **if** p is unrelated to $\text{cgf}_1 \Leftarrow cg$, or p is biased subject to $\text{cgf}_2(\cdot)$ **then**
5:        **output** $\mathcal{G}^s(p)$ to user
6:        **continue**
7:     **for** $k = CG_2$ to 1 **do**
8:        **if** $\exists$ distinct $cg_{21}, \ldots, cg_{2k} : c[cg_{21}] = c[cg_{22}] = \cdots = c[cg_{2k}] = k$ **then**
9:           $cg_2 \leftarrow$ random$\{cg_{21}, \ldots, cg_{2k}\}$
10:        $p \leftarrow p \cdot$ "Enforce the generated image such that $\text{cfg}_2(\cdot) = cg_2$"
11:        **break**
12:     **output** $img = \mathcal{G}^s(p)$ to user
13:     $cg \leftarrow \text{cgf}_2(img)$
14:     **for** $i = CG_2$ to 1 **do**
15:        **if** $cg = i$ **then** $c[i] \leftarrow \beta_i$
16:        **else** $c[i] \leftarrow c[i] - 1$

prompt p is unrelated to the condition where fairness shall be manifested, or if p is biased, then proceed by outputting the result (lines 4, 5, 6) as there is no need to take the generated image into fairness evaluation. In our evaluation, the checking at line 4 is done via querying a separate LLM. Otherwise, the for-loop and the following condition (lines 7, 8) try to detect if there are multiple concept group values whose deadline is approaching. When there exist k concept group values whose deadline equals k (line 8), it is then *mandatory* to use biased / non-neutral prompts to ensure one of the concept group values is selected in the corresponding image generation process, as reflected in lines 9 and 10. Note that the for-loop at line 7 iterates from $k = CG_2$ to 1 (not the other way round), as it is important to signal the issue as early as possible. Finally, an image is produced (line 12) and sent back to the user, and for the concept group value i matching the concept group value of the image cg (line 13, in our implementation via calling a vision-attribute identification model moondream[3]), the counter $c[i]$ is reset to β_i (line 15) while counters of other values are subtracted by 1 (line 16).

Example 7. Figure 2 illustrates an example on how Algorithm 1 is applied to enforce fairness under "successful business leader", where $\text{cgf}_{demographics} : \mathcal{I} \to [0 \cdots 4]$, with $\beta_1 = \beta_2 = \beta_3 = \beta_4 = 50$. Initially, $c[1] = c[2] = c[3] = c[4] = 50$. With the first prompt asking for a "cook", as it is unrelated to the concept group "successful business leader", the "if" statement at line 4 holds, so no additional action is needed apart from image synthesis at lines 5 and 6. For the second service request with prompt "Generate business leader", although it is related, enforcement is not triggered as the condition at line 8 does not hold. As the synthesized image has $\text{cgf}_2(img_2) = 1$ (Asian), $c[2], c[3], c[4]$ are decreased by 1

---
[3] https://github.com/vikhyat/moondream.

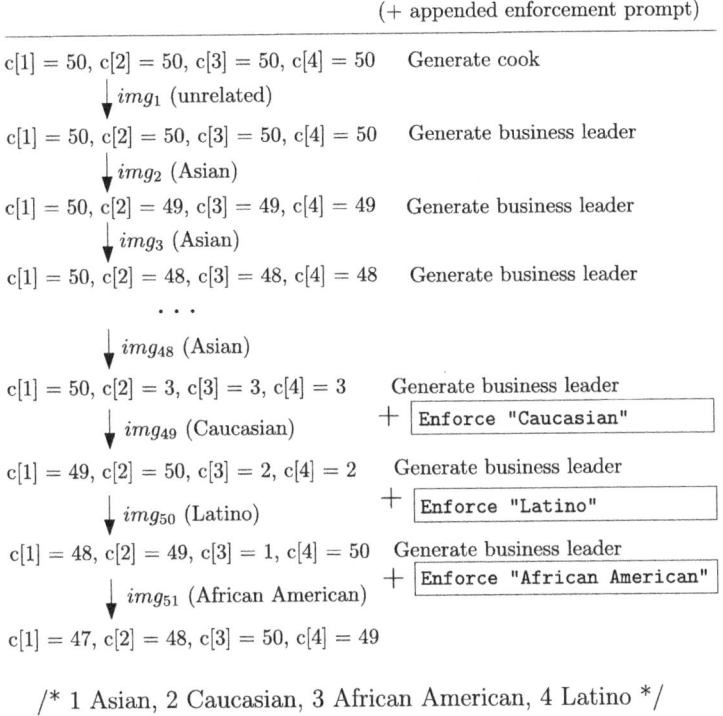

Fig. 2. Example illustrating how Algorithm 1 is applied.

to 49 while $c[1]$ is reset to 50. When the generator continuously produces images of Asians, it eventually leads to the case $c[1] = c[2] = c[3] = 3$. Consequently, the condition at line 8 holds, implying the need to enforce fairness. Then, one of the concept group values is taken from random to be enforced, whereas in Fig. 2, the first value being taken equals 2 (Caucasian).

For the correctness of the algorithm, the key insight is the use of the lookahead mechanism (lines 7 to 10), which reserves a buffer to react in a timely fashion. Provided that $\forall i \in [1 \cdots CG_2] : \beta_i > CG_2$ (at least possible to do round-robin), and the neural model performs correctly as intended (e.g., the LLM-based checking for prompt p at line 4 always returns the correct result, and the appended enforcement prompt always leads to the desired output), the correctness proof follows standard strategies that appear in the real-time scheduling theory textbook for proving the freeness of deadline violations.

6 Evaluation

We have evaluated fairness on two image-based generative AI tools, namely ChatGPT 4.0 connected with DALL·E3 from OpenAI as well as GLM-4 from ZHIPU AI, where Fig. 1 illustrates some of the image sequences produced by these tools. We have drawn multiple image sequences using neutral prompts, where the length of each image sequence is at least 40.

First, we observed that fairness is not universally enabled on all concepts in a generative AI model, as satisfaction can be conditional to certain concept group values. This confirms the appropriateness of our definition, which is always conditioned to a particular concept group value.

- (**Different degree of gender fairness**) When considering gender to be binary (male, female) based on the facial characteristics, for "successful business leader", within all sequences, the minimum β_k value that satisfies the finite version of Definition 5 is tightly centered around 5. However, for "poor person", female figures are substantially less presented, reflecting the minimum β_k value for image sequences being between 13 and 20.
- (**Different degree of demographic fairness**) For demographics, when it comes to "successful business leader", fairness with repeated appearance can be manifested, even for the concept group value "native American", as demonstrated in the 11th image at the second row of Fig. 1. This contrasts with the case of a "poor person" or "overweight person", where even fairness with eventual appearance can not be manifested due to missing images in the concept group value in some image sequences.

Second, we observed that even when using the approximate intersectional fairness criterion defined in Definition 9, generative AI models still struggle to include all combinations of pair-wise features. In our experiment, we generated multiple image sequences of length 80 using the GLM-4 model for "successful person", with explicit demands on diversity (using the neutral prompt "Generate an image being different from previously generated ones"), where we considered four concept group functions including demographics, gender, occupation, and the character being fuller-figured. The prompt explicitly hints the generative AI model to consider diversities at least in these four aspects. We normalize the value by dividing it with $\sum_{x \in [1 \cdots K]} \sum_{y \in [1 \cdots K], y > x} (\text{CG}_x)(\text{CG}_y)$ in Definition 9, as the denominator represents the number of all-paired combinations needed. The tendency increase is illustrated in Fig. 3, where each line corresponds to the behavior of one image sequence. With the maximum possible value being 1, we observed that the coverage is always below 0.4. Apart from one sequence, the coverage largely saturates after 25 images (reflected as a horizontal line), implying that the subsequent generated images highly resemble the first 25 images regarding concept group values (e.g., repeating doctors). Our results suggest a huge potential for the GLM-4 generative model to improve intersectional fairness in its image generation process.

Finally, we have also implemented the enforcement mechanism in Algorithm 1 to guarantee fairness, where the 5th row of Fig. 1 illustrates a clear improvement in ZHIPU GLM-4 in comparison to the original image sequence at the 4th row. In addition, we have the enforcement implemented as a web service connecting Gemma 2 LLM [29], Stable Diffusion[4] and moondream. The research prototype is made available at https://github.com/SEMTA-Group/FairGenAI.

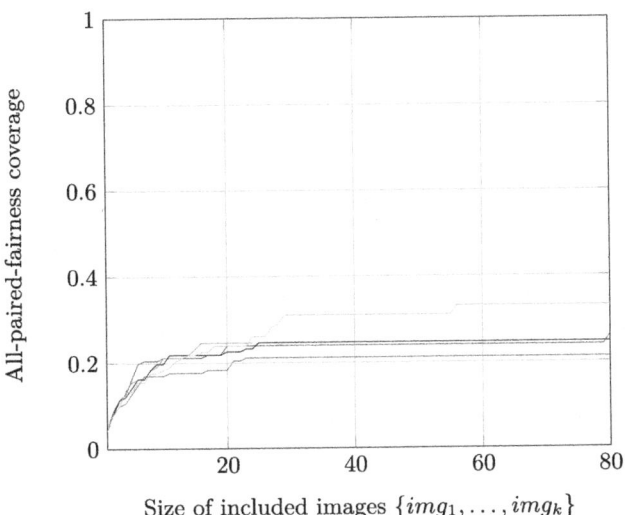

Fig. 3. The tendency of all-paired-fairness increase with GLM-4 generated image samples on "successful person"; the orange line is shorter as GLM-4 refuses to generate images further upon request.

7 Concluding Remarks

Our formal approach to fairness in generative AI uniquely defines fairness through the lens of infinite sequences of interactions between GenAI and its clients, allowing for a dynamic assessment and enforcement of fairness over time. By distinguishing between the fairness demonstrated in generated sequences and the inherent fairness of the AI system, we have established a comprehensive method that recognizes the nuanced nature of fairness as conditioned by specific concepts. In addition, our formal approach addresses the challenge of intersectional fairness through combinatorial testing, providing a scalable method for dealing with the combinatorial explosion of category combinations. This is critical to ensuring that the fairness measures remain effective even as the complexity of AI systems and the diversity of fairness dimensions increase. Initial experimental evaluations show that fairness enforcement techniques based on runtime monitoring of fairness conditions effectively manage inherent bias.

---

[4] https://huggingface.co/runwayml/stable-diffusion-v1-5.

A critical path forward is the practical application of GenAI fairness enforcement techniques within larger organizations and with active operational management at scale. Another important direction for future work is to extend the notion of conditional fairness to an *average arrival view*.

Acknowledgement. Funded by the European Union. Views and opinions expressed are however those of the author(s) only and do not necessarily reflect those of the European Union or the European Health and Digital Executive Agency (HADEA). Neither the European Union nor the granting authority can be held responsible for them. RobustifAI project, ID 101212818.

Appendix: Accessing Fairness on Finite Image Sequences

While the previously stated theoretical framework is based on infinite sequences of images, in practice, accessing fairness is commonly done on image sequences of finite length. In this situation, it is natural to change in Definition 4 from $\mathcal{I}^\omega$ (infinite word) to $\mathcal{I}^*$ (finite word) so that eventual appearance should be manifested in the finite image sequence.

The technical obscurity occurs in definitions related to the repeated occurrence (e.g., Definition 5), where manifesting repeated occurrence on finite traces is impossible.[5] On finite traces, defining fairness with repeated appearance requires *an assumption on extrapolating what happens if the finite image sequence is further extended*.

For Definition 5 on fairness with β-bounded repeated appearance, however, recall that bounded response $\Diamond_{\leq \beta} \phi$ in LTL over infinite words can be rewritten using the *neXt* ($\bigcirc$) operator, i.e., $\phi \vee \bigcirc \phi \vee \bigcirc \bigcirc \phi \vee \ldots \vee \bigcirc^\beta \phi$. To apply it in finite traces, the idea of the *weak-next* $\bigcirc_w$ operator as defined in LTL over finite traces [11] is useful, where $\bigcirc_w \phi$ holds automatically when considering being at the *last position* of the string (i.e., let π be a finite trace and $\text{len}(\pi)$ returns the length of the trace. Then $\pi, m \models \bigcirc_w \phi$ iff (i) $m < \text{len}(\pi) - 1$ and $\pi, m+1 \models \phi$, or (ii) $m = \text{len}(\pi) - 1$). This is based on the belief that if we extend the trace by 1, *it is possible* that the next symbol can satisfy ϕ. This leads to the following modified definition.

Definition 10. (Finite sequence fairness by β-bounded repeated appearance) *Let* cgf_1 *and* cgf_2 *be two concept grouping functions, and let* $\langle img_i \rangle \stackrel{\text{def}}{:=} img_1 \cdot img_2 \cdots \in \mathcal{I}^*$ *be the finite image sequence. Then* $\langle img_i \rangle$ *is **fair with β-bounded repeated appearance** for concept group 2 **conditional to** cgf_1 evaluated to cg, abbreviated as* $\langle \frac{\text{cgf}_2}{\text{cgf}_1 \Leftarrow cg} \rangle \; \Box \Diamond_{\leq \beta}$*-fair, if given* $\langle img'_i \rangle$ *defined by Eq. (1), (i)* $\text{len}(\langle img'_i \rangle) > \beta$*, and (ii) the condition characterized in Eq. (9) holds.*

---

[5] It is well known in the theory of linear temporal logic of finite traces [7] that the meaning of response property (i.e., $\Box \Diamond$ in LTL) has different interpretations when defining infinite and finite traces.

$$\forall k \in [1 \cdots CG_2] : \exists m : 1 \leq m \leq \beta_k \wedge \mathrm{cgf}_2(img'_m) = k$$
$$\wedge$$
$$\forall m_1 \geq 1 : (\mathrm{cgf}_2(img'_{m_1}) = k \rightarrow \quad (9)$$
$$((\exists m_2 : m_1 < m_2 \leq m_1 + \beta_k : \mathrm{cgf}_2(img_{m_2}) = k)$$
$$\vee$$
$$m_1 + \beta_k > \mathrm{len}(\langle img'_i \rangle)))$$

Comparing Eq. (3) and Eq. (9), the difference in the finite version lies in the disjunction ($\vee$) of condition ($m_1 + \beta_k > \mathrm{len}(\langle img'_i \rangle)$), reflecting that if the occurrence m_1 is close to the end of the image sequence, it is impossible to see β_k subsequent images. Similar to the semantic of $\bigcirc_w$, we opportunistically consider it can occur if the image sequence is prolonged.

$\langle img'_i \rangle$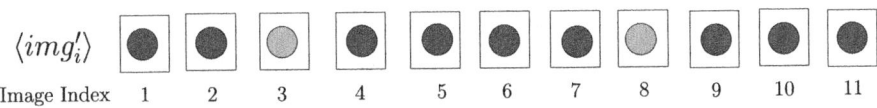

Image Index 1 2 3 4 5 6 7 8 9 10 11

Fig. 4. Example illustrating the concept of β-bounded repeated appearance in a finite sequence of 11 images after removal.

Example 8. Consider the finite image sequence as illustrated in Fig. 4, where let $\mathrm{cgf}_{\mathrm{shape}}$ maps to $\{0, 1(\mathrm{circle}), 2(\mathrm{square})\}$ and $\mathrm{cgf}_{\mathrm{color}}$ maps to $\{0, 1(\mathrm{blue}), 2(\mathrm{yellow})\}$. Then the image sequence in Fig. 4 is $\langle \frac{\mathrm{cgf}_{\mathrm{color}}}{\mathrm{cgf}_{\mathrm{shape}} \Leftarrow 1} \rangle$ $\Box\Diamond_{\leq (6,6)}$-fair. This is because the image sequence length is larger than 6, and for every yellow occurrence, the next occurrence occurs within a distance of 6. Note that for the final occurrence of "yellow" that makes $m_1 = 8$ in Eq. (9), the second term in the disjunction holds as $m_1 + \beta_2 = 8 + 6 = 14 > \mathrm{len}(\langle img'_i \rangle) = 11$.

References

1. Albarghouthi, A., Vinitsky, S.: Fairness-aware programming. In: Proceedings of the Conference on Fairness, Accountability, and Transparency, pp. 211–219 (2019)
2. Alur, R., Feder, T., Henzinger, T.A.: The benefits of relaxing punctuality. JACM **43**(1), 116–146 (1996)
3. Buolamwini, J., Gebru, T.: Gender shades: intersectional accuracy disparities in commercial gender classification. In: Conference on Fairness, Accountability, and Transparency (FAT), pp. 77–91. PMLR (2018)
4. Buyl, M., De Bie, T.: Inherent limitations of AI fairness. Commun. ACM **67**(2), 48–55 (2024)
5. Cano, F., Henzinger, T.A., Könighofer, B., Kueffner, K., Mallik, K.: Fairness shields: safeguarding against biased decision makers. In: Proceedings of the AAAI Conference on Artificial Intelligence, vol. 39, pp. 15659–15668 (2025)

6. Crenshaw, K.: Demarginalizing the intersection of race and sex: a black feminist critique of antidiscrimination doctrine, feminist theory and antiracist politics. In: Feminist Legal Theories, pp. 23–51. Routledge (2013)
7. De Giacomo, G., Vardi, M.Y., et al.: Linear temporal logic and linear dynamic logic on finite traces. In: International Joint Conference on Artificial Intelligence (IJCAI), vol. 13, pp. 854–860 (2013)
8. Ernst, J.S., et al.: Bias mitigation for large language models using adversarial learning. In: AEQUITAS Workshop on Fairness and Bias in AI (2023)
9. Fabbrizzi, S., Papadopoulos, S., Ntoutsi, E., Kompatsiaris, I.: A survey on bias in visual datasets. Comput. Vis. Image Underst. **223**, 103552 (2022)
10. Ferrara, E.: Fairness and bias in artificial intelligence: a brief survey of sources, impacts, and mitigation strategies. Science **6**(1), 3 (2023)
11. Fionda, V., Greco, G.: LTL on finite and process traces: complexity results and a practical reasoner. J. Artif. Intell. Res. **63**, 557–623 (2018)
12. Gohar, U., Cheng, L.: A survey on intersectional fairness in machine learning: notions, mitigation, and challenges. arXiv preprint arXiv:2305.06969 (2023)
13. He, H., Zha, S., Wang, H.: Unlearn dataset bias in natural language inference by fitting the residual. In: Workshop on Deep Learning Approaches for Low-Resource Natural Language Processing, DeepLo@ EMNLP-IJCNLP 2019, pp. 132–142. ACL (2021)
14. Henzinger, T.A., Karimi, M., Kueffner, K., Mallik, K.: Monitoring algorithmic fairness. In: International Conference on Computer Aided Verification, pp. 358–382. Springer (2023)
15. Huang, D., Bu, Q., Zhang, J., Xie, X., Chen, J., Cui, H.: Bias assessment and mitigation in LLM-based code generation. arXiv preprint arXiv:2309.14345 (2023)
16. Kearns, M., Neel, S., Roth, A., Wu, Z.S.: Preventing fairness gerrymandering: auditing and learning for subgroup fairness. In: International Conference on Machine Learning (ICML), pp. 2564–2572. PMLR (2018)
17. Kiritchenko, S., Mohammad, S.: Examining gender and race bias in two hundred sentiment analysis systems. In: Joint Conference on Lexical and Computational Semantics (*SEM), pp. 43–53 (2018)
18. Kirk, H.R.: Bias out-of-the-box: an empirical analysis of intersectional occupational biases in popular generative language models. Adv. Neural Inf. Process. Syst. (NeurIPS) **34**, 2611–2624 (2021)
19. Li, Y., Vasconcelos, N.: REPAIR: removing representation bias by dataset resampling. In: IEEE/CVF Conference on Computer Vision and Pattern Recognition (CVPR), pp. 9572–9581 (2019)
20. Limisiewicz, T., Mareček, D., Musil, T.: Debiasing algorithm through model adaptation. In: International Conference on Learning Representations (ICLR) (2023)
21. Nie, C., Leung, H.: A survey of combinatorial testing. ACM CSUR **43**(2), 1–29 (2011)
22. Pnueli, A.: The temporal logic of programs. In: Annual Symposium on Foundations of Computer Science (SFCS), pp. 46–57. IEEE (1977)
23. Ramezani, A., Xu, Y.: Knowledge of cultural moral norms in large language models. arXiv preprint arXiv:2306.01857 (2023)
24. Ranaldi, L., Ruzzetti, E.S., Venditti, D., Onorati, D., Zanzotto, F.M.: A trip towards fairness: bias and de-biasing in large language models. arXiv preprint arXiv:2305.13862 (2023)
25. Ruess, H.: Fairness analysis with Shapley-Owen effects. arXiv preprint arXiv:2409.19318 (2024)

26. Sheppard, B., et al.: Subtle misogyny detection and mitigation: an expert-annotated dataset. arXiv preprint arXiv:2311.09443 (2023)
27. Tan, Y.C., Celis, L.E.: Assessing social and intersectional biases in contextualized word representations. Adv. Neural Inf. Process. Syst. (NeurIPS) **32** (2019)
28. Tao, Y., Viberg, O., Baker, R.S., Kizilcec, R.F.: Auditing and mitigating cultural bias in LLMs. arXiv preprint arXiv:2311.14096 (2023)
29. Team, G., et al.: Gemma 2: improving open language models at a practical size. arXiv preprint arXiv:2408.00118 (2024)
30. Tommasi, T., Patricia, N., Caputo, B., Tuytelaars, T.: A deeper look at dataset bias. In: Domain Adaptation in Computer Vision Applications, pp. 37–55 (2017)
31. Torralba, A., Efros, A.: Unbiased look at dataset bias. In: IEEE/CVF Conference on Computer Vision and Pattern Recognition (CVPR), pp. 1521–1528 (2011)
32. Ungless, E., Rafferty, A., Nag, H., Ross, B.: A robust bias mitigation procedure based on the stereotype content model. In: Workshop on Natural Language Processing and Computational Social Science (NLP+CSS), pp. 207–217 (2022)

A ROS Adapter for RTLOLA

Jan Baumeister[2], Bernd Finkbeiner[2], Franz Jünger[1], Florian Kohn[2], Sebastian Schirmer[1(✉)], and Christoph Torens[1]

[1] German Aerospace Center (DLR), Braunschweig, Germany
{franz.juenger,sebastian.schirmer,christoph.torens}@dlr.de
[2] CISPA Helmholtz Center for Information Security, Saarbrücken, Germany
{jan.baumeister,finkbeiner,florian.kohn}@cispa.de

Abstract. This paper presents an adapter for RTLOLA that simplifies the integration of runtime verification into Robot Operating System (ROS) applications. While ROS is the standard middleware for robotic development, ensuring the safety and reliability of high-level tasks such as navigation and object recognition remains challenging. The adapter facilitates the use of RTLOLA, a stream-based specification language for defining complex real-time properties, by automatically connecting a generated RTLOLA monitor to ROS topics and services. As a use case, the adapter was deployed onboard of an unmanned aircraft to reduce false positives in detecting people near the landing site. Specifically, our RTLOLA monitor cross-validates machine-learning-based person detections against objects in LiDAR depth images using classical computer vision techniques. This experiment demonstrates that runtime verification improves robotic safety while requiring minimal integration effort.

Keywords: Runtime Verification · Stream-based Monitoring · ROS

1 Introduction

We present an adapter that simplifies the integration of RTLOLA into robotic applications running within the Robot Operating System (ROS). ROS is an open-source framework that provides essential middleware functionality and abstractions to manage the complexity of scaling autonomous robotic missions. For instance, ROS is designed with distributed computing in mind, where essential robotic functions are executed in *nodes* that receive data from other nodes and pass their results along. Such an essential function can be low-level as reading sensors but also more high-level such as navigation and object recognition. For a safe execution, ROS has basic monitoring capabilities. While sufficient for low-level tasks, these capabilities are too limited to ensure the safety of high-level autonomous functions, which often require monitoring complex temporal system properties with asynchronous inputs. As a result, users are typically forced to implement custom monitoring solutions using general-purpose code, increasing the likelihood of errors. To mitigate this risk, runtime verification (RV) offers a formal, lightweight alternative where complex properties are specified concisely using a formal language, from which executable monitors are automatically generated. RTLOLA is one such specification language. Based on stream computations, language features natively handle real-time and asynchronicity.

In this paper, we present a ROS adapter for RTLOLA[1]. This adapter enables seamless integration of a monitor generated with the RTLOLA framework [1] by wrapping it as a ROS node, eliminating the need for any manual adjustments. The key contributions of the paper are:

- *automatic input mapping*: inspecting the RTLOLA specification and automatically subscribing to ROS topics to match required streams;
- *automatic output mapping*: inspecting the RTLOLA ROS topic and automatically publish corresponding streams;
- *supports ROS service*: inspection of RTLOLA specification and stream mapping for direct request-reply communication;
- *implemented in Rust*: safe and efficient, compatible with any ROS 2 version;
- *tool validated in flight*: used for cross-validation of bounding boxes given by machine-learning-component and blobs detected in LiDAR image using traditional computer vision techniques.

Alongside the technical details presented in the subsequent sections, we also provide information on the experimental flight test, starting with the use-case.

Experimental Use-Case. We deployed the adapter for safeguarding a machine-learning (ML) component running onboard of an unmanned aircraft. This ML component is responsible for detecting people near a designated landing site. Figure 1 illustrates the scenario, where mannequins simulate people standing on a vertiport – the intended landing site for the hovering unmanned aircraft. Figure 2 depicts the unmanned aircraft equipped with a camera and a LiDAR. In the background, the "container city" is shown. Some mannequins were positioned within this city to provide occlusion scenarios. The aircraft's perspective is shown in Fig. 3, highlighting both correct detections (green) and challenging

  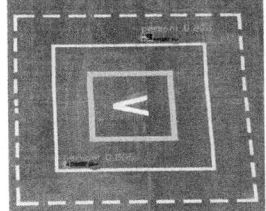

Fig. 1. Task: Safeguard detecting people at landing site.

Fig. 2. Compare detected persons with objects in a LiDAR depth image.

Fig. 3. True positives are shown in green, potential false positives in red. (Color figure online)

---

[1] https://github.com/DLR-FT/RTLola-ROS2-Adapter.

conditions that may lead to false positives (red) of the ML component. In this experiment, we use the adapter to integrate an RTLOLA monitor that cross-validates ML-based detections against objects in LiDAR depth images using a traditional Blob detector. In the following, we focus on the monitor integration, while referring to [7] for the experimental results where also other properties such as geofencing were considered for monitoring the operational design domain.

1.1 Related Work

In recent years, the integration of RV into ROS systems has received growing attention. ROS is widely used not only for developing robotic applications but also for supporting various simulation frameworks such as Gazebo [4] or Carla [3], as well as visualization tools like PlotJuggler. Several RV frameworks have been developed to support ROS. For example, RTAMT [8] integrates monitors based on Signal Temporal Logic into ROS applications. The Ogma [5] tool runs monitors specified in languages such as CoPilot, FRET, and Lustre as ROS nodes. Similarily, [2] uses the stream-based specification language TeSSLa to integrate monitors into ROS systems. Similar to them, we introduce the specification language RTLOLA to ROS. However, unlike prior tools, our tool supports not only topic-based communication, i.e., publishing and subscribing, but also introduces an RTLOLA service interface. This service enables request-response communication, thereby reducing the need for manual handling of monitoring responses using topic subscriptions. Although ROSMonitoring 2.0 [6] supports services by wrapping monitors in Python, we chose Rust for our adapter due to its advantages in safety and performance. Moreover, we refer to our tool as an "adapter" rather than a "bridge" because it incorporates logic that automatically derives the mappings between ROS and RTLOLA, offering more intelligent and robust integration.

2 RTLOLA Specification Language

In stream-based specification languages such as RTLOLA `input` streams capture observations of the system as a discrete sequence of measurements. `Output` streams aggregate, combine, and transform input streams to compute valuable statistics about the system. Special output streams called `trigger` streams can be declared to specify a Boolean verdict about the systems health based on these statistics. Output streams can be generalized to sets of stream instances that are uniquely identified by a set of parameters. Such parameterized output streams include a `spawn` and `close` condition, specifying when and how new stream instances are created and removed.

Experimental Setup. The specification used in the experiments[1] is given in Listing 1.1. The specification tests whether a blob exists within a given bounding

---

[1] The specification together with a toy trace can be tested within a playground: https://rtlola.cispa.de/playground/tutorial.

box, which should be the case for an actual person. First, in Line 2, four input streams are specified that characterize a single bounding box in the camera image by the x and y coordinate of its upper left corner and its width and height. Similarly, the input streams `blob_x`, `blob_y`, and `blob_r` describe the xy-position and the radius `r` of a single circular blob in the LiDAR image. Since the images of the camera and the LiDAR have different resolutions and only partially overlap w.r.t. their field of views, the two output streams `blob_x_in_cam` and `blob_y_in_cam` transform the coordinates of the detected blob in the LiDAR image into corresponding coordinates in the camera image. Note that due to lens curvature, the transformation is inherently non-linear. Furthermore, the solution depicted here represents a sub-optimal solution that is valid only within a specific altitude band. The next output stream in Line 10 is parameterized over the x and y coordinates of blobs and their radii `r`, specified by the parameter list followed after its stream name. The `spawn` condition of the stream (Line 11) instantiates these parameters with the (transformed) coordinate and radius of a blob, effectively creating an instance of the stream for each known blob. Each stream instance then validates whether the current bounding box contains the blob the stream instance corresponds to, specified in the `eval` clause of the stream (Line 12 to 13). Since memorizing every blob received at run-time is infeasible, we use the `close` condition: a stream instance (and with that a blob) becomes irrelevant after 200 milliseconds, using the instance's local clock starting upon creation (Line 14). Lastly, the `validate` stream in Line 16 tests whether the current bounding box intersects with any blob by aggregating over all instances of the `check` stream[2]. If such an instance exists, the stream evaluates to true.

```
// Service inputs: incoming bounding boxes                                      1
input bb_x, bb_y, bb_w, bb_h: Float64, Float64, Float64, Float64                2
// Subscribed inputs: detected blobs in depth image                             3
input blob_x, blob_y, blob_r: Float64, Float64, Float64                         4
// Transform depth image coordinates to camera coordinates                      5
output blob_x_in_cam := -0.01*blob_y**3.0 + 1.81*blob_y**2.0                    6
                       -66.24*blob_y + 1765.75                                  7
output blob_y_in_cam := 13.91*blob_x - 6627.13                                  8
// Whenever a new bounding box arrives compare it to all recent blobs           9
output check(x, y, r)                                                          10
    spawn with (blob_x_in_cam, blob_y_in_cam, blob_r)                          11
    eval with x - r > bb_x ∧ x + r < bb_x + bb_w ∧                             12
              y - r > bb_y ∧ y + r < bb_y + bb_h                               13
    close @Local(200ms) // recent is defined as 200ms                          14
// Service response                                                            15
output validate := check.aggregate(over_instances: all, using: ∃)              16
```

Listing 1.1. An RTLOLA specification matching bounding boxes to blobs.

3 ROS 2 Environment

ROS is a middleware that enables the execution of a distributed system made up of nodes, where each *node* typically handles a specific task in the robotic application. For example, one node may handle a sensor driver that collects

---

[2] In practice, bounding boxes are sent with a delay to not only consider past blobs.

sensor readings, another node may manage control tasks, and a third node may focus on monitoring. ROS supports different ways of communication between nodes. Most prominent are topics and services.

A *topic* is a named communication channel over which structured messages of a specific type are sent. To send data on a topic, a node must *publish* messages to it, while to receive, a node must *subscribe* to the topic. Multiple nodes can simultaneously publish to the same topic, and multiple nodes can subscribe. Each topic is strictly associated with one message type, and all publishers and subscribers must agree on this type. Listing 1.2 provides the interface file for the "blob" topic published by the Blob detector: a blob's xy-position and radius.

A *service* is a named communication channel that allows one node to request a specific response from another node. To initiate a service, a node must send a *request* message (client), while the node providing the service must process the request and sends a *response* (server). Each service is associated with a request and response message type, which must be defined beforehand, ensuring both the client and server nodes agree. Unlike topics, services operate in a one-to-one manner. A service call is blocking, meaning the client waits for a response before continuing. Listing 1.3 provides the interface file for the RTLOLA service that validates bounding boxes. The request and the response are separated by "---": the request specifies the xy-position, width, and height of the bounding box, while the response returns a single Boolean which indicates a matching blob.

Quality of Service (QoS) defines how data is exchanged between nodes. Some example settings include the *history* policy, which determines whether to keep only a limited number of recent messages ("keep last") or all messages ("keep all"), with the *queue size* applying only to the former; *reliability*, which defines whether messages are delivered with possible loss ("best effort") or guaranteed with retries ("reliable"); and *durability*, which controls if messages are persisted for late subscribers ("transient local") or discarded after publishing ("volatile").

ROS primarily support C++ and Python. C++ is widely used for performance-critical and hardware-related tasks, while Python is popular for scripting, rapid prototyping, and creating simpler nodes. Therefore, most core ROS components are written in C++. ROS comes with its own build system using CMake/Catkin, which makes the use of other compiling languages building on other build systems challenging, e.g., Rust using Cargo.

```
float64 x // x-position
float64 y // y-position
float64 r // radius
```
Listing 1.2. "blob" interface file

```
float64 x // x-position
float64 y // y-position
float64 w // width
float64 h // height
--- // Separates request and response
bool validate // is true positive
```
Listing 1.3. "bb" service interface file

Experimental Setup. The unmanned aircraft was a hexacopter with a maximal takeoff weight of 15.5 kg that followed a preprogrammed waypoint mission flying above the mannequins. To guarantee safety, a human remote pilot had always the possibility to takeover control when observing unintended drone behavior.

As hardware payload, the drone carries a Pixhawk 4 flight controller hardware, a Jetson jAi Go 2400 camera, an Ouster OS0 LiDAR, and a Nvidia Jetson AGX Orin companion computer. The companion computer is connected via 5 GHz Wlan to a ground control station for controlling the experiment and visualizing the validated bounding boxes.

Software-wise, the Pixhawk 4 runs the PX4 autopilot software and the Nvidia Jetson executes a ROS environment with multiple nodes. As PX4 and ROS provide a deep integration that directly allows to exchange information[3] numerous PX4 messages are directly available as ROS topics for the companion computer. This includes for instance information about battery, actuators, and sensor readings such as position[4]. The central ROS nodes for this experiments running on the companion computer were a node that publishes the camera images, a node for publishing the LiDAR depth images, a node that runs a OpenCV Blob detector on the depth images, an RTLOLA monitor, and DLR's UAVISION that runs a ML-based object detector and streams verified detections to a ground control station. The ML-component ran at ∼3 Hz and the Blob detector ran at around ∼20 Hz. UAVISION is subscribed to the images from the camera publisher. When UAVISION receives a camera image, it first runs the ML-based detector to obtain bounding boxes. It then uses a service provided by the RTLOLA monitor node to send each detected bounding box for cross-validation with the Blob detections subscribed to by the monitor If such a corresponding blob exists, the bounding box is validated; otherwise, it is falsified. This information, along with the bounding box, is transmitted to the ground control station. Validated bounding boxes are depicted in cyan, while falsified ones are shown in pink.

4 A ROS Adapter for RTLola

The adapter is written in Rust to ensure seamless integration with RTLOLA. It assumes a running ROS 2 workspace. To build and integrate the monitor for a given RTLOLA specification, the user simply needs to execute:
`cargo run - <specification>`.

Figure 4 shows the corresponding pipeline stages. During the "Generate" stage, the adapter collects information about available topics using ROS command-line tools. It starts by executing `ros2 topic list` to retrieve a list of currently available topics. Then, `ros2 interface show <topic/service>` is used to obtain the corresponding interface definitions. Finally, QoS details are accessed via `ros2 topic info <topic/service> -verbose`. This gathered information is used to generate Rust code instances of pre-defined templates, enabling topic subscription. These templates utilize the Rust crate `r2r`[5], which avoids the integration with the ROS build system and instead relies solely on `cargo`. By default, the subscriptions matches the QoS settings of the publisher to ensure compability. Whether the monitor publishes or provides a service depends on the presence of

---
[3] https://docs.px4.io/main/en/ros2/user_guide.html.
[4] https://github.com/PX4/px4_msgs.
[5] https://github.com/sequenceplanner/r2r.

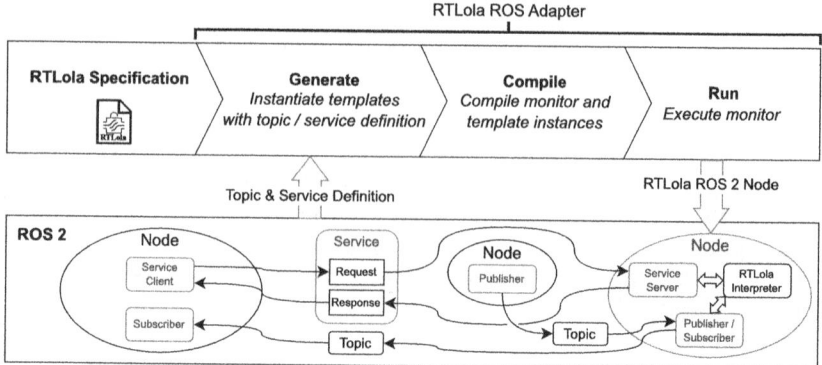

Fig. 4. Execution pipeline of the ROS adapter for RTLOLA.

the `RTLolaOutput` topic and the `RTLolaService` service interface in the running ROS workspace, respectively. If either interface is available, corresponding templates are instantiated to implement a publisher or a service server. Note that this stage is independent of the provided RTLOLA specification – the mapping of input/output RTLOLA streams are derived in a later stage. Further, a configuration file allows for QoS customization and includes a flag to "freeze" this stage's output, preventing overwriting of already generated code. During the next stage, the generated template instances and the monitor code are compiled. Finally, the wrapped RTLOLA monitor is executed as ROS node. An executed RTLOLA monitor first generates a mapping between RTLOLA input/output streams and corresponding topic members. This mapping adheres to a naming convention: <*package_name_lowercase*>_<*member*>, which is also applied during template instantiation. For example, the input stream `input adc_a0: Float32` maps to the float member a0 of topic `adc`. Moreover, fixed-length arrays in topics are unrolled, e.g., a topic *Gps* with member `float64[2] x` results in two streams: `gps_x_0` and `gps_x_1`. If any required stream is missing, the adapter will raise an error to notify the user. Note that the adapter only needs to be recompiled when topics or services are added or modified. Limitations: When responding to a service request, the adapter uses the immediate output stream values after processing the inputs. As a consequence, outputs of periodic streams may remain unchanged in the response. Additionally, topic members of unbounded array types are currently not supported and are therefore ignored.

Experimental Results. Prior to the flight test, the adapter was used during ground tests. The code generated during these tests was frozen by setting the respective flag to avoid code generation during flight tests. The PX4 autopilot provides over 50 topics. The adapter generated code for all necessary topics, so the user can focus fully on writing the specification while required topics are subscribed automatically.

The provided RTLOLA service simplified the implementation of the cross-validation called by UAVISION. If these requests were implemented using topics, additional boilerplate code would be required to handle the request-response pattern manually. Using a service avoids this overhead. Listing 1.4 shows a code snippet demonstrating how to integrate the service. Line 4 and 5 retrieve an image, detect persons, and create requests. For each detected bounding box, a blocking request `req_bb` is sent and handled asynchronously using a "future" response (Line 7). This response, once available, is passed to a callback function, responsible for forwarding the result to the ground control station (Line 8).

```
def callback(request, response):  # callback function
    ...
while True:
    frame = self.camera.read()  # reads camera frame
    req_bbs = self.ml.detect(frame)  # detection and creation of requests
    for req_bb in req_bbs:  # iterates over bounding box requests
        self.ros_client.call_async(req_bb).add_done_callback(
            functools.partial(self.callback, req_bb))  # bind request to callback
```

Listing 1.4. Excerpt of Python code demonstrating how the RTLOLA service simplifies monitor integration into UAVISION, avoiding explicit subscription handling.

The experiment also demonstrates that runtime verification improves the system's performance. Figure 5 illustrates a scenario where detections were successfully validated and could therefore be trusted. In contrast, Fig. 6 shows an example of a false positive detection that was identified as untrustworthy and subsequently discarded by the system.

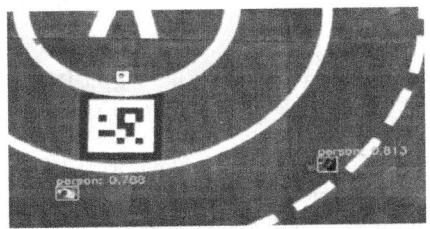

Fig. 5. The monitor validated two correct human bounding boxes (cyan).

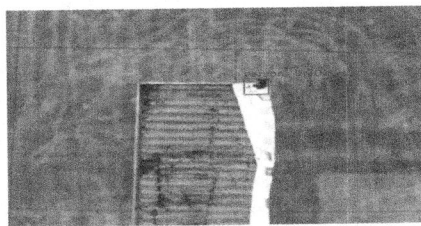

Fig. 6. Monitor flags a false positive (pink) with no matching blob. (Color figure online)

5 Conclusion

We presented a ROS adapter for RTLOLA, designed to simplify the integration of RTLOLA into ROS-based applications by automatically mapping ROS topics to RTLOLA streams. In real-flight experiments, the adapter successfully generated code for all required topics, significantly reducing user effort given the large number of available topics. Further, we demonstrated that providing a service interface by the monitor simplifies the usage of monitoring verdicts by eliminating manual request-response handling. In future, we plan to advance the cross-validation specification. Instead of checking if a blob is within a bounding box, we plan to test other metrics such as the Hausdorff distance or explicit overlap computation – thereby improving the accuracy of the cross-validation.

Acknowledgments. This work was partially supported by the German federal aviation research program (LuFo ID: 20D2111C, ID: 20Q1963B, and ID: 20Q1963C), German Research Foundation (DFG) as part of TRR 248 (No. 389792660), and by the European Research Council (ERC) Grant HYPER (No. 101055412). Sebastian Schirmer carried out this work as a member of the Saarbrücken Graduate School of Computer Science.

References

1. Baumeister, J., Finkbeiner, B., Kohn, F., Scheerer, F.: A tutorial on stream-based monitoring. CoRR arxiv:2501.15913 (2025). https://doi.org/10.48550/ARXIV.2501.15913
2. Begemann, M.J., Kallwies, H., Leucker, M., Schmitz, M.: TeSSla-ROS-bridge - runtime verification of robotic systems. In: Ábrahám, E., Dubslaff, C., Tarifa, S.L.T. (eds.) Theoretical Aspects of Computing - ICTAC 2023 - 20th International Colloquium, Lima, Peru, 4–8 December 2023, Proceedings. LNCS, vol. 14446, pp. 388–398. Springer, Heidelberg (2023). https://doi.org/10.1007/978-3-031-47963-2_23
3. Dosovitskiy, A., Ros, G., Codevilla, F., López, A.M., Koltun, V.: CARLA: an open urban driving simulator. In: 1st Annual Conference on Robot Learning, CoRL 2017, Mountain View, California, USA, 13–15 November 2017, Proceedings. Proceedings of Machine Learning Research, vol. 78, pp. 1–16. PMLR (2017). http://proceedings.mlr.press/v78/dosovitskiy17a.html
4. Koenig, N., Howard, A.: Design and use paradigms for gazebo, an open-source multi-robot simulator. In: 2004 IEEE/RSJ International Conference on Intelligent Robots and Systems (IROS) (IEEE Cat. No.04CH37566), vol. 3, pp. 2149–2154 (2004). https://doi.org/10.1109/IROS.2004.1389727
5. Perez, I., Mavridou, A., Pressburger, T., Will, A., Martin, P.J.: Monitoring ROS2: from requirements to autonomous robots. In: Luckcuck, M., Farrell, M. (eds.) Proceedings Fourth International Workshop on Formal Methods for Autonomous Systems (FMAS) and Fourth International Workshop on Automated and verifiable Software sYstem DEvelopment (ASYDE), FMAS/ASYDE@SEFM 2022, and Fourth International Workshop on Automated and verifiable Software sYstem DEvelopment (ASYDE)Berlin, Germany, 26–27 September 2022. EPTCS, vol. 371, pp. 208–216 (2022). https://doi.org/10.4204/EPTCS.371.15,
6. Saadat, M.G., Ferrando, A., Dennis, L.A., Fisher, M.: ROSMonitoring 2.0: extending ROS runtime verification to services and ordered topics. In: Luckcuck, M., Xu, M. (eds.) Proceedings Sixth International Workshop on Formal Methods for Autonomous Systems, FMAS@iFM 2024, Manchester, UK, 11–12 November 2024. EPTCS, vol. 411, pp. 38–55 (2024). https://doi.org/10.4204/EPTCS.411.3,
7. Torens, C.: Runtime-monitoring of operational design domain to safeguard machine learning components. Special Issue HorizonUAM, under review. CEAS Aeronaut. J (2023)
8. Yamaguchi, T., Hoxha, B., Ničković, D.: RTAMT – runtime robustness monitors with application to CPS and robotics. Int. J. Softw. Tools Technol. Transf. **26**(1), 79–99 (2023). https://doi.org/10.1007/s10009-023-00720-3,

DynSRV: Dynamically Updated Properties for Stream Runtime Verification

Morten Haahr Kristensen[✉], Thomas Wright, Cláudio Gomes, Lukas Esterle, and Peter Gorm Larsen

Department of Electrical and Computer Engineering, Aarhus University, Aarhus, Denmark
{mhk,thomas.wright,claudio.gomes,lukas.esterle,pgl}@ece.au.dk

Abstract. Systems that adapt to their environment or change based on new requirements pose challenges for runtime verification. Complexity is increased when the system needs to retain its internal state and continue monitoring while also updating properties or adding new ones during runtime. In this work, we propose DynSRV, a Stream Runtime Verification language that allows for dynamic updates of properties. A core benefit of this language is its capability to update properties at runtime without requiring a restart of the monitor, maintaining the internal state of the remaining properties. We formalise the semantics of our core primitives and demonstrate design patterns for allowing adaptations under certain constraints. Finally, we present an implementation of DynSRV and describe three memory strategies that balance memory usage and the ability to resolve dynamically added properties depending on historical data.

Keywords: Runtime Verification · Dynamic Properties · Stream Runtime Verification · Autonomous Systems · Dynamic Software Updating · Self-Adaptive Systems

1 Introduction

Motivation. How do we ensure continuous and accurate runtime monitoring when the system evolves during execution? If the system evolves in simple ways that can be captured in static Runtime Verification (RV) specifications then system evolution is not an issue. However, if significant behavioural changes are introduced by a human through Dynamic Software Updating (DSU) (see, e.g. [14]) or autonomously, then the RV specification must also be updated to ensure that the system is still being monitored correctly. Moreover, changes

---

The work presented here is supported by the RoboSAPIENS project funded by the European Commission's Horizon Europe programme under grant agreement number 101133807. In addition, the authors would like to thank Amalie Kaastrup-Hansen, Tobias Frejo Rasmussen, and Mikkel Kirkegaard for the fruitful discussions leading up to the paper.

often entail that the system requirements have evolved [14], and if so, then the RV specification must also evolve to reflect these new requirements. An example of this is shown in [19], where a self-adaptive cloud-edge-end power distribution system requires the deployment of a state-machine based monitor that changes to reflect requirement changes in real-time, as the system reacts to evolving load demands, sensors failure, or maintenance events. Naturally, one possibility is restarting the monitor with an updated specification, but this is not always possible, as it involves loss of internal state potentially leading to incorrect verdicts [22].

Contribution 1. We propose and formally define DynSRV, a Stream Runtime Verification (SRV) language that allows monitors to be updated at runtime without requiring restarts or manual rewriting. Specifically, we introduce two primitives to DynSRV which enable expressing Dynamically Updated Properties (DUPs).

- defer(p) allows a RV property p to be specified at a later point in time, enabling exactly one dynamic update.
- dynamic(p) extends the concept of defer(p) by permitting continual updates, allowing the dynamic property to be modified multiple times throughout execution.

DUPs extend the concept of DSU to SRV by allowing specifications to evolve alongside the system without restarting. Unlike traditional DSU, which modifies the functional aspects of a running system, DUPs focus on changing the RV properties that the system is expected to satisfy.

Contribution 2. While DynSRV enables flexible adaptation, allowing arbitrary dynamic expressions within a monitor introduces challenges in reasoning about specification correctness. Thus, we propose *design patterns* for the specification of DUPs, enabling controlled adaptations, refinements, and demonstrating common adaptation patterns within DSU.

Contribution 3. We highlight the unique challenge presented by allowing adaptive SRV with DynSRV, such as ensuring consistency in monitoring results despite evolving specifications, managing historical data for updated properties, and developing performant interpreters that allow evaluating unforeseen properties.

2 Background and Related Work

We begin by linking the fields of DSU and Self-Adaptive Systems (SASs), which provided the motivation for this work, and we discuss how they relate to DUPs. We then recap the basic concepts of SRV before introducing existing works that express special cases of DUPs in the context of RV.

2.1 Dynamic Software Updating and Self-Adaptive Systems

DSU enables modifying running systems without stopping them, which is critical for applications like financial systems or web servers where downtime is costly. Key challenges include maintaining safety, supporting flexible updates, minimising overhead, and easing the developer's burden. Hicks, Moore, and Nettles [14] address these with a DSU system for C-like languages using type-safe dynamic patches and tools to aid patch creation and application.

SASs autonomously manage and adjust themselves to meet high-level goals [16]. Inspired by biological autonomic systems, they reduce manual intervention through capabilities like self-configuration, optimisation, healing, and modular architectural updates [27]. SASs use feedback loops and distributed components to monitor, analyze, plan, and execute changes in dynamic environments. Key challenges include goal specification, ensuring safety, and handling emergent behaviour.

DSU and SASs are interrelated: DSU enables runtime adaptation for SASs, while SASs frameworks can manage DSU to maintain stability during updates. Virtual machine-based DSU approaches, such as those presented in [15,25,26], inspired our monitor architecture, offering runtime control and transformation of system structures.

At design time, formal verification ensures DSU maintains safety and liveness properties. A foundational model by Bierman et al. [2] uses a λ-calculus with an update primitive to enable formal reasoning about dynamic updates. Despite extensive research (see surveys [20,23,28]), runtime updating of verification properties remains an underexplored area. The following sections address existing work on this topic.

Other works have developed temporal logic-based controller synthesis techniques to generate dynamic updates to a controller which satisfy temporal logic properties specifying both the expected new behaviour and the manner of the update. Nahabedian et al. [21] introduced an approach to synthesising controllers which satisfy new specifications as well as update strategies which ensures correct behaviour during the update; this corresponds to a *guided adaptation strategy* as proposed by Zhang and Cheng [29]. Finkbeiner, Klein, and Metzger [11] introduced LiveLTL, an extension of Linear Temporal Logic (LTL) for specifying desired behaviour before and after a dynamic update, and introduced a synthesis algorithm for synthesising updated controllers which meet the new requirements as well as any outstanding unsatisfied old requirements.

2.2 Dynamically Updated Properties

SRV is a lightweight RV approach that monitors systems producing continuous data streams. It processes input streams, i.e., sequences of event values, into verdict streams following a given specification.

LOLA [8] is a SRV language, inspired by LUSTRE and ESTEREL, supporting basic operations, conditionals, and time-offsets to enable temporal monitoring. LOLA uses a dependency graph to determine if a specification is "Efficiently

Monitorable", ensuring bounded memory usage. LOLA pioneered SRV and has influenced many subsequent languages, including TeSSLa [18].

Lola 2.0 improves dynamic RV through dynamic parametrization, enabling quantification over objects and monitor spawning independent of observed instances, and retroactive parametrization, allowing monitors to revisit past events during execution [22]. While the new monitors support parameterizing existing expressions, DynSRV allows dynamically providing any syntactically valid expression that references valid input streams.

Barringer et al. [1] propose Eagle, a general logic framework supporting recursive monitoring rules with fixpoint semantics. Eagle supports dynamic monitor generation and logics like LTL, Metric Temporal Logic (MTL), and Statistical Contracts.

First order logic quantification in dynamically created objects in RV was explored by Havelund and Peled [13] and Sokolsky et al. [24] with LC_v. LC_v uses first-order and attribute quantifiers to track dynamic entities (e.g., tasks, sensors). This relates to Allocational Temporal Logic (ATL) using history-dependent automata [9].

Actor-based runtime verification [4–7] has previously been applied to self-adaptive systems, using independent monitor actors that observe and react to behaviour asynchronously.

The most relevant related work in terms of goals (but not methods) is by Carwehl et al. [3], who propose dynamically adapting monitors to changing requirements without restarting the monitor. Their monitors are synthesized as automata with error states based on structured English specifications translated into MTL, whereas we use stream-based properties. During execution, a Runtime Verifier checks for violations, and when requirements change, a Requirements Manager applies predefined Property Adaptation Patterns (e.g., updating a time guard or updating events). In contrast, we support arbitrary property expressions as long as they are syntactically valid and use existing input streams. While they argue that adhering to fixed patterns leads to safer adaptations and view fully dynamic RV as undesirable, we take a different stance, and demonstrate through Contribution 2 that we can address these valid concerns while prioritising expressiveness.

3 Specification Language

3.1 Motivational Example

To provide a motivational example (Fig. 1), we consider future production lines where different products are manufactured by autonomously moving robots. The robots move around in the production hall and utilise the different tools available in order to produce the desired items. The robot has an understanding of the production process and which tools to utilise for each product. However, while the robot and the production line are developed in parallel, the robot will only get knowledge of the final layout and the respective locations of the different tools upon completion of the production hall. Upon deployment, the robot will be given a product to manufacture, and it will start to move around the production hall. When the product is completed, the robot will receive a new product – potentially with a different requirement for the tools to be used. The robot will then have to adapt its plans, movement and overall behaviour to the new product. Finally, the robot is battery-operated and will need to recharge at certain intervals as well as undergo regular maintenance.

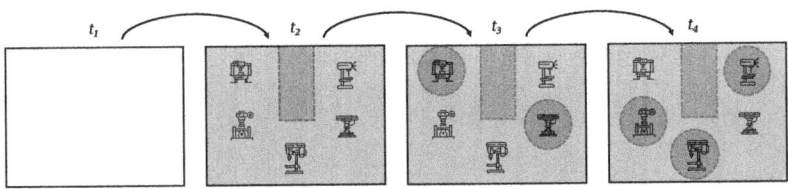

Fig. 1. Example of a production line at different time steps. First is the empty production hall, then the layout with the machines is added – a specific area is for robot maintenance (red square). Last two show which tools are allowed to be used during phases t_3 and t_4 (highlighted in purple). (Color figure online)

In this scenario, the robot uses the stream $l = \texttt{defer}(l_{in})$ for the layout of the production lines, respective locations of the different tools, and restricted areas, using defer since this configuration becomes immutable once it is made. At deployment time, $p = \texttt{dynamic}(p_{in})$ is used to change the rules determining which products the robot is allowed to manufacture as the production line evolves. Here, the new rules can use the information gathered from the layout stream. Finally, the verdict is available with $v = \texttt{update}(p_{init}, p)$ where an initial value of production rules is provided with update, which is detailed in Sect. 3.3.

This example highlights the need for DUPs in scenarios where the monitored system is subject to dynamic changes, and the monitoring properties must adapt accordingly. In addition, the specification can include static properties. For instance, the robot is also subject to regular maintenance and recharging within *at least* certain intervals (e.g., at least every 12 h), requiring stateful properties to be monitored. As the stateful maintenance information would be lost if the monitor is restarted, a simple restart for each product update is not feasible. While this is only a simple example, the reader can imagine more complex scenarios with multiple robots and multiple products operating in parallel and potentially creating conflicts around resources and tools during execution.

3.2 Syntax

DynSRV defines monitors that transform a set of input streams $I = \{p_1, \ldots, p_n\}$ into a set of output streams $O = \{o_1, \ldots, o_m\}$. Each stream $s = (s_1, s_2, \ldots)$ is a sequence of typed values s_i in some domain $\mathbb{D}$. These domains $\mathbb{D}$ include booleans $\mathbb{B}$, integers $\mathbb{Z}$, floating point numbers $\mathbb{F}$, and, recursively, stream expressions in the DynSRV *expression domain* $\mathbb{E}[\mathbb{D}]$ which we will shortly define with values in some domain $\mathbb{D}$. Streams may also take on a special value $\bot$ (pronounced *deferred*), denoting that no value was sent at the current time step.

A *specification* Φ over input streams and output streams $S = I \uplus O$ (where $\uplus$ denotes the *disjoint union*) consists of a set of equations

$$o_1 = \phi_{o_1} \quad \ldots \quad o_n = \phi_{o_n}$$

where the expressions ϕ_o are defined as stream expressions with output domain $\mathbb{D}$. Stream expressions $\phi \in \mathbb{E}[\mathbb{D}]$ are defined recursively to be a *basic expression*, a *DUP*, or a *DUP helper*. We elaborate on the precise semantics for DUPs in Sect. 3.3.

A *basic expression* is one of the following:
- a constant $\quad\quad\quad\quad \phi \triangleq c \quad\quad\quad\quad\quad\quad$ for $c \in \mathbb{D}$
- a stream variable $\quad\quad \phi \triangleq v \quad\quad\quad\quad\quad\quad$ for any $v \in S$
- a function application $\quad \phi \triangleq f(\psi_1, \ldots, \psi_n)$
  which lifts an arbitrary data-domain function $f : \mathbb{D}_1 \times \ldots \times \mathbb{D}_n \to \mathbb{D}$
- a temporal index $\quad\quad \phi \triangleq \psi[-j] \quad\quad\quad\quad$ for $\psi \in \mathbb{E}[\mathbb{D}], j \in \mathbb{N}$
  referring to the value of ψ at j time units in the past
- a conditional $\quad\quad\quad \phi \triangleq \text{if } \sigma \text{ then } \psi_1 \text{ else } \psi_2 \quad$ for $\sigma \in \mathbb{E}[\mathbb{B}]$
  $\quad\quad\quad\quad\quad\quad\quad\quad\quad\quad\quad\quad\quad\quad\quad\quad\quad\quad\quad\quad\quad \psi_1, \psi_2 \in \mathbb{E}[\mathbb{D}]$

A *DUP* is one of the following:
- a defer $\quad\quad\quad\quad \phi \triangleq \text{defer}(\psi) \quad\quad\quad\quad$ for $\psi \in \mathbb{E}[\mathbb{D}]$
  referring to a dynamic property which is $\bot$ until the first point at which ψ becomes available and behaves like ψ subsequently
- a dynamic $\quad\quad\quad \phi \triangleq \text{dynamic}(\psi) \quad\quad\quad$ for $\psi \in \mathbb{E}[\mathbb{D}]$
  referring to a dynamic property which behaves like the most recent value of ψ or is $\bot$ if none has been sent

A *DUP helper* is one of the following:
- a default $\quad\quad\quad \phi \triangleq \text{default}(\psi, c) \quad\quad\quad$ for $\psi \in \mathbb{E}[\mathbb{D}], c \in \mathbb{D}$
  which uses the default value c if ψ is $\bot$
- a when $\quad\quad\quad\quad \phi \triangleq \text{when}(\psi) \quad\quad\quad\quad\quad$ for $\psi \in \mathbb{E}[\mathbb{D}]$
  which is false until the first time ψ is not $\bot$ and true thereafter
- an update $\quad\quad\quad \phi \triangleq \text{update}(\psi_1, \psi_2) \quad\quad$ for $\psi_1, \psi_2 \in \mathbb{E}[\mathbb{D}]$
  which is ψ_1 until the first time ψ_2 is not $\bot$ and ψ_2 thereafter

Standard data-domain operators such as addition, multiplication, logical conjunction, disjunction, and comparison operators are supported as functions f lifted to stream expressions. These operators propagate $\bot$ values such that e.g. $42 + \bot = \bot$.

Furthermore, we define a specification to be *well-defined*, if it has no zero-time cycle of dependencies (similarly to [8]), that is, if any dependency cycle is guarded by a time index. This restriction is necessary for specifications to be monitorable.

3.3 Semantics of DUPs

In this section we define a mathematical semantics for DynSRV specifications Φ. We note that this follows a similar approach to the semantics of TeSSLa [18] and LOLA [8], whilst introducing novel definitions to handle DUPs.

First, we need to formalise the notion of streams, used for specification input and output. Streams s range over the time domain $\mathbb{T} \triangleq \mathbb{N}$ of natural numbers, and assign to each time point $t \in \mathbb{T}$ a stream value $s(t)$ in an appropriate data domain $\mathbb{D}$. We also need these to handle both deferred data $\bot$ (for dynamic properties) as well as *partiality*, which uses the special value ? to represent stream values which have not yet been computed.

Definition 1 (Stream). *A partial stream (or simply, stream) is a function $s : \mathbb{T} \to \mathbb{D} \cup \{?, \bot\}$ such that $s(i) = ?$ implies that for all $j > i$ we must have $s(j) = ?$. We denote the set of streams by $\text{STREAM} = [\mathbb{V} \to \mathbb{D} \cup \{?, \bot\}]$.*

Additionally, we call a partial stream *total* if $\forall i \in \mathbb{T} : s(i) \neq ?$.

We define the input namespace $\text{in}(\Phi)$ consisting of the set of input variables, the output namespace $\text{out}(\Phi)$ consists of the set of output variables, and we define $\text{vars}(\Phi) = \text{in}(\Phi) \cup \text{out}(\Phi)$. We also define $\text{vars}(\phi)$, for any stream expression ϕ to be the set of all stream variables appearing in ϕ, and define $\mathbb{V}$ to be the set of all variable names[1]. This allows us to introduce *contexts*, representing an assignment of partial streams to some stream variables v in the set of all stream variables $\mathbb{V}$.

Definition 2 (Context). *A context is a partial function $C : \mathbb{V} \rightharpoonup \text{STREAM}$. We denote the set of all such partial functions as*

$$\text{CONTEXT} \triangleq [\mathbb{V} \rightharpoonup \mathbb{T} \to \mathbb{D} \cup \{?, \bot\}] = [\mathbb{V} \rightharpoonup \text{STREAM}].$$

That is, within a given context, for a stream variable $v \in \mathbb{V}$ in the domain of stream variables for which it is defined, we have a stream for this stream variable $C(v) : \mathbb{T} \to \mathbb{D} \cup \{?, \bot\}$. In particular, the inputs to a specification Φ can be provided via an *input context* C_{in} such that $\text{dom}(C_{\text{in}}) = \text{in}(\Phi)$.

We also define the *refinement* partial order on data values by setting $u \sqsubseteq v$ iff $v = ?$ implies $u = ?$. This extends elementwise to a partial order $\sqsubseteq$ on streams, and on contexts sharing the same domain.

Using this, we define the semantics of a specification Φ as the least fixed-point of a *single-step semantics*, which expands one recursive step of the stream equations, using refinement to gradually build streams covering the whole time domain.

Definition 3. *We define the single-step semantics for a specification Φ to be the function $[\![\Phi]\!]_1 : \text{CONTEXT} \to \text{CONTEXT} \to \text{CONTEXT}$ defined such that*

$$[\![\Phi]\!]_1(C)(D)(v) = [\![\phi_v]\!]_1(C)(D \uplus C)$$

---

[1] To be concrete, we can set $\mathbb{V} = \mathbb{N}$ for countably many numerically-indexed variables.

for each $v \in \text{vars}(\phi)$, whilst the denotation function for a well-defined specification Φ given initial context $C = C_{\text{in}}$ to be the function $\llbracket \Phi \rrbracket : \text{CONTEXT} \to \text{CONTEXT}$ defined as the least-fixed point:

$$\llbracket \Phi \rrbracket(C) = \mu D. \llbracket \Phi \rrbracket_1(C)(D).$$

under the refinement order $\sqsubseteq$.

We also define the shorthand $\llbracket \psi \rrbracket(C) \triangleq \llbracket \Psi \rrbracket(C)$ for the semantics of ϕ within the specification $\Psi \triangleq v = \psi$ where v is any fresh variable name.

The fixed-point in the above definition exists and is unique for well-defined specifications Φ by Kleene's fixed-point theorem since the definitions of the single-step semantics for individual operators – which we will give shortly – are monotone in the refinement order $\sqsubseteq$, and hence so is $\llbracket \Phi \rrbracket_1(C)$.

This depends on the single-step semantics for individual operators, which we define as follows for basic operators,

$$\llbracket c \rrbracket_1(C)(D)(i) \triangleq c$$

$$\llbracket v \rrbracket_1(C)(D)(i) \triangleq D(v)(i)$$

$$\llbracket f(\psi_1, \ldots, \psi_k) \rrbracket_1(C)(D)(i) \triangleq f(\llbracket \psi_1 \rrbracket_1(C)(D)(i), \ldots, \llbracket \psi_k \rrbracket_1(C)(D)(i))$$

$$\llbracket \texttt{if } \sigma \texttt{ then } \psi_1 \texttt{ else } \psi_2 \rrbracket_1(C)(D)(i) \triangleq \begin{cases} \llbracket \psi_1 \rrbracket_1(C)(D)(i) & \text{if } \llbracket \sigma \rrbracket_1(C)(D)(i) = \text{true} \\ \llbracket \psi_2 \rrbracket_1(C)(D)(i) & \text{if } \llbracket \sigma \rrbracket_1(C)(D)(i) = \text{false} \\ \bot & \text{if } \llbracket \sigma \rrbracket_1(C)(D)(i) = \bot \\ ? & \text{if } \llbracket \sigma \rrbracket_1(C)(D)(i) = ? \end{cases}$$

$$\llbracket \psi[-j] \rrbracket_1(C)(D)(i) \triangleq \begin{cases} \llbracket \psi \rrbracket_1(C)(D)(i-j) & \text{if } i \geq j \\ \bot & \text{otherwise} \end{cases}$$

For the other functions, we first define duration restricted subsets of a context, which can be used to evaluate properties using only data available at a given point in time.

Definition 4. *Given a context C we define the duration-d prefix of C as the context $C|_d$ defined by*

$$C|_d(v)(i) \triangleq \begin{cases} C(v)(i) & \text{if } i \leq d \\ ? & \text{otherwise} \end{cases}$$

which we use to define the following two helper functions,

Definition 5. *For maximum duration i, expression ψ, and context C, we define the functions* $\text{first}, \text{last} : \mathbb{N} \times \mathbb{E}[\mathbb{D}] \times \text{CONTEXT} \to \mathbb{N} \cup \{\infty\}$ *defined by*

$$\text{first}(i, \psi, C) \triangleq \min\{ j \in \mathbb{N} \mid \llbracket \psi \rrbracket(C|_j)(j) \notin \{\bot, ?\} \wedge j \leq i \}$$
$$\text{last}(i, \psi, C) \triangleq \max\{ j \in \mathbb{N} \mid \llbracket \psi \rrbracket(C|_j)(j) \notin \{\bot, ?\} \wedge j \leq i \}$$

where each of these functions is set to ∞ if $\llbracket \psi \rrbracket(C|_j)(j) \in \{\bot, ?\}$ for all j.

Then we define the single-step semantics of dynamic properties by,

$$[\![\texttt{defer}(\psi)]\!]_1(C)(D)(i) \triangleq \begin{cases} [\![\psi_j]\!]_1(C)(D)(i) & \text{if } i \geq j \\ \bot & \text{if } j = \infty \end{cases}$$

$$[\![\texttt{dynamic}(\psi)]\!]_1(C)(D)(i) \triangleq \begin{cases} [\![\psi_k]\!]_1(C)(D)(i) & \text{if } i \geq k \\ \bot & \text{if } k = \infty \end{cases}$$

where $j = \text{first}(i, \psi, C)$, $k = \text{last}(i, \psi, C)$, $\psi_j \triangleq [\![\psi]\!]_1(C|_j)(D)(j)$, and $\psi_k \triangleq [\![\psi]\!]_1(C|_k)(D)(k)$.

Finally, we define the semantics of each of the DUP helper functions by

$$[\![\texttt{update}(\psi_1, \psi_2)]\!]_1(C)(D)(i) \triangleq \begin{cases} [\![\psi_1]\!]_1(C)(D)(i) & \text{if first}(i, \psi_2, D) = \infty \\ [\![\psi_2]\!]_1(C)(D)(i) & \text{otherwise} \end{cases}$$

$$[\![\texttt{when}(\psi)]\!]_1(C)(D)(i) \triangleq \begin{cases} \text{false} & \text{if first}(i, \psi, C) = \infty \\ \text{true} & \text{otherwise} \end{cases}$$

$$[\![\texttt{default}(\psi, c)]\!]_1(C)(D)(i) \triangleq \begin{cases} [\![\psi]\!]_1(C)(D)(i) & \text{if } [\![\psi]\!]_1(C)(D)(i) \neq \bot \\ c & \text{otherwise} \end{cases}$$

4 Design Patterns with DUPs

In practical RV scenarios, system requirements change. Supporting such changes with a first-class language construct allows specifications to adapt systematically, and allows expressing which parts are allowed to adapt. With DUPs, not only can the specification itself evolve over time, but it also becomes possible to express meta-properties, i.e., properties about how the specification may change. This section presents design patterns for writing specifications with DUPs in Dyn-SRV.

General Design Patterns

Open Property shows the most permissive use of dynamic, where the verdict v, directly reflects the incoming property p. In this case, it is up to the sender to ensure that the provided property is safe and valid.

$$v = \texttt{dynamic}(p)$$

Weaken allows dynamic properties to weaken an existing requirement. In this example, accepting a new goal g normally requires the robot's battery level b to be above 30%. However, in emergencies such as a fire, strictly enforcing this threshold could block critical actions, such as evacuating an area or saving material, thus custom rules p are allowed.

$$v = g \implies b > 30 \lor \texttt{default}(\texttt{dynamic}(p), \text{false})$$

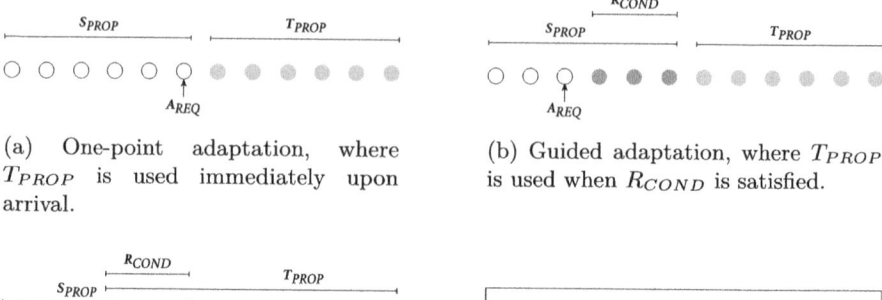

(a) One-point adaptation, where T_{PROP} is used immediately upon arrival.

(b) Guided adaptation, where T_{PROP} is used when R_{COND} is satisfied.

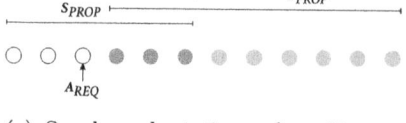

(c) Overlap adaptation, where T_{PROP} is used alongside S_{PROP} until the R_{COND} is satisfied, whereafter only T_{PROP} is used.

Fig. 2. Adaptation semantics proposed by Zhang and Cheng, figure adapted from [29] with minor modifications for SRV.

Strengthen allows dynamic properties to strengthen existing requirements. In the example, T is the current time, T_m is the scheduled maintenance time, and p represents dynamic rules that further constrain the maintenance window. For instance, these rules might shorten the service interval if the battery degrades or if the robot moves farther from its charging station.

$$v = T < T_m \wedge \texttt{default}(T < \texttt{dynamic}(p), \text{true})$$

Refinement allows refining an existing property with a new one, where the verdict reflects whether the refinement is valid. In this example, b represents an update of the original condition b_c to a new property p once sent. The refinement expression r evaluates whether the new property remains valid within the context of the original condition. Notably, r is a tautology ($b_c \implies b_c$) when no new property has been provided. The verdict v combines the updated condition b and the refinement r, where true means the requirements are met. If the new property evaluates to $\bot$, the verdict becomes false.

$$b_c = b_{in} > 30 \qquad b = \texttt{update}(b_c, \texttt{defer}(p))$$
$$r = b \implies b_c \qquad v = \texttt{default}(b \wedge r, \text{false})$$

Adaptation Patterns
In their works on A-LTL, Zhang and Cheng [29] formalised the semantics of three commonly occurring adaptation semantics: *one-point*, *guided*, and *overlap*

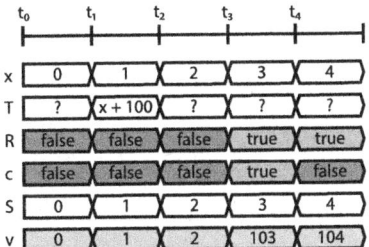
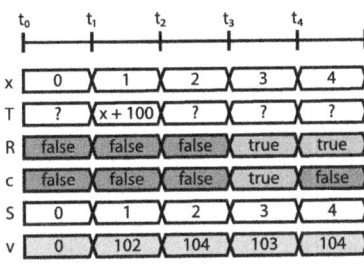

(a) Trace demonstrating guided adaptation. The verdict stream v switches to T after R is satisfied.

(b) Trace demonstrating overlap adaptation. The verdict stream v combines S and T until R is satisfied, after which it uses only T.

Fig. 3. Example traces for guided and overlap adaptation.

adaptation[2]. This is depicted in Fig. 2. To highlight the expressiveness of DynSRV, we demonstrate how the latter two can be expressed with DUPs. One-point adaptation is trivial with DynSRV, as it immediately applies the new property, which is the default behaviour of `defer` and `dynamic`.

Guided Adaptation allows a new property to not be used immediately but await for a restriction condition to be satisfied, as depicted in Fig. 2b. This allows the system to delay the application of a new property until appropriate.

The example below demonstrates a specification implementing guided adaptation in DynSRV, with the corresponding trace in Fig. 3a. An integer stream is used for the verdict to more clearly represent its distinct states.

$$S = x \qquad\qquad R = \mathtt{when}(T) \land c \lor \mathtt{default}(R[-1], \mathrm{false})$$
$$c = x == 3 \qquad\qquad v = \mathtt{if}\ R\ \mathtt{then}\ \mathtt{defer}(T)\ \mathtt{else}\ S$$

Here, x and T are input streams, with T representing a property received at time step 1. This property is not applied to the verdict v immediately but is gated by R, which becomes true when c holds after the property is received – at time step 3. The disjunction with $\mathtt{default}(R[-1], \mathrm{false})$ ensures that once R holds, it remains true thereafter. The verdict v switches to the deferred property $\mathtt{defer}(T)$ only after R holds; otherwise, it yields from S.

Overlap Adaptation allows a new property to be used alongside the original property until a condition is satisfied, as depicted in Fig. 2c. Once this condition holds, the new property is used exclusively.

---

[2] In Zhang and Cheng's [29] semantics, adaptation may involve a delay between receiving and applying an adaptation request to ensure the program is in a safe state. This is not required in DynSRV, as it is stateless.

The example below shows a DynSRV specification implementing this behaviour, with its trace depicted in Fig. 3b:

$S = x$ $R = \text{when}(T) \land c \lor \text{default}(R[-1], \text{false})$
$c = x == 3$ $v = \text{if } \neg\text{when}(T) \text{ then } S \text{ else if } \neg R \text{ then } S + T \text{ else } T$

Unlike guided adaptation, overlap adaptation introduces a transition phase where the original stream and the new one are combined $(S + T)^3$ until the condition R becomes true. Initially, the verdict v yields from S. When a new property is received at time step 1 via T, the verdict combines S and T until R is satisfied at time step 3. After that, the verdict uses only T.

5 Memory Management and History with DUPs

Efficient online monitoring with SRV has long been a focus of the community. Newer languages such as TeSSLa [18] guarantee Bounded Memory (BM) by disallowing future stream indexing – a restriction also adopted by DynSRV. Here, we define BM to mean that at each monitoring step, the monitor's memory usage does not grow with the length of the trace. While memory usage may change dynamically (e.g., when new properties are added), it must remain independent of the trace length. Allowing DUPs in DynSRV introduces a trade-off for ensuring BM, as dynamic expressions may require access to historical data that would otherwise be discarded as a part of the memory management strategy. In static SRV languages, the Dependency Graph (DG) can be used to safely discard unused history once it is no longer needed to resolve equations. In contrast, DUPs can introduce new data dependencies at runtime, potentially referencing historical values that have already been discarded to free memory. This dynamic behaviour makes it impossible to guarantee both BM usage and optimal resolution of expressions introduced by DUPs. Even if a dynamic expression at time t could be resolved to a non-$\bot$ value given the full trace, the monitor may still return $\bot$ if the necessary data has been discarded. This section defines *solvable* stream expressions in relation to memory management and presents three strategies that demonstrate the trade-off.

Solvable Stream Expressions
For this section, we use the notation that $\phi[-j]$ refer to a stream expression ϕ annotated with an optional temporal index $-j$, where $j = 0$ when no explicit index is given.

---

[3] Here, addition is used as an example; other operators may apply depending on context.

Definition 6 (Effective Index). *Given a stream expression $\phi[-j]$ and stream variable $s \in \text{vars}(\phi)$, the effective index $\text{index}(\phi, s, j)$ is defined as:*

$$\text{index}(\phi, s, j) = \begin{cases} j + j' & \text{if } \phi = s[-j'], s \in \text{vars}(\phi) \\ j & \text{if } \phi = \text{when}(\psi) \vee \\ & \quad \phi = \text{default}(\psi, c) \\ \text{index}(\psi, s, j) & \text{if } \phi = \text{defer}(\psi) \vee \\ & \quad \phi = \text{dynamic}(\psi) \\ \text{index}(\psi, s, j + j') & \text{if } \phi = \psi[-j'] \\ \max(\{\text{index}(\psi, s, j) \mid & \text{if } \phi = f(\psi_1, \ldots, \psi_n) \\ \quad \psi \in \{\psi_1, \ldots, \psi_n\}\}) \\ \max(\{\text{index}(\sigma, s, j), & \text{if } \phi = \text{if } \sigma \text{ then } \psi_1 \\ \quad \text{index}(\psi_1, s, j), \text{index}(\psi_2, s, j)\} & \quad \text{else } \psi_2 \\ \max(\{\text{index}(\psi_1, s, j), & \text{if } \phi = \text{update}(\psi_1, \psi_2) \\ \quad \text{index}(\psi_2, s, j)\}j & \text{otherwise} \end{cases}$$

Effective Index is useful for reasoning about expressions with nested temporal indices. We highlight the case with $\text{when}(\psi)$ and $\text{default}(\psi, c)$ expressions, which do not introduce new temporal indices and can therefore be used in practice to relax the requirements for *solvable* introduced below.

Definition 7 (Dependency Graph). *Let $s_x \in O, s_y \in S$ be streams and $\phi[-j]$ the expression assigned to s_x. A Dependency Graph (DG) is a weighted and directed multigraph $G = (S, E)$, with edges $(s_x, s_y, k, T) \in E$ iff the equations for s_x contains s_y as a subexpression with effective index $k = \text{index}(\phi, s_y, j)$, and the edge was introduced at monitor step T.*

The need for T in the DG definition becomes apparent when considering Dependency Graphs (DDGs) in strategy 3 below. Until then, it can be assumed that $T = 0$.

Note that if the specification contains DUPs, e.g., if $x = \text{dynamic}(p)$ then $(x, p, 0, 0) \in E$, but the properties sent at runtime to p are not. As a result, the DG must be extended to track new dependencies introduced by DUPs, as demonstrated with the strategies below, such that the dynamically received expressions can become *solvable*.

Definition 8 (Solvable). *Let $k = \text{index}(\phi, s, j)$ be the effective index of ϕ for stream variable $s \in \text{vars}(\phi)$. A stream expression $\phi[-j]$ is said to be solvable at monitor step t if there exists an edge $(s', s, j', T) \in E$ such that:*

$$t \geq T + k \wedge j' \geq k,$$

and s evaluated at monitor step $(t - k)$ is not equal to $\bot$.

Intuitively, the first term $t \geq T + k$ ensures that the monitor has progressed sufficiently in steps since the dependency was introduced to solve the expression.

The second term $j' \geq k$ ensures that there exists an edge in the DG with a sufficiently large effective index such that the kth last value of s is not discarded.

Theorem 1 claims that a solvable stream expression evaluates to a non-$\bot$ value at monitor step t. The proof follows by structural induction on ϕ and is written out below.

Theorem 1. *Let ϕ be a stream expression that is solvable at monitor step t and may contain DUPs instantiated with solvable stream expressions $(\psi_1, \ldots, \psi_N)$. Then, ϕ evaluated at monitor step t is not equal to $\bot$.*

Proof. Assume ϕ is a stream expression that is solvable at monitor step t, potentially containing DUPs receiving solvable subexpressions $(\psi_1, \ldots, \psi_N)$. We proceed by structural induction on the stream expression ϕ:

- Basic expressions: By definition of solvable, all stream variables referenced by ϕ at their respective time indices are not equal to $\bot$ at monitor step t. Therefore, if ϕ is a basic expression it cannot evaluate to $\bot$ at monitor step t, since basic expressions only evaluate to $\bot$ when a referenced stream variable is $\bot$ at that time step.
- default(ψ, c) never evaluates to $\bot$, because it yields ψ if $\psi \neq \bot$, and defaults to the constant $c \in \mathbb{D}$ otherwise.
- when(ψ) is guaranteed to evaluate to a value in $\mathbb{B}$.
- update(ψ_1, ψ_2) evaluates to ψ_2 if $\psi_2 \neq \bot$, which is guaranteed by the definition of solvable.
- DUPs: If ψ_i is a DUP, it is either $\psi_i = \text{defer}(\psi'_i)$ or $\psi_i = \text{dynamic}(\psi'_i)$. For ψ_i to be solvable, ψ'_i must also be solvable. By induction, this means that ψ'_i is either a non-DUP expression that evaluates to a non-$\bot$ value at step t or a DUP that is solvable, meaning it will evaluate to a non-$\bot$ value at step t.

Therefore, ϕ evaluated at monitor step t is not equal to $\bot$.

When writing DynSRV specifications, considering when a stream expression is not solvable is crucial, as an $\bot$ verdict at runtime may not be desirable. We now present three memory management strategies that have different trade-offs between memory efficiency and trace availability (keeping expressions solvable as often as possible).

Strategy 1 – Discard BM: Retain the Entire History
Favoring trace availability, this strategy introduces unbounded time dependencies to every other stream in the specification when a DUP is present:

$$E_{\text{DUP}} = \bigcup_{s \in O} \{(s, s', j, 0) \mid \text{hasDUP}(s), s' \in S \setminus \{s\}, j \in \mathbb{N}\}$$

$$G = (S, E \cup E_{\text{DUP}})$$

where hasDUP(s) indicates that stream s's expression contains a DUP.

Using this DG to retain data ensures that any stream expression received dynamically through a DUP is solvable at any monitor step t, if the monitor has progressed sufficiently and none of the referenced stream variables are $\bot$ at the specific monitor steps. That is, the condition $j' \geq k$ from Definition 8 is always met. However, this strategy sacrifices memory efficiency, as any specification involving DUPs will no longer have BM.

Strategy 2 – Preserve BM: Statically Specifying Dependencies of DUPs

To retain memory efficiency, an alternative approach is to restrict DUPs by requiring users to explicitly annotate their potential temporal dependencies in advance. For example, the expression `dynamic`$(p, \{(x, -4), (y, -2)\})$ declares that the dynamically introduced property p may depend on stream x up to 4 steps back in time, and on stream y up to 2 steps. A similar change could be made for `defer`. The DG is then defined as:

$$E_{\text{DUP}} = \bigcup_{s \in O} \text{declaredDUP}(s)$$

$$G = (S, E \cup E_{\text{DUP}})$$

where declaredDUP(s) returns the set of edges that are explicitly declared as dependencies of s. This strategy allows each property in the specification to maintain BM, even when using DUPs. However, this comes at the cost of expressiveness as it becomes possible to introduce expressions that never become solvable, specifically, expressions where the condition $j' \geq \text{index}(\phi, s, j)$ does not hold, causing them to always evaluate to $\bot$.

Strategy 3 – Preserve BM: Dynamically Update Dependencies

To balance memory efficiency and trace availability, we propose a DDGs, which extends static DGs by adding dependencies introduced by DUPs at runtime. The DG becomes a time-dependent structure, where the edges are updated based on the declared dependencies of received expressions.

We define the DDG as a stream of DGs that is updated according to the received expressions:

$$E_{\text{DUP}}(t) = \bigcup_{\substack{s \in O \\ \text{where } s \text{ is assigned } e}} \text{dep}(s, t, [\![s]\!](\text{last}(t, e, [\![\varPhi]\!]C_{in})))$$

$$G(t) = (S, E \cup E_{\text{DUP}}(t))$$

where $[\![s]\!](\text{last}(t, e, [\![\varPhi]\!]C_{in}))$ denotes the last received expression for stream s at time t in the context $[\![\varPhi]\!]C_{in}$, and $\text{dep}(s, T, e)$ returns the set of dependencies introduced by the expression e assigned to stream s at monitor step T.

The DDG is used in our DynSRV implementation, detailed in Sect. 6, to determine how much history to retain at each step. By updating the DDG accordingly, the condition $j' \geq \text{index}(\phi, s, j)$ from Definition 8 is guaranteed for new properties as there exists a j' equal to j. However, the monitor step T from Definition 7 is crucial here: If a new expression ψ referencing stream variable s at effective index k arrives at step T, and at step $T - 1$, s had no incoming edges in the DDG, then ψ is not solvable before time $T + k$, and may evaluate to $\bot$ until then. While this approach offers weaker trace availability than the previous two strategies, it preserves bounded memory and supports the full expressiveness of DUPs.

6 Implementation and Performance

DynSRV is implemented in Rust as part of the RoboSAPIENS trustworthiness language framework [17], which is a general framework for implementing stream-based languages. The framework is implemented as a modular runtime, with a parser layer that parses specifications into an Abstract Syntax Tree, an extensible execution layer that allows for multiple runtime engine and language semantics to be implemented, and a flexible IO layer allowing input and output streams to be transmitted several sources including files, MQTT, and ROS topics. The full source code is available at[4].

As discussed in Sect. 5, DUPs impose some additional requirements on the implementation of the language compared to existing SRV languages. We meet these requirements via two runtime engine implementations: a constraint-based similar to LOLA [8], and a novel stream-based which translates the specification into a collection of asynchronous Rust actors that communicate over channels. The latter engine features some key design decisions:

- Dependencies between stream variables are handled dynamically, with a publisher/subscriber model used to propagate input values to dependent streams.
- The lifetimes of stream values are handled automatically via Rust's ownership model and the use of channels to communicate between actors. This means that there is no central constraint store or garbage collection step.

This dynamic model does impose some performance challenges since specifications cannot easily be compiled to specifically optimized Rust code for a single specification (as in [12]) and has to keep track of dependencies at runtime.

In Fig. 4, we compare the monitoring of a dynamically introduced property to the same property introduced statically. We also compare the impact of the time during the run at which the dynamic property was introduced. This shows a significant, but constant overhead factor for the use of dynamic properties in this scenario, with this overhead factor increasing the later the dynamic property is introduced in the trace. However, in this case, the overall monitoring performance is still sufficient for real-time monitoring, with $100,000$ events being monitored in under 350 milliseconds in the worst case. All benchmarks use integer inputs read from a file and were carried out using an Intel i7-1370P CPU with 32 GiB RAM, and averaged over 10 runs.

---

[4] https://github.com/INTO-CPS-Association/robosapiens-trustworthiness-checker.

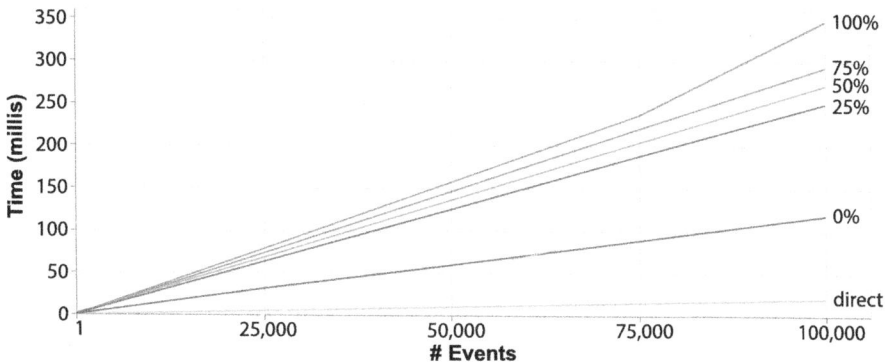

Fig. 4. Time taken to monitor a deferred property $z = \text{default}(\text{defer}(e), \text{true})$ with the property $e = x \wedge y$ introduced at a certain percentage of the run. This is compared to compared to directly monitoring the static property $z = x \wedge y$.

7 Conclusion

In this paper, we have demonstrated how DUPs can be supported with our SRV language DynSRV. Section 2 highlights how DynSRV differs from most related work by enabling truly dynamic expressions to the system's existing properties, whereas prior approaches primarily focus on adapting specific system behaviours.

The semantics presented in Sect. 3.3 define the denotational meaning of our DUPs primitives, while Sect. 5 compliments this by describing different memory management strategies based on the trade-off between memory usage and trace availability. Design patterns in Sect. 4 demonstrate how to weaken, strengthen, and refine properties, as well as describe how to express well-known DSU adaptation patterns.

We consider DynSRV to be especially relevant given the increasing number of systems that require DSU and SASs in our environment and the corresponding need for correctness and safety assurances. While the adaptation for some of these systems is simple enough to be specified statically, others may change in ways where we do not necessarily know what the behaviour in certain situations precisely looks like as shown by Esterle and Brown in [10]. Even if we could specify all possible adaptations in advance, state-space explosion makes it practically infeasible. Our language allows deferring certain parts of the verification to runtime, allowing users to specify new properties as the system evolves, similar to DSU, or allowing a SASs to autonomously specify updated properties as the system evolves.

In the future, we intend to further evaluate the language for industrial use cases, including the case studies provided by the RoboSAPIENS project [17]. We also hope to extend the core language to add full support for asynchronous, timed properties and distributed monitoring of properties. As an additional direction, more work could be carried out to understand and improve the performance characteristics of DUPs based on more realistic benchmarks and properties. For instance, techniques such as Just In Time compilation could potentially reduce the performance impact of dynamic properties compared to static properties.

References

1. Barringer, H., Goldberg, A., Havelund, K., Sen, K.: Rule-based runtime verification. In: Steffen, B., Levi, G. (eds.) VMCAI 2004. LNCS, vol. 2937, pp. 44–57. Springer, Heidelberg (2004). https://doi.org/10.1007/978-3-540-24622-0_5
2. Bierman, G., Hicks, M., Sewell, P., Stoyle, G.: Formalizing Dynamic Software Updating (2023)
3. Carwehl, M., Vogel, T., Rodrigues, G.N., Grunske, L.: Runtime verification of self- adaptive systems with changing requirements. In: IEEE/ACM Symposium on Software Engineering for Adaptive and Self-Managing Systems (SEAMS), pp. 104–114 (2023). https://doi.org/10.1109/SEAMS59076.2023.00024
4. Cassar, I., Francalanza, A.: On implementing a monitor-oriented programming framework for actor systems. In: Ábrahám, E., Huisman, M. (eds.) IFM 2016. LNCS, vol. 9681, pp. 176–192. Springer, Cham (2016). https://doi.org/10.1007/978-3-319-33693-0_12
5. Cassar, I., Francalanza, A.: Runtime adaptation for actor systems. In: Bartocci, E., Majumdar, R. (eds.) RV 2015. LNCS, vol. 9333, pp. 38–54. Springer, Cham (2015). https://doi.org/10.1007/978-3-319-23820-3_3
6. Clark, T., Kulkarni, V., Barat, S., Barn, B.: A homogeneous actor-based monitor language for adaptive behaviour. In: Ricci, A., Haller, P. (eds.) Programming with Actors. LNCS, vol. 10789, pp. 216–244. Springer, Cham (2018). https://doi.org/10.1007/978-3-030-00302-9_8
7. Clark, T., Kulkarni, V., Barat, S., Barn, B.: Actor monitors for adaptive behaviour. In: Proceedings of the Innovations in Software Engineering Conference, pp. 85–95 (2017). https://doi.org/10.1145/3021460.3021469
8. D'Angelo, B., et al.: LOLA: runtime monitoring of synchronous systems. In: Proceedings of the International Symposium on Temporal Representation and Reasoning, pp. 166–174 (2005). https://doi.org/10.1109/TIME.2005.26
9. Distefano, D., Rensink, A., Katoen, J.-P.: Model checking birth and death. In: Proceedings of IFIP International Conference on Theoretical Computer Science (TCS), pp. 435–447 (2002). https://doi.org/10.1007/978-0-387-35608-2_36
10. Esterle, L., Brown, J.N.: The competence awareness window: knowing what i can and cannot do. In: 2020 IEEE International Conference on Autonomic Computing and Self-Organizing Systems Companion (ACSOS-C), pp. 62–63 (2020). https://doi.org/10.1109/ACSOS-C51401.2020.00031
11. Finkbeiner, B., Klein, F., Metzger, N.: Live synthesis. Innov. Syst. Softw. Eng. **18**(3), 443–454 (2022). https://doi.org/10.1007/s11334-022-00447-5
12. Finkbeiner, B., Oswald, S., Passing, N., Schwenger, M.: Verified rust monitors for lola specifications. In: Deshmukh, J., Ničković, D. (eds.) RV 2020. LNCS, vol. 12399, pp. 431–450. Springer, Cham (2020). https://doi.org/10.1007/978-3-030-60508-7_24
13. Havelund, K., Peled, D.: Runtime verification: from propositional to first-order temporal logic. In: Colombo, C., Leucker, M. (eds.) RV 2018. LNCS, vol. 11237, pp. 90–112. Springer, Cham (2018). https://doi.org/10.1007/978-3-030-03769-7_7
14. Hicks, M., Moore, J.T., Nettles, S.: Dynamic software updating. ACM SIGPLAN Not. **36**(5), 13–23 (2001). https://doi.org/10.1145/381694.378798

15. Iftikhar, M.U.,Weyns, D.: ActivFORMS: active formal models for self-adaptation. In: Proceedings of the International Symposium on Software Engineering for Adaptive and Self-Managing Systems (SEAMS), pp. 125–134 (2014). https://doi.org/10.1145/2593929.2593944
16. Kephart, J., Chess, D.: The vision of autonomic computing. Computer **36**(1), 41–50 (2003). https://doi.org/10.1109/mc.2003.1160055
17. Larsen, P.G., et al.: Robotic safe adaptation in unprecedented situations: the RoboSAPIENS project. In: Research Directions: Cyber-Physical Systems, vol. 2 (2024). https://doi.org/10.1017/cbp.2024.4
18. Leucker, M., Sánchez, C., Scheffel, T., Schmitz, M., Schramm, A.: TeSSLa: runtime verification of non-synchronized real-time streams. In: Proceedings of the Annual ACM Symposium on Applied Computing, pp. 1925–1933 (2018). https://doi.org/10.1145/3167132.3167338
19. Li, Y., Duan, X., Xu, Y., Zhao, C.: Dynamic assessment approach for intelligent power distribution systems based on runtime verification with requirements updates. In: High-Confidence Computing (2024). https://doi.org/10.1016/j.hcc.2024.100255
20. Lounas, R., Mezghiche, M., Lanet, J.-L.: Formal methods in dynamic software updating: a survey. Int. J. Crit. Comput.-Based Syst. **9**(1–2), 76–114 (2019). https://doi.org/10.1504/IJCCBS.2019.098794
21. Nahabedian, L., et al.: Assured and correct dynamic update of controllers. In: 2016 IEEE/ACM 11th International Symposium on Software Engineering for Adaptive and Self-Managing Systems (SEAMS), pp. 96–107 (2016). https://doi.org/10.1145/2897053.2897056. https://ieeexplore.ieee.org/document/7830552. Accessed 25 July 2025
22. Pedregal, P., Gorostiaga, F., Sánchez, C.: A stream runtime verification tool with nested and retroactive parametrization. In: Runtime Verification, pp. 351–362 (2023). https://doi.org/10.1007/978-3-031-44267-4_19
23. Seifzadeh, H., Abolhassani, H., Moshkenani, M.S.: A survey of dynamic software updating. J. Softw. Evol. Process **25**(5), 535–568 (2012). https://doi.org/10.1002/smr.1556
24. Sokolsky, O., Sammapun, U., Lee, I., Kim, J.: Run-time checking of dynamic properties. Electron. Notes Theor. Comput. Sci. **144**(4), 91–108 (2006). https://doi.org/10.1016/j.entcs.2006.02.006
25. Subramanian, S., Hicks, M., McKinley, K.S.: Dynamic software updates: a VMcentric approach. In: Proceedings of the ACM SIGPLAN Conference on Programming Language Design and Implementation, pp. 1–12 (2009). https://doi.org/10.1145/1542476.1542478
26. Walton, C., Krl, D., Gilmore, S.: An abstract machine for module replacement. In: Proceedings of the Workshop on Principles of Abstract Machines (1998)
27. Weyns, D.: Engineering self-adaptive software systems an organized tour. In: Proceedings of the IEEE International Workshops on Foundations and Applications of Self* Systems (FAS*W), pp. 1–2 (2018). https://doi.org/10.1109/FASW.2018.00012
28. Wong, T., Wagner, M., Treude, C.: Self-adaptive systems: a systematic literature review across categories and domains. Inf. Softw. Technol. **148**, 106934 (2022). https://doi.org/10.1016/j.infsof.2022.106934
29. Zhang, J., Cheng, B.H.C.: Using temporal logic to specify adaptive program semantics. J. Syst. Softw. **79**(10), 1361–1369 (2006). https://doi.org/10.1016/j.jss.2006.02.062

Modular and Online Monitoring of Temporal Logic Specification with Integral and Filter

Simone Silvetti[1]($\boxtimes$), Michele Loreti[2], and Laura Nenzi[1]

[1] University of Trieste, Trieste, Italy
simone.silvetti@dia.units.it, lnenzi@units.it
[2] University of Camerino, Camerino, Italy
michele.loreti@unicam.it

Abstract. In a recent work, Bakhirkin and Basset [3] proposed a new specification language that extends STL. Their logic overcomes the syntactic restrictions of STL, enabling the production and manipulation of real-valued output signals and the expression of properties that have typically been described using other logics, such as STL*. In this contribution, we extend this specification language in three directions. First, we introduce a novel integral operator over sliding windows, allowing the specification of cumulative properties, for example, asserting that the integral of a signal over a time interval remains within a given threshold. Second, we introduce a filtering operator for the sliding window operator, enabling us to restrict the scope of aggregation to signal segments that satisfy the filtering condition. Third, we develop an efficient online monitoring algorithm for the extended logic. Finally, we test the logic on two case studies: an artificial pancreas controller and a monitoring of outdoor weather events.

Keywords: Signal Temporal Logic · Cumulative Temporal Properties · Runtime Verification · Monitoring

1 Introduction

As digitalization advances, smart cities and Industry 4.0 environments rely on sensors that generate massive amounts of data daily, capturing information on traffic, pollution, machine status, and energy usage [19]. These settings demand systems capable of real-time analysis and prompt reaction to critical changes. For instance, a smart insulin pump must continuously adapt insulin delivery based on fluctuating glucose levels, while an autonomous traffic management system dynamically adjusts signal timings to alleviate congestion. Ensuring the reliability and responsiveness of such systems requires formal specifications and verification methods that operate at runtime.

To this end, *temporal logics* such as Metric Interval Temporal Logic (MITL) and Signal Temporal Logic (STL) [20] have become standard tools for specifying temporal properties over real-valued signals. STL, in particular, has gained popularity due to its ability to express time-bounded properties over continuous signals and its efficient monitoring algorithms for both Boolean and quantitative (robustness) semantics [11,27].

However, despite these strengths, STL has significant expressiveness limitations. For example, it cannot naturally express cumulative temporal properties such as "the level of glucose is above the hyperglycemia threshold for more than 1 h", nor can it easily detect oscillatory behaviors or stabilization patterns. To overcome these limitations, several extended formalisms have been proposed. Signal Convolution Logic (SCL) [25] introduces convolution-based operators to express cumulative properties, while STL* [8] incorporates freeze quantifiers for referencing signal values at specific time points, allowing for expressing oscillatory or stabilizing behavior. A key challenge of these extensions is that their increased expressiveness often leads to more complex monitoring algorithms.

A notable recent contribution by Bakhirkin and Basset [3] introduces a specification language that extends STL by removing its syntactic constraints, allowing each formula to produce a real-valued output signal and combine them in a pointwise way with arithmetic operations, comparisons, etc. A key point of this work is that the extended logic preserves the linear-time (offline) monitoring complexity of STL while enabling more expressive specifications, such as stabilization and oscillatory behavior, typically described with STL*.

In this work, we extend the approach of Bakhirkin and Basset [3] in three directions. First, we introduce an *integral operator* over sliding windows, enabling the specification of cumulative properties, such as asserting that the integral of a signal over a time interval remains within a threshold. This addition supports reasoning about system behaviors that rely on accumulation or averaging, common in domains like energy systems and biomedical monitoring. Second, we introduce a *filtering operator* for the sliding windows operator, allowing us to reduce the scope of the aggregation to the signal satisfying the filtering condition. Third, we develop an efficient *online monitoring algorithm* for the extended logic. Unlike offline techniques that process entire traces post-execution, our algorithm processes signals incrementally as they arrive, making it suitable for real-time monitoring. Furthermore, we provide an efficient implementation for both piecewise-constant and piecewise-linear signals, proving that the property of finite variability is preserved. Our contribution thus bridges the gap between expressiveness and efficiency in runtime monitoring, enabling the specification and real-time evaluation of a richer class of temporal properties, essential for the dependable operation of modern Cyber-Physical Systems (CPS) applications.

Running Examples. We consider the following two representative examples to illustrate the types of temporal properties that motivate our work.

P1) *Weather Events* – The first example considers a network of Internet of Things (IoT) sensors capable of measuring temperature and CO_2 emissions [26], among other variables, to detect emerging issues during extreme weather events. A typical scenario, associated with a high risk of fire accident, arises when CO_2 and temperature sensors report average readings exceeding 400 ppm and 60°C over a one-hour interval. Formally, this can be written as:

$$\varphi_W(T, \theta_1, \theta_2) := \left(\frac{1}{T}\text{On}_{[0,T]} \text{ Int } CO_2 > \theta_1\right) \wedge \left(\frac{1}{T}\text{On}_{[0,T]} \text{ Int } temp > \theta_2\right)$$

with $\theta_1 = 400$, $\theta_2 = 60$, and $T = 3600$ sec. Note that this property cannot be expressed in SCL, because its cumulative operators act only on Boolean signals (e.g., $CO_2(t) > \theta_1$), rather than directly on the numerical value of $CO_2(t)$.

P2) *Artificial Pancreas* – It is a closed-loop system for treating type 1 diabetes, where a continuous glucose monitor (CGM) tracks blood sugar levels and a software-controlled insulin pump delivers insulin automatically.

To assess glycemic (concentration of glucose in the blood) control, standard CGM-derived metrics [7] are: the Time Above Range (TAR), representing glucose level exceeding 180 mg/dL (i.e., $\varphi_{AR} := G \geq 180$), and Time Below Range (TBR) where the glucose level is below 70 mg/dL (i.e., $\varphi_{BR} := G \leq 70$). Beyond these, the mean glucose level over a certain interval of time is a core indicator of overall glycemic status and can be represented with the following formulas:

$$\psi_{TAR} := \tfrac{1}{3h}\text{On}_{3h}\text{Int } \varphi_{AR}, \quad \psi_{TBR} := \tfrac{1}{3h}\text{On}_{3h}\text{Int } \varphi_{BR}$$

Furthermore, the conditional mean glucose values, restricted to periods of hyperglycemia and hypoglycemia, provide insight into the average glycemic burden during clinically significant excursions. These formulas can be formally written as:

$$\psi_{\mu GAR} := \tfrac{1}{3h}\text{On}_{3h}\text{Int } (G|\varphi_{AR}), \quad \psi_{\mu GBR} := \tfrac{1}{3h}\text{On}_{3h}\text{Int } (G|\varphi_{BR})$$

The utility of these conditional averages has been highlighted in recent CGM-based studies for their role in understanding the physiological impact of glucose extremes and tailoring individualized treatment strategies [12,15]. The rationale behind using a conditional glucose mean is straightforward: while TAR and TBR are important indicators for identifying hyperglycemia and hypoglycemia, respectively, they do not capture the severity of these conditions, something the proposed metrics characterize more effectively.

These examples underscore the need for a specification framework that supports both expressive and efficiently monitorable properties, particularly in safety-critical and time-sensitive domains. For other interesting properties regarding stabilization or oscillatory events, please refer to [3].

Related Work. Several works were introduced to extend the expressivity of STL, e.g., with existential quantification [4], or freeze quantification as in STL* [8]. With respect to the integral operator, Akazaki et al. [1] extend the syntax of STL with averaged temporal operators, specified time interval. The new operators require the definition of two types of robustness (positive and negative), which results in the loss of the correctness property. In [9], the authors introduce the integral operator but restricted to predicates; in [25], the authors presented the Signal Convolution Logic (SCL). The logic has a convolution operator that allows integration on Boolean constraints (i.e., it can specify the percentage of time a certain property is satisfied), but it does not permit describing properties as P1 and P2, averaging, and/or filtering directly the values of the signal.

An important challenge with these extensions is that the increased expressiveness of the new operators comes at the cost of more complex monitoring algorithms. The approach proposed by Bakhirkin and Basset [3] addresses this limitation by defining a specification language that is more expressive than STL, yet still efficient for offline monitoring. The core idea is to remove syntactic constraints from the temporal logic language. This enables the generation and manipulation of real-valued output signals, allowing for the direct expression of properties such as stabilization, local maxima, and linear growth. The logic supports aggregation using min and max functions, but does not include an integral and a filtering operator.

Online monitoring of Signal Temporal Logic (STL) has been explored to enable real-time verification of system behaviors during execution [11,27]. [11] introduces an approach to monitor STL robustness online by incrementally computing signal properties as new data arrives, considering an interval semantics. The tool RTAMT [27] supports online monitoring with efficient implementations. Despite these advances, full support for STL extensions in an online context remains an open challenge.

An interesting way to design online monitoring algorithms is to use transducers. The first contribution on this topic is [22], the paper introduces the temporal testers, a class of transducer automata that emit a Boolean signal at each step, indicating whether a temporal logic formula holds at that point in time. [21] presents a modular and algebraically founded approach to online monitoring of Metric Temporal Logic (MTL) formulas over continuous-time piecewise-constant signals, supporting both qualitative and quantitative semantics and managing uncertainty through compositional and deterministic signal transducers.

In the domain of stream-based monitoring, RTLola [14] supports sliding window aggregation. However, unlike our approach, it evaluates aggregates at a fixed, user-defined rate (e.g., integrating a signal every 10 ms). TeSSLa [18], on the other hand, provides a set of primitive operations that, when appropriately composed, can approximate the behavior of an integral operator. Nevertheless, it does not natively account for the *duration* a signal maintains a particular value during evaluation, limiting its ability to capture time-weighted integrals accurately.

2 Preliminaries

2.1 Dual Numbers

Dual numbers extend the real numbers $\mathbb{R}$ to the algebra $\mathbb{R}_\varepsilon = \{a + b\varepsilon \mid a, b \in \mathbb{R}\}$, where ε is a symbol satisfying the identity $\varepsilon^2 = 0$. Intuitively, ε represents an infinitesimal value, and $a + b\varepsilon$ for $b \neq 0$ is a number approaching a with slope b. Dual numbers, introduced in [10], have been applied to several topics ranging from geometry and mechanics to automatic differentiation. In this contribution, we use them to extend the concept of minimum and maximum to functions with discontinuities [3]. Consider indeed the following functions:

$$s_1(t) = \begin{cases} 1+t, & t \in [0.5, 1), \\ 1, & t \geq 1, \end{cases} \qquad s_2(t) = \begin{cases} 1+2t, & t \in [0.5, 1), \\ 2, & t \geq 1, \end{cases}$$

If we restrict to $\mathbb{R}$, the maximum of s_1 in $[0,2]$ is not defined because there always exists another point in the left neighbourhood of 1, with a higher value. Using dual numbers, instead, we define the maximum as $\max_{[0,2]} s_1 = \max(s_1(0), s_1(1-\varepsilon), s_1(2)) = 2 - \varepsilon$.

Dual numbers are particularly useful for computing relations among functions. Consider, for example, the requirement that $\forall t \in [0,2], s_1(t) < s_2(t)$. A standard approach to verify such a requirement is to verify if $\max_{[0,2]} s_1 < \min_{[0,2]} s_2$ which is true in $\mathbb{R}_\varepsilon$ considering that $\max_{[0,2]} s_1 = 2 - \varepsilon < 2 = \min_{[0,2]} s_2$. On the contrary, in $\mathbb{R}$ we cannot achieve the same with inf and sup operators.

2.2 Signal and Trace

Definition 1. (Symbolic State). *A symbolic state (or f-interval) $v = (I, f)$ is a pair where $I = [a, b) \subseteq \mathbb{R}$ is an interval and $f : \mathbb{R} \to \mathbb{R}$ a continuous function.*

We say that two symbolic states $v_1 = (I_1, f_1)$ and $v_2 = (I_2, f_2)$ are *adjacent* if the corresponding intervals are contiguous, i.e., $\sup(I_1) = \min(I_2)$ and that $(v_1; v_2)$ is a *refinement* of $v = (I, f)$ if v_1 and v_2 are adjacent, $I = I_1 \cup I_2$ and $f_1|_{I_1} = f|_{I_1}$ and $f_2|_{I_2} = f|_{I_2}$. Moreover, we say that v is *resolved* if it does not allow a refinement $(u; w)$ such that $f_u \neq f_w$.

We associate to any (adjacent) succession of symbolic states $v = (v_1, v_2, \dots)$ a function $f_v : \mathbb{R}_{\geq 0} \to \mathbb{R} \cup \{\texttt{NaN}\}$ such that if $v_i = (I_i, f_i)$ and $t \in I_i$ then $f_v(t) = f_i(t)$ while $f_v(t) = \texttt{NaN}$ if for any $i \in \mathbb{N}$ such that $t \notin I_i$, meaning that f_v assumes an undefined value represented by symbol NaN. As an example, consider succession $(([0,3), x), ([3, 10), 6 - x))$. It assumes defined values in $[0, 10)$ and the undefined value in $[10, +\infty)$. We impose that any function with NaN as one of its inputs produces NaN as output independently of the other input values. So for example $\texttt{NaN} \cdot 0 + 5 = \texttt{NaN}$.

Definition 2. (Signal). *A signal is a function $s : \mathbb{T} \subseteq \mathbb{R}_{\geq 0} \to \mathbb{R}$ that can be represented as a succession of symbolic states, meaning that there exists $v \in \mathcal{A}$ such that $s = f_v$.*

Remark 1. Let's consider two finite sequences of (adjacent) symbolic states, u and w. It is always possible to refine these sequences into new ones, $u' = \{(I_i, f_i)\}_{i \leq n}$ and $w' = \{(J_i, g_i)\}_{i \leq n}$, such that u' is equivalent to u and w' is equivalent to w, where equivalent means that they represent the same function. Moreover, this refinement can be done in such a way that $\forall i \leq n, I_i = J_i$, meaning the intervals are aligned (i.e., overlapping exactly) and $n \leq |u| + |v|$.

Definition 3. (Finite Variability Property). *A signal satisfies the finite variability property (fvp) if each of its restrictions to a finite length interval admits a representation as a finite succession of resolved symbolic states.*

The finite variability property was initially introduced for Boolean signals in [2] and later formalized for piecewise-constant signals in [20]. Different from the previous work, our definition is not saying that the signal assumes a finite number of states in a finite time window, but more generally, we are saying that the signals admit finite mathematical representations (as a continuous function) in a finite time window. This broader view motivates our use of the term symbolic state. In this sense, our definition aligns with the one proposed in [4] for piecewise-linear functions.

Definition 4. (Trace). *Let $n \in \mathbb{N}$, we define trace, or multi-valued signal, any function $s : \mathbb{R}_{\geq 0} \to \mathbb{R}^n$ such that $s = (s_1, \ldots, s_n)$ and $s_i : \mathbb{R}_{\geq 0} \to \mathbb{R}$ are signals.*

As an example, let's consider the first running example (P1) where the trace $s(t) = (temp(t), CO_2(t))$ is composed of two signals describing respectively the temperature and the level of CO_2.

3 Syntax and Semantics

The syntax of our language is given by

$$\varphi := X_i \mid \chi \mid op(\varphi_1, \ldots, \varphi_n) \mid \text{On}_T(\psi) \mid \psi \text{U}_T^d \chi \mid \varphi \downarrow \text{U}_T^d \chi$$
$$\psi := \text{Min}\,\varphi \mid \text{Max}\,\varphi \mid \text{Int}\,\varphi$$
$$\chi := \top \mid \bot \mid \varphi \bowtie 0 \mid \neg\chi \mid \chi \wedge \chi$$

where X_i is a variable indexed with $i \in \mathbb{N}$, op is a generic n-ary pointwise operator, $n \in \mathbb{N}$, On_T is the sliding window operator (or On-operator) with $T \subset \mathbb{R}_{\geq 0}$ a closed interval, $d \in \mathbb{R}$, U_T^d and $\downarrow \text{U}_T^d$ are respectively the find-first aggregation and the find-first pointwise until. Min, Max, and Int are, respectively, the minimum, maximum, and integral operators that serve as aggregation functions for the sliding window operator. Negation $\neg$ and conjunction $\wedge$ are the standard Boolean connectives, and $\bowtie \in \{>, \geq, <, \leq\}$. In addition, we can derive disjunction operator $\vee$ as usual, and the temporal operator of STL^1, as follows:

$$\chi_1 U_T \chi_2 := (\text{Min } \chi_1) \text{U}_T^0 \chi_2 \qquad G_T(\chi) := \text{On}_T \text{Min } \chi \qquad F_T(\chi) := \text{On}_T \text{Max } \chi$$

We also introduce the filtered version of the On-operator, defined as

$$\text{On}_T(\text{Agg }\varphi|\chi) := \text{On}_T(\text{Agg}(\varphi \text{ if } \chi \text{ else NaN})) \tag{1}$$

where (ψ if χ else NaN) is a pointwise operator useful to limit the scope of the sliding operator to the region of the time domain where a filtering condition (i.e., χ) holds, and Agg is a placeholder for Min, Max and Int.

The semantics of our logic is evaluated pointwise at each time.

---
[1] For a deeper discussion on this equivalence please refer to [3].

Definition 5. (Semantics). *We introduce the semantics function* $[\![\cdot]\!] : \mathcal{T} \times \mathbb{R}_{\geq 0} \times \mathcal{L} \to \mathbb{R}$, *where* $\mathcal{T}$ *is the trace domain, and* $\mathcal{L}$ *the logic, recursively as follows:*

$$[\![s, t, X_i]\!] := s_i(t)$$
$$[\![s, t, op(\varphi_1, \ldots, \varphi_n)]\!] := op([\![s, t, \varphi_1]\!], \ldots, [\![s, t, \varphi_n]\!])$$
$$[\![s, t, On_T(Agg\,\varphi)]\!] := Agg_{\tau \in t+T}[\![s, \tau, \varphi]\!]$$
$$[\![s, t, (Agg\,\varphi)\,U^d_T\chi]\!] := \begin{cases} Agg_{t \in F(t,T,\chi)}[\![s, \tau, \varphi]\!] & \text{if } F(t,T,\chi) \neq \emptyset \\ d & \text{otherwise} \end{cases}$$
$$[\![s, t, \varphi \downarrow U^d_T\chi]\!] := \begin{cases} [\![s, \tau, \varphi]\!] & \text{if } F(t,T,\chi) = [t,\tau] \neq \emptyset \\ d & \text{otherwise} \end{cases}$$
$$[\![s, t, \top]\!] := 1$$
$$[\![s, t, \bot]\!] := 0$$
$$[\![s, t, \varphi \bowtie 0]\!] := \begin{cases} 1 & \text{if } [\![s, t, \varphi]\!] \bowtie 0 \\ 0 & \text{otherwise} \end{cases}$$
$$[\![s, t, \neg \chi]\!] := 1 - [\![s, t, \psi]\!]$$
$$[\![s, t, \chi_1 \wedge \chi_2]\!] := \min([\![s, t, \chi_1]\!], [\![s, t, \chi_2]\!])$$

where $op : \mathbb{R}^n \to \mathbb{R}$ *are pointwise n-ary functions that map signals with finite variability property into signals with finite variability property,* $Agg_{t \in T}$ *is a placeholder for* $Int_{t \in T}, Min_{t \in T}$ *and* $Max_{t \in T}$ *which are the Riemann integral, minimum and maximum operator mapping real-valued functions into real values as* $Int_{t \in T}(s) = \int_T s(t)dt$, $Min_{t \in T}(s) = \min_{t \in T} s(t)$ *and* $Max_{t \in T}(s) = \max_{t \in T} s(t)$, *respectively.*

$$F(t, T, \chi) = \begin{cases} [t, \tau] & \text{if exists the smallest } \tau \in t + T \wedge \chi(\tau) \\ [t, \tau + \varepsilon] & \text{with } \tau \in \inf\{t' \mid t' \in t + T \wedge \chi(t')\} \\ \emptyset & \text{otherwise} \end{cases}$$

It is important to notice that $\bowtie 0$, and $\neg$ are two unary operators, respectively $\bowtie 0(x) := 1$ if $x \bowtie 0, 0$ otherwise and $\neg(x) := 1 - x$, as well as $\wedge$ is the minimum operator, i.e., $x \wedge y = \min(x, y)$. With a bit of redundancy, we decided to include them in the grammar because they allow us to define predicates.

A detailed description of the semantics follows.

Atomic Variables. Each atomic variable X_i is interpreted over the corresponding i-th signal s_i of the trace s in a specific time t.

n-ary (pointwise) Operators. The n-ary operators $op(\varphi_1, \ldots, \varphi_n)$ are interpreted with the corresponding op functions applied to the interpretation of $\varphi_1, \ldots, \varphi_n$. We are considering only pointwise operators in $\mathbb{R}^n \to \mathbb{R}$ obtained by lifting operators defined in $\mathbb{R}$. As an example, consider the summation defined as $(f + g)(x) = f(x) + g(x)$.

Sliding Window Operator. The On-operator $On_T(Agg\,\varphi)$ is interpreted as the application of the aggregation function (Agg), that can be Min, Max or Int, on the signal generated by the interpretation of φ in $t + T$.

Find-first Aggregation Until. The find-first aggregation until $(\text{Agg}\,\varphi)\text{U}_T^d\chi$ is interpreted as the application of the Aggregation operator (Agg) on the signal generated by the interpretation of φ on a time window that is not fixed a priori but depends on the satisfaction of χ. This time window corresponding to $F(t, T, \chi)$ as defined above, starts in t and ends as soon as χ is satisfied in $t + T$. If all the time locations in $t+T$ do not satisfy χ, the operator returns the default value d.

Find-first Pointwise Until. The find-first pointwise until $\varphi \text{U}_T^d \chi$ works as the previous one, but instead of performing a sliding window operator on the signal generated by the interpretation of φ, it returns the value of such interpretation on the upper bound of $F(t,T,\chi)$. If all the time locations in $t+T$ do not satisfy χ, and for this reason $F(t,T,\chi)$ is empty, the operator returns the default value d.

Negation and Conjunction Operators. Interpretation of negation and conjunction operators follows by considering them as unary and binary operators, respectively.

Filtered Sliding Window Operator. The semantic definition of the filtered sliding window operator (Eq. 1) poses a question. If indeed it is clear how NaN behaves with n-ary operators (see Sect. 2.2), we need to clarify how to interpret the aggregation on signals with undefined values. We opt for the following definition:

$$\text{Agg}_T(\varphi \text{ if } \chi \text{ else NaN}) := \text{Agg}_{T \cap \{t \in T | \chi(t)\}}\,\varphi$$

meaning that we are ignoring the values of signal φ where χ is false, which is coherent with the usual definition of filter. The well-foundedness of the previous definition depends on the aggregation function type and the structure of $T \cap \{t \in T \mid \chi(t)\}$. In Theorem 1 we show that the semantics of our logic preserves the finite variability property, meaning that χ has finite variability in any closed finite subset of $\mathbb{R}$, implying that $\{t \in T \mid \chi(t)\}$ consists in finite union of finite intervals, so that:

$$\text{Agg}_{T \cap \{t \in T | \chi(t)\}}\,\varphi = \text{Agg}_{\bigcup_{i \leq k} T_i}\,\varphi = \langle Agg \rangle(\varphi|_{T_0}, \ldots, \varphi|_{T_k})$$

with $\langle Min \rangle = \min$, $\langle Max \rangle = \max$, and $\langle Int \rangle = +$, which concludes the well-foundedness of the filtered sliding window operator definition.

3.1 Interpretation of Atomic Variables

In this paper, we interpret atomic variables either as piecewise-constant (pwc) functions, when modeling finite-state systems like gearshift dynamics that emit events only on state changes, or as piecewise-linear continuous (pwlc) functions, when representing physical quantities measured over time. This distinction reflects common practice: pwc signals are used for discrete systems, while pwlc (or pwl) signals suit continuous measurements under sufficiently high sampling rates. Under this assumption, our semantics can produce only piecewise-constant functions or *piecewise-polynomial functions (pwp)*, provided we restrict ourselves to n-ary operators that map polynomials to polynomials.

Since our semantics is defined recursively based on the semantics of simple formulae, it is crucial that the property of finite variability is preserved when applying logical operators. This preservation ensures the monitorability of the semantics and prevents the need to manage an infinite number of signal representations within a finite time horizon.

Theorem 1. *Let us consider a signal s with finite variability. For each formula $\varphi \in \mathcal{L}$, the semantics function $t \to [\![s,t,\varphi]\!]$ is a signal with finite variability.*

The proof is by induction on the complexity of the formula and follows the demonstration already proposed for MITL [2], which is then adapted to STL. The difference here is the presence of the integral operator, which generates piecewise-polynomial functions instead of piecewise-linear or piecewise-constant functions. We provide the full proof in Appendix A.1 [23].

4 Monitoring

Our online monitoring framework is based on transducers that accept signals as inputs and generate output signals which may not be synchronized with the inputs, leading to possible delays. Following the approach in [11], we use the Lemire running maximum filter [17], which was adapted for piecewise-constant signals in [13]. We extend this approach to handle piecewise-continuous functions and present a modular transducer architecture named *Monitoring Graph (MG)*. Each node is a *Monitoring Unit (MU)* that receives signals as inputs, performs an internal computation, and generates signals as outputs. Based on the Direct Acyclic Graph structures, the generated signals are then forwarded to other MUs. As an example, please consider Fig. 1, which reports the computational graph of property P1. There are two *leaf Monitoring Units* (ℓ-MUs), represented by the nodes CO_2 and *temp*, which receive as input measurement data and generate as output symbolic states with pwl functions. These symbolic states are then passed to MUs that perform integration ($On_{[0,3600]}$Int) without filtering and then to MUs that apply linear function operators ($\frac{\cdot}{3600} - 400$ and $\frac{\cdot}{3600} - 60$, respectively), and then to MUs that Booleanize the signal based on the inequality ($\cdot > 0$) and generate a pwc signal with the values 0 or 1 as output. These Boolean signals are then merged using the MUs ($\cdot \wedge \cdot$), which apply the min operator, and the resulting signal is provided as output. It is worth noting that, following our approach, online monitoring of specifications with future temporal operators can be performed without the use of *pastification* [27] and the need for past operators.

Definition 6. (Monitoring Units). *A Monitoring Unit (MU) $m = (Q, S, s_0, \lambda)$ is a tuple, where Q is an ordered list of n input (FIFO) queues that store symbolic states arriving from other MUs connected as input to m, S is the internal state (or memory) and s_0 is its initial value, $\lambda : S \times V^n \to S \times V$ is the state-output function that defines how the state and outputs are generated based on the current state, inputs and internal memory.*

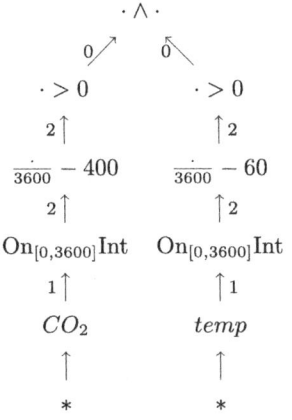

Algorithm 1 Step of monitoring unit $m = (Q, S, s_0, \lambda)$ receiving value v_{inp} on the i-th queue.

1: **procedure** $m[i \leftarrow v_{inp}]$
2: $\quad$ ADD$(Q[i], v_{inp})$
3: $\quad$ **while** ISFULL(Q) **do**
4: $\quad\quad v_{inp} \leftarrow$ DEQUEUE(Q)
5: $\quad\quad s, V_{out} \leftarrow \lambda(s, v_{inp})$
6: $\quad\quad$ **if** $V_{out} \neq \emptyset$ **then**
7: $\quad\quad\quad$ **for** $v_{out} \in V_{out}$ **do**
8: $\quad\quad\quad\quad$ **for** $j \in OE$ **do**
9: $\quad\quad\quad\quad\quad m[j \leftarrow v_{out}]$

Fig. 1. (Left) Monitoring graph of property $P1$: $\left(\frac{1}{3600}\text{On}_{[0,3600]} \text{ Int } CO_2 > 400\right) \wedge \left(\frac{1}{3600}\text{On}_{[0,3600]} \text{ Int } temp > 60\right)$. (Right) Computational step of a monitoring unit (Algorithm 1). The degree of monitoring units (Definition 9) is shown on output edges.

In our framework, special monitoring units, called leaf-monitoring units (ℓ-MU), interpret the sampled input values as pwlc or pwc signals. In Fig. 1, these units are represented by the nodes CO_2 and $temp$, which interpret inputs as pwlc signals.

Definition 7. (Leaf Monitoring Units.) *A leaf monitoring unit (ℓ-MU) is a special MU with $|Q| = 1$, which accepts sample values $v = (t_v, f_v)$ where t_v is a time and f_v a value representing the measured or collected value at time t_v. It is a transducer that transforms two consecutive sample values into symbolic states. In this paper, we define two types of ℓ-MU.*

1. *which return as output a pwc functions defined by (t_v, t_w, f_v)*
2. *which return as output a pwlc functions defined by $(t^v, t_w, \frac{f_w - f_v}{t_w - t_v}(t - t_v) + f_v)$*

where v and w represent two consecutive samples.

Definition 8. (Monitoring Graph). *A monitoring graph (MG) is a tuple (V, L, E, o) such that $(V \cup L, E)$ is a direct acyclic graph in which every vertex in V is a MU, and in L is a ℓ-MU, $o \in V$ is the terminal node.*

Below, we present how a monitoring graph is built from a formula and how the computations (i.e., what happens when a sample points arrive at a ℓ-MU) are performed.

Building Monitoring Graphs. The process begins by translating the *abstract syntax tree* of a formula into a monitoring tree by converting each logical operator into its corresponding monitoring unit. Identical sub-trees (if any) are merged to obtain the final monitoring graph. The leaf monitoring units are the input of this graph, while the node that was the root of the tree is the terminal node.

Computation of Monitoring Graphs. The computational steps of the entire graph are defined recursively, based on the computations of its individual MUs. When a new sample reaches an ℓ-MU, it is interpreted and forwarded to its connected MUs. These MUs receive the symbolic state, carry out their computations, and transmit their outputs to other connected MUs until a node without outgoing transitions is reached. Termination is guaranteed by the acyclic nature of the graph, and may or may not result in a final output. For simplicity, we do not include connection edges in the formal definition of an MU. Instead, we assume the existence of a routing mechanism that delivers outputs throughout the monitoring graph.

Computation of Monitoring Units (Algorithm 1). When a new value v_{inp} is received from the i-th input (line 1), it is added to the corresponding i-th input queue (line 2). If there is then at least one symbolic state in each input queue (line 3), the procedure DEQUEUE described below is executed in line 4. As a result, a vector $\boldsymbol{v}_{inp}$ of symbolic state with the same time intervals is generated and passed to the state-output function, which generates the new state (s) and a set of contiguous symbolic states (V_{out}) (line 5). If $V_{out} \neq \emptyset$, the monitoring unit propagates outputs through the rest of the monitoring graph (lines 7 – 9). This algorithm is generic and works for operators of any arity. However, it can be simplified for unary operators by keeping only lines 5 to 9 (and taking into account that the vector $\boldsymbol{v}_{inp}$ corresponds to the value v_{inp}).

Dequeue procedure (Algorithm 2). The dequeue procedure is a fundamental step in the calculation of a monitoring unit. It is responsible for retrieving values from the input queue (Q) and generating a vector input ($\boldsymbol{v}_{inp}$) that is then used by the output function (to generate a value that is passed to the rest of the monitoring graph). The Q is an ordered vector of queues, each storing a symbolic state as a top element with the same lower bound of the time interval as the others, but a different upper bound. For this reason, the first part of the procedure (lines 3 – 5) consists of identifying which is the minimum upper bound of those symbolic states ($\hat{t}$) so that it is always possible to extract a set of symbolic states with the same time bounds. This can be effectively done by removing the first chunk (of size depending on $\hat{t}$) of the symbolic state from each of the top symbolic states (lines 6 – 15). This new set of symbolic states corresponds to $\boldsymbol{v}_{inp}$, which is returned at line 16.

Remark 2. It is important to note that we assume each first element of the input queues has the same time lower bound. It is simple to show that this property is an invariant for the dequeue procedure and that, at the beginning, we initialized each ℓ-MUs with a sample value $(-\infty, \text{NaN})$ so that all the queues are initialized with a symbolic state with time lower bound equal to $-\infty$. We are assuming that any function with input NaN will return NaN, as already discussed in Sect. 2.2.

Algorithm 2. Dequeue procedure that considers as input the input queue (Q) of a monitoring unit.

1: **procedure** DEQUEUE(Q)
2: $\quad v_{inp} \leftarrow [], \hat{t} \leftarrow -\infty$
3: $\quad$ **for** $i < |Q|$ **do**
4: $\quad\quad v \leftarrow \text{PEAK}(Q[i])$
5: $\quad\quad \hat{t} \leftarrow \min(\hat{t}, t_v^e)$
6: $\quad$ **for** $i < |Q|$ **do**
7: $\quad\quad v \leftarrow \text{PEAK}(Q[i])$
8: $\quad\quad$ **if** $\hat{t} = t_v^e$ **then**
9: $\quad\quad\quad v_{inp} \leftarrow v_{inp} + [v]$
10: $\quad\quad\quad \text{POP}(Q[i])$
11: $\quad\quad$ **else**
12: $\quad\quad\quad v_{left} \leftarrow (t_v^s, \hat{t}, f_v)$
13: $\quad\quad\quad v_{right} \leftarrow (\hat{t}, t_v^e, f_v)$
14: $\quad\quad\quad \text{REPLACE}(Q[i], v_{right})$
15: $\quad\quad\quad v_{inp} \leftarrow v_{inp} + [v_{left}]$
16: $\quad$ **return** v_{inp}

Algorithm 3. Sliding window function customized for the Min aggregation function.

1: **procedure** $\text{SLIDE}_{MIN}(T, v_l, s)$
2: $\quad v_+, v_l \leftarrow \text{SPLIT}(T, v_l, s)$
3: $\quad v_+' \leftarrow \text{TRANSFORM}(v_+)$
4: $\quad k \leftarrow n$
5: $\quad$ **while** $s[k] \succ v_+'$ **do**
6: $\quad\quad \text{REMOVE}(s[k])$
7: $\quad\quad k \leftarrow k - 1$
8: $\quad$ **if** $k > 0$ **then**
9: $\quad\quad t' \leftarrow \text{SOLVE}(f_k(t) - f_+(a) = 0)$
10: $\quad\quad s[k] \leftarrow ([a_k, t'), f_k)$
11: $\quad$ **else**
12: $\quad\quad t' \leftarrow a_0$
13: $\quad s[k+1] \leftarrow ([t', a_+), t \to f_+(a_+))$
14: $\quad$ **if** $\forall t \in [a_+, b_+], \frac{\partial f_l}{\partial t} \leq 0$ **then**
15: $\quad\quad s[k+1] \leftarrow ([t, b), t \to f(a_+))$
16: $\quad$ **else**
17: $\quad\quad s[k+2] \leftarrow ([a, b), f_+)$
18: $\quad v_{out} \leftarrow \text{CUT}(\Delta_-, s)$
19: $\quad$ **return** v_{out}, v_l, s

We now describe all the monitoring units associated with the operators of our extended logic. *n-ary operator (op)*. This is a straightforward implementation of Algorithm 1 with empty memory and state-output function

$$\lambda((I, f_1), \ldots, (I, f_n)) := (I, op(f_1, \ldots, f_n))$$

All the other operators correspond to unary or binary application of Algorithm 1 where the λ function implements the sliding window algorithm or its customization. We now provide a general implementation of the sliding window algorithm, as well as custom implementations for the fixed-time window version (On-operator with Min/Max, Int) and the variable-time window version (for the two until operators).

Sliding Window Operator (Algorithm 4). The sliding window operator takes as input the window size T, the state s, which is the window queue storing symbolic states provided as inputs, the memory c, and the input symbolic state v. First, the set V_{out}, which will contain the resulting symbolic states, is initialized as the empty set (line 2), and v_l, which corresponds to the symbolic state we are trying to add to s, is initialized with v (line 3). While there is a symbolic state to add (line 4), the SLIDE procedure is executed (line 5). Based on the available space in the window queue s (which depends on the symbolic states already stored and the window size T), v_l can be added either completely or partially. In the first

Algorithm 4 Sliding window operator λ with window T and aggregator λ'.

1: **procedure** $\lambda(T, s, c, v)$
2:     $V_{out} \leftarrow \emptyset$
3:     $v_l \leftarrow v$
4:     **while** $v_l \neq \emptyset$ **do**
5:        $v_-, v_+, v_l, s \leftarrow \text{SLIDE}(T, v_l, s)$
6:        $c, v_{out} \leftarrow \lambda'(c, v_-, v_+)$
7:        $V_{out} \leftarrow V_{out} + [\text{SHIFT}(v_{out})]$
8:     **return** V_{out}, s, c

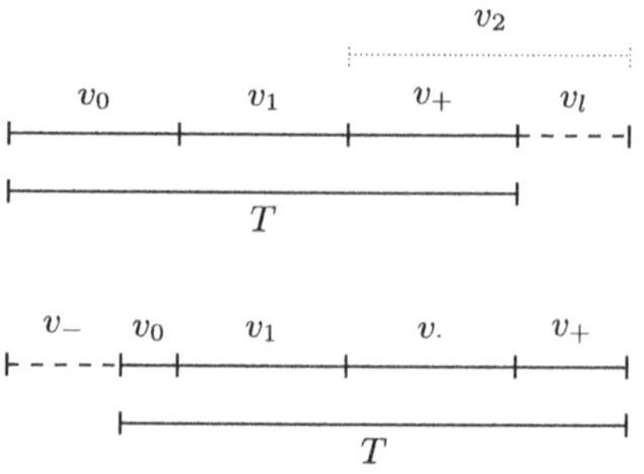

Fig. 2. (Left) Sliding window algorithm. (Right) Visualization of the SLIDE procedure when v_l is added chunk by chunk in more than one loop.

case, the SLIDE procedure returns $v_+ = v_l$ and $v_- = v_l = \emptyset$, meaning that the entire symbolic state is added to s. In the other case, v_l contains the portion that was rejected by s, v_+ is the portion of v_l that was added to s, and v_- is a portion of the first element in s that has been removed. Please refer to Fig. 2 (Right) for a visual representation of this second case. At line 6, the aggregation function computes the resulting updated memory (c) and the symbolic state (v_{out}), based on the current memory and the added (v_+) and removed (v_-) symbolic states. At line 7, v_{out} is shifted backward by a time units (SHIFT procedure) and added to a vector storing all output symbolic states (V_{out}), and finally, at line 8, V_{out}, s, and c are returned.

Sliding Window Operator with Integral Aggregation (On_TInt*).* Monitoring of this sliding window operator is a straightforward adaptation of Algorithm 4. Given two symbolic states $v_- = ([a_-, b_-], f_-)$ and $v_+ = ([a_+, b_+], f_+)$, the update function $\lambda'(c, v_-, v_+)$ returns a symbolic state v_{out} and an update of the memory c corresponding to:

$$v_{out} = \left([a_-, b_-], t \to c - \int_{a_-}^{t} f_-(\tau)\,d\tau + \int_{a_+}^{t} f_+(\tau)\,d\tau\right) \quad (2)$$

$$c \leftarrow c - \int_{a_-}^{M} f_-(\tau)\,d\tau + \int_{a_+}^{M} f_+(\tau)\,d\tau \quad (3)$$

with $M := \min(b_- - a_-, b_+ - a_+)$.

Considering that the sliding window operator must behave as specified at the end of Sect. 3, a slight change to the Algorithm 4 is required to handle symbolic states with undefined values. When a symbolic state with an undefined value is received, it is treated as a symbolic state with a constant function equal to zero, and a counter is initialized to keep track of the duration of such symbolic states. This counter recognizes whether a sequence of symbolic states with undefined values spans a time window longer than the window length T. The operator must return a symbolic state with an undefined value in such cases.

Sliding Window Operator with Min/Max Aggregation ($On_T Min$/$On_T Max$*).* A naive implementation consists of memorizing all the symbolic states of the running window (in memory c) and evaluating min and max directly on it. Here we propose an adaptation of Lemire's running maximum filter algorithm [17] to our modeling of signals as symbolic states. The key idea is to work directly on the way symbolic states are stored in the state vector s of Algorithm 4 by maintaining the so-called *monotonic edge property*. In Algorithm 3, we propose a customized version of the SLIDE procedure (Algorithm 4, line 5) for the minimum aggregation function[2] which returns directly the result of the aggregation (v_{out}) and does not consider the λ' (Algorithm 4, line 6). The fundamental property of this algorithm is to maintain a state vector s (or window queue) such that

$$\min([v_0, \ldots, v_n]) = \min([v'_0, \ldots, v'_m]) = f'_0(a'_0) \tag{4}$$

where $v'_0 = ([a'_0, b'_0), f'_0)$ and $s = [v_0, \ldots, v_n]$ are the signal passed to the monitoring unit and considered for the aggregation function, and $[v'_0, \ldots, v'_m]$ is the derived signal from s which has the same aggregating result (first equality of Eq. 4), but also has the monotonic edge property meaning that the result of the aggregation corresponds to its evaluation at the starting point (second equality of the same equation). The algorithm starts with the SPLIT procedure, which splits the input symbolic state (v_l) into the chunk added to the sliding window (v_+) and the chunk refused for the addition (stored using again v_l). At line 3, the TRANSFORM procedure will transform the $v_+ = ([a_+, b_+), f_+)$ into $v_+ = ([a_+, b_+), t \to f_+(b_+ - \epsilon))$ if $\forall t \in [a_+, b_+]$, $\frac{\partial f_t}{\partial t} \leq 0$, otherwise it will keep v'_+ as v_+. This transformation will make v'_+ itself satisfy the monotonic edge property, i.e., $\min_{t \in [a'_+, b'_+)} v'_+ = f'_+(a'_+)$. The algorithm continues by deleting all the symbolic states that are higher than the added v'_+. Since s satisfies the monotonic edge property, the while loop starts from the last element of s and goes backward until the first element not higher than v'_+ is identified (lines 5 – 7). If this element exists, the portion of the symbolic state $s[k]$ higher than v'_+ is identified and removed (lines 8 – 10); otherwise, all the elements of the queue are removed. Finally, all the removed elements are replaced with a constant symbolic state from t' to the beginning of v'_+, corresponding to a_+ (line 13), and v'_+ is added as the last symbolic state of s. The output symbolic state of this procedure is identified by removing exactly the timed portion of the first symbolic state of s, which is $([a_0, a_0 + (b_+ - a_+), f_0])$ corresponding to the timed portion of the added symbolic state v'_+.

Remark 3. The optimized sliding window algorithm for computing the minimum and maximum assumes that the added symbolic state is either increasing, decreasing, or constant (both in the TRANSFORM procedure and at line 14). This

---

[2] The version for the maximum aggregation function is a straightforward adaptation of the version of the minimum aggregation version.

is a property that must be enforced in order to use such an optimized procedure. Fortunately, this condition is naturally satisfied by leaf monitoring units of degree 0 and 1. It can also be preserved after applying an operator by evaluating the derivative of the signals and segmenting them based on whether this value is greater than or less than zero.

Find-first Aggregation Until $\psi U_T^d \chi$ *and Find-first Pointwise Until* $\varphi \downarrow U_T^d \chi$. This is a simple variation of the sliding window operator where the time window length is fixed. We report its description in Appendix A.2 [23].

The monitoring procedure described above sometimes requires finding the roots of polynomials. This occurs both in the evaluation of unary inequalities and when computing the minimum or maximum, both as binary operators or as an aggregation function of a sliding window operator. Since root-finding for polynomials of degree higher than 4 can be computationally expensive, often requiring approximation methods, and such approximations may compromise monitoring precision, we choose to consider only monitoring graphs where root-finding can be achieved algebraically, in closed form. For this purpose, it is convenient to introduce the following definition.

Definition 9. (Edge degree). *We introduce the degree function* $deg : \mathcal{V}_{M_G} \to \mathbb{N}$ *that associates to each edge of a monitoring graph (M_G) a natural number. It is defined recursively as follows:*

$$deg((m_a, m_b)) = p \text{ if } m_a \in \ell^p\text{-}MU$$
$$deg((m_a, m_b)) = \beta(m_a)(deg((m_0, m_a)), \ldots, deg((m_n, m_a)))$$

where $\{(m_i, m_a)\}_{i \leq n}$ *are the incoming edges of the monitoring unit* m_a, ℓ^p-*MU is the set of leaf monitoring units which interpret time-stamped values as pwp of degree p, and* $\beta : \mathcal{M}_G \to (\mathbb{N}^* \to \mathbb{N})$ *is a function taking as input a monitoring unit m (associated to an operator of arity, e.g. k) and producing as output a function* $\beta(m) : \mathbb{N}^k \to \mathbb{N}$ *which computes the degree of the polynomial generated as output, provided k polynomials as inputs.*

Please consider Fig. 1 (Right) as an example, where the degree of edges has been added. For more examples, refer to Table 1 in Appendix A.3 [23], where some beta functions have been reported.

Computational Complexity of the Monitoring Algorithm. Our algorithm's time complexity grows linearly with the number of symbolic states processed and with the size of the Monitoring Graph. Indeed, all monitoring units use the received symbolic states only once. This is also valid for the sliding-window operators for computing minima and maxima, as they rely on Lemire's optimal algorithm. Finally, the sliding-window integration operator is also linear with the number of received symbolic states, as we limit our attention to cases where the integration is purely symbolic.

5 Implementation and Experiments

We demonstrate our monitoring algorithm, implemented in Python and available online [24], on the two running examples.

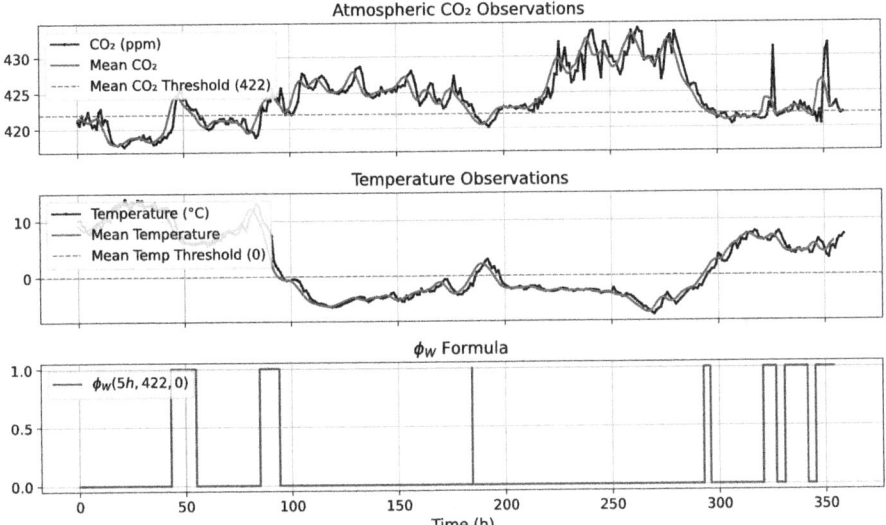

Fig. 3. Weather Case Study - The top chart displays the level of CO_2 in ppm, its rolling mean corresponding to evaluation of $\frac{1}{T}\text{On}_{[0,T]}$ Int CO_2, and the relative threshold of 422 ppm. The middle chart reports the level of air temperature in Celsius degrees, its rolling mean corresponding to evaluation of $\frac{1}{T}\text{On}_{[0,T]}$ Int $temp$, and the relative threshold of 0 °C. Finally, the bottom chart displays the evaluation of property $\varphi_W(5h, 422, 0)$.

Weather Events. This use case corresponds to the first running example. In weather monitoring, a typical requirement is defined by the property $\varphi_W(T, \theta_1, \theta_2)$ (P1, Sect. 1), which is typically used to specify a possible fire event in an outdoor environment, commonly with $\theta_1 = 400$ ppm and $\theta_2 = 60\,°\text{C}$, or an indoor environment to define an air-quality constraint typically with $\theta_1 = 1000$ ppm and $\theta_2 = 25\,°\text{C}$, each evaluated over an appropriate time window. In this case, we use real monitoring data collected at the Hohenpeissenberg, Germany, weather station, which is part of the Integrated Carbon Observatory System (ICOS) network [16]. In Fig. 3 we report results for monitoring of the property $\varphi_W(5h, 422, 0)$ and provide a video of the monitoring algorithm acting at runtime in the GitHub repository [24].

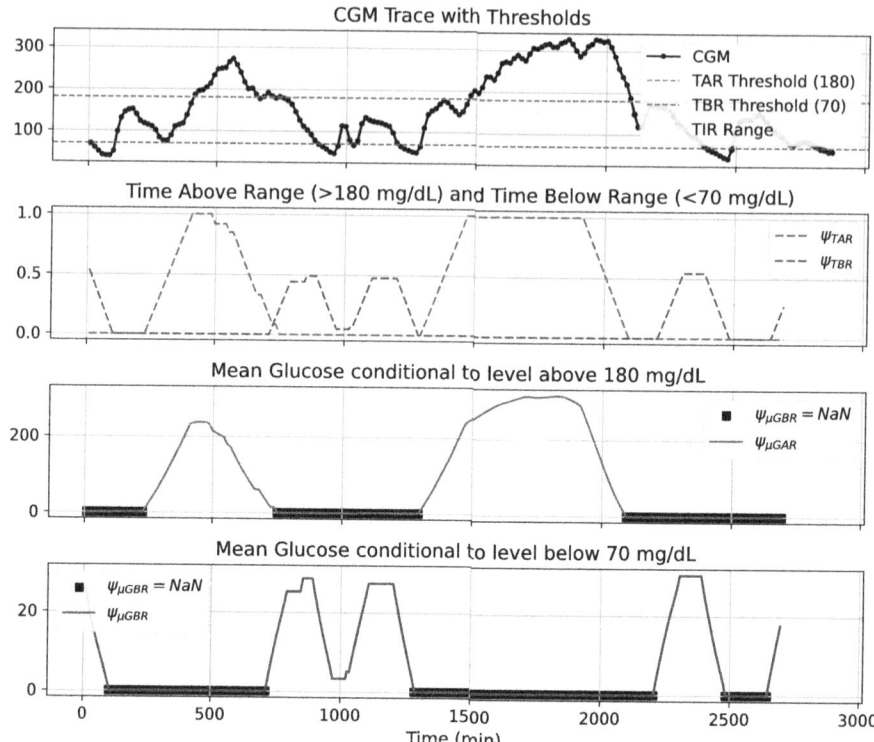

Fig. 4. CGM case study - The first chart shows glucose levels with Time in Range (TIR), Time Above Range (TAR), and Time Below Range (TBR) thresholds. The second shows evaluations of ψ_{TAR} and ψ_{TBR}. The third and fourth show $\psi_{\mu GAR}$ and $\psi_{\mu GBR}$, along with the portions of the time domain (represented with black squares) where these evaluations cannot be determined because the filter conditions are not satisfied across the entire sliding window.

Artificial Pancreas. This follows the second running example. We simulate the monitoring and evaluation of a deployed AP controller using the ShanghaiT1DM dataset [28], a publicly available collection of real-world clinical and monitoring data of adult patients with type 1 diabetes mellitus (T1DM), in Shanghai, China. We analyze the temporal evolution of glucose levels for a single patient over two consecutive days. Measurements are recorded every 15 min and modeled as a piecewise linear signal. Figure 4 presents the glucose trace alongside safe thresholds defining the Time in Range (TIR). The derived metrics ψ_{TAR} and ψ_{TBR}, representing the percentage of time spent above and below the safe range, respectively, and the mean glucose level conditioned during the occurrence of such events associated with Hyperglycemia and Hypoglycemia $\psi_{\mu GAR}$ and $\psi_{\mu GBR}$, are shown. These analyses offer valuable insight into both the severity and progression of glycemic events. For instance, we can observe that the second episode of hyperglycemia is not only longer but also more severe in terms of average glucose levels. For a demonstration video of the monitoring algorithm at runtime, refer to the GitHub repository [24].

6 Conclusions

We extend the specification language of Bakhirkin and Basset [3] by adding the integral operator as an aggregation function, allowing for the definition of cumulative properties and introducing also a filtering operator to constrain aggregation where specified conditions hold. We also generalize from piecewise-constant (pwc) to piecewise-polynomial (pwp) signals. Furthermore, we leverage transducers to propose a modular architecture for online monitoring of the extended logic, allowing property evaluation during target system execution. The proposed implementation of this architecture has a minor limitation: it may introduce delays in producing verdicts depending on the formula's time horizon, along with a trade-off in computational performance.

There are several directions for future work. First, we resolve the monitoring of future operators with the introduction of delays, meaning that we need to wait the entire time horizon of the formula to produce a verdict. It would be interesting to implement an interval value semantics that bounds the evaluation of the future operator at least for the maximum and minimum aggregation functions. Second, we currently restrict our monitoring framework to Monitoring Graphs so that the evaluation of the semantics is symbolic, meaning that no approximation technique is needed to evaluate zeros of polynomials (for example, when their degree is higher than 4). A promising direction is to incorporate efficient approximation routines when symbolic evaluation is infeasible. Third, a tool paper version of this contribution could be considered by including a more in-depth case study and a thorough comparison with stream-based approaches such as RTLola [14] and TeSSLa [18], as well as tools like VeriMon [5] and MonPoly [6] for monitoring discrete-time logic properties.

Acknowledgment. This study was carried out within the PRIN project n. 20228FT78M DREAM (modular software design to reduce uncertainty in ethics-based cyber-physical systems).

References

1. Akazaki, T., Hasuo, I.: Time robustness in MTL and expressivity in hybrid system falsification. In: Proc. of CAV, pp. 356–374. Springer (2015)
2. Alur, R., Feder, T., Henzinger, T.A.: The benefits of relaxing punctuality. J. ACM (JACM) **43**(1), 116–146 (1996)
3. Bakhirkin, A., Basset, N.: Specification and efficient monitoring beyond STL. In: International Conference on Tools and Algorithms for the Construction and Analysis of Systems, pp. 79–97. Springer (2019)

4. Bakhirkin, A., Ferrère, T., Henzinger, T., Nickovic, D.: The first-order logic of signals. In: International Conference on Embedded Software (EMSOFT) (2018)
5. Basin, D., et al.: VeriMon: a formally verified monitoring tool. In: International Colloquium on Theoretical Aspects of Computing, pp. 1–6. Springer (2022)
6. Basin, D.A., Klaedtke, F., Zalinescu, E.: The MonPoly monitoring tool. RV-CuBES **3**, 19–28 (2017)
7. Battelino, T., et al.: Clinical targets for continuous glucose monitoring data interpretation: recommendations from the international consensus on time in range. Diabetes Care **42**(8), 1593–1603 (2019)
8. Brim, L., Dluhoš, P., Šafránek, D., Vejpustek, T.: STL*: Extending signal temporal logic with signal-value freezing operator. Inf. Comput. **236**, 52–67 (2014)
9. Buyukkocak, A.T., Aksaray, D., Yazıcıoğlu, Y.: Control synthesis using signal temporal logic specifications with integral and derivative predicates. In: 2021 American Control Conference (ACC), pp. 4873–4878. IEEE (2021)
10. Clifford: Preliminary sketch of biquaternions. Proc. London Math. Soc. **1**(1), 381–395 (1871)
11. Deshmukh, J.V., Donzé, A., Ghosh, S., Jin, X., Juniwal, G., Seshia, S.A.: Robust online monitoring of signal temporal logic. Formal Methods Syst. Design **51**(1), 5–30 (2017). https://doi.org/10.1007/s10703-017-0286-7
12. Divani, M., et al.: Assessment of hyperglycemia, hypoglycemia and inter-day glucose variability using continuous glucose monitoring among diabetic patients on chronic hemodialysis. J. Clin. Med. **10**(18), 4116 (2021)
13. Donzé, A., Ferrere, T., Maler, O.: Efficient robust monitoring for STL. In: International Conference on Computer Aided Verification, pp. 264–279. Springer (2013)
14. Faymonville, P., et al.: StreamLAB: stream-based monitoring of cyber-physical systems. In: International Conference on Computer Aided Verification, pp. 421–431. Springer (2019)
15. Hoogendoorn, C.J., et al.: Dynamic relationships among continuous glucose metrics and momentary cognitive performance in diverse adults with type 1 diabetes. Diabetes Care **48**(5), 799–806 (2025)
16. Kubistin, D., Plaß-Dülmer, C., Arnold, S., Kneuer, T., Lindauer, M., Müller-Williams, J., Schumacher, M., ICOS RI: Icos atmosphere level 2 data, hohenpeissenberg, release 2024-1 (2024). https://doi.org/10.18160/QSDJ-P768, https://meta.icos-cp.eu/collections/jXIGuaTJJapMNE8XKAP4tC_d
17. Lemire, D.: Streaming maximum-minimum filter using no more than three comparisons per element. arXiv preprint cs/0610046 (2006)
18. Leucker, M., Sánchez, C., Scheffel, T., Schmitz, M., Schramm, A.: TeSSLa: runtime verification of non-synchronized real-time streams. In: Proceedings of the 33rd Annual ACM Symposium on Applied Computing, pp. 1925–1933 (2018)
19. Ma, M., Preum, S.M., Ahmed, M.Y., Tärneberg, W., Hendawi, A., Stankovic, J.A.: Data sets, modeling, and decision making in smart cities: a survey **4**(2) (2019). https://doi.org/10.1145/3355283
20. Maler, O., Nickovic, D.: Monitoring temporal properties of continuous signals. In: Lakhnech, Y., Yovine, S. (eds.) Formal Techniques, Modelling and Analysis of Timed and Fault-Tolerant Systems, pp. 152–166. Springer, Berlin Heidelberg, Berlin, Heidelberg (2004)
21. Mamouras, K., Chattopadhyay, A., Wang, Z.: A compositional framework for algebraic quantitative online monitoring over continuous-time signals. Int. J. Softw. Tools Technol. Transfer **25**(4), 557–573 (2023)
22. Pnueli, A., Zaks, A.: On the merits of temporal testers. 25 Years of Model Checking: History, Achievements, Perspectives, pp. 172–195 (2008)

23. Silvetti, S., Loreti, M., Nenzi, L.: Modular and Online Monitoring of Temporal Logic Specification with Integral and Filter (Extended Version). https://github.com/LogArtLab/gemon/blob/main/paper.pdf
24. Silvetti, S., Loreti, M., Nenzi, L.: Github repository (2025). https://github.com/LogArtLab/gemon
25. Silvetti, S., Nenzi, L., Bartocci, E., Bortolussi, L.: Signal convolution logic. In: International Symposium on Automated Technology for Verification and Analysis, pp. 267–283. Springer (2018)
26. Tsigkanos, C., Bersani, M.M., Frangoudis, P.A., Dustdar, S.: Edge-based runtime verification for the internet of things. IEEE Trans. Serv. Comput. **15**(5), 2713–2727 (2022). https://doi.org/10.1109/TSC.2021.3074956
27. Yamaguchi, T., Hoxha, B., Ničković, D.: Rtamt-runtime robustness monitors with application to cps and robotics. Int. J. Softw. Tools Technol. Transfer **26**(1), 79–99 (2024)
28. Zhao, Q., et al.: Chinese diabetes datasets for data-driven machine learning. Sci. Data **10**(1), 35 (2023)

Alignment Monitoring

Thomas A. Henzinger[2], Konstantin Kueffner[2(✉)], Vasu Singh[3], and I. Sun[1,3]

[1] University of Illinois Urbana-Champaign, Champaign, IL, USA
is16@illinois.edu
[2] ISTA, Klosterneuburg, Austria
{tah,kkeuffner}@ista.ac.at
[3] NVIDIA, Santa Clara, USA
vasus@nvidia.com

Abstract. Formal verification provides assurances that a probabilistic system satisfies its specification—*conditioned* on the system model being aligned with reality. We propose *alignment monitoring* to watch that this assumption is justified. We consider a probabilistic model well aligned if it accurately predicts the behaviour of an uncertain system in advance. An *alignment score* measures this by quantifying the similarity between the model's predicted and the system's (unknown) actual distributions. An alignment monitor observes the system at runtime; at each point in time it uses the current state and the model to predict the next state. After the next state is observed, the monitor updates the verdict, which is a high-probability interval estimate for the true alignment score. We utilize tools from sequential forecasting to construct our alignment monitors. Besides a monitor for measuring the expected alignment score, we introduce a differential alignment monitor, designed for comparing two models, and a weighted alignment monitor, which permits task-specific alignment monitoring. We evaluate our monitors experimentally on the PRISM benchmark suite. They are fast, memory-efficient, and detect misalignment early.

Keywords: Model alignment · Runtime verification · Statistical monitoring

1 Introduction

Probabilistic models such as Markov chains or Markov decision processes (MDPs) can be used to capture uncertainties in a system, for example, about the distribution of inputs. While many of these models are amenable to formal verification, the verification results are only as good as the models themselves: if some parameters of the actual system are different from the assumptions made by the probabilistic model, or change over time, then the properties of the model

---

K. Kueffner: Part of the work was conducted during an internship at NVIDIA.

become detached from reality. Hence, we must ensure that a probabilistic model is an accurate abstraction of the deployed system. This assurance can only be given by a runtime monitor.

We take the position that all models are "wrong," [8] irrespective of whether we obtain our model from an expert or by learning it from data. But some models are useful, and we formalize the "usefulness" of a model by its power to accurately predict how the system evolves. In this paper, we test the assumption that *a given probabilistic model accurately predicts the next state of a system* by constructing quantitative runtime monitors. In our setting, the system's states are fully observable, but its probabilistic next-state function is unknown.

Alignment Monitoring. An alignment monitor outputs, at every point in time, an "alignment score" that asserts how well-aligned the model is to the system, by measuring the prediction quality of the model. For stochastic models, the prediction quality for a given model and system state translates into some similarity measure between the model's and the system's successor distributions. Hence, the model's alignment score w.r.t. the current history must be some function mapping a sequence of pairs of distributions to a real value. However, without access to the system's distributions, this history is hidden and must be estimated from observations. Fortunately, we get these samples for free during runtime. At every point in time, we interpret the model's current successor distribution as a predictor for the next system state, which will be observed once the system transitions from the current to the next state. In alignment monitoring this sequence of predictions and observed states is the observed history and the input to the monitor. The observed states are realisations of the system's successor distributions, which are unknown but required for computing the alignment score. The monitor computes an interval estimate from the *observed history* to estimate the model's alignment score evaluated on the *hidden history*. We require that the sequence of interval estimates is correct at all times with high probability.

Average Alignment Monitor. In sequential forecasting scoring rules are used to quantify the quality of a prediction compared to an observation. The observed outcome is a sample from an unknown true distribution. The expected score w.r.t. to the true distribution provides a measure of how well the prediction is aligned with the true distribution. This is generalized to the sequential setting by taking the average over all predictions. This defines the *average expected score* (AES). The AES can be estimated from a sequence of predictions and observations using tools from sequential forecasting, where this problem is well-known [9]. The only assumption required is that the scoring rule be bounded and that the true distribution be determined before the prediction is made. We utilize these tools to construct a monitor that outputs, at every point in time, the average expected alignment score.

Extensions. We present two extensions to the average alignment monitor. The *weighted alignment monitor* allows the user to weigh predictions and outcomes depending on their importance for a particular task. For example, in probabilistic systems bottom strongly connected components (BSCCs), i.e., sets of states from which the system can never escape, are important, because once the system is in a safe BSCC, we are guaranteed to be safe indefinitely [7]. Therefore, if the monitor detects a transition away from a state that, according to the model, should be inside a BSCC, the safety guarantee of the system is in jeopardy. Hence, such transition should be of greater importance when assessing alignment. We can encode this using the weights of our weighted alignment monitor. Second, the *differential alignment monitor* allows the user to incorporate a reference model when evaluating the tested model's alignment. The monitor observes both the tested model's and the reference model's predictions, and computes interval estimates for the average expected score difference between the two models. If the reference model is already trusted, but may be overly conservative, a differential alignment monitor can be used to decide whether a tested model is better or worse on than the trusted reference model on the observed history.

Experiments. We evaluate our average and differential alignment monitor on slightly modified versions of the discrete-time Markov chains from the PRISM benchmark suit [26]. The computation time of our average alignment monitor depends linearly on the input dimension, i.e., the support of the prediction, but is constant w.r.t. the history. Even if the input dimension is large, e.g., 10^6, our monitor is fast, requiring roughly $260\mu s$ per iteration. We show that the differential alignment monitor can often decide which model is better after a few 100 observations. We evaluate our weighted alignment monitor on two toy examples, demonstrating its applicability to problems in formal verification.

Contributions

- We introduce and formalise the problem of alignment monitoring.
- We use tools from Choe et al. [9] to develop a runtime monitor that tracks the average expected alignment score using high-probability interval estimates.
- We present weighted and differential alignment monitoring as extension.

2 Preliminaries

Let $\mathbb{N}$ be the set of natural numbers, $\mathbb{N}^+$ be the set of natural numbers excluding zero, $\mathbb{R}$ be the set of real numbers. Let $a, b \in \mathbb{N}$ such that $a < b$. We define $[a;b]:=\{a, a+1, \ldots b\}$ as the interval from a to b over the natural numbers and as a shorthand we will use $[b]:=[1;b]$. Let $R \subseteq \mathbb{R}$ be a subset of the real-numbers, we denote the set of all interval over R as $I(R)$. Given a set countable $\mathcal{Z}$ and $n \in \mathbb{N}$ we denote the set of all sequences of length n as $\mathcal{Z}^n$. The set $\mathcal{Z}^*:=\bigcup_{n \in \mathbb{N}} \mathcal{Z}^n$ denotes the set of all finite sequences. We define $\Delta(\mathcal{Z})$ as the set of all probability distributions over $\mathcal{Z}$.

3 Alignment Monitoring

In this section we present the alignment monitoring problem.

Example 1. In quantitative model checking we are given a model of the environment represented as a Markov decision process (MDP) $\hat{\mathcal{M}}:=(\mathcal{S},\mathcal{A},\hat{P},\hat{\lambda})$ consisting of a state space $\mathcal{S}$, a set of actions $\mathcal{A}$, a transition probability function $\hat{P}\colon \mathcal{S}\times\mathcal{A}\to \Delta(\mathcal{S})$ where $\Delta(\mathcal{Z})$ denotes the set of all probability distributions over a set $\mathcal{Z}$, and an initial distribution $\hat{\lambda}\in\Delta(\mathcal{S})$. The nondeterminism introduced by the actions is resolved by a policy $\pi\colon \mathcal{S}\times\mathcal{A}$, resulting in a Markov chain (MC). Given a specification φ represented as an LTL formula, the probability that the policy satisfies the property w.r.t. the model is computed, i.e., $\mathbb{P}_\pi^{\hat{\mathcal{M}}}(S\models\varphi)$. This assures that the system, the environment and the policy, adhere to the specification. The setting above is fundamental to much of the work done in formal verification [7]. It relies on the assumption that model $\hat{\mathcal{M}}:=(\mathcal{S},\mathcal{A},\hat{P},\hat{\lambda})$ is aligned with the *actual* environment $\mathcal{M}^\star:=(\mathcal{S},\mathcal{A},P^\star,\lambda^\star)$.

We choose to measure the model's alignment with reality based on its predictive capabilities, e.g., how well can it predict the next state.

Example 2. Let $p^\star$ be the bias of an unknown coin and let $\hat{p}$ be the bias of the model coin given to us. We would consider the model coin well aligned with the actual coin, if $\hat{p}$ and $p^\star$ are close, e.g., if $|\hat{p}-p^\star|$ is small.

Example 3 (Ex. 1 cont.). We consider the model $\hat{\mathcal{M}}$ well aligned with reality $\mathcal{M}^\star$ for a state-action pair $(s,a)\in(\mathcal{S}\times\mathcal{A})$, if the respective successor distributions are "close", i.e., if $\hat{P}(s,a)\approx P^\star(s,a)$ for some notion of similarity.

Setting. Our objective is to monitor the alignment of the model with the environment. In monitoring, we are limited to watching reality unfold one step at a time, e.g., the monitor observes the state-action pairs generated by an agent interacting with the environment. We can model this as a stochastic process $X:=(X_t)_{t\in\mathbb{N}^+}$ over a given state space $\mathcal{X}$, e.g., the joint state-action space $\mathcal{S}\times\mathcal{A}$. The stochastic process is defined by the environment $\theta^\star\colon \mathcal{X}^\star\to\Delta(\mathcal{X})$ which is modelled as $\hat{\theta}\colon \mathcal{X}^\star\to\Delta(\mathcal{X})$. Together, the environment and the model define two stochastic processes, the hidden process $V:=(V_t)_{t\in\mathbb{N}^+}=(\hat{Y}_t,Y_t^\star)_{t\in\mathbb{N}^+}$ and the observed process $W:=(W_t)_{t\in\mathbb{N}^+}=(\hat{Y}_t,X_t)_{t\in\mathbb{N}^+}$ where for every $t\in\mathbb{N}^+$

$$\hat{Y}_t=\hat{\theta}(X_1,\ldots,X_{t-1})\quad\text{and}\quad X_t\sim Y_t^\star=\theta^\star(X_1,\ldots,X_{t-1}).$$

The hidden history $v:=v_1,\ldots,v_t$ at time t is a finite realisation of $V_1,\ldots,V_t$ consisting of model's predictions and environment's probability distribution. The observed history $w:=w_1,\ldots,w_t$ at time t is a finite realisation of $W_1,\ldots,W_t$ consisting of model's predictions and observed states. We can summarise the dynamics as follows. At time t the environment decides on the distribution $y_t^\star=\theta^\star(x_1,\ldots,x_{t-1})$, a prediction is made using the model $\hat{y}_t=\hat{\theta}(x_1,\ldots,x_{t-1})$, after which the next state x_t is obtained by sampling from $y_t^\star$.

Example 4 (Ex. 2 cont.). For the coins $p^\star$ and $\hat{p}$, the observed process $(\hat{Y}_t, X_t)_{t \in \mathbb{N}^+}$ and the hidden process $(\hat{Y}_t, Y_t^\star)_{t \in \mathbb{N}^+}$ are defined for every $t \in \mathbb{N}^+$ such that $Y_t^\star = \text{Bernoulli}(p^\star)$ and $\hat{Y}_t = \text{Bernoulli}(\hat{p})$ a.s., and $X_t \sim Y_t^\star$.

Example 5 (Ex. 3 cont.). Because π is deterministic we focus only on the states, i.e., $\mathcal{X} = \mathcal{S}$. The observed process $(\hat{Y}_t, X_t)_{t \in \mathbb{N}^+}$ and the hidden process $(\hat{Y}_t, Y_t^\star)_{t \in \mathbb{N}^+}$ are defined for every $t \in \mathbb{N}^+$ such that $\hat{Y}_{t+1} = \hat{P}(S_t, \pi(S_t))$, $Y_{t+1}^\star = P^\star(S_t, \pi(S_t))$, and $X_t = S_{t+1} \sim Y_{t+1}^\star$ with $\hat{Y}_1 = \hat{\lambda}$ and $Y_1^\star = \lambda^\star$.

Alignment Monitoring. Without any assumption on the environment $\theta^\star$, little can be said about the overall alignment of $\hat{\theta}$, by looking only at the observed history. We can, however, say something about the alignment thus far. Here we follow the intuition: if the model has shown a consistent track record of predicting the future, there is no reason to reject it; if the model consistently failed to predict the future, we should reject it. Formally, we measure the alignment of the model at every point in time using an alignment score function $d\colon (\Delta(\mathcal{X}) \times \Delta(\mathcal{X}))^* \to \mathbb{R}$, which computes an alignment score between two sequences of distributions. Our objective is to construct a monitor $\mathbf{M}\colon (\Delta(\mathcal{X}) \times \mathcal{X})^* \to I(\mathbb{R})$ computing an interval $[l_t, u_t] = \mathbf{M}(w_1, \ldots, w_t)$ from the observed history $w_1, \ldots, w_t$ at time $t \in \mathbb{N}^+$ estimating the quantity $d(v_1, \ldots, v_t)$ evaluated over the hidden history $v_1, \ldots, v_t$ with high probability.

Problem 1. Given an unknown environment $\theta^\star\colon \mathcal{X}^* \to \Delta(\mathcal{X})$, a model $\hat{\theta}\colon \mathcal{X}^* \to \Delta(\mathcal{X})$, an alignment score function $d\colon (\Delta(\mathcal{X}) \times \Delta(\mathcal{X}))^* \to \mathbb{R}$, and an error probability $\delta \in (0,1)$, find a monitor $\mathbf{M}\colon (\Delta(\mathcal{X}) \times \mathcal{X})^* \to I(\mathbb{R})$ such that

$$\mathbb{P}_{\theta^\star}\left(\forall t \in \mathbb{N}^+ : d(V_1, \ldots, V_t) \in \mathbf{M}(W_1, \ldots, W_t)\right) \geq 1 - \delta. \qquad (1)$$

The condition $\forall t \in \mathbb{N}^+ : d(V_1, \ldots, V_t) \in \mathbf{M}(W_1, \ldots, W_t)$ is an invariant guaranteeing that the monitor bounds the alignment score at every iteration during its infinite run. Equation 1 requires this invariant to hold with high-probability.

4 Average Alignment Monitor

In this section we present a monitor solving Problem 1 for the average alignment score, i.e., the average over individual alignment scores computed using scoring rules. The monitor is based on tools from the sequential forecasting literature [9].

Scoring Rule. A bounded scoring rule is a function $\ell\colon \Delta(\mathcal{X}) \times \mathcal{X} \to [a,b]$ for $a, b \in \mathbb{R}$ assessing the quality of the model's prediction at every time step w.r.t. the observation. The example below highlights two common scoring rules.

Example 6. For a distribution $y \in \Delta(\mathcal{X})$, and an observation $x \in \mathcal{X}$, the Brier score ℓ_B, bounded on $[0,2]$, and the spherical score ℓ_S, bounded on $[-1,0]$, are

$$\ell_B(y,x) := \sum_{x' \in \mathcal{X}} (y(x') - \mathbb{1}\{x' = x\})^2 \quad \text{and} \quad \ell_S(y,x) := \frac{-y(x)}{\sqrt{\sum_{x' \in \mathcal{X}} y(x')^2}}.$$

To assess the prediction quality w.r.t. the environment, we need to compute the expected score $\mathbb{E}_{X_t \sim y_t^\star}(\ell(\hat{y}_t, X_t))$. To ensure fair scoring, it is important that the scoring rule is proper, i.e., the expected score is minimised when the predicted distribution matches the true distribution, i.e., if all $y^\star, \hat{y} \in \Delta(\mathcal{X})$,

$$\mathbb{E}_{X \sim y^\star}[\ell(y^\star, X)] \leq \mathbb{E}_{X \sim y^\star}[\ell(\hat{y}, X)].$$

The expected score assesses the alignment of the model at every $t \in \mathbb{N}^+$. The average expected score (AES) extends this to sequences defined; it is defined over the hidden history $v := \hat{y}_1, y_1^\star, \ldots, \hat{y}_t, y_t^\star$ as

$$E^\ell(v) := \frac{1}{t} \sum_{i=1}^{t} \mathbb{E}_{X_i \sim y_i^\star}(\ell(\hat{y}_i, X_i)).$$

4.1 Monitor Construction

Computing the AES requires knowledge of the successor distributions as given by the environment. Because this is hidden from us, our monitor must estimate the AES during runtime.

Point Estimation. A natural estimator for the AES is the average score defined for every observed history $w := \hat{y}_1, x_1, \ldots, \hat{y}_t, x_t$ as

$$\hat{E}^\ell(w) := \frac{1}{t} \sum_{i=1}^{t} \ell(\hat{y}_i, x_i).$$

Confidence Sequences. We use confidence sequences to quantify how close our average score $\hat{E}_t := \hat{E}^\ell(W_1, \ldots, W_t)$ is to the AES $E_t := E^\ell(V_1, \ldots, V_t)$ for every $t \in \mathbb{N}^+$. A confidence sequence for the sequence of AESs $(E_t)_{t \in \mathbb{N}^+}$, is a sequence of lower and upper bounds $(L_t, U_t)_{t \in \mathbb{N}^+}$ containing $(E_t)_{t \in \mathbb{N}^+}$ with high probability, i.e., for $\delta \in (0,1)$ the confidence sequence $(L_t, U_t)_{t \in \mathbb{N}^+}$ ensures

$$\mathbb{P}(\forall t \in \mathbb{N}^+ : E_t \in [L_t, U_t]) \geq 1 - \delta.$$

Using techniques outlined in Howard et al. [23] and Choe et al. [9] we construct a confidence sequence centred around the point estimate, i.e., at every time $t \in \mathbb{N}^+$ the lower and upper bounds are defined as $L_t := \hat{E}_t - \varepsilon_t$ and $U_t := \hat{E}_t + \varepsilon_t$ respectively. The error ε_t is given by

$$\varepsilon_t(N_t, \delta, \sigma_\ell) := \frac{\sqrt{2.13 \cdot N_t \cdot g(N_t, \delta) + 1.76 \cdot \sigma_\ell^2 \cdot g(N_t, \delta)^2} + 1.33 \cdot \sigma_\ell \cdot g(N_t, \delta)}{t} \quad (2)$$

where $g(n, \delta) = (2 \cdot \log(\pi \log(n)/\sqrt{6}) + \log(2/\delta))$, $\sigma_\ell := b - a$ is the difference between the maximal and minimal value of the scoring rule, and N_t is the maximum between 1 and the empirical variance process, i.e.,

$$N_t := \max\left(1, \sum_{i=1}^{t} (\ell(\hat{Y}_i, X_i) - \hat{E}_{i-1})^2\right). \quad (3)$$

Implementation. The alignment monitor implemented in Algorithm 1 requires constant space and time w.r.t. the observed history. *Space:* the monitor uses three counters to incrementally compute the time t, the empirical variance process N, and the average score $\hat{E}$. *Time:* the monitor requires constant time to update the three counters. The only computationally demanding operation is computing the score stored in variable s. This depends on the scoring rule. For example, in the case of the Brier score and the spherical score this is in the order of $\mathcal{O}(|\mathcal{X}|)$. We denote $T_{\ell,\mathcal{X}}$ as the time required to evaluate the scoring rule.

Theorem 1. *Let V and W be the hidden and the observed process defined by the environment $\theta^\star$ and the model $\hat{\theta}$. Let ℓ be a scoring rule bounded on the interval $[a,b] \subset \mathbb{R}$, and let $\delta \in (0,1)$ be an error probability threshold, then the monitor $\mathbf{M}_{\ell,\delta}$ solves Problem 1 for $d{:=}E^\ell$. The monitor requires at each iteration $\mathcal{O}(1)$-space and $\mathcal{O}(T_{\ell,\mathcal{X}})$-time w.r.t. the history and the state space, where $T_{\ell,\mathcal{X}}$ is the time required to evaluate the scoring rule.*

Algorithm 1. Average Alignment Monitor $\mathbf{M}_{\ell,\delta}$

Require: Error probability $\delta \in (0,1)$, scoring rule $\ell \colon \Delta(\mathcal{X}) \times \mathcal{X} \to [a,b]$.
1: **function** INIT
2: $\quad t \leftarrow 0; \quad \hat{E} \leftarrow 0; \quad N \leftarrow 1; \quad \sigma_\ell \leftarrow b - a$
3: **end function**
4: **function** NEXT($\hat{y}, x$)
5: $\quad s \leftarrow \ell(\hat{y}, x); \quad t \leftarrow t + 1; \quad N \leftarrow \max(1, N + (s - \hat{E})^2)$
6: $\quad \hat{E} \leftarrow \frac{1}{t} \cdot (t-1) \cdot \hat{E} + s; \quad g \leftarrow 2\log\left(\frac{\pi \log(N)}{\sqrt{6}}\right) + \log\left(\frac{2}{\delta}\right)$
7: $\quad \varepsilon \leftarrow \frac{1}{t}\left(\sqrt{2.13 \cdot N \cdot g + 1.76 \cdot \sigma_\ell^2 \cdot g^2} + 1.33 \cdot \sigma_\ell \cdot g\right)$
8: $\quad$ **return** $[\hat{E} - \varepsilon, \hat{E} + \varepsilon]$
9: **end function**

---

5 Extensions

In Sect. 4 we presented a monitor for the average expected score (AES), i.e., the average of all past scores computed by a scoring function of a single model. In this section we extend our average alignment monitor by the differential alignment monitor, which compares the alignment scores of two models, and the weighted alignment monitor, which computes the weighted average of weighted scores.

5.1 Differential Alignment Monitor

Monitoring a single quantitative value may not be overly informative without a reference point. This is where differential alignment monitoring comes in.

Differential Alignment Monitoring. Assume that in addition to the model $\hat{\theta}$, we are given a reference model $\hat{\theta}^{\text{ref}}$. The reference model represents a benchmark against which we want to assess the performance of $\hat{\theta}$.

Example 7 (Ex 5 cont.). The reference model $\hat{\mathcal{M}}^{\text{ref}}:=(\mathcal{S}, \mathcal{A}, \hat{P}^{\text{ref}}, \hat{\lambda}^{\text{ref}})$ for the environment $\mathcal{M}^\star$ differs depending on the available knowledge. If little is known, a worst-case reference model is the uniform distribution, i.e., the model should be at least better than random chance. We distinguish between a black- and gray-box setting. In the black-box setting, $\hat{\mathcal{M}}^{\text{ref}}$ assigns *each state* the same probability, i.e., for all $s, s' \in \mathcal{S}$ and $a \in \mathcal{A}$ we have $\hat{P}^{\text{ref}}(s, a, s') = 1/|\mathcal{S}|$. In the gray-box setting, $\hat{\mathcal{M}}^{\text{ref}}$ assigns *each successor* the same probability, i.e., for all $s, s' \in \mathcal{S}$ and $a \in \mathcal{A}$ we have $\hat{P}^{\text{ref}}(s, a, s') = 1/|\mathcal{S}_{s,a}|$ if $s' \in \mathcal{S}_{s,a}$ where $\mathcal{S}_{s,a}:=\{s' \in \mathcal{S} \mid P^\star(s, a, s') > 0\}$, else $\hat{P}^{\text{ref}}(s, a, s') = 0$.

In the differential alignment monitoring setting, the monitor observes the predictions of both the model and the reference model at the same time, i.e., the hidden process $V^{\text{ref}}:=(V_t^{\text{ref}})_{t\in\mathbb{N}^+} = (\hat{Y}_t, \hat{Y}_t^{\text{ref}}, Y_t^\star)_{t\in\mathbb{N}^+}$ and the observed process $W^{\text{ref}}:=(W_t^{\text{ref}})_{t\in\mathbb{N}^+} = (\hat{Y}_t, \hat{Y}_t^{\text{ref}}, X_t)_{t\in\mathbb{N}^+}$ are defined analogously to V and W.

Problem 2. Given an unknown environment $\theta^\star: \mathcal{X}^* \to \Delta(\mathcal{X})$, a model $\hat{\theta}: \mathcal{X}^* \to \Delta(\mathcal{X})$, a reference model $\hat{\theta}^{\text{ref}}: \mathcal{X}^* \to \Delta(\mathcal{X})$, an alignment score function $d: (\Delta(\mathcal{X}) \times \Delta(\mathcal{X}))^* \to \mathbb{R}$, and an error probability $\delta \in (0, 1)$, find a monitor $\mathbf{M}: (\Delta(\mathcal{X}) \times \Delta(\mathcal{X}) \times \mathcal{X})^* \to I(\mathbb{R})$ such that

$$\mathbb{P}_{\theta^\star}\left(\forall t \in \mathbb{N}^+: D(V_1^{\text{ref}}, \ldots, V_t^{\text{ref}}) \in \mathbf{M}(W_1^{\text{ref}}, \ldots, W_t^{\text{ref}})\right) \geq 1 - \delta \quad (4)$$

where $D(V_1^{\text{ref}}, \ldots, V_t^{\text{ref}}) = d(\hat{Y}_1, Y_1^\star, \ldots, \hat{Y}_t, Y_t^\star) - d(\hat{Y}_1^{\text{ref}}, Y_1^\star, \ldots, \hat{Y}_t^{\text{ref}}, Y_t^\star)$.

Differential Alignment Monitor. We modify Algorithm 1 to solve Problem 2. The modification, presented in Algorithm 2, is limited to computing the score difference and adjusting the score value bounds to $[a - b, b - a]$.

Theorem 2. *Let V^{ref} and W^{ref} be the hidden and the observed process defined by the environment $\theta^\star$, the model $\hat{\theta}$, and the reference model $\hat{\theta}^{\text{ref}}$. Let ℓ be a scoring rule bounded on the interval $[a, b] \subset \mathbb{R}$, and let $\delta \in (0, 1)$ be an error probability, then the monitor $\mathbf{M}_{\ell, \delta}^D$ solves Problem 2 for $d:=E^\ell$. The monitor requires at each iteration $\mathcal{O}(1)$-space and $\mathcal{O}(T_{\ell, \mathcal{X}})$-time w.r.t. the history and the state space, where $T_{\ell, \mathcal{X}}$ is the time required to evaluate the score function.*

5.2 Weighted Alignment Monitor

The AES treats all predictions and all observations equally. In formal verification, this is not necessarily true. Some predictions may be high-stake. Some wrongly predicted outcomes are worse. Our monitor should be able to account for that.

Algorithm 2. Differential Alignment Monitor $\mathbf{M}^D_{\ell,\delta}$

Require: Error probability $\delta \in (0,1)$, scoring rule $\ell \colon \Delta(\mathcal{X}) \times \mathcal{X} \to [a,b]$.   ▷ σ_ℓ is scaled by 2.
1: **function** INIT
2:   $t \leftarrow 0$; $\hat{E} \leftarrow 0$; $N \leftarrow 1$; $\sigma_\ell \leftarrow 2 \cdot (b-a)$ ▷ σ_ℓ is scaled by 2.
3: **end function**
4: **function** NEXT($\hat{y}, \hat{y}^{\text{ref}}, x$)
5:   $s \leftarrow \ell(\hat{y},x) - \ell(\hat{y}^{\text{ref}},x)$; $t \leftarrow t+1$ ▷ s is the score difference.
6:   $N \leftarrow \max(1, N + (s-\hat{E})^2)$; $\hat{E} \leftarrow \frac{1}{t} \cdot (t-1) \cdot \hat{E} + s$
7:   **return** $[\hat{E} - \varepsilon_t(N,\delta,\sigma_\ell), \hat{E} + \varepsilon_t(N,\delta,\sigma_\ell)]$
8: **end function**

Example 8. The Markov chain below encodes a classical bank loan example from the fairness literature [19]. From the initial state (S) either a person from group A or group B is applying for a loan. If the loan is granted (G), the person can either repay the loan (R) or default on it (D). In all other cases we return back to the initial state S. For a common fairness measure, such as the difference of the loan grant probabilities between groups [19], we can evaluate the fairness from the model directly, i.e., $\mathbb{P}(G \mid A) - \mathbb{P}(G \mid B) = 0.7 - 0.4$. Naturally, we care more about the model's alignment on states A and B.

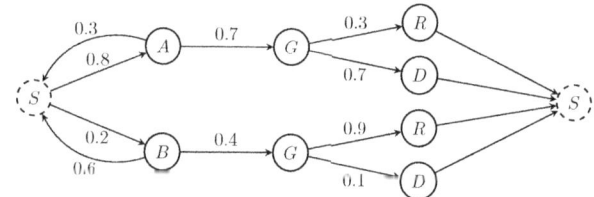

Quantifying the importance of states is a known concept [28,29]. However, as shown in the example below, it is necessary to consider transitions as well.

Example 9. Consider the Markov chain depicted below. The solid lines indicate the model; the environment is the union of the dashed and solid lines. Hence, during monitoring we will eventually observe two transitions not in the support of the model. Those two transitions are not equal. Take s_4 to be an unsafe state. In our model the probability of being safe when starting in s_1 is 0.9, while in reality the probability is 0. During monitoring we may observe the system transitioning from s_6 to s_5. Although this transition is not in the support of our model, the value of our verdict is not jeopardised. By contrast, if we observe the transition from s_6 to s_2 we should be alarmed, as it is vital for the validity of our verdict. Naturally, we care more about the latter than the former transition.

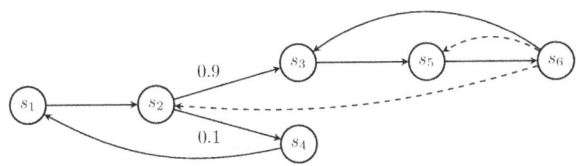

Weighted Alignment Monitoring. Assume the alignment score depends not only on the distributions, but also on the past observations, i.e., $d \colon (\Delta(\mathcal{X}) \times \Delta(\mathcal{X}) \times \mathcal{X})^* \to \mathbb{R}$. Our objective is to construct a monitor $\mathbf{M} \colon (\Delta(\mathcal{X}) \times \mathcal{X})^* \to I(\mathbb{R})$ computing an interval $[l_t, u_t] = \mathbf{M}(w_1, \ldots, w_t)$ from the observed history $w_1, \ldots, w_t$ at time $t \in \mathbb{N}^+$ estimating, with high probability, the quantity $d(v_1, x_1, \ldots, v_t, x_t)$ evaluated over the hidden history $v_1, \ldots, v_t$ and the observed states $x_1, \ldots, x_t$.

Problem 3. Given an unknown environment $\theta^\star \colon \mathcal{X}^* \to \Delta(\mathcal{X})$, a model $\hat{\theta} \colon \mathcal{X}^* \to \Delta(\mathcal{X})$, a weighted alignment score function $d \colon (\Delta(\mathcal{X}) \times \Delta(\mathcal{X}) \times \mathcal{X})^* \to \mathbb{R}$, and an error probability $\delta \in (0,1)$, find a monitor $\mathbf{M} \colon (\Delta(\mathcal{X}) \times \mathcal{X})^* \to I(\mathbb{R})$ s.t.

$$\mathbb{P}_{\theta^\star}\bigl(\forall t \in \mathbb{N}^+ \colon d(V_1, X_1, \ldots, V_t, X_t) \in \mathbf{M}(W_1, \ldots, W_t)\bigr) \geq 1 - \delta. \qquad (5)$$

Weighted Scoring Rules. Analogously to the average alignment monitor, the weighted alignment monitor uses weighted scoring rules, which are scoring rules $\ell_\omega \colon \Delta(\mathcal{X}) \times \mathcal{X} \to [c_\omega \cdot a, c_\omega \cdot b]$ defined by a weight function $\omega \colon \mathcal{X} \to [0, c_\omega]$ for $c_\omega > 0$. There are multiple approaches for creating weighted scoring rules [2,3,21]. The example below shows the outcome-based method of Holzmann et al. [21].

Example 10. Given a proper scoring rule $\ell \colon \Delta(\mathcal{X}) \times \mathcal{X} \to \mathbb{R}$ and a weight function $\omega \colon \mathcal{X} \to [0,1]$, we obtain a scoring rule ℓ_ω proper on $\{x \in \mathcal{X} \mid \omega(x) > 0\}$ by defining for $y \in \Delta(\mathcal{X})$ and $x \in \mathcal{X}$

$$\ell_\omega(y,x) := \omega(x)\ell(y_\omega, x) \quad \text{where} \quad y_\omega(x') := \frac{\omega(x')y(x')}{\sum_{x'' \in \mathcal{X}} \omega(x'')y(x'')} \quad \forall x'' \in \mathcal{X}.$$

Weighted Alignment Score. The weighted alignment score is the weighted average over scores computed by weighted scoring rules. For $c_\alpha, c_\beta > 0$ let $\alpha \colon \mathcal{X}^* \to [0, c_\alpha]$ be a function that assigns each prediction a weight based on the history, and let $\beta \colon \mathcal{X}^* \to (\mathcal{X} \to [0, c_\beta])$ be a function that defines a weight function for each outcome based on the history. Let $w := \hat{y}_1, x_1, \ldots, \hat{y}_t, x_t$ be a observed history, $z := x_1, \ldots, x_t$ the corresponding sequence of states, and $z_{1:k} := x_1, \ldots, x_k$ the prefix of z of length $k \in [t]$. We define the weighted alignment score as

$$\hat{F}^\ell_{\alpha,\beta}(w_1, \ldots, w_t) := \frac{1}{t_\alpha(z)} \sum_{i=1}^{t} \alpha(z_{1:i-1}) \cdot \ell_{\beta(z_{1:i-1})}(\hat{y}_i, x_i)$$

where $\ell_{\beta(z_{1:i-1})}$ is a weighted scoring function and $t_\alpha(z) := \sum_{i=1}^{t} \alpha(z_{1:i-1})$ is the weighted "progression of time". This is an estimator of the weighted expected score. It is defined for the corresponding hidden history $v:=\hat{y}_1,y_1^\star,\ldots,\hat{y}_t,y_t^\star$ as

$$F_{\alpha,\beta}^\ell(v_1,x_1,\ldots,v_t,x_t):=\frac{1}{t_\alpha(z)}\sum_{i=1}^t \alpha(z_{1:i-1})\cdot \mathbb{E}_{X_i \sim y_i^\star}(\ell_{\beta(z_{1:i-1})}(\hat{y}_i, X_i)).$$

Example 11 (Ex. 9 and 8). We present weight functions for the Markov chain in Example 9 and 8. We define them as a function of the current state and current transition, i.e., $\alpha\colon \mathcal{S} \to [0,1]$ and $\beta\colon \mathcal{S} \to (\mathcal{S} \to [0,1])$. In Example 8, we limit our alignment monitor to the states A and B, i.e., $\alpha(A)=\alpha(B)=1$ and 0 otherwise. In Example 9, we focus on the states in the bottom strongly connected component (BSCC), i.e., for all $s \in C := \{s_3, s_5, s_6\}$ we have $\alpha(s)=1$ and 0.1 otherwise. Moreover, we penalise transitions away from the BSCC, i.e., $\beta(s)(s')=1$ if $s \in C$ and $s' \notin C$, and 0.05 otherwise.

Weighted Alignment Monitor. We modify Algorithm 1 to solve Problem 3 for $d = F_{\alpha,\beta}^\ell$. We modify the almost sure bound to be $\sigma_\ell^{\alpha,\beta} := c_\alpha \cdot c_\beta \cdot (b-a)$, because multiplying the score changes its scale. We keep track of the weighted time t_α instead of the actual time, and have to remember the entire history because of the weight functions. Instead of the normal score, we compute the score weighted by both α and β. Details are in Algorithm 3.

Theorem 3. *Let V and W be the hidden and the observed process defined by the environment $\theta^\star$ and the model $\hat{\theta}$. Let ℓ be a scoring rule bounded on the interval $[a,b] \subset \mathbb{R}$, let $\alpha\colon \mathcal{X}^* \to [0, c_\alpha]$ and $\beta\colon \mathcal{X}^* \to (\mathcal{X} \to [0, c_\beta])$ be a prediction and an observation weight function, and $\delta \in (0,1)$ be an error probability, then the monitor $\mathbf{M}_{\ell,\delta}^W$ solves Problem 3 for $d:=F_{\alpha,\beta}^\ell$. The monitor requires at each iteration $\mathcal{O}(t)$-space and $\mathcal{O}(t + T_{\ell,\mathcal{X}})$-time w.r.t. the history $x_1,\ldots,x_t$ and the state space, where $T_{\ell,\mathcal{X}}$ is the time required to evaluate the score function.*

Algorithm 3. Weighted Alignment Monitor $\mathbf{M}_{\ell,\delta}^W$

Require: Error probability $\delta \in (0,1)$, scoring rule $\ell\colon \Delta(\mathcal{X}) \times \mathcal{X} \to [a,b]$, prediction and observation weight function $\alpha\colon \mathcal{X}^* \to [0,c_\alpha]$ and $\beta\colon \mathcal{X}^* \to (\mathcal{X} \to [0,c_\beta])$
1: **function** INIT
2:     $t \leftarrow 0;\ \hat{E} \leftarrow 0;\ N \leftarrow 1;\ z \leftarrow \epsilon$ ▷ Initialise Memory
3:     $\sigma_\ell^{\alpha,\beta} \leftarrow c_\alpha \cdot c_\beta \cdot (b-a)$ ▷ σ_ℓ scaled by max weights.
4: **end function**
5: **function** NEXT($\hat{y}, x$)
6:     $s \leftarrow \alpha(z) \cdot \ell_{\beta(z)}(\hat{y}, x);$ ▷ s is the score times the weights.
7:     $t \leftarrow t + \alpha(z)$ ▷ t is the sum of prediction weights.
8:     $z \leftarrow z \cdot x$ ▷ Increase memory
9:     $N \leftarrow \max(1, N + (s - \hat{E})^2);\ \hat{E} \leftarrow \frac{1}{t} \cdot (t-1) \cdot \hat{E} + s$
10:    **return** $[\hat{E} - \varepsilon_t(N, \delta, \sigma_\ell^{\alpha,\beta}), \hat{E} + \varepsilon_t(N, \delta, \sigma_\ell^{\alpha,\beta})]$
11: **end function**

Remark 1. In formal verification we commonly assume the environment to be Markovian. Here it is sensible to define the weights as a function of the current state and current transition, i.e., $\alpha\colon \mathcal{S} \to [0, c_\alpha]$ and $\beta\colon \mathcal{S} \to (\mathcal{S} \to [0, c_\beta])$. In this case, the monitor requires $\mathcal{O}(1)$-space and $\mathcal{O}(T_{\ell,\mathcal{X}})$-time per iteration.

6 Experiments

All experiments were run on an Apple M2 Pro with 16GB.

Expected Scoring Rules. We show the difference in behaviour between the two scoring rules, the Brier ℓ_B and the spherical score ℓ_S (see Example 6), using a discretised and truncated Gaussian distribution over 100 values. The environment distribution has mean 50 and standard deviation 5. The model uses the same distribution with different parameters. Figure 1 depicts the changes to the score when modifying the mean or the standard deviation of the model.

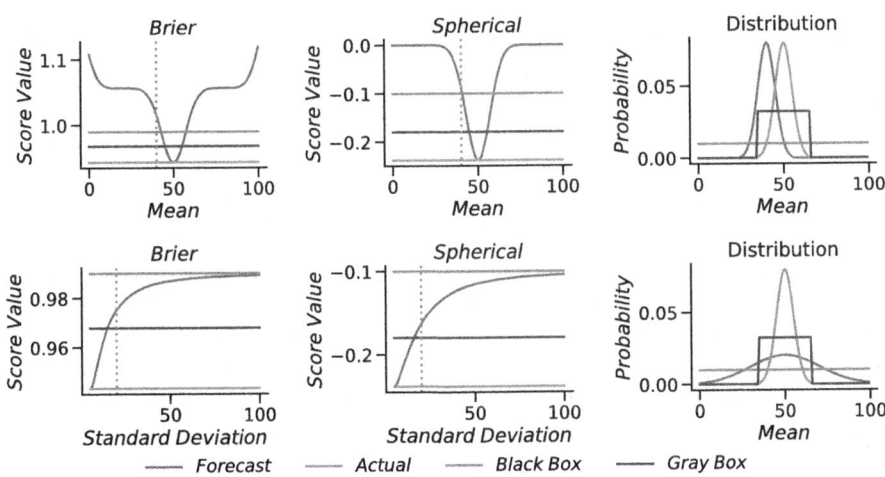

Fig. 1. Behaviour of the expected Brier and spherical score: if the forecast mean is changed (Top); if the forecast standard deviation is changed (Bot). The gray line indicates the corresponding example in the right column. (Color figure online)

Runtime. We evaluated the runtime of our monitor using the same discretised Gaussian distribution ranging from 10 to 10^6 values. Because our monitor is history-independent, we evaluated our monitor on a trace of length 10^4 and averaged the runtime per iteration. We observe linear scaling and similar behaviour for both scoring rules. For example, for the Brier score and 10 values, one iteration required on average $197 \pm 86\mu s$ of which $42 \pm 16\mu s$ is attributed to the scoring function. For 10^6 values we have $259 \pm 108\mu s$ and $72 \pm 40\mu s$ respectively.

6.1 Average and Differential Alignment Monitoring

We evaluate the average and the differential alignment monitor using the discrete-time Markov chains from the PRISM benchmark suite [26].

Environments. We consider the transition matrices Bench = {Brp(16,2), Conditional, Crowds(5,5), Crowds(4,3), Die, Leader(3,5), Nand(5,2), Quantiles}. To avoid bottom strongly connected components (BSCC), we add to each state a 0.01 probability of returning to the initial state.

Models. We considered two forecast models obtained by corrupting each transition matrix $P^\star$ in Bench. The corruption *additive noise* $\hat{P}_A$ adds a scaled centred uniformly distributed random variable to the transition matrix, i.e., for every $s, s' \in \mathcal{S}$ we have $P^\star(s,s') + 0.1 \cdot R$ where $R \sim \text{Uniform}([-0.5, 0.5])$, and normalise each row. The corruption *invert* $\hat{P}_I$ computes the multiplicative inverse for every non-zero transition probability, i.e., for every $s, s' \in \mathcal{S}$ we have $1/P^\star(s,s')$ if $P(s,s') > 0$, and normalise each row.

Reference Models. We consider three reference models obtained from each Markov chain in Bench. The black-box model $\hat{P}_B^{\text{ref}}$, i.e., a uniform distribution over $\mathcal{S}$, and the gray-box model $\hat{P}_G^{\text{ref}}$, i.e., a uniform distribution over the successor states, as defined in Example 7, an expert model $\hat{P}_E^{\text{ref}}$, and the environment model $P^\star$. The expert model is obtained by averaging the transition matrix of the environment and the gray-box model, i.e., $0.5 \cdot P^\star + 0.5 \cdot \hat{P}_G$.

Average Alignment Monitor. For each environment $P^\star \in$ Bench, each forecast model $\hat{P} \in \{\hat{P}_A, \hat{P}_I\}$, and each scoring function $\ell \in \{\ell_B, \ell_S\}$ we deploy our average alignment monitor once for 1000 steps. Example runs for Crowds(4,3) are depicted in the first row of Fig. 2. We add the average expected score for the reference models $\{\hat{P}_B^{\text{ref}}, \hat{P}_G^{\text{ref}}, P^\star\}$ in order to place the estimated score in context. The values for $\hat{P}_B^{\text{ref}}$ and $\hat{P}_G^{\text{ref}}$ can always be computed.

Differential Alignment Monitor. For each environment $P^\star \in$ Bench, each forecast model $\hat{P} \in \{\hat{P}_A, \hat{P}_I\}$, each reference model $\hat{P}^{\text{ref}} \in \{\hat{P}_B^{\text{ref}}, \hat{P}_G^{\text{ref}}, \hat{P}_E^{\text{ref}}, P^\star\}$, and each scoring function $\ell \in \{\ell_B, \ell_S\}$ we deploy our differential alignment monitor 5 times each for 1000 steps. We record the first point in time where the monitor can make a decision. That is, if the monitor's upper bound is below 0, then $\hat{P}$ is better aligned than $\hat{P}^{\text{ref}}$; if the lower bound is above 0, the inverse holds. We average the results and present them in Table 1. Example executions for Crowds(4,3) are depicted in the second row of Fig. 2. The inversion of the probability distribution performed for $\hat{P}_I$ is a severe corruption of the transition probabilities. As a consequence, the monitor declares in most cases that P^{ref} is the better performing model, after only a few observations. By contrast, $\hat{P}_A$ is obtained by adding additive noise, which is a less severe corruption. As a consequence, it is less clear whether P^{ref} or $\hat{P}_A$ is better, which is also reflected in the need for more observations. By construction, we know that the expert model is better aligned than the gray-box model, which is better aligned than the black-box model. This is reflected in the decisions of the monitor, e.g., if $\hat{P}$ outperforms $\hat{P}_G^{\text{ref}}$ then it must outperform $\hat{P}_B^{\text{ref}}$. The number of observations until a decision is a reflection of how difficult it is to distinguish the model from the reference model.

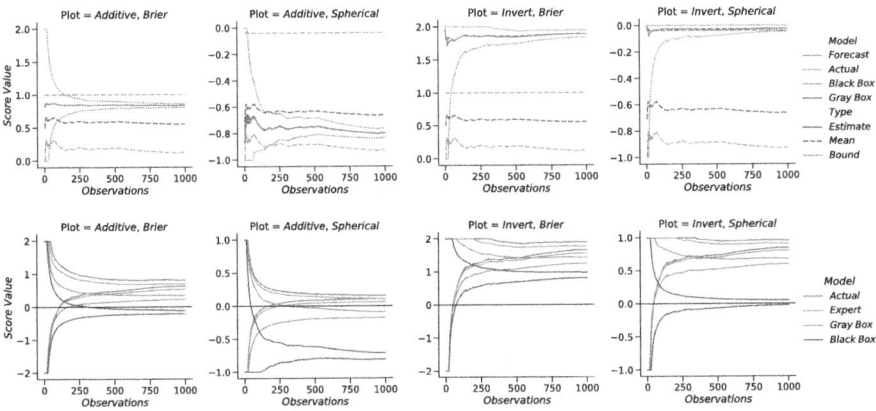

Fig. 2. Example executions of the average alignment monitor (top) and the differential alignment monitor (bot) on the PRISM benchmark Crowds(4,3).

6.2 Weighted Alignment Monitoring

We evaluate the weighted alignment monitor on Example 8 and Example 9, using both the weighted Brier and the weighted spherical scoring rule, obtained through the transformation in Example 10.

Fairness. The environment transition matrix $P^\star$ is taken from Example 8, the model transition matrix $\hat{P}$ is obtained by flipping the transition probabilities of S and the G states, e.g., $\mathbb{P}_{\hat{P}}(A \mid S) = 0.2$ instead of $\mathbb{P}_{P^\star}(A \mid S) = 0.8$. We use the alignment functions in Example 11, i.e., $\alpha(A) = \alpha(B) = 1$ and 0 otherwise. In Fig. 3 we observe that the weighted alignment monitor does not distinguish the model from the environment, i.e., the alignment score computed w.r.t. the actual environment is contained in the interval. By contrast, the average alignment monitor clearly distinguishes the two. We notice that the bounds converge slower for the weighted monitor.

Safety. The environment transition matrix $P^\star$ is taken from Example 9, the model transition matrix $\hat{P}$ is obtained by attributing 0.1 to each dotted transition, i.e., $\mathbb{P}(s_5 \mid s_6) = \mathbb{P}(s_2 \mid s_6) = 0.1$ and $\mathbb{P}(s_3 \mid s_6) = 0.8$. We use the alignment functions in Example 11, i.e., for all $s \in C := \{s_3, s_5, s_6\}$ we have $\alpha(s) = 1$ and 0.1 otherwise; $\beta(s, s') = 1$ if $c \in C$ and $s' \notin C$, and 0.05 otherwise. In Fig. 3

Table 1. Average number of observations until decision. ⊥ implies $\hat{P}^{\text{ref}}$ is better than $\hat{P}$, ⊤ implies $\hat{P}^{\text{ref}}$ is worse than $\hat{P}$, ? indicates indecision. A smaller number of observations is better, indicating an earlier differentiation of $\hat{P}^{\text{ref}}$ and $\hat{P}$.

Benchmark	Model Predictor	Environment	Expert	Gray Box	Black Box
Brp (16,2)	Additive	70.6 ± 17.17 (⊥)	72.8 ± 8.56 (⊥)	175.2 ± 2.49 (⊤)	236.0 ± 1.41 (⊤)
	Invert	39.0 ± 5.79 (⊥)	40.4 ± 4.16 (⊥)	52.0 ± 2.83 (⊥)	78.0 ± 9.46 (⊥)
Conditional	Additive	1000.0 ± 0.0 (?)	478.6 ± 68.11 (⊤)	113.0 ± 23.45 (⊤)	73.2 ± 17.17 (⊤)
	Invert	28.6 ± 5.81 (⊥)	29.4 ± 5.37 (⊥)	33.4 ± 5.37 (⊥)	40.6 ± 5.81 (⊥)
Crowds (5,5)	Additive	99.4 ± 15.92 (⊥)	100.8 ± 15.01 (⊥)	126.6 ± 15.37 (⊥)	1000.0 ± 0.0 (?)
	Invert	51.6 ± 4.22 (⊥)	51.2 ± 3.63 (⊥)	54.0 ± 4.36 (⊥)	68.0 ± 15.52 (⊥)
Die	Additive	1000.0 ± 0.0 (?)	540.0 ± 61.62 (⊤)	120.2 ± 26.35 (⊤)	63.0 ± 16.23 (⊤)
	Invert	31.0 ± 5.61 (⊥)	31.8 ± 5.17 (⊥)	34.4 ± 5.37 (⊥)	50.0 ± 8.22 (⊥)
Leader (3,5)	Additive	84.8 ± 18.09 (⊥)	94.8 ± 4.15 (⊥)	351.4 ± 3.44 (⊥)	125.0 ± 1.73 (⊤)
	Invert	34.2 ± 4.92 (⊥)	35.8 ± 4.02 (⊥)	40.0 ± 4.47 (⊥)	55.6 ± 10.41 (⊥)
Nand (5,2)	Additive	84.4 ± 9.94 (⊥)	79.8 ± 9.36 (⊥)	130.8 ± 2.59 (⊥)	561.6 ± 10.6 (⊤)
	Invert	42.6 ± 5.13 (⊥)	42.2 ± 4.15 (⊥)	52.0 ± 3.39 (⊥)	76.6 ± 9.45 (⊥)
Quantiles	Additive	1000.0 ± 0.0 (?)	525.6 ± 64.86 (⊤)	128.8 ± 33.57 (⊤)	82.2 ± 20.09 (⊤)
	Invert	40.2 ± 9.31 (⊥)	42.4 ± 9.79 (⊥)	47.8 ± 10.35 (⊥)	61.0 ± 14.88 (⊥)
crowds-4-3	Additive	105.0 ± 17.25 (⊥)	104.6 ± 17.34 (⊥)	168.8 ± 12.54 (⊥)	289.0 ± 18.64 (⊤)
	Invert	46.4 ± 3.65 (⊥)	44.6 ± 4.72 (⊥)	48.4 ± 4.27 (⊥)	63.6 ± 14.66 (⊥)

we observe that the weighted alignment monitor better distinguishes the model from the environment, i.e., the alignment score computed w.r.t. actual environment exits the interval earlier. We notice that the bounds converge slower for the weighted monitor.

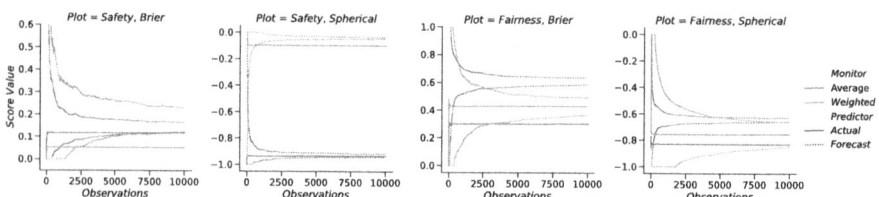

Fig. 3. Example executions of the weighted alignment monitor on Example 8 (Fairness) and 9 (Safety).

Discussion. Both of the above examples demonstrate how weighted alignment monitors enable specification-specific alignment monitoring. In the fairness setting, the model and the actual environment are aligned on the two states relevant for the property value. Hence, considering the specification, the two models should not be distinguished. The weighted alignment monitor demonstrates this behaviour, because it focuses only on the property relevant states, while the general alignment monitor does not. In the safety setting, our system is safe as long as the BSCC in the model remains a BSCC in reality. The weighted alignment monitor emphasises the transitions away from this BSCC, and is therefore more sensitive to safety critical model misalignments

7 Related Work

In this section we consider related work from verification and control, runtime methods, and (machine) learning.

Verification and control. Formal verification traditionally assumes that the model faithfully represents the real system. However, A recent line of work develops verification methods that can provide guarantees, even when the knowledge about the model is imprecise. This includes verification methods for robust MDPs, which are MDPs where the transition function is not known, but lies in an uncertainty set [34]. This class of MDPs includes models such as bounded-parameter MDPs [14] or interval MDPs [15,24]. Robust MDPs can be defined by experts or learned from data allowing sound probably approximately correct verification [4]. Even if learned from data, there is no guarantee that the sampled data is representative of reality–especially if the data is obtained from a simulator. In control theory, the alignment problem is known under model-plant mismatch, with works on quantifying model fidelity [6] and detecting a mismatch between model and reality [5]. In reinforcement learning it is known as the sim-to-real gap, which is concerned with bridging potential differences between reality and simulation [33,35].

Runtime Methods. There is work on monitoring the mismatch between the model and reality [16,22]. Both works address deterministic systems and detect misalignment using temporal logic specifications. In the verification of cyber-physical systems, the misalignment problem is also considered. For example Desai [10] utilise signal temporal logic monitors to detect the violation of assumptions made during the model checking process. In reinforcement learning, approaches such as model-ensembles and runtime model falsification are utilized to overcome the sim-to-real gap at runtime [13,36]. In our work, we are monitoring a hidden quantity, i.e., the expected score from realisations only. Hence, our monitor has to compute its verdict from partial observations. There is ample work on monitoring with imperfect or partial observations [12,25]. In our work the hidden quantity is the expected value of a distribution, which can therefore be inferred using statistical methods. This is similar to a recent line of work focused on monitoring group fairness [18,19].

Learning. A rich body of work addresses the problem of models facing changing data distributions or environments, often termed concept drift. Here they focus monitoring changes in a single distribution, e.g., a machine learning model is trained w.r.t. its training distribution. This distribution may shift over time [11,20]. Formal verification models are usually stateful, with drastic differences in the successor distribution between time steps. This is why techniques from the sequential forecasting literature are more appropriate. In our work, we directly apply the techniques developed by Choe et al. [9] and Howard et al. [23] to build our monitors. Choe et al. [9] uses the confidence sequences developed by Howard et al. [23] to evaluate whether one forecaster outperforms another on average, i.e., our differential alignment monitoring problem. Together with Henzi et al. [17], which develop a statistical test for detecting whether a forecaster outperforms another on every past prediction, they are the first to develop time-uniform statistical guarantees for forecaster evaluation.

Property Dependency. In formal verification, we are primarily interested in whether a system satisfies a given specification. Hence, we should be able to define alignment monitors with respect to a specification. Although weighted alignment monitors can adapt to a given property, this paper lacks a principled method for synthesizing a property-specific monitor. In developing such monitors, the literature on conformance testing may be particularly relevant. In conformance testing, the quality of a white-box model is assessed against a black-box model [32], potentially at runtime using monitors [27]. Model quality is evaluated using qualitative conformance relations [31] or distance measures [1] on their output traces. Most existing work, however, focuses on non-stochastic systems [32]. In a stochastic setting, approaches akin to reward scaling may support the development of property-specific alignment monitors—particularly because, similar to our weighted alignment monitors, reward scaling emphasizes or penalizes behaviors in reinforcement learning to enforce formal specifications, such as safety [30].

8 Conclusion

The guarantees obtained by formal verification rely on the fidelity of the model. If the model is misaligned with reality, those guarantees can no longer be trusted. We introduced alignment monitoring as a runtime technique to assess whether a model used in formal verification remains aligned with the actual system behaviour. Our method leverages scoring rules and confidence sequences to track the predictive capabilities of a model over time. This requires no assumptions on the environment. We extended this with a differential and a weighted alignment monitor. The differential alignment monitor, compares the model against a trusted baseline, and the weighted alignment monitor, allows the flexibility to emphasise critical predictions. We evaluated our monitors on synthetic examples and on the PRISM benchmark suite.

A clear extension is to develop more sophisticated alignment scores. This could include: utilising scoring rules defined over sequences of k prediction in the construction of our average alignment monitor, as suggested in Choe et al. [9]; or the development of alignment scores tailored to formal verification applications. Another line of extension is to enrich the setting by considering alignment monitoring under partial observability.

Acknowledgments. This work is supported by the European Research Council under Grant No.: ERC-2020-AdG 101020093.

Disclosure of Interests. The authors have no competing interests to declare that are relevant to the content of this article.

References

1. Abbas, H., Mittelmann, H., Fainekos, G.: Formal property verification in a conformance testing framework. In: 2014 Twelfth ACM IEEE Conference on Formal Methods and Models for Codesign (MEMOCODE), pp. 155–164 (2014)
2. Allen, S.: Weighted scoringrules: emphasizing particular outcomes when evaluating probabilistic forecasts. J. Stat. Softw. **110**, 1–26 (2024)
3. Allen, S., Ginsbourger, D., Ziegel, J.: Evaluating forecasts for high-impact events using transformed kernel scores. SIAM/ASA J. Uncertain. Quant. **11**(3), 906–940 (2023)
4. Ashok, P., Kwiatkowska, M.: Pac statistical model checking for Markov decision processes and stochastic games. In: TACAS (2019)
5. Badwe, A.S., Gudi, R.D., Patwardhan, R.S., Shah, S.L., Patwardhan, S.C.: Detection of model-plant mismatch in mpc applications. J. Process Control **19**(8), 1305–1313 (2009)
6. Badwe, A.S., Patwardhan, R.S., Shah, S.L., Patwardhan, S.C., Gudi, R.D.: Quantifying the impact of model-plant mismatch on controller performance. J. Process Control **20**(4), 408–425 (2010)
7. Baier, C., Katoen, J.P.: Principles of Model Checking. MIT press, Cambridge (2008)
8. Box, G.E.: Science and statistics. J. Am. Stat. Assoc. **71**(356), 791–799 (1976)
9. Choe, Y.J., Ramdas, A.: Comparing sequential forecasters. Oper. Res. **72**(4), 1368–1387 (2024)
10. Desai, A., Dreossi, T., Seshia, S.A.: Combining model checking and runtime verification for safe robotics. In: Lahiri, S., Reger, G. (eds.) RV 2017. LNCS, vol. 10548, pp. 172–189. Springer, Cham (2017). https://doi.org/10.1007/978-3-319-67531-2_11
11. Ditzler, G., Roveri, M., Alippi, C., Polikar, R.: Learning in nonstationary environments: a survey. IEEE Comput. Intell. Mag. **10**(4), 12–25 (2015)
12. Ferrando, A., Malvone, V.: Runtime verification with imperfect information through indistinguishability relations. In: International Conference on Software Engineering and Formal Methods, pp. 335–351. Springer, Heidelberg (2022). https://doi.org/10.1007/978-3-031-17108-6_21
13. Fulton, N., Platzer, A.: Verifiably safe off-model reinforcement learning. In: Vojnar, T., Zhang, L. (eds.) TACAS 2019. LNCS, vol. 11427, pp. 413–430. Springer, Cham (2019). https://doi.org/10.1007/978-3-030-17462-0_28
14. Given, R., Leach, S., Dean, T.: Bounded-parameter Markov decision processes. Artif. Intell. **122**(1–2), 71–109 (2000)
15. Haddad, S., Monmege, B.: Interval iteration algorithm for MDPS and IMDPS. Theoret. Comput. Sci. **735**, 111–131 (2018)
16. Hallé, S., Soueidi, C., Falcone, Y.: Leveraging runtime verification for the monitoring of digital twins. FMDT@ FM **3507** (2023)

17. Henzi, A., Ziegel, J.F.: Valid sequential inference on probability forecast performance. Biometrika **109**(3), 647–663 (2022)
18. Henzinger, T., Karimi, M., Kueffner, K., Mallik, K.: Runtime monitoring of dynamic fairness properties. In: Proceedings of the 2023 ACM Conference on Fairness, Accountability, and Transparency, pp. 604–614 (2023)
19. Henzinger, T.A., Karimi, M., Kueffner, K., Mallik, K.: Monitoring algorithmic fairness. In: International Conference on Computer Aided Verification, pp. 358–382. Springer, Heidelberg (2023). https://doi.org/10.1007/978-3-031-37703-7_17
20. Hinder, F., Vaquet, V., Hammer, B.: One or two things we know about concept drift–a survey on monitoring evolving environments. arXiv preprint arXiv:2310.15826 (2023)
21. Holzmann, H., Klar, B.: Focusing on regions of interest in forecast evaluation. Ann. Appl. Stat. **11**(4), 2404–2431 (2017). http://www.jstor.org/stable/26362191
22. Hosseinkhani, E., Leucker, M., Sachenbacher, M., Streichhahn, H., Vosteen, L.B.: A model-based approach for monitoring and diagnosing digital twin discrepancies. In: 35th International Conference on Principles of Diagnosis and Resilient Systems (DX 2024), pp. 2-1. Schloss Dagstuhl–Leibniz-Zentrum für Informatik (2024)
23. Howard, S.R., Ramdas, A., McAuliffe, J., Sekhon, J.: Time-uniform, nonparametric, nonasymptotic confidence sequences. Ann. Stat. **49**(2), 1055–1080 (2021)
24. Jonsson, B., Larsen, K.G.: Specification and refinement of probabilistic processes. In: Proceedings 1991 Sixth Annual IEEE Symposium on Logic in Computer Science, pp. 266–267. IEEE Computer Society (1991)
25. Junges, S., Torfah, H., Seshia, S.A.: Runtime monitors for Markov decision processes. In: Silva, A., Leino, K.R.M. (eds.) CAV 2021. LNCS, vol. 12760, pp. 553–576. Springer, Cham (2021). https://doi.org/10.1007/978-3-030-81688-9_26
26. Kwiatkowska, M., Norman, G., Parker, D.: The prism benchmark suite. In: 9th International Conference on Quantitative Evaluation of SysTems, pp. 203–204. IEEE CS press (2012)
27. Mitsch, S., Platzer, A.: Modelplex: verified runtime validation of verified cyber-physical system models. Formal Methods Syst. Des. **49**(1), 33–74 (2016)
28. Pouget, H., Chockler, H., Sun, Y., Kroening, D.: Ranking policy decisions. Adv. Neural. Inf. Process. Syst. **34**, 8702–8713 (2021)
29. Pranger, S., Chockler, H., Tappler, M., Könighofer, B.: Test where decisions matter: importance-driven testing for deep reinforcement learning. In: Conference on Neural Information Processing Systems (NeurIPS) (2024)
30. Qian, M., Mitsch, S.: Reward shaping from hybrid systems models in reinforcement learning. In: NASA formal methods symposium, pp. 122–139. Springer, Heidelberg (2023). https://doi.org/10.1007/978-3-031-33170-1_8
31. Roehm, H., Oehlerking, J., Woehrle, M., Althoff, M.: Reachset conformance testing of hybrid automata. In: Proceedings of the 19th International Conference on Hybrid Systems: Computation and Control, pp. 277–286 (2016)
32. Roehm, H., Oehlerking, J., Woehrle, M., Althoff, M.: Model conformance for cyber-physical systems: a survey. ACM Trans. Cyber-Phys. Syst. **3**(3), 1–26 (2019)
33. Stoffregen, T., et al.: Reducing the sim-to-real gap for event cameras. In: Vedaldi, A., Bischof, H., Brox, T., Frahm, J.-M. (eds.) ECCV 2020. LNCS, vol. 12372, pp. 534–549. Springer, Cham (2020). https://doi.org/10.1007/978-3-030-58583-9_32
34. Suilen, M., Badings, T., Bovy, E.M., Parker, D., Jansen, N.: Robust markov decision processes: a place where ai and formal methods meet. In: Principles of Verification: Cycling the Probabilistic Landscape: Essays Dedicated to Joost-Pieter Katoen on the Occasion of His 60th Birthday, Part III, pp. 126–154. Springer, Heidelberg (2024). https://doi.org/10.1007/978-3-031-75778-5_7

35. Trentsios, P., Wolf, M., Gerhard, D.: Overcoming the sim-to-real gap in autonomous robots. Procedia CIRP **109**, 287–292 (2022)
36. Yamagata, Y., Liu, S., Akazaki, T., Duan, Y., Hao, J.: Falsification of cyber-physical systems using deep reinforcement learning. IEEE Trans. Softw. Eng. **47**(12), 2823–2840 (2020)

Instrumenting Runtime Enforcement

François Hublet[1]($^{\boxtimes}$), David Basin[1], Linda Hu[1], Srđan Krstić[1],
and Lennard Reese[2]

[1] ETH Zürich, Zurich, Switzerland
{francois.hublet,basin,srdan.krstic}@inf.ethz.ch, lindhu@student.ethz.ch
[2] University of Copenhagen, Copenhagen, Denmark
lere@di.ku.dk

Abstract. Runtime enforcement ensures that a running system complies with a property by observing and modifying the system's actions. In practice, the property is often defined in terms of high-level, abstract events, while the system's behavior consists of low-level, concrete actions. The relationship between actions and events is established in the *instrumentation* process, where developers must ensure that (i) system actions report the right events, and (ii) the necessary modifications to the system's behavior are correctly enforced. However, the abstraction gap between a high-level property and low-level actions makes this process error-prone.

In this paper, we refine an existing formal model of runtime enforcement, which leaves instrumentation implicit, into a more precise model that explicitly accounts for instrumentation. We propose a correctness criterion for instrumentation and present a novel library, called INSTR-LIB, that instruments Python applications for runtime enforcement.

Keywords: Runtime Enforcement · Instrumentation · Edit Automata

1 Introduction

In 2022, personal data of roughly one third of Australia's population was stolen from the telecommunication provider Optus [26]. The attack was unsophisticated, involving the attacker exploiting a coding error in the instrumentation of an internet-facing, legacy API. Due to this error, the access control (AC) mechanism, while in place, was not invoked to protect the legacy API, allowing for the easy retrieval of millions of user records.

This data breach highlights a recurring theme: even when appropriate security mechanisms are in place, incorrect instrumentation can allow attackers to bypass the mechanisms entirely. A rigorous approach to instrumentation is especially crucial in applications where the property is a set of desired sequences of abstract events, with each event reflecting many possible concrete system actions. The prominent example of this is when enforcing requirements derived from privacy law [14,16]: if a regulation requires that "no user data is used without prior consent," then being able to ensure that "data usage" is blocked whenever "consent" has not been previously registered is insufficient to certify that an application complies with the law. The developers must also ensure that "data usage" is correctly identified by existing system instrumentation whenever low-level actions such as database reads and writes occur; furthermore, they must check that "consent" is only registered when users actually give consent in the UI.

Runtime enforcement generalizes AC by using execution monitors that observe the actions of a running system and modify these actions to ensure that only compliant behaviors are allowed. While, in recent years, increasingly powerful enforcement approaches and tools have been developed, much less attention has been devoted to the questions of how to properly instrument systems or how to audit existing instrumented systems to ensure correct enforcement.

Figure 1 (top) shows the idealized system model used in most previous work, which we call the *classical* model of runtime enforcement. In this model, the System under Enforcement (SuE) is a labeled transition system (LTS) with each transition labeled by some *event e*. When attempting to take a transition labeled by e (Step ①), the SuE sends the event e to a policy decision point (PDP) in charge of ensuring the SuE's compliance with a property P (Step ②). The PDP edits [21] the event e to a sequence of events e' compliant with P (Step ③). The modification can involve removing, replacing, or inserting events. The events e' are then returned as a command to the SuE (Step ④), which takes the appropriate transitions (Step ⑤). As it assumes that all events are correctly sent to the PDP and that the SuE always follows the PDP's commands, the classical model cannot capture non-compliance due to incorrect instrumentation.

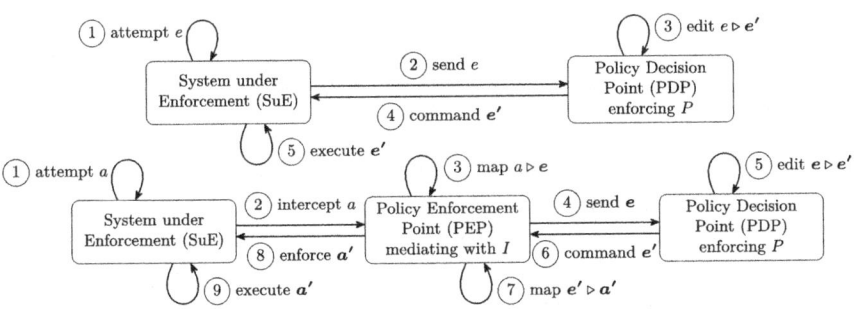

Fig. 1. The classical (top) and extended (bottom) enforcement models

We propose an *extended* model, shown in Fig. 1 (bottom), where the SuE is modeled as an LTS with transitions labeled by *actions* distinct from the events sent to the PDP. In addition to the SuE and PDP, our model introduces an explicit policy enforcement point (PEP) [9] that instruments the actions performed by the SuE, producing events processed by the PDP. Concretely, the PEP intercepts every action a attempted by the system (Step ②) and maps it to a sequence of events e (Step ③). This sequence is sent to the PDP (Step ④), which edits e to some e' (Step ⑤) and returns e' (Step ⑥). The PEP maps

e' back to a sequence of actions a' (Step ⑦) that the PEP enforces in the SuE (Steps ⑧ and ⑨).

In our extended model, the SuE's specification consists of two elements: the property P and a *mediator* I providing the desired interpretation of system actions in terms of PDP events. In the Optus data breach, the property P may have been "whenever a user u performs an API access (APIAccess(u) event), then u is authenticated," while the mediator I mapped both system actions `legacyAPIAccess`(u) and `modernAPIAccess`(u) to the event APIAccess(u). However, the PEP failed to map `legacyAPIAccess`(u) to APIAccess(u). As a result, although the PDP correctly enforced P, the composition of the SuE, PEP, and PDP did not provide the desired security guarantees.

Contributions. After reviewing the classical enforcement model (Sect. 2), we make the following contributions:

- We formally introduce our extended enforcement model and define the notions of PEP correctness that provide necessary and sufficient conditions for correct instrumentation, independent of any specific PDP (Sect. 3).
- We show how these conditions can be relaxed for properties where the occurrence of certain events can be soundly overapproximated (Sect. 4).
- We further specialize our theory to support state-of-the-art PDPs that process events in finite sets ('batches'). We provide a correct PEP algorithm for this setup and give auditing check-lists for ensuring compliance (Sect. 5).
- We implement our PEP algorithm in INSTRLIB, an open-source library for enforcing properties of Python applications using the state-of-the-art ENFGUARD [17] tool as the PDP. We illustrate our framework in a case study, enforcing privacy requirements in a micro-blogging application using INSTRLIB and then auditing our instrumentation's correctness (Sect. 6).

Related Work. Models of runtime enforcement mechanisms include security automata [11,27], edit automata [21], mandatory results automata (MRA) [22], and timed automata [3,24]. More recently, several frameworks for enforcing expressive first-order properties at runtime have also been developed [13,17,18]. Runtime enforcement can be performed both on high-level events and low-level system actions, e.g., through inlining [10]. Most models only consider the PDP's logic, without any guarantees of correct instrumentation. MRAs distinguish between system *actions* and enforced *results* and may fulfill the role of both a PDP and PEP, but do not provide for a clear separation between instrumentation and property enforcement. In contrast, several works from the security community discuss the composition of a PDP and PEP in the context of runtime enforcement without formally or precisely describing this composition [4,14,15,25]. Our account of the 'classical model' builds on work by Aceto et al. [1] and Falcone et al. [7,12], where an SuE modeled as an LTS and the PDP run in lockstep.

2 Preliminaries

After introducing notation, we review labeled transition systems and edit automata (Sect. 2.1). We then introduce the 'classical' enforcement model and its associated notions of PDP soundness and transparency (Sect. 2.2).

Notation. Given a set A, the set of all finite sequences of elements of A is denoted by A^*. We use Greek letters (e.g., α, σ, ρ, ...) or bold Latin letters (e.g., $\boldsymbol{a}$, $\boldsymbol{e}$, $\boldsymbol{\ell}$, ...) to denote sequences; bold Greek letters denote sequences of sequences. We denote the empty sequence as ε and finite sequences as $\langle a_1, a_2, \ldots, a_n \rangle$. The sequence $\sigma \setminus a$ stands for σ with all occurrences of a removed, $\sigma_{..i}$ for the prefix of σ of length i, and $\mathsf{pre}(\sigma)$ for the set of all prefixes of σ. Given $\sigma, \sigma' \in A^*$, the sequence $\sigma \cdot \sigma'$ is the concatenation of σ and σ'. Given a sequence of sequences $\boldsymbol{\sigma} = \langle \sigma_1, \ldots, \sigma_n \rangle \in (A^*)^*$, we denote by $\circ\boldsymbol{\sigma} \triangleq \sigma_1 \cdot \sigma_2 \cdot \ldots \cdot \sigma_n$ the concatenation of the σ_i.

For any set of labels $\mathcal{L}$, the set of *traces* over $\mathcal{L}$ is $\mathbb{T}_\mathcal{L} \triangleq \mathcal{L}^*$. A *property* $P_\mathcal{L}$ over $\mathcal{L}$ is a set of traces, i.e., a subset $P_\mathcal{L} \subseteq \mathbb{T}_\mathcal{L}$. To support *internal* (or 'silent') system actions, we use a distinguished label $\tau \notin \mathcal{L}$ and denote $\mathcal{L}_\tau \triangleq \mathcal{L} \cup \{\tau\}$.

2.1 Labeled Transition Systems and Edit Automata

As in previous work [1,2,6], we model systems as labeled transition systems:

Definition 1 (LTS). *A labeled transition system (LTS) over $\mathcal{L}$ is a quadruple $\mathcal{S} = (\mathbb{S}, \mathcal{L}, s^0, \rightarrow)$ such that $\mathbb{S}$ is a set of states, $\mathcal{L}$ is a set of labels, $s^0 \in \mathbb{S}$ is an initial state, and $\rightarrow \subseteq \mathbb{S} \times \mathcal{L}_\tau \times \mathbb{S}$ is a transition relation labeled by $\mathcal{L}_\tau$.*

We write $s \xrightarrow{\ell} s'$ for $(s, \ell, s') \in \rightarrow$. An LTS execution is of the form $s^0 \xrightarrow{\ell_1} s^1 \xrightarrow{\ell_2} \ldots \xrightarrow{\ell_n} s^n$ and the trace of such an execution is $\sigma = \langle \ell_1, \ell_2, \ldots \rangle \setminus \tau$, removing all internal τ actions. In this case, we also write $s^0 \xrightarrow{\sigma} s^n$.

Example 1. Figure 2 represents a social network application as an LTS over two different sets of labels, $\mathcal{E}$ ('events', left) and $\mathcal{A}$ ('actions', right) capturing the system's behavior at two levels of abstraction. For simplicity, we model the system for a single user. At a high level (events), the system can be described in terms of user interaction (give Consent for data usage, Revoke consent, Request data deletion), backend operations (Use/Delete user data), and clock ticks (Tick). At a lower level (actions), one can observe UI interactions (click_yes, click_no in a consent banner, clicks on a request button), database (read, write, delete) or authentication (Login, Logout) operations, and clock ticks (tick).

Edit automata (EA) [21] are a general model for PDPs, providing an abstract model for a large class of practical enforcement mechanisms. Edit automata are a special kind of LTS which, in each step, read a label ℓ^1 from some set of labels $\mathcal{L}^1$ and edit it deterministically into a possibly empty sequence of labels $\boldsymbol{\ell_2}$ from another set $\mathcal{L}^2$. If no $\boldsymbol{\ell_2}$ exists for a given ℓ_1, the execution of the LTS is terminated, similar to execution cutting in security automata [27].

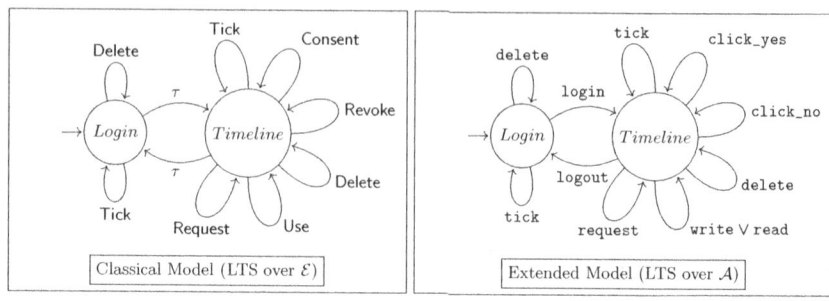

Fig. 2. Systems under Enforcement (SuE) in the Classical and Extended Model

Definition 2 (Edit Automaton). *An edit automaton (EA) over $(\mathcal{L}^1, \mathcal{L}^2)$ is an LTS $\delta = (\mathbb{S}_\delta, \mathcal{L}^1 \times \mathcal{L}^{2*}_\tau, s^0_\delta, \xrightarrow{\cdot \triangleright \cdot}_\delta)$ with a transition relation labeled with pairs of labels $(\ell_1, \boldsymbol{\ell_2}) \in \mathcal{L}^1 \times \mathcal{L}^{2*}_\tau$, also denoted as $\ell_1 \triangleright \boldsymbol{\ell_2}$, such that, for any $s_\delta \in \mathbb{S}_\delta$ and $\ell_1 \in \mathcal{L}^1$, there exists at most one pair $(s'_\delta, \boldsymbol{\ell_2}) \in \mathbb{S}_\delta \times \mathcal{L}^{2*}_\tau$ such that $s_\delta \xrightarrow{\ell_1 \triangleright \boldsymbol{\ell_2}} s'_\delta$.*

An edit automaton is input-enabled [23] iff for any ℓ^1, the automaton can always edit ℓ^1 to some $\boldsymbol{\ell_2}$. Written more formally:

Definition 3. *An edit automaton δ over $(\mathcal{L}^1, \mathcal{L}^2)$ is input-enabled iff for any $s_\delta \in \mathbb{S}_\delta$ and $\ell_1 \in \mathcal{L}^1$, there exists $s'_\delta \in \mathbb{S}_\delta$ and $\boldsymbol{\ell_2} \in \mathcal{L}^{2*}_\tau$ such that $s_\delta \xrightarrow{\ell_1 \triangleright \boldsymbol{\ell_2}} s'_\delta$.*

Note that there are two interpretations of an EA: the EA accepts a language of traces over pairs containing a label (from $\mathcal{L}^1$) and a sequence of labels (from $\mathcal{L}^{2*}_\tau$). Alternatively, it is a transducer, translating a sequence of labels from $\mathcal{L}^1$ into a sequence of labels from $\mathcal{L}^2$ by concatenating the $\boldsymbol{\ell_2}$. For $n \in \mathbb{N}$, $\xi = (x_i)_{1 \leq i < n}$, and $\upsilon = (y_i)_{1 \leq i < n}$, we denote by $\xi \triangleright \upsilon$ the zipped sequence $(x_i \triangleright y_i)_{1 \leq i < n}$. For any EA δ, we abuse notation and write δ as a partial function such that $\delta(\sigma) = \circ \boldsymbol{\sigma'} \iff \exists s'_\delta. s^0_\delta \xrightarrow{\sigma \triangleright \boldsymbol{\sigma'}} s'_\delta$, reflecting the view of δ as a trace transducer.

2.2 The Classical Model of Runtime Enforcement

In the classical enforcement model [1,6,21], an SuE (LTS) and a PDP (edit automaton) over the same set of labels are composed, progressing in lock-step. This can be formalized as follows in terms of LTS composition:

Definition 4. *An LTS $\mathcal{S}$ over $\mathcal{L}$ and an edit automaton δ over $(\mathcal{L}, \mathcal{L})$ serving as a PDP can be composed into an LTS $\langle \mathcal{S} | \delta \rangle = (\mathbb{S}_{\langle \mathcal{S} | \delta \rangle}, \mathcal{L}, s^0_{\langle \mathcal{S} | \delta \rangle}, \rightarrow_{\langle \mathcal{S} | \delta \rangle})$ by*

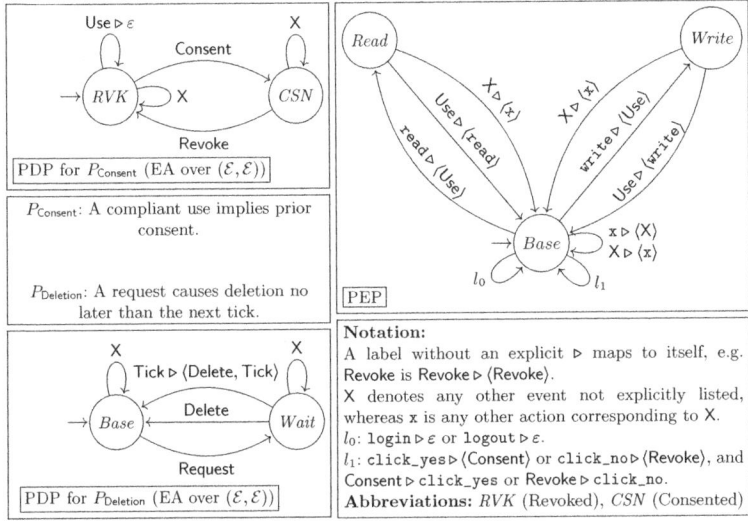

Fig. 3. Policy Decision Points (PDPs) and Policy Enforcement Point (PEP)

$$\mathbb{S}_{\langle S|\delta\rangle} \triangleq \mathbb{S}_S \times \mathbb{S}_\delta \times \mathcal{L}^* \qquad s^0_{\langle S|\delta\rangle} \triangleq (s^0_S, s^0_\delta, \varepsilon)$$

$$\dfrac{s_S \xrightarrow{\tau} s'_S}{(s_S, s_\delta, b) \xrightarrow{\tau}_{\langle S|\delta\rangle} (s'_S, s_\delta, b)}\, step_\tau \qquad \dfrac{s_S \xrightarrow{\ell' \neq \tau} s''_S \quad s_\delta \xrightarrow{\ell' \triangleright \varepsilon}_\delta s'_\delta}{(s_S, s_\delta, \varepsilon) \xrightarrow{\tau}_{\langle S|\delta\rangle} (s_S, s'_\delta, \varepsilon)}\, step_0$$

$$\dfrac{s_S \xrightarrow{\ell' \neq \tau} s''_S \quad s_\delta \xrightarrow{\ell' \triangleright (\langle\ell\rangle \cdot \boldsymbol{\ell})}_\delta s'_\delta \quad s_S \xrightarrow{\ell} s'_S}{(s_S, s_\delta, \varepsilon) \xrightarrow{\ell}_{\langle S|\delta\rangle} (s'_S, s'_\delta, \boldsymbol{\ell})}\, step_+ \qquad \dfrac{s_S \xrightarrow{\ell} s'_S}{(s_S, s_\delta, \langle\ell\rangle \cdot \boldsymbol{\ell}) \xrightarrow{\ell}_{\langle S|\delta\rangle} (s'_S, s_\delta, \boldsymbol{\ell})}\, buf$$

The states of the *enforced LTS* $\langle S|\delta\rangle$ have three components: the state of S, the state of δ, and a buffer in $\mathcal{L}^*$ used to temporarily store the sequences of labels returned by the PDP δ until corresponding transitions are taken by the system. The enforced LTS has four kinds of transitions:

- $step_\tau$ transitions mirror internal transitions in $\langle S|\delta\rangle$ without δ's intervention;
- $step_0$ transitions are triggered by the EA erasing the original label ℓ' of a transition of S, i.e., editing it to ε. In this case, the substate of $\langle S|\delta\rangle$ corresponding to the state of S does not change;
- $step_+$ transitions are triggered by the EA editing the original label ℓ' of a transition of S to a non-empty sequence of labels $\langle\ell\rangle \cdot \boldsymbol{\ell}$. In this case, a first transition labeled by ℓ is performed immediately in S, while $\boldsymbol{\ell}$ is buffered;
- *buf* transitions are performed while the buffer of the enforced LTS is not empty ($step_0$ and $step_+$ are disallowed in this case), performing one transition labeled with the first label in the buffer and removing it from the buffer.

This model allows PDPs to interrupt system execution: when the system can take a step $s_S \xrightarrow{\ell'} s'_S$ but there is no ℓ such that $s_\delta \xrightarrow{\ell' \triangleright \ell} s'_\delta$, the execution is blocked.

Example 2. We compose the SuE over $\mathcal{E}$ in Fig. 2 with the PDPs P_{Consent} and P_{Deletion} in Fig. 3. Consider our LTS on $\mathcal{E}$ in state *Timeline* (i.e., user is logged in) running together the PDP P_{Consent} in state RVK (i.e., user consent was revoked or never given). If the SuE attempts Use, the PDP receives Use in RVK and suppresses it by taking the step $RVK \xrightarrow{\text{Use} \triangleright \varepsilon} RVK$; by rule $step_0$, the state of the enforced LTS is left unchanged. Now, compose our LTS on $\mathcal{E}$ in the state *Timeline* with the PDP P_{Delete}. Assume that the LTS just executed Request, which put the PDP in state *Wait*. If the SuE attempts tick, the PDP takes a step $Wait \xrightarrow{\text{Tick} \triangleright \langle \text{Delete}, \text{Tick} \rangle}_\delta Base$, inserting Delete; the SuE executes $Timeline \xrightarrow{\text{Delete}} Timeline$ and buffers $\langle \text{Tick} \rangle$ by rule $step_+$; finally, since the buffer is not empty, the SuE takes a transition $Timeline \xrightarrow{\text{Tick}} Timeline$ by rule buf.

A PDP's correctness is expressed in terms of two well-known notions [21]: *soundness* and *transparency*. Soundness with respect to some property P states that any trace edited by the PDP is in P; transparency states that traces that already adhere to P are not modified by the PDP.

Definition 5 (Soundness). *An edit automaton δ over $(\mathcal{L}, \mathcal{L})$ is sound with respect to a property $P \subseteq \mathbb{T}_\mathcal{L}$ iff for any $\sigma \in \mathbb{T}_\mathcal{L}$, $\delta(\sigma) \subseteq P$.*

Definition 6 (Transparency). *An edit automaton δ over $(\mathcal{L}, \mathcal{L})$ is transparent with respect to a property $P \subseteq \mathbb{T}_\mathcal{L}$ iff for any $\sigma \in P$, $\delta(\sigma) = \sigma$.*

Next, we define the following variant of soundness: we say a PDP is *prefix-sound* if all prefixes of a trace edited by that PDP are in P. Prefix-soundness is stronger than standard soundness.

Definition 7 (Prefix-Soundness). *An edit automaton δ over $(\mathcal{L}, \mathcal{L})$ is prefix-sound with respect to $P \subseteq \mathbb{T}_\mathcal{L}$ iff for any $\sigma \in \mathbb{T}_\mathcal{L}$, $\mathsf{pre}(\delta(\sigma)) \subseteq P$.*

Runtime enforcement aims to ensure the compliance of the enforced LTS with some P. Another common requirement is that, if an execution of the original LTS already fulfills P, then this execution is not altered by the enforcement mechanism. The corresponding properties of the *enforced system* are as follows:

Definition 8 (Compliance). *An LTS $\mathcal{S} = (\mathbb{S}, \mathcal{L}, s^0, \rightarrow)$ complies with the property P iff for any execution $s^0 \xrightarrow{\sigma} s$, we have $\sigma \in P_\mathcal{L}$.*

Definition 9 (Preservation). *An LTS $\mathcal{S} = (\mathbb{S}, \mathcal{L}, s^0, \rightarrow)$ preserves the property $P_\mathcal{L}$ with respect to an LTS $\mathcal{S}_\star = (\mathbb{S}_\star, \mathcal{L}, s^0_\star, \rightarrow_\star)$ iff for any execution $s^0_\star \xrightarrow{\sigma}_\star s_\star$ of $\mathcal{S}_\star$ such that $\sigma \in P_\mathcal{L}$, we have an execution $s^0 \xrightarrow{\sigma} s$ of $\mathcal{S}$.*

The following theorems provide sufficient conditions for compliance and preservation. The first theorem shows that if a PDP δ is prefix-sound with respect to P, then any enforced system $\langle \mathcal{S}|\delta\rangle$ complies with P. The second theorem shows that if a PDP δ is transparent with respect to $\mathsf{pre}(P)$, then any enforced system $\langle \mathcal{S}|\delta\rangle$ preserves P with respect to $\mathcal{S}$. These theorems confirm that PDP soundness and transparency are useful properties as they guarantee that any system composed with a PDP complies to its specification. The first condition is necessary and sufficient. The second condition is sufficient, but not necessary.

Theorem 1. *The edit automaton δ is prefix-sound with respect to property P iff for any LTS $\mathcal{S}$, the LTS $\langle \mathcal{S}|\delta\rangle$ complies with P.*

Theorem 2. *Let $P \subseteq \mathbb{T}_\mathcal{L}$. If an automaton δ is transparent with respect to $\mathsf{pre}(P)$, then for any LTS $\mathcal{S}$, the LTS $\langle \mathcal{S}|\delta\rangle$ preserves P with respect to $\mathcal{S}$.*

As a corollary of Theorem 1, there exist sound (but not *prefix-sound*) edit automata that fail to ensure compliance when composed with certain systems. Such failures occur when an automaton inserts labels to restore compliance with P, but in doing so, creates intermediate trace prefixes that are not in P.

For example, let $\mathcal{L} = \{a, b\}$ and $P = \{\langle a, b\rangle\}$. Consider an edit automaton δ that (1) replaces the first symbol of any trace with $\langle a, b\rangle$, and then (2) blocks further execution. This automaton is sound with respect to P. When composed with a system, δ forces the system to execute a followed by b. However, after the first step, the system produces the intermediate trace $\langle a\rangle$, which is not in P. Thus, the enforced LTS does not comply with P.

Similarly, there exist edit automata that are transparent with respect to P (but not with respect to $\mathsf{pre}(P)$) and fail to ensure preservation. Using the same $\mathcal{L}$ and P, consider an edit automaton δ such that $\delta(\langle a\rangle) = \varepsilon$, $\delta(\langle b\rangle) = \varepsilon$, and $\delta(\langle a, b\rangle) = \langle a, b\rangle$. This automaton is transparent with respect to P. However, when composed with a system that has only two transitions $s_0 \xrightarrow{a} s_1 \xrightarrow{b} s_2$, this edit automaton prevents the generation of $\langle a, b\rangle$ by the enforced LTS, as it suppresses any initial a and thus prevents the LTS from reaching s_1.

To see why Theorem 2 is not an equivalence, consider the property $P = \{\varepsilon, \langle a\rangle, \langle a, a\rangle, \langle a, a, a\rangle, \ldots\}$ and a PDP δ with a single state s_δ^0 and transitions $s_\delta^0 \xrightarrow{\ell \triangleright \langle a, a\rangle} s_\delta^0$ for all ℓ. Since δ only ever inserts more a's, any trace $\sigma = \langle a, a, \ldots\rangle \in P$ of a system $\mathcal{S}$ is also a trace of $\langle \mathcal{S}|\delta\rangle$. However, δ is not transparent since, for example, $\delta(\langle a\rangle) = \langle a, a\rangle \neq \langle a\rangle$.

We conclude this discussion by noting that for prefix-closed properties, i.e., properties P such that $\mathsf{pre}(P) = P$, Theorems 1 and 2 can be expressed in terms of standard soundness and transparency with respect to P.

3 The Extended Enforcement Model

We now extend the classical model just presented to a model that explicitly distinguishes between low-level system actions and high-level PDP events. To this end, we first define a formal notion of a PEP that mediates between these two levels and introduce new notions of PEP soundness and transparency (Sect. 3.1); then, we describe the three-way composition of an SuE, PEP, and PDP and provide analogues of Theorems 1 and 2 in this extended setting (Sect. 3.2).

3.1 Formal Model of the Policy Enforcement Point (PEP)

Let $\mathcal{A}$ be a set of actions and $\mathcal{E}$ a set of events. A PEP η is a pair of edit automata, the *instrumentor* η_i and the *enforcer* η_e, that perform Steps ③ and ⑦ in Fig. 1 (bottom). The *instrumentor* η_i maps actions to sequences of events, while the *enforcer* η_e maps events back to sequences of actions. For the PEP to serve as a transducer between traces of actions and traces of events as they occur in the system, (i) the PEP's state after Step ⑥ may depend on the edited events it received in Step ⑤, but not on the attempted actions it had mapped in Step ①. Moreover, (ii) if the sequence of edited actions at the end of Step ⑥ is empty, the PEP's state must remain the same as before Step ①. Formally:

Definition 10. *A PEP over* $(\mathcal{A}, \mathcal{E})$ *is a pair* $\eta = (\eta_i, \eta_e)$, *where* $\eta_i = (\mathbb{S}_\eta, \mathcal{A} \times \mathcal{E}_\tau^*, s_\eta^0, \xrightarrow{\triangleright}_{\eta,i})$ *is an edit automaton over* $(\mathcal{A}, \mathcal{E})$ *and* $\eta_e = (\mathbb{S}_\eta, \mathcal{E} \times \mathcal{A}_\tau^*, s_\eta^0, \xrightarrow{\triangleright}_{\eta,e})$ *is an edit automaton over* $(\mathcal{E}, \mathcal{A})$, *with the same state space, such that for any*

$$s_\eta^1 \xrightarrow{a_1' \triangleright e_1'}_{\eta,i} s_\eta^{2,1} \xrightarrow{e_1 \triangleright \alpha_1}_{\eta,e} s_\eta^{3,1} \qquad s_\eta^1 \xrightarrow{a_2' \triangleright e_2'}_{\eta,i} s_\eta^{2,2} \xrightarrow{e_2 \triangleright \alpha_2}_{\eta,e} s_\eta^{3,2},$$

with $\circ \alpha_1 = \circ \alpha_2$, *then (i)* $s_\eta^{3,1} = s_\eta^{3,2}$, *and (ii) if* $\circ \alpha_1 = \varepsilon$, *then* $s_\eta^{3,1} = s_\eta^1$.

Definition 11. *A PEP* η *is input-enabled iff both* η_i *and* η_e *are input-enabled.*

For each sequence of alternating η_i and η_e transitions $s_\eta^0 \xrightarrow{a_1' \triangleright e_1'}_{\eta,i} s_\eta^1 \xrightarrow{\sigma_1 \triangleright \rho_1}_{\eta,e} s_\eta'^1 \xrightarrow{a_2' \triangleright e_2'}_{\eta,i} s_\eta^2 \xrightarrow{\sigma_2 \triangleright \rho_2}_{\eta,e} \cdots \to s_\eta'^n$, we denote by $s_\eta^0 \xrightarrow{\sigma \triangleright \rho_1 \cdots \rho_n}_\eta s_\eta^n$ the sequence of transitions generating the action trace $\circ(\rho_1 \cdot \ldots \cdot \rho_n)$ and the event trace $\circ \sigma$.

Example 3. The PEP in Fig. 3 mediates between $\mathcal{A}$ and $\mathcal{E}$, mapping the intercepted SuE actions into sequences of PDP events and the events edited by the PDP back into SuE actions. Note that (1) the PEP maps `login` and `logout`, which are irrelevant for enforcement, to ε; (2) the instrumentor non-injectively maps `read` and `write` to Use, going into state *Read* or *Write*, which allows the enforcer to transparently generate the original action if the PDP does not modify it.

3.2 A More Realistic Enforcement Model

Having formalized the PEP, we now compose it with an LTS and PDP:

Definition 12. *An LTS $\mathcal{S}$ over $\mathcal{A}$, a PEP η over $(\mathcal{A}, \mathcal{E})$, and a PDP δ over $\mathcal{E}$ can be composed into an LTS $\langle \mathcal{S}|\eta|\delta \rangle = (\mathbb{S}_{\langle \mathcal{S}|\eta|\delta \rangle}, \mathcal{L}, s^0_{\langle \mathcal{S}|\eta|\delta \rangle}, \rightarrow_{\langle \mathcal{S}|\eta|\delta \rangle})$ by*

$$\mathbb{S}_{\langle \mathcal{S}|\eta|\delta \rangle} \triangleq \mathbb{S}_\mathcal{S} \times \mathbb{S}_\eta \times \mathbb{S}_\delta \times \mathcal{L}^* \qquad s^0_{\langle \mathcal{S}|\eta|\delta \rangle} \triangleq (s^0_\mathcal{S}, s^0_\eta, s^0_\delta, \varepsilon)$$

$$\frac{s_\mathcal{S} \xrightarrow{\tau} s'_\mathcal{S}}{(s_\mathcal{S}, s_\eta, s_\delta, b) \xrightarrow{\tau}_{\langle \mathcal{S}|\eta|\delta \rangle} (s'_\mathcal{S}, s_\eta, s_\delta, b)} \; step_\tau \qquad \frac{s_\mathcal{S} \xrightarrow{a' \neq \tau} s''_\mathcal{S} \quad s_\eta \xrightarrow{a' \triangleright e'}_{\eta, i} s''_\eta \quad s_\delta \xrightarrow{e' \backslash \tau \triangleright \varepsilon}_\delta s'_\delta \quad s''_\eta \xrightarrow{e \backslash \tau \triangleright \varepsilon}_{\eta, e} s'_\eta \quad e' \backslash \tau \neq \varepsilon}{(s_\mathcal{S}, s_\eta, s_\delta, \varepsilon) \xrightarrow{\tau}_{\langle \mathcal{S}|\eta|\delta \rangle} (s_\mathcal{S}, s'_\eta, s'_\delta, \varepsilon)} \; step_0$$

$$\frac{s_\mathcal{S} \xrightarrow{a' \neq \tau} s''_\mathcal{S} \quad s_\eta \xrightarrow{a' \triangleright e'}_{\eta, i} s''_\eta \quad s_\delta \xrightarrow{e' \backslash \tau \triangleright e}_\delta s'_\delta \quad s''_\eta \xrightarrow{e \backslash \tau \triangleright (\langle a \rangle \cdot a)}_{\eta, e} s'_\eta \quad s_\mathcal{S} \xrightarrow{a} s'_\mathcal{S} \quad e' \backslash \tau \neq \varepsilon}{(s_\mathcal{S}, s_\eta, s_\delta, \varepsilon) \xrightarrow{a}_{\langle \mathcal{S}|\eta|\delta \rangle} (s'_\mathcal{S}, s'_\eta, s'_\delta, a)} \; step_+ \qquad \frac{s_\mathcal{S} \xrightarrow{a' \neq \tau} s'_\mathcal{S} \quad s_\eta \xrightarrow{a' \triangleright e'}_{\eta, i} s'_\eta \quad e' \backslash \tau = \varepsilon}{(s_\mathcal{S}, s_\eta, s_\delta, \varepsilon) \xrightarrow{\tau}_{\langle \mathcal{S}|\eta|\delta \rangle} (s'_\mathcal{S}, s_\eta, s_\delta, \varepsilon)} \; step_\varepsilon$$

$$\frac{s_\mathcal{S} \xrightarrow{a} s'_\mathcal{S}}{(s_\mathcal{S}, s_\eta, s_\delta, \langle a \rangle \cdot a) \xrightarrow{a}_{\langle \mathcal{S}|\eta|\delta \rangle} (s'_\mathcal{S}, s_\eta, s_\delta, a)} \; buf$$

The states of the enforced LTS $\langle \mathcal{S}|\eta|\delta \rangle$ have four components, and now also include the state of the PEP η. Rules $step_\tau$ and buf are similar to before, while $step_0$ and $step_+$ incorporate the mediation through η_i and η_e. We add a fifth rule $step_\varepsilon$ that covers the case where the instrumentor generates an empty sequence of events in response to an action, leading the enforced system to take the attempted transition without any intervention from δ.

Example 4. We compose our LTS on $\mathcal{A}$ with the PDP P_{Delete} and the PEP in Fig. 3. Assume that the SuE is in state *Timeline* and just executed a transition labeled by `request`, putting the PDP in state *Wait*. The PEP is in state *Base*. If the SuE attempts `tick`, the PEP takes a step *Base* $\xrightarrow{\texttt{tick} \triangleright \langle \text{Tick} \rangle}_{\eta, i}$ *Base*; the PDP takes a step *Wait* $\xrightarrow{\text{Tick} \triangleright \langle \text{Delete}, \text{Tick} \rangle}_\delta$ *Base*, inserting `delete`; the PEP takes steps *Base* $\xrightarrow{\text{Delete} \triangleright \texttt{delete}}_{\eta, e}$ *Base* $\xrightarrow{\text{Tick} \triangleright \texttt{tick}}_{\eta, e}$ *Base*; the SuE executes *Timeline* $\xrightarrow{\texttt{delete}}$ *Timeline* and buffers $\langle \texttt{tick} \rangle$ by rule $step_+$; since the buffer is non-empty, the SuE takes a transition *Timeline* $\xrightarrow{\texttt{tick}}$ *Timeline* by rule buf.

Now, we compose our LTS with the PDP P_{Consent} and the PEP as above, with the PDP in state *RVK*. If, in state *Timeline*, the SuE attempts `write`, then the PEP maps *Base* $\xrightarrow{\texttt{write} \triangleright \text{Use}}$ *Write*; the PDP receives `use` without prior consent and suppresses it, taking a step *RVK* $\xrightarrow{\text{Use} \triangleright \varepsilon}$ *RVK*; consequently, according to the rule $step_0$, the SuE does not take any transition.

The PEP mediates between traces of system actions and traces of PDP events. Hence, its correctness can only be assessed with regard to a mapping between these two sets of traces, which is part of the system's specification. We call such a mapping a *trace mediator*. We require trace mediators to be monotonic with respect to the prefix relation $\sigma' \in \text{pre}(\sigma)$.

Definition 13. *A* trace mediator *is a function* $I : \mathcal{A}^* \to \mathcal{E}^*$ *such that* $\forall \rho, \rho' \in \mathcal{A}^*$. $\rho \in \mathsf{pre}(\rho') \implies I(\rho) \in \mathsf{pre}(I(\rho'))$.

In practice, this is usually desirable, since otherwise I could arbitrarily map extensions of a given action trace to shorter or incomparable event traces.

We adopt the following definition of soundness. We later show that this definition ensures compliance of the three-way composition:

Definition 14. *A PEP* η *over* $(\mathcal{A}, \mathcal{E})$ *is* sound *with respect to a trace mediator* $I : \mathcal{A}^* \to \mathcal{E}^*$ *iff whenever* $s_\eta^0 \xrightarrow{\sigma \triangleright \rho} s_\eta'$, *then* $I(\circ \rho) \in \mathsf{pre}(\circ \sigma)$.

Note that the above definition only requires the action trace $I(\circ \rho)$ to be a prefix of the event trace $\circ \sigma$, rather than equal to it. Intuitively, we observe that, if the mapped action trace $I(\rho)$ is always a prefix of the event trace σ, then the fact that $\mathsf{pre}(\sigma) \subseteq P$ guarantees $I(\rho) \in P$.

Similarly, for transparency, we require that the instrumentor maps the action trace to a prefix of its image by I and that, whenever the edit automaton serving as a PDP does not modify the sequence of events in Step ④, the enforcer returns the same action that was originally passed to the instrumentor.

Definition 15. *A PEP* η *is* transparent *with respect to a trace mediator* I *iff it is input-enabled and, whenever* $s_\eta^0 \xrightarrow{\sigma \triangleright \rho} s_\eta' \xrightarrow{a' \triangleright e'}_{\eta, i} s_\eta'' \xrightarrow{e \triangleright \alpha}_{\eta, e} s_\eta'''$, *then* $\circ \sigma \cdot e' \in \mathsf{pre}(I(\circ \rho \cdot a'))$ *and* $e' = e \implies \circ \alpha = \langle a' \rangle$.

The following theorems provide analogues for the correctness results in Theorems 1–2 for our three-way composition. They show that an edit automaton δ is prefix-sound with respect to P if and only if its composition with a sound PEP η with respect to a trace mediator I and an arbitrary LTS complies with $I^{-1}(P)$, and, similarly, that an edit automaton δ that is transparent with respect to $\mathsf{pre}(P)$ guarantees that such an enforced system preserves $I^{-1}(P)$.

Theorem 3. *An edit automaton* δ *over* $\mathcal{E}$ *is prefix-sound with respect to* P *iff for any PEP* η *over* $(\mathcal{A}, \mathcal{E})$ *that is sound with respect to* I *and LTS* $\mathcal{S}$ *over* $\mathcal{A}$, *the LTS* $\langle \mathcal{S} | \eta | \delta \rangle$ *complies with* $I^{-1}(P) \triangleq \{\rho \in \mathcal{A}^* \mid I(\rho) \in P\}$.

Theorem 4. *For any edit automaton* δ *over* $\mathcal{E}$ *that is transparent with respect to* $\mathsf{pre}(P)$, *for any PEP* η *over* $(\mathcal{A}, \mathcal{E})$ *that is transparent with respect to* I, *and for any LTS* $\mathcal{S}$ *over* $\mathcal{A}$, *the LTS* $\langle \mathcal{S} | \eta | \delta \rangle$ *preserves* $I^{-1}(P)$ *with respect to* $\mathcal{S}$.

Note that Theorems 3–4 do not show that our definition of PEP soundness is 'minimal.' Under Theorem 3, there could in theory exist *weaker* notions of PEP soundness that would still ensure that any three-way composition is sound with respect to the PDP's property and PEP's trace mediator. Similarly, there could exist weaker notions of PEP transparency that still guarantee preservation. The following theorems show that such weaker definitions cannot exist:

Theorem 5. *Assume that* $|\mathcal{E}| \geq 2$. *A PEP* η *over* $(\mathcal{A}, \mathcal{E})$ *is sound with respect to* I *iff for any property* P, *for any edit automaton* δ *over* $\mathcal{E}$ *prefix-sound with respect to* P, *and for any LTS* $\mathcal{S}$ *over* $\mathcal{A}$, *the LTS* $\langle \mathcal{S} | \eta | \delta \rangle$ *complies with* $I^{-1}(P)$.

Theorem 6. *Assume that $|\mathcal{A}| \geq 2$. A PEP η over $(\mathcal{A}, \mathcal{E})$ is transparent with respect to I iff for any property P, for any edit automaton δ transparent with respect to $\mathsf{pre}(P)$, and for any LTS $\mathcal{S}$, the LTS $\langle \mathcal{S}|\eta|\delta\rangle$ preserves $I^{-1}(P)$ with respect to $\mathcal{S}$.*

4 Enforcement of Downward-Closed Properties

In the previous section, we have described how using a PEP that is sound with respect to a trace mediator I and a prefix-sound PDP for P ensures system compliance with $I^{-1}(P)$. In practice, however, PEPs that are not generally sound can still ensure compliance with more restricted classes of properties. For example, for property P_{Consent} above, a PEP preventing *too many* read actions can still guarantee compliance. In this case, what allows compliant behavior despite an unsound PEP is that P_{Consent} is *downward-closed* with respect to the relation $\preceq_{\mathsf{Use}-}$ such that $\sigma \preceq_{\mathsf{Use}-} \sigma'$ iff σ is obtained from σ' by removing Use events.

An "overapproximating" PEP such as the above has at several potential advantages: it may induce less runtime overhead because it produces fewer events; its implementation might be easier to audit for soundness as some checks (e.g., checking that the PEP does not prevent too many read actions) may become unnecessary. Next, we study this overapproximation by considering all properties $P \subseteq \mathcal{E}^*$ that are downward-closed with respect to some fixed relation $\preceq$ on $\mathcal{E}^*$:

Definition 16 (Downward Closure). *Let $\preceq \subseteq \mathcal{E}^* \times \mathcal{E}^*$. A property $P \subseteq \mathcal{E}^*$ is downward-closed under $\preceq$ iff $\forall \sigma, \sigma'. \sigma' \in P \land \sigma \preceq \sigma' \Longrightarrow \sigma \in P$.*

The following theorem follows straightforwardly from this definition:

Theorem 7. *Let I and I' be two trace mediators such that $\forall \rho.\ I'(\rho) \preceq I(\rho)$. If a system S complies with $I(\rho)$, it complies with $I'(\rho)$. If S preserves $I'(\rho)$ with respect to some $S_\star$, it preserves $I(\rho)$ with respect to $S_\star$.*

In the above example, one consequence of this theorem is that if we have a PEP η that is sound with respect to some I' such that I' produces *fewer* consent events than I, then any $\langle S|\eta|\delta_{\mathsf{Consent}}\rangle$ satisfies $I^{-1}(P_{\mathsf{Consent}})$. This is because the property P_{Consent} is downward-closed with respect to the relation $\preceq_{\mathsf{Consent}+}$ such that $\sigma \preceq_{\mathsf{Consent}+} \sigma'$ iff σ is obtained from σ' by adding Consent events.

Next, we consider the following notion of $\preceq$-soundness for PEPs:

Definition 17. *A PEP η is $\preceq$-sound with respect to I iff whenever $s_\eta^0 \xrightarrow{\sigma \triangleright \rho} s'_\eta$, then $\circ \boldsymbol{\sigma}$ is a prefix of some σ' with $\sigma' \preceq I(\circ \boldsymbol{\rho})$.*

The next theorem formalizes the overapproximation discussed above in the case of read: if a PEP η generates sequences of actions that are smaller (under $\preceq$) than the sequences of events edited by the PDP, then compliance is guaranteed.

Theorem 8. *Let η be a PEP over $(\mathcal{A}, \mathcal{E})$ and δ an edit automaton over $\mathcal{E}$ sound with respect to P. If η is $\preceq$-sound with respect to I and P is downward-closed under $\preceq$, then $\langle S|\eta|\delta\rangle$ complies with $I^{-1}(P)$.*

5 Practical Enforcement with Batches and Capabilities

The general model that we have described in Sects. 3–4 must be instantiated for specific classes of events, PDPs, and downward-closed relations to be used with real-world tools. In this section, we specialize our theory to enforcement mechanisms that work with sets of simultaneous events ('batches', sometimes also called *timepoints* [5] in the literature) and distinguish between events that the PDP can cause or suppress [13]. This will allow us to implement our framework with ENFGUARD [17] as PDP in Sect. 6. We first define batch edit automata, batch PEPs, and their properties, and introduce a relation $\preceq_{\mathsf{mono}}$ whose downward closure contains properties that cannot be violated by generating 'more' or 'fewer' of certain events (Sect. 5.1). Then, we give a concrete batch PEP algorithm and prove sufficient ($\preceq$-)soundness conditions (Sect. 5.2).

5.1 Batch Edit Automata and Batch PEPs

In this section, we consider the case where each $a \in \mathcal{A}$ and $e \in \mathcal{E}$ is a finite set, i.e., $\mathcal{A} \triangleq \mathcal{P}(A)_f$ and $\mathcal{E} \triangleq \mathcal{P}(E)_f$, where $\mathcal{P}(\cdot)_f$ denotes the set of all finite subsets. In contrast to the previous sections, we now refer to elements of $\mathcal{A}$ and $\mathcal{E}$ as *action batches* and *event batches*, and reserve the words *actions* and *events* for elements of A and E, respectively. As in previous work [17], we assume that the edit automaton serving as a PDP cannot insert or delete event batches, but only edit the *content* of the sets, and that which events can be caused or suppressed is known in advance: there is a set $C \subseteq E$ of *causable* events and a set $S \subseteq E$ of *suppressable* events. We call such automata *batch automata*; the pair (C, S) is called the automaton's *capabilities*.

We first specialize our definitions of edit automata and PEPs:

Definition 18. *A* batch edit automaton *(BEA) with capabilities (C, S) is an EA with transitions $s_\delta \xrightarrow{\ell \triangleright \langle \ell' \rangle} s'_\delta$ or $s_\delta \xrightarrow{\ell \triangleright \tau} s'_\delta$ only, where $\ell' - \ell \subseteq C$ and $\ell - \ell' \subseteq S$.*

Definition 19. *A* batch PEP *(BPEP) with capabilities (C, S) is an input-enabled PEP with transitions $s_\eta \xrightarrow{a \triangleright \langle e \rangle}_{\eta, i} s'_\eta$ and $s'_\eta \xrightarrow{e \triangleright \langle a \rangle}_{\eta, i} s''_\eta$ where, whenever $s_\eta^0 \xrightarrow{\sigma \triangleright \rho} s_\eta \xrightarrow{a' \triangleright \langle e' \rangle}_{\eta, i} s'_\eta \xrightarrow{e \triangleright \langle a \rangle}_{\eta, e} s''_\eta$, there exists $e'' \in \mathcal{E}$ and s'''_η such that $s_\eta \xrightarrow{a \triangleright \langle e'' \rangle} s'''_\eta$, $e'' - e' \subseteq C$, and $e' - e'' \subseteq S$.*

Next, we define classes of properties that are common in practice, namely those where adding or removing a given event e to any batch of a compliant trace can never yield a non-compliant trace. When a property P can never be violated by just adding e events to an already compliant trace, we call it *e-monotonic*; when it can never be violated by just removing e events from such a trace, we call it *e-antimonotonic*.

Definition 20. *A property $P \subseteq \mathcal{E}^*$ is* monotonic *with respect to $e \in E$ iff for all $\sigma, \sigma' \in \mathcal{E}^*$ such that for all $i \in \mathbb{N}$, $\sigma'_i \in \{\sigma_i, \sigma_i \cup \{e\}\}$, $\sigma \in P \implies \sigma' \in P$.*

Similarly, a property $P \subseteq \mathcal{E}^*$ is antimonotonic *with respect to $e \in E$ iff for all $\sigma, \sigma' \in \mathcal{E}^*$ such that for all $i \in \mathbb{N}$, $\sigma'_i \in \{\sigma_i, \sigma_i - \{e\}\}$, $\sigma \in P \implies \sigma' \in P$.*

For the rest of this section, we fix two sets $M^+, M^- \subseteq E$ of events and consider the following relation $\preceq_{\mathsf{mono}}$:

$$\sigma \preceq_{\mathsf{mono}} \sigma' \iff |\sigma| = |\sigma'| \wedge \forall i \in \{1, \ldots, |\sigma|\}.\ \sigma'_i - \sigma_i \subseteq M^+ \wedge \sigma_i - \sigma'_i \subseteq M^-.$$

The following proposition directly follows from Definition 20:

Theorem 9. *A property P is downward-closed with respect to $\preceq_{\mathsf{mono}}$ iff it is monotonic in every $e \in M^+$ and antimonotonic in every $e \in M^-$.*

5.2 A Batch PEP Algorithm

In this subsection, we present a concrete batch PEP algorithm and give sufficient conditions for it to be (i) sound and transparent or at least (ii) $\preceq_{\mathsf{mono}}$-sound.

The Algorithm. Our algorithm is defined via two functions $\mathsf{i}_\eta : \mathcal{A}^* \times \mathcal{A} \to \mathcal{E}$ and $\mathsf{e}_\eta : \mathcal{A}^* \times \mathcal{A} \times \mathcal{E} \to \mathcal{A}$ such that $s^0_\eta \xrightarrow{\sigma \triangleright \rho} s_\eta \xrightarrow{a' \triangleright \langle e' \rangle}_{\eta, \mathsf{i}} s'_\eta$ iff $e' = \mathsf{i}_\eta(\circ\rho, a')$ and $s^0_\eta \xrightarrow{\sigma \triangleright \rho} s_\eta \xrightarrow{a' \triangleright \langle e' \rangle}_{\eta, \mathsf{i}} s'_\eta \xrightarrow{e \triangleright \langle a \rangle}_{\eta, \mathsf{e}} s''_\eta$ iff $a = \mathsf{e}_\eta(\circ\rho, a', e)$. We call the resulting PEP $\mathcal{B}(\mathsf{i}_\eta, \mathsf{e}_\eta)$. The function i_η, called the *instrumentation mapping*, can be freely chosen. It maps an action to a sequence of events, which may depend on the history of past actions. The function e_η, called the *enforcement mapping*, is defined in terms of the instrumentation mapping as well as three *handlers*: the causation handler h_C, the preservation handler h_K ('K' stands for 'keep'), and the suppression handler h_S. Each handler is a partial map describing how the enforcer should handle the PDP's edits: when the original set of actions is a' and the PDP causes some set of events e, the handler generates the set of actions $\mathsf{h}_C(e, a')$; when the PDP does not modify some events e, the handler generates the actions $\mathsf{h}_K(e, a')$; and when it suppresses some events e, the handler generates the actions $\mathsf{h}_S(e, a')$. Since the first argument of each handler is a set of events, there may be several ways to use the same handler to cause, preserve, or suppress the same events. For instance, to cause $\{e_1, e_2, e_3\}$, one can either call $\mathsf{h}_C(\{e_1\}, a')$, $\mathsf{h}_C(\{e_2\}, a')$, and $\mathsf{h}_C(\{e_3\}, a')$ consecutively and collect the generated actions, call $\mathsf{h}_C(\{e_1, e_2\}, a')$ and $\mathsf{h}_C(\{e_2, e_3\}, a')$, call only $\mathsf{h}_C(\{e_1, e_2, e_3\})$, etc. For the PEP to be input-enabled, the domain of h_C (respectively, h_K, h_S) must *generate* C (respectively, E, S):

Definition 21. *Let Ω be an element set. A set $X \in \mathcal{P}(\mathcal{P}(\Omega))$ is a* generator *of another set $Y \in \mathcal{P}(\mathcal{P}(\Omega))$ iff for any $y \in Y$, there exists a finite subset $X' \subseteq X$ such that $y = \bigcup_{x \in X'} x$.*

Algorithm 1. Batch PEP Algorithm

$$
\begin{aligned}
\mathsf{e}_\eta(\rho, a', e) = \ &\text{let } e' = \mathsf{i}_\eta(\rho, a') \text{ in} \\
&(\text{if } e' = e \text{ then } a' \text{ else let } c_1, \ldots, c_{n_C} = \mathsf{choose}_{\mathrm{dom}(\mathsf{h}_C);C}(e - e'); \\
&\qquad k_1, \ldots, k_{n_K} = \mathsf{choose}_{\mathrm{dom}(\mathsf{h}_K);K}(e \cap e'); \\
&\qquad s_1, \ldots, s_{n_S} = \mathsf{choose}_{\mathrm{dom}(\mathsf{h}_S);S}(e' - e) \\
&\text{in } \bigcup_{i=1}^{n_C} \mathsf{h}_C(c_i, a') \cup \bigcup_{i=1}^{n_K} \mathsf{h}_K(k_i, a') \cup \bigcup_{i=1}^{n_S} \mathsf{h}_S(s_i, a') \ )
\end{aligned}
$$

In the case where several decompositions of the set of events into a union of elements of the domain exists, we can use any function $\mathsf{choose}_{Y;X} : Y \to \mathcal{P}(X)_f$ such that $\bigcup \mathsf{choose}_{X;Y}(y) = y$ to select a valid decomposition. Given such a choice function, the handlers provide a convenient way for developers to define (sound) PEP reactions to arbitrary PDP edits, without having to explicitly define the PEP's reaction to every combination of edits.

Algorithm 1 gives the pseudocode of e_η. First, the enforcer computes the events e' corresponding to the original actions and compares them to the edited events e returned by the PDP. If the PDP did not modify the events, the enforcer returns the original actions a'. Otherwise, it decomposes the sets of caused actions $e' - e$, preserved actions $e \cap e'$, and suppressed actions $e - e'$ over $\mathrm{dom}(\mathsf{h}_C)$, $\mathrm{dom}(\mathsf{h}_K)$, and $\mathrm{dom}(\mathsf{h}_S)$ respectively, and calls the corresponding handlers, returning the union of all generated actions.

Correctness. The following theorem provides a set of conditions that together guarantee that $\mathcal{B}(\mathsf{i}_\eta, \mathsf{e}_\eta)$ is a sound and transparent PEP with capabilities (C, S). We first state the theorem and then give an intuitive interpretation of each of the conditions in terms of instrumentation auditing:

Theorem 10. *Let $\mathsf{i}_\eta : \mathcal{A}^* \times \mathcal{A} \to \mathcal{E}$, $\mathsf{h}_C : \mathcal{P}(C)_f \to \mathcal{A} \to \mathcal{A}$, $\mathsf{h}_S : \mathcal{P}(S)_f \to \mathcal{A} \to \mathcal{A}$, $\mathsf{h}_K : \mathcal{P}(E)_f \to \mathcal{A} \to \mathcal{A}$ be given. Suppose that (1) $\mathrm{dom}(\mathsf{h}_C)$ is a generator of $\mathcal{P}(C)_f$ under $\cup$, (2) $\mathrm{dom}(\mathsf{h}_K)$ is a generator of $\mathcal{P}(E)_f$ under $\cup$, (3) $\mathrm{dom}(\mathsf{h}_S)$ is a generator of $\mathcal{P}(S)_f$ under $\cup$, (4) $\forall \rho, a, b.\ \mathsf{i}_\eta(\rho, a) \cup \mathsf{i}_\eta(\rho, b) = \mathsf{i}_\eta(\rho, a \cup b)$, where we set $\tau \cup s \triangleq s \cup \tau \triangleq s$, (5) $\forall \rho, c, a.\ \mathsf{i}_\eta(\rho, \mathsf{h}_C(c, a)) = c$, (6) $\forall \rho, k, a.\ \mathsf{i}_\eta(\rho, \mathsf{h}_K(k, a)) = k$, (7) $\forall \rho, s, a.\ \mathsf{i}_\eta(\rho, \mathsf{h}_S(s, a)) = \emptyset$, and (8) $\forall \rho, a.\ \mathsf{i}_\eta(\rho, a) = (I(\rho \cdot \langle a \rangle))_{|\rho|+1}$. Then $\mathcal{B}(\mathsf{i}_\eta, \mathsf{e}_\eta)$ is a batch PEP with capabilities (C, S) that is sound and transparent with respect to I.*

This theorem provides a checklist (1)–(8) that can be used to audit the correctness of the system's instrumentation when our PEP algorithm is used together with a sound PDP. The checks to be performed are as follows:

(1–3) Is the causation handler (respectively, preservation, suppression handler) defined for all causable events (respectively, for all events, for all suppressable events)?

(4) Does the instrumentation mapping map single actions to events independently, i.e., does a set of n actions map to the same events as the union of the events that each of the n actions maps to?

(5–6) When the causation (respectively, preservation) handler receives events, does it generate actions that map exactly (through i_η) to the events it received?

(7) Does the suppression handler only generate actions that map to $\emptyset$?

(8) Does the instrumentation mapping i_η implement exactly I?

For all events $e \in \mathcal{E}$ such that $e \in i_\eta(\rho, \{x\}) \implies i_\eta(\rho, \{x\}) = \{e\}$ (i.e., events that are never generated together with another event), note that the part of the preservation handler related to e can be straightforwardly defined as $a' \mapsto h_K(\{e\}, a') = \{x \in a' \mid e \in i_\eta(\rho, \{x\})\}$, triggering all actions in a' that map to e.

In practice, auditing these requirements, especially (6) and (8), can be challenging, as it requires checking correct instrumentation and enforcement for *all possible events*: the instrumentation must *always* provide *exactly* the right events *whenever necessary*; the enforcer must *always* generate *exactly* the right actions.

For $\preceq_{\mathsf{mono}}$ soundness, we can significantly weaken conditions (5)–(8):

Theorem 11. *Let i_η, h_C, h_S, and h_K be given. Suppose that (1)–(4) and (7) are as in Theorem 10, (5) $\forall\, c, a.\ i_\eta(\rho, h_C(c, a)) - c \subseteq C \cap M^+ \wedge c - i_\eta(\rho, h_C(c, a)) \subseteq M^-$, (6) $\forall \rho, k, a.\ i_\eta(\rho, h_K(k, a)) - k \subseteq C \cap M^+ \wedge k - i_\eta(\rho, h_K(k, a)) \subseteq S \cap M^-$, (8) $\forall \rho, a.\ i_\eta(\rho, a) \preceq (I(\rho \cdot \langle a \rangle))_{|\rho|+1}$. Then $\mathcal{B}(i_\eta, e_\eta)$ is $\preceq_{\mathsf{mono}}$-sound with respect to I.*

The questions to be answered for (5), (6), and (8) are now the following:

(5–6) a. When a handler receives an event that is *not both* antimonotonic *and* suppressable, does it always generate an action that maps to this event?
b. When a handler generates an action that maps to an event that is *not both* monotonic *and* causable, did it always receive this event originally?

(8) a. Does the implementation mapping i_η ensure that every event that is *not* monotonic is always logged when an action mapping to it occurs?
b. Does the implementation mapping i_η ensure that every event that is *not* antimonotonic is only ever logged when an action mapping to it occurs?

6 Case Study

INSTRLIB. We have implemented our batch PEP algorithm (Sect. 5) in a Python library called INSTRLIB [20]. The library consists of 1,500 lines of Python code with two instrumentation layers: a low-level layer, which allows for instrumenting arbitrary Python function calls and attributes, and a high-level layer providing off-the-shelf enforcement hooks for Django web applications. The latter uses a fixed set of actions (`read`, `write`, `input`, `output`, `execute`) to capture database reads and writes, user inputs and outputs, and calls to class members. The library allows developers to specify the PEP logic as in Algorithm 1 by providing an instrumentation mapping and handlers. Its architecture is shown in extended report [19]. It has bindings to the state-of-the-art ENFGUARD tool [17].

Minitwitter. We now showcase the usage of INSTRLIB by instrumenting a micro-blogging app for compliance with two privacy requirements. The target app has 435 lines of Python code and allows users to view their and other users' timeline, follow other users, and post short messages. Additionally, the app shows one of two advertisement messages on the user's timeline depending on the content of their posts. It also displays a privacy banner that prompts the user to accept or reject the use of their data for marketing purposes.

We enforce the two following requirements: (1) whenever data is used for marketing purposes, the user has given (and not revoked) consent; (2) if the user requests the deletion of all of their data, their data is deleted within one minute. Here, the events of interest are $\mathsf{use}(u,p)$, denoting "user u's data is used for purpose p;" $\mathsf{consent}(u,p)$ (respectively, $\mathsf{revoke}(u,p)$), denoting "user u gives (respectively, revokes) consent to use their data for purpose p;" $\mathsf{request}(u)$, denoting "user u requests deletion of their data;" and $\mathsf{delete}(u)$, denoting "user u's data is deleted:" The PDP is assumed to be able to cause delete and suppress use. The trace mediator I, which is part of the system specification, is shown in Table 1. As in most practical instances, this trace mediator is informal.

Table 1. The trace mediator I in Minitwitter

Actions	Event	Sets
Any reading or writing of some of user u's data for purpose p	$\mathsf{Use}(u,p)$	S, M^-
Any user input from u giving consent for purpose p	$\mathsf{Consent}(u,p)$	M^+
Any user input from u revoking consent for purpose p	$\mathsf{Revoke}(u,p)$	M^-
Any user input from u containing a deletion request	$\mathsf{Request}(u)$	M^-
Any call to a function that deletes all of user u's data	$\mathsf{Delete}(u)$	C, M^+

To instrument Minitwitter, developers proceed in three steps. *First*, they provide the property of interest in ENFGUARD's [17] property specification language: Metric First-Order Temporal Logic (MFOTL) [8]. Here, the property is

$\Box(\forall u.\ (\mathsf{Use}(u, \text{"marketing"}) \to (\neg\mathsf{Revoke}(u, \text{"marketing"}) \mathrel{\mathsf{S}} \mathsf{Consent}(u, \text{"marketing"})))$
$\land\ (\mathsf{Request}(u) \to \Diamond_{[0,60]}\mathsf{Delete}(u))).$

Second, the developers use the built-in Django bindings for INSTRLIB to associate actions to database reads and writes (actions `read` and `write`), user inputs to views (action `input`), and function calls (action `execute`). Functions with a specific processing can be marked with that purpose (here, "`marketing`"). At runtime, based on the current call stack, INSTRLIB injects the current purposes of processing into `read` and `write` actions. This step requires about 40 lines of code in the Python files describing the app's database models and URLs.

Third, the developers describe the instrumentation mapping and handlers. This requires about 50 lines of code in a single Python file. The instrumentation mapping maps database `read` or `write`s to Use events, consent banner clicks (captured by specific `input` actions) to either consent or revoke, clicks on a special 'Delete My Data' button (captured by other `input` actions) to request, and executions of a special function `delete_data(u)` that erases all of a user's data (captured by an `execute` action) to Delete. Two handlers are implemented: a suppression handler for use that returns None instead of the actual content of object fields and prevents their overwriting; and a causation handler for delete that calls `delete_data`. By default, INSTRLIB provides a simple preservation handlers as described in Sect. 5.2, which are sufficient when i_η maps each action to at most one event. All enforcement-related code is showed in extended report [19].

In Table 2, we report the latency of four of Minitwitter's views with and without instrumentation with INSTRLIB: viewing the **timeline**, **post**ing a message, giving **consent**, and **request**ing deletion of one's data, for different values of the number n of posts in the database. The runtime overhead is < 15 ms per request.

Table 2. Runtime latency (ms) over 20 repetitions

View	Baseline ($\propto n$)						Instrumented ($\propto n$)			
	10^2	10^3	10^4	10^5	10^6	10^2	10^3	10^4	10^5	10^6
timeline	54	54	58	58	66	56 +2	58 +4	69 +11	70 +12	75 +9
post	64	62	63	62	61	67 +4	68 +6	66 +3	67 +5	67 +6
consent	47	46	47	47	47	53 +6	54 +8	55 +8	54 +7	54 +7
request	–	–	–	–	–	58	59	59	58	72

Auditing Minitwitter's Implementation. In the property above, consent and delete are monotonic, whereas request, revoke, and use are antimonotonic. We can now go through the checklist provided by Theorem 11. For (1–3), we check the existence of a causation handler for delete, a suppression handler for use, and preservation handlers for all events. Regarding preservation handlers, we note that, as described above, INSTRLIB's default implementation provides simple preservation handlers that are sufficient with our choice of i_η—this also allows us to check (6). Condition (4) is implemented by INSTRLIB by design. For the delete causation handler, we answer (5a) positively by checking that the handler does call the delete_data function, whose behavior matches the informal description in Table 1. Condition (5b) is vacuous since delete is monotonic and causable. Condition (7) is trivially fulfilled since our suppression handlers return None. For (8a), we must check that request, use, and revoke events are always emitted when actions occur that map to them according to Table 1. Inspecting the interface of the application, we control that the buttons for revocation of consent and deletion requests map to the views whose inputs we have instrumented. Similarly, we check that all fields that contain personal data emit read and write events and that all functions performing marketing are marked as such. Finally, for (8b), we must check that consent and delete are only logged when the corresponding system actions as described in Table 1 happen. To this end, we control that consent is only generated by the input corresponding to clicking 'yes' in the banner and, similarly, that the delete event is only generated by the execute action of function delete_data.

7 Conclusions and Future Work

To the best of our knowledge, we have provided the first formal account of instrumentation in runtime enforcement. Besides a policy decision point (PDP), our extended enforcement model features a policy enforcement point (PEP) as an explicit component. Our model is general, independent of any specific PDP, and provides necessary and sufficient conditions for the correctness of the composition of a system, a PDP, and a PEP. We have demonstrated the applicability of our approach by implementing in the INSTRLIB instrumentation library and using it to enforce privacy requirements in a micro-blogging application.

Future work includes extending our auditing methodology to validate the implementation of runtime enforcement mechanisms in large applications with complex specifications and further optimizing INSTRLIB.

Acknowledgments. François Hublet is supported by the Swiss National Science Foundation grant "Model-driven Security & Privacy" (204796). We thank the anonymous RV reviewers for their insightful feedback.

References

1. Aceto, L., Cassar, I., Francalanza, A., Ingólfsdóttir, A.: On runtime enforcement via suppressions. In: Schewe, S., Zhang, L. (edis.) Conference on Concurrency Theory (CONCUR 2018), Leibniz International Proceedings in Informatics (LIPIcs), pp. 34:1–34:17, Dagstuhl, Germany, 2018. Schloss Dagstuhl – Leibniz-Zentrum für Informatik (2018)
2. Aceto, L., Cassar, I., Francalanza, A., Ingolfsdottir, A.: Bidirectional runtime enforcement of first-order branching-time properties. Logical Methods Comput. Sci. **19** (2023)

3. Alur, R., Dill, D.L.: A theory of timed automata. Theor. Comput. Sci. **126**(2), 183–235 (1994)
4. Bai, G., Gu, L., Feng, T., Guo, Y., Chen, X.: Context-aware usage control for android. In: Jajodia, S., Zhou, J. (eds.) SecureComm 2010. LNICST, vol. 50, pp. 326–343. Springer, Heidelberg (2010). https://doi.org/10.1007/978-3-642-16161-2_19
5. Basin, D., Klaedtke, F., Müller, S., Zalinescu, E.: Monitoring metric first-order temporal properties. J. ACM (JACM) **62**(2), 15:1–15:45 (2015)
6. Cassar, I., Francalanza, A., Aceto, L., Ingólfsdóttir, A.: Developing theoretical foundations for runtime enforcement. CoRR arxiv:1804.08917 (2018)
7. Charafeddine, H., El-Harake, K., Falcone, Y., Jaber, M.: Runtime enforcement for component-based systems. In: Symposium on Applied Computing, pp. 1789–1796. ACM (2015)
8. Chomicki, J.: Efficient checking of temporal integrity constraints using bounded history encoding. Trans. Datab. Syst. (TODS) **20**(2), 149–186 (1995)
9. OASIS XACML Technical Committee. eXtensible Access Control Markup Language (XACML) Version 1.0. Technical Report oasis-xacml-1.0, OASIS (2003)
10. Erlingsson, Ú.: The inlined reference monitor approach to security policy enforcement. PhD thesis, Cornell University (2004)
11. Erlingsson, U., Schneider, F.B.: Sasi enforcement of security policies: a retrospective. In: New Security Paradigms, pp. 87–95 (1999)
12. Falcone, Y., Jaber, M.: Fully automated runtime enforcement of component-based systems with formal and sound recovery. J. Softw. Tools Technol. Transf. (STTT) **19**(3), 341–365 (2017)
13. Hublet, F., Basin, D., Krstić, S.: Real-time policy enforcement with metric first-order temporal logic. In: European Symposium on Research in Computer Security (ESORICS), pp.211–232. Springer, Heidelberg (2022). https://doi.org/10.1007/978-3-031-17146-8_11
14. Hublet, F., Basin, D., Krstić, S.: Enforcing the GDPR. In: European Symposium on Research in Computer Security (ESORICS), pp. 400–422. Springer, Heidelberg (2023). https://doi.org/10.1007/978-3-031-51476-0_20
15. Hublet, F., Basin, D., Krstić, S.: User-controlled privacy: Taint, track, and control. Proc. Priv. Enhancing Technol. **2024**(1), 597–616 (2024)
16. François Hublet, Alexander Kvamme, and Srdan Krstic. Towards an enforceable GDPR specification. *CoRR*, abs/2402.17350, 2024
17. Hublet, F., Lima, L., Basin, D., Krstić, S., Traytel, D.: Scaling up proactive enforcement. In: Piskac, R., Rakamarić, Z. (eds.) Computer Aided Verification (CAV), pp. 370–392. Springer, Heidelberg (2025). https://doi.org/10.1007/978-3-031-98682-6_19
18. Hublet, F., Lima, L., Basin, D., Krstić, S., Traytel, D.: Proactive real-time first-order enforcement. In: Gurfinkel, A., Ganesh, V. (eds.) Computer Aided Verification (CAV), vol. 14682 of LNCS, pp. 156–181. Springer, Heidelberg (2024). https://doi.org/10.1007/978-3-031-65630-9_8
19. Hublet, F., Basin, D., Hu, L., Krstić, S., Reese, L.: Instrumenting runtime enforcement. Technical report, ETH Zürich (2025). Extended version. https://doi.org/10.5281/zenodo.16530943
20. Hublet, F., Basin, D., Hu, L., Krstić, S., Reese, L.: InstrLib (2025). https://github.com/runtime-enforcement/instrlib
21. Ligatti, J., Bauer, L., Walker, D.: Edit automata: enforcement mechanisms for run-time security policies. J. Inf. Secur. **4**, 2–16 (2005)

22. Ligatti, J., Reddy, S.: A theory of runtime enforcement, with results. In: Gritzalis, D., Preneel, B., Theoharidou, M. (eds.) ESORICS 2010. LNCS, vol. 6345, pp. 87–100. Springer, Heidelberg (2010). https://doi.org/10.1007/978-3-642-15497-3_6
23. Lynch, N.A., Tuttle, M.R.: An introduction to input/output automata. Laboratory for Computer Science, Massachusetts Institute of Technology (1988)
24. Pinisetty, S., Falcone, Y., Jéron, T., Marchand, H., Rollet, A., Nguena Timo, O.L.: Runtime enforcement of timed properties. In: Qadeer, S., Tasiran, S. (eds.) RV 2012. LNCS, vol. 7687, pp. 229–244. Springer, Heidelberg (2013). https://doi.org/10.1007/978-3-642-35632-2_23
25. Rasthofer, S., Arzt, S., Lovat, E., Bodden, E.: Droidforce: enforcing complex, data-centric, system-wide policies in android. In: Availability, Reliability and Security, pp. 40–49. IEEE (2014)
26. Sarraf, S.: Optus breach occurred due to a coding error, alleges ACMA. CSO Online (2022)
27. Schneider, F.: Enforceable security policies. Trans. Inf. Syst. Sec. **3**(1), 30–50 (2000)

Active Monitoring with RTLola: A Specification-Guided Scheduling Approach

Jan Baumeister[✉][iD], Bernd Finkbeiner[iD], and Frederik Scheerer[iD]

CISPA Helmholtz Center for Information Security, Saarbrücken, Germany
{jan.baumeister,finkbeiner,frederik.scheerer}@cispa.de

Abstract. Stream-based monitoring is a well-established runtime verification approach which relates input streams, representing sensor readings from the monitored system, with output streams that capture filtered or aggregated results. In such approaches, the monitor is a passive external component that continuously receives sensor data from the system under observation. This setup assumes that the system dictates what data is sent and when, regardless of the monitor's current needs. However, in many applications – particularly in resource-constrained environments like autonomous aircraft, where energy, size, or weight are limited – this can lead to inefficient use of communication resources. We propose making the monitor an active component that decides, based on its current internal state, which sensors to query and how often. This behavior is driven by scheduling annotations in the specification, which guide the dynamic allocation of bandwidth towards the most relevant data, thereby improving monitoring efficiency. We demonstrate our approach using the stream-based specification language RTLola and assess the performance by monitoring a specification from the aerospace domain. With equal bandwidth usage, our approach detects specification violations significantly sooner than monitors sampling all inputs at a fixed frequency.

Keywords: Stream-based Monitoring · Constraint-Based Scheduling · Real-time Properties

1 Introduction

Cyber-physical systems are increasingly prevalent, and many now operate fully autonomously in complex, real-world environments. These systems are often deployed in safety-critical domains, such as autonomous vehicles or drones, where incorrect behavior can lead to catastrophic outcomes. Runtime monitoring is a well-established technique for checking the system's behavior at runtime against a formal specification and, therefore, ensuring its correct behavior [15,19,23].

A prominent class of runtime monitoring frameworks is stream-based monitoring [6,17,22]. There, the system continuously supplies a monitor with data

© The Author(s), under exclusive license to Springer Nature Switzerland AG 2026
B. Könighofer and H. Torfah (Eds.): RV 2025, LNCS 16087, pp. 181–201, 2026.
https://doi.org/10.1007/978-3-032-05435-7_11

about its current state via input streams. Output streams compute new values by aggregating and filtering the inputs, often leveraging temporal operators to express rich, time-dependent specifications. This makes stream-based monitoring particularly suitable for complex safety requirements of cyber-physical systems.

However, in modern autonomous systems, monitors must process data from a diverse set of sources in real-time. For example, an autonomous vehicle or drone might rely on GPS, camera feeds, and many other sensors to assess its environment and maintain safety. Here, the monitor is a passive component, consuming the updates about the current state of the system under observation. A key challenge in such settings is limited bandwidth: the connection between sensors and the monitor cannot support arbitrarily high-frequency updates from all sources due to factors like energy consumption, physical size, or weight constraints. Consequently, it is not feasible to transmit all sensor data at its highest possible frequency. However, reducing the sampling frequency leads to increased latency in detecting critical events and dangerous situations, undermining the effectiveness of the monitor.

We propose that, since the monitor has a comprehensive view of all received data, it has a better understanding of which data is currently needed than the different sources individually. For instance, consider a drone equipped with both an altitude sensor and a camera. When the drone is landed, altitude readings are irrelevant, while the ground-level camera might be more important for monitoring the surrounding ground. Conversely, at higher altitudes, the camera data becomes less informative, whereas altitude measurements become more significant as the drone is approaching predefined upper altitude limits. We present an active monitoring approach in which the system adaptively queries the sensors based on the drone's current altitude. This enables dynamic prioritization of sensor data, emphasizing ground-level visual input when near the ground and focusing on altitude measurements when high up in the sky – therefore making more effective use of the limited bandwidth between the sensors and the monitor.

Such an approach is especially interesting for applications that are designed for actively requesting individual sensors' data. A prominent example is the OBD-II interface present in all modern vehicles, which must be explicitly queried for individual sensors of the car, instead of receiving a stream of new sensor data on its own.

Given the availability of well-established monitoring tools [6,22,25,26], we chose not to develop a new monitoring framework from scratch. Instead, our approach builds on existing monitoring tools by introducing a scheduling component that interfaces between the monitor and the sensors. This scheduler observes the current monitoring state and determines which sensors to query next. Once the selected data has been acquired, the scheduler forwards it to the underlying monitor to initiate the next monitoring cycle. This architecture allows our method to remain independent of the monitor implementation and be compatible with a wide range of existing monitoring infrastructures.

We demonstrate our approach through an implementation based on the stream-based monitoring language RTLola [6], which has previously been successfully applied to the monitoring of unmanned aircraft [5,9] or for increasing trust in automatic decision and prediction systems [8]. We extend RTLola by introducing scheduling annotations that can be attached to individual streams in the specification. These annotations guide the scheduling process by indicating which inputs should be prioritized under certain conditions of the monitor. The annotated specification is then automatically transformed into a "regular" RTLola specification compatible with all existing RTLola implementations [3,10,16]. The schedule is embedded into this transformed specification through additional output streams, which are then interpreted by the scheduler to determine which inputs should be queried in the next cycle.

We evaluated our approach using data obtained through the Microsoft AirSim simulator. Our results demonstrate that the proposed method can significantly reduce bandwidth consumption without compromising monitoring quality, or, on the other hand, detect violations earlier compared to a fixed-frequency approach, while utilizing the same amount of bandwidth.

Contribution. To summarize, we make the following contributions:

- We define a formal semantics for stream-based specification languages that incorporate scheduling of streams,
- We extend RTLola with an annotation mechanism to express scheduling constraints directly within the specification,
- We present a translation from annotated specifications to regular ones, which integrate the scheduling information as additional streams, and
- We implement our approach on top of RTLola and evaluate it in an online setting using simulated drone data.

The remainder of this paper is structured as follows: In Sect. 2, we provide a background on the RTLola monitoring language and define formal semantics for stream-based specification languages. In Sect. 3, we extend these semantics to incorporate the scheduling mechanism. Section 4 introduces our active monitoring framework and discusses challenges specific to integrating scheduling into RTLola. Finally, we present our evaluation in Sect. 5.

1.1 Related Work

Many monitoring frameworks assume that every change in the system is observable by the monitor. However, this assumption does not hold in bandwidth-constrained environments, where the monitor must instead periodically sample the system state. Bonakdarpour et al. [11] propose a time-driven monitoring approach that samples the system at a fixed frequency to reduce overhead. This frequency is statically determined to guarantee that no violations are missed, but it treats all inputs equally throughout execution. Navabpour et al. [24] extend this work by making the sampling path-aware, allowing the frequency to vary over time. Stoller et al. [27] also aim to reduce monitoring overhead by sampling the system periodically and use Hidden Markov Models to estimate unobserved states between samples. In contrast to the previous approaches which sample the system, our setting allows explicitly querying individual sensor, giving us the potential to prioritze inputs according to their importance. Huang et al. [21] take a different approach by dynamically adjusting the amount of monitoring to stay within a user-specified target overhead. Instead of sampling, they temporarily disable the monitoring of certain events when the limit is exceeded otherwise.

Our approach is designed for the stream-based specification language RTLola [6], a successor of the synchronous stream-based specification language Lola [13]. RTLola has been successfully applied to the monitoring of cyber-physical systems, such as unmanned aircraft [5,9]. However, our approach is also transferable to other asynchronous stream-based languages, including Tessla [22] and Striver [17]. While there exist stream-based approaches that utilize annotations in specifications for correctness guarantees [4,18], we use annotations to represent timing constraints.

Another relevant area of research is scheduling in real-time systems, assigning tasks to processors – a topic comprehensively overviewed by Buttazzo [12] – and various approaches also consider bandwidth constraints (e.g., [1,2,14,28]). In this paper, we adapted these concepts to stream-based languages, by defining the scheduling semantics in the context of stream-based monitoring and integrating them into the specification language. While scheduling of real-time systems defines dependencies between tasks, stream-based settings provide a different kind of dependency constraints, relating jointly evaluated tasks. Our approach is closest to non-preemptive scheduling with dynamic priorities and hard aperiodic deadlines.

2 RTLola

Stream-based monitors operate over a set of *streams*, each representing an infinite sequence of values. RTLola specifications define these streams through stream-equations, which describe how the values in the sequences are computed. We distinguish between *input streams*, which are populated with data from the monitored system, and *output streams*, which compute new values by aggregating and filtering the inputs.

Consider the following example of an RTLola specification:

```
1  input alt : Float64
2  output alt_diff
3      eval @alt with abs(alt - alt.offset(by:-1).defaults(to: 0.0))
4  trigger alt_diff > 10.0
```

The specification defines one input stream `alt` which is automatically populated with new readings from the drone's altitude sensor as they arrive at the monitor. Next, the specification defines the output stream `alt_diff`, which computes the absolute difference between two consecutive altitude readings. This is achieved using the offset operator, which allows access to past stream values. Because such previous values are unavailable at the startup of the monitor, a default value must be provided that is used instead in this case. Finally, a trigger is defined to check whether the altitude difference exceeds 10. If the expression evaluates to true, the trigger activates, indicating a violation of the specification.

2.1 Types

Each stream in RTLola has two associated types: a value type and a pacing type. The *value type* specifies the kind of data contained in the stream, such as integers, floating-point numbers, or booleans. The *pacing type* defines *when* new values of a stream are computed and is indicated using the @-symbol following the eval keyword. In this paper, all output streams are *event-driven*, meaning they are evaluated whenever new inputs arrive. For example, the alt_diff stream always computes a new value whenever the alt stream receives a new value, as indicated by its pacing type.

Next, consider the following extension of the previous specification:

```
output num_high_alt
    eval @alt when alt > 20.0
        with num_high_alt.offset(by:-1).defaults(to: 0) + 1
```

This stream is evaluated whenever the alt input stream receives a new value. Here, the evaluation is further conditioned by the dynamic filter condition provided after the when keyword: A new value is computed only if the condition evaluates to true. In this case, the stream counts how often a high-altitude reading occurs. RTLola also allows multiple eval clauses per stream. Clauses are checked from top to bottom, and the stream is evaluated using the with expression of the first clause whose when condition is satisfied.

For a more detailed explanation of the RTLola monitoring language – including features such as time-driven streams, aggregations, and parametrization – we refer the reader to the RTLola Tutorial [6].

2.2 Semantics

We use the following semantics for stream-based monitors. Although the formulation is applied to RTLola, the semantics are transferable to accommodate other stream-based specification languages. We define the semantics via an *evaluation model* $\omega \in \mathbb{W}$, which assigns stream references ID, consiting of input stream references $\text{ID}^\uparrow$ and output stream references $\text{ID}^\downarrow$, to a timed series of values. We write $\omega(t)$ to refer to the real-time timestamp at discrete timestep $t \in \text{Time}$, and $\omega(sid)(t)$ to refer to the value of the stream sid at time t. If this stream did not calculate a new value at that time because of its pacing or filter conditions, $\bot$ is returned instead.

The semantics ensure that each output stream value in the evaluation model is correctly computed according to the specification's defining equations. Formally, given an RTLola specification φ, we define its semantics as the set:

$$\llbracket\varphi\rrbracket = \{\omega \in \mathbb{W} \mid \forall sid \in \text{ID}^\downarrow.\forall t \in \text{Time}.\varphi(sid) \Downarrow_\omega^t \omega(sid)(t) \\ \wedge \forall t \in \text{Time}.\omega(t) < \omega(t+1)\},$$

In the formula, $\varphi(sid) \Downarrow_w^t v$ denotes that the defining stream equations $\varphi(sid)$ of stream sid evaluate to v at time t. This evaluation yields the result of the with-expression of the first eval clause whose pacing and when condition is satisfied at time t. If no clause is evaluated, the result is $\bot$.

An evaluation model is considered valid with respect to a specification if, at every time step, all output stream values are correctly computed according to the defining stream equations and the time map is strictly monotonically increasing.

An RTLola specification φ is considered *well-defined*, if for every possible input trace $I \in \text{Time} \to \text{InputValues}$ with $\text{InputValues} : \text{ID}^\uparrow \to \mathbb{V}_\bot$, there exists a unique evaluation model $\omega \in [\![\varphi]\!]$ with $\forall t \in \text{Time}. \forall i \in \text{ID}^\uparrow. \omega(i)(t) = I(t)(i)$.

3 Scheduled Monitor Semantics

This section introduces the general concept for stream-based scheduling, where a scheduler must dynamically adapt to the current state of the monitor. We describe a valid schedule with a set of static constraints and later determine whether a scheduler satisfies them. We start by defining dynamic schedule constraints to decide at each time point if the evaluation violates the constraint. Then, we describe how to transform a static schedule into its dynamic counterpart – the transformation later implemented by the scheduling component.

In our setting, the scheduler determines at each time step which tasks are evaluated in the next step. The set of possible tasks defines the space of scheduling decisions available to the scheduler at each time step.

Definition 1 (Task). *For each $\tau \in \text{Tasks}$ there exists: 1. a predicate $\omega \models_t \tau$ to dermine if the evaluation model $\omega \in \mathbb{W}$ satisfies the task τ at time t, 2. a partial order $\preceq$ representing dependencies between tasks, and 3. a predicate $iv \models \mathcal{T}$ to determine if an input $iv : \text{InputValues}$ reflects the set of tasks $\mathcal{T}$.*

To illustrate different choices for the task space, consider two examples.

Example 1 (Individual Streams). For this example, consider a scheduler that selects individual streams during evaluation. Then Tasks = ID consisting of all stream's references and

$$\omega \models_t sref \quad \text{iff} \quad \omega(sref)(t) \neq \bot$$
$$\tau_1 \preceq \tau_2 \quad \text{iff} \quad \tau_1 = \tau_2$$
$$iv \models \mathcal{T} \quad \text{iff} \quad \forall i \in \text{ID}^\uparrow. iv(i) \neq \bot \Leftrightarrow \exists sref \in \mathcal{T}. sref = i.$$

In this case, tasks are satisfied at time t whenever their stream receives a value, i.e., is not $\bot$ at time t. There exist no dependencies between tasks, and an input reflects a set of tasks if each input receives a new value iff it is contained in the set of tasks.

Example 2 (Stream Sets). Alternatively, consider a scheduler selecting groups of streams to be jointly evaluated. We then set Tasks = $\mathcal{P}(\text{ID})$ and

$$\omega \models_t \tau \quad \text{iff} \quad \forall sref \in \tau. \omega(sref)(t) \neq \bot$$
$$\tau_1 \preceq \tau_2 \quad \text{iff} \quad \tau_1 \subseteq \tau_2$$
$$iv \models \mathcal{T} \quad \text{iff} \quad \forall i \in \text{ID}^\dagger. iv(i) \neq \bot \Leftrightarrow \exists \tau \in \mathcal{T}. i \in \tau.$$

In this representation, tasks have dependencies through a subset relation, and an input reflects a set of tasks if at least one task updates each input.

3.1 Dynamic Schedule Constraints

Next, we introduce the concept of dynamic scheduling constraints, which specify how each task is expected to be evaluated:

Definition 2 (Dynamic Schedule Constraint). *A dynamic schedule constraint is a function that maps the current monitor state ($\mathbb{W}$, Time) to a scheduling decision over tasks:*

$$S : (\mathbb{W} \times \text{Time}) \to \text{Tasks} \to \mathbb{S} \quad \mathbb{S} = \{Y, M, N\}$$

For each task, the constraint assignes whether the task must (Y), may (M), or must not (N) be evaluated at that time.

The semantics of stream-based languages ensure that all stream values are computed in accordance with their defining stream equations. We extend this semantics to account for scheduling constraints, requiring the evaluation model to also satisfy the tasks according to a constraint. In addition, we introduce a *bandwidth bound* B, which encodes the bandwidth limitations between sensors and the monitor. Formally, given a specification φ, a schedule constraint $\psi \in S$, and a bandwidth constraint B, the *scheduled semantics* is defined as:

$$[\![(\varphi, \psi, B)]\!] = \{\omega \in \mathbb{W} \mid \omega \in [\![\varphi]\!] \wedge \omega \in [\![\psi]\!] \wedge \forall t \in \text{Time}. B(\omega, t)\}.$$

Intuitively, an evaluation model is valid if it: 1. correctly computes all stream values according to φ, 2. adheres to the scheduling decisions made by ψ, and 3. respects the bandwidth constraint B at all times.

For an evaluation model to satisfy a constraint $\psi \in S$, the satisfaction or non-satisfaction of tasks must always align with ψ:

$$[\![\psi]\!] = \left\{ \omega \in \mathbb{W} \mid \forall t \in \text{Time}. \forall \tau \in \text{Tasks}. \begin{cases} \omega \models_{t+1} \tau & \text{if } \psi(\omega,t)(\tau) = Y \\ \top & \text{if } \psi(\omega,t)(\tau) = M \\ \omega \not\models_{t+1} \tau & \text{if } \psi(\omega,t)(\tau) = N \end{cases} \right\}.$$

If the schedule constraints assign Y to τ at time t, the evaluation model must satisfy that task at time $t + 1$. If the decision is N, it must not satisfy that task, while for M, both outcomes are permitted.

Last, we define the bandwidth constraints imposed by the communication between sensors and the monitor. These constraints are formalized as a predicate $B : (\mathbb{W} \times \text{Time}) \to \mathbb{B}$, which determines whether the inputs received by the monitor at time t conform to the bandwidth limitations. In this paper, we consider a simple constraint model InputEventBound_b that limits the number of input streams that can receive a value at the same time to a fixed threshold b:

$$\text{InputEventBound}_b(\omega, t) = |\{i \in \text{ID}^\uparrow \mid \omega(i)(t) \neq \bot\}| \leq b.$$

Other constraints could account for the varying bit widths of individual input types or enforce protocols that require specific combinations of inputs.

3.2 Static Scheduling Constraints

This section introduces three *static schedule constraints* – deadlines, priorities, and their combination – and presents a translation deriving their dynamic counterpart. Static schedule constraints contain *conditions* Cond, which can be evaluated to a boolean under a given evaluation state $\Downarrow_t^\omega$: Cond $\to \mathbb{B}$, to constrain a task differently at runtime. In the following paragraphs, we describe these static schedules individually.

Deadline. The first static schedule constraints describe deadlines. The constraints assign upper bounds to tasks, which indicate that a task should not be evaluated later than its deadline. It is defined as

$$\text{Deadline} : \text{Tasks} \to \mathcal{P}\,(\text{Cond} \times \mathbb{R})$$

and assigns each task to a set of pairs, each consisting of conditions and a corresponding deadline. Given such a static schedule constraint $\xi \in$ Deadline, we derive a dynamic schedule $\psi \in S$ as follows:

$$\psi(\omega, t)(\tau) = \begin{cases} Y & \text{if } \exists (c, dl) \in \xi(\tau) \land \exists t' < t.c \Downarrow_{t'}^\omega \top \\ & \quad \land \forall t'' \in (t', t].\omega \not\models_{t''} \tau \\ & \quad \land \omega(t+2) > \omega(t') + dl \\ M & \text{otherwise} \end{cases}$$

Intuitively, assuming tasks represent individual streams, a stream must be evaluated at time $t+1$ (i.e., $\psi(\omega, t)(\tau) = Y$) if there exists a condition in the static schedule that was satisfied at an earlier time t' and no new value has been produced for that stream since. Then, $t+1$ is the last chance to produce a value for that stream before violating its deadline. Otherwise, the scheduling decision defaults to M, allowing the stream's evaluation to be postponed.

Priority. We may want to fully utilize the available bandwidth without manually assigning explicit deadlines. To support this use case, we introduce the *priority*-based static schedule constraint. In this case, each task is assigned a priority depending on conditions, dynamically determining its importance:

$$\text{Priority} : \text{Tasks} \to \mathcal{P}\left(\text{Cond} \times \mathbb{N}\right).$$

At each time step, the scheduler must select the streams with the highest priority. Given a static schedule constraint $\xi \in \text{Priority}$, we determine the current priority of a task with $Prio_\xi$:

$$Prio_\xi : \text{Tasks} \times \mathbb{W} \times \text{Time} \to (\text{Cond} \times \mathbb{N})_\perp$$

$$Prio_\xi(\tau, \omega, t) = \begin{cases} \arg\max_{(c,p) \in S}(\max\{t' \mid t' \leq t \land c \Downarrow_{t'}^{\omega} \top\}) & \text{if } (c, p) \text{ exists} \\ \perp & \text{otherwise} \end{cases}$$

$Prio_\xi$ returns the most recent priority assignment of a task (if any) whose condition evaluates to true in ω at some time point $t' \leq t$. Using this function, we translate a static schedule $\xi \in \text{Priority}$ into a dynamic schedule $\psi \in S$ with

$$\psi(\omega, t)(\tau) = \begin{cases} \text{Y} & \text{if } (c_1, p_1) = Prio_\xi(\tau, \omega, t) \\ & \land \exists \tau'.(c_2, p_2) = Prio_\xi(\tau', \omega, t) \\ & \land \omega \models_{t+1} \tau' \land p_1 > p_2 \\ & \land \neg \exists \tau'' \succeq \tau.\omega \models_{t+1} \tau'' \\ \text{M} & \text{otherwise} \end{cases}$$

With this definition, a task must be selected if another, lower-priority task is selected for evaluation at the next step. This restriction, however, does not hold if the task is part of a larger, high-priority task, indicated by the dependency relation.

Deadline and Priority. The priority schedule allows specifying the relative importance of tasks without explicitly reasoning about individual deadlines. However, this can lead to starvation: a lower-priority task may never be evaluated if higher-priority tasks continuously occupy all available bandwidth. To address this issue, we propose a combined schedule that merges priorities with deadlines. By default, the schedule behaves like the priority schedule. However, each τ is assigned a deadline dl_τ, which defines the maximum duration it may remain unevaluated before it is considered *overdue*:

$$\text{overdue} : \text{Tasks} \times \mathbb{W} \times \text{Time} \to \mathbb{B}$$
$$\text{overdue}(\tau, \omega, t) = \exists \tau' \subseteq \tau.$$
$$\omega(t) - \omega(\max\{t' \in \text{Time} \mid t' < t \land \omega \models_{t'} \tau'\}) > dl_\tau$$

An overdue stream should be evaluated, regardless of the assigned priority. We translate a static schedule constraint $\xi \in \text{Priority}$ into a dynamic schedule constraint $\psi \in S$ with:

$$\psi(\omega, t)(\tau) = \begin{cases} Y & \text{if } \exists \tau'.overdue(\tau, \omega, t+1) \wedge \neg overdue(\tau', \omega, t+1) \\ & \wedge \omega \models_{t+1} \tau' \\ Y & \text{if } (\_, p_1) = Prio_s(\tau, \omega, t) \\ & \wedge \exists \tau'.(\_, p_2) = Prio_s(\tau', \omega, t) \\ & \wedge \omega \models_{t+1} \tau' \wedge p_1 > p_2 \wedge \neg overdue(\tau', \omega, t+1) \\ & \wedge \neg \exists \tau'' \succeq \tau.\omega \models_{t+1} \tau'' \\ M & \text{otherwise} \end{cases}$$

This definition assigns overdue tasks an even higher priority, but in general, it follows the previous definition.

3.3 Valid Scheduler

A scheduler is a program that, given schedule and bandwidth constraints, decides at each time point which set of tasks to evaluate. If all selections respect the constraints, the scheduler is considered valid:

Definition 3 (Valid Scheduler). *Given a static schedule constraint ξ over a set of Tasks, a specification φ and a bandwidth bound B, a scheduler $SA_{\xi,B}$: $\mathbb{W} \times Time \to \mathcal{P}(Tasks)$ that decides at each timepoint which streams are evaluated at the next time step, is* valid *if*

1. $\forall \omega \in [\![(\varphi, \xi, B)]\!].\forall t \in Time.\forall T \subseteq Tasks.\forall i \in InputValues.$
$prefix_{SA_{\xi,B}}(\omega, t) \wedge SA_{\xi,B}(\omega, t) = T \wedge i \models T$
$\to \exists \omega' \in [\![(\varphi, \xi, B)]\!].validTasks(\omega', t+1, T) \wedge \omega'[..t] = \omega[..t] \wedge \omega'[t+1] = i.$
2. $\forall \omega \in [\![(\varphi, \xi, B)]\!].\forall t \in Time.\exists t' > t.|SA_{\psi,B}(\omega, t')| \geq 1$

with

$$validTasks : \mathbb{W} \times Time \times \mathcal{P}(Tasks) \to \mathbb{B}$$
$$validTasks(\omega, t, T) = \forall \tau \in T.\omega \models_t \tau \wedge \forall \tau \notin T.\omega \not\models_t \tau$$
$$\wedge \forall \tau_1, \tau_2 \in Tasks.\tau_1 \preceq \tau_2 \wedge \tau_2 \in T \to \tau_1 \in T$$
$$prefix_{SA_{\xi,B}} : \mathbb{W} \times Time \to \mathbb{B}$$
$$prefix_{SA_{\xi,B}}(\omega, t) = \forall t' < t.validTasks(\omega, t'+1, SA_{\xi,B}(\omega, t'))$$

A scheduler is considered valid if it satisfies two properties: 1. The scheduler must never get stuck. That is, for every point in time and any possible choice of input values consistent with the selected tasks, the evaluation model must be able to continue as a correctly scheduled evaluation model. 2. The scheduler may not indefinitely select empty tasks. These conditions ensure that the scheduler defines a sound evaluation strategy.

4 Active Scheduling in RTLola

This section demonstrates how our scheduling approach is integrated with the stream-based monitoring language RTLola. The overall architecture is illustrated in Fig. 1. First, we allow users to augment RTLola specifications with scheduling annotations, as shown on the left side of the figure. These annotations assign deadlines or priorities to individual streams or clauses, and are detailed in Sect. 4.1. A translator then processes the annotated specification and produces a transformed RTLola specification. During this step, the translator interprets the scheduling annotations and adds helper streams that encode the scheduling constraints. We describe the translation process in Sect. 4.2 in more detail. The resulting specification is compatible with existing RTLola implementations, while a separate scheduling component interfaces between the backend and the sensors to issue sensor queries at runtime. We further explain this scheduler interface in Sect. 4.3.

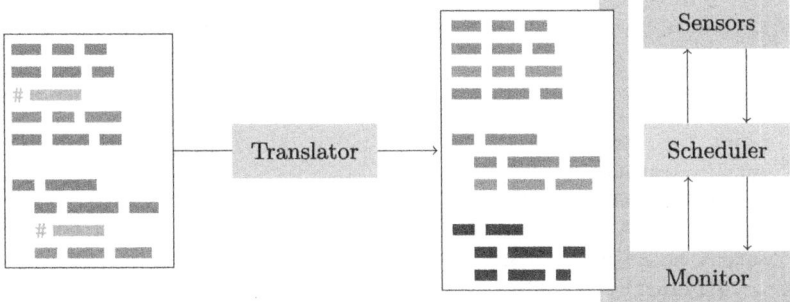

Fig. 1. Overview of the scheduling process.

4.1 Annotations

For the configuration of the scheduler, we embed the scheduling-related information as annotations directly within the specification. These annotations attach constraints to streams – either directly on input streams or on the eval-clause of output streams. Each annotation defines either a *priority* or a *deadline* – following the idea from Sect. 3.2. We represent the annotations as a mapping $a \in \text{ID} \to \mathcal{P}(\text{Cond} \times \mathbb{V})$. The conditions are a combination of the pacing of the stream and an expression derived from the when-conditions of the annotated eval clause. However, since when-conditions are evaluated top-to-bottom, the effective condition for each clause includes not only its own when-condition but also the negation of all preceding ones. This ensures that conditions are mutually exclusive, reflecting the semantics of sequential when evaluation. Depending on the kind of static schedule used for scheduling, the value $\mathbb{V}$ is either a deadline

∈ ℝ or a priority ∈ ℕ. For deadline-priority scheduling, annotations consist of priorities, while deadlines of individual tasks are configured globally.

Example 3. The specification in Fig. 2 monitors two conditions: 1. whether the current latitude and longitude violate a geofence, and 2. whether the current altitude exceeds an upper bound. The annotations result in the following representation:

$$s(\texttt{bound\_violation}) = \{(\texttt{@lat\&\&lon}, \texttt{distance\_to\_bound} < 12.0), 10),$$
$$(\texttt{@lat\&\&lon}, \texttt{distance\_to\_bound} >= 12.0), 1)\},$$
$$s(\texttt{altitude\_violation}) = \{(\texttt{@alt}, \texttt{true}), 5)\}$$

The specification assigns the output `bound_violation` a high priority, numerically represented as 10, if the distance to the bound is smaller than 12. If it is further away from the bound, the bound check is assigned a low priority, a 1. The altitude check is assigned a constant medium priority, represented as a 5. As a result, when the system is far away from a geofence boundary, the altitude has a higher priority and is therefore checked more frequently. Conversely, as the system approaches a potential geofence violation, geofence monitoring is prioritized.

```
1  input lat, lon, alt : Float64
2  output distance_to_bound
3     eval @lat&&lon
4        with min(lat - 3, UPPER_LAT - 8, lon - 5, UPPER_LON - 10)
5  output bound_violation
6     #[priority="high"]
7     eval @lat&&lon when distance_to_bound < 12.0
8        with distance_to_bound < 0.0
9     #[priority="low"]
10    eval @lat&&lon when distance_to_bound >= 12.0
11       with false
12 output altitude_violation
13    #[priority="medium"]
14    eval @alt with altitude > 50.0
```

Fig. 2. Example of scheduling annotations in RTLola.

4.2 Translation

A translator converts the annotated specification into a standard RTLola specification that any existing implementation can process. This translation aims to ensure that the resulting monitor satisfies the specified scheduling constraints by guiding the scheduling component to supply the necessary inputs at appropriate times. For this, it adds additional output streams to the resulting specification, which are in turn read by the scheduling component.

At first glance, one expects the scheduling annotations to correspond directly to the static schedule. However, setting Tasks = ID leads to an issue, as illustrated in Fig. 3. Assume the scheduler is restricted to providing a new value to only one input stream at a time. In this scenario, there is no valid schedule that updates any inputs. If stream a receives a new value due to its high priority, stream c is also evaluated, triggered by its pacing. Yet, a stream with higher priority, namely b, is not evaluated, contradicting the scheduling semantics.

```
1  #[priority="high"]
2  input a : UInt64
3  #[priority="medium"]
4  input b : UInt64
5  output c
6    #[priority="low"]
7    eval @a when true with a + 1
```

Fig. 3. Example specification.

The root of the issue is, that while output streams can be annotated with scheduling constraints, in practice, the evaluation of output streams is controlled by the underlying monitor and determined by its pacing type – the scheduler can only decide when to emit new input values to the monitor – and not prevent the evaluation of outputs. Consequently, the scheduler must supply inputs at a frequency that respects the scheduling annotations of all outputs streams, by satisfying their pacing at the right times. To support this idea, we restrict tasks to sets of input streams, i.e., Tasks = $\mathcal{P}\left(\text{ID}^\dagger\right)$, and propagate all annotations from output streams to the corresponding sets of inputs necessary for their evaluation.

Definition 4 (RTLola Tasks). *Given an RTLola specification φ containing input streams* $\text{ID}^\dagger$, *we define the task set* Tasks = $\mathcal{P}\left(\text{ID}^\dagger\right)$ *with*

$$\omega \models_t \tau \quad \text{iff} \quad \forall i \in \tau. \omega(i)(t) \neq \bot$$
$$\tau_1 \preceq \tau_2 \quad \text{iff} \quad \tau_1 \subseteq \tau_2$$
$$i \models \mathcal{T} \quad \text{iff} \quad \forall s \in \text{ID}^\dagger. i(s) \neq \bot \Leftrightarrow \{i\} \in \mathcal{T}.$$

Given annotations $a : \text{ID} \to \mathcal{P}(\text{Cond} \times \mathbb{V})$, we construct the static schedule ξ_a as the following, where $pac(s)$ returns the pacing of stream $s \in \text{ID}$:

$$\xi_a : \mathcal{P}\left(\text{ID}^\dagger\right) \to \mathcal{P}(\text{Cond} \times \mathbb{V})$$
$$\xi_a(\tau) = \left\{(c, v) \mid v = \max\left\{v' \mid \exists s \in \text{ID}.pac(s) \subseteq \tau \land (c', v') \in a(s) \land c' \Rightarrow c\right\}\right\}$$

In other words, for each task – i.e., set of input streams – the schedule includes all constraint-condition pairs (c, v) such that v is the maximal value out of all annotations of streams whose pacing is implied by τ, and whose conditions imply c. The maximal value is chosen according to the domain $\mathbb{V}$: it represents the most restrictive constraint, e.g., the highest priority, or the shortest deadline.

Through pacing types in RTLola, the task dependency relation is not sufficient to determine if a task set is valid. Consider the following example where we have two input streams, i and i', and a task set containing the tasks i and i'. When both input streams are updated, the pacing consisting of their combination also activates because of the RTLola semantics. Therefore, we need to ensure that the task containing the combination is also part of the task set. We therefore have to strengthen the notion of valid task sets introduced in Definition 3 with the additional constraint

$$\forall \tau_1, \tau_2 \in \text{Tasks}.\tau_1, \tau_2 \in \mathcal{T} \to \tau_1 \cup \tau_2 \in \mathcal{T}.$$

To represent this static schedule as additional RTLola streams, we construct a single stream for each task, i.e., each pacing type. We utilize different clauses guarded by the corresponding condition to dynamically assign the schedule value of a task based on the current state. The clauses are ordered by their schedule value in ascending order, so that more restrictive schedules are considered first. Further, for each task, separate output streams are added, which note the time of the task's last evaluation, and if needed, additional streams to indicate if a task is overdue. For the specification in Fig. 2, the translation process would add the following output streams to the specification:

```
output schedule_lat_lon
    eval @lat&&lon when distance_to_bound < 10.0 with 10
    eval @lat&&lon when distance_to_bound >= 10.0 with 1
output last_lat_lon eval @lat&&lon with now
output schedule_alt eval @alt with 5
output last_alt eval @alt with now
```

4.3 Scheduler

While all previous steps occur before the monitor is executed, the scheduler is the runtime component responsible for querying new inputs and passing them to the underlying monitor. In each cycle, the scheduler queries sensors and forwards the obtained values to the monitor, triggering a new evaluation step. As usual, the monitor computes new output stream values, including the schedule streams that guide the scheduling decisions. The scheduler uses these newly computed values to decide which inputs to query in the next cycle.

The strategy the scheduler uses to populate the available bandwidth depends on the type of scheduling constraints. For all strategies, the bandwidth is specified as the number of input values per event b and the number of events per second f_e. At runtime, the scheduler emits events to the monitor at the specified frequency and populates each event with the predefined number of inputs according to the scheduling strategy.

For deadline scheduling, the scheduler $DS_{\xi,B}$ employs an earliest-deadline-first strategy [20]. In this mode, each task is associated with a deadline representing the maximum allowable timestamp of the next update. The scheduler tracks the current time and selects the task with the most urgent deadlines first until the bandwidth is fully utilized. In contrast, for priority scheduling, the scheduler $PS_{\xi,B}$ fills the event with tasks, selected in decreasing order of priority. It is the same for the deadline-priority scheduler $DPS_{\xi,B}$, only that overdue tasks are assigned to a new, highest priority. If multiple streams share the same priority level, the scheduler resolves this by choosing the stream that was updated the longest time ago. The formal definition of these schedulers can be found in the full version [7]. With some restrictions, these schedulers satisfy the validity conditions in Definition 3:

Theorem 1 (Valid RTLola Schedulers). *Given a well-defined specification φ, an annotation $a \in \mathtt{ID} \to \mathcal{P}(\mathit{Cond} \times \mathbb{V})$, and a bound $B = \mathit{InputEventBound}_b$:*

- *The schedulers $PS_{S_a,B}$ and $DPS_{S_a,B}$ are valid if $b \geq \max_{\tau \in \mathit{Tasks}} |\tau|$,*
- *The scheduler $DS_{\xi_a,B}$ is valid if $\forall \tau \in \mathit{Tasks}. \forall (c,dl) \in \xi(\tau).dl > n$ and $b \geq \max_{\tau \in \mathit{Tasks}} |\tau|$, with:*

$$n = \min\{n' \mid \forall \mathcal{T} \in \mathit{Permutations}_{|\mathit{Tasks}|}(\mathit{Tasks}).\mathit{splits}_B(\mathcal{T},\varepsilon) = n'\}$$

$$\mathit{Permutations}_{|\mathit{Tasks}|}(\mathit{Tasks}) = \left\{ \tau_1 \tau_2 \ldots \in \mathit{Tasks}^{|\mathit{Tasks}|} \;\middle|\; \forall i,j. i = j \vee \tau_i \neq \tau_j \right\}$$

$$\mathit{splits}_B(\varepsilon, \mathit{cur}) = 1$$

$$\mathit{splits}_B(\tau_1 \circ \mathcal{T}, \mathit{cur}) = \begin{cases} 1 + \mathit{splits}_B(\tau_1 \circ \mathcal{T}, \varepsilon) & \text{if } |\mathit{cur} \cup \tau_1| > b \\ \mathit{splits}_B(\mathcal{T}, \mathit{cur} \cup \tau_1) & \text{otherwise} \end{cases}$$

Generally, the bandwidth bound b needs to be large enough to accommodate each task individually. For the priority and deadline-priority schedulers, in each step, the tasks can be selected purely on the current priority assignments, and there are no constraints from previous evaluations. The schedule selects the highest priority tasks. Our construction can trigger tasks with a potentially lower priority; however, the dependency relation, together with the construction through the scheduling annotations, ensures that these priorities do not conflict with the semantics. For the deadline scheduler, we need to account for constraints from previous cycles. There, the bound ensures that previously imposed deadlines can't conflict with newly added ones. Detailed proof sketches for the validity of each scheduler can be found in the full version [7].

5 Implementation and Evaluation

We have implemented our approach[1] from Sect. 4 on top of the RTLola monitoring framework [6]. For the evaluation, we use the AirSim simulator, a simulation environment for drones and cars developed by Microsoft. AirSim exposes various sensors through an API, including GPS coordinates, altitude readings, camera images, and LIDAR data.

For our evaluation, we investigate the following setting with the deadline-priority constraints. A drone is tasked to collect barometer data during flight for an experiment in a restricted airspace. It relies on four sensors, which must share the limited available bandwidth of the drone: the GPS and altitude sensor for

---

[1] The artifacts can be found on https://github.com/reactive-systems/rtlola-active-monitoring.

enforcing their respective bounds, and two barometers, whose data collection for the experiment is the primary target of the flight. We use stream annotations as presented in Sect. 4.1 to represent different priorities for the tasks in the specification. The closer the drone comes to the geofence border, threatening a violation, the higher the assigned priority of the geofence task becomes. Likewise, the closer the drone comes to an altitude violation, the higher the assigned priority. The barometers, which serve the experiment, are assigned a constant medium priority. As a result, they receive most of the bandwidth if there is no immediate danger of a boundary violation. We employ overdue deadlines to ensure the geofence bounds are checked at least every 3 s to prevent violations from being missed because of higher priority tasks. The annotated specification can be found in Fig. 4.

In our experiments, we compare the behavior of our scheduled monitoring approach against a set of baseline monitors that query all inputs at fixed frequencies. Each baseline monitor queries all sensors at the same frequency, but we vary this frequency across baselines to explore the trade-off between bandwidth and responsiveness. To ensure a fair comparison, all monitors observe the same drone flight in parallel.

The goal of the evaluation is to assess the effectiveness of actively scheduling the inputs in runtime monitoring under bandwidth constraints. Specifically, we aim to answer the following questions: 1. Can we reduce the overall bandwidth consumption while maintaining a comparable level of monitoring quality? 2. Can we detect specification violations earlier by allocating the bandwidth more intelligently – focusing on data that is more likely to reveal a violation?

We evaluate the performance of our scheduling approach over 10 flights with the simulator by analyzing two metrics obtained from the evaluation. Figure 5a shows the average number of values that occupy the bandwidth for each sensor. For each monitor, we group the sensors into two categories, represented by the horizontal bars: The blue bar captures the bandwidth used for geofence and altitude checks, while the red bar shows the bandwidth used for collecting barometer data for the experiment. In the fixed-frequency monitors, bandwidth is distributed evenly across all sensors. In contrast, the scheduled monitor dynamically adjusts the frequency of sensor queries based on the current state of the system, resulting in an uneven allocation of bandwidth. As shown in the figure, the scheduled monitor allocates more bandwidth to the barometer sensors, aligning with the experiment's objective of maximizing barometer data collection. Meanwhile, the sensors responsible for enforcing the geofence and altitude boundaries are queried less frequently. In contrast, Fig. 5 presents a boxplot of the delay in detecting violations. Delays are measured relative to the earliest point in time any monitor detects the same violation.

To answer the first question, the results show that our scheduled monitor detects violations as early as the fastest fixed-frequency monitor operating at 2 Hz. Notably, it achieves this while consuming half the bandwidth, as evident from the comparison in the previous figure.

```
 1  #![frequency="2Hz",bound="2"]
 2  import math
 3  #[deadline="3s"]
 4  input gps_lat_long : (Float64, Float64)
 5  #[deadline="3s"]
 6  input gps_altitude : Float64
 7  #[priority="medium",deadline="3s"]
 8  input barometer_pressure : Float64
 9  #[priority="medium",deadline="3s"]
10  input barometer_altitude : Float64
11  output lat := gps_lat_long.0
12  output long := gps_lat_long.1
13  output start_lat @gps_lat_long :=
        start_lat.offset(by:-1).defaults(to: lat)
14  output start_long @gps_lat_long :=
        start_long.offset(by:-1).defaults(to: long)
15  output start_altitude @gps_altitude :=
        start_altitude.offset(by:-1).defaults(to: gps_altitude)
16  output distance_to_start := sqrt((lat-start_lat)*(lat-start_lat)
17    + (long-start_long)*(long-start_long))*10000.0
18  output altitude_above_ground := gps_altitude - start_altitude
19  output geofence := distance_to_start ≥ 8.0
20  output scheduled_geofence
21    #[priority="low"]
22    eval @gps_lat_long when distance_to_start ≤ 4.0
23                     with geofence
24    #[priority="medium"]
25    eval @gps_lat_long when distance_to_start ≤ 6.0
26                     with geofence
27    #[priority="high"]
28    eval @gps_lat_long with geofence
29  trigger scheduled_geofence "outside geofence"
30  output altitude_bound := altitude_above_ground ≥ 10.0
31  output scheduled_altitude_bound
32    #[priority="low"]
33    eval @gps_altitude when altitude_above_ground ≤ 5.0
34                     with altitude_bound
35    #[priority="medium"]
36    eval @gps_altitude when altitude_above_ground ≤ 7.5
37                     with altitude_bound
38    #[priority="high"]
39    eval @gps_altitude with altitude_bound
40  trigger scheduled_altitude_bound "altitude too high"
```

Fig. 4. Evaluation Specification

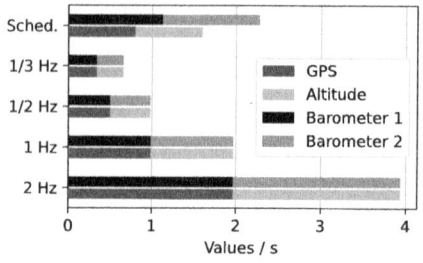 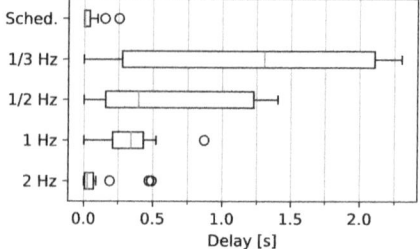

(a) Bandwidth consumption of each sensor. (b) Delay until trigger is detected.

Fig. 5. Comparison between the scheduled monitor and four fixed-frequency ones. (Color figure online)

To answer the second question, we compare the scheduled monitor against a fixed-frequency monitor with equal bandwidth usage. The scheduled monitor consumes four values per second – equivalent to the bandwidth of a 1 Hz fixed-frequency monitor. Despite this, the scheduled monitor detects violations significantly earlier than the 1 Hz monitor, because in critical situations, the scheduled monitor focuses on the more critical inputs. This demonstrates that our approach makes more effective use of the available bandwidth through our scheduling approach.

6 Conclusion

We addressed the challenge of runtime monitoring in bandwidth-constrained environments by presenting an approach to dynamically allocating the available bandwidth to different sensors depending on the monitor's current state. This approach enables the monitor to prioritize inputs and allocate bandwidth to data most likely to reveal specification violations. To facilitate this, we define a formal semantics for scheduled monitors and introduce several static schedules. Scheduling annotations, embedded directly within the specification, offer an intuitive and flexible mechanism to express constraints guiding the scheduler. A scheduler interfacing between the monitor and the sensors is responsible for querying sensors at the appropriate times and passing the values to the underlying monitor. We evaluated our approach using simulations in the AirSim drone simulator. The results demonstrate the effectiveness of scheduled monitoring in detecting violations early on, while consuming significantly less bandwidth compared to a monitor receiving all inputs at a fixed frequency.

For future work, we want to evaluate our approach in a real-world setting to assess the overhead introduced by querying sensors with the active role of the monitor. Furthermore, many real-world settings involve sensors producing multiple values, leading to more complex task dependencies. We want to investigate how our approach can be extended to handle such cases.

Acknowledgments. This work was partially supported by the German Research Foundation (DFG) as part of TRR 248 (No. 389792660) and by the European Research Council (ERC) Grant HYPER (No. 101055412).

References

1. Afshar, S., Behnam, M., Bril, R.J., Nolte, T.: Resource sharing under global scheduling with partial processor bandwidth. In: 10th IEEE International Symposium on Industrial Embedded Systems, SIES 2015, Siegen, Germany, June 8-10, 2015, pp. 195–206. IEEE (2015). https://doi.org/10.1109/SIES.2015.7185061
2. Agrawal, A.: Hardware Contention-Aware Real-Time Scheduling on Multi-Core Platforms in Safety-Critical Systems. Ph.D. thesis, Kaiserslautern University of Technology, Germany (2019). https://kluedo.ub.rptu.de/frontdoor/index/index/docId/5612
3. Baumeister, J., Correnson, A., Finkbeiner, B., Scheerer, F.: An intermediate program representation for optimizing stream-based languages. In: Piskac, R., Rakamarić, Z. (eds.) Computer Aided Verification, pp. 393–407. Springer, Cham (2025). https://doi.org/10.1007/978-3-031-98682-6_20
4. Baumeister, J., Dauer, J.C., Finkbeiner, B., Schirmer, S.: Monitoring with verified guarantees. Int. J. Softw. Tools Technol. Transf. **25**(4), 593–616 (2023). https://doi.org/10.1007/S10009-023-00712-3
5. Baumeister, J., et al.: Monitoring unmanned aircraft: specification, integration, and lessons-learned. In: Gurfinkel, A., Ganesh, V. (eds.) Computer Aided Verification - 36th International Conference, CAV 2024, Montreal, QC, Canada, July 24-27, 2024, Proceedings, Part II. Lecture Notes in Computer Science, vol. 14682, pp. 207–218. Springer, Cham (2024). https://doi.org/10.1007/978-3-031-65630-9_10
6. Baumeister, J., Finkbeiner, B., Kohn, F., Scheerer, F.: A tutorial on stream-based monitoring. In: International Symposium on Formal Methods, pp. 624–648. Springer, Cham (2024)
7. Baumeister, J., Finkbeiner, B., Scheerer, F.: Active monitoring with rtlola: a specification-guided scheduling approach (2025). https://arxiv.org/abs/2507.20615
8. Baumeister, J., Finkbeiner, B., Scheerer, F., Siber, J., Wagenpfeil, T.: Stream-based monitoring of algorithmic fairness. In: Gurfinkel, A., Heule, M. (eds.) Tools and Algorithms for the Construction and Analysis of Systems, pp. 60–81. Springer, Cham (2025). https://doi.org/10.1007/978-3-031-90643-5_4
9. Baumeister, J., Finkbeiner, B., Schirmer, S., Schwenger, M., Torens, C.: RTLola cleared for take-off: monitoring autonomous aircraft. In: Lahiri, S.K., Wang, C. (eds.) CAV 2020. LNCS, vol. 12225, pp. 28–39. Springer, Cham (2020). https://doi.org/10.1007/978-3-030-53291-8_3
10. Baumeister, J., Finkbeiner, B., Schwenger, M., Torfah, H.: FPGA stream-monitoring of real-time properties. ACM Trans. Embed. Comput. Syst. **18**(5s), 88:1–88:24 (2019). https://doi.org/10.1145/3358220
11. Bonakdarpour, B., Navabpour, S., Fischmeister, S.: Sampling-based runtime verification. In: Butler, M., Schulte, W. (eds.) FM 2011. LNCS, vol. 6664, pp. 88–102. Springer, Heidelberg (2011). https://doi.org/10.1007/978-3-642-21437-0_9
12. Buttazzo, G.: Hard Real-Time Computing Systems: Predictable Scheduling Algorithms and Applications. Real-Time Systems Series, Springer, Boston (2011)

13. d'Angelo, B., et al.: LOLA: runtime monitoring of synchronous systems. In: 12th International Symposium on Temporal Representation and Reasoning (TIME 2005), pp. 166–174. IEEE (2005)
14. Eremeev, A.V., Malakhov, A.A., Sakhno, M.A., Sosnovskaya, M.Y.: Multi-core processor scheduling with respect to data bus bandwidth. CoRR **abs/2010.16058** (2020). https://arxiv.org/abs/2010.16058
15. Falcone, Y., Havelund, K., Reger, G.: A tutorial on runtime verification. In: Broy, M., Peled, D.A., Kalus, G. (eds.) Engineering Dependable Software Systems, NATO Science for Peace and Security Series, D: Information and Communication Security, vol. 34, pp. 141–175. IOS Press (2013). https://doi.org/10.3233/978-1-61499-207-3-141
16. Faymonville, P., et al.: Streamlab: stream-based monitoring of cyber-physical systems. In: Dillig, I., Tasiran, S. (eds.) Computer Aided Verification - 31st International Conference, CAV 2019, New York City, NY, USA, July 15-18, 2019, Proceedings, Part I. LNCS, vol. 11561, pp. 421–431. Springer, Cham (2019). https://doi.org/10.1007/978-3-030-25540-4_24
17. Gorostiaga, F., Sánchez, C.: Striver: Stream runtime verification for real-time event-streams. In: International Conference on Runtime Verification, pp. 282–298. Springer, Cham (2018)
18. Hagen, G., Tinelli, C.: Scaling up the formal verification of lustre programs with SMT-based techniques. In: Cimatti, A., Jones, R.B. (eds.) Formal Methods in Computer-Aided Design, FMCAD 2008, Portland, Oregon, USA, 17-20 November 2008, pp. 1–9. IEEE (2008). https://doi.org/10.1109/FMCAD.2008.ECP.19
19. Havelund, K., Goldberg, A.: Verify your runs. In: Meyer, B., Woodcock, J. (eds.) VSTTE 2005. LNCS, vol. 4171, pp. 374–383. Springer, Heidelberg (2008). https://doi.org/10.1007/978-3-540-69149-5_40
20. Horn, W.: Some simple scheduling algorithms. Naval Res. Logistics Q. **21**(1), 177–185 (1974)
21. Huang, X., et al.: Software monitoring with controllable overhead. Int. J. Softw. Tools Technol. Transf. **14**(3), 327–347 (2012). https://doi.org/10.1007/S10009-010-0184-4
22. Kallwies, H., Leucker, M., Schmitz, M., Schulz, A., Thoma, D., Weiss, A.: Tessla–an ecosystem for runtime verification. In: International Conference on Runtime Verification, pp. 314–324. Springer, Cham (2022)
23. Leucker, M., Schallhart, C.: A brief account of runtime verification. J. Log. Algebraic Methods Program. **78**(5), 293–303 (2009). https://doi.org/10.1016/J.JLAP.2008.08.004
24. Navabpour, S., Bonakdarpour, B., Fischmeister, S.: Path-aware time-triggered runtime verification. In: Qadeer, S., Tasiran, S. (eds.) RV 2012. LNCS, vol. 7687, pp. 199–213. Springer, Heidelberg (2013). https://doi.org/10.1007/978-3-642-35632-2_21
25. Perez, I., Goodloe, A.E., Dedden, F.: Runtime verification in real-time with the copilot language: a tutorial. In: Platzer, A., Rozier, K.Y., Pradella, M., Rossi, M. (eds.) Formal Methods - 26th International Symposium, FM 2024, Milan, Italy, September 9-13, 2024, Proceedings, Part II. LNCS, vol. 14934, pp. 469–491. Springer, Cham (2024). https://doi.org/10.1007/978-3-031-71177-0_27
26. Rozier, K.Y., Schumann, J.: R2U2: tool overview. In: Reger, G., Havelund, K. (eds.) RV-CuBES 2017. An International Workshop on Competitions, Usability, Benchmarks, Evaluation, and Standardisation for Runtime Verification Tools, September 15, 2017, Seattle, WA, USA. Kalpa Publications in Computing, vol. 3, pp. 138–156. EasyChair (2017). https://doi.org/10.29007/5PCH

27. Stoller, S.D., Bartocci, E., Seyster, J., Grosu, R., Havelund, K., Smolka, S.A., Zadok, E.: Runtime verification with state estimation. In: Khurshid, S., Sen, K. (eds.) Runtime Verification - Second International Conference, RV 2011, San Francisco, CA, USA, September 27-30, 2011, Revised Selected Papers. Lecture Notes in Computer Science, vol. 7186, pp. 193–207. Springer (2011). https://doi.org/10.1007/978-3-642-29860-8_15
28. Xu, D., Wu, C., Yew, P.: On mitigating memory bandwidth contention through bandwidth-aware scheduling. In: Salapura, V., Gschwind, M., Knoop, J. (eds.) 19th International Conference on Parallel Architectures and Compilation Techniques, PACT 2010, Vienna, Austria, September 11-15, 2010, pp. 237–248. ACM (2010). https://doi.org/10.1145/1854273.1854306

The Power of Reframing: Using LLMs in Synthesizing RV Monitors

Itay Cohen[1], Klaus Havelund[2], Doron Peled[1(✉)], and Yoav Goldberg[1]

[1] Bar Ilan University, 52900 Ramat Gan, Israel
doron.peled@gmail.com
[2] Jet Propulsion Laboratory, California Institute of Technology, Pasadena, USA

Abstract. We present a method and an interactive tool named LLMon that utilizes an LLM for synthesizing RV monitors from temporal or natural language (NL) specifications. Our focus is on allowing the flexibility of defining further temporal constructs on top of the standard ones; it helps to better customize the temporal formalism for expressing requirements originally given in NL. Our method allows the user to define new temporal operators through interaction with the tool. The LLM reframes the given descriptions of new operators, provided by the user in natural language, and synthesizes code for each alternative description. It performs analysis that compares the alternative generated codes, based on searching for traces with distinguishing verdicts. It then generates verbal descriptions that help the user to select the correct semantic interpretation. The tool can be used to synthesize monitors either directly from specifications in the extended temporal logic, or from NL descriptions.

1 Introduction

We study here the synthesis of Runtime Verification (RV) monitors from Natural Language (NL) descriptions with the help of Large Language Models (LLMs) [3,14,16,17]. Such a monitor can follow the execution of a process, based on captured events, and provide a verdict w.r.t. given requirements. The requirements are often written using a fixed formalism such as temporal logic, automata, or rule systems [4–6,12,15]. In typical scenarios, users who wish to utilize RV technology must be familiar with the native formalism supported by the tool that is used. Often, the constructs of such formalisms may not directly align precisely with the engineer's needs, and the user must therefore engage in a complicated *encoding*.

The research performed by Itay Cohen and Doron Peled was partially funded by Israeli Science Foundation grant 2454/23: "Validating and controlling software and hardware systems assisted by machine learning". The research performed by Klaus Havelund was carried out at Jet Propulsion Laboratory, California Institute of Technology, under a contract with the National Aeronautics and Space Administration.

In this work, we focus on the translation of requirements that are originally formulated in natural language into RV monitors. This poses some challenges. The natural language description may contain phrases that are far removed from the constructs of the formalism used by a given tool. This may result in unreliable translations. Further, a natural language description may contain some ambiguity. Even for simple temporal constructs there can sometimes be alternative interpretations that make sense. Suppose that we want to use a temporal operator $q_1 HB q_2$, where HB stands for *happened before*, which we will use as a running example. One interpretation can be that if q_2 holds then q_1 has happened before or at the same timestep. An alternative interpretation is that q_1 has happened strictly before q_2.

In this work, we present a method and the interactive translation tool LLMon [1] based on using LLMs combined with RV synthesis algorithms (e.g., [13]). It can be used to (a) define and implement a monitoring logic in a stepwise manner, and (b) act as a corresponding monitor synthesizer from natural language requirements. This approach differs from similar works that employ LLMs in a more direct manner [8–10], translating requirements to an existing fixed temporal formalism. A fundamental feature of our method is that it allows the flexibility of *adding new operators* to the temporal logic used as specification formalism. It synthesizes a monitor from a specification that uses these constructs. The semantics for these new operators is acquired through interaction in natural language between our tool and the user, rather than only through formal artifacts. One can consider many dozens of such operators, to mention only a few of them: since, previously, historically, previous-time, every k steps, value alternation, all except k times, stable-in-the-past, changes-only-once, initially, never, exactly-once, etc.

We exploit in our method the fact that the ambiguity that appears in natural language is also inherent in LLMs, which are trained on human texts. This ambiguity is a main challenge in automatically translating natural language descriptions into a formal notation. The fact that the ambiguity weakness is shared by both humans and LLMs is turned by our method into a strength by letting the LLM suggest different interpretations of a construct, which the user can then choose between. We employ the following tactic for the selection of the correct interpretation for a new construct. When the user wants to introduce a new temporal construct together with its short natural language description, the LLM suggests several alternative interpretations for the construct, including code for each of these. Based on the user's preferences, the tool compares pairs of such interpretations by synthesizing code for the different interpretations, and compares exhaustively the verdicts they provide on short traces. With such *distinguishing traces*, which possess *different* verdicts for the distinct (re)formulation of the semantics for the new construct, the LLM explains to the user the difference between the definitions, thus assisting the user in choosing between alternative interpretations.

We limit the target specification logic to propositional constructs with past-time semantics, encompassing past-time propositional LTL, but allowing also user-defined constructs that are not directly expressive in this logic (e.g., a past version of Wolper's example in [18]). Our approach is compositional in that the code generated from individual constructs can be combined with code that is independently constructed for other constructs and form a composite specification. Besides using the newly defined constructs, obtained through interaction with the tool in a structured formula, we can include them as part of an NL requirement, which can be translated to a formula and monitored by the code synthesized by our tool. Ultimately, the use of the suggested methodology and tool is a step in the direction of allowing RV users to write the specification in natural language, as close as possible to the given requirement in a design document.

2 Preliminaries

Our method uses LLMs to facilitate synthesizing monitors for temporal specifications. It combines the abilities of LLMs with RV techniques. Specifically, it generates monitors in the style of the past-time LTL monitors in [13]. We describe here that logic and the classical RV algorithm for it.

Propositional Past-Time Linear Temporal Logic. Propositional past-time linear temporal logic (PLTL) is a specification formalism that allows expressing safety properties [2]. The formulas of PLTL are defined using the following grammar:

$$\varphi ::= true \mid q \mid \neg\varphi \mid (\varphi \vee \psi) \mid (\varphi \; \mathcal{S} \; \psi) \mid \ominus\varphi$$

The symbol q denotes a Boolean proposition over some finite set A of *propositions*. The temporal operators have the following informal meaning: the formula $(\varphi \; \mathcal{S} \; \psi)$, which reads as φ *since* ψ, means that ψ holds in some past and φ has been holding since. The property $\ominus\varphi$ (previous-time φ) means that φ is true in the current trace if φ is true in the trace obtained from the current one by omitting the last event. We can also define the following additional derived operators: $(\varphi \wedge \psi) = \neg(\neg\varphi \vee \neg\psi)$, $(\varphi \rightarrow \psi) = (\neg\varphi \vee \psi)$, $\diamondsuit\varphi = (true \; \mathcal{S} \; \varphi)$ ("past" or "once"), and $\boxminus\varphi = \neg\diamondsuit\neg\varphi$ ("always in the past" or "historically").

The Synthesis Algorithm The synthesis algorithm for past-time LTL translates the formula into a syntax tree. The monitor uses a *summary* with one bit per each node of the tree, corresponding to a subformula. The truth value of each such bit corresponds to the truth value (0 or 1) of each subformula after the current sequence of observed events.

Upon intercepting a new event, the summary is updated. The updates propagate bottom up according to the syntax tree and depending on the Boolean values of the new event. Figure 1 depicts the syntax tree and summary generated for the formula $\varphi = ((a \vee b) \mathcal{S} c)$. The left tree is the summary after observing an event with the Boolean values $\langle a=1, b=0, c=1 \rangle$, and the right tree is the summary after further observing an event with $\langle a=0, b=1, c=0 \rangle$. The evaluation of the current right tree will refer to the previous left tree for temporal operator nodes. The update of the summary is according to the algorithm below, with η as its input formula. We denote by $\mathsf{pre}(\varphi)$ the summary

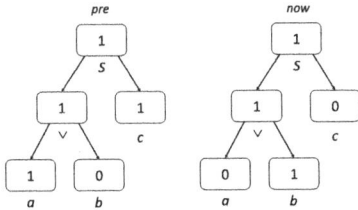

Fig. 1. Syntax tree and summary for $((a \lor b)\,\mathcal{S}\,c)$, given the trace $\langle a = 1,\, b = 0,\, c = 1 \rangle; \langle a = 0,\, b = 1,\, c = 0 \rangle$

value corresponding to the subformula φ before the update (left tree), and by $\mathsf{now}(\varphi)$ the value after the update (right tree). The order of updates is bottom up, according to the syntax tree.

```
now(φ) ← false for each subformula φ of η.
loop
    Observe a new event s ⊆ A as input.
    pre(φ) ← now(φ) for each subformula φ.
    for all subformulas φ of η do
    # If φ is a subformula of ψ then update now(φ) before now(ψ).
        now(true) ← true
        now(p) ← (p ∈ s)
        now(φ ∨ ψ) ← now(φ) ∨ now(ψ)
        now(¬φ) ← ¬ now(φ)
        now(φ S ψ) ← now(ψ) ∨ (now(φ) ∧ pre(φ S ψ))
        now(⊖ φ) ← pre(φ)
    end for
    if now(η) = false then report violation; exit
    end if
end loop
```

One previously explored alternative way to increase the expressiveness of past-time LTL is by adding *transition rules* to the temporal logic [11]. The rules use new propositions B, disjoint of the set of propositions A, and a set of rules of the form $b := L$, where $b \in B$ and L is a Boolean expression that can include propositions from $A \cup B$ and the non-nested previous-time operator $\ominus$; when a proposition from B occurs, it must appear within the scope of the operator $\ominus$. For instance, an example by Wolper [18] shows that one cannot in LTL express that some property holds in every odd state. But this property becomes expressible when adding the following simple rule to past-time LTL: $q := \neg \ominus q$. Then, one can express that p holds in every odd state as $\boxminus(q \to p)$.

3 LLM Synthesis of Monitors with User Defined Temporal Constructs

We present in this section our method for synthesizing RV monitors from NL requirements and the tool LLMon. This involves adding new temporal constructs to a specification formalism. We do this using a running example that showcases the interaction between a prospective user and the tool. We display here only the core content of the prompts given by the tool to the LLM. Note that the user is never interacting directly with the LLM.

Formalism Translation Stage. Assume that the user intends to define a new construct that captures "the occurrence of one event *before* another". The tool asks the user to provide a name, a notation, and a natural language description for the construct. The input from the user is obtained by the interaction with the tool's user interface. The construct information provided by the user does not need to follow a specific format, as it will be embedded in a prompt generated from their response and sent to the LLM, which can infer the user's intent from the free-form text. An interaction can look as follows.

Tool

Please provide a new temporal construct description (name, notation, natural-language semantics), and I will suggest some interpretations for it.

User

Construct name: "happened before".
Notation: q_1 HB q_2
Description: at any timestep, if q_2 holds, q_1 happened before that (or at the same timestep).

Based on this information, the tool assembles a prompt of the following form, that asks the LLM to create multiple (by default four) NL interpretations ("reframings") that are slightly different from the original description. In addition, a Python code is requested in the prompt for every NL interpretation

```
Consider the following construct description: {user description}. Create
four different Python codes that calculate the truth value of the construct.
Each code should be based on a slightly different natural language
interpretation...
Important: the code should update the truth value of the operator in an
efficient way.
```

The emphasis on efficiency in the prompt leads the LLM to generate code that updates the construct truth value with minimal memory overhead, aligning with the classical RV algorithm. According to this prompt, the tool presents the LLM response. We show here only the first two generated interpretations and their code snippets. By default, the tool's user interface displays code snippets in a collapsed state, but users can expand them if they wish to view the code alongside the natural language interpretations.

Tool

Interpretation #1: q_1 can occur at the same timestep or before q_2 for the operator to be true.

```
def __init__(self):
    self.q1_occurred = False
    self.operator_truth = True
def update(self, q1, q2):
    if q2:
        if not self.q1_occurred and not q1:
            self.operator_truth = False
    if q1:
        self.q1_occurred = True
    return self.operator_truth
```

Interpretation #2: q_1 must occur strictly before q_2 for the operator to be true.

```
def __init__(self):
    self.q1_occurred = False
    self.operator_truth = True
def update(self, q1, q2):
    if q2:
        if not self.q1_occurred:
            self.operator_truth = False
    if q1:
        self.q1_occurred = True
    return self.operator_truth
```

At this point, the user needs to select a *primary interpretation*, which is the one whose natural language description most likely reflects their original intent. This interpretation will be compared to the others. Since interpretations are compared in pairs, choosing a primary interpretation reduces the number of comparisons and allows the user to focus on the most relevant ones. The user may also choose to ignore some of the provided versions at this step, or supply their own interpretation in addition to the existing ones. Here, we assume that the user selected the first interpretation as the primary version. Next, in a separate prompt, the LLM is instructed to generate code that compares the user-selected primary version with the alternative versions that remained. Each pairwise comparison should return all short traces of length k (a configurable parameter set up by the user, which should be at least 3) that may differentiate between pairs of the generated code implementations. Since we test the construct codes *in isolation*, it is often sufficient to generate traces of limited length, say with 3–5 events, to capture all the differences in behaviors.

```
Generate Python code that compares the primary version to all the other
versions, based on all the possible traces of length <k>...
```

Subsequently, the tool extracts the code from the LLM response, executes it, and displays the results (distinguishing traces) to the user. This information is available for the user, who, however, may just pass directly to the next step, where the LLM generates insights on these distinguishing traces.

Tool

Comparison: interpretation #1 vs. interpretation #2
Trace: [(q1=F, q2=F); (q1=F, q2=F); (q1=T, q2=T)] ⇒ V1: T, V2: F
▸ Expand for more traces

Comparison: interpretation #1 vs. interpretation #3
..

In the following step, the tool generates a prompt that directs the LLM to examine the given distinguishing traces for each pairwise comparison and identify the key differences between the versions. Note that the tool uses all the distinguishing traces generated per pair of interpretations (the primary one against the alternatives) to generate the text explaining the key differences. This explanation is more intuitive for the user than inspecting the distinguishing traces directly, enabling them to understand how their primary interpretation compares to the alternatives. In the listing below we show an example of such a generated text for a single pair of interpretations.

Tool

Trace analysis:
- Version 1: the operator is true even if q_1 occurs at the same timestep as q_2, allowing more flexibility in satisfying the condition.
- Version 2: the operator is false if q_2 occurs without q_1 having occurred strictly before it. This means that even if q_1 and q_2 occur simultaneously, the operator will be false.

Following this analysis, the user can either select a preferred version, choose a new primary version for additional comparisons, or revise their original description and restart the stage. Let us assume that the user selects Version 1. Now, the tool prompts the LLM to return relevant details about the selected construct version in a JSON format, structured for seamless integration into the tool's knowledge base. The stored attributes include the chosen interpretation description, construct arity (unary or binary), construct symbol (notation), and the Python code implementing its update rule. To maintain compatibility with the upcoming monitor synthesis stage, the LLM is instructed to adhere to specific code design guidelines:

```
The construct class must define:
(1) An __init__ method that sets initial auxiliary variables, current
verdict and previous verdict.
(2) An update(arg) or update(arg1, arg2) method that updates and returns the
verdict. Make sure to actively update the verdict after every new event...

This function will have one argument for an unary operator and two for a
binary operator.
```

Once the LLM returns all construct attributes, the new construct is added to a file containing a JSON array of all constructs generated by the tool. This array serves as the tool's construct knowledge base. At this point, the user may choose to define another construct or continue to the next stage.

NL Specification Translation Stage. This stage focuses on translating a user-provided natural language specification into a structured formula built from the previously introduced constructs. To offer greater flexibility, the user can choose to describe the specification either in natural language or as a structured formula. If the specification is already provided as a structured formula, this stage is bypassed, and the tool moves directly to the monitor synthesis stage.

To handle the translation, the tool issues a dedicated prompt to the LLM that contains the notations and descriptions of the new supported constructs. Given that the new constructs are defined in natural language, the LLM is able to align requirements with those definitions and produce structured formulas using the constructs. This prompt also contains three few-shot examples of illustrative input-output pairs, as done in [7]. These examples focus on the four standard past-time LTL constructs and primarily illustrate the expected output format given a natural language specification. We demonstrate how the tool applies this dedicated translation prompt using the natural language specification shown below.

User
"Whenever a user writes to a file, it must have been created beforehand. The same requirement applies to reading from a file."

The tool appends this specification, together with the JSON array that was built for the constructs, to the translation prompt. The prompt contains two sequential tasks for the LLM to carry out: (1) identify events in the natural language specification and associate them with Boolean variables and (2) translate the NL specification into a structured formula over the available constructs and the Boolean variables that represent the different identified events. Below is the LLM translation for the natural language specification entered by the user.

Tool
The following events were identified and associated with Boolean variables:
q_1 – file was created, q_2 – user writes to a file, q_3 – user reads from a file.
The specification formula: $(q_1 \text{ HB } q_2)$ && $(q_1 \text{ HB } q_3)$

Monitor Synthesis Stage. The tool generates an RV monitor from the structured formula, using a synthesizer component that integrates the features of the new constructs into the classical algorithm. The synthesizer component utilizes a pre-defined parser that extracts all construct symbols and their arities (assumed to be unary or binary) from the tool's knowledge base. This allows it to correctly parse formulas that include newly added constructs and generate an abstract syntax tree (AST). For each construct encountered, the tool retrieves and embeds its corresponding Python code (describing its update rule) into the synthesized monitor file. The monitor generation then proceeds largely in line with the classical algorithm.

4 Experiments

We used LLMon to define new temporal constructs based on natural language descriptions. We report here on experiments with thirteen constructs that were created, each with an associated name, notation and description. The first ten constructs, shown in Table 1, have a corresponding form in past-time LTL, presented in the rightmost column of the table. The latter three are beyond the scope of past-time LTL, but can be expressed using the addition of transition rules [11], as shown in Table 2. For all the constructs that we experimented with, their natural language description often reveals inherent ambiguity. We evaluated our tool using GPT-4o as the underlying LLM (via calls to OpenAI's API), setting the temperature to 0.1. Although we also tested a temperature value of 0, we found that introducing slight randomness encouraged more useful interpretation suggestions compared to fully deterministic outputs. In the cases marked by '∗' in Table 1, through using the interactions with the tool, our given initial description for a new construct turned out not to match our intended meaning of the new construct; this required us to provide an alternative description.

Table 1. Temporal constructs with past-time LTL equivalent expressions.

Construct name	Notation	Natural language description	PLTL equivalence
weak since	$q_1 \text{ WS } q_2$	q_1 has been true since the last time q_2 was true (one step after that). If q_2 never became true, q_1 must hold for the entire sequence.	$(q_1 \mathcal{S} q_2) \vee \boxminus q_1$
previous-time historically*	$\text{PTH}(q_1)$	q_1 was true from the beginning until one step before the most recent event.	$\ominus \boxminus q_1$
value alternation	$\text{VA}(q_1)$	q_1 should change its value at every step.	$\boxminus (\ominus true \rightarrow (q_1 \leftrightarrow \ominus(\neg q_1)))$
consistent Boolean value	$\text{CBV}(q_1)$	true if q_1 is the same across all timesteps.	$\boxminus q_1 \vee \boxminus (\neg q_1)$
never	$\text{N}(q_1)$	q_1 never holds.	$\boxminus(\neg q_1)$
happened before*	$q_1 \text{ HB } q_2$	at any given timestep it is true that if q_2 holds, q_1 happened before that (or at the same timestep).	$\boxminus (q_2 \rightarrow \diamondsuit q_1)$
false since*	$q_1 \text{ FS } q_2$	since one step after the latest occurrence of q_2, q_1 has been false. If q_2 was never true, $q_1 \text{ FS } q_2$ is true.	$\diamondsuit q_2 \rightarrow (\neg q_1 \mathcal{S} q_2)$
false before*	$q_1 \text{ FB } q_2$	Before the current q_2, q_1 was always false.	$q_2 \rightarrow \boxminus(\neg q_1)$
at least once from start	$\text{OAS}(q_1)$	q_1 has been true at least once from start.	$\diamondsuit (\boxminus q_1)$
changes only once	$\text{COO}(q_1)$	q_1 changes its value once in the sequence.	$(q_1 \wedge (q_1 \mathcal{S} \boxminus \neg q_1)) \vee (\neg q_1 \wedge (\neg q_1 \mathcal{S} \boxminus q_1))$

After obtaining the desired update rules for each construct in Table 1, we aimed at verifying their correctness: for each construct, we randomly generated one hundred structured formulas composed of standard logical connectives, the four standard past-time LTL temporal constructs, and the new construct. The formulas varied in size, ranging from ten to twenty syntax tree nodes. We first used the tool's synthesizer component to generate RV monitors for each formula. Then, for each generated formula, we created an equivalent formula by replacing the new construct with its corresponding past-time LTL expression. We utilized the tool's synthesizer component again to generate an additional RV monitor, given the past-time LTL formula where our constructs were translated into their standard past-time LTL form. We compared the two monitors using 10,000 randomly generated traces of 50 events each. In all the constructs tested, no discrepancies were detected in any of the generated formulas.

The last three constructs cannot be expressed as past-time LTL formulas. Consequently, to properly verify them, we had to be able to synthesize RV monitors that support *transition rules*, as presented in Sect. 2. We extended the tool's synthesizer component to support auxiliary Boolean variables, each defined by a transition rule. After verifying the correctness of each construct as done with the previously mentioned constructs, no discrepancies were observed.

Table 2. Temporal constructs beyond the scope of past-time LTL used in our experiments. ($\ominus true$ means that there *is* a previous state)

Construct name	Notation	NL description	Auxiliary variables	Equivalent formula
holds at odd	$ODD(q_1)$	q_1 holds at odd timesteps.	$a_1 := \neg \ominus a_1$	$\boxminus(a_1 \rightarrow q_1)$
holds at some divisible by 3	$DIV3(q_1)$	q_1 holds at some timestep divisible by 3.	$a_1 := \neg(\ominus^2(true) \rightarrow (\ominus^3(true) \land \neg \ominus^3(a_1)))$	$\Diamondsuit(a_1 \land q_1)$
consistent odd and once even	$COOE(q_1)$	q_1 has the same value at all odd timesteps, and holds in at least one even timestep.	$a_1 := \neg \ominus a_1;\ a_2 := \neg(\ominus(true) \rightarrow \ominus a_1)$	$(\boxminus(a_1 \rightarrow q_1) \lor \boxminus(a_1 \rightarrow \neg q_1)) \land (\Diamondsuit(a_2 \land q_1))$

5 Discussion

This work explored a stepwise LLM-assisted workflow for building RV monitors directly from natural language requirements. LLM translation is not perfect. Thus, our approach keeps the human in the loop for selecting the semantics of suggested temporal constructs. It exploits a procedure that facilitates the selection between alternative semantic interpretations for the new constructs. This is based on comparing the verdicts provided on input traces by the different alternative interpretations. Although our method is designed to reduce the reliance on the code generation capabilities of the LLM by performing smaller, human-assisted steps, such a use of LLMs is still not entirely resilient. In our experiments, however, the LLM code generation performed quite reliably. We did not evidence any issues with the LLM automatic generation of code used for the tool to make its internal comparison analysis[1]. Additionally, we observed no issues with the tool's ability to translate NL requirements using the constructs from our experiments. However, we acknowledge that performance in this step may decline if more constructs are introduced or if less capable LLMs are used. Also, the translation of NL requirements to temporal logic may potentially be flawed, which however, may not be much different from how LLMs are used today in code generation.

References

1. LLMon tool source code (2025). https://github.com/itay99988/LLMon
2. Alpern, B., Schneider, F.B.: Recognizing safety and liveness. Distrib. Comput. **2**(3), 117–126 (1987)
3. Anil, R., Borgeaud, S., Wu, Y., Alayrac, J., et al.: Gemini: a family of highly capable multimodal models. CoRR **abs/2312.11805** (2023)

---

[1] We could have guaranteed further reliability by programming these parts, which are not dependent on the user input, ourselves, although we decided to benefit from the LLM's ability to synthesize this code.

4. Barringer, H., Rydeheard, D.E., Havelund, K.: Rule systems for run-time monitoring: from eagle to RuleR. J. Log. Comput. **20**(3), 675–706 (2010)
5. Bartocci, E., Falcone, Y., Francalanza, A., Reger, G.: Introduction to runtime verification. In: Bartocci, E., Falcone, Y. (eds.) Lectures on Runtime Verification. LNCS, vol. 10457, pp. 1–33. Springer, Cham (2018). https://doi.org/10.1007/978-3-319-75632-5_1
6. Basin, D.A., Klaedtke, F., Müller, S., Zalinescu, E.: Monitoring metric first-order temporal properties. J. ACM **62**(2), 15:1–15:45 (2015)
7. Cohen, I., Peled, D.: End-to-End AI generated runtime verification from natural language specification. In: Steffen, B. (ed.) Bridging the Gap Between AI and Reality, pp. 362–384. Springer, Cham (2025)
8. Cosler, M., Hahn, C., Mendoza, D., Schmitt, F., Trippel, C.: nl2spec: interactively translating unstructured natural language to temporal logics with large language models. In: Enea, C., Lal, A. (eds.) Computer Aided Verification - 35th International Conference, CAV 2023, Paris, France, July 17-22, 2023, Proceedings, Part II. LNCS, vol. 13965, pp. 383–396. Springer, Cham (2023)
9. Fuggitti, F., Chakraborti, T.: NL2LTL - a python package for converting natural language (NL) instructions to linear temporal logic (LTL) formulas. In: Williams, B., Chen, Y., et al. (eds.) Thirty-Seventh AAAI Conference on Artificial Intelligence, AAAI 2023, Thirty-Fifth Conference on Innovative Applications of Artificial Intelligence, IAAI 2023, Thirteenth Symposium on Educational Advances in Artificial Intelligence, EAAI 2023, Washington, DC, USA, February 7-14, 2023, pp. 16428–16430. AAAI Press (2023)
10. Hahn, C., Schmitt, F., Tillman, J.J., Metzger, N., Siber, J., Finkbeiner, B.: Formal specifications from natural language. CoRR **abs/2206.01962** (2022)
11. Havelund, K., Peled, D.: An extension of first-order LTL with rules with application to runtime verification. Int. J. Softw. Tools Technol. Transf. **23**(4), 547–563 (2021)
12. Havelund, K., Peled, D., Ulus, D.: First-order temporal logic monitoring with BDDs. Formal Methods Syst. Des. **56**(1), 1–21 (2020)
13. Havelund, K., Roşu, G.: Synthesizing monitors for safety properties. In: Katoen, J.P., Stevens, P. (eds.) Tools and Algorithms for the Construction and Analysis of Systems, pp. 342–356. Springer, Heidelberg (2002)
14. Jiang, A.Q., Sablayrolles, A., Mensch, A., Bamford, C., Chaplot, D.S., et al.: Mistral 7B. CoRR **abs/2310.06825** (2023)
15. Leucker, M., Schallhart, C.: A brief account of runtime verification. J. Log. Algebraic Methods Program. **78**(5), 293–303 (2009)
16. Radford, A., Narasimhan, K., Salimans, T., Sutskever, I., et al.: Improving language understanding by generative pre-training. OpenAI (2018)
17. Touvron, H., Lavril, T., Izacard, G., Martinet, X., Lachaux, M., et al.: LLaMA: open and efficient foundation language models. CoRR **abs/2302.13971** (2023)
18. Wolper, P.: Temporal logic can be more expressive. In: 22nd Annual Symposium on Foundations of Computer Science, Nashville, Tennessee, USA, 28-30 October 1981, pp. 340–348. IEEE Computer Society (1981)

Conformal Safety Shielding for Imperfect-Perception Agents

William Scarbro[1], Calum Imrie[2], Sinem Getir Yaman[2], Kavan Fatehi[2], Corina Păsăreanu[3], Radu Calinescu[2], and Ravi Mangal[1](✉)

[1] Colorado State University, Fort Collins, USA
ravi.mangal@colostate.edu
[2] University of York, York, UK
[3] Carnegie Mellon University, Pittsburgh, USA

Abstract. We consider the problem of safe control in discrete autonomous agents that use learned components for *imperfect* perception (or more generally, state estimation) from high-dimensional observations. We propose a *shield* construction that provides run-time safety guarantees under perception errors by restricting the actions available to an agent, modeled as a Markov decision process, as a function of the state estimates. Our construction uses *conformal prediction* for the perception component, which guarantees that for each observation, the predicted set of estimates includes the actual state with a user-specified probability. The shield allows an action only if it is allowed for *all* the estimates in the predicted set, resulting in *local safety*. We also articulate and prove a *global safety* property of existing shield constructions for perfect-perception agents bounding the probability of reaching unsafe states if the agent always chooses actions prescribed by the shield. We illustrate our approach with a case-study of an experimental autonomous system that guides airplanes on taxiways using high-dimensional perception DNNs.

Keywords: Imperfect Perception · Shielding · Conformal Prediction

1 Introduction

The computational capabilities unlocked by neural networks have made it feasible to build autonomous agents that use learned neural components to interact with their environments for achieving complex goals. As an example, consider an autonomous airplane taxiing system that senses the environment through a camera and is tasked with following the center-line on taxiways [7,12]. The agent *observes* the environment through sensors, *perceives* its underlying state with respect to its environment (position on the taxiway) from the sensor readings via neural components, *chooses* actions (go left, right, or straight) based on the perceived state using either symbolic or neural components, and *executes* the

---
W. Scarbro and C. Imrie—Equal contribution.

actions to update the agent state. The use of neural components for perception can cause the agents to make mistakes when perceiving the underlying state from the sensor readings. We refer to this phenomenon as *imperfect perception*.

Autonomous agents with imperfect perception are often intended to be deployed in safety-critical settings. Accordingly, one would like to ensure that all actions taken by the agent come with safety guarantees. Shielding [11,13] is a promising technique that restricts the set of actions available to the agent at run-time in a manner that guarantees safety. Existing methods, however, either assume that perception is *perfect* [11] or they require mathematically modeling the complex processes of generating observations and perceiving them [3,23].

MDP Formulation. We model agents and their environments together as Markov Decision Processes (MDPs) with safety expressed as a specification in a probabilistic temporal logic. Our MDP formulation is generic and can model any discrete agent that follows the observe-perceive-choose-execute loop while exhibiting stochasticity and non-determinism. Our formulation accounts for the fact that the agent can only access the underlying state through stochastic observations by defining a state of the MDP as a triple of the actual agent state, the observation corresponding to the state, and the estimate of the actual state.

Safety through Conformal Perception and Shielding. In this work, we enforce safety for imperfect-perception agents by constructing, either offline [11] or online [14], a *conformal shield* that restricts the set of available actions in each state of the MDP as a function of the perceived or estimated states. The shield is independent to the actual state and observations resulting from it. Importantly, constructing the shield does not require us to model either the complex generative process mapping actual states to observations or the perception process that maps observations to estimates. Our key insight is to leverage existing methods [11,21] to construct shields for perfect-perception MDPs, i.e., MDPs modeling agents that are able to perceive the underlying states from observations without any errors (thereby making it unnecessary to model the observation and perception processes). Given such a shield, our next idea is to *conformalize* [1,25] the neural perception component so that, given an observation (for instance, an image), it predicts a set of state estimates instead of a single estimate of the underlying actual state. This set is guaranteed to contain the actual state with a user-specified probability, assuming that training and future data are *exchangeable*—a weaker variant of the i.i.d. assumption. Our final step is to use the perfect-perception shield to compute the set of actions that it deems safe with respect to all the states in a predicted set. Since the actual state is guaranteed to be in the predicted set with a user-specified probability (due to conformalization), the resulting set of actions comes with a notion of safety, even under imperfect perception.

Figure 1 gives an overview of our approach. A *conformalizer* constructs the conformalized perception deep neural network (DNN) from the original perception DNN using calibration data in the form of (actual state, observations) pairs. A *shield synthesizer* is used to construct a shield for the perfect-perception agent modeled as the MDP Γ_{Perf}. The synthesized shield and the conformal-

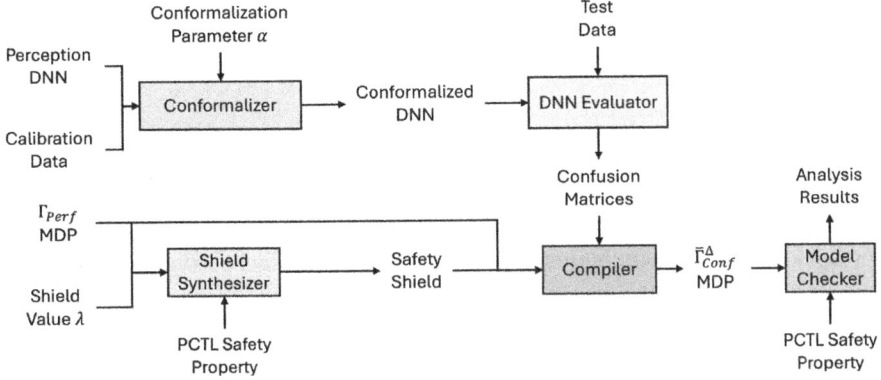

Fig. 1. Overall pipeline for our approach. Γ_{Perf} refers to the MDP formulated for the perfect-perception agent (Sect. 2.2) while $\overline{T}^{\Delta}_{Conf}$ refers to the MDP for the imperfect-perception agent with the conformalized shield and a probabilistic abstraction of the observation and perception processes (Sect. 2.4).

ized perception can then be combined to construct our conformal shield suitable for imperfect-perception agents. Although our shield comes with a local safety guarantee, in our empirical evaluation, we also measure the overall safety of the shielded imperfect-perception agent via model checking. To do so, we formulate an MDP ($\overline{T}^{\Delta}_{Conf}$) representing the shielded, imperfect-perception agent. Due to the complexity of the observation and perception processes, they are replaced in $\overline{T}^{\Delta}_{Conf}$ with a probabilistic abstraction that maps actual states to a distribution over sets of estimated states. This abstraction is constructed using existing methods [2,19] that consume a confusion matrix reporting the performance of the perception component. The *compiler* puts all the pieces together to generate the $\overline{T}^{\Delta}_{Conf}$ MDP from the Γ_{Perf} MDP, the perfect-perception shield, and the confusion matrices representing the performance of the conformalized perception.

Safety Guarantees. Our shield construction provides finite-horizon, probabilistic safety properties where safety is characterized by a set of states to be avoided. In particular, our construction aims for a notion of *local safety*—from any state of the imperfect-perception MDP, if one takes actions as prescribed by the shield, then from the resulting successor states, there very likely exist policies[1] (or strategies or controllers) such that finite-horizon probabilistic safety is guaranteed, even though the shield does not have access to the actual state. We also precisely express and prove the *global safety* guarantees granted by existing shielding methods for perfect-perception MDPs when considering finite-horizon, probabilistic safety properties. A global guarantee ensures that, starting from the initial state, if the agent always chooses actions prescribed by the shield, then the probability of reaching unsafe states in a finite number of steps can be

---

[1] A map from states to actions.

bounded. Our proof also highlights that, in general, shields can cause agents—even under perfect perception—to reach *stuck* states, i.e., states where the shield is empty.

Case Study. We implement our approach and evaluate it using the case study of autonomous airplane taxiing system. We also evaluate the effect of different hyperparameters associated with conformalization and shielding on the safety outcomes. We show that our shield can reduce the probability of imperfect-perception agents reaching unsafe states compared to shields constructed assuming perfect perception.

Contributions. In summary, we make the following contributions: (i) a formal model of imperfect-perception agents as MDPs; (ii) a shield construction for imperfect-perception MDPs that does not require a precise model of the observation and perception processes (iii) statement and proof of global safety guarantees granted by existing shield constructions for perfect-perception agents; (iv) an implementation and evaluation of our ideas via a case study.

2 Theoretical Foundations

In this section, we give MDP formulations of discrete autonomous agents with perfect as well as imperfect perception, with and without shields. We also state and prove local and global safety guarantees for the shielded agents.

2.1 Imperfect-Perception MDP

In this work, an autonomous system (or agent) is a tuple $(S, O, A, \iota, \rho, \eta, \omega)$ where S is the finite system state space, O is the finite observation space (for instance, the space of images of a fixed size), A is the finite action space, $\iota \in S$ is the initial system state, $\omega : S \times O \to [0, 1]$ is the observation function that maps actual states to observations, $\rho : O \to S$ is the perception function mapping observations to state estimates, and $\eta : S \times A \times S \to [0, 1]$ describes the system dynamics. For technical convenience, we assume O has a *null* element (denoted as $\perp_O$).

The system can be formulated as a Markov Decision Process (MDP), $\Gamma := (\hat{S}, A, \hat{\iota}, P)$, where $\hat{S} := S \times O \times S$ is the set of MDP states, $\hat{\iota} := \iota \times \perp_O \times \iota$ is the initial MDP state, and $P : \hat{S} \times A \times \hat{S} \to [0, 1]$ is the (partial) probabilistic transition function defined as:

$$P := \forall s, s', s'' \in S, \forall o, o' \in O.$$
$$(s, o, s') \xrightarrow{\sum_{a' \in A} \eta(s, a', s'') \cdot \omega(s'', m')} (s'', m', \rho(m')) \quad (1)$$

where $\hat{s} \xrightarrow{a, p} \hat{s}'$ denotes $P(\hat{s}, a, \hat{s}') := p$. A controller (or policy or strategy) $\pi : \hat{S} \to A$ fixes the action to take in each state of the MDP. Given a policy π for an MDP Γ, the set of all possible system *paths*, starting from a state $\hat{s}$ is given by $\texttt{Paths}_{\Gamma,\pi}(\hat{s}) := \{(\hat{s}_t)_{t=0}^{\infty} \in \hat{S}^* \mid \forall t \in \mathbb{N}. \ P(\hat{s}_t, \pi(\hat{s}_t), \hat{s}_{t+1}) > 0 \wedge \hat{s}_0 = \hat{s}\}$. Γ with a fixed π gives rise to a probability space over the set $\texttt{Paths}_{\Gamma,\pi}(\hat{s})$ of system paths from the state $\hat{s}$. We use $\mathbb{P}^{\hat{s}}_{\Gamma,\pi}$ to denote the probability measure associated with this space. The probability of a finite path $p \in \texttt{Paths}_{\Gamma,\pi}(\hat{s})$ consisting of states $(\hat{s}_0, ..., \hat{s}_{n-1})$ may be calculated from the transition function P and the policy π as,

$$\mathbb{P}^{\hat{s}}_{\Gamma,\pi}(p) = \prod_{t=0}^{n-2} P(\hat{s}_t, \pi(\hat{s}_t), \hat{s}_{t+1}) \qquad (2)$$

For a set of paths **p** which start from $\hat{s}$, one may compute the probability of observing any path within this set by summing over the probability of all paths within **p** as,

$$\mathbb{P}^{\hat{s}}_{\Gamma,\pi}[\mathbf{p}] = \sum_{p \in \mathbf{p}} \mathbb{P}^{\hat{s}}_{\Gamma,\pi}(p) \qquad (3)$$

Safety Property. We are interested in finite and infinite horizon probabilistic safety properties. Given a set of unsafe system states $S_U \subseteq S$, the set of unsafe states in MDP Γ is given by $\hat{S}_U := \{\hat{s} \in \hat{S} \mid \forall s \in S_U. \ \hat{s} = (s, \_, \_)\}$ and the set of paths that reach unsafe states within n steps from a state $\hat{s}$ is $\texttt{Unsafe}_{\hat{S}_U,n}(\hat{s}) := \{(\hat{s}_t)_{t=0}^{\infty} \in \texttt{Paths}_{\Gamma,\kappa}(\hat{s}) \mid \exists t \leq n. \ \hat{s}_t \in \hat{S}_U\}$. The system is *safe* with respect to a finite horizon of length n and probability p if,

$$\max_{\pi \in \hat{S} \to A} \mathbb{P}^{\hat{\iota}}_{\Gamma,\pi}[\texttt{Unsafe}_{\hat{S}_U,n}(\hat{\iota})] \leq p \qquad (4)$$

A safety property ψ of this form can be expressed in Probabilistic Computational Tree Logic (PCTL) as the property $\mathbb{P}_{\leq p}[F^{\leq n} \hat{S}_U]$ where $\mathbb{P}$ is PCTL's probabilistic operator, F is the eventually modality, and, abusing notation, $\hat{S}_U$ is the proposition that the MDP state is in the set $\hat{S}_U$. We write $\Gamma, \hat{s} \models \phi$ to refer to the fact that the set of paths of the MDP Γ starting from state $\hat{s}$ satisfy the property ψ. If the MDP Γ satisfies Eq. 4, then $\Gamma, \hat{\iota} \models \psi$.

2.2 Perfect-Perception MDP with Shield

An autonomous system is a *perfect-perception* system if

$$\forall s \in S. \ \forall o \in \{o' \in O \mid \omega(s, o') > 0\}. \ \rho(o) = s \qquad (5)$$

Intuitively, this says that the agent is always able to perceive the underlying actual state from the observations. Under this condition, we can define the MDP corresponding to the perfect-perception variant of the autonomous system as $\Gamma_{Perf} := (S, A, \iota, P)$ where $P : S \times A \times S \to [0,1]$ is defined as:

$$P := \forall s, s' \in S. \\ (s) \xrightarrow{a \in A, \ \eta(s,a,s')} (s') \qquad (6)$$

Note that this MDP does not need to track the observations and state estimates due to perfect perception. Given the perfect-perception MDP Γ_{Perf} and a PCTL safety property ψ of the form $F^{\leq n}\hat{S}_U$, a *shielded* perfect-perception MDP Γ_{Perf}^{Δ} is the tuple (S, A, ι, P) where $P : S \times A \times S \to [0,1]$ is defined as:

$$P := \forall s, s' \in S.$$
$$(s) \xrightarrow{a \in \Delta_{\psi,\lambda}(s),\ \eta(s,a,s')} (s') \tag{7}$$

where $\Delta_{\psi,\lambda} : S \to 2^A$ is referred to as the shield and it restricts the actions available in the MDP in a state-dependent manner. In this work, we only consider *absolute* shields constructed as follows:

$$\Delta_{\psi,\lambda}(s) := \{a \in A \mid \sigma_\psi(s,a) \leq \lambda\} \tag{8}$$

$$\text{where } \sigma_\psi(s,a) := \min_{\pi \in S \to A} \sum_{s' \in S} P(s,a,s') \cdot \mathbb{P}^{s'}_{\Gamma_{Perf},\pi}[\texttt{Unsafe}_{S_U,n}(s')] \tag{9}$$

Theorem 1 (Global Safety of Perfect-Perception MDP with Shield). *Given a shielded perfect-perception MDP Γ_{Perf}^{Δ} where the shield is constructed with respect to a safety property $\psi := F^{\leq n} S_U$, starting from the initial state ι of Γ_{Perf}^{Δ}, and under the assumptions that ι is safe (**initially safe**) and the system does not encounter stuck states (**no stuck**), the maximum probability of reaching unsafe states S_U in n' steps is given by,*

$$\max_{\pi \in S \to A} \mathbb{P}^{\iota}_{\Gamma_{Perf}^{\Delta},\pi}[\texttt{Unsafe}_{S_U,n'}(\iota)] \leq 1 - (1-\lambda)^{n'} \tag{10}$$

Proof. The following provides a summary of a complete proof found in Appendix A of the extended version of the paper [22]. This proof relies on the assumptions *initially safe* and *no stuck*, which are referenced in Theorem 1 and precisely defined in Appendix A. For ease of construction, we prove a lower bound on safety using an equivalent statement of Theorem 1: $\min_{\pi \in S \to A} \mathbb{P}^{\iota}_{\Gamma_{Perf}^{\Delta},\pi}[\texttt{Safe}_{S_U,n'}(\iota)] \geq (1-\lambda)^{n'}$. This proof uses *occupancy vectors* of type $\mathbb{R}^S$ which represent the probability the system is in each state at a given time. First, we define a ψ-preserving transformation of a system Γ_{Perf}, which we call Γ_{Perf}^{ψ}, which allows one to measure the probability of achieving ψ on Γ_{Perf} by simply considering the probability of Γ_{Perf}^{ψ} ending in S_U. Defining this transformation allows us to reason about the satisfaction of ψ in Γ_{Perf} by only considering individual time-steps of Γ_{Perf}^{ψ} rather than entire paths on Γ_{Perf}. Then, we build an inductive argument over d_i, the occupancy vector achieved by Γ_{Perf}^{ψ} at timestep i, and a particular function $g : \mathbb{R}^S \to \mathbb{R}$. By showing that any policy π allowed by the shield implies $g(d_{i+1}) \geq (1-\lambda)g(d_i)$ and assuming $g(d_0) = 1$, we conclude $g(d_{n'}) \geq (1-\lambda)^{n'}$ via an inductive argument. We use the property that $g(d_{n'})$ is a lower bound on the safety of $d_{n'}$ to conclude the probability of Γ_{Perf}^{ψ} ending in a safe state must be greater than $(1-\lambda)^{n'}$ after n' time-steps. Using the correspondence of Γ_{Perf}^{ψ} and Γ_{Perf} described above, this implies the restatement of Theorem 1. □

It is important to note the distinction between n and n' in Theorem 1. The parameter n represents the lookahead used to construct the shield Δ, while the parameter n' represents the horizon of the system considered for safety verification. It is somewhat counterintuitive that n does not appear in the safety condition provided by Theorem 1. Figure 5 in the extended version [22] and its discussion show why increasing lookahead does not improve the safety guarantee of shielded control on an arbitrary system. However, increasing lookahead may improve safety for a fixed system through mechanisms not captured by Theorem 1.

We note that *stuck* states are those states where the shield is empty and therefore, no further actions are allowed by the agent. Such stuck states are distinct from safe and unsafe states. As we show in Appendix A.5 [22], if the shield is synthesized with respect to a fixed horizon, there exist certain state topologies for which actions allowed by the shield are guaranteed to result in stuck states. In practice, for systems which can abort operation or revert to manual control, it is reasonable to assume that autonomous control will be terminated when a state is reached where no actions are allowed by the shield. Alternately, detecting that a system is in a stuck state can be viewed as an *early-warning* indicating that further use of autonomous control is fraught with risks. A pre-deployment analysis of the frequency of reaching stuck states can also serve as useful feedback to system designers. Note that, for a particular system, the likelihood of reaching stuck states can be changed by increasing the shielding lookahead n or modifying the shielding parameter λ.[2]

Theorem 1 represents a significant advancement of the theoretical foundations of shielded control. Previous methods [8,11] shield actions according to their safety relative to the safest action from the same state. This strategy does not produce a global guarantee of safety because even the safest action from a state may be entirely unsafe. Instead, we apply the shielding criterion uniformly across all actions to produce a global guarantee of safety, but this comes at the cost of possible stuck states with no available actions allowed by the shield. In the absence of these stuck states, Theorem 1 gives a global guarantee of safety relative to the parameters of the shield.

2.3 Imperfect-Perception MDP with Conformal Shield

The shielded, conformalized version of the system with imperfect perception is the tuple $(S, O, A, \hat{\iota}, \hat{\rho}_\alpha, \eta, \omega, \hat{\Delta}_{\psi,\lambda})$ where $\hat{\rho}_\alpha : O \to 2^S$ is the conformalized perception function and $\hat{\Delta}_{\psi,\lambda} : 2^S \to 2^A$ is a shield that acts on a set of states. This system can be formulated as a Markov Decision Process (MDP), $\Gamma^\Delta_{Conf} := (\hat{S}, A, \hat{\iota}, P)$, where $\hat{S} := S \times O \times 2^S$ is the set of MDP states, $\hat{\iota} := \iota \times \bot_O \times \{\iota\}$ is the initial MDP state, and $P : \hat{S} \times A \times \hat{S} \to [0, 1]$ is the (partial) probabilistic transition function defined as:

$$P := \forall s, s'' \in S, \forall \overline{s} \in 2^S, \forall o, o' \in O.$$
$$(s, m, \overline{s}) \xrightarrow{a \in \hat{\Delta}_{\psi,\lambda}(\overline{s}),\ \eta(s,a',s'') \cdot \omega(s'',o')} (s'', o', \hat{\rho}(o')) \tag{11}$$

---

[2] In the case study found in Fig. 6 of the extended version [22], either of these modifications are sufficient to make stuck states unreachable by a shielded controller.

The shield $\hat{\Delta}_{\psi,\lambda}$ is constructed from the shield $\Delta_{\psi,\lambda}$ for the perfect-perception MDP Γ_{Perf} as:

$$\hat{\Delta}_{\psi,\lambda}(\overline{s}) := \bigwedge_{s \in \overline{s}} \Delta_{\psi,\lambda}(s) \tag{12}$$

Conformalized Perception. To construct the conformalized perception function $\hat{\rho}_\alpha$, we use existing methods for conformalizing classifiers [1]. We assume access to a *calibration dataset* consisting of i.i.d. pairs (o_i, s_i) of observations $o_i \in O$ and corresponding actual system states $s_i \in S$, unseen during training of the perception function $\pi : O \to S$. The conformalized perception function $\hat{\rho}_\alpha$, constructed using this data, comes with the following probabilistic guarantee:

$$\mathbb{P}[s_{\text{test}} \in \hat{\rho}_\alpha(o_{\text{test}})] \geq 1 - \alpha \tag{13}$$

where $(o_{\text{test}}, s_{\text{test}})$ is a fresh observation-state pair from the same distribution as the calibration dataset.

Ideally, we would like to provide a *local safety* guarantee for imperfect-perception MDPs with conformal shields. Given an imperfect-perception MDP Γ^Δ_{Conf} with conformal shield $\hat{\Delta}_{\psi,\lambda}$ where the shield is constructed with respect to a safety property $\psi := F^{\leq n}\hat{S}_U$, we would like to guarantee (14) where $a \in \hat{\Delta}_{\psi,\lambda}(\hat{s})$, $\sigma_\psi(\hat{s}, a) := \min_{\pi \in S \to A} \sum_{s' \in S} P(s, a, s') \cdot \mathbb{P}^{s'}_{\Gamma_{Perf}, \pi}[\texttt{Unsafe}_{S_U,n}(s')]$, $\hat{s} := (s, m, \overline{s})$.

$$\mathbb{P}[\sigma_\psi(\hat{s}, a) \leq \lambda] \geq 1 - \alpha \tag{14}$$

The probability measure in Eq. 14 corresponds to the distribution over (o_i, s_i) pairs induced by the distribution $\mathbb{P}^i_{\Gamma^\Delta_{Conf}, \pi}$ over paths of the MDP Γ^Δ_{Conf} where π is the worst-case policy for safety.

Intuitively, this would guarantee that after applying an action prescribed by the shield in the current state $\hat{s}$, there exists a policy from the resulting successor states such that, assuming perfect perception in the future, the statement that the probability of reaching unsafe in the future is bounded holds with a high probability. While such a guarantee assumes a best-case scenario in the future, it can be helpful to know that the chosen action is at least safe in an optimistic setting.

Establishing such a guarantee would be straightforward if the calibration dataset were drawn from the same distribution over (o_i, s_i) pairs as in Eq. 14. In practice, however, the calibration dataset is initially drawn from the distribution over (o_i, s_i) pairs induced by the path distribution for the imperfect-perception MDP Γ that is neither shielded nor conformalized and where the actions in each step are drawn uniformly at random. One can then use the following iterative procedure to improve the calibration dataset: (i) use the initial calibration dataset to construct the conformalized perception function; (ii) construct a shielded, conformalized MDP and use this MDP (via simulations) to collect more calibration data; (iii) use the new calibration dataset to construct a new conformalized perception function, and repeat. We leave the investigation of such a procedure and its ability to help establish the desired local safety guarantee as future work. Ideally, we would also like to provide a global safety guarantee, similar to Theorem 1, that bounds the probability of reaching unsafe states as long as the agent takes actions prescribed by the shield. We leave this also for future work.

2.4 Probabilistic Abstractions of Conformalized Perception

The observation function $\omega : S \times O \to [0,1]$ is very complex in practice and infeasible to model mathematically. To be able to model check Γ^Δ_{Conf}, we leverage past work [2,19] to construct a probabilistic abstraction of the composition of the conformalized perception function $\hat{\rho}$ and ω. The resulting shielded, conformalized system with imperfect perception is the tuple $(S, A, \hat{\iota}, \nu, \eta, \hat{\Delta}_{\psi,\lambda})$ where $\nu : S \times 2^S \to [0,1]$ is the probabilistic abstraction that describes a distribution over sets of estimated system states given an actual system state. This system can be formulated as a Markov Decision Process (MDP), $\overline{\Gamma}^\Delta_{Conf} := (\hat{S}, A, \hat{\iota}, P)$, where $\hat{S} := S \times 2^S$ is the set of MDP states, $\hat{\iota} := \iota \times \{\iota\}$ is the initial MDP state, and $P : \hat{S} \times A \times \hat{S} \to [0,1]$ is the (partial) probabilistic transition function defined as:

$$P := \forall s, s' \in S, \forall \overline{s} \in 2^S.$$
$$(s, \overline{s}) \xrightarrow{a \in \hat{\Delta}_{\psi,\lambda}(\overline{s}),\ \eta(s,a,s') \cdot \nu(s', \overline{s}')} (s', \overline{s}') \quad (15)$$

3 Empirical Evaluation

We evaluate our proposed approach on a simulated case study that mimics the autonomous airplane taxiing system from prior works [7,12,19]. Note that all of our empirical evaluation is with respect to imperfect-perception systems for which Theorem 1 is not applicable.

3.1 Implementation

Figure 1 describes our overall pipeline.[3] It is implemented in Python along with external tools such as the PRISM model checker [15]. The *conformalizer* implements a standard conformal prediction algorithm (Fig. 2 from [1]) and yields the conformalized perception DNN from the original perception DNN of the agent. The *shield synthesizer* is implemented using PRISM. In particular, for each state $s \in S$ and each action $a \in A$ of the perfect-perception MDP, we issue a PRISM query as described in Eq. 9 and construct the shield using Eq. 8. The *DNN evaluator* simply evaluates the conformalized DNN on the test data to construct a confusion matrix that records, for each actual state, the number of times each set of estimated states is predicted. We also implement a simple *compiler* in Python that converts perfect-perception MDPs expressed in a domain specific language to imperfect-perception MDPs with a conformal shield and a

---
[3] Code available at https://github.com/CSU-TrustLab/cp-control.

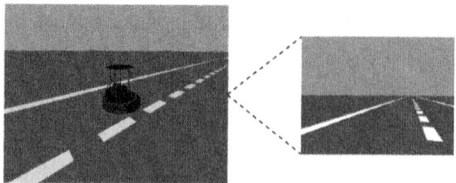

Fig. 2. The simulation setup of the Turtlebot4 in Gazebo (left), and a sample image captured by the Turtlebot4's camera (right). These captured images represent the images that would be passed to the perception DNN.

probabilistic abstraction, i.e., $\overline{T}_{Conf}^{\Delta}$ (as in Sect. 2.4) expressed in the PRISM modeling language. The compiler ingests the shield computed by the shield synthesizer and the confusion matrix for this translation. Finally, we use PRISM as our *model checker* to model check the resulting MDP.

3.2 Details of Autonomous Taxiing Case Study

For our case study, we consider an experimental system for autonomous centerline tracking on airport taxiways [7,12]. It takes as input a picture of the taxiway and estimates the plane's position with respect to the centerline in terms of two outputs: cross-track error (cte), which is the distance in meters of the plane from the centerline and heading error (he), which is the angle of the plane with respect to the centerline. The state estimation or perception is performed by a neural network. The resulting state estimates are fed to a controller, which maneuvers the plane to follow the centerline. Error is defined as excessive deviation from the centerline, either in terms of cte or he values. We consider a discretized version of the system as in prior work [19].

Simulation Setup. To explore with realistic data, we devised a simulated setup which has the same objective as the autonomous airplane taxiing problem. Specifically, we implemented a simulated setup of a Turtlebot4 robot in the Gazebo simulator operating on a taxiway. In our simulation, the Turtlebot4 serves the role of the airplane and it is equipped with an RGB camera which can capture 240 × 320 pixel images. We use the simulator to collect a dataset of images that would be captured by the camera. This collected dataset is used for training the perception DNN and also for conformalizing the DNN.

Data Processing Pipeline. To generate a dataset of images, we place the Turtlebot4 randomly on the taxiway, and save the resulting image taken from the camera. Along with this image, we capture the true pose of the robot, (x, y, θ), where (x, y) are the robot's coordinates and θ is the angle with respect to the centerline. We collected a total of 5500 images. Figure 2 contains screenshots of the simulated setup and an example image taken from the camera. Input preprocessing normalizes RGB values using ImageNet statistics ($\mu = [0.485, 0.456, 0.406]$, $\sigma = [0.229, 0.224, 0.225]$) to leverage pre-trained backbone weights for perception

DNNs. For training the DNN, we further augment the dataset using strategies such as random horizontal flipping ($p = 0.5$), color jittering with brightness and contrast variations (± 0.2), and Gaussian noise injection ($\sigma = 0.01$) to improve model robustness and generalization. We use 60% of the collected data for training the DNN, 10% for validation, 15% for calibration, and 15% for testing. The dataset is split using stratified sampling to maintain balanced class distributions across all cte and he categories. This ensures representative learning across all states and prevents bias toward more frequent state configurations.

State Space Representation. As in past work [19], we consider a discretized state space where the safe range of cross-track error (cte) is discretized into 5 buckets and safe range of heading error (he) into 3 buckets. This yields a total of 15 discrete system states that perception must classify from visual input.

Neural Architecture. The perception function ρ is implemented as a multi-task convolutional neural network processing RGB images of size $240 \times 320 \times 3$. The architecture employs a MobileNetV2 backbone utilizing depthwise separable convolutions with inverted residual blocks for computational efficiency. Feature extraction layers progressively reduce spatial dimensions from 240×320 to 7×10 while expanding the channel depth to 1280. The global average pooling aggregates spatial features into a unified 1280-dimensional representation. The shared processing backbone applies dropout regularization ($p = 0.3$), batch normalization, and ReLU activation, with linear transformations that reduce dimensionality through $1280 \rightarrow 512 \rightarrow 256$ neurons.

The architecture then branches into task-specific classification heads from the 256-dimensional shared representation. The cte head implements a ($256 \rightarrow 128 \rightarrow 5$) structure with ReLU activations, computing probability distributions over the five lateral position states. The he head follows an identical architecture ($256 \rightarrow 128 \rightarrow 3$) for the three heading states. Both heads employ softmax activation to produce normalized probability distributions over their respective state spaces.

The trained model outputs joint probability distributions $P(\text{cte}|o)$ and $P(\text{he}|o)$ for each input observation o, providing both point predictions through argmax selection and uncertainty estimates through probability values. These probabilistic outputs $\hat{f}$ serve as input to the conformalization process.

Neural Training. The network jointly optimizes both classification tasks with independent cross-entropy losses: $\mathcal{L}_{\text{cte}} = -\sum_i y_i^{\text{cte}} \log(p_i^{\text{cte}})$ and $\mathcal{L}_{\text{he}} = -\sum_i y_i^{\text{he}} \log(p_i^{\text{he}})$, where y_i represents one-hot encoded ground truth labels and p_i denotes predicted probabilities. The combined objective $\mathcal{L}_{\text{total}} = \mathcal{L}_{\text{cte}} + \mathcal{L}_{\text{he}}$ enables the simultaneous learning of both navigation parameters.

For training, we use Adam optimization with $\beta_1 = 0.9$, $\beta_2 = 0.999$ which provides adaptive learning rate control with initial rate 0.001. The learning rate scheduler monitors the validation loss with patience=5 epochs, applying multiplicative decay (factor=0.1) when improvement stagnates. Regularization of weight decay (factor $= 1 \times 10^{-4}$) prevents overfitting, while gradient clipping (max_norm = 1.0) ensures training stability. Mini-batch processing with batch_size = 16 balances memory efficiency with gradient estimation quality.

MDP Formulation. We formulate a perfect-perception MDP corresponding to our case study where the state space $S := \{0, \ldots, 4\} \times \{0, 1, 2\}$ representing the five possible cte values and three possible he values and the action space $A := \{0, 1, 2\}$ corresponds to the three actions available for each state, namely, go straight, go left, and go right. In each time-step, the agent continues to move forward even if it executes the command to go left or go right. We define a stochastic dynamics for the agent where the source of stochasticity is in the action execution. For instance, the agent controller might choose to go straight in a particular state, but we model a small probability of this choice actually resulting in the agent going left or right due to windy conditions or actuator errors. For all our experiments, we assume that the agent starts at the centerline, facing straight ahead (i.e., in the initial state, cte=0 and he=0). A PRISM model of the perfect-perception MDP is available in Appendix B in the extended version [22]. Note that while the PRISM model makes some changes for ease of expression, in essence it models a perfect-perception MDP as explained here.

The autonomous taxiing agent fails the mission if it moves off the taxiway, or if the agent rotates too far left or right. These states will be referred to as *fail* state and are terminal states in the model. Moreover, the imperfect-perception agent with a conformal shield may find itself in a state where the set of predicted states (output by the conformalized perception) are such that the shield (as constructed using Eq. 12) has no safe actions available for the predicted set. Such states are referred to as *stuck* states and are also terminal states in our MDP.[4] In practice, once the agent encounters a stuck state, it may employ a failsafe action (take another reading, go straight, halt the agent, raise an alarm to a human operator, etc.) but this is outside the scope of our current work.

For our experiments, we construct the imperfect-perception MDP with conformal shielding and probabilistic abstractions (as defined in Sect. 2.4) using our compiler. The perfect-perception shield is constructed with respect to the PCTL property, $F^{\leq 5} S_U$ where S_U are the fail states for the case study. We construct multiple MDPs by varying the conformalization hyperparameter α $((1 - \alpha) = \alpha' \in \{0.95, 0.99, 0.995\})$, and the shield hyperparameter λ $((1 - \lambda) = \lambda' \in \{0.7, 0.8, 0.9\})$. With each of the imperfect-perception MDP, we employ three different versions:

1. An MDP that has non-determinism intact for selecting actions (referred to as *worst-case*)
2. An MDP where we fix the policy to choose actions allowed by the shield uniformly at random (referred to as *random*)
3. An MDP where where we fix the policy to choose the safest action as per the shield; given a set of predicted states $\bar{s}$, the safest action a_{safe} is the action

---

[4] An empty shield is a commonality between this definition of *stuck* and the one given in Sect. 2.2 in the perfect-perception context. However, the conditions which produce stuck states in the two cases are different because of the distinct shield constructions.

with the smallest maximum probability of unsafety across the set of states, i.e., $a_{safe} := \text{argmin}_{a \in \hat{\Delta}_{\psi,\lambda}(\overline{s})} \max_{s \in \overline{s}} \sigma_\psi(s, a)$ where $\sigma_\psi(s, a)$ is as defined in Eq. 9 (referred to as *safest*)

We use the PRISM model checker to analyse the models constructed with respect to the following PCTL properties:

$$\mathbf{P}_{\text{fail}} : \mathbb{P}_? \, [F^{\leq n'} \text{ "fail"}]$$
$$\mathbf{P}_{\text{stuck}} : \mathbb{P}_? \, [F^{\leq n'} \text{ "stuck"}] \quad (16)$$
$$\mathbf{P}_{\text{success}} : \mathbb{P}_? \, [F \, t = n']$$

where n' is the length of the agent paths (i.e., number of time-steps) and t is a variable denoting the number of steps taken by the agent. $\mathbf{P}_{\text{success}}$ captures the situation where the agent successfully operates for n' steps without failing or getting stuck. In our experiments, we consider values of n' in $\{1, \ldots, 30\}$. For the MDP models using non-determinism for action selection (*worst-case*), the properties were slightly modified; $\mathbf{P}_{\text{fail}}$ and $\mathbf{P}_{\text{stuck}}$ are aimed at finding the strategy which maximizes these values, and $\mathbf{P}_{\text{success}}$ is aimed at finding the minimal value. This is to find the worst case scenario, i.e. where the system chooses the worst possible action allowed by the shield at each step.

As a baseline, we consider an imperfect-perception MDP formulation of the autonomous taxiing agent where the perception DNN is not conformalized and the shield is constructed assuming perfect perception.

3.3 Empirical Results

As the length of the operation increases, the probabilities of encountering either the fail state or the stuck state increases, therefore a decrease of mission success (see Fig. 3). The conformaliser hyperparameter α' (i.e., $1 - \alpha$) has a substantial effect on the performance of the agent. As expected, higher α' decreases the probability of going to the fail state. Increasing α', however, results in the conformalized perception predicting larger sets of states. This in turn increases the probability of the shield being empty, i.e., no safe action being available and the agent getting stuck as reflected in the results. Note that, in our baseline setup, for all states, there was a minimum of one action allowed by the shield, meaning the system would never get stuck.

The shield hyperparameter λ' (i.e., $1 - \lambda$) also affects the agent significantly. As λ' increases, fewer actions are included in the shield. This therefore increases the number of sets of states where the shield is empty, resulting in an increase of probability of encountering the stuck state as seen in the results. A consequence of getting stuck often is that the probability of encountering the fail state as well as succeeding in the mission are reduced. That said, when the conformalizer guarantee is set to 0.95, there is only a small increase to the probability of encountering the stuck state. It is then seen that the probability of going to a fail state decreases as the shield value increases, demonstrating the shield is further filtering unsafe actions.

We also compare our results with a baseline imperfect-perception MDP model of the agent where the perception is not conformalized and the shield is constructed assuming perfect perception. The baseline results demonstrate that the inclusion of conformalization generally reduces the probability of crashing ($\mathbf{P}_{\text{fail}}$). While the baseline has a higher probability of succeeding ($\mathbf{P}_{\text{success}}$) in some instances, this is due to the impossibility of getting stuck. For instance, when $\alpha' = 0.95$, the conformalized MDP demonstrates a smaller probability of getting stuck and outperforms baseline with respect to $\mathbf{P}_{\text{success}}$. In contrast, for higher values of α', probability of success is lower compared to the baseline because the agent is very likely to get stuck; for the same reason, the conformalized agent demonstrates a lower probability of failure compared to the baseline.

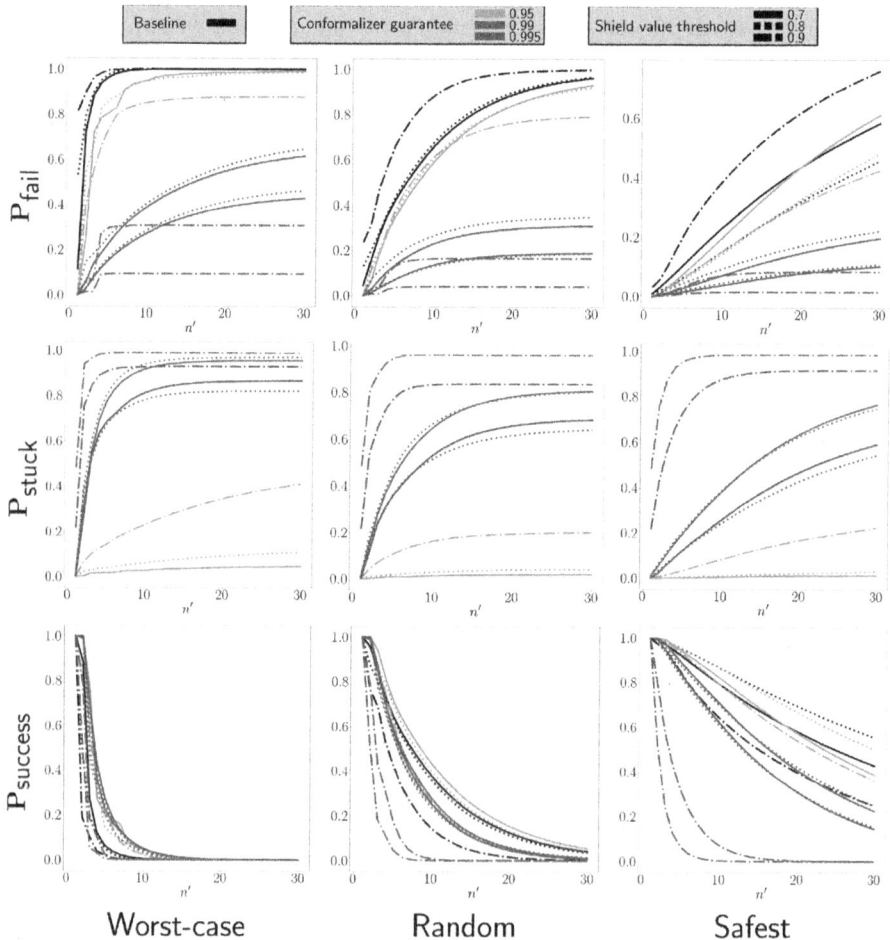

Fig. 3. Results for properties $\mathbf{P}_{\text{fail}}$, $\mathbf{P}_{\text{stuck}}$, and $\mathbf{P}_{\text{success}}$ as n' increases. Black lines represent the baseline results.

We also evaluate the time to perform model checking for each property across n', see Fig. 4. Expectedly, as n' increases the model checking time also increases, with $n' = 1$ on average being less than 0.01 s, and $n' = 30$ ranging between 0.2 and 1.5 s depending upon property and setup. As α' increases, more states are included in the sets, increasing the overall model size. Though, continuing to increase α' will inevitably result in fewer unique sets being produced as a result of the sets including more and more of the states. Therefore, this will result in a smaller model for analysis purposes. This is observed as α' increases from 0.95 to 0.99 with the accompanying increase in time, and then a decrease in time when α' increases from 0.99 to 0.995. Increasing λ' can reduce the number of available actions for each set of states and can lead to a reduction in model checking time as the number of possible transitions decreases, specially if the shield value threshold generates substantially more empty action sets for the predicted sets of states.

3.4 Discussion

We note that our proposed shield can be used either in an offline or online fashion. Similar to existing works on shielding [3,11], the shielded imperfect-perception MDP can be used when learning an optimal policy via reinforcement learning (RL) to ensure safe exploration while accelerating learning. Once an optimal policy is learned, the shield may be discarded. In contrast to this offline usage, the shield may also be used online as a run-time monitor that ensures no actions are taken by the agent that violate local safety. This mode of usage is particularly useful when the optimal policy does not come with any safety guarantees. The synthesis of the shield itself can also be carried out in an offline [11] or online [14] fashion as has been noted in prior works. Since our conformal shield maps sets of predicted states to sets of actions, the size of the shield grows exponentially with the number of possible classes that the original perception predicts over. Consequently, online shield construction can be particularly effective since the shield is only computed for the sets of predicted states observed in operation. We also note that, as in existing works on shielding, our construction also assumes that the safety-relevant fragment of the MDP can be mathematically modeled. However, our work does not require modeling the observation or perception processes. Finally, we already note in Sect. 2.3 that the conformalization guarantee requires distributional assumptions and careful collection of calibration data.

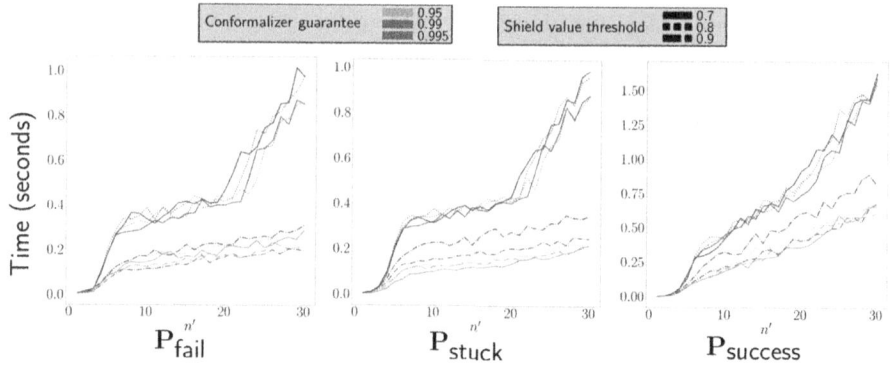

Fig. 4. Time to perform model checking on each property as n' increases. For each variation of α' and λ', the average time was computed over the three different model variations—worst-case, random, and safest.

4 Related Work

Shielding. The work on shielding Partially Observable Markov Decision Processes (POMDPs) [3,23] is closely related to our approach. Like MDPs, POMDPs model decision-making settings that involve both stochasticity and non-determinism. However, in contrast to MDPs, POMDPs also capture the fact that the underlying state can only be accessed through stochastic observations. Safety is ensured by constructing a shield that restricts the set of available actions in each belief state of the POMDP.[5]

While promising, POMDP-based shielding faces several limitations. First, it requires modeling the stochastic process of generating observations from underlying states. For the airplane taxiing example, one would need to model the complex process of generating images corresponding to the airplane's position on the taxiway, which can be infeasible in practice.[6] Second, a POMDP formulation assumes that agents compute belief states before choosing actions. However, this assumption often does not hold for realistic systems. Third, existing works on POMDP shielding [3,23] only consider infinite-horizon, almost-sure safety properties (i.e., the probability of violation tends to zero as the run length increases). However, for many agents, including the autonomous taxiing system, the probability of violating safety over an infinite horizon is often one. Therefore, we are interested in finite-horizon, probabilistic safety guarantees.

On the other hand, [9] address the challenge of achieving safe reinforcement learning (RL) in complex, continuous environments. They implement a

---

[5] A *belief state* is a distribution over the underlying states that reflects the agent's current best estimate based on the history of observations.

[6] [3] slightly relax this requirement by only needing to know the transitions from states to observations that have non-zero probability, rather than the exact probabilities.

counterexample-guided policy optimization based on reward computation. However, this study only provides approximate safety guarantees. [13] explore shielding for RL to synthesize a correct-by-construction reactive system and further extend this with a formal "probabilistic shield" approach. This method computes per-state/action safety constraints via shielding, filtering the RL agent's actions focusing on the tradeoffs between sufficient progress in exploration of the environment and ensuring safety [11]. Nevertheless, they do not formally guarantee a global safety of existing shield constructions for perfect- perception.

Conformal Prediction and Control. Conformal prediction offers a powerful framework for generating finite-sample, distribution-free error bounds for perception, which can then be integrated into robust control pipelines. End-to-end probabilistic safety guarantees for perception-based control with sequential, time-uniform conformal bounds have been explored by Yang et al. [30] using barrier functions. Building on this, Lindemann et al. [17] effectively represent uncertainty via conformal prediction and formalize safety through linear programming. These approaches focus on continuous time and therefore provide weaker formal guarantees. State-dependent (heteroskedastic) conformal bounds have been introduced by Waite et al. [26] to achieve tighter and less conservative safety guarantees. This work also differs from our approach, as it provides guarantees of reaching a particular state while in continuous space. While Fulton and Platzer [8] presented formal model-based safety proofs with reinforcement learning via runtime monitoring, this work doesn't explicitly address learned vision, neural perception, or the direct propagation of perception uncertainty into control safety. [5] utilizes a learned perception map to predict a linear function of the system's state to design a safe set and a robust controller for the closed-loop system. They demonstrate that, given suitable smoothness assumptions on both the perception map and the generative model, the parameters of the safe set can be learned through dense sampling of the state space.

Safety Certificates. Safety certificates, particularly Control Barrier Functions (CBFs), are widely used for run-time enforcement of safety [6]. Differentiable and neural CBFs enable their integration into end-to-end pipelines to filter out unsafe actions and intervene to preserve safety, as in robotics [24]. Works by Xiao et al. [28,29] evaluate the efficacy of CBFs in end-to-end vision-based autonomous driving and control. However, their formal guarantees primarily rely on the CBF layer itself and often do not explicitly model or formally bound vision-induced uncertainty. While these methods apply to autonomous driving with RGB camera images and may require explicit error bounds for estimators, they typically do not derive these bounds directly from learned vision or conformal prediction methods, unlike approaches such as Lindemann et al. [16]. More recently, Dawson et al. [4] proposed a learning-enabled hybrid controller with neural safety certificates, providing formal safety and liveness guarantees for systems using learned perception directly in observation space, thus not relying on explicit state estimation. An automated, formal, counterexample-based approach to synthesizing Barrier Certificates (BCs) as a neural network for the safety verification of continuous and hybrid dynamical models is introduced in [20].

Analysis of Autonomous Systems with Learned Perception. Formal analysis of autonomous systems that incorporate learned perception components is a growing area [18]. Approaches such as DeepDECS [2] integrate DNN verification and uncertainty quantification into formal (Markov model-based) controller synthesis to create formal, system-level safety-aware controllers. Similarly, probabilistic abstractions (via confusion matrices) and DNN-specific runtime guards for systems like airplane taxiing with vision DNNs have been explored [19]. While Hsieh et al. [10] approximated high-dimensional vision perception with low-dimensional surrogates for system-level verification, its safety is primarily verified empirically and through program analysis, lacking formal guarantees that connect actual perception errors directly to safety; it relies on empirical "precision" without formal coverage bounds. Another line of work involves scenario-based probabilistic compositional verification with symbolic abstractions, as seen in applications to airplanes and F1Tenth cars with DNN vision. However, these methods, like Watson et al. [27], often focus on assumption generation for compositional verification rather than formally modeling vision uncertainty or providing finite-sample coverage guarantees or explicit set-based safety through conformal approaches.

5 Conclusion

In this paper, we study the problem of designing safe controllers (or policies) for discrete autonomous agents with imperfect perception. We present MDP formulations of such agents and propose a shield construction for such agents that restrict, at run-time, the actions available to the agent in each state as a function of state estimates. The construction combines the shield computed for a perfect-perception agent with conformalization of the perception component, with the aim of providing probabilistic, local safety guarantees with respect to finite horizons. Importantly, our construction does not require mathematical models of the complex process for generating observations from actual states and of the perception component. We also present a result proving *global safety* of existing shield constructions for perfect-perception agents. We evaluate our constructions using the case study of an autonomous airplane taxiing system. Our experiments demonstrate that while the shield can improve safety, it comes at the cost of the system getting *stuck*, i.e., reaching states where the shield is empty. In general, reaching stuck states is unavoidable under shielding, even with perfect perception. In future work, we plan to develop a proof of global safety for imperfect-perception agents using our conformal shield.

References

1. Angelopoulos, A.N., Bates, S.: A gentle introduction to conformal prediction and distribution-free uncertainty quantification. arXiv preprint arXiv:2107.07511 (2021)

2. Calinescu, R., Imrie, C., Mangal, R., Rodrigues, G.N., Păsăreanu, C., Santana, M.A., Vázquez, G.: Controller synthesis for autonomous systems with deep-learning perception components. IEEE Trans. Softw. Eng. (2024)
3. Carr, S., Jansen, N., Junges, S., Topcu, U.: Safe reinforcement learning via shielding under partial observability. In: Proceedings of the AAAI Conference on Artificial Intelligence, vol. 37, pp. 14748–14756 (2023)
4. Dawson, C., Lowenkamp, B., Goff, D., Fan, C.: Learning safe, generalizable perception-based hybrid control with certificates. IEEE Rob. Autom. Lett. **7**(2), 1904–1911 (2022)
5. Dean, S., Matni, N., Recht, B., Ye, V.: Robust guarantees for perception-based control. In: Learning for Dynamics and Control, pp. 350–360. PMLR (2020)
6. Dean, S., Taylor, A., Cosner, R., Recht, B., Ames, A.: Guaranteeing safety of learned perception modules via measurement-robust control barrier functions. In: Conference on Robot Learning, pp. 654–670. PMLR (2021)
7. Fremont, D.J., Chiu, J., Margineantu, D.D., Osipychev, D., Seshia, S.A.: Formal analysis and redesign of a neural network-based aircraft taxiing system with VERIFAI. In: Lahiri, S.K., Wang, C. (eds.) CAV 2020. LNCS, vol. 12224, pp. 122–134. Springer, Cham (2020). https://doi.org/10.1007/978-3-030-53288-8_6
8. Fulton, N., Platzer, A.: Safe reinforcement learning via formal methods: toward safe control through proof and learning. In: Proceedings of the AAAI Conference on Artificial Intelligence, vol. 32, no. 1 (2018). https://doi.org/10.1609/aaai.v32i1.12107. https://ojs.aaai.org/index.php/AAAI/article/view/12107
9. Goodall, A.W., Belardinelli, F.: Leveraging approximate model-based shielding for probabilistic safety guarantees in continuous environments. In: Proceedings of the 23rd International Conference on Autonomous Agents and Multiagent Systems, AAMAS '24, pp. 2291–2293. International Foundation for Autonomous Agents and Multiagent Systems, Richland (2024)
10. Hsieh, C., Li, Y., Sun, D., Joshi, K., Misailovic, S., Mitra, S.: Verifying controllers with vision-based perception using safe approximate abstractions (2021). https://doi.org/10.1109/TCAD.2022.3197508
11. Jansen, N., Könighofer, B., Junges, S., Serban, A.C., Bloem, R.: Safe reinforcement learning via probabilistic shields (2019). https://arxiv.org/abs/1807.06096
12. Kadron, I.B., Gopinath, D., Pasareanu, C.S., Yu, H.: Case study: analysis of autonomous center line tracking neural networks. In: Bloem, R., Dimitrova, R., Fan, C., Sharygina, N. (eds.) Software Verification - 13th International Conference, VSTTE 2021, New Haven, CT, USA, October 18-19, 2021, and 14th International Workshop, NSV 2021, Los Angeles, CA, USA, 18–19 July 2021, Revised Selected Papers. LNCS, pp. 104–121. Springer, Heidelberg (2021). https://doi.org/10.1007/978-3-030-95561-8_7
13. Könighofer, B., Lorber, F., Jansen, N., Bloem, R.: Shield synthesis for reinforcement learning. In: Margaria, T., Steffen, B. (eds.) ISoLA 2020. LNCS, vol. 12476, pp. 290–306. Springer, Cham (2020). https://doi.org/10.1007/978-3-030-61362-4_16
14. Könighofer, B., Rudolf, J., Palmisano, A., Tappler, M., Bloem, R.: Online shielding for reinforcement learning. Innov. Syst. Softw. Eng. **19**(4), 379–394 (2023)
15. Kwiatkowska, M., Norman, G., Parker, D.: PRISM 4.0: verification of probabilistic real-time systems. In: Gopalakrishnan, G., Qadeer, S. (eds.) CAV 2011. LNCS, vol. 6806, pp. 585–591. Springer, Heidelberg (2011). https://doi.org/10.1007/978-3-642-22110-1_47

16. Lindemann, L., Robey, A., Jiang, L., Tu, S., Matni, N.: Learning robust output control barrier functions from safe expert demonstrations (2021). https://doi.org/10.1109/OJCSYS.2024.3385348
17. Lindemann, L., Zhao, Y., Yu, X., Pappas, G.J., Deshmukh, J.V.: Formal verification and control with conformal prediction. arXiv preprint arXiv:2409.00536 (2024)
18. Mitra, S., et al.: Formal verification techniques for vision-based autonomous systems–a survey. In: Principles of Verification: Cycling the Probabilistic Landscape: Essays Dedicated to Joost-Pieter Katoen on the Occasion of His 60th Birthday, Part III, pp. 89–108. Springer, Heidelberg (2024). https://doi.org/10.1007/978-3-031-75778-5_5
19. Pasareanu, C.S., Mangal, R., Gopinath, D., Getir-Yaman, S., Imrie, C., Calinescu, R., Yu, H.: Closed-loop analysis of vision-based autonomous systems: A case study. In: Enea, C., Lal, A. (eds.) Computer Aided Verification - 35th International Conference, CAV 2023, Paris, France, 17–22 July 2023, Proceedings, Part I. LNCS, vol. 13964, pp. 289–303. Springer, Heidelberg (2023). https://doi.org/10.1007/978-3-031-37706-8_15
20. Peruffo, A., Ahmed, D., Abate, A.: Automated and formal synthesis of neural barrier certificates for dynamical models (2020). https://arxiv.org/abs/2007.03251
21. Pranger, S., Könighofer, B., Posch, L., Bloem, R.: TEMPEST - synthesis tool for reactive systems and shields in probabilistic environments. In: Hou, Z., Ganesh, V. (eds.) ATVA 2021. LNCS, vol. 12971, pp. 222–228. Springer, Cham (2021). https://doi.org/10.1007/978-3-030-88885-5_15
22. Scarbro, W., et al.: Conformal safety shielding for imperfect-perception agents. arXiv preprint arXiv:2506.17275 (2025)
23. Sheng, S., Parker, D., Feng, L.: Safe pomdp online planning via shielding. In: 2024 IEEE International Conference on Robotics and Automation (ICRA), pp. 126–132. IEEE (2024)
24. Tong, M., Dawson, C., Fan, C.: Enforcing safety for vision-based controllers via control barrier functions and neural radiance fields. In: 2023 IEEE International Conference on Robotics and Automation (ICRA), pp. 10511–10517. IEEE (2023)
25. Vovk, V., Gammerman, A., Shafer, G.: Algorithmic Learning in a Random World, vol. 29. Springer, Heidelberg (2005)
26. Waite, T., Geng, Y., Turnquist, T., Ruchkin, I., Ivanov, R.: State-dependent conformal perception bounds for neuro-symbolic verification of autonomous systems (2025). https://doi.org/10.48550/arXiv.2502.21308
27. Watson, C., Alur, R., Gopinath, D., Mangal, R., Pasareanu, C.S.: Scenario-based compositional verification of autonomous systems with neural perception (2025). https://arxiv.org/abs/2504.20942
28. Xiao, W., Wang, T.H., Chahine, M., Amini, A., Hasani, R.M., Rus, D.: Differentiable control barrier functions for vision-based end-to-end autonomous driving (2022). https://doi.org/10.48550/arXiv.2203.02401
29. Xiao, W., et al.: Barriernet: differentiable control barrier functions for learning of safe robot control (2023). https://doi.org/10.1109/TRO.2023.3249564
30. Yang, S., Pappas, G.J., Mangharam, R., Lindemann, L.: Safe perception-based control under stochastic sensor uncertainty using conformal prediction. In: 2023 62nd IEEE Conference on Decision and Control (CDC), pp. 6072–6078. IEEE (2023)

Extended Timed Regular Expressions

Marco Muñiz[✉], Marius Mikučionis, and Kim G. Larsen

Aalborg University, Aalborg, Denmark
{muniz,marius,kgl}@cs.aau.dk

Abstract. The behavior of complex organisms or systems is often stored as time series data. Time series data is valuable because it contains valuable information in the form of timed patterns. However, this patterns are difficult to formalize and to detect. We present Extended Timed Regular Expressions (ETRE) to express complex timed patterns which can be systematically and efficiently matched in large sets of time series data. We translate ETRE to Timed Automata (TA), where pattern matching is computed by reachability analysis in TA. We implement our theory using C++ in the new tool TIMEREX. Our tool can be used for online (run time) or offline (post processing) pattern matching. We run extensive experiments on real data. We have been able to efficiently match a number of relevant patterns.

1 Introduction

Time series data is present everywhere, it can be produced by a Cyber Physical System (CPS), by sensors monitoring the human body, communication protocols, etc. As an example consider Fig. 1a shows an example of time series data from an ECG from the PhysioNet MIT-BIH Arrhythmia Database [10]. Time series data is valuable because it contains valuable information in the form of timed patterns. These patterns can be used to classify the data, to do predictions, and when possible to control the behavior of a system. As example consider Fig. 1a where it is of interest to find early occurrence of a QRS complex (peak) a sign of arrhythmia.

Regular Expressions (RE) is a fundamental formalism in Computer Science developed in formal language theory by Kleene [11] and formalizes the concept of a regular language. An equivalent – similarly fundamental – formalism is that of Finite State Automata. By now RE are commonly used to specify patterns in a text with supporting search and replace engines of word processors and text editors and with support in many programming languages. Timed patterns can be expressed in a number of formalisms including Timed Regular Expressions [3], Signal Temporal Logic [14,15], Linear Temporal Logic [18] , and Timed Automata [1] (TA).

This work introduces Extended Timed Regular Expressions (ETRE) which generalizes Timed Regular Expressions in two principles ways: events are value constraints (e.g. intervals) on one or more of the continuous signals present in the time-series, and sub-expressions may be subject to timing-constraints. Inspired on the equivalence notion between TRE and TA [3] we translate ETRE to Extended TA (XTA) where ETRE pattern matching can be decided as reachability in XTA. Our translation carefully exploits the notion of urgency to allow for a discrete-time engine. We have implemented our theory using C++ in the new tool TIMEREX. Our tool supports both online (run time) and offline pattern matching. Later in this paper we present an extensive experimental evaluation with encouraging results.

As an example consider Fig. 1a which shows an ECG from the MIT-BIH arrhythmia database [10]. A QRS complex is a sophisticated temporal pattern with several points of inflection. Therefore, a high degree polynomial could be an initial approximation. Figure 1b describes a tube generated by the ETRE $\langle f_{\delta=0.38}^{\text{MLII}} \rangle_{[d_1=0.039\,s, d_2=0.045\,s]}$ where f is a seventh degree polynomial. A seventh degree polynomial is an approximation based on our experiments. It will correctly match on a one to one relation all QRS complex in the given data. Finally, the more complex ETRE $\langle f_{\delta=0.38}^{\text{MLII}} \rangle_{[0.039\,s, 0.045\,s]} \cdot \langle \Sigma^* \rangle_{[0.04\,s, 0.65\,s]} \cdot \langle f_{\delta=0.38}^{\text{MLII}} \rangle_{[0.039\,s, 0.045\,s]}$ approximates a QRS complex followed by any value (Σ^*) for a period of in less than 0.65s and then followed by another QRS complex (a sign of arrhythmia). The red rectangle in Fig. 1a shows a match of this ETRE in the signal from our tool TIMEREX. This ETRE can be used to systematically detect all premature heart beats on the given signal.

Finally, the notions of ETRE and TA provide an unambiguous (explainable) formalism for the domain expert to specify important patterns (for matching) as well evaluate possibly learned patterns. Learning formulae is an active research area e.g. LTL learning [20], RE learning [13], parametric timed pattern matching [2,16].

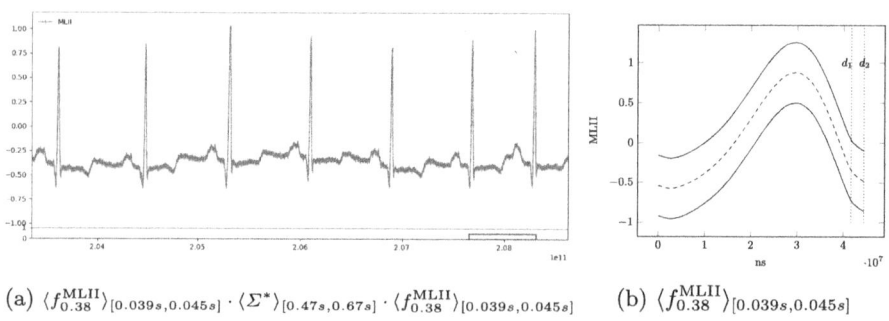

(a) $\langle f_{0.38}^{\text{MLII}} \rangle_{[0.039s, 0.045s]} \cdot \langle \Sigma^* \rangle_{[0.47s, 0.67s]} \cdot \langle f_{0.38}^{\text{MLII}} \rangle_{[0.039s, 0.045s]}$ (b) $\langle f_{0.38}^{\text{MLII}} \rangle_{[0.039s, 0.045s]}$

Fig. 1. Pattern Matching ETRE to detect Arrhythmia. Red rectangle is a match. (Color figure online)

Related Work. ETRE are based on the seminal work for Timed Regular Expressions TRE [3]. ETRE syntax allows for arbitrary functions with a tolerance for noise. ETRE extend the alphabet by allowing tuples of real valued events. ETRE semantics align with those from TRE [3] (time event sequence semantics). In the following we compare our approach with the state of the art.

Timed Pattern Matching. The work in [19] introduces Timed Pattern Matching for TRE. The semantics of TRE in [19] are over boolean signals (signal semantics) and it is believed that the semantics do not coincide with the time event sequence semantics from [3]. The authors introduce the notion of match set. A match set contains the start and stop points of uncountably many matches. The authors show that for finite variability signals a match set can be computed and represented by a finite union of zones. The algorithms are based on operations on zones. The main differences with our approach are that ETRE semantics are the so called time event sequence semantics which align with the semantics from [3]. In addition, as input (corpus) we require finite timed words (discrete time series) with no finite variability constraints. As a result there is only finitely many sub-words which match the given ETRE. We do not compute a match set. We only compute the start and stop indexes of the first sub-word which matches. Further, our assumptions and construction allow for a discrete time engine implementation avoiding complex operations on zones.

Existing Formalisms. Signal Temporal Logic (STL) [14,15] allows for predicates over real values. The semantics are over continuous time signals. ETRE are interpreted over time series data and arbitrary functions are supported by the syntax. Regular Expressions are widely used in industry. In the industrial context, we expect a smoother transition from RE to ETRE than from RE to STL. *Signal Regular Expressions (SRE).* The work in [5] introduces SRE together with qualitative and quantitative semantics. SRE allows to compare variables on signals against real numbers. The main differences with our approach are that SRE are interpreted in the signal semantics where as ETRE are interpreted using time event sequence semantics. Further the semantics for the Kleene star operator are different. In addition, ETRE support the use of functions. *Shape Expressions* [8,17] allows RE over parameterized signal shapes. Shape expressions translate to Shape Automata which act as recognisers. While Shape Expressions and ETRE aim at describing complex patterns, the underlying assumptions and techniques are different. A simple inspection could suggest that both formalisms complement. However, a formal comparison is be needed.

Online Monitoring Using Automata. In [6] and [22,23] patterns are specified as Timed Automata. TA is then used for timed pattern matching on continuous signals. The underlying algorithms perform symbolic reachability using zones. On the contrary, our translation from ETRE yields a subset of TA for which a discrete engine implementation is possible. Further our construction enables efficient application of Partial Order Reduction.

Parametric Timed Pattern Matching. The works in [2] and Parametric TRE [16] study parametric pattern matching. Here specifications allow parameters to cope with uncertainty. An extended match set is computed using reachability synthesis in parametric Timed Automata. In our case studies e.g. ECG for arrhythmia detection, identifying the right durations is challenging. We believe that this approach could complement nicely with ETRE for identifying adequate durations.

Skipping Techniques. The work in [22] applies Boyer-Moore pattern matching method. In contrast to our work, the procedure in [22] requires pre-computing the region graph. The same authors improve this result in [23], by using a more efficient skipping method and by replacing the region automaton by the zone graph. Our results ensure that we only need to construct a discrete transition system. Therefore, it should be possible to profit from such advanced techniques. As future work, we aim at including these techniques in our framework.

Quantitative Timed Pattern Matching. The work in [5] introduces robust semantics for pattern matching of SRE. The semantics shows how robustly a signal satisfies (or violates) the given specification. The work in [21] presents and online method for computing robust semantics where the specification is given as a Timed Automata. Robust semantics for ETRE is interesting and relevant for many industrial applications.

2 Preliminaries

We apply our method to the theory of timed automata [1]. Our formal model is *extended timed automata* and it is an abstract representation of modeling formalism used in the tool UPPAAL [7]. *Clocks and Variables.* Let X be a set of *clocks*. A *clock valuation* is a function $\mu : X \to \mathbb{R}_{\geq 0}$. We use $\mathcal{V}(X)$ to denote the sets of all valuations for clocks in X. We use μ_{ini} to denote the valuation where all clocks in X are assign the value 0. Let V be a set of *variables*. A *variable valuation* is a function $\nu : V \to \mathbb{R}$ that maps variables to real numbers. We use $\mathcal{V}(V)$ to denote the set of all variable valuations. We use ν_{ini} to denote the valuation where all variables are assign the value 0. *Constraints.* The set $B(X)$ is the set of *clock constraints* generated by the grammar $\phi ::= x \bowtie c \mid \phi_1 \wedge \phi_2$, where $x \in X$, $\bowtie \in \{<, \leq, \geq, >\}$, and $c \in \mathbb{Q}$. The set $B(V)$ is a set of *Boolean variable constraints* over V. The set $B(X, V)$ of constraints comprises $B(X)$, $B(V)$, and conjunctions over clock and variable constraints. *Updates.* A *clock update* is of the form $x := 0$. A *variable update* is of the form $v := c$ where $c \in \mathbb{R}$. The set $U(X, V)$ of *updates* contains all finite, possibly empty sequences of clock and variable updates. We let $[\![r^\nu]\!] : \mathcal{V}(X) \cup \mathcal{V}(V) \to \mathcal{V}(X) \cup \mathcal{V}(V)$ be a map from valuations to valuations. We use $\mu[r]$ to denote the updated clock valuation $[\![r]\!](\mu)$. Analogously, for variable valuations. *Channels.* Given a set C of *channels*, the set $H(C)$ of synchronizations over channels is $\{h!, h?, \tau\}$ where $h \in C$, and τ represents an internal action.

Definition 1 (Extended Timed Automata XTA). *An* extended timed automaton $\mathcal{A}$ *is a tuple* $(L, L^u, L^f, l^{\text{ini}}, X, V, H(C), E, I)$ *where:* L *is a set of locations,* $L^u \subseteq L$ *denotes the set of urgent locations,* $L^f \subseteq L$ *denotes the set of accepting locations,* $l^{\text{ini}} \in L$ *is the initial location,* X *is a set of clocks,* V *is a set of variables,* $H(C)$ *is a set of channel synchronizations for set of channels* C, $E \subseteq L \times H(C) \times B(X) \times B(V) \times U(X, V) \times L$ *is a set of edges between locations* with a channel expressions, a clock guard, a variable guard, an update set, and $I : L \to B(X)$ assigns clock invariants to locations.

Definition 2 (Network of XTA). *A network $\mathcal{N}$ of XTA consists of a finite sequence $\mathcal{A}_1, \ldots, \mathcal{A}_n$ of XTA, where $\mathcal{A}_i = (L_i, L_i^u, L_i^f, l_i^{\text{ini}}, X_i, V_i, H(C)_i, E_i, I_i)$ for $1 \leq i \leq n$. Locations are pairwise disjoint i.e. $L_i \cap L_j = \emptyset$ for $1 \leq i, j \leq n$ and $i \neq j$. The set of locations is $L = \cup_{i=1}^n L_i$, analogously for urgent L^u locations. The set of clocks is $X = \bigcup_{i=1}^n X_i$ and the set of variables is $V = \cup_{i=1}^n V_i$. The set of channel expressions is $H(C) = \cup_{i=1}^n H(C)_i$. The set of edges is $E = \cup_{i=1}^n E_i$. A location vector is a vector $\vec{l} = (l_1, \ldots, l_n)$, and $\vec{l}_0 = (l_1^0, \ldots, l_n^0)$ is the initial location vector. The invariant function over location vectors is $I(\vec{l}) = \bigwedge_i I_i(l_i)$.*

We write $\vec{l}[l'_i/l_i]$ to denote the vector where the i-th element l_i of $\vec{l}$ is replaced by l'_i. We write $\vec{l}^i$ to denote the i-th element of $\vec{l}$. We write $\vec{l}_{\text{ini}}$ to denote the vector where for all $1 \leq i \leq n$ we have $\vec{l}_{\text{ini}}^i = l_i^{\text{ini}}$.

Definition 3 (Semantics of a Network of XTA). *Let $\mathcal{N} = \mathcal{A}_1, \ldots, \mathcal{A}_n$ be a network of TA. Its semantics is defined as a transition system $(S, s_0, \to)$, where $S \subseteq (L_1 \times \cdots \times L_n) \times \mathcal{V}(X) \times \mathcal{V}(V)$ is the set of states comprising a location vector, a zone, and a variable valuation, $s_{\text{ini}} = (\vec{l}_{\text{ini}}, \mu_{\text{ini}}, \nu_{\text{ini}})$ is the initial state, and $\to \subseteq S \times (\mathbb{R}_{\geq 0} \cup 2^E) \times S$ is the transition relation defined by:*

- *Delay transition, $(\vec{l}, \mu, \nu) \xrightarrow{d} (\vec{l}, \mu + d, \nu)$ iff $\vec{l}^i \notin L_i^u$ for $1 \leq i \leq n$, $d \in \mathbb{R}_{\geq 0}$ and $\mu + d' \models I(\vec{l})$ holds for all $d' \in [0, d]$.*
- *Internal transition, $(\vec{l}, \mu, \nu) \xrightarrow{\{e_i\}} (\vec{l}[l'_i/l_i], \mu', \nu')$ iff exits $e_i = (l_i, \tau, \phi, \psi, r, l'_i) \in E_i$ with $\mu' = \mu[r]$, $\mu' \models I(\vec{l}[l'_i/l_i])$, $\nu' = \nu[r]$, and $\nu \models \psi$.*
- *Broadcast transition, $(\vec{l}, \mu, \nu) \xrightarrow{E'} (\vec{l'}, \mu', \nu')$ iff $E' = \{e, e_1, e_2, \ldots, e_m\} \subseteq E$, $|E'| > 1$, and E' is such that $e = (l, h!, \phi, \psi, r, l')$ is a sender and for $1 \leq i \leq m$ $e_i = (l_i, h?, \phi_i, \psi_i, r_i, l'_i)$ is a receiver. Where*
  - *edges $e, e_1, e_2, \ldots, e_m$ are from different components,*
  - *$e_1, e_2, \ldots, e_m$ are ordered according the component ordering $\mathcal{A}_1, \ldots, \mathcal{A}_n$,*
  - *$\vec{l'} = \vec{l}[l/l'][l'_1/l_1] \ldots [l'_m/l_m]$,*
  - *$\mu \models \phi$ and for $1 \leq i \leq m$ $\mu \models \phi_i$, $\mu' = \mu[r][r_1] \ldots [r_m]$, $\mu' \models I(\vec{l'})$,*
  - *$\nu \models \psi$ and for $1 \leq i \leq m$ $\nu \models \psi_i$, $\nu' = \nu[r][r_1] \ldots [r_m]$.*

Additional Notation. In the following, we are given a network of TA $\mathcal{N} = \mathcal{A}_1, \ldots, \mathcal{A}_n$ with locations L, clocks X, variables V, edges E, and induced symbolic transition system $(S, s_0, \to)$. Given state $s = (\vec{l}, \mu, \nu) \in S$ we use $\vec{l}(s) = \vec{l}$, $\mu(s) = \mu$, $\nu(s) = \nu$ to denote the location vector, clock valuation, and variable valuation of s. A finite *run* ρ of $\mathcal{N}$ is a finite sequence $\rho = (\vec{l}_0, \mu_0, \nu_0) \xrightarrow{\lambda_0} (\vec{l}_1, \mu_1 \nu_1) \xrightarrow{\lambda_1} \ldots \xrightarrow{\lambda_{n-1}} (\vec{l}_n, \mu_n, \nu_n)$. An *accepting run* is a run starting from the initial configuration s_{ini} and terminating at state s such that for all $1 \leq i \leq n$, $\vec{l}(s)^i \in L_i^f$ i.e. all locations in $\vec{l}$ are accepting locations. Network $\mathcal{N}$ is accepting if there exists an accepting run.

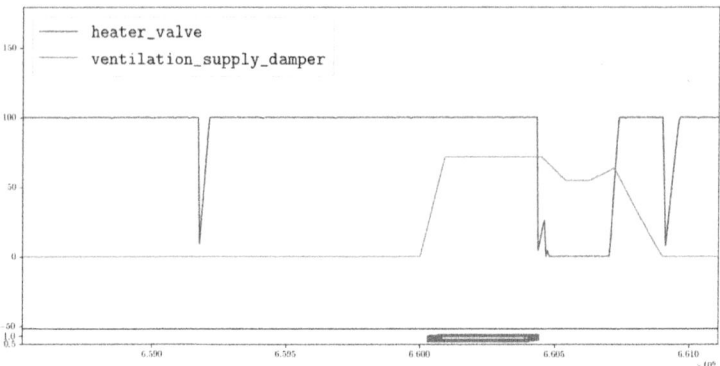

Fig. 2. Heating and ventilation in Thomas Manns vej 23. in Aalborg University. Red rectangles at the bottom indicates the matches of the ETRE $\langle (80_{20}^{heat})^* \rangle_{[3600\,s, 7200\,s]} \cap \langle (60_{40}^{vent})^* \rangle_{[3600\,s, 7200\,s]}$. This are instances where the heater and the ventilator are ON at the same time for a period between 1 to 2 h. (Color figure online)

A state $s \in S$ is *zero time* if it can not delay, denoted by $\mathsf{zt}(s)$ and defined by $\mathsf{zt}(s)$ iff $\forall s' \in S, \lambda \in \mathbb{R}_{\geq 0} \cup 2^E$. $s \xrightarrow{\lambda} s' \implies \lambda \in 2^E$. We write $s_0 \rightarrow^* s_n$ iff exists run $s_0 \xrightarrow{\lambda_0} s_1 \xrightarrow{\lambda_1} s_1 \dots s_n$. We write $s_0 \xrightarrow[\mathsf{zt}]{}^* s_n$ iff exists run $s_0 \xrightarrow{\lambda_0} s_1 \xrightarrow{\lambda_1} s_1 \dots s_n$ such that $\lambda_i \in 2^E$ and if $n > 0$ we have $\mathsf{zt}(s_i)$ for $0 \leq i < n$.

Time-additivity. For any $d_1, d_2 \in \mathbb{R}_{\geq 0}$, $s, s' \in S$ it holds that $s \xrightarrow{d_1} \cdot \xrightarrow{d_2} s'$ iff $s \xrightarrow{d_1 + d_2} s'$ Given any run we can use time-additivity to produce a run which consists of alternations of delays and discrete transitions. We denote such runs as *runs closed under time-additivity*.

3 Extended Timed Regular Expressions (ETRE)

Our intention is to extend the applicability of Timed Regular Expressions to the context of time series data and to industrial applications involving large magnitudes of data. First we use timed words to formalize time series data. Then we define ETRE by keeping in mind the nature of time series data and computational efficiency. We describe timed words and Extended Timed Regular Expressions in the spirit of [4].

3.1 Timed Words

A monoid is a triple $(M, \cdot, \epsilon)$ where M is a set, $\cdot$ is an associative binary operation on M and ϵ is the identity element of M satisfying $\epsilon \cdot m = m \cdot \epsilon = m$ for every $m \in M$. Time passage is described by the *time monoid* $(\mathbb{R}_{\geq 0}, +, 0)$ of positive real numbers under addition. Events are described by the *event monoid* $(\Sigma, +, \mathbf{0})$ of vectors $\Sigma \subseteq \mathbb{R}^n$ under vector addition. As described in [4] the *time-event monoid* $\mathcal{T} = (\mathbb{R}_{\geq 0} \uplus \Sigma, \cdot, \varepsilon)$ is obtained as the free product of the time and event monoids, where · is concatenation and ε is the empty word. A *timed word* $w = t_0 \cdot a_0 \cdot t_1 \cdot a_1 \cdots$, is an element of the time-event monoid with $t_i \in \mathbb{R}_{>0}$ and $a_i \in \Sigma$ for $i > 0$. Given timed word w its duration is given by $\mathsf{dur}(w) \in \mathbb{R}_{\geq 0}$.

Figure 1a shows a finite timed word on a single dimension i.e. $\Sigma = \mathbb{R}^1$. Figure 2 shows a finite timed word on two dimensions. Dimensions correspond to the valve position for the heating and the ventilation of a room in a building at Aalborg University. Our goal is to define and match complex patterns in time series data, for this we define Extended Timed Regular Expressions.

Definition 4 (Extended Timed Regular Expressions (ETRE)). *The set $\mathcal{E}$ of ETRE is given by the following grammar:*

$$\varphi ::= \phi \mid \varphi \cap \varphi$$
$$\phi ::= \varepsilon \mid c^i_\delta \mid \Sigma \mid \langle f^i_\delta \rangle_J \mid \phi \cup \phi \mid \phi \cdot \phi \mid \phi^+ \mid \phi^* \mid \langle \phi \rangle_J$$

where $c \in \mathbb{R}$, $0 \leq i < n$, $\delta \in \mathbb{R}_{\geq 0}$, J is an integer-bounded interval, and f is a real-valued computable function.

Definition 4 is similar to that given in [4]. The main differences include, events are vectors in $\mathbb{R}^n$, we include functions, and intersections are only allowed at the top level. Restriction on intersections is to avoid the expensive automata product construction (allowing nesting of intersections would not affect our theoretical results). Instead, intersections will be translated to networks of XTA which will be explored on the fly.

Definition 5 (ETRE semantics). *The semantics of a regular expression φ is given by a set of elements of the time-event monoid. Formally, $[\![\ ]\!] : \mathcal{E} \to 2^T$.*

$[\![\varepsilon]\!] = \{\varepsilon\}$
$[\![c^i_\delta]\!] = \{r \cdot (a^0, \ldots, a^n) \mid r \in \mathbb{R}_{\geq 0}, a^i \in [c - \delta, c + \delta], a^k \in \mathbb{R} \text{ for } k \neq i\}$
$[\![\Sigma]\!] = \{r \cdot (a^0, \ldots, a^n) \mid r \in \mathbb{R}_{\geq 0}, a^i \in \mathbb{R}\}$
$[\![\langle f^i_\delta \rangle_{[d_1, d_2]}]\!] = \{w \mid w = t_0 \cdot a_0 \cdots t_m \cdot a_m \text{ with } \mathsf{dur}(w_{0:m-1}) < d_1,$
$\quad \mathsf{dur}(w) \in [d_1, d_2], \text{ and for } 0 \leq j \leq m \text{ and } k \neq i \text{ we have }$
$\quad 0 < t_j, a^k_j \in \mathbb{R}, a^i_j \in [f(\mathsf{dur}(w_{0:j})) - \delta, f(\mathsf{dur}(w_{0:j})) + \delta]\}$
$[\![\phi_1 \cdot \phi_2]\!] = [\![\phi_1]\!] \cdot [\![\phi_2]\!]$
$[\![\phi_1 \cup \phi_2]\!] = [\![\phi_1]\!] \cup [\![\phi_2]\!]$
$[\![\langle \phi \rangle_J]\!] = [\![\phi]\!] \cap \{w \mid \mathsf{dur}(w) \in J\}$
$[\![\phi^*]\!] = \bigcup_{i=0}^{\infty} ([\![\underbrace{\phi \cdots \phi}_{i \text{ times}}]\!])$
$[\![\phi^+]\!] = \phi \cdot \phi^*$
$[\![\varphi_1 \cap \varphi_2]\!] = [\![\varphi_1]\!] \cap [\![\varphi_2]\!]$

As an example consider the ETRE $\langle f^{\mathrm{MLII}}_{\delta=0.38} \rangle_{[d_1=0.039\,s, d_2=0.045\,s]}$ we use MLII instead of 1 for readability. The function f is a 7th degree polynomial as illustrated by the dashed line in Fig. 1b. The semantics of this expression is the set of timed words inside the tube induced by f and δ with duration in the interval $[d_1, d_2]$. The semantics of the more complex expression

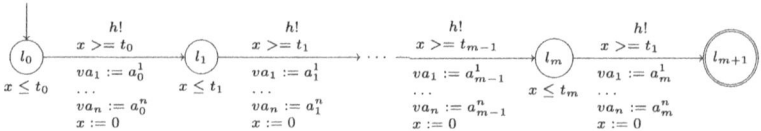

Fig. 3. XTA $\mathcal{A}_w$ for timed word $w = t_0 \cdot a_0 \cdot t_1 \cdot a_1 \cdot t_2 \cdot a_2 \cdot \ldots t_m \cdot a_m$

$\langle f_{0.38}^{\text{MLII}} \rangle_{[0.039\,s, 0.045\,s]} \cdot \langle \Sigma^* \rangle_{[0.47\,s, 0.67\,s]} \cdot \langle f_{0.38}^{\text{MLII}} \rangle_{[0.039\,s, 0.045\,s]}$ is the set of timed words in $\langle f_{0.38}^{\text{MLII}} \rangle_{[0.039s, 0.045s]}$ concatenated with any word (Σ^*) with duration in $[0.47s, 0.67s]$ followed by timed words in $\langle f_{0.38}^{\text{MLII}} \rangle_{[0.039s, 0.045s]}$. This set of timed words hint to a QRS complex followed by another QRS complex too early, a sign of arrhythmia.

As another example consider ETRE $\langle (80_{20}^{\text{heat}})^* \rangle_{[1h,2h]} \cap \langle (60_{40}^{\text{vent}})^* \rangle_{[1h,2h]}$ from Fig. 2. The semantics of the ETRE $\langle (80_{20}^{\text{heat}})^* \rangle_{[1h,2h]}$ is the set of all timed words with value 80 ± 20 in the dimension heat with duration between 1 and 2 h. This ETRE indicate that the heater has been ON for the given duration. An intersection with the set $\langle (60_{40}^{\text{vent}})^* \rangle_{[1h,2h]}$ indicates that both heater and ventilation have been ON for the duration. Note that computing matches for every conjunct independently, will require to merge the results while satisfying the time constraints. Table 1 shows a number of ETRE used in our case studies.

4 Timed Word Membership for ETRE

The work in [4] shows the language equivalence between Timed Regular Expressions and Timed Automata. The expressiveness of ETRE goes beyond that of Timed Automata. However, we are interested in matching patterns in finite time series data (finite timed words) i.e. given a finite timed word w with non-zero delays and ETRE φ we need to decide if $w \in [\![\varphi]\!]$. We show that we can decide this problem by translating w and φ to a network of XTA, and then checking if the resulting network is accepting.

Definition 6 (XTA for a word). *Given non-empty finite word $w = t_0 \cdot a_0 \cdot t_1 \cdot a_1 \cdot \ldots t_m \cdot a_m$ with $t_i > 0$ the corresponding XTA is given by $\mathcal{A}_w = (L, \emptyset, L^f, l_0, \{\hat{x}, x\}, \{va_1, \ldots, va_n\}, H(C), E, I)$ where: $L = \{l_0, \ldots, l_{m+1}\}$, $C = \{h\}$, $E = \{(l_j, h!, x \geq t_j, \text{true}, [va_0 := a_j^0, \ldots va_n := a_j^n, x := 0], l_{j+1}) \mid 0 \leq j \leq m\}$, $I(l_j) = x \leq t_j$ for $0 \leq j \leq m$ and $I(l_{m+1}) = \text{true}$.*

Figure 3 describes $\mathcal{A}_w$. The automaton for the empty word ε is the automaton consisting of a unique location which is initial and accepting. Given ETRE φ the next step is to construct a network of XTA $\mathcal{N}_\varphi$ which accepts and produces finite words in φ. Note that $\mathcal{A}_w$ will generate inputs on which $\mathcal{N}_\varphi$ will synchronize. We carefully design $\mathcal{N}_\varphi$ to be input enabled by using urgent locations.

Definition 7 (Network of XTA for an ETRE). *Given ETRE φ the corresponding network $\mathcal{N}_\varphi = \mathcal{A}_1, \ldots, \mathcal{A}_n$ with channel $C = \{h\}$ is defined inductively as follows. The network for $\varphi \equiv \phi$ consist of a single automaton given by:*

- $\phi \equiv \varepsilon$ then $\mathcal{A}_\varepsilon = (\{l_0, l_1\}, \{l_0\}, \{l_1\}, l_0, \emptyset, \emptyset, H(C), E, I)$ where $E = \{(l_0, \tau,$ true, true, $[], l_1)\}$ and $I(l) =$ true for $l \in \{l_0, l_1\}$.
- $\phi \equiv c_\delta^i$ then $\mathcal{A}_\phi = (L, \{l_1\}, \{l_2\}, l_0, \emptyset, \{va_i\}, H(C), E, I)$ where $L = \{l_0, l_1, l_2\}$, $E = \{(l_0, h?, \text{true}, \text{true}, l_1), (l_1, \tau, \text{true}, c - \delta \leq va_i \leq c + \delta, [], l_2)\}$ and $I(l) =$ true for $l \in \{l_0, l_1, l_2\}$.
- $\phi \equiv \Sigma$ then $\mathcal{A}_\phi = (L, \{l_1\}, \{l_2\}, l_0, \emptyset, \emptyset, H(C), E, I)$ where $L = \{l_0, l_1, l_2\}$, $E = \{(l_0, h?, \text{true}, \text{true}, l_1), (l_1, \tau, \text{true}, \text{true}, [], l_2)\}$ and $I(l) =$ true for $l \in \{l_0, l_1, l_2\}$.
- $\phi \equiv \langle f_\delta^i \rangle_{[d_1, d_2]}$ then $\mathcal{A}_\phi = (L, \{l_1\}, \{l_2\}, l_0, \{x\}, \{va_i, \delta, f, d_1, d_2\}, H(C), E, I)$, $L = \{l_0, l_1, l_2\}$, $I(l) =$ true for $l \in L$, and $E = \{(l_0, h?, \text{true}, \text{true}, [], l_1), (l_1, \tau, x < d_1, f(x) - \delta \leq va_i \leq f(x) + \delta, [], l_0), (l_1, \tau, d_1 \leq x \leq d_2, f(x) - \delta \leq va_i \leq f(x) + \delta, [], l_2)\}$.
- $\phi \equiv \phi_1 \cdot \phi_2$ then $\mathcal{A}_\phi = (L, L^u, L_2^f, l_1^{\text{ini}}, X_1 \cup X_2, V_1 \cup V_2, H(C), E' \cup E_2, I_1 \cup I_2)$ where E' is obtained from E_1 by replacing every edge of the form $(l, \alpha, \phi, \psi, r, l')$ with $l' \in L_1^f$ by an edge $(l, \alpha, \phi, \psi, r', l_2^{\text{ini}})$ where r' appends to r reset $x := 0$ for every clock $x \in X_2$, $L = (L_1 \setminus L_1^f) \cup L_2$, and $L^u = (L_1^u \setminus L_1^f) \cup L_2^u$.
- $\phi \equiv \phi_1 \cup \phi_2$ then $\mathcal{A}_\phi = (L_1 \cup L_2 \cup \{l\}, L_1^u \cup L_2^u \cup \{l\}, L_1^f \cup L_2^f, l, X_1 \cup X_2, V_1 \cup V_2, H(C), E' \cup E_1 \cup E_2, I)$ where $E' = \{(l, \tau, \text{true}, \text{true}, [], l_i^{\text{ini}}) \mid 1 \leq i \leq 2\}$ and $I = I_1 \cup I_2 \cup \{(l, \text{true})\}$.
- $\phi \equiv \phi_1^+$ then $\mathcal{A}_\phi = (L_1, L_1^u, L_1^f, l_1^{\text{ini}}, X_1, V_1, H(C), E_1 \cup E', I_1)$ where E' is obtained by adding for every edge $(l', \alpha, \phi, \psi, r, l_f)$ in E_1 with $l_f \in L_1^f$ an edge of the form $(l', \alpha, \phi, \psi, r', l_1^{\text{ini}})$. Where r' appends to r reset $x := 0$ for every clock $x \in X_1$.
- $\phi \equiv \phi_1^*$ then $\mathcal{A}_{\varepsilon \cup \phi_1^+}$ results of the union of $\varepsilon \cup \phi_1^+$.
- $\phi \equiv \langle \phi_1 \rangle_{[d_1, d_2]}$ then $\mathcal{A}_\phi = (L_1, L_1^u, L_1^f, l_1^{\text{ini}}, X_1 \cup \{x\}, V_1, H(C), E, I)$ where E is obtained from E_1 by replacing every edge of the form $(l', \alpha, \phi, \psi, r, l_f) \in E_1$ where $l_f \in L_1^f$ with an edge $(l', \alpha, \phi \wedge d_1 \leq x \leq d_2, \psi, r, l_f)$.

The network for $\varphi \equiv \varphi_1 \cap \varphi_2$ consists of the automata in the network for φ_1 and in the network for φ_2.

Figure 4 illustrates our construction. Note that some locations can delay "wait" for inputs in channel h. We call such locations *input locations*.

Definition 8 (Input Locations). *Given network with locations L and edges E. Location l is an* input location *iff exists edge $(l, h?, \phi, \psi, r, l')$ in E.*

The network $\mathcal{N}_\varphi$ has a number of syntactic structural invariants. These invariants are key to our results, proofs, and algorithms.

Lemma 1. *Given ETRE φ and the induced network $\mathcal{N}_\varphi = \mathcal{A}_1, \ldots, \mathcal{A}_n$. Then the network $\mathcal{N}_\varphi$ has the following structural invariants:*

1. *Initial locations are not accepting locations.*
2. *Accepting locations have no outgoing edges.*

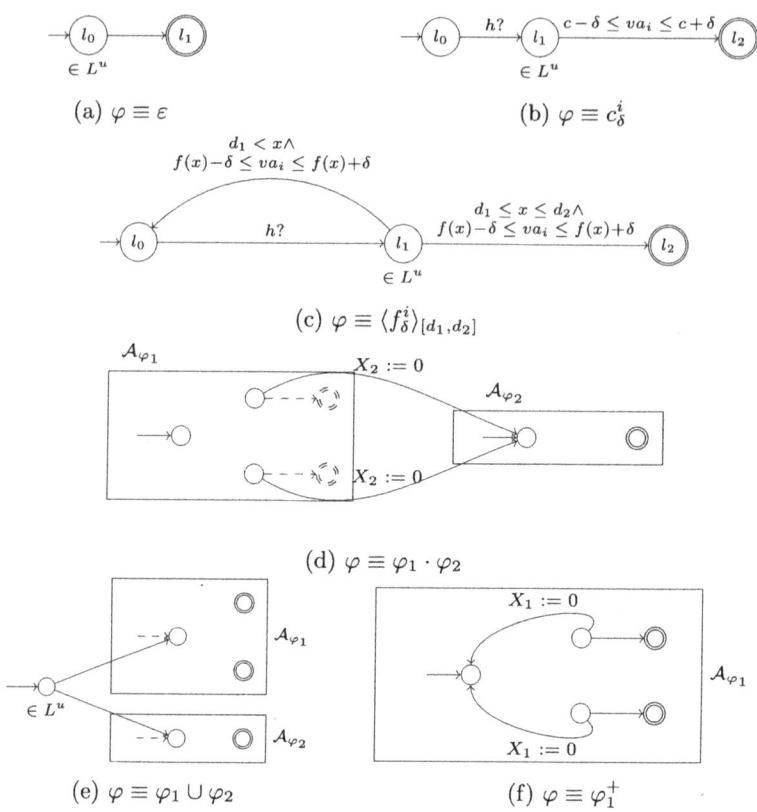

Fig. 4. XTA for ETRE

3. Input locations have a unique outgoing edge e. The destination location of e is not an accepting or input location.
4. For any location l. Location l is not urgent iff l is accepting or l is an input location.

Given a finite timed word w Lemma 1 implies that accepting runs of the network including $\mathcal{A}_w$ and the automata in $\mathcal{N}_\varphi$ have a particular form. Informally, $\mathcal{A}_w$ delays and send an input, then $\mathcal{N}_\varphi$ consumes the input and urgently (a sequence $\xrightarrow{}_{zt}^*$) checks if the corresponding prefix of w is inside $[\![\varphi]\!]$.

Lemma 2. *Given finite timed word $w = t_0 \cdot a_0 \cdot t_1 \cdot a_1 \cdot \ldots \cdot t_m \cdot a_m$, ETRE φ, induced network $\mathcal{A}_w, \mathcal{A}_1, \ldots, \mathcal{A}_n$, and closed under time-additivity accepting run ρ. Then ρ is of the form:*

$$s_{ini} \xrightarrow{}_{zt}^* s_0 \xrightarrow{t_0} \cdot \xrightarrow{E_{a_0}} s'_0 \xrightarrow{}_{zt}^* s_1 \xrightarrow{t_1} \cdot \xrightarrow{E_{a_1}} s'_1 \xrightarrow{}_{zt}^* \ldots \xrightarrow{}^* s_m \xrightarrow{t_m} \cdot \xrightarrow{E_{a_m}} s'_m \xrightarrow{}_{zt}^* s_{m+1}$$

where $E_{a_i} \subseteq 2^E$ for $0 \le i \le m$ is the set of edges participating in the broadcast induced by the edge going from l_i to l_{i+1} in $\mathcal{A}_w$.

Lemma 2 implies that for accepting runs, the only possible delays (closed under time-additivity) are the ones in $\mathcal{A}_w$. This will allow us to implement an efficient discrete-time engine avoiding the expensive difference-bound matrices (DBM) operations. Note, that Lemma 2 indicates that there can be urgent behavior from the initial state before automaton $\mathcal{A}_w$ has updated the shared variables va and sent a synchronization. If an operation e.g. concatenation of $\varphi_1 \cdot \varphi_2$ is applied, the variable valuation after executing $\mathcal{A}_{\varphi_1}$ will differ from the initial valuation for $\mathcal{A}_{\varphi_2}$ and could potentially block $\mathcal{A}_{\varphi_2}$. The following lemma ensures that the initial urgent behavior can not be blocked by variable guards.

Lemma 3. *Let $s_{\mathsf{ini}} \xrightarrow{u}_{zt} s_0$ be a prefix of an accepting run with $u \in (E_1 \cup \cdots \cup E_n)^*$. For any edge $u_i = (l, \alpha, \phi, \psi, r, l')$ in u the variable guard ψ is true.*

In the following we are given a finite timed word w and ETRE φ. We use $\mathcal{N}_\varphi^w$ to denote the network $\mathcal{A}_w, \mathcal{A}_1, \ldots, \mathcal{A}_n$.

Lemma 4. *Given finite timed word w. If $w \in [\![\varphi]\!]$ then $\mathcal{N}_\varphi^w$ is accepting.*

Lemma 5. *Given finite timed word w. If $\mathcal{N}_\varphi^w$ is accepting then $w \in [\![\varphi]\!]$.*

The proofs are quite technical and long. Detailed proofs for all the lemmas and theorems can be found in the extended version of this paper. Informally, for the above lemmas. We apply Lemma 2 and use structural induction on φ. For the case when $\varphi \equiv \phi$ we use induction on the length of w (accepting run ρ respectively). For the case when $\varphi \equiv \varphi_1 \cap \varphi_2$ we use the structural I.H. together with the fact that after receiving an input from $\mathcal{A}_w$, the actions in automata φ_1, φ_2 are urgent and commute (only read shared variables). The following theorem indicates that we can perform a reachability analysis in $\mathcal{N}_\varphi^w$ to decide if $w \in [\![\varphi]\!]$.

Theorem 1. *Given finite timed word w then $w \in [\![\varphi]\!]$ iff $\mathcal{N}_\varphi^w$ is accepting.*

5 Timed Pattern Matching with ETRE

Our goal is to efficiently match complex timed patterns described as an ETRE in time series data. An additional step is to transform a given time series into a timed word. This can be easily done by replacing the time stamps in the data by the induced delays. We require that the delays are not 0. Note that in [19] timed pattern matching returns a match set with uncountably many points where the expression matches. In contrast our algorithm will only return the start (and stop) indexes of the first sub-word that matches the expression. Our pattern matching method is described in Algorithm 1 presented in the spirit of [9]. For illustration purposes and clarity Line 1 ask to compute $\mathcal{A}_w$. As expected our implementation will not construct $\mathcal{A}_w$ but only inject the events and delays from w. Our implementation supports injection of events online (run time) and off-line for e.g. post processing.

Our method exploits the form of the runs as described in Lemma 2. The lemma indicates that there is an alternation among non-urgent and urgent

Algorithm 1. Timed Pattern Matching for ETRE using XTA

Input Word $w = t_0 \cdot a_0 \ldots t_m \cdot a_m$, ETRE φ.
Output First position k with $w_{0:k} \in [\![\varphi]\!]$, or $\perp$ if no match exists.

1: compute $\mathcal{A}_w, \mathcal{A}_1, \ldots, \mathcal{A}_n$ from φ using Definition 7
2: **if** $\mathsf{zt}(s_{\mathsf{ini}})$ **then** $W := UrgentExploration(s_{\mathsf{ini}})$
3: **else** $W := \{s_{\mathsf{ini}}\}$
4: **for** $k = 0$ to m **do**
5: $\quad W' := \emptyset$
6: $\quad$ **for all** $s \in W$ **do**
7: $\quad\quad$ **if** s is accepting for $\mathcal{A}_1, \ldots, \mathcal{A}_n$ **then return** k
8: $\quad\quad$ **if** exists s' with $s \xrightarrow{t_k} \cdot \xrightarrow{E'} s'$ **then** $W' := W' \cup UrgentExploration(s')$
9: $\quad W := W'$
10: **if** exists $s \in W$ s.t. s is accepting for $\mathcal{A}_1, \ldots, \mathcal{A}_n$ **then return** m
11: **return** $\perp$

Algorithm 2. $UrgentExploration(s)$

Input urgent state s
Output a pair with a set with non urgent states and a boolean indicating if an accepting state was found

1: $W_{\mathsf{zt}} := \{s\}$, $P := \emptyset$, $W_{\neg \mathsf{zt}} := \emptyset$
2: **while** $W_{\mathsf{zt}} \neq \emptyset$ **do**
3: $\quad$ pick $s \in W_{\mathsf{zt}}$, $W_{\mathsf{zt}} := W_{\mathsf{zt}} \setminus \{s\}$
4: $\quad$ **if** $s \in P$ **then continue**
5: $\quad P := P \cup \{s\}$
6: $\quad$ compute stubborn set $\mathsf{St}(s)$
7: $\quad Succs := \{s' \mid \exists i \in \{1, \ldots, n\}, e \in E_i . s \xrightarrow{e} s'$ and $\{e\} \in \mathsf{St}(s)\}$
8: $\quad$ **for all** $s \in Succs$ **do**
9: $\quad\quad$ **if** $\mathsf{zt}(s)$ **then** $W_{\mathsf{zt}} := W_{\mathsf{zt}} \cup \{s\}$
10: $\quad\quad$ **else** $W_{\neg \mathsf{zt}} := W_{\neg \mathsf{zt}} \cup \{s\}$
11: **return** $W_{\neg \mathsf{zt}}$

---

behavior. For this reason, after delaying and injecting an event, Algorithm 1 calls Algorithm 2 for urgent exploration in Line 8 (or if the initial state is urgent Line 2). Algorithm 2, is the well known reachability algorithm for model checking. An invariant of this algorithm is that all the states in the waiting list W_{zt} are urgent. In addition, since automata $\mathcal{A}_1, \ldots, \mathcal{A}_n$ do not share clocks and only read shared variables (they are independent) it is an ideal scenario for application of urgent partial order reduction techniques [12] Line 6.

The intuition for the correctness of our method is as follows. Algorithm 1 simulates w in the network $\mathcal{N}_\varphi$. If Line 7 returns k then all locations in $\mathcal{N}_\varphi$ are accepting. From the algorithm execution we can construct an accepting run indicating that $\mathcal{N}_\varphi^{w_{[0:k]}}$ is accepting. By Lemma 5 we have that $w_{[0:k]} \in [\![\varphi]\!]$. In the case where $w_{[0:k]} \in [\![\varphi]\!]$ for the first k. By Lemma 4, we have that exits

Table 1. ETRE expressions for case studies.

Property	ETRE
qrs-const$_\delta$	1_δ^{MLII}
qrs-const-verify$_\delta$	qrs-const$_\delta \cap (1_{0.1}^{\text{annot}} \cup -0.5_{0.1}^{\text{annot}})$
early-const$_\delta$	qrs-const$_\delta \cdot \langle \Sigma^* \rangle_{[0.04s, 0.65s]} \cdot$ qrs-const$_\delta$
early-const-verify	early-const$_\delta \cap \langle \Sigma^* \rangle_{[0.47s, 0.77s]} \cdot 1.0_{0.1}^{\text{annot}} \cdot \langle \Sigma^* \rangle_{[0, 03s]}$
qrs-func$_\delta$	$\langle f_\delta^{\text{MLII}} \rangle_{[0.039s, 0.045s]}$
qrs-func-verify$_\delta$	qrs-func$_\delta \cap (\langle \Sigma^* \rangle_{[0\,s, 0.45\,s]} \cdot 1_{0.1}^{\text{annot}} \cup -0.5_{0.1}^{\text{annot}} \cdot \langle \Sigma^* \rangle_{[0, 03\,s]})$
early-func$_\delta$	qrs-func$_\delta \cdot \langle \Sigma^* \rangle_{[0.47\,s, 0.67\,s]} \cdot$ qrs-func$_\delta$
early-func-verify$_\delta$	early-func$_\delta \cap \langle \Sigma^* \rangle_{[0.47\,s, 0.77\,s]} \cdot 1_{0.1}^{\text{annot}} \cdot \langle \Sigma^* \rangle_{[0\,s, 0.03\,s]}$
sto-gates-closed$_\delta$	$300_{270}^{\text{havn}} \cap 77_\delta^{\text{port}}$
sto-safe-fjord-ub$_\delta$	50_δ^{fjord}
sto-close-diff	$(-200_{100}^{\text{diff}} \cup 200_{100}^{\text{diff}}) \cap 51_{50}^{\text{port}}$
sto-water-levels$_\delta$	$0_{25}^{\text{diff}} \cap 0_\delta^{\text{port}}$
tmv-energy$_J$	$\langle (80_{20}^{\text{heat}})^* \rangle_J \cap \langle (60_{40}^{\text{vent}})^* \rangle_J$
tmv-solar$_J$	$\langle (f(t) = 268.2 + 0.1t)_{100}^{\text{solar}} \rangle_J$

accepting run ρ in $\mathcal{A}_{w_{[0:k]}}, \mathcal{A}_1, \ldots, \mathcal{A}_n$. By Lemma 2 we have the form of ρ and we can easily see that the algorithm can execute ρ (or equivalent if POR is applied).

Theorem 2 (Total Correctness). *Given $w = t_0 \cdot a_0 \ldots t_m \cdot a_m$ and ETRE φ. Algorithm 1 terminates and if Algorithm 1 returns $k \geq 0$ then $w_{[0:k]} \in [\![\varphi]\!]$ otherwise $w \notin [\![\varphi]\!]$.*

6 Evaluation

We have implemented our theory using C++ in the tool TIMEREX. Our tool supports both online (run time) and offline pattern matching. The online version uses C++20 coroutines and ranges to compose lazy reading from a JSON-formatted stream of records, parsing and matching, and a buffer to store the passed records for a limited backtracking. Our tool includes a simple python GUI to enter ETRE and visualize the matches in the corresponding data. We run our experiments using a HPC cluster with AMD EPYC 9334 CPUs. For every experiment we allocate a single CPU with 10GB or RAM. Table 2 gives information on the time series data for each case study.

6.1 Arrhythmia

We consider the PhysioNet MIT-BIH Arrhythmia Database [10][1]. We analyze the data for patient 100 which contains 650000 samples and 2274 annotations.

---
[1] https://physionet.org/content/mitdb/1.0.0/.

Annotations classify ventricular myocardial depolarization called the *QRS complex* as normal (value -0.5) and arrhythmia (value 1). From the 2274 annotations 33 are classified as arrhythmia. We use ETRE to approximate the QRS complex, and arrhythmia. Table 1 presents the ETRE we use for matching and Table 2a presents our results. We briefly describe the properties:

1. qrs-const$_\delta$ approximates a QRS complex using the constant 1 (a peak) on the dimension MLII.
2. qrs-const-verify$_\delta$ verifies qrs-const$_\delta$ by checking (the second conjunct) that the corresponding annotation is either normal -0.5 or arrhythmia 1.
3. early-const$_\delta$ approximates arrhythmia by matching a peak qrs-const$_\delta$ followed by any value (Σ) in the given interval and then followed by another peak.
4. early-const-verify verifies early-const$_\delta$ by checking that during the duration of early-const$_\delta$ the value 1 appears in the annotation.
5. qrs-func$_\delta$ approximates a QRS complex using ETRE $\langle f_\delta^{\mathrm{MLII}} \rangle_{[0.039s, 0.045s]}$ where function f is a 7th degree polynomial illustrated in Fig. 1b.
6. qrs-func-verify$_\delta$ verifies qrs-func$_\delta$ by checking that during the duration of qrs-func-verify$_\delta$ values -0.5 or 1 appear in the annotation signal.
7. early-func$_\delta$ approximates arrhythmia by matching a QRS complex (using qrs-func$_\delta$) followed by any sequence of values with a duration between 0.47 to 0.67 s and then followed by another QRS complex. Figure 1a shows a match for this expression when $\delta = 0.38$.
8. early-func-verify$_\delta$ verifies early-func$_\delta$ by checking that during the duration of early-func$_\delta$ the value 1 appears in the annotation.

Table 2a presents our results of matching the ETRE described above for different δ values. We observe that execution times are below 2 min (we consider it fast given the number of samples), even in the presence of Σ^* which might cause a quadratic number of calls (in the number of samples) to Algorithm 1.

Consider early-const$_{0.4}$ with 177 matches of which 155 were also annotated qrs-const-verify$_{0.4}$. Remember that there is a total of 33 arrhythmia annotations. A visual inspection shows that there are repetitions (an arrhythmia detected more than once). We also observe that 1 arrhythmia annotation is not matched and few QRS complex are matched but not annotated as arrhythmia. We obtain a similar result with expression early-func. However, with few more false positives in a period where the heart rate of the patient is slightly higher. Note that the duration of the unconstrained time word (Σ^*) in early-const an in early-func is different and has a big impact in the matches. We report that finding the appropriate ETRE and their parameters such as δ or duration is involved and can greatly affect the number of matches (Fig. 5).

6.2 Storm Surge Barriers

The data comes from sea water gates provided by Danish Coastal Authorities[2] through STORM_SAFE project[3]. The gate installation consists of 14 identical

---
[2] https://kyst.dk/hav-og-anlaeg/maalinger-og-data/.
[3] https://www.interregnorthsea.eu/stormsafe.

Table 2. ETRE experiments. Time in seconds. Memory usage for all experiments with mean 5.5MB and standard deviation 0.158MB

(a) Arrhythmia.

δ	ETRE	Matches	Time	ETRE	Matches	Time
0.32		9545	1.7		2253	2.8
0.34		9918	1.7		2263	2.8
0.36	qrs-const$_\delta$	10274	1.8	qrs-const-verify$_\delta$	2265	2.8
0.38		10591	1.8		2268	2.8
0.40		10875	1.8		2271	2.8
0.32		153	6.9		136	20.3
0.34		158	7.2		140	20.9
0.36	early-const$_\delta$	165	7.3	early-const-verify$_\delta$	145	21.5
0.38		169	7.5		148	22.1
0.40		177	7.9		155	23.9
0.32		2409	30.5		2409	109.4
0.34		2681	33.1		2681	118.6
0.36	qrs-func$_\delta$	2930	35.1	qrs-func-verify$_\delta$	2930	126.7
0.38		3189	37.0		3189	133.4
0.40		3469	37.9		3469	136.1
0.32		94	41.2		29	63.7
0.34		105	46.1		34	69.9
0.36	early-func$_\delta$	115	50.9	early-func-verify$_\delta$	39	77.9
0.38		128	54.0		40	84.3
0.40		143	57.8		44	92.1

(b) Storm Surge Barriers.

δ	ETRE	Match	Time
73		39473	7.7
74	sto-gates-closed	41049	7.5
75		144246	7.7
76		147210	7.7
20		41429	7.2
21		45668	7.3
22	sto-safe-fjord-ub	50116	7.3
23		55152	7.5
24		61829	7.2
25		68631	7.3
100	sto-close-diff	3074	8.9
0		72937	7.7
1	sto-water-levels	76733	7.7
2		214435	8.0
3		219446	8.0

(c) Thomas Manns Vej 23.

J in s.	ETRE	Match	Time
[1800, 3600]		172	2.7
[3600, 5400]	tmv-energy$_J$	81	2.7
[5400, 7200]		43	2.7
[7200, 9000]		13	2.7
[300, 600]		8142	2.5
[600, 900]	tmv-solar$_J$	5648	2.7
[900, 1200]		3845	2.9
[1200, 1500]		2619	3.0

(d) Time series data for case studies.

Data	Dimensions	Size,MB	Samples	Annotations
Arrhythmia	3	60	650000	2274
Storm-safe	19	50	764572	–
TMV 23	13	23	23360	–

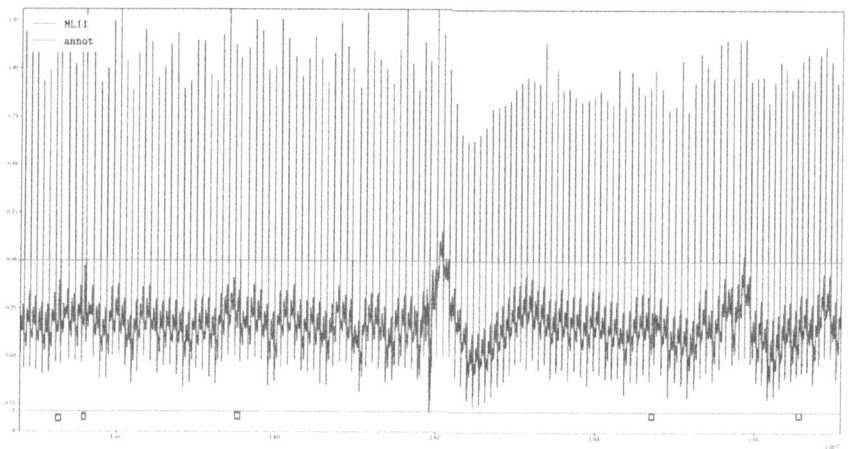

Fig. 5. early-const$_{0.4}$ missing one arrhythmia and matching one non annotated.

gates at Hvide Sande harbor controlling the flow of water between North Sea and Ringkøbing fjord, with the following objectives:

1. Protect the fjord coasts from North Sea storms: all gates must be closed during storms. Query for finding counter examples: sto-gates-closed$_\delta$.
2. Protect the fjord coasts from (precipitation and melting snow) floods by letting the fjord water out into North Sea and maintain the water levels below 25cm. Counter example query: sto-safe-fjord-ub$_\delta$.
3. Protect the installation and harbor navigation from strong water currents by allowing the gates to open only if the difference between sea and fjord water levels is less than 100cm. Counter example query: sto-close-diff.
4. Support the fish migration by opening all gates when the sea and fjord levels are the same. Counter example query: sto-water-levels$_\delta$.

The prepared data consists of a time series of: timestamp, North Sea water level, Ringkøbing fjord level (both at Hvide Sande harbor), state of each gate (0cm means fully closed, 550cm means fully open) and a reason behind the gate control command. The water levels are sampled every 10 min from a 4 min running average and the gate state changes according to the control commands.

The algorithm has detected tens of thousands of requirement violations over the 14 years worth of data (see Table 2b). The violations were minor, stemming from underestimating the storm magnitude (e.g. sea water levels exceeding the fjord levels just a little above 1 m, and/or operator closing the last fish water passage right after the sea levels were reported above the limit), making the tool useful for both local operator alerts and monitoring transparency. Even though the log files contain millions of records (hundreds of megabytes) the memory consumption stays very limited (up to 5.7MB), which makes the tool suitable for embedded platforms, responsible for safe and autonomous operations close to the physical gates.

6.3 Smart Building

As example we consider the time series data from the AAU Civil Engineering building (Thomas Manns Vej 23, Aalborg). The building is highly automated and provides interfaces for automatic control of e.g. blinds, heaters, ventilation, etc. In spite of the buildings high level of automation, current controllers are not collaborative and energy consumption or user comfort can be improved.

1. tmv-energy$_J$ identifies instances where the heater and the ventilation (cooling) are open (about 80% or 60%) simultaneously for a duration in the interval J seconds.
2. tmv-solar$_J$ matches when the solar radiation is increasing according to a first degree polynomial for a duration in the interval J, this information can be used to control the automatic blinds to improve user comfort.

Table 2c shows the number of matches, time and memory usage for both ETRE. There are 23360 data points, memory usage is below 6Mb and computing times below 3 s. Figure 2 shows some matches for tmv-energy$_J$. For every sample, our implementation only returns the start and stop indexes of the first match. However, we observe that many consecutive matches are found. While not incorrect it can be redundant. In deed, it would be interesting to apply parametric techniques e.g. [2,16] to find the maximal interval J where both the heating and the cooling are active.

7 Discussion

We presented Extended Timed Regular Expressions (ETRE) which extend TRE to the context of time series data. Events are vectors over signals. We present a sound and complete translation for finite words from ETRE to Timed Automata. We have implemented our approach in the tool TIMEREX. We conduct experiments on 3 case studies with real world time series data. Our experiments are encouraging with fast execution times for complex ETRE in large time series data. We observe that finding the appropriate ETRE which contains several parameters e.g. for arrhythmia detection is complex task and requires domain expertise. Future work includes learning ETRE expressions, studying complement of ETRE expressions, and studying automata based optimizations.

Acknowledgments. We thank MD. Ernesto Barrientos and DVM. Gonzalo Malaga for their feedback on ECG and arrhythmia detection. We are also grateful to Ole Skovsgaard Daniel and the rest of DCA team for explaining storm barrier data and requirements. We thank the reviewers for their thorough and constructive comments and suggestions.

References

1. Alur, R., Dill, D.L.: A theory of timed automata. Theoret. Comput. Sci. **126**(2), 183–235 (1994)
2. André, É., Hasuo, I., Waga, M.: Offline timed pattern matching under uncertainty. In: 23rd International Conference on Engineering of Complex Computer Systems, ICECCS 2018, Melbourne, Australia, December 12-14, 2018, pp. 10–20. IEEE Computer Society (2018). https://doi.org/10.1109/ICECCS2018.2018.00010
3. Asarin, E., Caspi, P., Maler, O.: A Kleene theorem for timed automata. In: Proceedings of the 12th Annual IEEE Symposium on Logic in Computer Science, pp. 160–171. LICS '97, IEEE Computer Society, Washington, DC, USA (1997). http://portal.acm.org/citation.cfm?id=788019.788856
4. Asarin, E., Caspi, P., Maler, O.: Timed regular expressions. J. ACM **49**(2), 172–206 (2002)
5. Bakhirkin, A., Ferrère, T., Maler, O., Ulus, D.: On the quantitative semantics of regular expressions over real-valued signals. In: Abate, A., Geeraerts, G. (eds.) Formal Modeling and Analysis of Timed Systems, pp. 189–206. Springer, Cham (2017)
6. Bakhirkin, A., Ferrère, T., Nickovic, D., Maler, O., Asarin, E.: Online timed pattern matching using automata. In: Jansen, D.N., Prabhakar, P. (eds.) Formal Modeling and Analysis of Timed Systems, pp. 215–232. Springer, Cham (2018)
7. Behrmann, G., David, A., Larsen, K.G.: A tutorial on UPPAAL. In: Bernardo, M., Corradini, F. (eds.) SFM-RT 2004. LNCS, vol. 3185, pp. 200–236. Springer (2004)
8. Dejan Ničković, X.Q.: Shape expressions for specifying and extracting signal features. In: Runtime Verification. RV 2019. LNCS, vol. 11757 (2019). https://par.nsf.gov/biblio/10199912
9. Esparza, J., Blondin, M.: Automata Theory: An Algorithmic Approach. MIT Press (2023). https://books.google.dk/books?id=SP2nEAAAQBAJ
10. Goldberger, A., et al.: Components of a new research resource for complex physiologic signals. PhysioNet, vol. 101 (2000)
11. Goyvaerts, J., Levithan, S.: Regular Expressions Cookbook - Detailed Solutions in Eight Programming Languages, Second Edition. O'Reilly (2012). http://www.oreilly.de/catalog/9781449319434/index.html
12. Larsen, K.G., Mikučionis, M., Muñiz, M., Srba, J.: Urgent partial order reduction for extended timed automata. In: Hung, D.V., Sokolsky, O. (eds.) ATVA 2020. LNCS, vol. 12302, pp. 179–195. Springer, Cham (2020). https://doi.org/10.1007/978-3-030-59152-6_10
13. Lee, M., So, S., Oh, H.: Synthesizing regular expressions from examples for introductory automata assignments. In: Proceedings of the 2016 ACM SIGPLAN International Conference on Generative Programming: Concepts and Experiences, pp. 70–80. GPCE 2016, Association for Computing Machinery, New York, NY, USA (2016). https://doi.org/10.1145/2993236.2993244
14. Maler, O., Nickovic, D.: Monitoring temporal properties of continuous signals. In: Lakhnech, Y., Yovine, S. (eds.) Formal Techniques, Modelling and Analysis of Timed and Fault-Tolerant Systems, pp. 152–166. Springer, Berlin, Heidelberg (2004)
15. Maler, O., Nickovic, D., Pnueli, A.: From MITL to timed automata. In: Asarin, E., Bouyer, P. (eds.) FORMATS 2006. LNCS, vol. 4202, pp. 274–289. Springer, Heidelberg (2006). https://doi.org/10.1007/11867340_20

16. Mambakam, A., Asarin, E., Basset, N., Dang, T.: Pattern matching and parameter identification for parametric timed regular expressions. In: Proceedings of the 26th ACM International Conference on Hybrid Systems: Computation and Control. HSCC '23, Association for Computing Machinery, New York, NY, USA (2023). https://doi.org/10.1145/3575870.3587115
17. Ničković, D., Qin, X., Ferrère, T., Mateis, C., Deshmukh, J.: Shape expressions for specifying and extracting signal features. In: Finkbeiner, B., Mariani, L. (eds.) RV 2019. LNCS, vol. 11757, pp. 292–309. Springer, Cham (2019). https://doi.org/10.1007/978-3-030-32079-9_17
18. Pnueli, A.: The temporal logic of programs. In: 18th Annual Symposium on Foundations of Computer Science, Providence, Rhode Island, USA, 31 October – 1 November 1977, pp. 46–57. IEEE Computer Society (1977). https://doi.org/10.1109/SFCS.1977.32
19. Ulus, D., Ferrère, T., Asarin, E., Maler, O.: Timed pattern matching. In: Legay, A., Bozga, M. (eds.) FORMATS 2014. LNCS, vol. 8711, pp. 222–236. Springer, Cham (2014). https://doi.org/10.1007/978-3-319-10512-3_16
20. Valizadeh, M., Fijalkow, N., Berger, M.: LTL learning on GPUs. In: Gurfinkel, A., Ganesh, V. (eds.) Computer Aided Verification – 36th International Conference, CAV 2024, Montreal, QC, Canada, July 24–27, 2024, Proceedings, Part III. Lecture Notes in Computer Science, vol. 14683, pp. 209–231. Springer (2024). https://doi.org/10.1007/978-3-031-65633-0_10
21. Waga, M.: Online quantitative timed pattern matching with semiring-valued weighted automata. In: André, É., Stoelinga, M. (eds.) Formal Modeling and Analysis of Timed Systems, pp. 3–22. Springer, Cham (2019)
22. Waga, M., Akazaki, T., Hasuo, I.: A Boyer-Moore type algorithm for timed pattern matching. In: Fränzle, M., Markey, N. (eds.) Formal Modeling and Analysis of Timed Systems, pp. 121–139. Springer, Cham (2016)
23. Waga, M., Hasuo, I., Suenaga, K.: Efficient online timed pattern matching by automata-based skipping. In: Abate, A., Geeraerts, G. (eds.) Formal Modeling and Analysis of Timed Systems, pp. 224–243. Springer, Cham (2017)

Monitoring Distributed Systems Based on Partial Order Executions with Global States

Moran Omer[1], Doron Peled[1(✉)], Ely Porat[1], and Vijay K. Garg[2]

[1] Department of Computer Science, Bar Ilan University, Ramat Gan, Israel
doron.peled@gmail.com
[2] Department of Electrical and Computer Engineering, UT Austin, Austin, USA

Abstract. Runtime Verification (RV) allows monitoring the behaviors of a system while checking them against a formal specification. The executions of *distributed systems* are often modeled using interleaving semantics, where events of different processes are interleaved into a total order. However, certain behavioral properties are difficult to express using interleaving semantics, whereas they can be naturally expressed in terms of partial order semantics. We study the problem of runtime verification for distributed systems based on the global states structure associated with a partial order execution. We present two algorithms for RV with branching temporal specifications and study the complexity of this problem. The first algorithm is for a global temporal logic with past operators we term PaCTL (for *Past* CTL). It involves constructing the branching structure of global states. We then show a second, more efficient, algorithm, for a subset of this logic that we term PaBTL. This algorithm does not require constructing the branching structure. We present implementations for both algorithms with experimental results.

1 Introduction

Runtime verification (RV) [5,6,20] monitors an execution trace consisting of events emitted by the observed system and verifies it against a given formal specification. RV for distributed systems poses a non-trivial challenge, since it depends on combining information related to events that are executed on different processes. In system verification (e.g., RV and model checking), concurrent systems are typically modeled using interleaving semantics, imposing a *total order* between the executed events; occurrences of independently executed events from different processes are *interleaved* in either order in different execution sequences. In contrast, a model that assumes a *partial order* [28,48] among the events sometimes offers a more direct and intuitive view of executions that

---

The research performed by the first two authors was partially funded by Israeli Science Foundation grant 2454/23: "Validating and controlling software and hardware systems assisted by machine learning". The research performed by the fourth author was partially funded by the Cullen Trust for Higher Education Endowed Professorship.

© The Author(s), under exclusive license to Springer Nature Switzerland AG 2026
B. Königshofer and H. Torfah (Eds.): RV 2025, LNCS 16087, pp. 252–273, 2026.
https://doi.org/10.1007/978-3-032-05435-7_15

can be distributed among different processes. There, events executed independently by different processes, which can also overlap in time with each other, are unordered; dependencies between events in different processes can result from message passing or the access of variables shared between multiple processes.

The interleaving model is rather simple and enjoys the benefit of using common mathematical tools for verification, e.g., based on finite automata over infinite words [45]. Specification over this model is often given using Linear Temporal Logic (LTL) [25]. Practice shows that for most purposes, the interleaving model is sufficient for modeling concurrent systems as a basis for temporal specification; the fact that concurrently executed events are interleaved is often not restrictive, in particular if the specification is not sensitive to the relative order of such interleavings [37]. On the other hand, there are cases where properties of a distributed system are lost when interleaving their executed events and it is beneficial to use the partial order execution model.

In this paper, we study runtime verification of distributed systems, based on the partial order semantics. The verification is with respect to a temporal logic specification that asserts about the *branching structure* over *global states* related to a partial order execution of the monitored system. The global states in the partial order model correspond to *cuts*, where a cut is a *history closed* subset of events of the partial order. The RV monitoring in our case is centralized, which is in accordance with the global state based specification.

An example of a property that calls for the use of the partial order model is related to the detection of global *snapshots* [9] of a distributed system, i.e., a consistent collection of local states of the system. Such a snapshot corresponds to a cut of the partial order execution, while in the interleaving model such a snapshot may not appear directly as a global state of the modeled interleaving sequence[1]. Another example is from distributed databases, where *transactions*, i.e., pieces of the execution that involve multiple events, are designed to behave *as if* executed one after another in some linearizations [8,13,21,33], while in other linearizations of these events the transactions may (partially) overlap; this allows achieving some concurrency between the events of the transactions, and, on the other hand, simplifying the design, based on the sequential-like behavior. A similar idea can be used for describing properties of concurrent data objects or systems implemented without a centralized control (e.g., based on blockchains).

Contributions. We present a runtime verification algorithm for distributed systems, based on the global states construction over the partial order execution model. The specification formalism that we use is a past time version of the temporal logic we call PaCTL, applied to the branching time structure of global states. This logic contains past operators such as $EP\varphi$ (φ holds sometimes in the past) and $E(\varphi S \psi)$ (φ holds along some linearization since ψ held). We provide an algorithm for the complete logic, whose worst case complexity is exponential

---

[1] If one groups together all the interleaving sequences that are consistent with the partial order execution as in *Mazurkiewicz traces* [28], there is at least one interleaving on which this global state appears.

in the number of processes, with the base of the exponent being the number of events, and a corresponding tool called PoET [50]. We provide a related hardness result. We then present a second algorithm, for a subset of this logic, which we call PaBTL, confined to the past operators EP (and its dual AH) together with the Boolean operators. We present a corresponding tool called Kairos [51]. The complexity of this algorithm is linear in the number of events and quadratic in the number of processes, but is exponential in the size of the property. We show experimental results comparing the two tools.

Related Work. Several logics are interpreted over partial order executions, see, e.g., the survey [34]. The branching time temporal logic POTL [38] includes both future and past branching operators, in the style of the logic CTL [11]. The interpretation is over local states and events; all the possible partial order executions are combined into a *single* structure, as in *event structures* [48]. Some other temporal logics that are interpreted over partial order executions are defined over the *global states* (cuts) rather than directly over the *local states* of the partial order between events; for each partial order execution, a *branching* structure between the global states is separately constructed. In that category of logics, the temporal logic ISTL [23,36] uses the operators of CTL, applied to each such branching structure. The logic LTrL [43] uses the syntax of linear temporal operators but applies them to branching structures of global states that are constructed from partial order executions. Model checking various subsets of ISTL [36] is studied in [1,3,35,44] and of LTrL in [44]. A logic that uses the LTL constructs over Mazurkiewicz traces and a translation from specifications to automata are presented in [7].

An RV verification algorithm, where a past time CTL specification is interpreted directly over the *local states* associated with the events of the partial order execution, rather than over the related structure of *global states* as in our work, was described in [4]; thus, the same formula has a completely different interpretation in [4] than in our work. Another past time logic defined over the partial order between events is MTTL [41]; a distributed algorithm (and implementation) was given based on the ability to pass information between processes when accessing shared variables. In [10,40,42], procedures are presented for deciding whether a partial order execution satisfies properties that can be written as a *restricted* version of the logic ISTL [1]. These works identify also cases of specifications with lower complexity. Ogale and Garg [32] have proposed a logic called Basic Temporal Logic (BTL), which is also a subset of ISTL; they presented a decision procedure for checking whether a partial order execution satisfies a BTL property based on *predicate slicing*, with time complexity exponential in the size of the formula but polynomial in the size of the computation. Another line of works on verification, related to the partial order model, is aimed at proving that a property holds for a *representative* interleaving of a partial order execution assuming synchronous clocks with a small bounded maximal drift. This limits the number of possible interleavings. This is done for LTL specification based on SMT solving [15] and for a stream-based specification [12].

2 Preliminaries

The Partial Order Model (Local View). In the *partial order execution model* [26,39,48], events of disjoint processes may be unordered with respect to each other, while the events that involve the same process must be totally ordered. Interactions between processes, e.g., events mutual to a pair of processes, which can model synchronous message passing, can induce order between events of different processes. This results in a partial order, i.e., a transitive, antisymmetric and irreflexive relation, between the events, rather than a total order (linearization of the events) as in the more commonly used interleaving model. A *partial order execution* $\mathcal{E} = \langle \mathcal{P}, E, Pr, \prec, \iota, A, L \rangle$, has the following components:

- $\mathcal{P}$ is a finite set of *processes*.
- E is a (finite or infinite) set of *events*.
- $Pr : E \mapsto 2^{\mathcal{P}}$ maps each event to a set of processes that are *involved* in its execution.
- $\prec \subset E \times E$ is a *partial order* relation over E. In addition, $\prec$ is well-founded, i.e., E does not have an infinite decreasing chain of events $e_1 \succ e_2 \succ \ldots$. The relation $\prec$ is the *minimal* partial order such that for each $p \in \mathcal{P}$, the events that involve a process p, i.e., $\{e \in E | p \in Pr(e)\}$ are totally ordered; the transitivity of $\prec$ and the fact that events can involve multiple processes induce further order between events from different processes.
- $\iota \in E$ is the *initial event* of E. It is *minimal* w.r.t. $\prec$ and $Pr(\iota) = \mathcal{P}$.
- $A = \biguplus_{p \in \mathcal{P}} A_p$ is a finite set of *propositions*. The set A is partitioned into subsets A_p, one for each process $p \in \mathcal{P}$. Thus, each proposition can represent some property (predicate) *local* to some process.
- $L(e, p) \in 2^{A_p}$ for $p \in Pr(e)$. L maps each event and process that participates in it to a subset of propositions from A_p. This represents the propositions that hold (i.e., are set to *true*) in process p *immediately after* e is executed.

We can also denote the labeling $L(e, p)$ as a minterm, i.e., a conjunction of literals, over the propositions A_p; the propositions in $L(e, p)$ appear non-negated, while the propositions of $A_p \setminus L(e, p)$ appear negated. In a short form for denoting minterms, conjunctions are removed and negated propositions are marked with an overbar, hence $t_1 \wedge \neg t_2$ is denoted as $t_1 \overline{t_2}$. If $Pr(e) \cap Pr(f) = \emptyset$, we say that e and f are *independent*. If both $e \not\prec f$ and $e \not\succ f$, we say that e and f are *concurrent*; in this case, e and f are also independent. We say that f is an *immediate successor* of e if $e \prec f$ and there is no g such that $e \prec g \prec f$.

Typically, events involve either only a single process, i.e., *local* to a single process, or a pair of processes, representing *synchronous* or *handshake* communication. The described model can represent handshake communication as in the programming language CSP [19]. The model and subsequently the RV algorithm can be adapted to deal with asynchronous message passing.

Figure 1 shows an execution that contains three processes, p_1, p_2 and p_3, with seven events: $\{\iota, \alpha_1, \alpha_2, \alpha_3, \beta_1, \beta_2, \beta_3\}$. The event α_2 involves both processes p_1 and p_2, while β_2 involves p_2 and p_3. The rest of the events involve only a single process each. We have $A_{p_1} = \{t_1, t_2\}$, $A_{p_2} = \{r_1, r_2\}$ and $A_{p_3} = \{q_1, q_2\}$. Then, $L(\alpha_1, p_1) = \{t_2\}$, $L(\alpha_2, p_1) = \{t_1\}$ and $L(\alpha_2, p_2) = \{r_1\}$, which are represented, correspondingly, by the minterms $\overline{t_1}t_2$, $t_1\overline{t_2}$ and $r_1\overline{r_2}$.

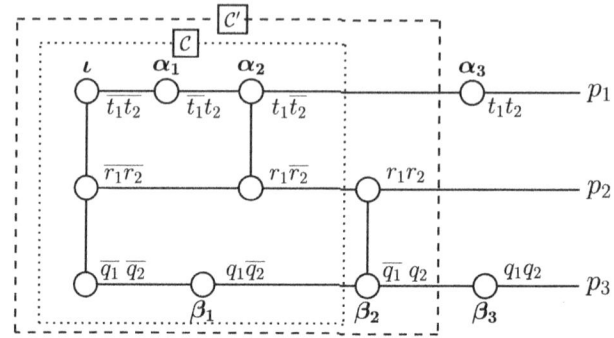

Fig. 1. A partial order execution

The Global View. Based on the local view, we further define the *global view*, which contains *cuts* (and *frontiers*) that correspond to *global states* [26]. These global states form a branching structure.

A *cut* $\mathcal{C}$ of a partial order execution $\mathcal{E}$ is a nonempty (as it always includes the initial event ι) *history-closed* finite subset of its events E. That is, if $f \in \mathcal{C}$ and $e \prec f$ then $e \in \mathcal{C}$. Intuitively, a cut represents a potential *global state* of the modeled or inspected system, where the events in the cut appeared in its past and the other events have not happened yet. The set of cuts of a partial order is closed under unions and intersections.

Denote by $max(\mathcal{C}, p)$ the maximal event in $\mathcal{C}$ of the process p w.r.t. the order $\prec$ (such a maximum exists, since $\iota \in \mathcal{C}$). A *frontier* $\mathcal{F}_\mathcal{C}$ of a cut $\mathcal{C}$ is[2] the set of *maximal* events from $\mathcal{C}$ for the different processes in $\mathcal{P}$ i.e., $\bigcup_{p \in \mathcal{P}}\{max(\mathcal{C}, p)\}$. A single event can play the role of a maximal event for *multiple* processes that it involves. We assign to a cut $\mathcal{C}$, or, equivalently to the frontier $\mathcal{F}_\mathcal{C}$, a global interpretation of the propositions A that agrees with the local maximal interpretations of each process in the cut, formally, $L(\mathcal{C}) = \biguplus_{p \in \mathcal{P}} L(max(\mathcal{C}, p), p)$ and $L(\mathcal{F}_\mathcal{C}) = L(\mathcal{C})$. In Fig. 1, the marked cut $\mathcal{C}$, whose events are enclosed within an inner *dotted* box, contains the events $\{\iota, \alpha_1, \alpha_2, \beta_1\}$. The corresponding frontier $\mathcal{F}_\mathcal{C}$ is $\{\alpha_2, \beta_1\}$, where α_2 is maximal for both processes p_1 and p_2 and β_1 is maximal for p_3. The global interpretation (state) of the cut $\mathcal{C}$ (and frontier $\mathcal{F}_\mathcal{C}$) is $t_1\overline{t_2}r_1\overline{r_2}q_1\overline{q_2}$.

Note that a pair of events that are *not independent* of each other *may* be maximal w.r.t. different processes, hence can belong to the same frontier. For

---

[2] Denoting the corresponding cut $\mathcal{C}$ as a subscript in $\mathcal{F}_\mathcal{C}$ is optional, and we may simply write $\mathcal{F}$.

example, in the cut $\mathcal{C}'$, which appears within the outer *dashed* box in Fig. 1, the frontier $\mathcal{F}_{\mathcal{C}'}$ includes both α_2, which is maximal for p_1, and β_2, which is maximal for p_2 and p_3, where $\alpha_2 \prec \beta_2$. The interpretation of frontiers depends for each process on the event maximal for that process, hence, $L(\mathcal{F}_{\mathcal{C}'}) = t_1 \bar{t}_2 r_1 r_2 \bar{q}_1 q_2$.

We can now define, based on the (local) partial order execution, a corresponding *global* partial order between the cuts and, correspondingly, between the corresponding frontiers of $\mathcal{E}$. Let $\mathcal{C}_1 < \mathcal{C}_2$ if $\mathcal{C}_1 \subset \mathcal{C}_2$ and, correspondingly, $\mathcal{F}_{\mathcal{C}_1} < \mathcal{F}_{\mathcal{C}_2}$. We also denote $\mathcal{C}_1 \twoheadrightarrow \mathcal{C}_2$, or, more informatively, $\mathcal{C}_1 \stackrel{e}{\twoheadrightarrow} \mathcal{C}_2$ if $\mathcal{C}_2 = \mathcal{C}_1 \cup \{e\}$ for some $e \in E$. We say that $\mathcal{C}_2$ is an *immediate successor* of $\mathcal{C}_1$. Accordingly, the corresponding frontier $\mathcal{F}_{\mathcal{C}_2}$ of $\mathcal{C}_2$ is the immediate successor of the frontier $\mathcal{F}_{\mathcal{C}_1}$ of $\mathcal{C}_1$, and we also denote that $\mathcal{F}_{\mathcal{C}_1} \twoheadrightarrow \mathcal{F}_{\mathcal{C}_2}$ (or $\mathcal{F}_{\mathcal{C}_1} \stackrel{e}{\twoheadrightarrow} \mathcal{F}_{\mathcal{C}_2}$). Hence, the relation $<$ is the transitive closure of the relation $\twoheadrightarrow$. In the example in Fig. 1, $\mathcal{F}_\mathcal{C} \stackrel{\beta_2}{\twoheadrightarrow} \mathcal{F}_{\mathcal{C}'}$.

The relation $\twoheadrightarrow$ forms a *branching structure*, over which our specification can be interpreted. The maximal paths in the constructed graph are the *equivalent* linearizations of the (local) partial order execution (see also Mazurkiewicz trace semantics [28]). The diagram in Fig. 2 represents the global partial order execution obtained from the local partial order execution in Fig. 1. Each circle represents a global state, and the filled circle corresponds to the frontier $\mathcal{F}_\mathcal{C}$. This is a *Hasse diagram* of the global view, where the depicted edges represent the "immediate successor" relation $\twoheadrightarrow$.

In the branching structure formed from a partial order, if $\mathcal{C} \stackrel{e}{\twoheadrightarrow} \mathcal{C}_1$ and $\mathcal{C} \stackrel{f}{\twoheadrightarrow} \mathcal{C}_2$, where $e \neq f$, then e and f are independent; furthermore, we also have $\mathcal{F}_\mathcal{C} \stackrel{e}{\twoheadrightarrow} \mathcal{F}_{\mathcal{C}_1} \stackrel{f}{\twoheadrightarrow} \mathcal{F}_{\mathcal{C}'}$ and $\mathcal{F}_\mathcal{C} \stackrel{f}{\twoheadrightarrow} \mathcal{F}_{\mathcal{C}_2} \stackrel{e}{\twoheadrightarrow} \mathcal{F}_{\mathcal{C}'}$. Vice versa, if $\mathcal{F}_\mathcal{C} \stackrel{e}{\twoheadrightarrow} \mathcal{F}_{\mathcal{C}_1} \stackrel{f}{\twoheadrightarrow} \mathcal{F}_{\mathcal{C}'}$ and e and f are independent, then we also have $\mathcal{F}_\mathcal{C} \stackrel{f}{\twoheadrightarrow} \mathcal{F}_{\mathcal{C}_2} \stackrel{e}{\twoheadrightarrow} \mathcal{F}_{\mathcal{C}'}$; we then say that e and f *commute* with each other from $\mathcal{F}_\mathcal{C}$. Similarly, if $\mathcal{F}_{\mathcal{C}_1} \stackrel{e}{\twoheadrightarrow} \mathcal{F}_\mathcal{C}$ and $\mathcal{F}_{\mathcal{C}_2} \stackrel{f}{\twoheadrightarrow} \mathcal{F}_\mathcal{C}$, then e and f are independent.

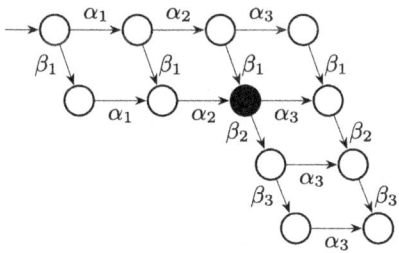

Fig. 2. A Hasse diagram of the global states view of the partial order execution

Collecting Events from the Monitored Processes. During the runtime of a distributed system by a centralized monitor, events from the different processes need to be collected and processed by the monitor. An immediate difficulty is that these events may be reported out of order. For example, in Fig. 1, the event α_2 may be reported to the monitor process by process p_1, while the event β_2 may be reported to the monitor by p_3; it can happen that the information about β_2 will be received by the monitor after the information about α_2, although $\alpha_2 \prec \beta_2$. A reported event cannot be processed by the monitor until all events that happened before it according to $\prec$ were also reported; otherwise, the situation will be similar to trying to analyze a linear execution while there are holes in the sequence observed so far.

We assume the absence of a global physical clock, which synchronizes between the events of the monitored system. Instead, we use *logical clocks* [26]. As done in [22], we adopt the use of Fidge and Mattern [14,27] *vector* clocks, where each event keeps a vector of values, one per each involved process. Comparing the order between vector clocks of a pair of events e and f allows to check whether $e \prec f$; furthermore, they also allow one to check if, for a reported event f, there is some $e \prec f$ that is not yet reported to the monitor process. Reported events can be kept in a queue before all their predecessors are reported. Then, they can be processed by the RV algorithm. This also guarantees that when a new event e is processed, the set of events processed so far forms a cut that is an immediate *successor* of the cut that was formed by the set of events processed before, according to the order $\xrightarrow{e}$. Consequently, these cuts (and their corresponding frontiers) are formed in an order that is a *linearization* of the monitored partial order. The RV algorithm can calculate each time a verdict for the current cut/frontier, which will be reported according to the order of this linearization. This applies to both our algorithms in Sect. 3 and Sect. 4.

The Logic and the Interpretation Over the Global View. We use a *past* time branching temporal logic, in the style of CTL [11], to specify properties of the global view of a partial order execution. The restriction to past time allows interpreting the formulas on finite structures. As in CTL, each temporal operator consists of a pair of operators: the first is a *path quantifier*, either A (forall paths) or E (there exists a path). The second operator is temporal; the temporal operators used here are the past mirror images of the corresponding CTL operators: $\mathcal{S}$ (*since*) instead of $\mathcal{U}$ (*until*) and Y (*yesterday*) instead of X (*next time*). We call this logic PaCTL (for *past* CTL). The syntax is as follows, where q is a proposition:

$$\varphi ::= q \mid (\varphi \wedge \varphi) \mid \neg \varphi \mid EY\varphi \mid A(\varphi \mathcal{S} \varphi) \mid E(\varphi \mathcal{S} \varphi)$$

The semantics is as follows, where S, S' represent cuts (or frontiers):

- $S \models q$ if $q \in L(S)$.
- $S \models (\varphi_1 \wedge \varphi_2)$ if $S \models \varphi_1$ and $S \models \varphi_2$.
- $S \models \neg \varphi$ if not $S \models \varphi$.
- $S \models EY\varphi$ if there exists $S' \twoheadrightarrow S$ such that $S' \models \varphi$.
- $S \models E(\varphi \mathcal{S} \psi)$ if either $S \models \psi$ or both $S \models \varphi$ and there exists $S' \twoheadrightarrow S$ such that $S' \models E(\varphi \mathcal{S} \psi)$.

- $S \models A(\varphi \mathcal{S} \psi)$ if either $S \models \psi$ or both $S \models \varphi$ and for each $S' \twoheadrightarrow S$ it holds that $S' \models A(\varphi \mathcal{S} \psi)$, where at least one such predecessor S' exists.

We can also define additional Boolean and temporal operators: $true = (q \vee \neg q)$ for some proposition q, $false = \neg true$, $(\varphi \vee \psi) = \neg(\neg \varphi \wedge \neg \psi)$, $EP\varphi = E(true\mathcal{S}\varphi)$, $AY\varphi = \neg EY \neg \varphi$, $AP\varphi = A(true\mathcal{S}\varphi)$, $EH\varphi = \neg AP \neg \varphi$ and $AH\varphi = \neg EP \neg \varphi$, where P reads as *previously* and H reads as *historically*.

Remark. We show that some properties expressed over the global view cannot be expressed using local properties. The branching logic TLC in [4] is defined directly over the local view. It contains both past and future operators (and in addition to the CTL modalities, an operator $\|$ for *concurrently*). It was shown in [4] that the logic TLC can be translated into an automaton, hence represents a regular language. On the other hand, PaCTL can express properties that cannot be expressed as regular languages by comparing (essentially, counting the length of) subsequences of events along independently (concurrently) executing processes. This can be done by a zigzagging argument, as will be presented in the lower bound proof in Sect. 3.

3 An RV Algorithm for Global Partial Order Executions

Our RV algorithm is based on a *centralized* monitor, which checks a partial order execution against a branching logic PaCTL specification. Upon processing a new event[3], the algorithm calculates a new verdict, comparing the specification against the set of events collected so far. The sequence of issued verdicts follows a linearization of the collected events. For each processed event α, the monitor obtains the involved processes, i.e., $Pr(\alpha)$, the assignment to their propositions immediately after the execution of α, i.e., $\bigcup_{p \in Pr(\alpha)} L(\alpha, p)$ and the vector clock. For example, the event α_2 in Fig. 1 involves the processes p_1 and p_2 and its associated minterm is $t_1 \overline{t_2} r_1 \overline{r_2}$.

The RV algorithm constructs a *subgraph* of the global view; the nodes represent frontiers and the edges correspond to the relation $\twoheadrightarrow$ between the corresponding adjacent frontiers (hence we use the same notation $\twoheadrightarrow$ for edges as we used between frontiers). Each edge is labeled with an event that forms the transition between the corresponding frontiers. With each newly processed event, the graph is updated, adding new nodes and edges. Some old nodes may become redundant, in which case they can be removed. We can consider the constructed graph, obtained after a sequence of processed events, as a *sliding window* into the global view graph, which slides with each new event.

Updating the Sliding Window Graph. During runtime verification, the monitor performs updates, based on the reported events, to the sliding window graph whose nodes are *frontiers* of the partial order execution.

---

[3] As described in Sect. 2, we can process a new event only after all the events preceding according to the order $\prec$ were reported to the monitor.

As part of the algorithm, we use the following procedure to construct for a given frontier $\mathcal{F}$ its f successor $\mathcal{F}'$, i.e., $\mathcal{F} \xrightarrow{f} \mathcal{F}'$. This successor exists provided that all the immediate predecessors of f according to $\prec$ are in $\mathcal{F}$. This is done as follows: after adding f to the events of $\mathcal{F}$, events of $\mathcal{F}$ that are no longer maximal for *at least* one process, are removed. The order $\prec$ between events can be checked based on the vector clocks attached to the events. For example, in Fig. 1, the frontier $\mathcal{F}_\mathcal{C} = \{\alpha_2, \beta_1\}$, which corresponds to the cut $\mathcal{C}$, is created after the sequence $\iota\alpha_1\beta_1\alpha_2$ was observed. Then if an event β_2 occurs, the successor frontier $\mathcal{F}_{\mathcal{C}'}$, which corresponds to the cut $\mathcal{C}'$, such that $\mathcal{F}_\mathcal{C} \xrightarrow{\beta_2} \mathcal{F}_{\mathcal{C}'}$, is constructed as follows: first we add β_2 to $\mathcal{F}_\mathcal{C}$ and then we remove from it β_1 since β_1 is not any more maximal for process p_3, as $\beta_1 \prec \beta_2$. Thus, $\mathcal{F}_{\mathcal{C}'} = \{\alpha_2, \beta_2\}$. The event α_2 is *not* removed from $\mathcal{F}_{\mathcal{C}'}$, since it is still maximal w.r.t. the process p_1 even after adding β_2.

We now describe how to update the sliding window graph G. At each point, a node s_m represents the maximal frontier $\mathcal{F}_m$ of G according to the global order $<$. This is the frontier that corresponds to the cut containing all the events processed so far by the algorithm. Initially, the graph consists of a single node, representing the frontier $\{\iota\}$, where ι is the initial event. With each new observed event, the graph G is transformed, where new nodes are added, and some nodes may also be removed.

When a new event e is added, we first add to G an edge $s_m \xrightarrow{e} s_n$, where s_n represents the new maximal frontier $\mathcal{F}_n$ and $\mathcal{F}_m \xrightarrow{e} \mathcal{F}_n$. Further, new nodes and edges are added to G as follows. For edges $s \xrightarrow{\alpha} s' \xrightarrow{\beta} s''$, where α and β are independent ($Pr(\alpha) \cap Pr(\beta) = \emptyset$), β can *propagate backwards* over the edge $s \xrightarrow{\alpha} s'$ in the following manner: new edges $s \xrightarrow{\beta} r \xrightarrow{\alpha} s''$ are added where r is a new node (unless such edges and node already exist from previous updates). Both the β successor of the frontier corresponding to s and the α successor of the frontier corresponding to r exist due to the commutativity between α and β, as described in Sect. 2. The addition of the node r may induce, through commutativity, further backward propagations. This chain of propagations repeats until no further edges can be added.

After finishing a phase of extending the graph G with new nodes and edges due to observing a new event e, a phase of removing *redundant* nodes (and all of their connected edges) from G starts. A node s becomes redundant when the occurrence of future events cannot generate further successors to s, hence it can no longer affect the RV verdict. A sufficient condition for this is that for each process $p \in \mathcal{P}$, the algorithm has already processed an event α involving p (i.e., $p \in Pr(\alpha)$) that generates a successor to s. To implement this, for each state s in G, we accumulate the processes involved in generating its successors in the set R_s, which is initialized to the empty set when the node s is generated. We remove s when $R_s = \mathcal{P}$. Furthermore, if there is an edge $s \xrightarrow{\alpha} s'$ and the node s' has become redundant and was removed, then s can also be removed. The reason for this is that no *new* edge $s \xrightarrow{\beta} s''$ can be further added to the graph.

To see this, recall that if there is a β successor to the frontier corresponding to s, then α and β are independent. Hence there is a β successor to the frontier associated with s', thus an edge labeled with β emanates from s'. Since s' was redundant, the β successor of s' was already constructed before s' was removed, by induction on the order of removing redundant nodes and edges. Moreover, by the construction of the sliding window, the edge labeled β from s' has already been propagated backwards over $s \xrightarrow{\alpha} s'$. Thus, an edge $s \xrightarrow{\beta} s''$ has already been constructed before s' was removed.

We demonstrate in Fig. 3 the first few steps of the construction windows for the observation $\sigma = \iota\alpha_1\alpha_2\beta_1$, which is a prefix of the linearization $\sigma = \iota\alpha_1\alpha_2\beta_1\alpha_3\beta_2\beta_3$ of the partial order execution in Fig. 1. The steps are denoted as **A-G**. In every step, the node corresponding to the maximal frontier is shaded. New edges, added due to backward propagation (in steps **E** and **F**) appear dashed. The backward propagation in Step **E** causes another backward propagation that appears in Step **F**. The two nodes in Step **F** with dotted border become redundant and are removed, with their corresponding edges, resulting in Step **G**.

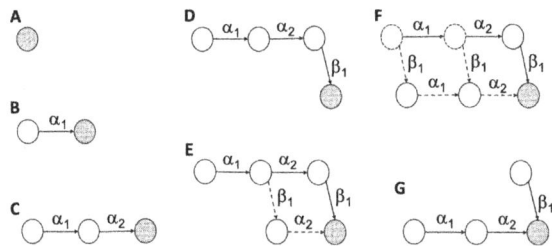

Fig. 3. Graphs constructed for the trace $\sigma = \alpha_1\alpha_2\beta_1\alpha_3$.

Calculating the Values of Subformulas on the Nodes. The following procedure calculates the truth value for each subformula for each new frontier (global state) constructed by the sliding window graph-updating algorithm. This can be compared to updating the *summary vector* used in the case of past time LTL [20]. For each subformula η of the specification φ and each node representing a frontier $\mathcal{F}$ we keep a bit $val(\mathcal{F}, \eta)$ that is *true* if η holds in $\mathcal{F}$. Calculating the truth value for a subformula η may depend on the values calculated for subformulas of η; hence the calculation of the truth values progresses *bottom up* according to the syntax tree of φ. Further, the calculations also use the values of truth values previously calculated for the *predecessor* frontiers according to the sliding window graph. The calculation of the truth values is performed as follows.

$val(\mathcal{F}, q) = true$ for a proposition q, iff $q \in L(\mathcal{F})$.

$val(\mathcal{F}, \neg\eta) = true$ iff $val(\mathcal{F}, \eta) = false$.

$val(\mathcal{F}, (\eta_1 \wedge \eta_2)) = true$ iff $val(\mathcal{F}, \eta_1) = true$ and $val(\mathcal{F}, \eta_2) = true$.

$val(\mathcal{F}, EY\eta) = true$ iff there exists a predecessor frontier $\mathcal{F}'$ of $\mathcal{F}$ such that $val(\mathcal{F}', \eta) = true$.

$val(\mathcal{F}, E(\eta_1 S \eta_2)) = true$ iff either $val(\mathcal{F}, \eta_2) = true$ or both $val(\mathcal{F}, \eta_1) = true$ and there exists a predecessor frontier $\mathcal{F}'$ of $\mathcal{F}$ in the graph such that $val(\mathcal{F}', E(\eta_1 S \eta_2)) = true$.

$val(\mathcal{F}, A(\eta_1 S \eta_2)) = true$ iff either $val(\mathcal{F}, \eta_2) = true$ or both $val(\mathcal{F}, \eta_1) = true$ and for each predecessor frontier $\mathcal{F}'$ of $\mathcal{F}$, (where there must be at least one such predecessor) in the graph it holds that $val(\mathcal{F}', A(\eta_1 S \eta_2)) = true$.

The RV verdict for the specification φ over the processed events is $val(\mathcal{F}_m, \varphi)$.

Complexity. The overall number of constructed global states is $O((|E|/k)^k)$, where $|E|$ is the overall number of events and $k = |\mathcal{P}|$ (i.e., the number of processes). This worst case bound occurs when the events are distributed evenly ($|E|/k$ per process) and all the events of different processes are independent, maximizing the number of global state combinations. Constructing a new frontier from its predecessor is done in time $O(k)$. Calculating the vector of Boolean values for subformulas related to a frontier is done in time $O(k\,|\varphi|)$. This gives a complexity of $O(k\,|\varphi|\,(|E|/k)^k)$, which is exponential in the number of processes with a base proportional to the number of events, and linear in the size of the property.

Runtime verification can be performed online or offline. For online verification, an important complexity measure is the *incremental time complexity*, which measures the computation performed after each new event that is monitored. This is a critical measure if a verdict needs to be given as soon as possible, based on the prefix seen so far. Unfortunately, the incremental complexity of the RV algorithm presented here is still very hard. In particular, after each newly observed event, the number of nodes (frontiers) added to G can be $O((|E|/k)^{k-1})$, where the local state of the new event can be combined with all the local states of the other (independent) events.

It should be noted that such a centralized setting makes the speed of the monitor process a bottleneck for the RV process, as it needs to process the events from all the participating processes. The global nature of the specification formalism does not easily lend itself to an efficient distributed RV algorithm that may be implemented on the monitored processes themselves (which can be the subject of further research). This, and the complexity results described, may in fact limit the *online* application of runtime verification in some cases.

Hardness of RV Problem. We present a hardness result for the RV problem of making a verdict for the logic PaCTL over a partial order execution. The overall complexity of the described RV algorithm is $O((|E|/k)^k)$, when ignoring the linear factors involving updating each frontier. We employ a reduction from a fine-grained complexity problem that does not belong to the standard complexity hierarchy, such as P, NP, or PSPACE. Fine-grained complexity [46] is a rapidly growing area of research that seeks to establish tight computational bounds for specific problems by exploring their precise relationships. This field examines a variety of foundational problems that are considered computationally hard. This approach allows us to capture the complexity in terms of *two* parameters: the number of processes and the total number of events. We show that, under some known complexity assumption, when the length of the formula is linear in the number of processes, this is also the lower bound up to a poly-logarithmic factor in the base, i.e. in the number of events. Specifically, we establish a lower bound that shows that the complexity is not only exponential in k, but that the *base* of the exponent grows with $\Omega(\frac{|E|}{k \log^2 \frac{|E|}{k}})$, rather than remaining a fixed constant such as 2 or 3.

We will describe a fine-grained reduction from the k-OV framework [47], which connects the complexity of our target problem to this hypothesis. The Boolean vectors $a_1, a_2, \ldots, a_k$ are *orthogonal* if no bit position contains a 1 in all vectors simultaneously. Formally, this condition holds if $\bigvee_{i=1}^{d} \bigwedge_{j=1}^{k} a_j[i] = 0$, where $a_j[i]$ denotes the i-th bit of vector a_j, $\wedge$ represents bitwise conjunction (logical *and*), and $\vee$ represents disjunction (logical *or*) over the bit positions. In the k-OV problem, there are k sets $E_1, E_2, \ldots, E_k$, each contains n d-bit vectors, where $d = O(\log^2 n)$. One needs to decide whether there exists a selection of vectors $a_1 \in E_1, a_2 \in E_2, \ldots, a_k \in E_k$ such that the chosen vectors are orthogonal. A widely believed conjecture in complexity theory [47] states that the k-OV problem requires time at least $\Omega\left(n^{k-\epsilon}\right)$ for any constant $\epsilon > 0$.

We describe an encoding of the sets of vector as processes and a temporal logic formula that implements the orthogonality constraint using local propositions. Each set E_i of vectors is encoded as a sequence of $|E_i| = O(n \log^2 n)$ events, which is $1/k$ of the total number of events $|E| = \sum_{i=1}^{k} |E_i| = O(k n \log^2 n)$. The vectors are encoded one after the other, separated by a delimiter as will be explained below. Therefore in our case $n = \Omega(\frac{|E|}{k \log^2 \frac{|E|}{k}})$ and we get a lower bound of $\Omega\left(\left(\frac{|E|}{k \log^2 \frac{|E|}{k}}\right)^{k-\epsilon}\right)$. As stated above, the base of the exponent is within a polylogarithmic factor of the upper bound $O((|E|/k)^k)$.

- **Vector encoding:** Each bit vector is encoded as a sequence of events within its corresponding process. For example, to represent a bit vector 101 in process p_i, we generate three consecutive events where proposition v_i holds *true*, *false*, and *true*, respectively. This proposition v_i reflects the current bit value represented at each sequence position. All bit vectors are assumed to have uniform length d across all processes, though this is a global convention not explicitly enforced by our formula.
- **Vector separation:** We introduce a delimiter proposition δ_i for each process p_i to mark boundaries between consecutive vector encodings. When $\delta_i = 1$, the current event represents a transition between vectors.

- **Synchronization mechanism:** A trinary counter l_i is associated with each process.[4] This counter cycles through the values 0, 1, and 2 across successive non-delimiter events within the same process and can be implemented using two bits. To align delimiters with $l_i = 0$, we pad each vector with $v_i = 0$ until its length is a multiple of 3.

The structural constraints described above are enforced when constructing each single process p_i from a given set of vectors E_i. We express the orthogonality condition in PaCTL using a formula of the form $EP(\psi \wedge EY\, E(\varphi \mathcal{S} \psi))$ of size $O(k)$, where:

1. ψ identifies global states where all processes are at delimiter events, expressed as $\bigwedge_{1 \leq i \leq k} \delta_i$.
2. The formula φ constrains the path satisfying $(\varphi \mathcal{S} \psi)$ to follow a specific *zigzagging* pattern: either all processes hold the same value, or there exists an index i such that $1 \leq i < k$, where processes 1 through i hold some value $v \in \{0,1,2\}$, and processes $i+1$ through k hold the value $(v+1) \bmod 3$.
   To encode this, we proceed in two steps. First, we restrict the state so that all processes use up to two of the three possible values. Second, we enforce that for each adjacent pair of processes, the value of l_{i+1} is either equal to l_i or to $(l_i + 1) \bmod 3$. Both conditions can be encoded using a formula of size $O(k)$.
3. Further, φ asserts that when all $\delta_i = 0$ and all the counters l_i have identical values, at least one process must satisfy $v_i = 0$. This enforces the core orthogonality condition by ensuring the bitwise conjunction across all processes equals zero.

4 An Efficient Algorithm for a Subset of the Logic

The logic PaBTL (for *Past Basic Temporal Logic*) is obtained by restricting PaCTL to the operators EP and AH (where $AH\varphi = \neg EP\neg\varphi$) and the Boolean operators ($\wedge, \vee, \neg$). This restriction enables a more efficient algorithm while still capturing many practical properties. Several works suggested RV algorithms for logics that use *future* versions of the temporal operators [10,32,40,42]; so, instead of the EP operator in PaCTL one has its future mirror EF ("sometimes in the future for some path") and instead of the AH operator, one has AG ("for every state in all paths in the future"). A model checking algorithm for a logic with the future versions of the temporal operators is described in [1], based on imposing conditions on linearizations of the partial order into an automaton.

Converting to Normal Form. A *disjunctionless normal form* or DLNF formula is defined as follows:

- Atomic propositions.
- $EP(\varphi_1 \wedge \ldots \wedge \varphi_n)$, if $\varphi_1 \ldots \varphi_n$ are in DLNF.

---

[4] The use of bit patterns to compare events across different processes appears in [44].

– If φ is in normal form, then so is $\neg\varphi$.

Our algorithm starts by translating the PaBTL specification into a DNF (Disjunctive Normal Form) combination of DLNF subformulas; while DLNF formulas have no disjunctions internally, we convert the entire PaBTL specification into a DNF of DLNF formulas, hence allowing disjunction at the top level only. The translation follows [1], where a similar translation is applied to the logic BTL. The translation is based on the equivalence $EP(\varphi \vee \psi) = (EP\varphi \vee EP\psi)$. To increase efficiency of the algorithm, the translation can rewrite the formulas into a DAG rather than in linear form (as in text). Each node of the DAG contains an operator (Boolean or EP), open or close parenthesis or a proposition. Traversing each subgraph in depth-first-search order, left to right, corresponds to a subformula. Subformulas that are *repeated* under the translation can be represented *once* (hence the *DAG* structure, rather than an abstract syntax *tree* representation). The translation can result in an exponential explosion in the size of the specification [1].

Detecting a Frontier That Satisfies a Conjunction of Minterms. Our algorithm for RV of PaBTL properties first employs a procedure for *detecting* a frontier F that satisfies a conjunction of minterms $\eta = \bigwedge_{1 \leq i \leq n} \gamma_i$, where each minterm γ_i contains only propositions from A_{p_i}. Further, F is the minimum such frontier that satisfies $P \leq F$ for some given frontier P. This procedure modifies a procedure presented in [30] for finding a frontier satisfying a minterm: on top of which we added the condition $P \leq F$ and on-the-fly processing, which performs updates based on the arrival of new events.

We now show that if such a frontier F exists, there is a minimum one with respect to the order $<$. It is sufficient to show that if two frontiers F and F' satisfy the above conditions, then the frontier that is obtained by taking the intersection of their corresponding cuts C_F and $C_{F'}$ has a frontier Q (hence $Q \leq F$ and $Q \leq F'$) satisfying η. We denote the maximal event involving p_i in F by F_i. For each process p_i, let $Q_i = \min_{\prec}(F_i, F'_i)$. Then Q_i must be in the cut $C_F \cap C_{F'}$. In addition, Q_i must be maximal with respect to $\prec$ among events $C_F \cap C_{F'}$ that involve p_i; this is because by the selection of Q_i, it is impossible that both C_F and $C_{F'}$ have a mutual event (thus, in their intersection) involving p_i that is bigger than Q_i. Hence Q forms the frontier of $C_F \cap C_{F'}$. Since Q_i is either F_i or F'_i, it satisfies γ_i. Consequently, Q satisfies η.

Our procedure uses a vector M to store events, such that $M[i]$ is an event of p_i. Since events may involve multiple processes, it is possible that different components of M may represent the same event. We initialize M to the events in P. When a new event α is processed, the procedure is called to perform updates to M as detailed below. When no more updates are available, the value of the vector M is kept for the next call of the procedure. When for each i, $M[i] \models \gamma_i$ then M forms a frontier satisfying η and it is not updated further.

With a new event α, we check if $M[i] \models \gamma_i$ for each process $p_i \in Pr(\alpha)$. If this is the case, there is no need to update M until the next event is processed. Otherwise, we perform *component correction*: for each $p_i \in Pr(\alpha)$ we set $M[i]$ to α. As a consequence, M may not form a frontier anymore. In this case, some components of M need to be updated in order to advance M to the frontier of the minimum cut that contains the current events in M. We call this *frontier update*: each time some element $M[i]$ is updated, we may need to progress an event in other components $M[j]$, for some $j \neq i$. This happens when there is an immediate successor β of $M[j]$ such that $\beta \preceq M[i]$ (because in this case, $M[j]$ cannot be the maximal element involving p_j in a frontier that contains also $M[i]$). In this case we advance $M[j]$ to β. This update may cause a chain of similar updates to other elements of M. When no further such an update is possible, M has become a frontier again.

In the process of frontier update of M, we may have changed some component $M[l]$ such that previously $M[l] \models \gamma_l$ but not anymore. In this case, we need to check if we can perform further component corrections, progressing $M[l]$ to some successor ν. We can pick as ν either the minimal observed event involving p_l that satisfies γ_l and is bigger than $M[l]$, or, if no such event exists, the maximal observed event involving p_l. If such progress is possible, then frontier update may become necessary again. An induction on the order of the updates to M shows that whenever M forms a frontier, there is no frontier F that satisfies $P \leq F < M$ such that $F \models \eta$.

The process of alternately performing component corrections and frontier updates repeats until one of the following two cases occur: (1) for each i, $M[i]$ satisfies γ_i; then $M \models \eta$ and we are done, or (2) all the components of $M[l]$ such that $M[l] \not\models \gamma_l$ are maximal among the events involving p_l w.r.t. $\prec$. In the latter case, a further call to the procedure, upon processing the next event, will advance M further towards achieving a frontier satisfying η.

Table 1. Monitoring Algorithm Steps and Conditions

Step	Types	M Initialization / fixing	Success Condition
(1)	$\mathbb{P}$ only	Fix $M \triangleq P$ after (a) holds.	(a)
(2)	$\mathbb{P} + \mathbb{M}$	Init $M = P$ after (a) holds.	(a) and (b)
(3)	$\mathbb{P} + \mathbb{M} + \mathbb{N}$	Init $M = P$ after (a) holds.	(a) and (b) and (c)
(4)	$\mathbb{P} + \mathbb{N}$	Fix $M \triangleq P$.	(a) and (c)
(5)	$\mathbb{M} + \mathbb{N}$	Init M as initial event ι.	(b) and (c)
(6)	$\mathbb{N}$ only	Fix M as the initial event ι.	(d)
(7)	$\mathbb{M}$ only	Init M as initial event ι.	(b)

(a) All $EP\varphi_i$ ($1 \leq i < k$) already hold.
(b) The minterm η_k is satisfied for detected frontier M.
(c) For each $EP\psi_l$ ($k \leq l \leq n$) that already holds, not $N_l \leq M$ for detected frontier M.
(d) ι is not yet satisfying $EP\psi_l$ for each $k < l \leq n$.

An RV Algorithm for DLNF Formulas. The following algorithm is applied to each subformula of the form $EP\varphi$ in DLNF, including those nested within other $EP\varphi$ subformulas. The algorithm for different such subformulas is not applied consecutively, but is first initiated for all such subformulas and then updates are performed each time a new event is added for processing to the partial order. The updates for $EP\varphi$ must follow the updates for all the subformulas in φ. For each such subformula $EP\varphi$, where, according to the DLNF form, $\varphi = \eta_1 \wedge \ldots \wedge \eta_n$, we rearrange the conjuncts η_i in the formula according to the following order:

ℙ For $1 \leq j < k$, $\eta_j = EP\varphi_j$. These are the *positive* conjuncts. We denote the minimum frontier satisfying η_j by P_j.

𝕄 Let η_k be a conjunction of literals, i.e., a *minterm*, collected together (i.e., we do not consider each literal in the conjunction separately).

ℕ For $k < l \leq n$, $\eta_l = \neg EP\varphi_l$. These are the *negative* conjuncts. We denote the minimum frontier satisfying $EP\varphi_l$ by N_l.

Not all the above three types of components have to exist in $EP\varphi$. For each such $EP\varphi$ subformula, we keep a *separate* vector M that is used to calculate the minimum frontier that satisfies $EP\varphi$. (To simplify the presentation, we denoted M and P rather than M_φ and P_φ per each DLNF subformula.) The vector M is updated by calls to the procedure described above, synchronizing the calls with the processing of new events. We also keep an indication of whether $EP\varphi$ was found to already hold ("success condition"). Otherwise, the truth value of $EP\varphi$ is *false*. Note that $EP\varphi$ is *stable*, i.e., when it holds, it will continue to hold when new events are added to the partial order. The evaluation of $EP\varphi$ depends on the components ℙ, 𝕄 and ℕ that are included in φ. At least one such component must exist; hence there are seven cases, detailed in Table 1, where the included types of components are listed in the second column.

The third column for each row of the table specifies the initialization of the corresponding vector M. We distinguish in the table between the case where M is *fixed* upon initialization, or may be achieved later than the time it is initialized, after the occurrence of further events. Let P_j refer to the minimum frontier that satisfies the subformula $EP\varphi_j$, for $1 \leq j < l$, that appears positively (i.e., of the form ℙ *within $EP\varphi$*). For initializations, we need to calculate the minimum frontier P such that $P_j \leq P$. In lattice theory, P is the *least upper bound* with respect to $\leq$ among the set of frontiers P_i, denoted $P = \bigsqcup_{1 \leq j < k} P_j$. The frontier P can be calculated as follows: for each process p_i, $P[i]$ is the maximal event involving the process p_i among the different frontiers P_j. (This follows from the fact that taking the set of cuts C_j for which P_j is a frontier, we have that P is the frontier of $C = \bigcup_{1 \leq j < k} C_j$). The initialization (including fixing) of M to the frontier $P = \bigsqcup_{1 \leq j < k} P_j$ takes place when all components of the form P_j required to calculate P were detected. The fourth column specifies conditions under which the subformula $EP\varphi$ (stably) holds, based on conditions (a), (b), (c) and (d), which are defined at the bottom of the table.

After a vector of the form M for a subformula of type $EP\varphi$ was initialized (but *not* fixed), if it does not already satisfy the subformula η_k of φ, then M

is updated upon processing a new event added to the partial order. This is done according to the procedure described at the beginning of this section for detecting a frontier satisfying η_k; each γ_i in that procedure corresponds to the part of the minterm η_k that consists of variables of the process p_i. Updating M can affect conditions (a)–(d). One can optimize the algorithm by removing events that cannot contribute further to the verdict: an event α can be removed if *for each* frontier M calculated according to Table 1 for some subformula of the form $EF\varphi$, either M is already detected, or M contains an event β such that $\alpha \prec \beta$.

We now explain in some detail the case (3) in the table, which is the most involved. The subformula $EP\varphi$ requires that (a) for each of its immediate subformulas of the form $EP\varphi_i$ of φ (i.e., of type $\mathbb{P}$), we have already found a minimum frontier P_i satisfying it. In addition, it requires in (b) that we have found a frontier M that satisfies η_k (type $\mathbb{M}$), where $P_i \leq M$. The latter is enforced by initializing M to P, calculated as explained above. Finally, it requires in (c) that if for some $EP\psi_l$ subformula of φ (i.e., of type $\mathbb{N}$) we have already found a satisfying frontier N_l, then this frontier must not satisfy $N_l \leq M$. Condition (c) refers only to the frontiers N_l that were detected when M that satisfies η_k was already detected; a frontier N_l that will be detected after M is detected will not satisfy $N_l \leq M$.

To complete the verdict of the verified specification, recall that it was translated into a DNF combination of DLNF subformulas. We apply the Boolean operators as appearing in the DNF to the external level subformulas of the form $EP\varphi$ (i.e., those that are not proper subformulas of $EP\varphi$ subformulas).

The overall complexity of the algorithm is $O(|E|\,k^2\,2^{|\varphi|})$. where $|E|$ is the number of events, k is the number of processes, and $|\varphi|$ is the size of the specification. The problem of detecting a frontier that satisfies a Boolean formula φ was shown in [32] to be NP-Complete using a reduction from SAT. The reduction constructs a set of processes, one per each variable of φ. Each process consists of two events, independent of the events of all other processes. The truth value assigned to the propositional variable associated with a process is set to *true* for one of these events and to *false* for the other. This reduction can be trivially adapted to PaBTL by setting the verified property to $EP\varphi$.

5 Implementations and Experiments

We developed two runtime verification tools implementing the monitoring algorithm presented in this paper. PoET [50] implements the complete PaCTL algorithm described in Sect. 3, supporting the full branching temporal logic with past operators including complex nesting and arbitrary formula structures. Kairos [51] (from the ancient Greek concept of opportune time) implements the PaBTL algorithm from Sect. 4, supporting the restricted subset of PaCTL limited to EP operators and Boolean connectives. This tool achieves complexity that is linear in the size of the partial order execution and quadratic in the number of processes, but exponential in the size of the formula due to DLNF transformation.

We conducted comparative performance evaluation to assess the efficiency and scalability of both monitoring approaches across diverse temporal logic patterns, using an Apple MacBook Pro (M1, 16 GB RAM, macOS Sequoia). We evaluated four representative PaBTL properties (Fig. 4), covering different cases, with results shown in Table 2. For each property evaluation, we generated four distinct trace files (1K–500K events per trace) with 3–6 concurrent processes. The generated traces used in our experiments are available as part of the PoET and Kairos GitHub repositories [50,51].

1. $EP(status\_ok \land load\_lt\_100 \land \neg critical\_alarm)$
2. $EP(EP(a) \land EP(b) \land EP(c) \land \neg EP(d))$
3. $EP((aX \land EP(pX)) \lor (aY \land EP(pY)))$
4. $EP((EP(s1) \land \neg EP(j1)) \lor (EP(j2) \land ms \land \neg EP(s2)))$

Fig. 4. Properties in the PaBTL formalism.

Table 2. Experimental Results: Performance Comparison (∗ means > 1 h)

Property	Tool	Parameters	Trace 1K	Trace 10K	Trace 100K	Trace 500K
1	Kairos	Time	0.12 s	0.29 s	2.64 s	13.23 s
		Memory	18MB	27MB	126MB	557MB
	PoET	Time	0.59 s	5.55 s	1032.77 s	∗
		Memory	40MB	85MB	652MB	
2	Kairos	Time	0.12 s	0.37 s	3.55 s	19.39 s
		Memory	19MB	33MB	177MB	803MB
	PoET	Time	5.90 s	∗	∗	∗
		Memory	190MB			
3	Kairos	Time	0.09 s	0.33 s	3.22 s	13.93 s
		Memory	19MB	29MB	143MB	650MB
	PoET	Time	20.03 s	1941.84 s	∗	∗
		Memory	237MB	1.52GB		
4	Kairos	Time	0.10 s	0.47 s	4.62 s	25.45 s
		Memory	19MB	33MB	190MB	882MB
	PoET	Time	∗	∗	∗	∗
		Memory				

We now present further experiments that demonstrate the full expressiveness of the PoET tool *beyond* the PaBTL-compatible.

> 5. $EH((s_{p_1} \rightarrow AY(A(\neg s_{p_2} \ S \ e_{p_2}))) \vee (s_{p_2} \rightarrow AY(A(\neg s_{p_1} Se_{p_1}))))$
> 6. $E((EH((((a \leftrightarrow a') \wedge (b \leftrightarrow b')) \wedge ((t_1 \leftrightarrow t_1') \wedge (t_2 \leftrightarrow t_2'))) \vee ((t_2 \leftrightarrow \neg t_2') \wedge ((t_1 \leftrightarrow \neg t_2) \leftrightarrow \neg t_1')))) \ S \ init)$
> 7. $EH(COM \rightarrow (AH(c_{p_3} \rightarrow (EP((c_{p_1} \vee c_{p_2}) \wedge EY(COM))))))$
> 8. $EH(s_{p_1} \rightarrow AH(s_{p_1} \rightarrow EP(e_{p_1} \wedge EY sr_{p_1}))) \vee EH(s_{p_2} \rightarrow AH(s_{p_2} \rightarrow EP(e_{p_2} \wedge EY sr_{p_2})))$

Fig. 5. PaCTL Properties demonstrating full temporal logic expressiveness

The following four properties in Fig. 5 require operators beyond the PaBTL subset (e.g., AY, AS, ES) and showcase scenarios where complete PaCTL expressiveness is useful. Table 3 presents results for properties 5–8 across trace sizes from 50 to 1000 events. Due to the exponential complexity of the algorithm, traces were limited to 1K events maximum.

Table 3. PoET Experimental Results for PaCTL Properties

Property	Metric	Trace 50	Trace 100	Trace 500	Trace 1000
5	Time	0.44 s	0.41 s	18.91 s	204.02 s
	Memory	34MB	37MB	126MB	328MB
6	Time	0.38 s	0.57 s	23.64 s	230.27 s
	Memory	34MB	38MB	134MB	430MB
7	Time	0.35 s	0.51 s	21.78 s	233.33 s
	Memory	34MB	39MB	138MB	474MB
8	Time	0.34 s	0.23 s	0.48 s	0.80 s
	Memory	34MB	35MB	38MB	49MB

6 Conclusions

We studied RV for partial order executions. Specifically, we used as a specification formalism a past time branching time temporal logic PaCTL, interpreted over the partial order structure between frontiers/cuts obtained from a partial order execution. We presented a runtime verification algorithm with complexity that grows exponentially in the number of processes with a base proportional to the number of events. We implemented this algorithm in a tool named PoET.

We also presented an algorithm for PaBTL, a subset of PaCTL restricted to temporal operator EP and Boolean operators (including $AH\varphi = \neg EP\neg\varphi$). This algorithm has linear complexity in events, quadratic in processes, and exponential in specification size. We implemented this in a tool named Kairos.

Experimental comparison shows that Kairos significantly outperforms PoET in both time and memory. While PoET becomes infeasible for larger traces, Kairos maintains reasonable performance up to 500K events. This conforms well with the complexity results of the two algorithms. On the other hand, PoET allows more expressive specifications, including the *ES*, *AS* and *EY* operators.

References

1. Alur, R., McMillan, K., Peled, D.: Deciding global partial-order properties. Formal Methods Syst. Des. **26**(1), 7–25 (2005)
2. Alur, R., Peled, D., Penczek, W.: Model-checking of causality properties. In: LICS 1995, San Diego, CA, pp. 90-100
3. Alur, R., Peled, D.: Undecidability of partial order logics. Inf. Process. Lett. **69**(3), 137–143 (1999)
4. Audrito, G., Damiani, F., Stolz, V., Torta, G., Viroli, M.: Distributed runtime verification by past-CTL and the field calculus. J. Syst. Softw. **187**, 111251 (2022)
5. Bartocci, E., Falcone, Y. (eds.): Lectures on Runtime Verification – Introductory and Advanced Topics. LNCS, vol. 10457. Springer, Cham (2018). https://doi.org/10.1007/978-3-319-75632-5
6. Bauer, A., Leucker, M., Schallhart, C.: The good, the bad, and the ugly, but how ugly is ugly? In: Sokolsky, O., Taşıran, S. (eds.) RV 2007. LNCS, vol. 4839, pp. 126–138. Springer, Heidelberg (2007). https://doi.org/10.1007/978-3-540-77395-5_11
7. Bollig, B., Leucker, M.: Deciding LTL over Mazurkiewicz traces. Data Knowl. Eng. **44**(2), 219–238 (2003)
8. Chakraborty, S., Henzinger, T.A., Sezgin, A., Vafeiadis, V.: Aspect-oriented linearizability proofs. Logical Methods Comput. Sci. **11**(1) (2015)
9. Chandy, K.M., Lamport, L.: Distributed snapshots: determining the global state of distributed systems. ACM Trans. Comput. Syst. **3**, 63–75 (1985)
10. Chase, C.M., Garg, V.K.: Detection of global predicates: techniques and their limitations. Distrib. Comput. **11**, 191–201 (1998)
11. Clarke, E.M., Emerson, E.A.: Design and synthesis of synchronization skeletons using branching time temporal logic. In: Kozen, D. (ed.) Logic of Programs 1981. LNCS, vol. 131, pp. 52–71. Springer, Heidelberg (1982). https://doi.org/10.1007/BFb0025774
12. Danielsson, L.M., Sanchez, C.: Decentralized stream runtime verification for timed asynchronous networks. IEEE Access **11**, 84091–84112 (2023)
13. Dominguez, J., Nanevski, A.: Visibility and separability for a declarative linearizability proof of the timestamped stack. In: CONCUR 2023, pp. 1–16 (2023)
14. Fidge, C.: Timestamps in message-passing systems that preserve the partial ordering. In: Raymond, K. (ed.) Proceedings of the 11th Australian Computer Science Conference (ACSC'88), vol. 10, pp. 56–66 (1987)
15. Ganguly, R., Momtaz, A., Bonakdarpour, B.: Distributed runtime verification under partial synchrony. OPODIS **20**, 1–17 (2020)
16. Garg, V.K.: Elements of Distributed Computing. Wiley (2002)
17. Garg, V.K., Skawratananond, Ch., Mittal, N.: Timestamping messages and events in a distributed system using synchronous communication. Distrib. Comput. **19**(5–6), 387–402 (2007)
18. Genest, B., Kuske, D., Muscholl, A., Peled, D.: Snapshot verification. In: TACAS 2005. LNCS, vol. 3440, pp. 510–525. Springer, Verlag (2005)

19. Hoare, C.A.R.: Communicating Sequential Processes. Prentice-Hall (1985)
20. Havelund, K., Rosu, G.: Synthesizing monitors for safety properties. In: Tools and Algorithms for the Construction and Analysis of Systems (TACAS'02). LNCS, vol. 2280, pp. 342–356. Springer, Verlag (2002)
21. Herlihy, M., Wing, J.M.: Linearizability: a correctness condition for concurrent objects. ACM Trans. Program. Lang. Syst. **12**(3), 463–492 (1990)
22. Jard, C., Jourdan, G.V., Jeron, T., Rampon, J.X.: A general approach to trace-checking in distributed computing systems. In: 14th International Conference on Distributed Computing Systems, Pozman, Poland, pp. 396–403 (1994)
23. Katz, S., Peled, D.: Interleaving set temporal logic. Theoret. Comput. Sci. **75**(3), 263–287 (1990)
24. Kupferman, O., Vardi, M.Y.: Model checking of safety properties. Formal Methods Syst. Des. **19**(3), 291–314 (2001)
25. Manna, Z., Pnueli, A.: The temporal logic of reactive and concurrent systems - specification. Springer (1992)
26. Lamport, L.: Time, clocks, and the ordering of events in a distributed system. In: Concurrency: The Works of Leslie Lamport, pp. 179–196 (2019)
27. Mattern, F.: Virtual time and global states of distributed systems. In: Proceedings of Workshop on Parallel and Distributed Algorithms, Chateau de Bonas, France, Elsevier, pp. 215–226 (1988)
28. Mazurkiewicz, A.: Trace semantics. In: Proceedings of Advances in Petri Nets 1986, Bad Honnef. LNCS, vol. 255, pp. 279–324. Springer, Verlag (1987)
29. Mittal, N., Garg, V.K.: Computation slicing: techniques and theory. In: Welch, J. (ed.) DISC 2001. LNCS, vol. 2180, pp. 78–92. Springer, Heidelberg (2001). https://doi.org/10.1007/3-540-45414-4_6
30. Mittal, N., Garg, V.K.: Techniques and applications of computation slicing. Distrib. Comput. **17**(3), 251–277 (2005)
31. Niebert, P., Peled, D.: Efficient model checking for LTL with partial order snapshots. Theor. Comput. Sci. **410**(42), 4180–4189 (2009)
32. Ogale, V.A., Garg, V.K.: Detecting temporal logic predicates on distributed computations. In: Pelc, A. (ed.) DISC 2007. LNCS, vol. 4731, pp. 420–434. Springer, Heidelberg (2007). https://doi.org/10.1007/978-3-540-75142-7_32
33. Papadimitriou, C.H.: The Theory of Database Concurrency Control. Computer Science Press (1986)
34. Penczek, W., Kuiper, R.: Traces and Logic. In: The Book of Traces, pp. 307–390 (1995)
35. Penczek, W.: On undecidability of propositional temporal logics on trace systems. Inf. Process. Lett. **43**(3), 147–153 (1992)
36. Peled, D., Pnueli, A.: Proving partial order properties. Theoret. Comput. Sci. **126**, 143–182 (1994)
37. Peled, D., Wilke, T., Wolper, P.: An algorithmic approach for checking closure properties of temporal logic specifications and omega-regular languages. Theoret. Comput. Sci. **195**(2), 183–203 (1998)
38. Pinter, S.S., Wolper, P.: A temporal logic for reasoning about partially ordered computations (extended abstract). In: PODC, pp. 28–37 (1984)
39. Reisig, W.: Partial order semantics versus interleaving semantics for CSP-like languages and its impact on fairness. In: ICALP 1984. LNCS, vol. 172, pp. 403–413. Springer, Verlag (1984)
40. Sen, A., Garg, V.K.: Detecting temporal logic predicates in distributed programs using computation slicing. In: OPODIS 2003, pp. 171–183 (2003)

41. Sen, K., Vardhan, A., Agha, G., Rosu, G.: Decentralized runtime analysis of multithreaded applications. In: IPDPS 2006, 25–29 April 2006, Rhodes Island, Greece (2006)
42. Stoller, S., Liu, Y.A.: Efficient symbolic detection of global properties in distributed systems. In: CAV 1998. LNCS, vol. 1427, pp. 357–368. Springer, Verlag (1998)
43. Thiagarajan, P.S., Walukiewicz, I.: An expressively complete linear time temporal logic for Mazurkiewicz traces. Inf. Comput. **179**(2), 230–249 (2002)
44. Walukiewicz, I.: Difficult configurations – on the complexity of LTrL. In: International Colloquium on Automata, Languages and Programming, ICALP 1998. LNCS, vol. 1443, pp. 140–151. Springer, Verlag (1998)
45. Vardi, M.Y., Wolper, P.: Reasoning about infinite computations. Inf. Comput. **115**, 1–37 (1994)
46. Willams, V.V.: On some fine-grained questions in algorithms and complexity. In: ICM 2018, pp. 3447–3487 (2018)
47. Williams, R.: A new algorithm for optimal 2-constraint satisfaction and its implications. Theoret. Comput. Sci. **348**(2–3), 357–365 (2005)
48. Winskel, G.: Event structures. In: Advances in Petri Nets, pp. 325–392 (1986)
49. Wolper, P., Vardi, M.Y., Sistla, A.P.: Reasoning about infinite computation paths (extended abstract). In: FOCS 1983, pp. 185–194 (1983)
50. PoET tool source code. https://github.com/moraneus/PoET
51. Kairos tool source code. https://github.com/moraneus/kairos

Hidden-Layer Monitoring for Out-of-Distribution Localization in Image Segmentation

Jan Křetínský[1,2](✉)[iD], Sabine Rieder[1,2](✉)[iD], Gesina Schwalbe[3](✉)[iD], and Youssef Shoeb[4,5](✉)[iD]

[1] Masaryk University, Brno, Czech Republic
{139914,sabine.rieder}@mail.muni.cz
[2] Technical University of Munich, Munich, Germany
[3] University of Lübeck, Lübeck, Germany
gesina.schwalbe@uni-luebeck.de
[4] Continental AG, Hanover, Germany
shoeb@campus.tu-berlin.de
[5] Technical University of Berlin, Berlin, Germany

Abstract. The superior performance of neural networks (NNs) in safety-critical situations like automated driving (AD) vision is challenged by so-called *out-of-distribution* (OoD) examples: These are samples that are improbable according to the training data's distribution, such as novel object classes. In such unusual cases, NNs are prone to produce erroneous predictions with high confidence. Therefore, real-time capable localization of OoD areas in input images is needed, enabling appropriate caution if OoD locations conflict with the AD trajectory. A promising direction is computationally efficient hidden-layer "distribution-based" OoD monitoring methods. They model the activation values of neurons in a given hidden layer of the NN (so-called latent features) using probability distributions. During runtime, they then flag images yielding low probability as OoD. These methods have been successfully applied to classification, but neither to OoD *localization* nor object *segmentation* NNs. This paper investigates how far these monitoring techniques can be adapted to OoD localization and performs an extensive case study with several monitoring techniques. Additionally, we examine potential influence factors like NN architecture and training data. Our results demonstrate that this is a promising direction for efficient OoD localization.

1 Introduction

Neural Networks (NNs) achieve remarkable results on complex tasks like image classification [9], object detection [26,50] and semantic segmentation [32,45]. Due to their capabilities, they have also found their way into safety-critical domains such as computer vision for autonomous driving [4,13,49]. However, NNs rely on the assumption that the data used during inference is generated from the same data distribution as the training data – they are *in-distribution (ID)* data. It is

© The Author(s), under exclusive license to Springer Nature Switzerland AG 2026
B. Könighofer and H. Torfah (Eds.): RV 2025, LNCS 16087, pp. 274–295, 2026.
https://doi.org/10.1007/978-3-032-05435-7_16

well known that NNs are prone to incorrect predictions when this assumption is violated [44], i.e., when the NN is presented with data that is *out-of-distribution (OoD)* with respect to the training-data distribution. This highlights the need for runtime monitoring, so-called **OoD detection** [19,23,27,48]: OOD detection aims to recognize when the NN is presented with an input that is considerably different from what has been seen during training, hence increasing the risk of an erroneous output.

Common approaches directly observe a NN fulfilling the target task and utilize gradient information [30] and/or (near-to-)final outputs [18,46]. This, however, makes them specific to the training task and adds computational overhead due additionally needed backwards passes during runtime. A recently flourishing research direction for runtime-capable OoD monitoring are the **distribution-based methods**, e.g. [16,22,33]. These generally aim to model the distribution of training samples with one (or more) probability distributions. Typically, it is not the distribution of *input features* that is considered, but the distribution of NN *latent features* obtained for the training samples, i.e., the intermediate outputs from a hidden layer of the NN. As compared to other approaches, distribution-based methods are agnostic to the output task, are post-hoc applicable and usually require little computational overhead, because they utilize the available NN intermediate outputs. Besides, they are a convenient choice in the setting where we only have positive data (ID from training) and no negative data (unknown OoD yet to appear during runtime).

These methods have been successfully applied to **OoD classification** (see related work below), i.e., classifying a complete input as unusual. However, in practical object detection and *segmentation* as required for, e.g., automated driving (recognizing what objects are where), each area of the input, e.g., each pixel or voxel, is assigned a class by an NN. In such applications, it is of interest *which areas* in the inputs are anomalous (**OoD localization**), as compared to simply flagging the complete image as OoD or ID (OoD classification). For example, in object segmentation for automated driving, anomalies in regions far off the targeted trajectory would not require corrective action. A false alarm could be avoided by more fine-grained OoD localization instead of OoD classification.

In contrast to OoD classification, OoD localization for segmentation NNs has not been studied well in the literature. Existing methods often either require known OoD data [3,34,39,41] just the input [25], or only consider the last layers for uncertainty estimation [18,21]. In this paper, we therefore investigate to what extent the distribution-based methods so far used in OoD classification are also suitable for runtime-capable OoD localization in object segmentation NNs. In particular, the question arises which distribution modeling methods can be carried over and which factors influence their capabilities.

Our contribution can be summarized as follows:

- We extend runtime-capable OoD classification methods based on distribution modeling to OoD localization on segmentation NNs.

- We systematically evaluate the influence of several factors such as model size, training data, and depth of the monitored layer on OoD localization quality, demonstrating the potential of this light-weight technique.
- Our experiments show that, against our expectations and the literature, the last hidden layers are not always the best for monitoring and the diversity of the NN training dataset influences monitor performance with less diverse training datasets leading to better results.

2 Related Work

OoD Detection for Semantic Segmentation. OoD detection methods for semantic segmentation NNs can be divided into those that use "known unknowns" as a proxy for OoD data during training [3,34,35,39,41] and those which do not [11,18,21,22,25]. The general notion behind *using proxy OoD* samples is to learn certain behaviors of the network when encountering inputs that differ from the training distribution. This behavior is then expected to generalize to unseen OoD samples at test time. In this work, we avoid using proxy OoD data as it requires prior knowledge of potential OoD categories and may not generalize well to unseen distributions. Instead, we focus on methods that rely solely on the ID raining data to identify OoD regions at runtime time.

Among the methods that do *not use proxy OoD* data for OoD segmentation, there are two approaches. Firstly, *uncertainty estimation* methods assume that OoD objects result in low-confidence predictions. The uncertainty of the model can be estimated through softmax probabilities [18], ensembles [21], or Monte Carlo dropout [11]. However, the probabilities produced by a closed-set model are often poorly calibrated and result in overconfident predictions for inputs that belong to OoD objects [46]. Secondly, *generative* models have been used for OoD segmentation either through density estimation [22] or by reconstructing the input [25]. Generative methods are typically impractical for real-time applications due to high computational costs and long inference times. PostâĂŞhoc open-set detection work developed for image classification [40,47], could be naively applied to segmentation NN by per-pixel passes, however, this either collapses spatial context that is indispensable for dense prediction, or multiplies memory and runtime by the number of pixels, violating real-time constraints.

Therefore, in this work, we focus on methods that are both fast and do not rely on proxy OoD samples. Lastly, our methods differ from the ones named above as these methods operate at pixel-level. In practical applications like autonomous driving, this is often not required. While information on the position of the OoD area is needed, a single pixel holds little significance. In contrast, knowing that several pixels in the same region are OoD is more useful as this indicates a greater issue in the prediction and needs to be assessed before making safety-critical decisions. For a more detailed review on different methods for OoD segmentation, we refer the reader to [42].

Hidden-Layer-Based Methods. Monitors in this category base their decision on the neuron activation values of at least one hidden layer of the NN. During training, the monitor observes the activation values computed for ID inputs. Then, at runtime, the monitor compares the values from the current input to the previously observed activation values. If they are similar by some notion dependent on the monitor, the current input is said to be ID; otherwise, OoD.

Cheng et al. [5] derive patterns from the activation values of hidden layers by capturing the activation status (zero or above zero) of ReLU neurons for known safe data and expect new ID inputs to result in similar patterns. The Box Monitor [19] considers the numerical values instead of just the patterns. It clusters these values into hyper-rectangles. During runtime, ID inputs are expected to produce activation values contained within these hyper-rectangles. Lukina et al. [29] extend this approach with a quantitative measure of how unknown the new sample is when compared to the hyper-rectangles. Additionally, they propose a method to adapt the monitor at runtime to new classes. He et al. [17] compute hyper-rectangles for the YOLO models. The Gaussian Monitor [16] models the activation value of each neuron as a Gaussian distribution. ID inputs are expected to produce values close to the mean. This method was later extended to object detection NNs [15] and combined to first compute hyper-rectangles [19] and then adjust the width of the hyper-rectangles based on the Gaussian distribution of each neuron [14]. Lee et al. [22] model the observed activation values as a multivariate Gaussian distribution. They compute OoD scores for samples based on the Mahalanobis distance. Morteza and Li [33] use Gaussian mixtures for modeling the distribution of ID data in the feature space and propose a new scoring method based on the energy score [27]. Sun et al. [43] focus on the density of training samples around a newly obtained input. They treat the distance to the k-nearest neighbor as an OoD score. Corbière et al. [6] suggest training an NN on the neuron activation values and use it as a monitor. Yang et al. [48] present a survey of different OoD detection methods.

In this paper, we focus on the Box Monitor [19], and variants of the Gaussian Monitors [14,15,22,33]. All these methods have in common that they require little additional memory and computational overhead at runtime.

3 Preliminaries

3.1 Neural Networks

General Structure. In general, a *neural network (NN)* consists of L consecutive layers $1, \ldots, L$. Layer 1 is called the input layer and layer L the output layer, from which we can derive the prediction of the NN. The layers in between are called *hidden layers*. For an input x, each hidden layer i with N_i neurons computes so-called *activation values* h_i based on a weighted sum of the activation values h_{i-1} of the previous layer $(i-1)$.

$$h_1(x) = x \tag{1}$$

$$h_i(x) = \sigma_i(W_i h_{i-1}(x) + b_i) \tag{2}$$

We call $W_i \in \mathbb{R}^{N_i \times N_{i-1}}$ the *weights* of layer i, $b_i \in \mathbb{R}^{N_i}$ is the bias, and σ_i its *activation function*, for example $ReLU(x) = max(0, x)$. This basic architecture can be extended with several more advanced layers, for example, convolutions or self-attention layers.

Segmentation Neural Networks. The task of semantic *segmentation* is to assign each pixel in a given image to one of pre-defined classes $\mathcal{C}$. The training dataset $\{(x_m, y_m)\}_{m=0}^{M}$ consists of a set of M images $x \in \mathcal{X}$ with $\mathcal{X} = \mathbb{R}^{H \times W \times 3}$ for images of $H \times W$ pixels and 3 color channels, and their corresponding labels $y \in \mathcal{Y}$ with $\mathcal{Y} = \mathcal{C}^{H \times W}$. The training objective of a segmentation neural network is to learn a mapping $f : \mathcal{X} \to \mathbb{R}^{H \times W \times |\mathcal{C}|}$ from image space $\mathcal{X}$ to a vector z that is normalized using the softmax function to obtain the output $\hat{y}$.

Vision Transformers. A *vision transformer (ViT)* [10,28,36,38] is a special type of NN used for segmentation tasks. It first divides an input with height H and width W into *patches* of size p_H, p_W with $p_h < H$, $p_W < W$. These patches, therefore, contain only information about a particular part of the input. The patches are projected into a c-dimensional space and processed by an encoder NN. From the intermediate layers of this encoder architecture, several connections lead to a decoder that uses the collection of information from different layers to make a prediction. As encoders are often only trained once with large datasets, they are considered frozen. However, this also means that the encoders might contain information irrelevant to the current task at hand. To reduce information, a projection is learned that maps the features of the encoder into a new space that only contains the features relevant for the decoder.

3.2 Dimensionality Reduction

Principal Component Analysis. The main goal of *principal component analysis (PCA)* [20] is to find the orthogonal vector directions into which a sample $\mathcal{S} \subset \mathbb{R}^k$ of data points exhibits the largest statistical variance, the so-called *principal components*. This is typically formulated using the sample's covariance matrix $Cov(\mathcal{S})$, which holds in the i, jth entry the covariance between the ith and the jth dataset feature, and allows to calculate the variance $Var(u^T \mathcal{S})$ of $\mathcal{S}$ along any feature direction $u \in \mathbb{R}^k$:

$$Cov(\mathcal{S}) = \left(\mathbb{E}_{x \sim \mathcal{S}}\left[(x_i - \overline{x}_i)(x_j - \overline{x}_j)\right]\right)_{i,j} \qquad (3)$$

$$= \frac{1}{|\mathcal{S}|} \sum_{x \in \mathcal{S}} (x - \overline{x})(x - \overline{x})^T \in \mathbb{R}^{k \times k} \qquad (4)$$

$$Var(u^T \mathcal{S}) = \frac{1}{N} \sum_{x \in \mathcal{S}} (u^T x - u^T \overline{x})^T (u^T x - u^T \overline{x}) = u^T Cov(\mathcal{S}) u \qquad (5)$$

where $\bar{x} = \mathrm{E}_{x \sim \mathcal{S}}[x] = \mathrm{mean}_{x \in \mathcal{S}} x$. The m directions u_i of largest variance

$$(u_1, \ldots, u_m)^\star = \underset{\substack{v_1, \ldots, v_m \in \mathbb{R}^k \\ \|v_i\|_2 = 1}}{\arg\max} \sum_{i=1}^m v_i^T \mathrm{Cov}(\mathcal{S}) v_i \qquad (6)$$

turn out to be the m normalized eigenvectors u_i of $\mathrm{Cov}(\mathcal{S})$ with the largest eigenvalues $\lambda_i = \mathrm{Var}(u_i^T \mathcal{S})$.

Projecting to these normalized eigenvectors via $\mathcal{S}' = (u_1, \ldots, u_m)^T \mathcal{S} \subset \mathbb{R}^m$ discards directions of low variance, and essentially projects the data to a hyperplane where most of the data's variance is maintained. This makes it ideal for dimensionality reduction before applying distribution modeling techniques, since as little as possible of the distribution information is lost. Furthermore, even when all dimensions are kept, PCA has the advantage that it rotates the data into a new space where the axes align with the directions of maximum variance of the data.

Contrastive PCA. PCA captures directions of high variance of one set $\mathcal{S}$ of samples (the *foreground*). *Contrastive PCA (cPCA)* [2] instead aims to capture those directions where a foreground dataset $\mathcal{S}$ exhibits higher variance than a *background* dataset $\widehat{\mathcal{S}}$. This only requires a slight adaptation to the PCA formulation. Namely we search for eigenvectors and -values of the *contrasted covariance* $\mathrm{Cov}(\mathcal{S}) - \alpha \mathrm{Cov}(\widehat{\mathcal{S}})$ instead of the plain foreground covariance matrix:

$$(u_1, \ldots, u_m)^\star = \underset{\substack{v_1, \ldots, v_m \in \mathbb{R}^k \\ \|v_i\|_2 = 1}}{\arg\max} \sum_{i=1}^m v_i^T \left(\mathrm{Cov}(\mathcal{S}) - \alpha \mathrm{Cov}(\widehat{\mathcal{S}}) \right) v_i \qquad (7)$$

where $\alpha \geq 0$ is a balancing hyperparameter, empirically set to 1 [12]. Note that due to the contrasting, also negative eigenvalues can be obtained where the variance of the background data exceeds that of the foreground.

These contrasted principal components tend to highlight statistical differences between the foreground and the background data sample when using them for dimensionality reduction. cPCA is by now a common method for data exploration and visualization.

3.3 Probability Distributions

Gaussian Mixture Models. *Gaussian mixture models (GMMs)* are probabilistic models that assume all the data points are generated from a mixture of a finite number of Gaussian distributions. Formally, a GMM is a weighted mixture of M multivariate Gaussians which define a probability density function over a sample space $\mathcal{S} \subset \mathbb{R}^k$ as:

$$p(x) = \sum_{i=1}^M \pi_i \cdot \mathcal{N}(x \mid \mu_i, \Sigma_i) \qquad (8)$$

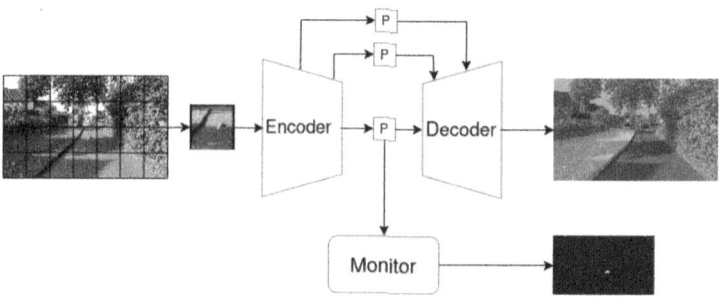

Fig. 1. Abstract process for the monitoring of segmentation NNs.

where $\pi_i \in [0,1]$ are the mixing coefficients such that $\sum_{i=1}^{M} \pi_i = 1$, and $\mathcal{N}(x \mid \mu_i, \Sigma_i)$ denotes the multivariate Gaussian density with mean $\mu_i \in \mathbb{R}^k$ and covariance matrix $\Sigma_i \in \mathbb{R}^{k \times k}$. GMMs are particularly useful for modeling complex distributions that are not well-approximated by a single Gaussian. Each component can capture a local mode of the data distribution.

Von-Mises-Fisher Distribution. When samples are unit-norm vectors that live on the $k-1$-dimensional hypersphere $\mathbb{S}^{k-1} = \{x \in \mathbb{R}^k \mid ||x||_2 = 1\}$, the von-Mises-Fisher (vMF) distribution [31] captures the mean direction μ of the samples and measures how closely the samples are concentrated around μ through the concentration parameter κ. The probability density function for a sample is:

$$f(x|\mu,\kappa) = \mathcal{C}_k(\kappa)\exp(\kappa\mu^T x), \quad \mathcal{C}_k(\kappa) = \frac{\kappa^{k/2-1}}{(2\pi)^{k/2} I_{k/2-1}(\kappa)} \tag{9}$$

where $I_v(\cdot)$ is the modified Bessel function of the first kind at order v.

4 Methodology

Problem Statement. In this paper, we investigate whether hidden-layer monitoring techniques that only rely on ID samples for training can be applied to OoD localization in segmentation NNs. We have two main requirements for our methods. (1) All considered monitoring techniques ought to impose little computational overhead and require little additional memory. This ensures that they can be applied in practice during runtime. (2) We are interested in finding OoD areas in the image. Neither do we want to classify the entire image as OoD, nor a single pixel, as errors in single pixels are often not of relevance for practical purposes. An area is a rectangular selection of pixels in the input image. We considered an area as OoD if the majority of its pixels belongs to an OoD object.

Based on these requirements, we extend existing monitoring techniques and investigate the influence of various factors, such as NN architecture, layer selection, and monitoring algorithm, on detection accuracy.

4.1 Monitoring for Segmentation NNs

We build our monitoring method on top of a ViT architecture as shown in Fig. 1. First, the input is divided into patches. For visibility, we divide into large **patches** in Fig. 1. In practice, smaller sizes are used, e.g., 14×14 pixels. These patches are then separately processed by the ViT, consisting of an encoder and a decoder. This is the key insight that allows us to perform OoD localization. The patches contain information that, on the one hand, *summarizes an area* of the image and, on the other hand, is *not restricted to a single pixel*. Consequently, a single pixel having an unusual value due to, e.g., a sensor failure does not affect the monitoring prediction. The monitor will only alarm when the patch as a whole is unusual. As we know the exact position of each patch in the image, we can then highlight problematic patches in the image resulting in OoD localization. The size of the patches influences how fine-grained the OoD-localization is. In Fig. 1, the monitor has identified several patches as OoD and propagated their position in the input image.

The question, in **which layers** of the NN architecture we should apply monitoring, remains. The encoder is often trained on a large dataset, which allows application to several different tasks. Only the decoder is fine-tuned for a particular application. Therefore, data that is OoD to the decoder is not necessarily also OoD for the encoder. As we need to identify inputs for which the overall prediction is wrong, we cannot monitor in the encoder. However, the decoder immediately after receiving information from the encoder starts to construct the prediction for each single pixel in the patch. As we want information on the patch as a whole, we need to apply monitoring before this process starts. The only position in the pipeline where we can receive condensed patch-level information that is fine-tuned to our task at hand are the connections from the encoder to the decoder. These connections occur at various depths of the encoder and pass through a projection layer that removes information not relevant for the task the decoder was fine-tuned on. Consequently, we monitor the output of these projection layers.

4.2 Monitoring Techniques

In this paper, we consider a variety of *hidden-layer distribution-based monitoring* techniques. In general, these monitoring methods observe the activation values

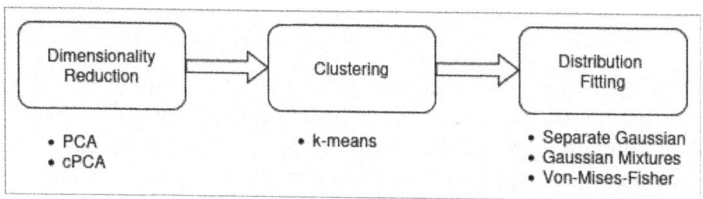

Fig. 2. The process of learning our monitors.

of a hidden layer on known ID training data. Based on these activation values, the monitors fit a probability distribution to model the behavior observed on ID data. During runtime, the monitor observes for each new input the activation values in the hidden layer and compares it to the known behavior. If it is "too different" compared to the distribution learned by the monitor, the input is considered to be OoD. In this section we detail on the first part of this process, i.e., constructing the distribution representing the activation values. For the second part, i.e., setting the threshold heuristic used during runtime, we refer to the related work section for standard techniques and our experimental evaluation for their comparison.

Figure 2 shows the steps our monitors follow for modeling the activation values of a hidden layer. We introduce the idea of dimensionality reduction and utilize clustering as suggested in [14].

Step 1: Dimensionality Reduction. As the first step, we apply PCA or cPCA to the observed activation values. PCA and cPCA both can reduce the dimensions of the data they are applied to, which increases computation speed for the following steps. Furthermore, even if we choose not to reduce the dimensions of the observed activation values, PCA and cPCA still transform the activation values into a space where the axes align with the directions of maximum variance, which might improve later steps and ease the fitting of probability distributions.

When applying cPCA, the choice of background in comparison to which the contrast is computed is important. We consider two variants. In the first case, we assume that we are computing a monitor for one particular class, for example class Human, while other classes, e.g., Vehicle and Sky, are available. Then, we can compute the contrast of images of class Human in comparison to the other classes. In the second case, we assume that all available data is used to train the monitor. Therefore, no meaningful data is available for computing contrast. We then randomly draw features from a Gaussian distribution.

Step 2: Clustering. Similar to the Box monitor [19], we focus on k-means clustering, as the k-means algorithm creates clusters centered around a single point. While this does not always capture data perfectly, it is beneficial for the next step in our pipeline, distribution modeling. However, a large number of clusters also increases computation time as a new input needs to be compared to several clusters instead of just a single probability distribution. We find the final number of clusters through a hyperparameter search.

Step 3: Distribution Fitting. As the third step, the clusters are modeled using a probability distribution. We consider independent Gaussians for each neuron, Gaussian mixture models with different types of covariance matrices, and the von-Mises-Fisher distribution, which has not been considered in the literature before.

5 Evaluation

To evaluate the performance of different runtime monitoring techniques and investigate the importance of different influence factors, we consider the following research questions:

RQ1: How does the NN architecture influence the monitoring algorithms? We expect that different NN architectures result in changed performance of the monitoring algorithms. In particular, we expect the size of a model to be an influential factor. Larger models might contain more irrelevant information in their hidden layers. Furthermore, we question whether the architecture influences which layer is well-suited for monitoring. In the OoD detection literature, oftentimes the monitors focus on the last layers which were empirically shown to work well [16,19]. We expect similar behavior for OoD localization.

RQ2: What influence do the training data have? We focus on two parts of the question. First, we ask whether OoD localization is influenced by the diversity of the dataset the NN was trained on. We also question which classes are harder to distinguish for monitors. When a monitor cannot separate two classes, this indicates that the NN treats them similarly.

RQ3: What is the structure of the latent space? This question aims to find which monitors work well in practice. The question is, which distribution models should be used, and how many clusters are necessary for the different distributions. Furthermore, we want to know whether dimensionality reduction reduces performance drastically.

5.1 Experimental Setup and Implementation

Datasets. For our experiments, we focus on the well-known Cityscapes [7] datasets. As this dataset is large, we only consider the cities of Stuttgart, Ulm, and Mönchengladbach. Due to their different size, we expect that they provide us with a good coverage of the entire dataset. The Cityscapes dataset contains pixel-wise annotations for each image, assigning each of the pixels to one class. The classes are grouped together in 8 categories shown in Table 1. The last category, void, also contains objects that are rare within the dataset.

We consider OoD objects of the Lost-And-Found [37] dataset for our evaluation. Furthermore, to increase the diversity of OoD data in our experiments, we train separate NNs on only one of the categories of the Cityscapes dataset and compare them to objects from the other categories.

Considered NNs. We evaluate different encoders, DINOv2-S (30.9M parameters), Dinov2-B(96.2M parameters), Dinov2-L (314.5M parameters) [36], CLIP (654.9M parameters) [38], and Swin-T (95.9M parameters) [28] in different sizes. We concentrate on ViT-style encoders because their intrinsic patch-token representation mirrors the granularity required by our OoD localization task, without

Table 1. Grouping of Classes in Cityscapes

Group	Classes
Flat	Road, Sidewalk, Parking, Rail Track
Construction	Building, Wall, Fence
Object	Pole, Traffic Light, Traffic Sign,
Nature	Vegetation, Terrain
Sky	Sky
Human	Person, Rider
Vehicle	Car, Truck, Bus, Train, Motorcycle, Bicycle
Void	Unlabeled, Ego Vehicle, Rectification Border, Out of Roi, Static, Dynamic, Ground, Guard Rail, Bridge, Tunnel, Polegroup, Caravan, Trailer

an additional patch-extraction step. For each encoder, we train a Feature Pyramid Network [24] decoder on the Cityscapes [8] dataset, freezing all encoder layers except the projection layers. This allows us to preserve the strong features learned during pretraining, while adapting only the final projection layers of the encoder to better capture the in-distribution classes. The different segmentation NNs had a mean Intersection over Union (mIoU) score ranging from 80–83% on the Cityscapes validation set.

For each encoder, we monitor one early layer (l0), two from intermediate stages (l1, l2), and the final layer (l3). These layers were selected to capture a range of semantic abstraction levels, since early layers tend to encode low-level features, while deeper layers encode high-level object semantics.

Considered Monitors. For our experiments, we consider 8 different monitors:

- *GAUSS* trains separate Gaussian distributions for each neuron and counts the number of neurons for which the new value falls within two times the standard deviation [16]. The number of neurons needed to raise an alarm is usually set according to some heuristics. Instead of choosing a particular threshold, we evaluate the whole trade-off between False Positive and True Positive Rate for different thresholds.
- *C-GAUSS* clusters the values and for each cluster and neuron computes the above Gaussian distributions [14].
- *PCA-C-GAUSS* performs PCA, and then behaves as C-GAUSS.
- *P-GAUSS* performs PCA and then applies GAUSS without clustering.
- *cPCA-C-GAUSS* applies cPCA and then behaves as C-GAUSS. This monitor is only trained on one of the ID groups and uses all others as background.
- *N-cPCA-C-GAUSS* behaves as above, but the background is random noise.
- *GMM* trains a standard GMM from the sklearn [1] to fit the training data. The implementation applies k-means clustering before fitting the GMM. The probability prediction is the score. Again, we do not set a fixed threshold.

– *VMF* normalizes the data and fits a vMF distribution.

Monitors are trained on a maximum of 1000 randomly chosen patches per class (fewer if not as many are available) and evaluated on a maximum of 5000 randomly chosen patches. We ensure that the evaluation dataset is balanced by restricting the size if fewer patches are available for ID or OoD data.

When comparing monitor performance on different layers or NNs, we use the best monitor configuration we found, i.e., we experimentally choose the best number of clusters and, potentially, the most suitable layer.

Quality Measure and Plots. We use the well-established notion of Receiver Operating Characteristic (ROC), Precision-Recall Curve (PRC) and FPR@95TPR. ROC and PRC are used to compare the performance of a binary classifier for different decision thresholds. ROC plots the True Positive Rate (TPR), also known as sensitivity or recall, against the False Positive Rate (FPR):

$$\text{TPR} = \frac{\text{True Positives}}{\text{True Positives} + \text{False Negatives}}$$

$$\text{FPR} = \frac{\text{False Positives}}{\text{False Positives} + \text{True Negatives}}$$

In our case, we consider an ID example as negative and an OoD example as positive. The TPR measures how many OoD instances out of all OoD instances were captured, i.e., how many times the monitor flagged an image compared to how often it should have. The FPR tells us how many times the monitor did not raise an alarm when it should have. Reversing the definition of what is positive and negative reflects the ROC curve at the diagonal. Additionally, reversing the score leads to the same curve. For comparing several ROCs, we use the Area Under the ROC (AUROC). A value of 1 for the AUROC indicates a perfect trade-off between TPR and FPR, whereas a value of 0.5 is achieved by a random classifier, assuming the evaluation dataset is balanced.

The PRC plots Precision against TPR:

$$\text{Precision} = \frac{\text{True Positives}}{\text{True Positives} + \text{False Positives}}$$

Precision measures how many times the monitor raised a correct alarm compared to the overall number of alarms. Therefore, the PRC compares the number of correct alarms versus all alarms to the number of correct alarms versus all OoD inputs. It is highly dependent on which class is seen as positive, and reversing the labeling can change the shape drastically. The Area Under the PRC (AUPRC) quantifies the overall performance of different classifiers and allows comparison.

FPR@95TPR reports on the FPR when the TPR is fixed to be at least 95%. While for the other scores we aim for high values, in this case, lower values are preferable and the worst possible value is 1. For some experiments, we choose to omit the FPR@95TPR as it mostly correlates with the AUROC score.

Execution Environment. While the execution of monitors only requires limited resources, the resources for training them depend on the model. As we consider rather large NNs and need to store the activation values of several inputs at once, we use a powerful machine. All executions were run on a server with 96 AMD EPYC 9274F CPUs and 380GB RAM.

5.2 RQ1: Influence of the NN

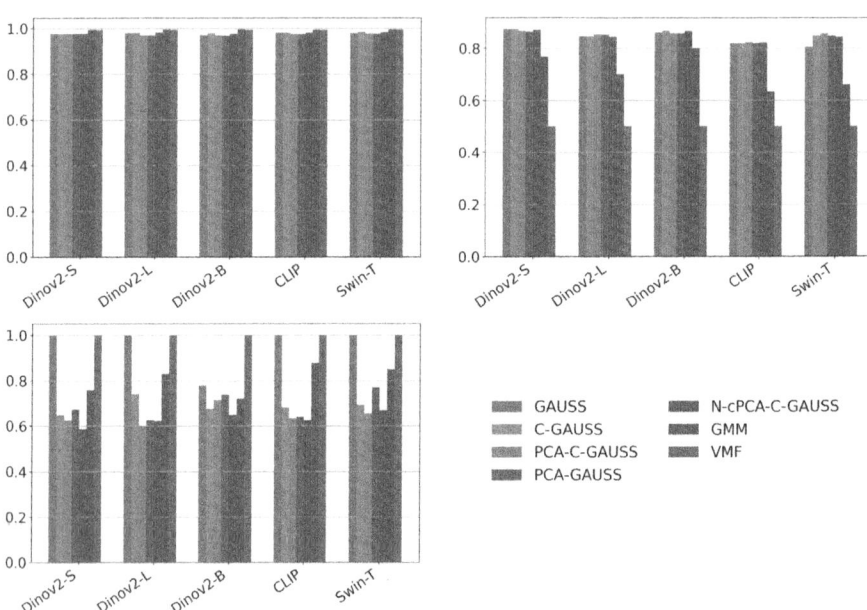

Fig. 3. AUPRC (left), AUROC (right) and FPR@95TPR (bottom) for different architectures and sizes.

NN Architecture and Size. Figure 3 shows monitoring results for the different architectures. For each monitor, we take the best configuration and the most fitting layer. All monitors were trained on all groups, which excludes the N-cPCA-C-GAUSS, and are evaluated on the Lost-And-Found dataset. We can see that the performance over all different architectures and NN sizes is relatively stable, especially for the AUPRC. When considering the AUROC, we find that most monitors perform slightly better on Dinov2-S than on other models and slightly worse on CLIP. The only exception is the GAUSS, which performs worse on Swin-T compared to its performance on other models. For FPR@95TPR, the results are not as clear, but generally Dinov2-S is a good choice for most monitors. This indicates that larger hidden layers do not necessarily coincide with increased performance of runtime monitors. We conjecture that all NNs considered in the experiments have large enough layers to be able to provide a separation of features for different input data. How clear this separation is, is most likely influenced by other factors, like training.

Monitored Layers. In a second experiment, we aim to check whether later layers are also better suited for OoD localization, as has been found for OoD detection [16,19]. Figure 4 shows the monitor performance averaged over all NNs together with the standard deviation. Again, the AUROC shows slightly more diverse values than the AUPRC. The difference between the layers is not large, indicating that monitoring is possible in all of them. As expected, the last layer seems promising. When investigating the large standard deviations, we found that, while on average the last layer is a good choice, this is not necessarily true for each monitor and each architecture. For example, Fig. 5 shows the same data restricted Swin-T. In this case, the third observed layer is preferable for most monitors when considering AUROC. The best layer according to FPR@95TPR differs for each monitor. Furthermore, for some monitors, the last observed layer provided the worst trade-off between FPR and TPR. The PCA experiments showed that, somewhat reasonably, OoD cases are rather off in the direction of low-variance dimensions. NNs develop invariances and abstractions with increasing depth, that might simply remove information about these OoD directions. Thus, there seems to be a sweet-spot of layer depth between richness of the representation and learned invariances.

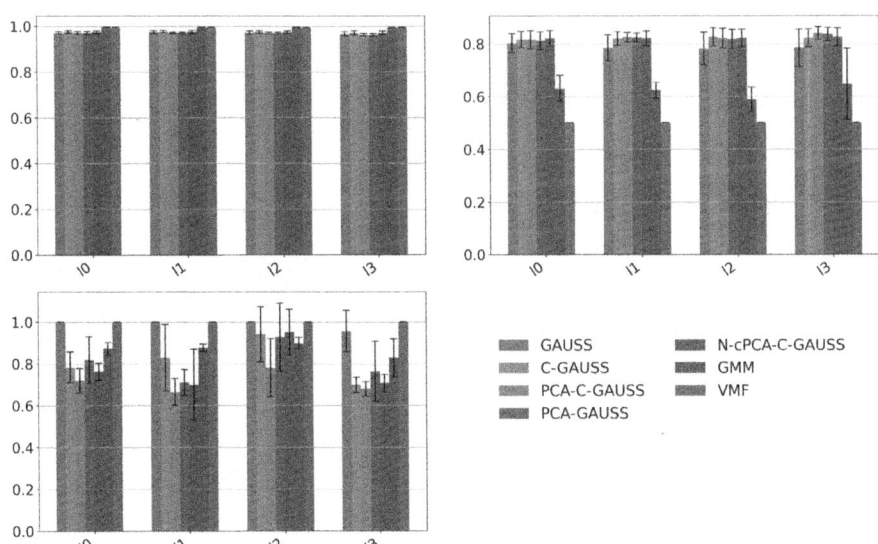

Fig. 4. AUPRC (left), AUROC (right) and FPR@95TPR (bottom) for different layers averaged over all NN architectures and sizes.

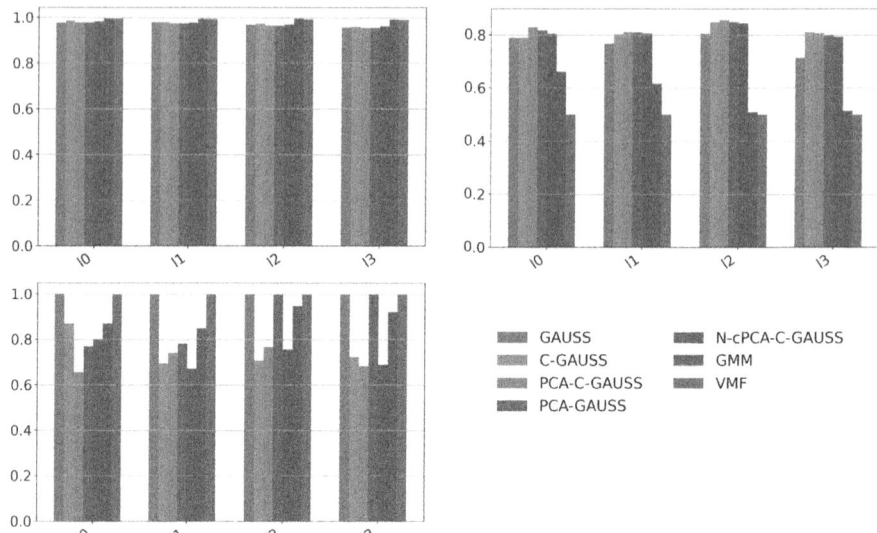

Fig. 5. AUPRC (left) and AUROC (right) for different layers for Swin-T.

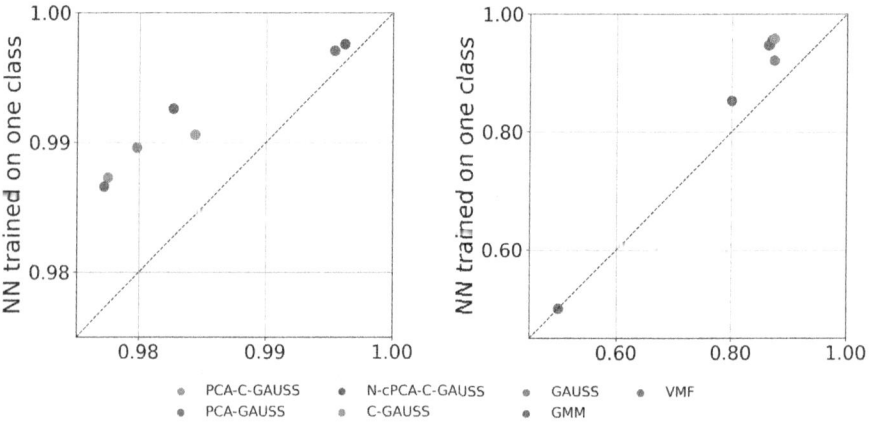

Fig. 6. Comparison of AUPRC (left) and AUROC (right) when training NNs on all or one group.

5.3 RQ2: Influence of the Data

Training on Diverse Datasets. We train the Swin-T architecture and the Dinov2-S architecture on only one group. This results in six different NNs for each architecture. We then compare the performance of monitors in detecting the OoD objects of the Lost-And-Found dataset for the new NNs to the monitor's performance for the original NNs. For each monitor, we take the best configuration and average over the different NNs. Figure 6 shows the result in the form of a scatter plot. As all points lie above the diagonal, we can see that training on a more diverse dataset results, on average, in worse performance.

Semantic Similarity of Groups. From a human understanding, all of our groups as shown in Table 1 are well distinguishable. We depict the performance of our monitors on average over all NNs and monitors for distinguishing these groups in Fig. 2 and Fig. 3. A monitor trained on Flat (column Flat) achieves, on average, a high score for both AUPRC and AUROC, indicating that the group Flat can easily be distinguished from other classes. Nevertheless, the AUPRC reflects the closeness to the group Construction, which appears to be the most similar one. On the other hand, most monitors trained on other classes have issues separating Flat from their own group data. Most monitors can distinguish a human well from their own group. This indicates that the NNs have learned a representation of Humans that is different from objects or general surroundings. However, monitors trained for Humans do not perform as well. We further see, as expected, that Construction and Object have a lower AUROC value than other classes for the respective monitors. As objects like traffic signs often occur in front of Construction, this is to be expected. Lastly, we also find that the standard deviation is high in nearly the entire table. We conclude that the performance drastically depends on the chosen monitors and optimizations are necessary (Tables 2 and 3).

Table 2. AUPRC (Mean ± Std) when distinguishing different groups. Monitors are trained on the column classes and evaluated on row classes.

	Flat	Construction	Object	Nature	Sky	Human	Vehicle
Flat	–	0.56 ± 0.14	0.30 ± 0.17	0.47 ± 0.15	0.27 ± 0.20	0.27 ± 0.17	0.48 ± 0.14
Construction	0.60 ± 0.16	–	0.28 ± 0.17	0.48 ± 0.16	0.28 ± 0.21	0.24 ± 0.19	0.43 ± 0.16
Object	0.92 ± 0.04	0.90 ± 0.04	–	0.86 ± 0.06	0.66 ± 0.14	0.51 ± 0.14	0.82 ± 0.07
Nature	0.65 ± 0.14	0.59 ± 0.14	0.27 ± 0.19	–	0.31 ± 0.20	0.24 ± 0.20	0.46 ± 0.16
Sky	0.84 ± 0.08	0.81 ± 0.08	0.42 ± 0.16	0.76 ± 0.09	–	0.36 ± 0.18	0.68 ± 0.13
Human	0.93 ± 0.04	0.91 ± 0.04	0.63 ± 0.11	0.88 ± 0.05	0.70 ± 0.13	–	0.87 ± 0.05
Vehicle	0.74 ± 0.11	0.67 ± 0.12	0.30 ± 0.18	0.60 ± 0.14	0.36 ± 0.20	0.27 ± 0.19	–

5.4 RQ3: Structure of the Latent Space

Comparison of the Monitors. Figure 3 shows a comparison of monitors over the different NNs. We can see that most monitors perform nearly equally well. However, the VMF monitor archives an AUROC value similar to a random classifier. Therefore, we conclude that this is not a suitable representation of the ID distribution. The GMM monitor also performs surprisingly badly, albeit not as badly as the VMF monitor. We investigated further and found that the standard implementation oftentimes results in one Gaussian distribution with

Table 3. AUROC (Mean ± Std) when distinguishing different classes. Monitors are trained on the column classes and evaluated on row classes.

	Flat	Construction	Object	Nature	Sky	Human	Vehicle
Flat	–	0.73 ± 0.15	0.64 ± 0.16	0.70 ± 0.13	0.77 ± 0.16	0.67 ± 0.10	0.70 ± 0.12
Construction	0.84 ± 0.16	–	0.57 ± 0.06	0.74 ± 0.12	0.80 ± 0.15	0.69 ± 0.09	0.76 ± 0.13
Object	0.87 ± 0.17	0.76 ± 0.13	–	0.80 ± 0.14	0.84 ± 0.16	0.75 ± 0.13	0.80 ± 0.14
Nature	0.85 ± 0.16	0.78 ± 0.14	0.69 ± 0.12	–	0.82 ± 0.15	0.74 ± 0.12	0.78 ± 0.14
Sky	0.89 ± 0.17	0.84 ± 0.16	0.77 ± 0.16	0.86 ± 0.16	–	0.79 ± 0.15	0.83 ± 0.16
Human	0.88 ± 0.17	0.85 ± 0.15	0.77 ± 0.16	0.83 ± 0.15	0.86 ± 0.17	–	0.81 ± 0.15
Vehicle	0.87 ± 0.16	0.82 ± 0.15	0.73 ± 0.14	0.80 ± 0.15	0.85 ± 0.17	0.73 ± 0.12	–

high variance spanning nearly the entire space and several small ones tightly fitted to outliers. The number of clusters we allow for the GMM mostly only influences the number of smaller clusters while one main cluster maintains high variance. While this represents the data well, it is not what we require for OoD localization, where several Gaussians with smaller variance are preferred.

Number of Clusters. Furthermore, we investigate the number of clusters needed to represent the data. Figure 7 shows the AUPRC and AUROC for different numbers of clusters on Dinov2-S and layer 13. We observe that the number of clusters only has a minor influence on the AUPRC and a higher influence on the AUROC value. Therefore, aiming for fewer clusters to improve computation efficiency is possible. We further see that AUPRC and AUROC are different metrics, as GMM performs best with regard to AUPRC and worst for AUROC. As AUROC also considers True Negatives, which AUPRC does not, this indicates that the number of True Negatives is comparably low for the GMM monitors.

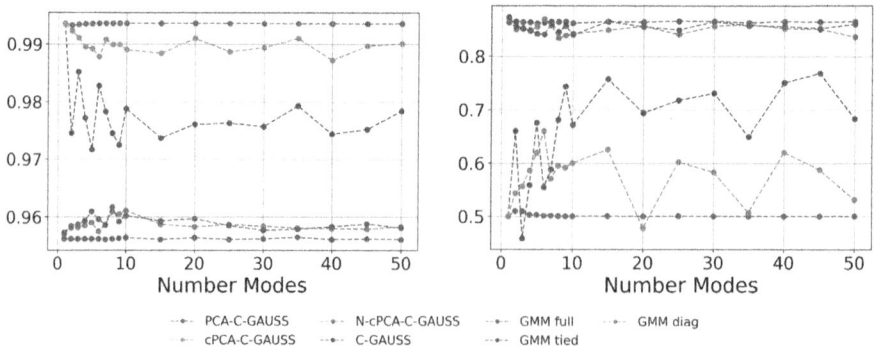

Fig. 7. AUPRC (left) and AUROC (right) for a different number of clusters for the last considered layer of Dinov2-S.

Influence of Dimensionality Reduction. Lastly, we investigate the influence of dimensionality reduction. We apply PCA or cPCA to rotate the data and order the dimensions according to their variance. Then, we only consider a subset of these dimensions for monitoring. In detail, we divide the dimensions into 10 groups of equal size. Figure 8 shows the AUPRC and AUROC for Dinov2-S. The AUROC decreases when considering fewer dimensions. This behavior is consistent when looking at other NNs. Interestingly, the first 10% of dimensions do not achieve the best results even though they capture the most variance. Other dimensions might be equally important, hinting that misbehavior in directions that usually have lower variance is an indicator of OoD data.

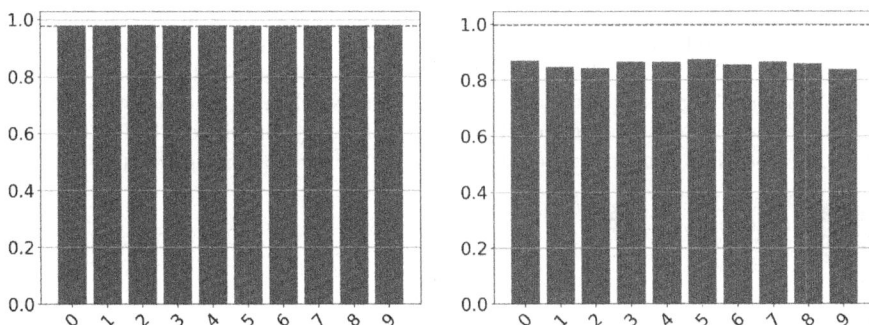

Fig. 8. AUPRC (left) and AUROC (right) for the different deciles of PCA components for PCA-C-GAUSS on Dinov2-S. The red line shows the best configuration when monitoring all dimensions. (Color figure online)

6 Conclusion and Future Work

In this paper, we applied distribution-based hidden-layer runtime monitoring to segmentation NNs in the form of Vision Transformers. We investigated different factors that could influence the performance of the monitors. We found that monitors achieve good results on smaller NNs, which are often preferable for real-time applications. Additionally, we saw that, against our expectations and the literature, the last hidden layers are not always the best layers for monitor. Nevertheless, monitors on this layer perform well on average making it a good choice when training time for the monitors is limited. We also found that monitors for NNs that were trained on a less diverse dataset performed better in detecting OoD data. Overall, the proposed type of monitors achieved good results for the task of OoD localization.

As a next step, we want to apply the monitoring techniques to a wider variety of datasets to see whether our findings carry over. As the Cityscapes dataset contains a diverse set of objects, we expect similar behavior. In parallel, we will investigate how well the proposed monitors transfer to CNN-based segmentation backbones in order to disentangle architecture-specific effects from task-intrinsic limitations. Additionally, future work can utilize our findings for creating new types of monitors. Especially the fact that some classes are hard to distinguish from others could be considered.

Acknowledgments. This research has received funding from the European Union under Grant Agreement No. 101171844, project Intelligence-Oriented Verification&Controller Synthesis (InOVationCS), and from the European Union's Horizon Europe program under Grant Agreement No. 101212818, Robustifying Generative AI Through Human-Centric Intergration of Neural and Symbolic Methods (RobustifAI). Views and opinions expressed are, however, those of the authors only and do not necessarily reflect those of the European Union or European Research Executive Agency. Neither the European Union nor the granting authority can be held responsible for them. This research has also received funding from the MUNI Award in Science and Humanities MUNI/I/1757/2021 of the Grant Agency of Masaryk University.

G.S. acknowledges support through the junior research group project "chAI" funded by the German Federal Ministry of Research, Technology and Space (BMFTR), grant no. 01IS24058. The authors are solely responsible for the content of this publication.

References

1. GaussianMixture. https://scikit-learn.org/stable/modules/generated/sklearn.mixture.GaussianMixture.html. Accessed 20 May 2025
2. Abid, A,, Zhang, M.J., Bagaria, V.K., Zou, J.: Exploring patterns enriched in a dataset with contrastive principal component analysis. Nat. Commun. **9**(1), 2134 (2018)
3. Chan, R., Rottmann, M., Gottschalk, H.: Entropy maximization and meta classification for out-of-distribution detection in semantic segmentation. In: Proceedings of the IEEE/CVF International Conference on Computer Vision, pp. 5128–5137 (2021)
4. Chen, L., et al.: Deep neural network based vehicle and pedestrian detection for autonomous driving: a survey. IEEE Trans. Intell. Transp. Syst. **22**(6), 3234–3246 (2021). https://doi.org/10.1109/TITS.2020.2993926
5. Cheng, C.H., Nührenberg, G., Yasuoka, H.: Runtime monitoring neuron activation patterns. In: 2019 Design, Automation & Test in Europe Conference & Exhibition (DATE), pp. 300–303 (2019). https://doi.org/10.23919/DATE.2019.8714971
6. Corbière, C., Thome, N., Bar-Hen, A., Cord, M., Pérez, P.: Addressing failure prediction by learning model confidence. In: Proceedings of the 33rd International Conference on Neural Information Processing Systems. Curran Associates Inc., Red Hook, USA (2019). https://doi.org/10.5555/3454287.3454548
7. Cordts, M., et al.: The cityscapes dataset for semantic urban scene understanding. In: Proceedings of the IEEE Conference on Computer Vision and Pattern Recognition (CVPR) (2016)
8. Cordts, M., et al.: The cityscapes dataset for semantic urban scene understanding. In: Proceedings of the IEEE Conference on Computer Vision and Pattern Recognition, pp. 3213–3223 (2016)

9. Deng, J., Dong, W., Socher, R., Li, L.J., Kai Li, Li Fei-Fei: ImageNet: a large-scale hierarchical image database. In: Proceedings of 2009 IEEE Conference Computer Vision and Pattern Recognition, pp. 248–255. IEEE, Miami, FL (2009). https://doi.org/10.1109/CVPR.2009.5206848
10. Dosovitskiy, A., et al.: An image is worth 16 × 16 words: transformers for image recognition at scale. In: 9th International Conference on Learning Representations, ICLR 2021, Virtual Event, Austria, May 3-7, 2021. OpenReview.net (2021). https://openreview.net/forum?id=YicbFdNTTy
11. Gal, Y., Ghahramani, Z.: Dropout as a Bayesian approximation: representing model uncertainty in deep learning. In: International Conference on Machine Learning, pp. 1050–1059. PMLR (2016)
12. Gerolymatos, S., Evangelopoulos, X., Gusev, V.V., Goulermas, J.Y.: Cluster exploration using informative manifold projections. In: ECAI 2024, pp. 2011–2018. IOS Press (2024). https://doi.org/10.3233/FAIA240717
13. Grigorescu, S., Trasnea, B., Cocias, T., Macesanu, G.: A survey of deep learning techniques for autonomous driving. J. Field Robot. **37**(3), 362–386 (2020)
14. Hashemi, V., Křetínský, J., Rieder, S., Schön, T., Vorhoff, J.: Gaussian-based and outside-the-box runtime monitoring join forces. In: International Conference on Runtime Verification, pp. 218–228. Springer (2024)
15. Hashemi, V., Křetínský, J., Rieder, S., Schmidt, J.: Runtime monitoring for out-of-distribution detection in object detection neural networks. In: International Symposium on Formal Methods, pp. 622–634. Springer (2023)
16. Hashemi, V., Křetínský, J., Mohr, S., Seferis, E.: Gaussian-based runtime detection of out-of-distribution inputs for neural networks. In: Runtime Verification: 21st International Conference, RV 2021, Virtual Event, October 11–14, 2021, Proceedings, pp. 254–264. Springer, Berlin and Heidelberg, Germany (2021). https://doi.org/10.1007/978-3-030-88494-9_14
17. He, W., Wu, C., Bensalem, S.: Box-based monitor approach for out-of-distribution detection in YOLO: an exploratory study. In: International Conference on Runtime Verification, pp. 229–239. Springer (2024)
18. Hendrycks, D., Gimpel, K.: A baseline for detecting misclassified and out-of-distribution examples in neural networks. In: International Conference on Learning Representations (2017)
19. Henzinger, T.A., Lukina, A., Schilling, C.: Outside the box: abstraction-based monitoring of neural networks. In: De Giacomo, G., Catala, A., Dilkina, B. (eds.) ECAI 2020 : 24th European Conference on Artificial Intelligence, pp. 2433–2440. No. 325 in Frontiers in Artificial Intelligence and Applications, IOS Press, Amsterdam, Netherlands (2020). https://doi.org/10.3233/FAIA200375
20. Hotelling, H.: Analysis of a complex of statistical variables into principal components. J. Educ. Psychol. **24**, 498–520 (1933)
21. Lakshminarayanan, B., Pritzel, A., Blundell, C.: Simple and scalable predictive uncertainty estimation using deep ensembles. Adv. Neural Inf. Process. Syst. **30** (2017)
22. Lee, K., Lee, K., Lee, H., Shin, J.: A simple unified framework for detecting out-of-distribution samples and adversarial attacks. Adv. Neural Inf. Process. Syst. **31** (2018)
23. Liang, S., Li, Y., Srikant, R.: Enhancing the reliability of out-of-distribution image detection in neural networks. In: International Conference on Learning Representations (2018)

24. Lin, T.Y., Dollár, P., Girshick, R., He, K., Hariharan, B., Belongie, S.: Feature pyramid networks for object detection. In: Proceedings of the IEEE Conference on Computer Vision and Pattern Recognition, pp. 2117–2125 (2017)
25. Lis, K., Nakka, K., Fua, P., Salzmann, M.: Detecting the unexpected via image resynthesis. In: Proceedings of the IEEE/CVF International Conference on Computer Vision, pp. 2152–2161 (2019)
26. Liu, L., et al.: Deep learning for generic object detection: a survey. Int. J. Comput. Vision **128**(2), 261–318 (2019). https://doi.org/10.1007/s11263-019-01247-4
27. Liu, W., Wang, X., Owens, J., Li, Y.: Energy-based out-of-distribution detection. Adv. Neural. Inf. Process. Syst. **33**, 21464–21475 (2020)
28. Liu, Z., et al.: Swin transformer: hierarchical vision transformer using shifted windows. In: Proceedings of the IEEE/CVF International Conference on Computer Vision, pp. 10012–10022 (2021)
29. Lukina, A., Schilling, C., Henzinger, T.A.: Into the unknown: active monitoring of neural networks. In: International Conference on Runtime Verification, pp. 42–61. Springer (2021)
30. Maag, K., Riedlinger, T.: Pixel-wise gradient uncertainty for convolutional neural networks applied to out-of-distribution segmentation. arXiv preprint arXiv:2303.06920 (2023)
31. Mardia, K.V., Jupp, P.E.: Directional statistics. John Wiley & Sons (2009)
32. Mo, Y., Wu, Y., Yang, X., Liu, F., Liao, Y.: Review the state-of-the-art technologies of semantic segmentation based on deep learning. Neurocomputing **493**, 626–646 (2022). https://doi.org/10.1016/j.neucom.2022.01.005, https://www.sciencedirect.com/science/article/pii/S0925231222000054
33. Morteza, P., Li, Y.: Provable guarantees for understanding out-of-distribution detection. In: Proceedings of the AAAI Conference on Artificial Intelligence. vol. 36, pp. 7831–7840 (2022)
34. Nayal, N., Shoeb, Y., Güney, F.: A likelihood ratio-based approach to segmenting unknown objects. Int. J. Comput. Vis. 1–13 (2025)
35. Nayal, N., Yavuz, M., Henriques, J.F., Güney, F.: RBA: segmenting unknown regions rejected by all. In: Proceedings of the IEEE/CVF International Conference on Computer Vision, pp. 711–722 (2023)
36. Oquab, M., et al.: DINOv2: learning robust visual features without supervision. Transactions on Machine Learning Research (2024)
37. Pinggera, P., Ramos, S., Gehrig, S., Franke, U., Rother, C., Mester, R.: Lost and found: detecting small road hazards for self-driving vehicles. In: 2016 IEEE/RSJ International Conference on Intelligent Robots and Systems (IROS), pp. 1099–1106. IEEE (2016)
38. Radford, A., et al.: Learning transferable visual models from natural language supervision. In: International Conference on Machine Learning, pp. 8748–8763. PmLR (2021)
39. Rai, S.N., Cermelli, F., Fontanel, D., Masone, C., Caputo, B.: Unmasking anomalies in road-scene segmentation. In: Proceedings of the IEEE/CVF International Conference on Computer Vision, pp. 4037–4046 (2023)
40. Salehi, M., Mirzaei, H., Hendrycks, D., Li, Y., Rohban, M.H., Sabokrou, M.: A unified survey on anomaly, novelty, open-set, and out-of-distribution detection: Solutions and future challenges. arXiv preprint arXiv:2110.14051 (2021)
41. Shoeb, Y., Nayal, N., Nowzad, A., Güney, F., Gottschalk, H.: Segment-level road obstacle detection using visual foundation model priors and likelihood ratios. arXiv preprint arXiv:2412.05707 (2024)

42. Shoeb, Y., Nowzad, A., Gottschalk, H.: Out-of-distribution segmentation in autonomous driving: problems and state of the art. In: Proceedings of the Computer Vision and Pattern Recognition Conference (CVPR) Workshops, pp. 4310–4320 (2025)
43. Sun, Y., Ming, Y., Zhu, X., Li, Y.: Out-of-distribution detection with deep nearest neighbors. In: International Conference on Machine Learning, pp. 20827–20840. PMLR (2022)
44. Szegedy, C., Zaremba, W., Sutskever, I., Bruna, J., Erhan, D., Goodfellow, I.J., Fergus, R.: Intriguing properties of neural networks. In: Bengio, Y., LeCun, Y. (eds.) 2nd International Conference on Learning Representations, ICLR 2014, Banff, AB, Canada, April 14-16, 2014, Conference Track Proceedings (2014). http://arxiv.org/abs/1312.6199
45. Thisanke, H., Deshan, C., Chamith, K., Seneviratne, S., Vidanaarachchi, R., Herath, D.: Semantic segmentation using vision transformers: a survey. Eng. Appl. Artif. Intell. **126**, 106669 (2023). https://doi.org/10.1016/j.engappai.2023.106669, https://www.sciencedirect.com/science/article/pii/S0952197623008539
46. Vaze, S., Han, K., Vedaldi, A., Zisserman, A.: Open-set recognition: a good closed-set classifier is all you need. In: International Conference on Learning Representations (2022)
47. Yang, J., et al.: OpenOOD: benchmarking generalized out-of-distribution detection. Adv. Neural. Inf. Process. Syst. **35**, 32598–32611 (2022)
48. Yang, J., Zhou, K., Li, Y., Liu, Z.: Generalized out-of-distribution detection: a survey. Int. J. Comput. Vision **132**(12), 5635–5662 (2024)
49. Zhao, J., Wu, Y., Deng, R., Xu, S., Gao, J., Burke, A.: A survey of autonomous driving from a deep learning perspective. ACM Comput. Surv. **57**(10), 1–60 (2025)
50. Zhao, Z.Q., Zheng, P., Xu, S.T., Wu, X.: Object detection with deep learning: a review. IEEE Trans. Neural Netw. Learn. Syst. **30**(11), 3212–3232 (2019). https://doi.org/10.1109/TNNLS.2018.2876865

CoCAI: Copula-Based Conformal Anomaly Identification for Multivariate Time-Series

Nicholas Andrea Pearson[1]([✉]) [iD], Francesca Zanello[2], Davide Russo[2], Luca Bortolussi[1] [iD], and Francesca Cairoli[1] [iD]

[1] University of Trieste, Trieste, Italy
nicholasandrea.pearson@phd.units.it
[2] Idrostudi srl, Trieste, Italy

Abstract. We propose a novel framework that harnesses the power of generative artificial intelligence and copula-based modeling to address two critical challenges in multivariate time-series analysis: delivering accurate predictions and enabling robust anomaly detection. Our method, Copula-based Conformal Anomaly Identification for Multivariate Time-Series (CoCAI), leverages a diffusion-based model to capture complex dependencies within the data, enabling high quality forecasting. The model's outputs are further calibrated using a conformal prediction technique, yielding predictive regions which are statistically valid, i.e., cover the true target values with a desired confidence level. Starting from these calibrated forecasts, robust outlier detection is performed by combining dimensionality reduction techniques with copula-based modeling, providing a statistically grounded anomaly score. CoCAI benefits from an offline calibration phase that allows for minimal overhead during deployment and delivers actionable results rooted in established theoretical foundations. Empirical tests conducted on real operational data derived from water distribution and sewerage systems confirm CoCAI's effectiveness in accurately forecasting target sequences of data and in identifying anomalous segments within them.

Keywords: Multivariate Time-Series · Anomaly Detection · Generative AI · Copula Modeling · Conformal Prediction

1 Introduction

Recent advances in sensor, network and storage technology have expanded opportunities for critical system monitoring and control, while also reducing data collection costs [1]. As a result, such campaigns have been carried out in a variety of critical domains, from urban and environmental engineering [16,27,40] to industrial applications [28,39], healthcare [15,20,36] and finance [22]. The data recorded over time by these systems allows for the creation of an ordered sequence of multiple interrelated values, commonly referred to as a multivariate time-series (MTS). These time-series play an essential role in monitoring the correct behavior of the system as they offer a near-real time representation of its state. These data can further facilitate the implementation of predictive alert systems designed to detect critical events at an early stage, enabling timely and targeted mitigating measures that reduce their operational costs and the likelihood of major failures [14]. In most fields of application, the sensors responsible for data collection are placed in challenging and uncontrolled locations, increasing the risk of environmental and operational damage, interference or total failure. If these factors are overlooked, the data recorded by these sensors may be corrupted or anomalous, yielding readings that do not fully reflect the system's true state. Undetected anomalous readings undermine the monitoring system's reliability, potentially generating false alarms or, more critically, failing to identify high-risk events. This degradation directly compromises the integrity of downstream data-driven decision-making processes. From a theoretical standpoint, an anomaly can be defined as "*an observation that deviates so much from other observations as to arouse suspicion that is was generated by a different mechanism*" [12]. More specifically, in the domain of MTS, anomalies may take the form of punctual observations or sequences of points which present patterns and characteristics which fail to conform to the expected behavior [9] and the available historic data. Anomalies and outliers in time-series data generally fall into two categories: measurement errors/noise or system events like failures or operational changes [4]. An accurate and timely identification of both is crucial. For noise, removing such artifacts ensures data integrity. For system events, early detection offers valuable diagnostic information, enabling data-driven interventions that can prevent operational disruptions or optimize system performance.

We propose CoCAI (Copula-based Conformal Anomaly Identification), a novel framework for multivariate time-series which allows for both a statistically valid imputation of any missing segment of the time-series and for the detection of anomalous patterns via a copula-based modeling approach. CoCAI's predictive component utilizes a score based diffusion model designed for time-series data [35] to generate imputations for any target segment of the multivariate sequence. To provide rigorous coverage guarantees, these imputations are then adjusted using a conformal prediction technique tailored for time-series [34]. After the predictive step, CoCAI computes deviations between predicted and observed values using a suitable distance metric, yielding a sequence that quantifies the differences from the predicted behavior. This sequence of discrepancies is then compressed via a dimensionality reduction technique that preserves temporal dependencies. By applying this procedure to a held-out dataset, we derive empirical distributions for each term in the low-dimensional representation. These distributions form the basis for estimating their joint distribution using copula modeling. Building on established theoretical results, including the Mahalanobis distance and the inferred joint distribution, CoCAI produces an intuitive, interpretable anomaly score. The *main advantages* of the proposed method are:

i. CoCAI provides accurate imputations for target data by leveraging score-based diffusion models in combination with conformal prediction, ensuring both high accuracy and statistically valid coverage guarantees.

ii. CoCAI offers significant flexibility, as imputations can be performed and calibrated across highly variable target windows, allowing it to adapt to different use cases and requirements.
iii. CoCAI provides a statistically sound anomaly score, allowing for flexibility in threshold selection and for ease of interpretation of the results. Furthermore, the anomaly detection step remains agnostic to the selected predictive model.
iv. Given the use of dimensionality reduction techniques, CoCAI scales well to longer forecasting windows.
v. At runtime, CoCAI introduces minimal computational overhead and can be deployed instantaneously after a one-time offline calibration.

Related Works. *Conformal prediction* has been widely applied to calibrate the output of runtime monitoring tasks [5–8,18,41]. Our work directly conforms the temporal outputs rather than a scalar assurance metric. *Anomaly detection* in time-series has been explored via next-step prediction [31] and statistical methods, including majority-voting in ensembles [37], copula-based approaches [17] and variational techniques [38]. Surveys [19,32] and domain-specific criteria [3] further contextualize the challenge of detecting distributional shifts.

Building on Sect. 2, we introduce the full CoCAI methodology in Sect. 3 and validate it through two real-world case studies (water distribution and sewerage systems) in Sect. 4.

2 Background

In this section, we first present the predictive model used for time-series imputation – a score-based diffusion model – along with the conformal inference framework which allows for the calibration of its predictions into statistically valid regions. We then introduce copulas and their role in modeling dependency structures, which is crucial for time-series analysis in both calibration and anomaly detection. Lastly, we provide a definition of the Mahalanobis distance and summarize its properties under known distributions. While diffusion models were selected for their flexibility and robustness, our method is general and can be adapted to other predictive models.

2.1 Diffusion Models for Time-Series Imputation

As probabilistic models, generative models learn to estimate the underlying data distribution from samples while preserving key statistical characteristics. Once trained, these models can be used to generate new synthetic observations which resemble the training data. Sampling from the learned probabilistic model involves drawing from a base distribution and transforming it into the desired output. Here, the neural network serves as a distribution transformer.

Denoising Diffusion Probabilistic Models (DDPMs) [13] are a type of deep generative models that have been shown to produce high quality samples in a variety of fields. DDPMs are trained in a two step procedure to learn an approximation of a true data distribution. In the initial forward process, data is gradually and iteratively corrupted by adding small amounts of Gaussian noise via a Markov chain ($\mathcal{K}$ iterative diffusion steps). In the complementary backwards process, a neural network is trained to gradually estimate and remove the noise at each step, learning an iterative procedure that allows the generation of clean samples starting from pure random noise.

More formally, let x_0 be data belonging to the unknown target data distribution $q(x_0)$, and let $p_\theta(x_0)$ be a model distribution that aims to approximate $q(x_0)$. As k approaches $\mathcal{K}$, the distribution of x_k converges to a standard Gaussian distribution. Starting from pure random noise, a data sample is generated by iteratively sampling from the reverse transition kernel $p_\theta(x_{k-1} \mid x_k)$ until $k = 1$. The learnable transition kernel introduced in [13] takes the form of a Gaussian whose variance is uniquely determined by the noise-injection parameter used in the forward process. Its mean additionally depends on a learnable denoising function, typically implemented as a neural network, that estimates the noise added to x_t.

With their work on Conditional Score-based Diffusion Models for Probabilistic Time Series Imputation (CSDI) [35], Tashiro et al. adapted DDPMs specifically for the task of time-series imputation. Let $x \in \mathbb{R}^{D \times L}$ be a multivariate time-series with missing values, where D and L represent the numbers of channels and timesteps respectively. It is possible to identify the missing values of x using a binary mask $M \in \{0, 1\}^{D \times L}$, where $M_{i,j} = 0$ if the corresponding element of x is missing. The task of time-series imputation focuses on estimating these missing values given the remaining observed values of the time-series. More specifically, the CSDI model takes as input the observed values of the multivariate time-series x, identified via the binary mask M, and a random noise initialization. Its output is a sampled realization of the target values of x, corresponding to the unobserved entities specified by M.

2.2 Conformal Prediction

Given the growth in popularity of predictive models in high-risk scenarios, it is often important not only to obtain an accurate forecast for the values of interest but also an estimate of the uncertainty associated with those predictions [2], in other words, a measure of their reliability. Uncertainty can be estimated via *conformal prediction* (CP), a framework that constructs predictive regions that offer statistically sound guarantees of covering the ground truth with a desired probability. CP is flexible enough to produce these regions starting from the output of most predictive models, requiring minimal assumptions on the data, namely exchangeability. A dataset of size n is said to be exchangeable if any of its $n!$ possible permutations are equally likely [34]. We here focus on regression problems. Let $\mathcal{I} = \{(x_i, y_i)\}_{i=1}^n$ be a dataset of exchangeable samples, where $x_i \in \mathcal{X}$ represents input variables and $y_i \in \mathcal{Y}$ denotes the corresponding target value. In *split CP* [2] we divide $\mathcal{I}$ into a training dataset $\mathcal{I}_T = \{(x_i, y_i)\}_{i=1}^m$ and a calibration set $\mathcal{I}_C = \{(x_i, y_i)\}_{i=m+1}^n$. Let $\hat{f}$ be a predictive model fitted on the training dataset.

CP revolves around a notion of nonconformity defined by a function that quantifies the discrepancy between the values predicted by the model and the ground truth. Let $\mathtt{ncf} : \mathcal{X} \times \mathcal{Y} \to \mathbb{R}$ be the selected non-conformity function (NCF) and let $\mathcal{S}_C$ be the set of non-conformity scores $s_i = \mathtt{ncf}(x_i, y_i)$ for all samples of the calibration set $\mathcal{I}_C$. Given an error probability $\alpha \in (0,1)$, under the assumption that $(x,y), (x_{m+1}, y_{m+1}), \ldots, (x_n, y_n)$ are exchangeable, CP computes a bound $b_\alpha : \mathbb{R}^{n-m} \to \mathbb{R}$ such that $\mathbb{P}(\mathtt{ncf}(x,y) \leq b_\alpha(s_{m+1}, \ldots, s_n)) \geq 1 - \alpha$, where $s_i = \mathtt{ncf}(x_i, y_i)$. From this bound over nonconformity scores, we can build a *prediction region* over target values, $\Gamma^\alpha(x; \mathcal{I}_C)$, by including all targets y' whose nonconformity scores are likely to follow the distribution of nonconformity scores for the true targets, i.e., have a nonconformity score lower than $b_\alpha(s_{m+1}, \ldots, s_n)$:

$$\Gamma^\alpha(x; \mathcal{I}_C) := \{y' \in \mathcal{Y} : \mathtt{ncf}(x, y') \leq b_\alpha(s_{m+1}, \ldots, s_n)\}. \tag{1}$$

This region is guaranteed to contain the true value y with confidence $1 - \alpha$:

$$\mathbb{P}\big(y \in \Gamma^\alpha(x; \mathcal{I}_C)\big) \geq 1 - \alpha. \tag{2}$$

We stress that the above guarantees are marginal, meaning averaged over the test and calibration data. They hold when (x,y) is exchangeable w.r.t. calibration data $\mathcal{I}_C$, i.e., when the joint probability of $(x_{m+1}, y_{m+1}), \ldots, (x_n, y_n), (x, y)$ is invariant to permutations. A natural choice to derive the upper bound b_α from the calibration nonconformity scores $s_{m+1}, \ldots s_n$ is the quantile function, i.e., $b_\alpha(s_{m+1}, \ldots, s_n) := \mathcal{Q}_{1-\alpha}(\mathcal{F}_C)$.

More precisely, given $\alpha \in (0,1)$, $\mathcal{Q}_{1-\alpha}(\mathcal{F}_C)$ denotes the $(1-\alpha)$-th quantile over the empirical distribution $\mathcal{F}_C = \frac{1}{n-m+1}\big(\sum_{(x_i, y_i) \in \mathcal{I}_C} \delta_{s_i} + \delta_\infty\big)$, with δ_{s_i} being the Dirac distribution centered at $s_i = \mathtt{ncf}(x_i, y_i)$ and ∞ is added as a correction to obtain finite sample guarantees.

For a generic real-valued random variable T, the quantile function $\mathcal{Q}$ is formally defined as $\mathcal{Q}_{1-\alpha}(T) = \inf\{t \in \mathbb{R} \mid \mathbb{P}(T \leq t) \geq 1 - \alpha\}$. A common choice as NCF for *regression* problems is the Euclidean distance, i.e., $\mathtt{ncf}(x_i, y_i) = \|y_i - \hat{f}(x_i)\|_2$. In *quantile regression* problems [29], where the model outputs a quantile range, i.e., $\hat{f}(x) = [\hat{q}_l(x), \hat{q}_u(x)] \subseteq \mathbb{R}$, a common NCF is $\mathtt{ncf}(x_i, y_i) = \max\{\hat{q}_l(x_i) - y_i, y_i - \hat{q}_u(x_i)\}$. For these particular NCF choices, the predictive interval is defined as:

$$\Gamma^\alpha(x; \mathcal{I}_C) = [\hat{q}_l(x) - \mathcal{Q}_{1-\alpha}(\mathcal{F}_C), \hat{q}_u(x) + \mathcal{Q}_{1-\alpha}(\mathcal{F}_C)], \tag{3}$$

where $\hat{q}_l(\cdot) = \hat{q}_u(\cdot) = \hat{f}(\cdot)$ in case of deterministic predictors. Intuitively, $\Gamma^\alpha(x; \mathcal{I}_C)$ enlarges or shrinks the quantile range by adding a value of $\mathcal{Q}_{1-\alpha}(\mathcal{F}_C)$ to both quantiles to correct for miscoverage. The guarantees in (2) hold regardless of the underlying data distribution, the choice of predictive model $\hat{f}$, or the accuracy of the chosen model [2].

2.3 Copulas and the Mahalanobis Distance

Let $X = (X_1, \ldots, X_d)$ be a multivariate random vector, with $F(x) = P(X_1 \leq x_1, \ldots, X_d \leq x_d)$ its joint Cumulative Distribution Function (CDF). Additionally, let $F_1, \ldots, F_d$ be the marginal CDFs of $X_1, \ldots, X_d$. By applying the probability integral transform to each element of X, we obtain the random vector $(U_1, \ldots, U_d) = (F_1(X_1), \ldots, F_d(X_d))$ whose marginals follow a uniform distribution on $[0, 1]$. With his work in 1959 [33], Sklar investigated the relation between joint CDFs and their marginals through copulas.

Definition 1. *A copula is a function $C : [0,1]^d \to [0,1]$ which satisfies the following properties:*

1. *For every $u = (u_1, \ldots u_d) \in [0,1]^d$, if there exists $j \in \{1, \ldots, d\}$ such that $u_j = 0$, then $C(u) = 0$.*
2. *For any $j \in \{1, \ldots, d\}$ and for any $u_j \in [0,1]$, if $u = (1, \ldots, 1, u_j, 1, \ldots, 1)$, then $C(u) = u_j$.*
3. *C is d-increasing: for any $a = (a_1, \ldots, a_d)$ and $b = (b_1, \ldots, b_d)$ in $[0,1]^d$ such that $a_j \leq b_j$ for all $j \in \{1, \ldots, d\}$, the C-volume $\Delta_{(a,b)} C$ of the hyper-rectangle defined between a and b is non negative. $\Delta_{(a,b)} C$ is computed as: $\Delta_{(a,b)} C = \sum_{v \in V} sign(v) \cdot C(v)$, where V is the set of 2^d vertices of the hyper-rectangle defined between a and b and $sign(v) := (-1)^{\sum_{j=1}^{d} \mathbb{I}(v_j = a_j)}$, with $\mathbb{I}(v_j = a_j)$ being an indicator function which is equal to 1 if $v_j = a_j$, and 0 otherwise [23,24].*

Sklar's Theorem [33] establishes that copulas link marginal distributions to their joint distribution, enabling flexible modeling of multivariate dependencies independent of individual marginals. Specifically, given a d-dimensional CDF F with marginals $F_1, \ldots, F_d$, there exists a copula C such that $F(x_1, \ldots, x_d) = C(F_1(x_1), \ldots, F_d(x_d))$. Since marginals are often easier to estimate, copulas alone suffice to model the joint distribution, allowing practitioners to choose from diverse copula families to capture varying dependency structures. We here introduce three different types of copula, defined for any $(u_1, \ldots, u_d) \in [0,1]^d$.

- **Independence Copula** represents the dependence structure of independent random variables and corresponds to the scenario in which the joint distribution is simply the product of its marginals: $C^I(u_1, \ldots, u_d) = \prod_{i=1}^{d} u_i$.
- **Gaussian Copula** models the full joint distribution as a multivariate normal entirely defined by the correlation matrix $\Sigma \in [-1, 1]^{d \times d}$:

$$C_{\Sigma}^{Gauss}(u_1, \ldots, u_d) = \Phi_{\Sigma}\left(\Phi^{-1}(u_1), \ldots, \Phi^{-1}(u_d)\right), \tag{4}$$

where $\Phi^{-1}(\cdot)$ is the inverse of a univariate standard normal CDF and $\Phi_{\Sigma}(\cdot)$ is the joint CDF of a multivariate normal distribution with mean vector zero and covariance matrix equal to the correlation matrix Σ.
- **Student's t Copula** models the full joint distribution as a joint CDF of the multivariate Student's t CDF with a zero mean vector, ν degrees of freedom, and a scale or covariance matrix equal to the correlation matrix Σ:

$$C_{\Sigma,\nu}^{Stud}(u_1, \ldots, u_d) = t_{\Sigma,\nu}\left(t_{\nu}^{-1}(u_1), \ldots, t_{\nu}^{-1}(u_d)\right), \tag{5}$$

where $t_{\nu}^{-1}(\cdot)$ is the inverse of a univariate Student's t CDF with ν degrees of freedom.

Remark 1. The Gaussian copula assumes symmetric dependencies but lacks tail dependence, limiting its ability to model joint extreme events. In contrast, Student's t copula captures symmetric tail dependence, controlled by its degrees of freedom (ν). Lower ν strengthens tail dependence, while $\nu \to \infty$ recovers the Gaussian copula with vanishing tail dependence.

The *Mahalanobis distance* measures how far an observation deviates from a known multivariate distribution. For a point $x \in \mathbb{R}^d$ and a distribution with mean μ and a covariance matrix Σ, the Mahalanobis distance $D_M(x) : \mathbb{R}^d \to \mathbb{R}$ is defined as $D_M(x) = \sqrt{(x-\mu)^T \cdot \Sigma^{-1} \cdot (x-\mu)}$. By using the inverse covariance matrix, it accounts for variable correlations, making it effective for outlier detection. If the distribution is multivariate normal, $D_M^2(x)$ follows a χ^2-distribution with d degrees of freedom [11]; for a multivariate Student's t-distribution, it follows a scaled $\mathcal{F}$-distribution with d, ν degrees of freedom [30].

3 Methodology

The proposed methodology (CoCAI) presents a novel and flexible framework which allows practitioners to obtain accurate predictive regions which offer statistically sound coverage guarantees for any target segment in a MTS. Starting from these regions, CoCAI also provides a statistically meaningful indicator allowing for the identification of out-of-distribution, and thus potentially anomalous, observations. CoCAI's main advantage lies in its flexible, three-phase pipeline, which can be tailored to better suit the specifics of the problem at hand. In the first part of the procedure, the *predictive phase*, an imputation model is used to obtain predictions for the target segments of the MTS. For this, we adopt the modified CSDI model from [25] to perform quantile regression on target data. In the subsequent *conformalization phase*, the resulting empirical quantile range is adjusted through a CP procedure specifically tailored for time-series, yielding a predictive region which offers statistically rigorous coverage guarantees. Figure 1-(a) shows the ground truth (blue), the quantile regressor outputs (dashed orange) and the conformal predictive region (orange shaded), which provides coverage guarantees. In the final *anomaly detection phase*, the distances between predicted and observed values are computed using a metric of choice (green dots in Fig. 1-(b)).

A dimensionality reduction technique which preserves temporal dependencies is then used on the resulting series, which, combined with copula models, provides a statistically sound indicator on how out-of-distribution, and thus potentially anomalous, a datapoint is, as depicted in Fig. 1-(b, c, d). It is important to note that the predictive phase is independent from the rest of the procedure, meaning that any kind of imputation model can be used as long as a suitable distance metric is used in the anomaly detection phase. Additionally, both the conformalization and anomaly detection phases require a one-time offline calibration step that does not require repetition during deployment. In the following, each component of the proposed pipeline will be described in detail.

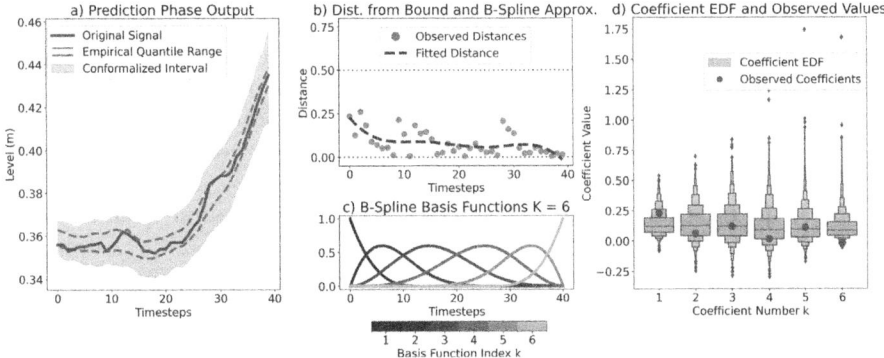

Fig. 1. (a): Ground truth (blue line), outputs of the quantile regressor (orange dashed line) and conformalized predictive region (orange shading); **(b, c)**: observed distances between predicted and observed values (green dots) vs. fitted using B-splines (purple dashed line); **(d)**: Empirical distribution of spline coefficients over an held out dataset (orange), observed coefficients for a test point (blue dots). (Color figure online)

3.1 Prediction Phase

Given a dataset of n elements $\mathcal{D} = \{\bar{x}^i_{1:T}\}_{i=1}^n$, where each $\bar{x}^i_{1:T} \in \mathbb{R}^{T \times d}$ is a multivariate time-series with d channels and T time steps, let $\mathcal{J} \subseteq \{1, \ldots, d\}$ be a non-empty index set such that $|\mathcal{J}| = d'$ and $d' \leq d$. Given $t \in \mathbb{N}$, where $1 \leq t \leq T$, we can define a prediction target as $y^i_{1:t,\mathcal{J}} = \{\bar{x}^i_{\tau,j} : \tau \in \{T-t, \ldots, T\}, j \in \mathcal{J}\}$ with $y^i_{1:t,\mathcal{J}} \in \mathbb{R}^{t \times d'}$ and $\bar{x}^i_{\tau,j}$ being the value of the j-th channel of the i-th series at time step τ. For simplicity, in the following we will refer to the i-th complete MTS $\bar{x}^i_{1:T}$ as $\bar{x}^i$, while its prediction target $y^i_{1:t,\mathcal{J}}$ will be referred to as y^i. Lastly we denote all of the elements of $\bar{x}^i$ which are not included in y^i as x^i. In this way we can express the full MTS as $\bar{x}^i = x^i \cup y^i$, with $x^i \cap y^i = \emptyset$, and allowing for a clear separation between the conditioning information x^i from the prediction targets y^i. As shown in Fig. 2, the full dataset $\mathcal{D}$ is split into a training set $\mathcal{D}_T$, used to train an imputation model, and two calibration sets $\mathcal{D}_{CP}$ and $\mathcal{D}_{AD}$ used respectively in the conformal prediction and the anomaly detection phase.

Generative Model. Following [25], the CSDI framework is used to obtain plausible predictions for our multivariate time-series data, with the objective of obtaining imputations for the target data y^i, conditioned on the observed values x^i. At training time CSDI learns an estimate for $p_\theta(y^i \mid x^i)$, the conditional probability distribution of the target values of the time-series conditioned on the observed ones, from $\mathcal{D}_T$. This is achieved using a self-supervised procedure where various portions of the MTS are masked or obscured and the model attempts to reconstruct them given the remaining observations. The choice of which parts to mask plays an essential role in defining what data patterns the model will be able to reconstruct in the inference phase and should ideally match the objective of the target application and the expected missing data patterns.

At inference time, the model generates multiple plausible imputations for the target data by repeatedly sampling from the estimated conditional distribution, using different random noise initializations. Each sample produces a distinct realization of the target value y^i, naturally capturing the uncertainty in the imputation process. From these imputations, we can derive either point estimates (using aggregate statistics like the mean or median) or uncertainty estimates (through empirical quantile ranges). While our methodology focuses on quantile-based approaches due to their ability to capture imputation uncertainty, the pipeline remains equally applicable to point estimates with minimal modifications.

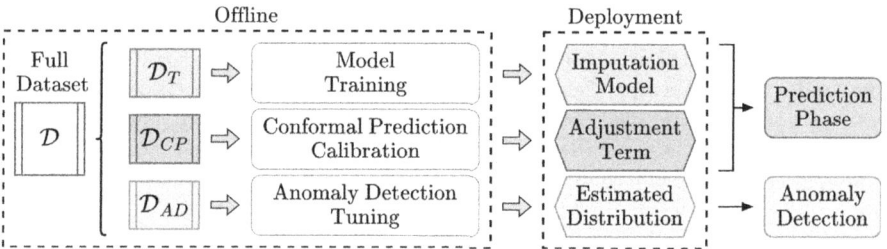

Fig. 2. Scheme of the CoCAI pipeline highlighting the offline and deployment steps

More precisely, for each target channel $j \in \mathcal{J}$ and each time step $\tau \in \{T - t, \ldots, T\}$, the ϵ-th quantile function, $\hat{q}_\epsilon^{\tau,j}(x^i)$, is computed as the ϵ-th empirical quantile extracted from the learned probabilistic output $p_\theta(y^i|x^i)$ at time τ and channel j. Given a desired confidence level $1 - \alpha$, we can denote an empirical quantile range (EQR) as $[\hat{q}_l(x^i), \hat{q}_u(x^i)]$ obtained by extracting, from the set of sampled imputations, the quantiles of order $\alpha/2$ and $1 - \alpha/2$ for each target channel and time step independently. In practice, $\hat{q}_l(x^i)$ and $\hat{q}_u(x^i)$ are two ($t \times d'$)-dimensional objects, i.e., $\hat{q}_*(x^i) = \{\hat{q}_*^{\tau,j}(x^i)\}_{\tau,j}$ for $* \in \{l, u\}$. The predictive region constructed in this way is a sequence of length t of d'-dimensional hyper-rectangles and, in general, does not provide the coverage guarantee of containing the ground truth with the desired confidence level.

Conformal Prediction. More formally, the extracted quantile range does not satisfy $\mathbb{P}\left(y^i \in [\hat{q}_l(x^i), \hat{q}_u(x^i)]\right) \geq 1 - \alpha$, where the condition $y^i \in [\hat{q}_l(x^i), \hat{q}_u(x^i)]$ is true only if, for every $\tau \in \{T - t, \ldots, T\}$, the true target y^i_τ falls inside the hyper-rectangle defined by the quantile range at time τ. To address this limitation, we use CopulaCPTS [34], a CP copula based approach tailored for multivariate and multi time-step time-series imputation tasks. CopulaCPTS leverages copula models to provide confidence intervals which are as small as possible while still satisfying the formal coverage guarantee. We adapt CopulaCPTS to operate on the probabilistic output of CSDI, constructing intervals starting from empirical quantile ranges. More specifically, we utilize the non-conformity score proposed in [29]: $\texttt{ncf}(x^i, y^i) = \max\{\hat{q}_l(x^i) - y^i, y^i - \hat{q}_u(x^i)\}$.

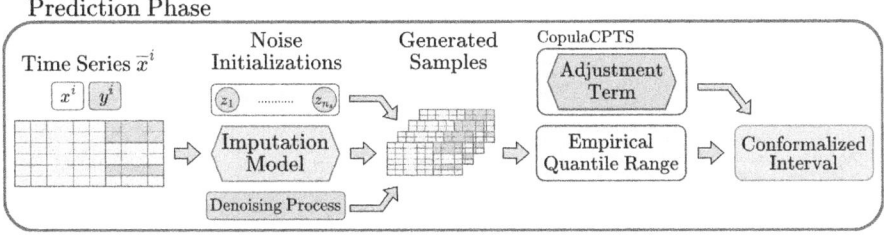

Fig. 3. Pipeline of the full prediction phase. Starting from a MTS, a set of samples is obtained for the target data using the imputation model. An EQR is then obtained from this set and further adjusted using CopulaCPTS to provide coverage guarantees.

In our experiments, the gradient-descent optimization proposed in Eq. 8 of [34] often led to unstable results, providing adjustment terms which present high variability over the time window. To address this issue, we employed the Trust-Region Constrained optimization algorithm [10], explicitly encoding efficiency as the objective to maximize, while still enforcing validity constraints. Further details on how our solution outperforms the gradient-based implementation proposed in [34] can be found in the appendix of [26].

By applying this adapted version of CopulaCPTS in the conformalization process on $\mathcal{D}_{CP}$, we obtain an adjustment term (assuming different values at each time step) that, when added to and subtracted from the upper and lower bounds of the original quantile range, provides the predictive interval $[\hat{q}_l^c(x^i), \hat{q}_u^c(x^i)]$. This interval is guaranteed to contain the ground truth values y^i over all time steps with the desired confidence level $1-\alpha$, while requiring the smallest possible adjustments to the original bounds. The main theoretical results presented so far can be summarized as follows:

Theorem 1. *Let $\mathcal{D}_{CP}$ be a dataset of exchangeable observations defined as in Sect. 3.1, and let (x^*, y^*) be a test observation such that $\mathcal{D}_{CP} \cup \{(x^*, y^*)\}$ remains exchangeable. Let $[\hat{q}_l(\cdot), \hat{q}_u(\cdot)]$ be an EQR derived from any pre-trained predictive model. The CopulaCPTS procedure calibrated on $\mathcal{D}_{CP}$ for a given confidence level $1-\alpha$ and the EQR produces an adjustment term yielding a predictive interval $[\hat{q}_l^c(x^*), \hat{q}_u^c(x^*)]$, as per Eq. 3, such that $\mathbb{P}(y^* \in [\hat{q}_l^c(x^*), \hat{q}_u^c(x^*)]) \geq 1-\alpha$. The condition $y^* \in [\hat{q}_l^c(x^*), \hat{q}_u^c(x^*)]$ holds if and only if, for every timestep τ in the target window, the true value y_τ^* falls within the hyper-rectangle defined by the corresponding predictive interval at time τ.*

3.2 Anomaly Detection Phase

Offline Tuning. Let $\mathcal{D}_{AD} = \{\bar{x}^i\}_{i=1}^m$ be a held-out dataset of MTS that do not present anomalies in their target data $\{y^i\}_{i=1}^m$. Following the pipeline described in Sect. 3.1, we obtain a conformalized predictive region $[\hat{q}_l^c(x^i), \hat{q}_u^c(x^i)]$ for each observation of $\mathcal{D}_{AD}$.

Distance Evaluation. For each observation $\bar{x}^i$, we compute the distance between the ground truth y^i and the closest bound of the corresponding interval for each target channel j and target time-step τ using $\delta^i_{\tau,j}$ defined as:

$$\delta^i_{\tau,j} = -\frac{d^i_{\tau,j}}{w^i_{\tau,j}} + 0.5, \text{ with } d^i_{\tau,j} = \max\left(\hat{q}^c_l(x^i)_{\tau,j} - y^i_{\tau,j}, y^i_{\tau,j} - \hat{q}^c_u(x^i)_{\tau,j}\right), \quad (6)$$

and where $w^i_{\tau,j} = \hat{q}^c_u(x^i)_{\tau,j} - \hat{q}^c_l(x^i)_{\tau,j} > 0$ is the width of the conformalized interval at target time-step τ and target channel j for observation i. This formulation ensures that $\delta^i_{\tau,j}$ is non-negative, taking values close to 0 when $y^i_{\tau,j}$ is near the midpoint of the interval and reaching a value of 0.5 as $y^i_{\tau,j}$ gets closer to either bound. Values greater than 0.5 indicate that the observation is outside the interval. For each observation i and target channel j, we can define a time-series $\Delta^i_j = \left(\delta^i_{1,j}, \ldots, \delta^i_{t,j}\right)$ which represents the relative position of the ground truth with respect to its predictive interval over the full target window.

Dimensionality Reduction. As the length of the target window increases, so does the value of t, leading to higher computational costs. In order to reduce the dimensionality of Δ^i_j, we choose a set of B-splines consisting of K cubic functions $\{\phi_k(\cdot)\}^K_{k=1}$ defined over the full target window with uniformly distributed knots. These basis functions are kept constant for all observations and target channels. By using $\{\phi_k(\cdot)\}^K_{k=1}$, we can obtain a smooth curve that approximates each term of the sequence Δ^i_j as:

$$\hat{\delta}^i_{\tau,j} = \sum_{k=1}^{K} \beta^i_{k,j} \cdot \phi_k(\tau). \quad (7)$$

The resulting curve maintains the structure of the original sequence Δ^i_j and is entirely defined by the coefficient array $B^i_j = \left(\beta^i_{1,j}, \ldots, \beta^i_{K,j}\right)$ of length K, with $K \leq t$. Given that by construction each basis function $\phi_k(\cdot)$ is non-zero only over a specific portion of the time domain, as is visible in Fig. 1-(c), the corresponding coefficient $\beta^i_{k,j}$ captures the behavior of Δ^i_j in that particular segment. This approach effectively preserves existing temporal dependencies as each coefficient $\beta^i_{k,j}$ maintains localized temporal information corresponding to the region of the target window where the basis function is non-zero. Given that the basis functions are fixed, each coefficient consistently represents the same temporal region across all sequences, with the full coefficient set providing a lower-dimensional representation. To determine the optimal number of basis functions K, we compute the residual sum of squares between the observed value $\delta^i_{\tau,j}$ in $\mathcal{D}_{AD}$ and its estimate $\hat{\delta}^i_{\tau,j}$ obtained with a range of different values of K. By representing these values with an elbow plot, we can identify the optimal value of K that balances reconstruction accuracy and number of parameters.

Empirical Distribution Function Estimation. By performing this procedure for each observation of $\mathcal{D}_{AD}$, we obtain m K-dimensional sequences B^i_j which approximate the original t-dimensional Δ^i_j. It is crucial to remark that $\mathcal{D}_{AD}$

exclusively consists of series which have been deemed to be anomaly-free. Consequently, the derived coefficient sequences B_j^i provide a low-dimensional representation of normal system behavior, capturing the patterns which can be observed in ordinary, non-anomalous conditions. Provided that the tuning dataset $\mathcal{D}_{AD}$ contains a sufficiently large number of representative observations, it is possible to accurately approximate the distribution of each coefficient $\beta_{k,j}$ using its empirical distribution function (EDF) $\hat{F}_{k,j}(\cdot)$.

Copula Modelling. Although these EDFs accurately capture the behavior of each coefficient $\beta_{k,j}$ independently, they fail to account for correlations or dependencies that may exist with other elements of the full coefficient vector. To address this limitation, we use the estimated EDFs $\hat{F}_{k,j}(\cdot)$ as a starting point for fitting Gaussian and Student's t copula models, providing an approximation of the joint distribution of the coefficients and preserving their dependency structure. Each observed coefficient $\beta_{k,j}^i$ is transformed using its corresponding EDF, yielding values $u_{k,j}^i = \hat{F}_{k,j}(\beta_{k,j}^i)$ which are, by construction, uniformly distributed on the interval $[0,1]$. By repeating this procedure for each observation i and each coefficient index k, we obtain a set of m sequences $U_j^i = (u_{1,j}^i, \ldots, u_{K,j}^i)$ which offer a suitable input for modeling both Gaussian and Student's t copulas.

In the case of the Gaussian copula the sequences U_j^i are further transformed by applying the inverse of a univariate standard normal cumulative density function (CDF) to each of their elements, obtaining $Z_j^i = (z_{1,j}^i, \ldots, z_{K,j}^i)$, where $z_{k,j}^i = \Phi^{-1}(u_{k,j}^i)$. The normalized values Z_j^i are used to estimate the empirical covariance matrix $\hat{\Sigma}_j \in \mathbb{R}^{K \times K}$, obtained by computing the Pearson correlation across all m observations for each pair of coefficients. In this setting, we assume that the dependence structure of the transformed scores Z_j can be adequately described by a multivariate Gaussian distribution. Recalling Sect. 2.3 and Eq. 4, the resulting Gaussian copula, which is uniquely determined by the correlation matrix $\hat{\Sigma}_j$, provides an estimate for the joint distribution of the coefficient set B_j by coupling the estimated EDFs with the multivariate Gaussian dependence structure. The resulting estimate for the joint distribution follows a multivariate Gaussian with mean vector zero and covariance matrix $\hat{\Sigma}_j$.

A similar procedure can also be employed for the estimation of Student's t copula, only requiring minor adjustments, namely the usage of the inverse Student's t CDF with ν degrees of freedom when computing $z_{k,j}^i = t_\nu^{-1}(u_{k,j}^i)$. In addition to the correlation matrix $\hat{\Sigma}_j$, this kind of copula also requires the estimation of the degrees of freedom parameter $\hat{\nu}$, determined through maximum likelihood estimation. In this scenario, we assume that the dependence structure of the transformed scores Z_j can be adequately described by a multivariate Student's t distribution. The resulting estimate for the joint distribution of B_j, as per Eq. 5, takes the form of a multivariate Student's t CDF with a zero mean vector, $\hat{\nu}$ degrees of freedom, and a scale parameter $\hat{\Sigma}_j$.

Deployment. Starting from these estimated joint distribution functions, it is possible to provide an anomaly score for a selected channel j of the target data

y^* of a previously unseen MTS $\bar{x}^*$. To ensure the validity of the process, it is essential that the target data y^* is defined using the same subset of channels $\mathcal{J}$ and target length t as in the previous calibration procedure.

Following the predictive procedure described in Fig. 3, we obtain a conformalized predictive region $[\hat{q}_l^c(x^*), \hat{q}_u^c(x^*)]$, which is then used to compute the series of distances to the target data y^*, as defined in Eq. 6. Using the B-spline basis functions described in Eq. (7), we obtain a K-dimensional representation of our distance series in the form of the coefficient series B_j^*. Each of its elements is transformed into a uniform value $u_{k,j}^* = \hat{F}_{k,j}(\beta_{k,j}^*)$ using the EDFs estimated in the tuning phase. These uniform values are then further transformed, yielding a score array Z_j^*, where $z_{k,j}^* = \Phi^{-1}(u_{k,j}^*)$ when a Gaussian copula is selected and $z_{k,j}^* = t_{\hat{\nu}}^{-1}(u_{k,j}^*)$ when a Student's t copula is used.

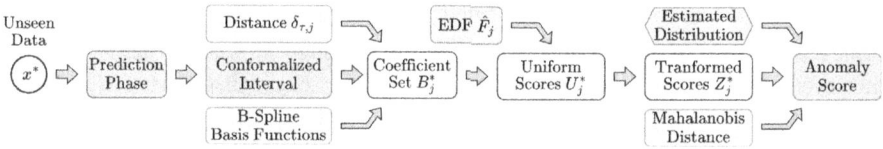

Fig. 4. Schema representing the full deployment pipeline of our methodology. Starting from a MTS, conformalized intervals are obtained via the prediction phase. A coefficient set providing a low-dimensional representation of the distances between target data and predicted interval is then obtained and transformed via the estimated EDFs, and then normalized wrt the selected copula model. Lastly, the Mahalanobis distance between the transformed coefficients and the estimated distribution yields an anomaly score.

We finally use these transformed values to compute an anomaly score by means of the Mahalanobis distance, a distance metric which quantifies the deviation of an observation from an existing and known distribution [21]. If the assumptions made on the dependence structure of the transformed scores Z_j introduced during the tuning phase are satisfied, the chosen copula model will provide an estimate for the joint distribution either in the form of a multivariate Gaussian or of a multivariate Student's t. Given that both these distributions have zero mean vector and $\hat{\Sigma}_j$ covariance matrix, following the definition in Sect. 2.3 it is possible to define the squared Mahalanobis distance for an observation Z_j^* as $D_M^2(Z_j^*) = (Z_j^*)^T \cdot \hat{\Sigma}_j^{-1} \cdot (Z_j^*)$. Known theoretical results demonstrate that in the case of a K-dimensional multivariate normal $D_M^2(Z_j^*) \sim \chi_K^2$ while for a Student's t with ν degrees of freedom it holds that $1/\nu \cdot D_M^2(Z_j^*) \sim \mathcal{F}_{K,\nu}$. These distributions allow us to set statistical thresholds for out-of-distribution detection. The complete deployment pipeline is illustrated in Fig. 4.

4 Experiments

To demonstrate the practical applicability of our approach, we now present experimental results using real-world data. Idrostudi srl has provided us with two real-world datasets which contain operational data from urban infrastructure monitoring campaigns. We have deliberately focused our experimental analysis on this data as it presents greater complexity and reflects the challenges encountered in real-world scenarios. The first dataset focuses on a Water Distribution System (WDS), while the second one is made of time-series derived from sewerage systems, also referred to as wastewater networks. Both systems are essential for local communities, but rely on aging networks which are difficult to maintain. Urban population growth, combined with more frequent extreme weather events due to climate change and widespread soil sealing are additional stressors for sewerage systems, potentially causing overflows with significant environmental and health risks. For WDSs, undetected leakages and pipe breaks can cause water loss, contamination and soil erosion, posing structural risks to nearby infrastructure. To monitor these systems, Idrostudi srl teams conduct campaigns which leverage strategically placed sensors, recording physical parameters every six minutes and providing MTS which accurately reflect the networks behavior.

4.1 Case Studies

Water Distribution Systems. For the WDS section of our experimental analysis, we focus on monitoring campaigns performed in Northern Italy, using data recorded by groups of three sensors which are placed in topologically connected locations within the same network. For each sensor, the physical parameters of interest are water *pressure* and *flow-rate* which were both used in our analysis, yielding a MTS with a total of six channels (as depicted in Fig. 5–left). This grouping strategy was selected to exploit both the correlations existing between different physical parameters measured by the same sensor and the spatial and temporal correlations between the recordings of topologically connected sensors.

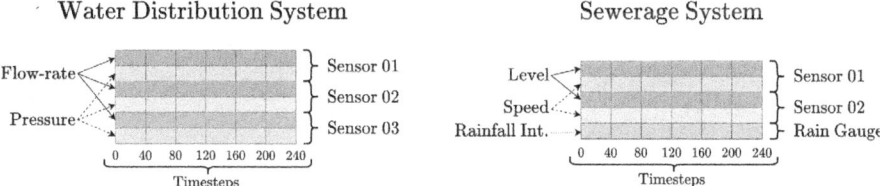

Fig. 5. Graphical representation of the multivariate time-series used in the experimental section for water distribution (left) and sewerage (right) systems.

Sewerage Systems. For the sewerage system we adopt a similar grouping strategy, pairing sensors which are placed in topologically connected sites within the same network into groups of two. In this scenario, the physical parameters of interest are the sewage's *level* and *speed*. Moreover, given that wastewater networks are also responsible for collecting stormwater, we also include rainfall intensity measurements taken from a surface rain gauge placed in proximity to the selected sensors. This setup results in a MTS with a total of five channels (as depicted in Fig. 5-right), which captures both the physical dynamics of the network and the effect of external environmental factors.

4.2 Experimental Setup

For both the WDSs and sewerage systems scenarios, we construct datasets composed by MTS covering a 24-h period. Given that a measurement is taken every six minutes, this translates into series with a total of 240 time steps (Fig. 5). The presented experiments focus on the task of contextual forecasting, a predictive approach that generates forecasts using historical values of target variables while leveraging both historical and known current information from other variables as additional context. Specifically, we perform imputations over the final four hours, or 40 timesteps, of a single target channel at the time. The chosen time window was selected in order to simulate the frequency of data transmissions from the data-loggers connected to the sensors and to emulate a near real-time anomaly detection framework. It is important to note that in the sewerage system case study, the channel containing rainfall intensity measurements only operates as contextual information and is not considered as a possible target channel. For the imputation task, we trained two separate CSDI models, one for WDSs and one for sewerage systems. To increase imputation flexibility, during training, the masking procedure is extended to allow for concurrent imputations on multiple channels and longer target windows. Considering that during precipitation events runoff is drained by wastewater networks, these systems present markedly different hydraulic behaviors in dry and wet weather conditions, with significantly higher recorded *level* and *speed* values during wet periods. Given these differences, we perform the CP calibration procedure separately for the two scenarios. This ensures that the calibration provides adjustments which are not over-inflated in dry weather and too conservative in wet conditions. This partition also remains in place for the AD tuning procedure of sewerage data in order to ensure consistency within the results.

4.3 Results

We present here results derived from applying the CoCAI framework to both test cases. For each scenario, we selected one sensor and separately applied the full procedure on both *level* and *speed* measurements for sewerage data, and *flow-rate* and *pressure* for WDSs. For brevity, for the sewerage system, we only present results in dry conditions. Hyperparameter selection was performed independently for the four test cases, with a value of $\alpha = 0.1$ always being used in the CP procedure. This value was chosen as it offered a reasonable trade-off between high coverage and small interval size. The other hyperparameters, i.e. the number of basis functions K and the value of the degrees of freedom parameter $\hat{\nu}$, were selected following what was presented in Sect. 3.2 and the chosen values are visible in Table 2. The degree of abnormality for each observation is

Table 1. Comparison of the median, average width, average relative width and data coverage percentage between the Empirical Quantile Range (EQR) and conformalized intervals across the considered datasets. The results highlight superior coverage for the conformalized interval, while only requiring minor adjustments.

	Obs	Median	EQR Avg. Width	Avg. Rel. Width (%)	Cov. (%)	Conformalized Interval Avg. Width	Avg. Rel. Width (%)	Cov. (%)
Sew. - Level	1295	0.452	0.008	1.92	1.62	0.026	6.10	**91.58**
Sew. - Speed	1301	0.358	0.024	6.84	2.77	0.058	17.05	**90.70**
WDS - Flow-rate	1613	53.27	2.82	5.14	0.25	7.14	13.24	**90.45**
WDS - Pressure	1604	7.50	0.03	0.35	2.24	0.07	0.92	**89.29**

quantified by two *anomaly scores* $a_G := 1 - p_G$ and $a_S = 1 - p_S$, where p_G and p_S correspond respectively to the p-values associated with the Mahalanobis distance of the transformed observation from the distribution derived from the test case-specific Gaussian and Student's t copula models. This formulation provides interpretable scores bounded within the interval $[0, 1]$, with values closer to 1 indicating stronger evidence for an anomaly. We evaluate the performance of the CoCAI pipeline from two complementary perspectives. First, we assess the quality of the predictive phase by evaluating the predicted conformalized regions. Table 1 shows the coverage rates for both the EQR and conformalized regions. These values represent the percentage of test time-series for which the target sequence falls within the respective interval over all timesteps simultaneously. The results show that the conformalized regions not only provide a significant improvement over the EQR, but also achieve the desired coverage rate for all four test cases. While this increase in coverage comes at the cost of marginally wider intervals, their width remains within satisfactory limits when compared to the target value. This is evident from a comparison between the absolute widths of the EQR and conformalized interval, where only a limited increment can be observed. An additional comparison of the relative widths, which also account for the scale the target values, confirms that the increase in interval size remains proportionally limited, as can also be seen in Fig. 6. The figure presents a qualitative evaluation of a selection of examples from all four test cases, where the left plot in each panel shows the ground truth for the target segment (blue line), the EQR (orange dashed line) and conformalized interval (orange shading). Green and red borders indicate if the observed values are fully covered by the conformalized interval or not. Additional plots with supplementary results can be found in the appendix of [26].

Second, we evaluate the anomaly detection component by analyzing which observations are flagged as anomalous by the computed scores. For both anomaly scores a_G and a_S, we select a threshold value of 0.9 and consider as potentially anomalous all series for which at least one of the scores is greater than 0.9. This value was selected for all four test cases in order to increase comparability between different datasets. Results presented in Table 2 and Fig. 6 show that there is generally strong agreement between the two anomaly scores, with a_S

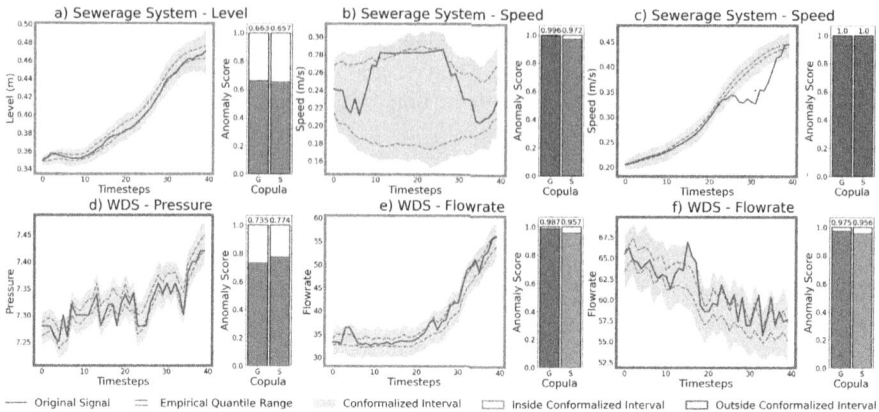

Fig. 6. Prediction and anomaly detection results for a set of time-series derived from sewerage networks (**a, b, c**) and WDSs (**d, e, f**). The left side of each panel shows the conformalized interval (orange shading), EQR (orange dashed line) and the observed target sequence (blue line). Green/red borders indicate if the observed values are fully covered by the conformalized interval. The bar plots in the right side of each panel represent the anomaly scores derived from Gaussian (left) and Student's t (right) copulas. (Color figure online)

usually proposing a more conservative output. This is to be expected given the heavier tails of the underlying distribution and results in the Student's t copula flagging as anomalous a number of series which is more aligned with what would be expected given the selected threshold. Limited variability within the proportion of flagged series across different test cases can also be observed, likely due to differences in the underlying characteristics of the time-series. In particular, noisier signals such as *speed* in sewerage systems and *flow-rate* for WDS data (Fig. 6-(b, f)), are more likely to be flagged as anomalous, especially by the Gaussian score. If necessary, this issue can be mitigated by setting case-specific threshold values as it enables tuning the sensitivity of the anomaly detection process based on the specific context and operational constraints. From Table 2 is also possible to note that a target segment which is not fully covered by the conformalized interval is more likely to have a high anomaly score than one which is. However, this is not the only criterion influencing anomaly detection. Figure 6 contains a collection of illustrative cases showing different combinations of anomaly scores and interval coverage. In particular we can observe that panels (b, e) show time-series which are fully covered by the conformalized interval but are flagged as potentially anomalous. Conversely, panel (d) shows an example which is not flagged as anomalous even if the observed value falls outside of the interval for at least one time step. This highlights the benefits of using both approaches concurrently, as they offer complementary insights in potentially anomalous data behavior. Lastly, domain experts from Idrostudi srl have

Table 2. Comparison of flagging rates for the anomaly scores of both Gaussian and Student's t Copula models while accounting for conformalized interval coverage rates over the considered datasets. Results for series which are not flagged are also shown.

	# obs	# basis	$a_G > 0.9$		$a_S > 0.9$		$a_G \leq 0.9 \land a_S \leq 0.9$	
			Inside Interval (%)	Outside Interval (%)	Inside Interval (%)	Outside Interval (%)	Inside Interval (%)	Outside Interval (%)
Sew. - Level	1295	15	110 (8.49)	73 (5.64)	25 79 (6.10)	63 (4.86)	1076 (83.09)	36 (2.78)
Sew. - Speed	1301	13	119 (9.15)	89 (6.84)	20 73 (5.61)	76 (5.84)	1061 (81.55)	32 (2.46)
WDS - Flow-rate	1613	15	163 (10.11)	85 (5.27)	11 91 (5.64)	70 (4.34)	1293 (80.16)	68 (4.22)
WDS - Pressure	1604	15	105 (6.55)	73 (5.55)	23 72 (4.49)	66 (4.11)	1327 (82.73)	99 (6.17)

examined representative results, including those in Fig. 6, validating the system's effectiveness, and confirming the presence of anomalies in Fig. 6-(b, c, e, f).

5 Conclusions

In this work we have proposed CoCAI, a novel and flexible framework for multivariate time-series. CoCAI leverages denoising diffusion probabilistic models combined with conformal prediction techniques to provide accurate predictive regions that offer statistically grounded coverage guarantees. These regions are then used alongside copula-based modeling to derive interpretable anomaly scores, enabling the detection of observations that deviate from the expected pattern. Through practical experiments on real-world operational data derived from sewerage and water distribution systems, we have demonstrated the pipeline's effectiveness in identifying potential anomalies. Furthermore, having the ability to set custom threshold values allows practitioners to tailor the flagging mechanism according to the constraints of the specific application. It is important to note that the current implementation of CoCAI applies the conformal prediction and anomaly detection phases separately for each channel of the multivariate time-series, as it does not yet support a fully multivariate approach for these stages. Given that the underlying predictive model already supports multivariate imputations, extending the full pipeline to operate in a full multivariate setting presents a promising direction for future work. Additionally, we also plan to evaluate the performance of CoCAI on multivariate time-series from other domains, such as medical data, as well as on standardized benchmark datasets.

Acknowledgments. This work has been supported by Idrostudi srl, who is funding the PhD scholarship of Nicholas A. Pearson. The authors also wish to thank Idrostudi srl for providing the operational datasets that enabled the experimental evaluation presented in this work and for their constant support and interest in this project.

This work has been partially supported by the PNRR project iNEST (Interconnected North-Est Innovation Ecosystem) funded by the European Union NextGenerationEU (Piano Nazionale di Ripresa e Resilienza (PNRR) – Missione 4 Componente 2, Investimento 1.5 – D.D. 1058 23/06/2022, ECS_00000043).

Disclosure of Interests. The authors have no competing interests to declare that are relevant to the content of this article.

References

1. Ahmed, S.F., et al.: Industrial internet of things enabled technologies, challenges, and future directions. Comput. Electr. Eng. **110**, 108847 (2023)
2. Angelopoulos, A.N., Bates, S.: Conformal prediction: a gentle introduction. Found. Trends Mach. Learn. **16**(4), 494–591 (2023). https://doi.org/10.1561/2200000101
3. Bertrand-Krajewski, J.L., Clemens-Meyer, F., Lepot, M.: Metrology in Urban Drainage and Stormwater Management: Plug and Pray. IWA Publishing (2021)
4. Boniol, P., Liu, Q., Huang, M., Palpanas, T., Paparrizos, J.: Dive into time-series anomaly detection: a decade review. arXiv preprint arXiv:2412.20512 (2024)
5. Cairoli, F., Bortolussi, L.: Scalable and reliable stochastic parametric verification with stochastic variational smoothed model checking. Int. J. Syst. Sci., 1–29 (2025)
6. Cairoli, F., Bortolussi, L., Paoletti, N.: Learning-based approaches to predictive monitoring with conformal statistical guarantees. In: Katsaros, P., Nenzi, L. (eds.) RV 2023. LNCS, vol. 14245, pp. 461–487. Springer, Cham (2023). https://doi.org/10.1007/978-3-031-44267-4_26
7. Cairoli, F., Kuipers, T., Bortolussi, L., Paoletti, N.: Conformal quantitative predictive monitoring of stochastic systems with conditional validity. Nonlinear Anal. Hybrid Syst. **57**, 101606 (2025)
8. Cairoli, F., Paoletti, N., Bortolussi, L.: Conformal quantitative predictive monitoring of STL requirements for stochastic processes. In: Proceedings of the 26th ACM International Conference on Hybrid Systems: Computation and Control, pp. 1–11 (2023)
9. Chandola, V., Banerjee, A., Kumar, V.: Anomaly detection: a survey. ACM Comput. Surv. (CSUR) **41**(3), 1–58 (2009)
10. Conn, A.R., Gould, N.I.M., Toint, P.L.: Trust region methods. Soc. Ind. Appl. Math. (2000). https://doi.org/10.1137/1.9780898719857. https://epubs.siam.org/doi/abs/10.1137/1.9780898719857
11. Ghorbani, H.: Mahalanobis distance and its application for detecting multivariate outliers. Facta Universitatis Seri. Math. Inform., 583–595 (2019)
12. Hawkins, D.M.: Identification of Outliers, vol. 11. Springer, Dordrecht (1980)
13. Ho, J., Jain, A., Abbeel, P.: Denoising diffusion probabilistic models. In: NIPS 2020. Curran Associates Inc., Red Hook (2020)
14. Hu, Z., Chen, W., Wang, H., Tian, P., Shen, D.: Integrated data-driven framework for anomaly detection and early warning in water distribution system. J. Clean. Prod. **373**, 133977 (2022)
15. Ketu, S., Mishra, P.K.: Internet of healthcare things: a contemporary survey. J. Netw. Comput. Appl. **192**, 103179 (2021)
16. Lanzolla, A., Spadavecchia, M.: Wireless sensor networks for environmental monitoring. Sensors **21**(4) (2021). https://doi.org/10.3390/s21041172. https://www.mdpi.com/1424-8220/21/4/1172
17. Li, Z., Zhao, Y., Botta, N., Ionescu, C., Hu, X.: COPOD: copula-based outlier detection. In: 2020 IEEE International Conference on Data Mining (ICDM), pp. 1118–1123. IEEE (2020)

18. Lindemann, L., Qin, X., Deshmukh, J.V., Pappas, G.J.: Conformal prediction for STL runtime verification. In: Proceedings of the ACM/IEEE 14th International Conference on Cyber-Physical Systems (with CPS-IoT Week 2023), pp. 142–153 (2023)
19. Liu, Q., Paparrizos, J.: The elephant in the room: towards a reliable time-series anomaly detection benchmark. Adv. Neural. Inf. Process. Syst. **37**, 108231–108261 (2024)
20. Majumder, S., et al.: Smart homes for elderly healthcare–recent advances and research challenges. Sensors **17**(11), 2496 (2017)
21. McLachlan, G.J.: Mahalanobis distance. Resonance **4**(6), 20–26 (1999)
22. Mhlanga, D.: The role of big data in financial technology toward financial inclusion. Front. Big Data **7**, 1184444 (2024)
23. Nelsen, R.B.: An Introduction to Copulas. Springer, New York (2006)
24. Okhrin, O.: Fitting high-dimensional copulae to data. In: Duan, JC., Härdle, W., Gentle, J. (eds.) Handbook of Computational Finance. Springer Handbooks of Computational Statistics, pp. 469–501. Springer, Heidelberg (2011). https://doi.org/10.1007/978-3-642-17254-0_17
25. Pearson, N.A., Cairoli, F., Bortolussi, L., Russo, D., Zanello, F.: Diffusion-based time series forecasting for sewerage systems (2025). https://arxiv.org/abs/2506.08577
26. Pearson, N.A., Zanello, F., Russo, D., Bortolussi, L., Cairoli, F.: CoCAI: lopula-based conformal anomaly identification for multivariate time-series (2025). https://arxiv.org/abs/2507.17796
27. Rashid, B., Rehmani, M.H.: Applications of wireless sensor networks for urban areas: a survey. J. Netw. Comput. Appl. **60**, 192–219 (2016)
28. Ren, S., Kim, J.S., Cho, W.S., Soeng, S., Kong, S., Lee, K.H.: Big data platform for intelligence industrial IoT sensor monitoring system based on edge computing and AI. In: 2021 International Conference on Artificial Intelligence in Information and Communication (ICAIIC), pp. 480–482. IEEE (2021)
29. Romano, Y., Patterson, E., Candès, E.J.: Conformalized Quantile Regression. Curran Associates Inc., Red Hook (2019)
30. Roth, M.: On the Multivariate T Distribution. Linköping University Electronic Press (2012)
31. Russo, S.A., et al.: Robust anomaly detection for time series data in sensor-based critical systems (2025)
32. Schmidl, S., Wenig, P., Papenbrock, T.: Anomaly detection in time series: a comprehensive evaluation. Proc. VLDB Endow. **15**(9), 1779–1797 (2022)
33. Sklar, M.: Fonctions de repartition an dimensions et leurs marges. Publ. Inst. Statist. Univ. Paris **8**, 229–231 (1959)
34. Sun, S.H., Yu, R.: Copula conformal prediction for multi-step time series prediction. In: The Twelfth International Conference on Learning Representations (2023)
35. Tashiro, Y., Song, J., Song, Y., Ermon, S.: CSDI: conditional score-based diffusion models for probabilistic time series imputation. In: Advances in Neural Information Processing Systems (2021)
36. Taylor, K.I., Staunton, H., Lipsmeier, F., Nobbs, D., Lindemann, M.: Outcome measures based on digital health technology sensor data: data-and patient-centric approaches. NPJ Digi. Med. **3**(1), 97 (2020)
37. Torfah, H., Joshi, A., Shah, S., Akshay, S., Chakraborty, S., Seshia, S.A.: Learning monitor ensembles for operational design domains. In: Katsaros, P., Nenzi, L. (eds.) RV 2023. LNCS, vol. 14245, pp. 271–290. Springer, Cham (2023). https://doi.org/10.1007/978-3-031-44267-4_14

38. Wang, X., Pi, D., Zhang, X., Liu, H., Guo, C.: Variational transformer-based anomaly detection approach for multivariate time series. Measurement **191**, 110791 (2022)
39. Wright, R.F., Lu, P., Devkota, J., Lu, F., Ziomek-Moroz, M., Ohodnicki, P.R., Jr.: Corrosion sensors for structural health monitoring of oil and natural gas infrastructure: a review. Sensors **19**(18), 3964 (2019)
40. Zanella, A., Bui, N., Castellani, A., Vangelista, L., Zorzi, M.: Internet of things for smart cities. IEEE Internet Things J. **1**(1), 22–32 (2014). https://doi.org/10.1109/JIOT.2014.2306328
41. Zhao, Y., Hoxha, B., Fainekos, G., Deshmukh, J.V., Lindemann, L.: Robust conformal prediction for STL runtime verification under distribution shift. In: 2024 ACM/IEEE 15th International Conference on Cyber-Physical Systems (ICCPS), pp. 169–179. IEEE (2024)

Monitoring Progress and Failure in Autonomous Robot Navigation: A Case Study

Vladislav Nenchev(✉) and Prodromos Sotiriadis

Department of Electrical and Computer Engineering, University of the Bundeswehr
Munich, Neubiberg, Germany
{vladislav.nenchev,prodromos.sotiriadis}@unibw.de

Abstract. As the deployment of autonomous robots expands, relying on complex decision-making policies – whether handcrafted or learned – raises concerns about their reliability. These policies are susceptible to vulnerabilities and bugs that can compromise operational integrity. This case study focuses on monitoring robotic navigation tasks, where a robot, driven by a black-box controller, must navigate towards a target. We compare three progress criteria – a simple distance metric and two variants of a stability certificate – and three finite horizon roll-out failure criteria. In laboratory experiments in both a free-space and an obstacle-field environment, one criterion combination detects true failures early with a low number of false alarms and outperforms classical heuristics at minimal computational cost. Our monitor uses only the filtered state and a finite horizon roll-out, providing formal progress/failure guarantees with low computational overhead.

Keywords: Monitoring · Progress evaluation · Failure detection · Autonomous vehicles · Robot navigation · Runtime verification for autonomy and runtime assurance

1 Introduction

The increased application of autonomous vehicles and robotic platforms across industrial, commercial, and consumer domains has been driven by advances in perception, learning, and control algorithms. However, as these systems grow in complexity, the operational reliability of their decision-making policies becomes increasingly difficult to guarantee [5]. In many deployed autonomous systems the navigation stacks include learned, proprietary or black-box components. Unanticipated disturbances, sensor faults, and software vulnerabilities can lead to navigation stalls, collisions, or mission-critical failures. These failures may compromise safety, undermine public trust, and hinder wider adoption of autonomy.

Runtime monitoring has emerged as a promising "second" layer of defense against these risks, providing an independent check on system behavior without requiring modification of the underlying controllers. By observing the robot's sensed or estimated state and comparing it against a safety or liveness specification, a monitor can raise alerts or trigger a safe fallback before a failure occurs. Traditional approaches use heuristic metrics such as distance-to-goal [26]), model-based certificates [22], and reachability analysis [34], but either lack anticipatory detection, assume white-box access to controller code and system architecture, or impose heavy computational burdens that hinder real-time onboard implementation. Traditional runtime-verification metrics were designed for logic-based monitoring and often fail to capture the behavior of Artificial Intelligence (AI)-driven systems, motivating the development of new performance measures and broader experimental validation [21]. Lyapunov-based stability certificates provide a scalar value, which must monotonically decrease along a safe execution. Because the stability certificate depends only on the robot's state and other external mission parameters, it can be evaluated without access to the controller's internals to obtain an analytically grounded indicator of whether the closed-loop system is converging or diverging from its goal [8]. Safety of a legacy controller can be achieved by enforcing these bounds, requiring to solve a Quadratic Programming (QP) online [2] and having access to the controller's input and output interfaces. However, using stability-based certificates as lightweight anticipatory runtime-verification metrics for black-box navigation has remained underexplored so far.

In this case study, we present a progress-and-failure monitoring approach using stability certificates for goal-oriented robot navigation. The monitor integrates key components into a unified approach: a discrete-time unicycle model capturing the robot's kinematics under bounded linear and angular velocities; a Candidate Lyapunov Function (CLF) computed offline to guarantee nominal decrease towards the goal; required data pre-processing, e.g., by an Extended Kalman Filter (EKF) for real-time state estimation under Gaussian noise; and checking criteria for progress and failure. We investigate *three* alternative progress checks and *three* alternative failure checks, each under quantified state uncertainty. Specifically, to monitor progress, we compare a lower distance bound (**P1**), a lower CLF bound (**P2**), and a lower CLF bound with horizon term (**P3**). Failure is checked in an anticipatory manner using a nominal goal-attainment and obstacle-avoidance controller to predict the robot's behavior over a finite horizon and evaluating an upper predicted distance (**F1**), an upper CLF bound with horizon term (**F2**), and an upper predicted CLF value (**F3**). Experiments on a four-wheeled ground robot in free-space and obstacle-cluttered scenarios show that both **P3** and **F3** incur few false positives and **F3** detects true failures earliest. By contrast, options **P1**, **P2**, **F1** and **F2** suffered from false positives, and **F1** and **F2** from later failure detection times. Thus, in the absence of policy assumptions, Lyapunov-based metrics may serve as promising indicators of progress or lack thereof.

This work advances runtime verification for embodied autonomy through the following contributions:

(i) A runtime monitor approach that requires only measured motion-relevant states and an offline-computed safety certificate, which avoids the need for white-box controller access or extensive online computation.
(ii) Presenting three alternative progress and three alternative failure criteria for reliable progress monitoring and early detection of failure under Gaussian-noise uncertainty.
(iii) Experimental validation and comparison on a ground robot in a laboratory environment that demonstrates earlier detection and fewer false positives compared to classical monitoring heuristics.

This paper considers static obstacles, planar motion, and Gaussian sensor noise. Extensions are possible for dynamic environments, more complex robotic platforms, and other disturbance classes. The primary focus of this case study is on empirical evaluation, while formal proofs of soundness and completeness are currently under development.

The remainder of the paper is organized as follows. Section 2 reviews related work in runtime verification and monitoring. Section 3 details the system model, the safety certificate design, required sensor data pre-processing, and the investigated progress/failure criteria. Section 4 presents our experimental protocol and results. Section 5 discusses advantages of the approach and possible future extensions, and Sect. 6 concludes the work.

2 Related Work

Runtime monitoring for autonomous robots utilizes a variety of techniques that trade off formal guarantees, computational cost, controller transparency, and assumptions about system and data access interfaces. Safety and security properties are typically defined in a formal specification language, and ensured by automatically generated monitors that compute a robustness score over observed states, e.g., [17,37]. Monitoring frameworks such as [12] allow portability across Robot Operating System (ROS) distributions and agnosticism w.r.t. the specification formalism, or adaptation to changing deployment requirements [4,15]. Interpretable rule-based monitors can check at run-time if the vehicle may become unsafe and plan safe corrective actions if found unsafe [13]. Runtime monitoring of safety requirements for time-bounded serial tasks has been enabled using time window temporal logic [3]. Although these monitors offer rigorous safety guarantees, they require at least gray-box system models and non-negligible onboard computation resources.

Reachability analysis typically computes backward-reachable sets offline using Hamilton–Jacobi partial differential equations, which yield a safe tube of states guaranteed to reach the goal without violating constraints [6]. During execution runtime monitoring reduces to a table lookup to verify state inclusion. However, the dimensionality of realistic vehicle models and the memory footprint of the lookup tables limit feasibility on resource-constrained embedded platforms.

Runtime monitoring for robotic perception, including anomaly detection in learned vision models and consistency checks on sensor outputs has received considerable attention recently [31]. Online model-based monitoring of spatiotemporal properties for imprecise signals [35] and of Signal Temporal Logic (STL) specifications [38] have also been addressed. Model-based runtime monitors that combine learning an expert policy and comparing it to the robot's actual action to flag deviations before safety is compromised have also been proposed [24]. Consistency and progress in generative controllers have been monitored using large-language or vision models to detect spurious or regressing behavior [1], but remain largely exploratory and require further validation on robot platforms.

Optimization-based planning frameworks have also incorporated runtime monitoring loops to correct potential future specification violations. *Control Barrier Functions* (CBFs) can be used to enforce forward invariance of safe sets by solving a quadratic program at each timestep (e.g., [2]). Model Predictive Control (MPC)-based safety envelopes generate short-horizon predictions under bounded disturbances, thus, translating feasibility of reaching the goal into a receding-horizon safety certificate, e.g., [20]. STL specifications have been translated into mixed-integer linear constraints, to generate reference trajectories, and then use an event-triggered MPC to correct planned trajectories on-the-fly [23]. While these monitors can handle complex constraints and nonlinearities, real-time optimization imposes significant computational overhead or may require specialized hardware.

Lyapunov-based certificates are typically used offline to assess controller stability and safety. A unicycle-based path-following controller in cluttered environments extends Lyapunov arguments to incorporate forward invariance around a given path [33]. However, these methods often require full controller knowledge or entail continuous optimization, making them ill-suited for black-box navigation policies or noisy sensor data. Data-driven Lyapunov learning approaches train a parameterized Lyapunov function on demonstration data, followed by offline validation to ensure decrease properties [32]. Learned certificates [9,16] avoid the dependence on closed-form mathematical models but may lack formal guarantees outside the training data distribution.

In the context of autonomous driving, analytical safety bounds were used for trajectory-following controllers by quantifying model mismatch and disturbance effects at the trajectory level [19]. Code-level verification was achieved by model checking embedded adaptive cruise controllers [27,29], which also enabled software portability checking across different vehicle hardware configurations [28] and compositional reasoning of simultaneously operating automated driving controllers [30]. These methods yield correctness proofs but are infeasible when source code or internal models are inaccessible.

Our work differentiates itself from classical runtime verification monitors, which rely on temporal-logic robustness, incur significant buffering/evaluation overhead, and provide logical guarantees, in two key ways: (i) we employ an offline-computed closed-form stability candidate certificate that incorporates actuator limits, a nominal robot motion model and sensor-based state estimates at runtime, thus, avoiding expensive online computation, and (ii) we derive and compare multiple progress checks and finite horizon failure checks under Gaussian-noise uncertainty, ultimately selecting the best performing variants (with low false positives, earliest failure detection). This yields a lightweight monitor requiring only state estimates and no white-box controller access, well suited for black-box robotic navigation under both static and dynamically discovered obstacles.

3 Monitor Design

The goal of this work is to monitor progress and failure in robot navigation. This section presents the key components of the approach as shown in Fig. 1, integrating a discrete-time robot motion model, state estimation, designing a stability certificate, and deriving criteria. The progress and failure criteria are checked under Gaussian noise and bounded control inputs. Further, failure criteria are evaluated over a finite horizon.

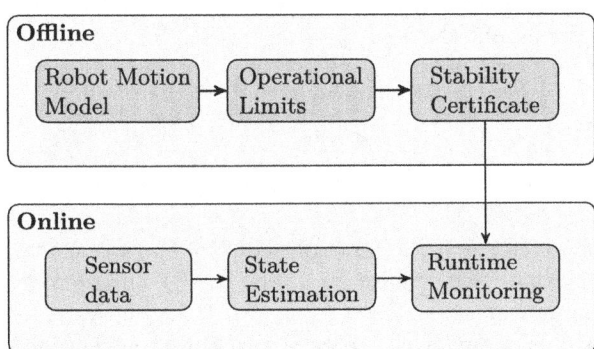

Fig. 1. Overview of the monitoring pipeline: In the *Offline* stage (top) the stability certificate is synthesized from the robot motion model and input limits; in the *Online* stage (bottom) the estimated state is used to compute the certificate value to perform runtime monitoring.

3.1 System Model and Operational Limits

At time k, the robot's state contains its two-dimensional position x_k, y_k and heading (yaw) angle θ_k, measured from the global x-axis. The control signals are the linear velocity v_k and the angular velocity ω_k.

As a system model, we adopt the discrete-time unicycle with:

$$\xi_k = \begin{bmatrix} x_k \\ y_k \\ \theta_k \end{bmatrix}, \quad u_k = \begin{bmatrix} v_k \\ \omega_k \end{bmatrix}, \quad \xi_{k+1} = f(\xi_k, u_k) = \begin{bmatrix} x_k + v_k \cos\theta_k \, \Delta t \\ y_k + v_k \sin\theta_k \, \Delta t \\ \theta_k + \omega_k \, \Delta t \end{bmatrix}, \quad (1)$$

where Δt is the sampling time interval. The system's operation is constrained, where the state is bounded by $\xi_{min} \leq \xi_k \leq \xi_{max}$ and the control is bounded by $u_{min} \leq u_k \leq u_{max}$.

Obstacles are modeled as a finite set of m circular regions in the plane:

$$\mathcal{O} = \bigcup_{i=1}^{m} \left\{ p = [x,y]^T \mid \|p - c_i\| \leq r_i \right\},$$

where each obstacle i is centered at $c_i \in \mathbb{R}^2$ with radius $r_i > 0$. We define the *free workspace* as

$$\mathcal{W}_{\text{free}} = \left\{ p \in \mathbb{R}^2 \mid \forall i, \|p - c_i\| > r_i \right\},$$

and require the robot's planar position $[x_k, y_k]^T \in \mathcal{W}_{\text{free}}$ at all times. These circular obstacles enter the employed stability certificate as repulsive barrier terms as shown in the following.

3.2 Stability Certificate

We apply a stability certificate directly to the state ξ. We adopt the rotated-error quadratic function about the goal $\xi_g = [x_g, y_g, \theta_g]^T$:

$$\begin{aligned}L(x,y,\theta) =& (\cos\theta_g\,(x - x_g) + \sin\theta_g\,(y - y_g))^2 \\ &+ (-\sin\theta_g\,(x - x_g) + \cos\theta_g\,(y - y_g))^2 \\ &+ \frac{1}{\gamma}\,\mathrm{wrapToPi}(\theta - \theta_g)^2,\end{aligned} \quad (2)$$

where γ is a parameter and the function wrapToPi wraps the angle to $(-\pi, \pi]$. The function (2) is positive definite about (x_g, y_g, θ_g) – it is zero at the goal pose, and grows when moving away. For it to be a CLF for the system (1), we want to empirically verify that under the robot's (black-box) navigation controller, the function will decrease.

To handle static obstacles, we augment the function (2) with repulsive barrier terms. Let there be m circular obstacles with centers $c_i \in \mathbb{R}^2$ and radii $r_i > 0$. Then, we define the extended CLF

$$V(\xi) = L(\xi) + \sum_{i=1}^{m} \frac{\alpha_i}{\|p - c_i\|^2 - r_i^2 + \varepsilon}, \quad p = [x,y]^T, \quad (3)$$

where $L(\xi)$ comes from (2), $\alpha_i > 0$ is a repulsion and $\varepsilon \ll 1$ a regularization parameter. Each barrier term $\alpha_i/(\|p - c_i\|^2 - r_i^2 + \varepsilon)$ increases as the robot approaches the obstacle boundary, thus penalizing unsafe states.

By construction, $V(\xi)$ is positive definite with respect to the goal and diverges only in the close vicinity of an obstacle. At runtime, we compute the one-step increment $\Delta V = V(\hat{\xi}_{k+1}) - V(\hat{\xi}_k)$ and its standard deviation $\sigma = \sqrt{g^\top \Sigma_k g}$, where $g = \nabla_\xi V(\hat{\xi}_k)$ includes both goal-error and barrier gradients. This composite certificate simultaneously encourages convergence to the goal and avoidance of obstacles under quantified estimation uncertainty.

3.3 Sensor Data and State Estimation

For onboard deployment, filtered state estimates (e.g., pose and covariance) may be available (e.g., from the robot's built-in localization module) and the monitor can subscribe directly to these. However, if additional redundancy and independence from the onboard software stack are desired, or if the monitor is to be deployed offboard, sensor fusion approaches have to be used to produce state $\hat{\xi}_k$ and covariance Σ_k estimates at each timestep. Appendix A summarizes how these can be obtained using an EKF and the model (1).

3.4 Progress Criteria

Define at time k:

$$V_k = V(\hat{\xi}_{k|k}), \quad \mu_k = V_{k+1} - V_k, \quad g_k = \nabla_\xi V(\hat{\xi}_{k|k}), \quad \sigma_k = \sqrt{g_k^T \Sigma_{k|k} g_k},$$

and let β denote the corresponding Gaussian quantile factor. Let the robot have at most N discrete steps for maximal mission execution, e.g., imposed by battery limitations. At time k, there are only $(N-k)$ steps remaining. We assume a nominal horizon of length M to bring the CLF to zero. Thus, we define the prediction horizon

$$H_k = \min\{M, N-k\}. \quad (4)$$

We consider the following three progress checks with a small threshold ε_P:

P1 (Lower distance bound): Define $e_{x,k} = x_k - x_g, e_{y,k} = y_k - y_g, e_{\theta,k} = \text{wrapToPi}(\theta_k - \theta_g)$, and

$$d_k = \sqrt{e_{x,k}^2 + e_{y,k}^2 + \kappa^2 e_{\theta,k}^2} + \sum_{i=1}^{m} \frac{\alpha_i}{\|p - c_i\|^2 - r_i^2 + \varepsilon}, \quad p = [x, y]^\top. \quad (5)$$

Linearize $d(\hat{\xi}_{k|k})$ to obtain gradient $h_k = \nabla_\xi d(\hat{\xi}_{k|k})$ and variance $\sigma_{d,k}^2 = h_k^T (\Sigma_{k|k} + \Sigma_{k+1|k}) h_k$. Then, progress is sufficient, if the lower bound of the distance change $\Delta d(k) = d_{k+1} - d_k - \beta \sigma_{d,k} < \varepsilon_P$.

P2 (Lower CLF bound): Let the one-step lower bound quantile of ΔV_k be given by

$$\Delta V_l(k) = \mu_k - \beta \sigma_k.$$

Then, progress is sufficient, if $\Delta V_l(k) < \varepsilon_P$.

P3 (Lower CLF bound with Horizon Term): With the one-step lower bound quantile of ΔV_k given by $\Delta V_l(k)$, in order for $V_{k+1} \leq V_k - V_k/H_k$, we additionally require at least a fraction of a decrease per step of the CLF value, i.e.,

$$\Delta V_{l,\text{ext}}(k) = \Delta V_l(k) + \frac{V_k}{H_k},$$

where H_k is as specified in (4). If $\Delta V_{l,\text{ext}}(k) > 0$, even the best-case one-step drop cannot force V to zero in H_k steps. Thus, progress is sufficient, if $\Delta V_{l,\text{ext}}(k) < \varepsilon_P$.

3.5 Failure Criteria

As the robot may operate in dynamic or partially-known environments, computing full reachable sets can be prohibitively expensive and overly conservative whenever obstacles move or new information arrives. Therefore, at each step, we opt for a finite horizon roll-out of a nominal controller to adapt to newly sensed obstacles, which requires only a few milliseconds to simulate on embedded hardware and captures likely future behavior sufficiently accurate to predict failure. We use a standard reactive controller $\pi(\xi)$ (Appendix B) for the model (1) to generate finite horizon predictions. Note that the main requirement for this controller is that it guarantees reliable navigation to the goal x_g and avoids obstacles on the way. Assuming the upper bound of the considered state quantile $\xi_{k|k} = \hat{\xi}_{k|k} + \beta \sigma_k$ and the uncertainty $\Sigma_{k|k}$ as initial values, we simulate forward both the state and covariance for H_k steps:

$$\xi_{i+1|k} = f\big(\xi_{i|k}, \pi(\xi_{i|k})\big), \quad \Sigma_{i+1|k} = A_i \, \Sigma_{i|k} \, A_i^T + Q_w, i = k, \ldots, k + H_k - 1. \tag{6}$$

Then, we compare the following failure criteria evaluated with a small threshold ε_F:

F1 (Upper predicted distance): With (5) and the horizon length (4), failure is likely, if the distance to the goal after H_k steps is $\|d_{k+H_k}(k)\| > \varepsilon_F$.

F2 (Upper CLF bound with horizon term): Let the one-step pessimistic quantile of ΔV_k be augmented by a horizon term, yielding

$$\Delta V_{u,\mathrm{ext}}(k) - \mu_k + \beta \sigma_k - \frac{V_k}{H_k},$$

When the final deadline nears, but the CLF does not approach zero, failure is likely, i.e., formally, $\|\Delta V_{u,\mathrm{ext}}(k)\| > \varepsilon_F$.

F3 (Upper predicted CLF value): At time $k + H_k$, failure is likely, if when starting at the upper bound of the state estimate quantile, the predicted CLF value after H_k steps is $\|V_{k+H_k}(k)\| > \varepsilon_F$.

3.6 Runtime Monitoring Algorithm

At runtime, the monitor executes two checks at each step – one for dynamic progress and one for finite horizon failure – both accounting for state-estimate uncertainty.

Here, the *progress check* ensures that even the best-case Lyapunov drop remains negative, filtering out spurious spikes; the *failure check* predicts the system evolution over a finite horizon to catch stall behavior. This loop runs in real time, requires only EKF outputs, and raises an alert as soon as either condition is violated.

Algorithm 1. Model-Based Runtime Monitor

1: **Offline:**
2:   Choose horizon M, sampling time Δt, confidence factor β.
3: **Init:**
4:   Initialize filter $\hat{\xi}_0, \Sigma_0$, compute $V_0 = V(\hat{\xi}_0)$.
5: **for** $k = 1, 2, \ldots$ **do**
6:   Run filter to obtain $\hat{\xi}_k, \Sigma_k$.
7:   Compute CLF value $V_k = V(\hat{\xi}_k)$ and one-step increment $\mu_k = V_k - V_{k-1}$.
8:   Compute gradient $g_k = \nabla_\xi V(\hat{\xi}_k)$ and $\sigma_k = \sqrt{g_k^\top \Sigma_k g_k}$.
9:   **Check progress by evaluating** $P \in \{\mathbf{P1, P2, P3}\}$
10: **Check failure by evaluating** $F \in \{\mathbf{F1, F2, F3}\}$
11: **end for**

4 Experimental Evaluation

To demonstrate the reliability of our runtime-monitoring approach, we conducted an extensive evaluation of all six candidate checks (three for progress, three for failure) on a differential-drive robot navigating toward a fixed goal in a laboratory environment. We defined two distinct test scenarios – free-space and obstacle-field motion – and in each scenario varied both the robot's initial pose and the length of the prediction horizon. In every trial, the robot's task was to drive from its start pose to a specified target while maintaining collision-free operation. We recorded whether and when each monitor variant issued an alert, measured detection lead time relative to the true event, and produced false alerts.

4.1 Experimental Setup

(a) Freespace navigation.   (b) Navigation with obstacles.

Fig. 2. Laboratory arena with four-wheeled differential-drive robot moving to a goal area (marked in red, upper right) in (a) free-space and (b) obstacle field. (Color figure online)

Robot Platform. Tests were run on a four-wheeled differential-drive robot [10] (shown in Figs. 2a and 2b) developed at our institute at the University of the Bundeswehr Munich – with a footprint 0.44×0.4 m and mass of 5 kg. Its main onboard hardware relevant for the data generation includes:

- Quadrature wheel encoders (in single edge mode by one channel with 16 pulses/rev) for odometry
- An ITG-3200 gyroscope providing data at 10 Hz for full-scale $\pm 2000\,°/s$
- A Hokuyo URG-04LX 2D LiDAR (0.06–4.095 m range, 0.36° angular resolution and Field of View 240°) measuring at a rate 10 Hz;
- Onboard STM32F746ZG-Nucleo board with an ARM® 32-bit Cortex®-M7 CPU with FPU, configured for real-time control 1000 Hz;
- A Raspberry Pi 4B with 8 GB RAM running ROS 2;
- Actuator bounds $v \in [-0.26, 0.26]$ m/s, $\omega \in [-1, 1]$ rad/s;
- Operation state space limited to $x, y \in [-4, 4] \times [-3, 3]$ m, $\theta \in [-\pi, \pi]$.

Based on the described sensor setup and computing units, we set $\Delta t = 0.1$ s. We ran the ROS 2 stack [25] as a baseline planner and interfaced our monitor as an independent lifecycle node running offboard.

Filter Tuning. The process-noise covariance is empirically set to $Q_w = 10^{-3}I_3$, the measurement covariance to $R_v = \mathrm{diag}(10^{-3}, 10^{-3}, 10^{-3}, 10^{-2}I_m)$, where m is the number of LiDAR ranges. The resulting EKF state-estimate uncertainty $\Sigma_{k|k}$ is used to compute σ_k.

Parameters. The angle-error weight was chosen as $\gamma = 2.0$. The obstacle-barrier terms (3) use $\alpha_i = 0.5$ and $\varepsilon = 10^{-4}$. Controller repulsion influence distance is $d_{\mathrm{rep}} = 0.5$ m with $\eta_i = 0.1$ and a blending parameter $\alpha = 1$. The following thresholds were used: $\varepsilon_P = 0.01$, $\varepsilon_F = 0.02$ m. A trace length of $N = 100$ was recorded and a horizon length of $M = 25$ was selected. As a confidence factor, we chose $\beta = \sqrt{\chi^2_{3, 0.95}} \approx 2.796$ to form 95% quantile bounds on ΔV.

4.2 Navigation Scenarios

We tested two distinct scenarios within the robot's operating state space (Fig. 2):

(i) **Free-Space:** Start at $(-0.005, -0.0015)$ m, goal at $(2.3564, 0.6611)$ m, no obstacles in the direct line of sight.
(ii) **Obstacle Field:** Same start and goal positions, but with static obstacles along the straight-line corridor.

For each scenario, four different initial vehicle orientations were chosen to ensure robustness to pose variation and three different goals as shown in Fig. 3 to cover different operation failure types, resulting in an overall 12 runs.

Table 1. Experimental metrics by progress and failure criteria

Free-Space Scenario			
Criterion	Lead Time (s)	False Pos. (%)	False Neg. (%)
P1 (low-dist)	–	40.0	0.0
P2 (low-Lyap)	–	0.0	3.3
P3 (low–Lyap-horizon)	–	0.0	0.0
Failure criterion	Lead Time (s)	False Pos. (%)	False Neg. (%)
F1 (upper-pred-dist)	0.1 ± 0.1	6.7	10.0
F2 (upper-Lyap-horizon)	0.2 ± 0.1	3.3	6.7
F3 (upper-pred-Lyap)	0.5 ± 0.2	0.0	0.0
Obstacle-Field Scenario			
Progress criterion	Lead Time (s)	False Pos. (%)	False Neg. (%)
P1 (low-dist)	–	50.0	0.0
P2 (low-Lyap)	–	3.3	6.7
P3 (low-Lyap-horizon)	–	3.3	0.0
Failure criterion	Lead Time (s)	False Pos. (%)	False Neg. (%)
F1 (upper-pred-dist)	0.2 ± 0.1	10.0	13.3
F2 (upper-Lyap-horizon)	0.3 ± 0.2	6.7	6.7
F3 (upper-pred-Lyap)	0.7 ± 0.2	0.0	3.3

4.3 Results

Table 1 reports the results for each scenario, for the three progress criteria **P1, P2, P3** and the three failure criteria **F1, F2, F3**. For each one, we show:

- **Detection Lead Time (s):** average time (relative to the actual alert) at which an alert was raised (higher = earlier warning). Not evaluated for progress.
- **False Positives (%):** percentage of trials in which the monitor raised an alert although no true failure occurred.
- **False Negatives (%):** percentage of trials in which a true failure (collision or missed deadline) occurred but no alert was raised in advance.

In the **Free-Space** scenario:

- In terms of progress criteria, **P1** produced 40% false positives (spurious progress alerts caused by sensor noise briefly increasing Δd_k) and it never missed a true stall (0% false negatives).
- **P2** produced no false positives but introduced false negatives (cases where the quantile-plus-horizon term stayed negative despite an actual stall).
- **P3** eliminated false positives and caught all true stalls.
- Among failure checks, **F1** signaled about 0.1 s before actual failure on average, but incurred 6.7% false positives and 10% false negatives.

- **F2** yielded 3.3% false positives and 6.7% false negatives, with lead time ≈ 0.2 s.
- **F3** achieved no false positives, no false negatives, and the earliest warnings (≈ 0.5 s on average).

In the **Obstacle-Field** scenario:

- **P1** again suffered from high noise sensitivity yielding 50% false positives.
- While **P2** fared better than **P1** with respect to false positives, it yielded 6.7% false negatives.
- **P3** performed best among the evaluated progress criteria.
- For failures, **F1** produced 10% false positives and 13.3% false negatives, with only ≈ 0.2 s lead time.
- **F2** exhibited error rates at 6.7% each, and a lead time of ≈ 0.3 s.
- **F3** again had no false positives, only 3.3% false negatives, and the earliest warning (≈ 0.7 s). The false negative occurred because the predicted nominal detour underestimated the actual extra path length, causing the predicted final CLF value to remain below the bound until one step before impact.

Overall, the combination (**P3, F3**) yields the best performance: it detects stalls or collisions the earliest, with a low number of false alarms, in both free-space and obstacle field environments.

4.4 Trajectory Examples

Figure 3 illustrates typical trajectories for the considered scenarios clusters with corresponding monitor signals shown in Fig. 4. Only in (a) do all criteria detect progress and do not indicate failure toward the true goal 1. In (d–f), the reactive controller detours around obstacles, and only the predictor **F3** flags failures correctly. In addition, across both free-space and obstacle maneuvers, the horizon-predicted standard deviation (6) remains within 10% of the EKF-estimated covariance.

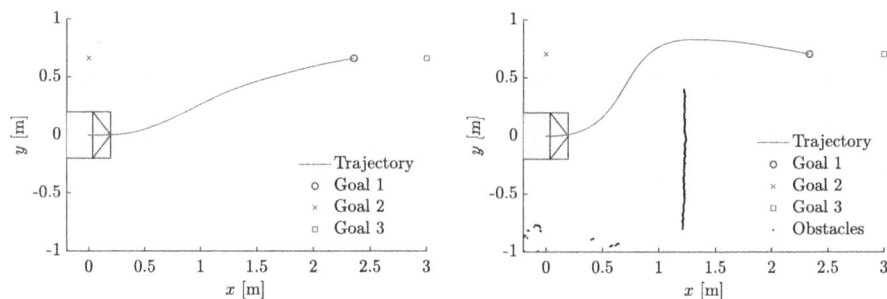

(a) Freespace navigation toward goal 1.   (b) Moving toward goal 1 with obstacles.

Fig. 3. Sample runs showing real trajectory and obstacles. Different goal locations are indicated in each case: goal 1 is the true goal, goal 2 denotes a divergence, goal 3 is a stall case.

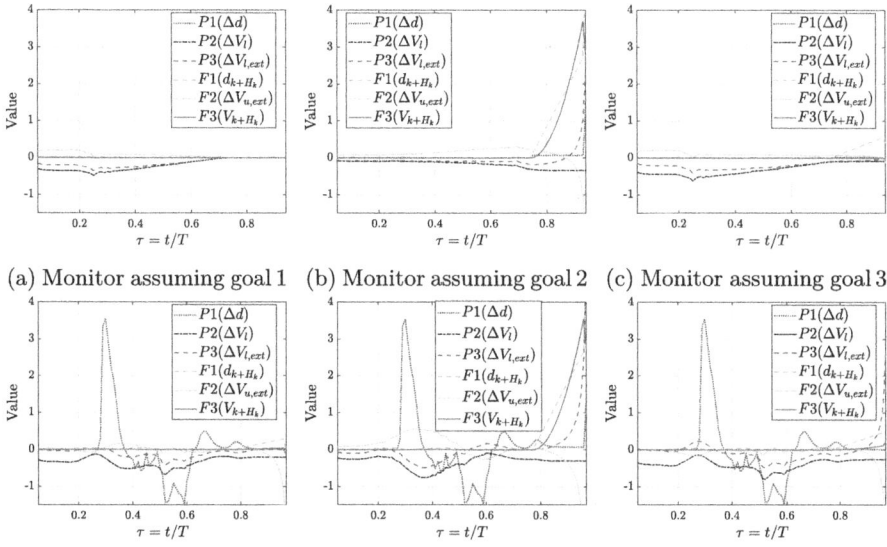

Fig. 4. Runtime monitoring of a free-space (a–c) and obstacle field (d–f) scenario when hypothesizing each of three possible goals.

5 Discussion

We now summarize the advantages and potential extensions of the presented approach.

5.1 Key Benefits

Early Warnings with Low False Alarms. Our experimental evaluation has shown that across both free-space and obstacle-field scenarios the combination of the progress criterion **P3** (lower CLF bound with horizon term) and the failure criterion **F3** (predicted final CLF value) consistently outperforms the other alternatives, yielding early failure detection and low false alarms for both progress and failure.

Quantile-Based Bounds Improve Robustness. By focusing on Gaussian quantile bounds, we avoid spurious progress alerts when estimated state covariance Σ_k is large. As mentioned in the previous section, the uncertainty propagation (6) remained close to the estimate, which confirms that the predicted values reliably bound the observed ones. These findings reassure that quantile statistics remain valid despite the approximation errors inherent in finite horizon EKF-linearization (Appendix A).

Integration Ready for a Safe Navigation Stack. Our monitor requires only pose and obstacle estimates. As such, it can seamlessly integrate as an independent ROS 2 node. The considered navigation task is included in many real-world robotic missions, ranging from surveillance and environmental monitoring to infrastructure inspection and search-and-rescue. Moreover, the approach is equally suitable for safeguarding AI-based navigation policies (e.g., neural planners or reinforcement-learning agents) without any changes to their internal logic. All proposed monitoring checks require only a handful of arithmetic operations per cycle and a short state buffer. Therefore, they are suitable for direct usage on resource-constrained embedded platforms, which will be a subject of future work.

5.2 Extensions

Finite Horizon Evaluation. While evaluating over a fixed finite horizon proved sufficient in our scenarios, it may be too short if the robot must navigate around many obstacles or operate at slower speeds. A longer horizon yields earlier "no-reach" warnings but incurs more computation and may be overly conservative in environments with dense obstacles. Mitigation strategies may include using a time-varying horizon when the uncertainty or obstacle density is high, running a coarse simulation for a longer horizon at lower frequency, or combining a short horizon for collision checks with a medium horizon for goal-reach viability.

Use-Case Scalability. Our safety certificate extends naturally to aerial drones by adding a third position coordinate z and using a similar rotated-error. Manipulator arms (e.g. 6-DOF) allow similar certificates in joint-space or task-space. Learning suitable certificates (e.g. via sum-of-squares programs for polynomial dynamical models, or neural-Lyapunov approaches for learned models), using simplified roll-out models and using more advanced filtering and uncertainty propagation techniques might be feasible alternatives, particularly for high-dimensional systems. The proposed method can be extended to support richer objectives described by temporal logic specifications, e.g., using high-order control Lyapunov-barrier functions [36].

Dynamic & Uncertain Operating Conditions. Our current evaluation assumed static obstacles. When obstacles move with relatively high speed, we must incorporate short-term obstacle motion forecasts into the obstacle-avoidance controller and the roll-out, update the barrier term weights or even the certificate's structure as new obstacles appear, e.g., using [14]. Dynamic re-allocation of goals in a multi-agent system to preserve safe formation and progress [7] is another possible extension. In addition, sensor noise or unmodeled disturbances may deviate from the assumed Gaussian distribution. Mitigation strategies may include adaptive noise tuning, where online residual checks can adjust the covariance parameters of the noise whenever innovation statistics drift outside expected bounds.

Formal Guarantees. The present study focused on empirical validation and comparison of the monitor with different progress and failure criteria. Providing formal proofs of soundness or completeness for the monitor's decisions is ongoing work. A possible approach could be to use reachability tools, such as [11], to automate the derivation of bounds under disturbances. Completing this proof pipeline would convert the current monitor into a formally verifiable safety layer without altering the navigation system, which could support compliance with safety standards such as ISO 26262 [18].

6 Conclusion

In this work, we have presented a lightweight monitoring approach for progress and failure in autonomous robot navigation using black-box policies. In indoor experiments on a four-wheeled ground robot we have systematically evaluated three candidate progress checks and failure checks in both free-space and obstacle-field scenarios. We identified that the combination of a lower candidate Lyapunov function bound with horizon term for progress and a predicted final candidate Lyapunov function value for failure offers the best empirical performance with respect to early reliable detection and minimal false alarms with a small computational overhead. Our results demonstrate that principled Lyapunov-based monitoring, when combined with probabilistic thresholds, provides a practical and formally grounded runtime-verification solution for safety-critical autonomous navigation.

A State Filtering

Assuming a typical robotic sensor suite consisting of a wheel-encoder odometry providing $(x_k^{\text{odo}}, y_k^{\text{odo}})$, an IMU yielding yaw θ_k^{imu}, and a 2D LiDAR (or rangefinder) producing m range measurements $\{r_k^i\}_{i=1}^m$ along known bearings, the measurement vector and the sensor map are

$$z_k = \begin{bmatrix} x_k^{\text{odo}} & y_k^{\text{odo}} & \theta_k^{\text{imu}} & r_k^1 & \ldots & r_k^m \end{bmatrix}^T, \quad h(\xi_k) = \begin{bmatrix} x_k & y_k & \theta_k & h_{\text{lidar}}(\xi_k) \end{bmatrix}^T,$$

where $h_{\text{lidar}}(\xi_k) \in \mathbb{R}^m$ computes the expected range readings to known obstacles or landmarks in the environment. Let $\hat{\xi}_{k-1|k-1}$, $\Sigma_{k-1|k-1}$ denote the state estimate and covariance after incorporating measurement z_{k-1}. Upon receiving control input $u_{k-1} = [v_{k-1}, \omega_{k-1}]^T$, the *prediction* step is

$$\hat{\xi}_{k|k-1} = f(\hat{\xi}_{k-1|k-1}, u_{k-1}),$$
$$\Sigma_{k|k-1} = A_{k-1} \Sigma_{k-1|k-1} A_{k-1}^\top + Q_w,$$

where $Q_w \in \mathbb{R}^{3\times 3}$ is the process-noise covariance and A_{k-1} for (1) is given by:

$$A_k = \left.\frac{\partial f}{\partial \xi}\right|_{\hat{\xi}_k, u_k} = \begin{bmatrix} 1 & 0 & -v_k \sin\theta_k \Delta t \\ 0 & 1 & v_k \cos\theta_k \Delta t \\ 0 & 0 & 1 \end{bmatrix} \quad \text{evaluated at } (\hat{\xi}_k, u_k).$$

When a new measurement z_k arrives, we compute

$$y_k = z_k - h(\hat{\xi}_{k|k-1}), H_k = \left.\frac{\partial h}{\partial \xi}\right|_{\hat{\xi}_{k|k-1}} \in \mathbb{R}^{(m+3)\times 3}.$$

Given measurement noise covariance $R_v \in \mathbb{R}^{(m+3)\times(m+3)}$, the *update* step is

$$S_k = H_k \Sigma_{k|k-1} H_k^\top + R_v, \qquad \hat{\xi}_{k|k} = \hat{\xi}_{k|k-1} + L_k y_k,$$
$$L_k = \Sigma_{k|k-1} H_k^\top S_k^{-1}, \qquad \Sigma_{k|k} = (I - L_k H_k)\Sigma_{k|k-1}.$$

B Nominal Controller

At each time step k, given the estimated pose $\hat{\xi}_k = [\hat{x}_k, \hat{y}_k, \hat{\theta}_k]^T$, the controller [33] computes (v_k, ω_k) as follows:

1. **Compute Attractive Vector to Goal**

$$p_k = \begin{bmatrix}\hat{x}_k \\ \hat{y}_k\end{bmatrix}, \quad g = \begin{bmatrix}x_g \\ y_g\end{bmatrix}, \quad \delta g = g - p_k,$$

$$\phi_k = \operatorname{atan}(\delta g_y, \delta g_x), \quad d_{g,k} = \|\delta g\|.$$

   The "goal-oriented" heading is ϕ_k, the Euclidean distance to the goal – $d_{g,k}$.

2. **Compute Obstacle Repulsion.** For each circular obstacle i with center c_i and radius r_i, compute the vector from the robot to obstacle center:

$$\delta o_k^i = \hat{p}_k - c_i, \quad \rho_k^i = \|\delta o_k^i\|,$$

   and a repulsive force magnitude

$$u_k^i = \begin{cases} \eta_i \left(\dfrac{1}{\rho_k^i - r_i} - \dfrac{1}{d_{\text{rep}}}\right)\left(\dfrac{1}{(\rho_k^i - r_i)^2}\right), & \text{if } \rho_k^i < r_i + d_{\text{rep}}, \\ 0, & \text{otherwise,}\end{cases}$$

   where d_{rep} is a tunable "influence distance" and $\eta_i > 0$ scales obstacle i's repulsion. The total repulsive vector is

$$F_k^{\text{rep}} = \sum_{i=1}^{m}\left(u_k^i \cdot \frac{\delta o_k^i}{\rho_k^i}\right).$$

   Its angle is $\psi_k = \operatorname{atan}(F_y^{\text{rep}}, F_x^{\text{rep}})$ and magnitude $\|F_k^{\text{rep}}\|$.

3. **Combine Attractive and Repulsive Directions.** We form a weighted heading θ_k^{des} that combines goal attraction and obstacle repulsion:

$$\theta_k^{\text{des}} = \operatorname{wrapToPi}\bigl(w^{\text{att}}\phi_k + w^{\text{rep}}\psi_k\bigr), \quad w^{\text{att}} = \frac{d_{g,k}}{d_{g,k}+\alpha}, \quad w^{\text{rep}} = \frac{\alpha}{d_{g,k}+\alpha},$$

   where $\alpha > 0$ is a blending parameter.

4. **Compute Control Velocities.** We choose a linear speed v_k that decreases near obstacles or as we approach the goal:

$$v_k = \begin{cases} v_{\max} \dfrac{d_{g,k}}{d_{\text{slow}}}, & \text{if } d_{g,k} < d_{\text{slow}}, \\ v_{\max}, & \text{otherwise,} \end{cases} \quad v_k \in [\,0,\, v_{\max}\,],$$

where d_{slow} is a threshold distance to begin slowing. The angular speed ω_k steers the heading toward θ_k^{des}:

$$e_{\theta,k} = \text{wrapToPi}\bigl(\theta_k^{\text{des}} - \hat{\theta}_k\bigr), \quad \omega_k = \text{sat}\,\bigl(k_\omega\, e_{\theta,k},\, -\omega_{\max},\, \omega_{\max}\bigr),$$

with gain $k_\omega > 0$ and $|\omega_k| \leq \omega_{\max}$.

Finally, the control pair (v_k, ω_k) is sent to the robot's low-level controllers.

References

1. Agia, C., et al.: Unpacking failure modes of generative policies: runtime monitoring of consistency and progress. In: Proceedings of the 8th Conference on Robot Learning. Proceedings of Machine Learning Research, vol. 270, pp. 689–723. PMLR (2025)
2. Ames, A.D., Xu, X., Grizzle, J.W., Tabuada, P.: Control barrier function based quadratic programs for safety critical systems. IEEE Trans. Autom. Control **62**(8), 3861–3876 (2017). https://doi.org/10.1109/TAC.2016.2638961
3. Bonnah, E., Hoque, K.A.: Runtime monitoring of time window temporal logic. IEEE Robot. Autom. Lett. **7**(3), 5888–5895 (2022). https://doi.org/10.1109/LRA.2022.3160592
4. Bozhinoski, D., et al.: MROS: runtime adaptation for robot control architectures. Adv. Robot. **36**(11), 502–518 (2022). https://doi.org/10.1080/01691864.2022.2039761
5. Caldas, R., García, J.A.P., Schiopu, M., Pelliccione, P., Rodrigues, G., Berger, T.: Runtime verification and field-based testing for ROS-based robotic systems. IEEE Trans. Software Eng. **50**(10), 2544–2567 (2024). https://doi.org/10.1109/TSE.2024.3444697
6. Chen, M., Tomlin, C.J.: Hamilton–Jacobi reachability: some recent theoretical advances and applications in unmanned airspace management. Ann. Rev. Control Robot. Auton. Syst. **1**(Volume 1, 2018), 333–358 (2018). https://doi.org/10.1146/annurev-control-060117-104941. https://www.annualreviews.org/content/journals/10.1146/annurev-control-060117-104941
7. Choudhury, S., Gupta, J.K., Kochenderfer, M.J., Sadigh, D., Bohg, J.: Dynamic multi-robot task allocation under uncertainty and temporal constraints. Auton. Robots **46**(1), 231–247 (2022). https://doi.org/10.1007/s10514-021-10022-9
8. Cohen, M., Belta, C.: Adaptive and Learning-Based Control of Safety-Critical Systems. Synthesis Lectures on Computer Science, 1 edn. Springer, Cham (2023). https://doi.org/10.1007/978-3-031-29310-8
9. Dawson, C., Qin, Z., Gao, S., Fan, C.: Safe nonlinear control using robust neural Lyapunov-barrier functions. In: Faust, A., Hsu, D., Neumann, G. (eds.) Proceedings of the 5th Conference on Robot Learning. Proceedings of Machine Learning Research, vol. 164, pp. 1724–1735. PMLR (2022). https://proceedings.mlr.press/v164/dawson22a.html

10. Englberger, F., Latzel, T., Sotiriadis, P.: An autonomous robot for embedded systems and robotics. In: 2018 12th European Workshop on Microelectronics Education (EWME), pp. 35–39 (2018). https://doi.org/10.1109/EWME.2018.8629475
11. Fan, C., Qi, B., Mitra, S., Viswanathan, M.: DryVR: data-driven verification and compositional reasoning for automotive systems. In: Majumdar, R., Kunčak, V. (eds.) CAV 2017. LNCS, vol. 10426, pp. 441–461. Springer, Cham (2017). https://doi.org/10.1007/978-3-319-63387-9_22
12. Ferrando, A., Cardoso, R.C., Fisher, M., Ancona, D., Franceschini, L., Mascardi, V.: ROSMonitoring: a runtime verification framework for ROS. In: Mohammad, A., Dong, X., Russo, M. (eds.) TAROS 2020. LNCS (LNAI), vol. 12228, pp. 387–399. Springer, Cham (2020). https://doi.org/10.1007/978-3-030-63486-5_40
13. Franco, C.D., Bezzo, N.: Interpretable run-time monitoring and replanning for safe autonomous systems operations. IEEE Robot. Autom. Lett. **5**(2), 2427–2434 (2020). https://doi.org/10.1109/LRA.2020.2972828
14. Fu, R., Quan, Q., Li, M., Cai, K.Y.: Practical distributed control for cooperative multicopters in structured free flight concepts. IEEE Trans. Intell. Transp. Syst. **24**(4), 4203–4216 (2023). https://doi.org/10.1109/TITS.2022.3229386
15. Hochgeschwender, N.: Adaptive deployment of safety monitors for autonomous systems. In: Romanovsky, A., Troubitsyna, E., Gashi, I., Schoitsch, E., Bitsch, F. (eds.) SAFECOMP 2019. LNCS, vol. 11699, pp. 346–357. Springer, Cham (2019). https://doi.org/10.1007/978-3-030-26250-1_28
16. Hsieh, C., Waga, M., Suenaga, K.: Certifying Lyapunov stability of black-box nonlinear systems via counterexample guided synthesis. In: Proceedings of the 28th ACM International Conference on Hybrid Systems: Computation and Control, HSCC 2025. Association for Computing Machinery, New York (2025). https://doi.org/10.1145/3716863.3718047
17. Huang, J., et al.: ROSRV: runtime verification for robots. In: Bonakdarpour, B., Smolka, S.A. (eds.) RV 2014. LNCS, vol. 8734, pp. 247–254. Springer, Cham (2014). https://doi.org/10.1007/978-3-319-11164-3_20
18. International Organization for Standardization: ISO 26262: Road vehicles - functional safety (2018). https://www.iso.org/standard/68383.html
19. Jacumet, R., Rathgeber, C., Nenchev, V.: Analytical safety bounds for trajectory following controllers in autonomous vehicles. In: Proceedings of the International Conference on Control, Decision and Information Technologies (CoDIT), pp. 730–735 (2023)
20. Koller, T., Berkenkamp, F., Turchetta, M., Krause, A.: Learning-based model predictive control for safe exploration. In: 2018 IEEE Conference on Decision and Control (CDC), pp. 6059–6066 (2018). https://doi.org/10.1109/CDC.2018.8619572
21. Könighofer, B., Bloem, R., Ehlers, R., Pek, C.: Correct-by-construction runtime enforcement in AI - a survey. In: Raskin, J.F., Chatterjee, K., Doyen, L., Majumdar, R. (eds.) Principles of Systems Design. LNCS, vol. 13660, pp. 650–663. Springer, Cham (2022). https://doi.org/10.1007/978-3-031-22337-2_31
22. Li, B., Wen, S., Yan, Z., Wen, G., Huang, T.: A survey on the control Lyapunov function and control barrier function for nonlinear-affine control systems. IEEE/CAA J. Automatica Sinica **10**(3), 584–602 (2023). https://doi.org/10.1109/JAS.2023.123075
23. Lin, Z., Baras, J.S.: Optimization-based motion planning and runtime monitoring for robotic agent with space and time tolerances**this work was partially supported by the ONR grant n00014-17-1-2622. IFAC-PapersOnLine **53**(2), 1874–1879 (2020). https://doi.org/10.1016/j.ifacol.2020.12.2606. https://www.sciencedirect.com/science/article/pii/S2405896320333590. 21st IFAC World Congress

24. Liu, H., Dass, S., Martín-Martín, R., Zhu, Y.: Model-based runtime monitoring with interactive imitation learning. In: 2024 IEEE International Conference on Robotics and Automation (ICRA), pp. 4154–4161 (2024). https://doi.org/10.1109/ICRA57147.2024.10611038
25. Macenski, S., Martín, F., White, R., Ginés Clavero, J.: The marathon 2: a navigation system. In: 2020 IEEE/RSJ International Conference on Intelligent Robots and Systems (IROS) (2020). https://github.com/ros-planning/navigation2
26. Mohanan, M., Salgoankar, A.: A survey of robotic motion planning in dynamic environments. Robot. Auton. Syst. **100**, 171–185 (2018). https://doi.org/10.1016/j.robot.2017.10.011. https://www.sciencedirect.com/science/article/pii/S0921889017300313
27. Nenchev, V.: Model checking embedded adaptive cruise controllers. Robot. Auton. Syst. **167**, 104488 (2023)
28. Nenchev, V.: One stack, diverse vehicles: checking safe portability of automated driving software. In: 2025 IEEE/SICE International Symposium on System Integration (SII), pp. 764–769 (2025). https://doi.org/10.1109/SII59315.2025.10870905
29. Nenchev, V., Imrie, C., Gerasimou, S., Calinescu, R.: Code-level safety verification for automated driving: a case study. In: Platzer, A., Rozier, K.Y., Pradella, M., Rossi, M. (eds.) FM 2024. LNCS, vol. 14934, pp. 356–372. Springer, Cham (2024). https://doi.org/10.1007/978-3-031-71177-0_22
30. Nenchev, V., Imrie, C., Gerasimou, S., Calinescu, R.: Compositional code-level safety verification for automated driving controllers. J. Syst. Softw. **230**, 112499 (2025). https://doi.org/10.1016/j.jss.2025.112499. https://www.sciencedirect.com/science/article/pii/S0164121225001670
31. Rahman, Q.M., Corke, P., Dayoub, F.: Run-time monitoring of machine learning for robotic perception: a survey of emerging trends. IEEE Access **9**, 20067–20075 (2021). https://doi.org/10.1109/ACCESS.2021.3055015
32. Richards, S.M., Berkenkamp, F., Krause, A.: The Lyapunov neural network: Adaptive stability certification for safe learning of dynamical systems. In: Proceedings of Machine Learning Research, vol. 87, pp. 466–476 (2018)
33. Rimon, E., Koditschek, D.: Exact robot navigation using artificial potential functions. IEEE Trans. Robot. Autom. **8**(5), 501–518 (1992). https://doi.org/10.1109/70.163777
34. Shao, Y.S., Chen, C., Kousik, S., Vasudevan, R.: Reachability-based trajectory safeguard (RTS): a safe and fast reinforcement learning safety layer for continuous control. IEEE Robot. Autom. Lett. **6**(2), 3663–3670 (2021). https://doi.org/10.1109/LRA.2021.3063989
35. Visconti, E., Bartocci, E., Loreti, M., Nenzi, L.: Online monitoring of spatio-temporal properties for imprecise signals. In: 2021 19th ACM-IEEE International Conference on Formal Methods and Models for System Design (MEMOCODE), pp. 78–88 (2021). https://doi.org/10.1145/3487212.3487344
36. Xiao, W., Belta, C.A., Cassandras, C.G.: High order control Lyapunov-barrier functions for temporal logic specifications. In: 2021 American Control Conference (ACC), pp. 4886–4891 (2021). https://doi.org/10.23919/ACC50511.2021.9483028
37. Yalcinkaya, B., Torfah, H., Desai, A., Seshia, S.A.: ULGEN: a runtime assurance framework for programming safe cyber–physical systems. IEEE Trans. Comput. Aided Des. Integr. Circuits Syst. **42**(11), 3679–3692 (2023). https://doi.org/10.1109/TCAD.2023.3246386
38. Yamaguchi, T., Hoxha, B., Ničković, D.: RTAMT – runtime robustness monitors with application to CPS and robotics. Int. J. Softw. Tools Technol. Transfer **26**, 79–99 (2024). https://doi.org/10.1007/s10009-023-00720-3

Conformal Predictive Monitoring for Multi-modal Scenarios

Francesca Cairoli[1](✉)[iD], Luca Bortolussi[1][iD], Jyotirmoy V. Deshmukh[2], Lars Lindemann[2], and Nicola Paoletti[3][iD]

[1] University of Trieste, Trieste, Italy
francesca.cairoli@units.it
[2] University of Southern California, Los Angeles, CA, USA
[3] King's College London, London, UK

Abstract. We consider the problem of quantitative predictive monitoring (QPM) of stochastic systems, i.e., predicting at runtime the degree of satisfaction of a desired temporal logic property from the current state of the system. Since computational efficiency is key to enable timely intervention against predicted violations, several state-of-the-art QPM approaches rely on fast machine-learning surrogates to provide prediction intervals for the satisfaction values, using conformal inference to offer statistical guarantees. However, these QPM methods suffer when the monitored agent exhibits multi-modal dynamics, whereby certain modes may yield high satisfaction values while others critically violate the property. Existing QPM methods are mode-agnostic and so would yield overly conservative and uninformative intervals that lack meaningful mode-specific satisfaction information. To address this problem, we present GenQPM, a method that leverages deep generative models, specifically score-based diffusion models, to reliably approximate the probabilistic and multi-modal system dynamics without requiring explicit model access. GenQPM employs a mode classifier to partition the predicted trajectories by dynamical mode. For each mode, we then apply conformal inference to produce statistically valid, mode-specific prediction intervals. We demonstrate the effectiveness of GenQPM on a benchmark of agent navigation and autonomous driving tasks, resulting in prediction intervals that are significantly more informative (less conservative) than mode-agnostic baselines.

1 Introduction

Predictive monitoring is an advanced form of runtime verification that leverages forecasts of a system's future behavior to detect safety violations before they occur. Traditional runtime verification checks whether a system trace satisfies a temporal logic property in real time but only considers the observed prefix of the trajectory, i.e., it cannot reason about possible future evolutions of the system [19]. In contrast, predictive monitoring incorporates a model of system dynamics to predict future trajectories and assess, in an online manner, whether

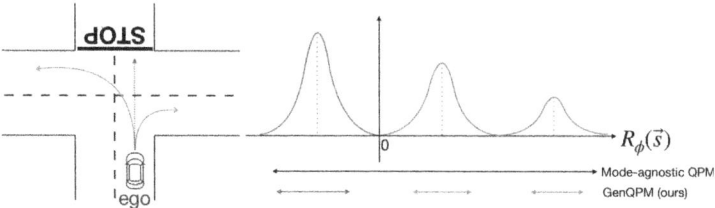

Fig. 1. Left: Vehicle facing multiple possible choices. Right: Distribution of the robustness values of these choices/modalities w.r.t. an STL safety requirement. Bottom-right: uninformative mode-agnostic prediction interval vs informative mode-specific intervals.

a violation is imminent from the current state, thereby enabling preemptive and timely safety interventions.

This paper focuses on predictive monitoring for *stochastic systems*, where future behavior is inherently uncertain. In such systems, the satisfaction of temporal logic specifications becomes a stochastic quantity (some evolutions can be safe, others unsafe). Although probabilistic model checking (PMC) [2] can provide exact satisfaction probabilities, it requires full knowledge of the system model and becomes intractable for large or continuous state spaces. Statistical Model Checking (SMC) [34] alleviates some of these problems by estimating satisfaction probabilities from sampled trajectories, but it must be run at each state during execution. This makes both PMC and SMC impractical for online predictive monitoring. In particular, we focus on correctness specifications given as *Signal Temporal Logic (STL)* formulas [14,23] and on monitoring STL robustness, i.e., the logic's quantitative semantics indicating the degree of satisfaction of an STL formula by a trajectory. We call this problem *Quantitative Predictive Monitoring (QPM)*. Our work builds on recent QPM methods [10,12,21,36], which rely on machine-learning models for trajectory predictions and employ the conformal prediction framework [1,32] to produce prediction intervals for STL robustness with guaranteed coverage. However, these methods fail to provide useful results in scenarios with *multi-modal dynamics*.

The main concern in this paper is the predictive monitoring of multi-modal systems, i.e., systems that can evolve along qualitatively different future behaviors (or "modes"). For instance, consider the example in Fig. 1-left, where we see an autonomous vehicle approaching an intersection. The vehicle might turn left, turn right, or go straight—each representing a distinct mode. The first two modes lead to safe scenarios, i.e., scenarios that satisfy the safety requirements (positive STL robustness), whereas the latter mode violates safety/traffic rules (negative STL robustness). Figure 1-right highlights the multi-modal distribution of STL robustness values in such an environment. In such settings, the above-mentioned methods would fail to capture the impact of different modes. So, they would produce overly conservative regions that cover a broad range of outcomes, losing valuable information about which modes are safe or unsafe.

To address this limitation, our goal is to develop a predictive monitor that can quantify the mode-specific satisfaction of STL requirements. That is, rather than providing a single large prediction interval over possible robustness values, we aim to produce separate prediction intervals for each mode, offering insights into which modes are likely to lead to violations or satisfaction, thus enhancing the decision-making process of the agent.

To this purpose, we propose *GenQPM*, a novel *dynamics-aware quantitative predictive monitor* that leverages deep generative models and conformal inference to provide reliable and mode-specific prediction intervals. First, we use *score-based diffusion models* [16], a class of state-of-the-art generative models, to learn a probabilistic surrogate of the stochastic system dynamics and generate possible future trajectories. Second, we partition these trajectories into distinct dynamical modes using a *mode classifier*, which may be known or learned from data (in either a supervised or unsupervised fashion). For each mode, we estimate the distribution of STL robustness values and compute prediction intervals by applying *conformalized quantile regression (CQR)* [26]. Doing so, our approach ensures statistically valid coverage, even if the generative surrogate model is approximate. In summary, the main contributions of this paper are:

1. We introduce GenQPM, a method that combines diffusion models with conformal inference to enable STL predictive monitoring for multi-modal stochastic systems.
2. GenQPM provides probabilistic guarantees and supports both known and learned mode predictors.
3. We evaluate GenQPM on four case studies, including a 2D navigation task and a multi-agent cross-road scenario. Our method yields mode-specific robustness intervals that are more interpretable and substantially tighter than mode-agnostic QPM baselines.

2 Problem Statement

Stochastic Process. We consider systems that can be described as stochastic processes (as in [12]), defined by a collection of random variables $\mathbf{S}(i,\omega)_{i\in\mathcal{I},\omega\in\Omega}$ over a probability space $(\Omega, \mathcal{F}, \mathbb{P})$. Here, Ω is the sample space (all possible outcomes), $\mathcal{F}$ is the event space (all subsets of Ω), and $\mathbb{P}$ is the probability function, assigning each event a value in $[0,1]$. $\mathcal{I} = 0, 1, \ldots$ is a discrete-time index set, and each $\mathbf{S}(i,\omega)$ maps to a measurable state space $S \subseteq \mathbb{R}^n$. A realization $\mathbf{S}(\cdot,\omega) : \mathcal{I} \to S$ is a sample trajectory. For a horizon H, $\vec{s}$ denotes a realization of the random sequence $\vec{\mathbf{S}} = (\mathbf{S}(0,\cdot), \ldots, \mathbf{S}(H-1,\cdot))$, where $\mathbf{S}(k,\cdot)$ is the state – a random variable – at time k.

Signal Temporal Logic (STL). STL [14,23] specifies properties of real-valued signals via the syntax: $\phi := true \mid \mu \mid \neg\phi \mid \phi \wedge \phi \mid \phi\ U_I\ \phi$, where predicates $\mu \equiv g(\cdot) > 0$ are evaluated based on a predicate function $g : S \to \mathbb{R}$ and where $I = [a,b] \subseteq \mathbb{T}$ are time intervals. Derived operators include *false*, $\vee$, $F_I \phi$ (eventually), and $G_I \phi$ (globally). The Boolean semantics is defined as follows:

$$(\vec{s},t) \models \mu \quad \Leftrightarrow \quad g(\vec{s}(t)) > 0$$
$$(\vec{s},t) \models \neg\phi \quad \Leftrightarrow \quad \neg((\vec{s},t) \models \phi)$$
$$(\vec{s},t) \models \phi_1 \wedge \phi_2 \quad \Leftrightarrow \quad (\vec{s},t) \models \phi_1 \wedge (\vec{s},t) \models \phi_2$$
$$(\vec{s},t) \models \phi_1 U_{[a,b]}\phi_2 \quad \Leftrightarrow \quad \exists\, t' \in [t+a,t+b]\ \text{s.t.}\ (\vec{s},t') \models \phi_2 \ \forall\, t'' \in [t,t'],\ (\vec{s},t'') \models \phi_1$$

Let S^H denote the space of trajectories $\vec{s}$ of length H and let $\mathcal{I}_H = \{0, 1, \ldots, H-1\}$ denote the discrete time interval, the quantitative semantics, or robustness, is defined as a function $\text{Rob} : S^H \times \mathcal{I}_H \to \mathbb{R}$:

$$\text{Rob}_\mu(\vec{s},t) = g(\vec{s}(t))$$
$$\text{Rob}_{\neg\phi}(\vec{s},t) = -\text{Rob}_\phi(\vec{s},t)$$
$$\text{Rob}_{\phi_1 \wedge \phi_2}(\vec{s},t) = \min(\text{Rob}_{\phi_1}(\vec{s},t), \text{Rob}_{\phi_2}(\vec{s},t))$$
$$\text{Rob}_{\phi_1 U_{[a,b]} \phi_2}(\vec{s},t) = \sup_{t' \in [t+a,t+b]} \left(\min\left(\text{Rob}_{\phi_2}(\vec{s},t'),\ \inf_{t'' \in [t,t']} \text{Rob}_{\phi_1}(\vec{s},t'') \right) \right).$$

The robustness of a trajectory quantifies the level of satisfaction with respect to ϕ. Positive robustness means that the property is satisfied, whereas negative robustness means that the property is violated. In this paper, we focus on the above quantitative semantics, but our framework could accommodate alternative semantics as well (e.g., temporal robustness [25] or space-time robustness [14]).

Quantitative Predictive Monitoring. Given a stochastic process $\mathbf{S} = \{\mathbf{S}(t,\omega), t \in \mathcal{I}\}$, an STL requirement ϕ and a state $s_0 \in S$, the robustness over future evolutions of the system starting from s_0 is distributed according to the conditional distribution $\mathbb{P}_{\vec{s} \sim \mathbf{S}}\big(\text{Rob}_\phi(\vec{s},0) \mid \vec{s}(0) = s_0\big)$. This conditional distribution captures the distribution of the STL robustness values for trajectories of length H starting in s_0.

The quantitative predictive monitoring (QPM) problem can be expressed as follows. From any state $\vec{s}(0)$ of the *unknown* stochastic process, we aim to construct a prediction interval guaranteed to include, with arbitrary probability, the true STL robustness of any (unknown) stochastic trajectory starting at $\vec{s}(0)$. QPM builds on the only assumption of having access to a set D of observed realizations of the random sequence $\vec{\mathbf{S}}$, i.e., a set of trajectories of length H coming from an unknown stochastic process $\mathbf{S}$. The trajectories in D are split into a training set D_t and a calibration set D_c. Formally, the guarantees offered by QPM in [12] can be expressed as: for a significance level $\alpha \in (0,1)$

$$\mathbb{P}_{\vec{s} \sim \vec{\mathbf{S}}}\Big(\text{Rob}_\phi(\vec{s},0) \in \text{Int}\big(\vec{s}(0)\big)\Big) \geq 1 - \alpha, \tag{1}$$

where $\text{Int}(\cdot)$ is a monitoring function producing prediction intervals guaranteed to cover the true STL robustness values of trajectories $\vec{s} \sim \vec{\mathbf{S}}$ with a probability greater than $1 - \alpha$. The QPM problem has been solved in [12] as a conditional quantile regression problem. This boils down to learning, for a generic state $\vec{s}(0)$, an upper and a lower quantile of the random variable $\text{Rob}_\phi(\vec{s}, 0)$ induced by $\vec{s}$. These two quantiles build the output of the function Int in $\vec{s}(0)$. Conformal prediction is then used to ensure that such an interval is well-calibrated—meaning that the probabilistic guarantees are satisfied theoretically and empirically.

A big limitation of the presented QPM problem is that the monitoring function only quantifies how much the requirement is satisfied in the near future, no information about the dynamics that cause the predicted violations can be retrieved from such a monitor. Additionally, the intervals obtained in [12] are not mode-specific and may hence be conservative. We also note that the quantile regressor has to be retrained when the specification changes.

In this paper we tackle the aforementioned issues, and the first step to do so is to learn a surrogate model of the system dynamics—meaning that we learn a conditional parametric distribution $p_\theta(\vec{s}|\vec{s}(0))$ over observations D_t that approximates the unknown distribution $p(\vec{s}|\vec{s}(0))$. The surrogate model is used to gain insights into system dynamics in cases where a model of the stochastic system is either unavailable or computationally too expensive to integrate with a monitor that needs to operate efficiently in real-time.

Instead of using an end-to-end approach, i.e. directly mapping the current state to an interval over the values of the STL robustness as in [12], we solve the QPM problem by leveraging deep generative models to learn the approximate distribution $p_\theta(\vec{s}|\vec{s}(0))$ from realizations of $\vec{\mathbf{S}}$. In particular, we use score-based diffusion models to train a generator function $\text{gen}_\theta(z, \vec{s}(0))$ acting as a distribution transformer, mapping latent samples z from a standard latent distribution $p(z|\vec{s}(0))$ into samples over the target space S^H (more details in Sect. 3). To evaluate the monitoring function Int at $\vec{s}(0)$, we compute the empirical quantiles of the robustness values computed over trajectories sampled from $p_\theta(\vec{s}|\vec{s}(0))$, followed by a calibration step based on conformal prediction.

Another important consideration is that trajectories $\vec{s}$ may belong to different dynamical modes. Assume that the monitored agent may choose between G different dynamical modes. A mode assignment is defined as a total function that maps trajectories into a finite set of application-specific labels $\{1, \ldots, G\}$. Some modes may be rare to observe, some may always be safe, whereas others may be more prone to violations. For instance, in the crossroad scenario, depicted in Fig. 1, the agent, meaning the ego vehicle, may choose between three different dynamical modes, namely going straight, a left or right turn. The QPM guarantees of (1) are marginal, meaning that predictors $\text{Int}(\cdot)$ are guaranteed to have coverage that on average is higher than $1 - \alpha$. This means that modes with accurate predictions may compensate for rare and error-prone ones. We aim at obtaining mode-specific predictors $\text{Int}^{(\text{mode})}(\cdot)$ such that the coverage guarantees hold for every mode, i.e., we may require that the prediction intervals are $1 - \alpha$ accurate regardless of the mode that they belong to. We can also discern safer modes from risky ones. To achieve such mode-conditional predictors, we assume that the calibration trajectories are labelled with the dynamical mode they belong to. Mode-conditional guarantees can be stated as follows.

Problem 1 (Mode-conditional Quantitative Predictive Monitoring). Given two sets of trajectories D_t and D_c from an unknown discrete-time stochastic process $\vec{S}$ with the set of modes $\{1, \ldots, G\}$ that are labelled by a, potentially unknown, mode assignment function $\mathcal{M} : S^H \to \{1, \ldots, G\}$. Then, for a significance level $\alpha \in (0, 1)$, an STL formula ϕ, and every mode $\in \{1, \ldots, G\}$, we want to derive a mode-specific monitoring function $\text{Int}^{(\text{mode})}$ producing intervals that cover the STL robustness of trajectories belonging to mode with a probability of no less than $1 - \alpha$. Mathematically, we want to achieve

$$\mathbb{P}_{\vec{s} \sim \vec{S}}\Big(\text{Rob}_\phi(\vec{s}, 0) \in \text{Int}^{(\text{mode})}(\vec{s}(0)) \mid \mathcal{M}(\vec{s}) = \text{mode}\Big) \geq 1 - \alpha, \qquad (2)$$

for all mode $\in \{1, \ldots, G\}$; above, $\mathcal{M}$ maps every realization of length H of the stochastic process into one of the G modes.

To solve Problem 1, we will use the class-conditional version of conformal inference to obtain conditional guarantees determined by the mode-conditional calibration sets $D_c^{(\text{mode})} = \{\vec{s} \in D_c | \mathcal{M}(\vec{s}) = \text{mode}\}$, for mode $\in \{1, \ldots, G\}$. In general, the mode predictor $\mathcal{M}$ may be known or learned from data either in a supervised or unsupervised fashion, depending on the availability of ground truth labels, denoting the correct mode, for a pool of trajectories. The machine-learning techniques used to tackle the problems stated above are introduced in the next section.

3 Background

3.1 Generative Models and Diffusion Models

Every dataset can be considered as a set of observations $\mathbf{x}$ drawn from an unknown distribution $p(\mathbf{x})$. Generative models aim at learning a model that mimics this unknown distribution as closely as possible, i.e., learn a parametric distribution $p_\theta(\mathbf{x})$ as similar as possible to $p(\mathbf{x})$. The parametric distribution p_θ is chosen so that one knows how to efficiently sample from it. A generative model acts as a distribution transformer, i.e., a map $\text{gen}_\theta : Z \to X$ transforming a simple distribution $p(z)$ over a latent space Z into a complex distribution over the target space X. Given a noise sample $\mathbf{z} \sim p(\mathbf{z})$, $\text{gen}_\theta(\mathbf{z})$ is thus a sample in X. For our monitoring application, we are interested in generating stochastic trajectories conditioned, for instance, on the starting position of the system. To approximate such conditional distribution $p(\mathbf{x} \mid \mathbf{y})$, we use conditional deep generative models [30], which can be seen as maps $\text{gen}_\theta : Z \times Y \to X$, where Y is the conditioning space. We can generate samples in X conditioned on $\mathbf{y} \in Y$, $\text{gen}_\theta(\mathbf{z}, \mathbf{y}) \in X$, resulting in a distribution $p_\theta(\mathbf{x}|\mathbf{y})$ approximating $p(\mathbf{x}|\mathbf{y})$.

Diffusion models [16,29] are a class of generative models that learn to synthesize data by gradually denoising random noise. We focus on Denoising Diffusion Probabilistic Models (DDPMs) [16], which operate through two key processes.
Forward Process: the datapoint $\mathbf{x}^0$ is sequentially corrupted by noise over a finite number of steps (indexed by τ) according to a so called noise schedule

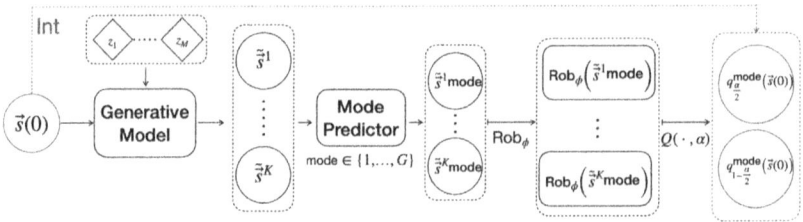

Fig. 2. GenQPM: dynamic-aware quantitative predictive monitor with mode-conditional guarantees.

$\beta_1, \ldots, \beta_T$: $p(\mathbf{x}^\tau \mid \mathbf{x}^{\tau-1}) = \mathcal{N}\left(\sqrt{1-\beta_\tau}\mathbf{x}^{\tau-1}, \beta_\tau \mathbf{I}\right)$. After $\mathcal{T}$ steps, $\mathbf{x}^\mathcal{T}$ approximates pure noise, i.e., a Gaussian distribution $\mathcal{N}(\mathbf{0}, \mathbf{I})$.

Reverse Process: a neural network $\epsilon_\theta(\mathbf{x}^\tau, \tau)$ then learns to recursively denoise $\mathbf{x}^\tau$ by predicting the noise added at each step as follows: $\min_\theta \mathbb{E}_{\mathbf{x}^0, \epsilon, \tau} |\epsilon - \epsilon_\theta(\mathbf{x}^\tau, \tau)|_2^2$, where $\mathbf{x}^\tau = \sqrt{\alpha_\tau}\mathbf{x}^0 + \sqrt{1-\alpha_\tau}\epsilon$ ($\alpha_\tau := \prod_{i=1}^\tau (1-\beta_i)$). Sampling generates data by iteratively denoising $\mathbf{x}^\mathcal{T} \sim \mathcal{N}(\mathbf{0}, \mathbf{I})$.

For conditional generation (e.g., $p(\mathbf{x}^0|\mathbf{y})$), the model learns $\epsilon_\theta(\mathbf{x}^\tau, \tau \mid \mathbf{y})$ via: $\min_\theta \mathbb{E}_{\mathbf{x}^0, \mathbf{y}, \epsilon, \tau} |\epsilon - \epsilon_\theta(\mathbf{x}^\tau, \tau \mid \mathbf{y})|_2^2$. A more flexible approach to controlling the generation process is *guidance* [4,28].

3.2 Conformal Inference

Conformal inference [1,3,22] is a lightweight statistical tool for uncertainty quantification that can be applied on top of any supervised learning algorithm for constructing distribution-free prediction regions with guaranteed marginal coverage. The conformal framework requires minimal adaptation to suit the problem at hand. For instance, probabilistic predictors call for *Conformalized Quantile Regression* (CQR) [26]. Consider a probabilistic function $q(\mathbf{x})$ mapping an input $\mathbf{x} \in X$ into a quantile interval over $\mathbb{R}$, i.e., $q(\mathbf{x}) = [q_{lo}(\mathbf{x}), q_{hi}(\mathbf{x})] \subseteq \mathbb{R}$. The goal is to calibrate such predictive intervals to have marginal guarantees of coverage. Starting from a dataset $D_c = \{(\mathbf{x}_i, t_i)\}_i$ of pairs sampled i.i.d. from an unknown distribution $p(\mathbf{x}, t)$. CQR performs the following steps:

1. Define a non-conformity score function $E: X \times \mathbb{R} \to \mathbb{R}$, such that $E(\mathbf{x}, t)$ quantifies the discrepancy between t and the prediction interval $q(\mathbf{x})$:

$$E(\mathbf{x}_i, t_i) = \max\{q_{lo}(\mathbf{x}_i) - t_i, \; t_i - q_{hi}(\mathbf{x}_i) \mid (\mathbf{x}_i, t_i) \in D_c\}. \tag{3}$$

2. Use D_c to define the calibration distribution $\mathcal{F}_c = \sum_{i=1}^{|D_c|} \frac{1}{|D_c|+1} \delta_{e_i} + \frac{1}{|D_c|+1} \delta_\infty$, where δ_e is the Dirac distribution with parameter e and $e_i = E(\mathbf{x}_i, t_i)$ is the score of the i-th calibration point;

3. For a given test point $\mathbf{x}$ and an error rate α, construct the prediction region as $C_\alpha(\mathbf{x}) = \{t : E(\mathbf{x}, t) \leq Q(\mathcal{F}_c; 1-\alpha)\}$, where $Q(\mathcal{F}_c; 1-\alpha)$ is the $1-\alpha$ quantile

of $\mathcal{F}_c$. Such prediction region satisfies the following coverage guarantee w.r.t. unseen test data $(\mathbf{x}, t) \sim p(\mathbf{x}, t)$:

$$Pr_{(\mathbf{x},t) \sim p(\mathbf{x},t)}(t \in C_\alpha(\mathbf{x})) \geq 1 - \alpha. \qquad (4)$$

Note that the above holds in the more general case when $(\mathbf{x}, t)$ is exchangeable w.r.t. calibration data, i.e. when the joint probability of $(\mathbf{x}_1, t_1), \ldots, (\mathbf{x}_{|D_c|}, t_{|D_c|}), (\mathbf{x}, t)$ remains the same for any permutation of the data points. In practice, $C_\alpha(\mathbf{x})$ corresponds to a recalibration of the predictive interval $q(\mathbf{x})$, i.e., $C_\alpha(\mathbf{x}) = [q_{lo}(\mathbf{x}) - \tau_\alpha, q_{hi}(\mathbf{x}) + \tau_\alpha]$, where $\tau_\alpha := Q(\mathcal{F}_c; 1 - \alpha)$.[1]

4 Methods

We present GenQPM a method to solve Problem 1. Let $\vec{s}(0) \in S$ denote the current state of the system, from which the future evolutions are stochastically distributed with probability $p(\vec{s}|\vec{s}(0))$, which is a conditional distribution over the space of trajectories of length H. The system's evolution should satisfy given requirements, expressed by a Signal Temporal Logic (STL) formula ϕ. We aim to monitor such satisfaction in real-time, i.e., as the system evolves. An important consideration is that we monitor a stochastic system, meaning that satisfaction values will be stochastic too.

4.1 Generative QPM

The GenQPM monitoring algorithm is outlined in Algorithm 1 and illustrated in Fig. 2. A generative model is trained over the observed trajectories D_t (step 1) resulting in a surrogate model $p_\theta(\vec{s}|\vec{s}(0))$ of the system dynamics, i.e. a model that can predict the future evolutions of the system from any current state (see Sect. 3.1). The surrogate generates multiple possible realizations for each calibration state (step 2.b). For each mode $\in \{1, \ldots, G\}$, we compute the STL robustness of the surrogate trajectories mapped to mode by the mode predictor $\mathcal{M}$ (step 2.c) and use these values to extract the empirical quantiles, $q_{lo}^{\phi,\text{mode}}(\vec{s}(0))$ and $q_{hi}^{\phi,\text{mode}}(\vec{s}(0))$, associated respectively to $\alpha/2$ and $1 - \alpha/2$ (step 2.d). Such mode-specific quantile predictor, resulting from the composition of the generative model $p_\theta(\vec{s}|\vec{s}(0))$ and the mode predictor $\mathcal{M}$, produces a mode-specific prediction interval $PI^{\phi,\text{mode}}(\vec{s}(0)) = [q_{lo}^{\phi,\text{mode}}(\vec{s}(0)), q_{hi}^{\phi,\text{mode}}(\vec{s}(0))]$, that quantifies how much the realizations of the system belonging to mode are expected to meet the desired property ϕ. The true robustness values of the calibration set $D_c^{(\text{mode},\phi)}$

---

[1] The chosen nonconformity function E assumes real values and thus τ_α can be negative. The conformalized prediction interval $C_\alpha(\cdot)$ can therefore be tighter than the original prediction interval $q(\cdot)$. The calibrated intervals can be more efficient than the uncalibrated ones, where the efficiency is the average width of the prediction intervals over a test set. Moreover, unlike $q(\cdot)$, $C_\alpha(\cdot)$ has guaranteed coverage.

Algorithm 1. GenQPM — Illustrated in Fig. 2

Inputs
- Dataset $D_t = \{(\vec{s}_i(0), \vec{s}_i), i = 1, \ldots, N_t\}$ where $\vec{s}_i(0) \in S$ is the initial condition and $\vec{s}_i$ is a trajectory of length H.
- Mode-conditional calibration sets $D_c^{(\text{mode})}$.
- Mode predictor $\mathcal{M} : S^H \to \{1, \ldots, G\}$
- STL property ϕ to monitor.
- Significance level $\alpha \in (0, 1)$, q_{lo} and q_{hi} are the $\frac{\alpha}{2}$-th and $(1 - \frac{\alpha}{2})$-th quantiles.

Training
1. Train a generative model $p_\theta(\vec{s}|\vec{s}(0))$ that approximates $p(\vec{s}|\vec{s}(0))$, the conditional distribution over the trajectory space, using D_t.
2. *Property-specific calibration.* For every mode $\in \{1, \ldots, G\}$:
   (a) Compute $D_c^{(\phi,\text{mode})} := \{(\vec{s}_i(0), \text{Rob}_\phi(\vec{s}_i)) \mid \vec{s}_i \in D_c^{(\text{mode})}\}$ where $\text{Rob}_\phi(\vec{s}_i)$ denotes the robustness of $\vec{s}_i$ w.r.t. ϕ.
   (b) Sample K trajectories $\tilde{\vec{s}}_i^1, \ldots, \tilde{\vec{s}}_i^K$ from $p_\theta(\vec{s}|\vec{s}_i(0))$ for each $\vec{s}_i(0)$ from $\vec{s}_i \in D_c^{(\text{mode})}$.
   (c) Keep only the trajectories mapped to mode by $\mathcal{M}$, i.e. keep $\tilde{\vec{s}}_i^j$ if $\mathcal{M}(\tilde{\vec{s}}_i^j) = \text{mode}$, and compute their robustness values $\text{Rob}_\phi(\tilde{\vec{s}}_i^j)$ for $j \in \{1, \ldots, K_{\text{mode}}\}$, where $K_{\text{mode}} < K$ denotes the number of generated trajectories mapped to mode by $\mathcal{M}$.
   (d) Use the computed robustness values to retrieve the mode-specific lower and upper empirical quantiles:
   $$q_{lo}^{\phi,\text{mode}}(\vec{s}_i(0)) = Q(\{\text{Rob}_\phi(\tilde{\vec{s}}_i^j)\}_{j=1}^{K_{\text{mode}}}; \alpha/2);\ q_{hi}^{\phi,\text{mode}}(\vec{s}_i(0)) = Q(\{\text{Rob}_\phi(\tilde{\vec{s}}_i^j)\}_{j=1}^{K_{\text{mode}}}; 1 - \alpha/2)$$
   obtaining the mode-specific prediction interval $PI^{\phi,\text{mode}}(\vec{s}_i(0)) = [q_{lo}^\phi(\vec{s}_i(0)), q_{hi}^\phi(\vec{s}_i(0))]$, where $Q(\cdot; \alpha)$ denotes the quantile function.
   (e) Compute the calibration nonconformity scores $e_i^{\phi,\text{mode}}$ by comparing the true $\text{Rob}_\phi(\vec{s}_i)$ in $D_c^{(\phi,\text{mode})}$ with $q_{lo}^{\phi,\text{mode}}(\vec{s}_i(0))$ and $q_{hi}^{\phi,\text{mode}}(\vec{s}_i(0))$:
   $$e_i^{\phi,\text{mode}} := \max\{q_{lo}^{\phi,\text{mode}}(\vec{s}_i(0)) - \text{Rob}_\phi(\vec{s}_i), \text{Rob}_\phi(\vec{s}_i) - q_{hi}^{\phi,\text{mode}}(\vec{s}_i(0))\}.$$
   (f) Identify $\tau^{\phi,\text{mode}}$ as the $(1 - \alpha)$-th empirical quantile of the distribution of calibration scores $\{e_i^{\phi,\text{mode}} \mid (\vec{s}_i(0), \text{Rob}_\phi(\vec{s}_i)) \in D_c^{(\phi,\text{mode})}\}$ computed at the previous step.

Test
(3) Given a test point $\vec{s}(0)$, compute, for each mode $\in \{1, \ldots, G\}$, the quantile estimates $q_{lo}^{\phi,\text{mode}}(\vec{s}(0))$ and $q_{hi}^{\phi,\text{mode}}(\vec{s}(0))$ (as in the calibration step) and return:
$$CPI^{\phi,\text{mode}}(\vec{s}(0)) = [q_{lo}^\phi(\vec{s}(0)) - \tau^{\phi,\text{mode}},\ q_{hi}^{\phi,\text{mode}}(\vec{s}(0)) + \tau^{\phi,\text{mode}}].$$

(built at step 2.a) are compared with the predictive intervals $PI^{\phi,\text{mode}}$ to obtain a set of nonconformity scores $e_i^{\phi,\text{mode}}$ (step 2.e) from which we extract the $(1-\alpha)$-th empirical quantile which results in the property and mode-specific critical score $\tau^{\phi,\text{mode}}$ (step 2.f). This $\tau^{\phi,\text{mode}}$ score is then used to recalibrate the predictive intervals computed over test data (step 3) to guarantee a coverage of $1 - \alpha$. The guarantees follow from the conformalized quantile regression theory introduced in Sect. 3.2 and state that the calibrated prediction interval $CPI^{\phi,\text{mode}}$ is guaranteed to contain the true unknown robustness values of trajectories belonging to mode with probability $(1 - \alpha)$. It represents the monitoring function $\text{Int}^{(\text{mode})}$ we asked for in Problem 1. Mathematically,

$$Pr_{\vec{s} \sim \vec{S}}(\text{Rob}_\phi(\vec{s}) \in CPI^{\phi,\text{mode}}(\vec{s}(0)) \mid \mathcal{M}(\vec{s}) = \text{mode}) \geq 1 - \alpha, \quad (5)$$

where $\vec{s}(0)$ is the current state of the system and $\vec{\mathbf{S}}$ denotes the random variable induced by the stochastic process $\mathbf{S} = \{\mathbf{S}(t,\omega), t \in \mathcal{I}\}$ defined before. We stress that guarantees hold under the assumption of exchangeability between calibration and test samples.

These mode-conditional guarantees allow us to obtain a range of robustness values for each possible dynamical mode. This information can be used to understand which decisions are safer than others and to identify modes that result in intervals with very high robustness, as well as those that cause potential violations. Moreover, the generative model could offer dynamics-aware insights into why the monitor is issuing an alarm. These insights can guide users in making informed decisions in response to the alarms. In particular, by analyzing the surrogate trajectories that result in negative robustness values, users can identify common undesirable behaviours potentially leading to safety violations. It is important to note that while these trajectories offer valuable insights into the causes of the alarms, they may not accurately depict potential scenarios—the statistical guarantees hold w.r.t. the robustness values calculated from them. Note that the generative model $p_\theta(\vec{s}|\vec{s}(0))$ is trained once and for all in step (1) (independently of the property), whereas step (2) is done only once (one for each mode) after we know the property and it should be repeated only if the property changes.

Unbalanced Generation. The process of filtering through the mode predictor $\mathcal{M}$ (step 2.c) could lead to unbalanced datasets as the number $K_{\texttt{mode}}$ of trajectories generated per mode may considerably vary based on the likelihood of observing that specific dynamics. This may affect the quality of the empirical quantiles $q_{lo}^{\phi,\texttt{mode}}(\vec{s}_i(0))$ and $q_{hi}^{\phi,\texttt{mode}}(\vec{s}_i(0))$. A solution would be to train a mode-conditional generative model so that we can generate the same number of trajectories for each mode. Mathematically, $p_\theta(\vec{s}|\vec{s}(0),\texttt{mode})$ produces samples trajectores $\vec{s}$ belonging to class $\texttt{mode} \in \{1,\ldots,G\}$. However, such a solution would limit the flexibility of the generative model, as adding a dynamical mode would require a retraining of the generative model. Alternatively, one can use guidance strategies [4,28] to impose soft constraints over the generation of trajectories that are likely to belong to the desired mode and with no need to even retrain the model.

Remark 1. The mode predictor, $\mathcal{M}$, can be either known a priori or learned from data. If labeled trajectories are available, where each label corresponds to the ground truth mode, supervised learning techniques can be employed to approximate the (unknown) true mode predictor. Conversely, in the absence of labels, unsupervised learning methods can be used, and the resulting learned predictor will serve as the true mode predictor. Regardless of how $\mathcal{M}$ is obtained, the mode-specific validity condition in Eq. (5) applies to the mode predictor used to partition the calibration set. However, experiments may reveal deviations from the target coverage level of $1-\alpha$ when evaluating the approximate mode predictor against a labeled test set. This occurs because the calibration data (classified by the approximate predictor) and the test data (classified by ground truth labels) lack exchangeability.

The union of the G mode-conditional calibrated prediction intervals, $CPI^\phi(\vec{s}(0)) := \bigcup_{\text{mode}=1}^{G} CPI^{\phi,\text{mode}}(\vec{s}(0))$, has a guaranteed marginal coverage of $1-\alpha$ over the robustness values of all trajectories (here, using the law of total probability):

$$Pr_{\vec{s}\sim\mathbf{S}}\big(\text{Rob}_\phi(\vec{s}) \in CPI^\phi(\vec{s}(0))\big) = \sum_{\text{mode}=1}^{G} Pr_{\vec{s}\sim\mathbf{S}}(\mathcal{M}(\vec{s}) = \text{mode}) \cdot \qquad (6)$$
$$\cdot Pr_{\vec{s}\sim\mathbf{S}}\big(\text{Rob}_\phi(\vec{s}) \in CPI^{\phi,\text{mode}}(\vec{s}(0)) \mid \mathcal{M}(\vec{s}) = \text{mode}\big) \geq 1-\alpha.$$

The need for a generative model lies in that it allows approximating the conditional distribution of trajectories $p(\vec{s}|\vec{s}(0))$, from which it is then trivial to compute empirical upper and lower quantiles of $p(\text{Rob}_\phi(\vec{s}) \mid \vec{s}(0))$. An autoregressive/recurrent trajectory model, that predicts only $\mathbb{E}[\vec{s}|\vec{s}(0)]$ (as in [21]), does not allow us to access the full distribution and thus we cannot extract quantiles. An alternative would be to directly predict quantiles of $p(\text{Rob}_\phi(\vec{s}) \mid \vec{s}(0))$ (as in [12]). The advantage is that the predictor is tailored to the property and may lead to better accuracy but that is also a disadvantage in that one needs to train a predictor for any property of interest. The above approach instead requires only making a pass to the calibration distribution (step 2) whenever we know the property and need no retraining of the generative model.

4.2 Dynamic Multi-agent Dynamic Environments

GenQPM adapts efficiently to dynamically changing environments. Consider, for instance, a scenario such as the one depicted in Fig. 3, where an ego vehicle approaches a crossroad. Property ψ should enforce that the ego vehicle always keeps a safety distance from pedestrians and other vehicles and does not go the wrong way down a one-way street, e.g. it should not turn right from the state depicted in the figure. Some requirements are static, e.g., staying in the lane and not turning right. Some others may change dynamically over time, for instance, those when new obstacles appear or when obstacles move unpredictably. Looking at Fig. 3, we see how the car coming from the right lane could either go straight, turn left or turn right and this choice affects the safety of the monitored ego vehicle. The same applies to the pedestrian who, moreover, can become invisible to the ego vehicle when covered by the big tree. Even when the environment changes, the mode predictor itself remains fixed (e.g., the dynamical modes of the ego vehicle are still limited to turning left, turning right, or going straight).

However, in multi-agent environments, where interactions are highly unpredictable, the distribution of robustness values becomes significantly more complex. In GenQPM we face such dynamic environments as follows. For each agent that enters the scene, we train a dedicated generative model capable of emulating all possible behavioural outputs. By doing so the unpredictable evolutions of the dynamic agents can be incorporated into the monitoring scheme. More precisely, as soon as the ego vehicle detects a new agent in the scene (a car, a bike or a pedestrian) it updates the property ϕ to account for such new agent and evaluate its robustness by simulating a pool of synthetic evolutions of all the agents present in the scene. As the environment dynamically evolves, we must periodically update the calibration sets $D_c^{\phi,1}, \ldots, D_c^{\phi,G2}$ as the robustness values also depend on the unrolling of other agents' dynamics, which can be efficiently emulated to extract the mode-specific calibration scores $\tau^{\phi,\text{mode}}$. In other words, the process necessitates additional surrogate simulations for all the new agents and it involves calculating new robustness values, given that the property being monitored has changed. Furthermore, once an agent is detected, GenQPM continues to track it within a defined time window. This allows the monitor to account for agents temporarily obscured from view, such as a pedestrian hidden behind a tree, who might suddenly re-enter the scene and pose a collision risk. This approach enhances system safety and improves the reliability of our monitor in managing partially observable obstacles.

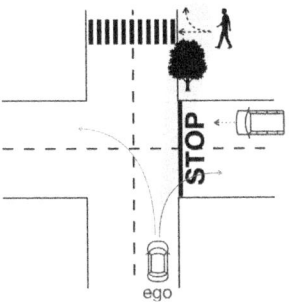

Fig. 3. Example of an uncertain multi-agent environment: pedestrian following a stochastic behavior with an obstacle (the tree) partially hiding its position to the ego vehicle.

5 Experimental Results

We experimentally evaluate the proposed GenQPM over a variety of multi-modal stochastic scenarios. We consider a one-dimensional signal showing multiple stable equilibria, a crossroad scenario, and a 2D planning scenario with obstacles to avoid.

---

[2] The introduction of new agents introduces a distribution shift. While there are other ways to address distribution shifts in CP, we choose to update the calibration datasets to obtain coverage guarantees over the shifted distribution and restore exchangeability between the calibration and test set.

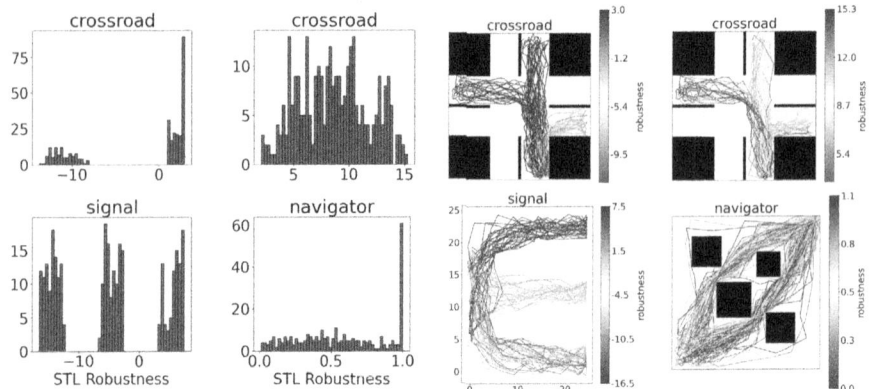

Fig. 4. Left: distribution of STL robustness values for Crossroad-ϕ_{right}, ϕ_{car}, ϕ_{multi}, Signal and Navigation respectively. Right: Simulated trajectories with colour denoting the STL robustness for the same case studies.

5.1 Case Studies

Signal. One-dimensional signal evolving over time showing three different stable equilibria. The STL property states that the signal will eventually reach and stay in the equilibrium with a value higher than 17.5: $\phi = F_{[0,22]}G_{[0,22]}(\vec{s} \geq 17.5)$. The scenario shows three dynamical modes.

Navigation. Agent navigating in a 2D room with square obstacles. The STL property specifies that the agent should avoid all the obstacles including the walls: $\phi = G_{[0,H]}\left(\wedge_{i=1}^{4} (\|\vec{s} - c_i\|_\infty \geq \ell_i) \wedge \|\vec{s} - (15,15)\|_\infty \leq 14\right)$ where (c_i, ℓ_i) denotes the obstacles' centre and radius. The scenario shows four dynamical modes, two of which are rarely visited by the agent.

Crossroad. Crossroad scenario shown in Fig. 3, where the ego vehicle approaches the crossroad from the bottom and there is another moving car approaching from its right. We enforce two different STL properties: ϕ_{right} states that turning right is forbidden (as it is a one-way road), $\phi_{\text{right}} = G_{[0,20]}(x \leq 37)$, and ϕ_{car} states that ego should keep a safe distance from the moving car, $\phi_{\text{car}} = G_{[0,20]}(d(\vec{s}_{ego}, \vec{s}_{car}) > 5)$. The scenario shows three dynamical modes. In this simpler example, we assume no pedestrian populating the scene and the other car is assumed to go straight because the no-turn signal was used to indicate a possible turn.

Multi-agent Crossroad. The crossroad scenario in Fig. 3 features multiple obstacles with varying degrees of uncertainty. For example, the no-right-turn sign represents a static obstacle (property ϕ_{right}), while the other car follows a deterministic path (property ϕ_{car}). In contrast, the pedestrian's future position is probabilistic, as they may decide to cross the street or not. Additionally, the pedestrian's movements are only partially observable as a tree temporarily blocks the ego vehicle's view. The STL property is $\phi_{\text{multi}} = G_{[0,20]}\Big((d(\vec{s}_{ego}, \vec{s}_{ped}) >$

5))$\land \phi_{\text{car}} \land \phi_{\text{right}}$, where ϕ_{right} and ϕ_{car} are the properties defined above stating respectively not to turn right and to keep a safety distance from the moving car. The dynamics of the moving obstacles are replaced by deep generative models acting as surrogates informing the ego vehicle about the possible evolutions of the multi-agent system. In this particular framework, we train a deep generative model capturing the possible choices of a pedestrian as it approaches a crossroad. Once the ego vehicle detects a pedestrian, it continues to track the pedestrian even if it temporarily loses sight of it for a short period.

Figure 4 and 5 show a visualization of the three case studies. Figure 4 shows trajectories with the respective STL robustness values, where blue denotes higher values and red denotes lower values. Figure 5 shows the same trajectories classified according to their dynamical mode. The Signal case study presents a scenario where trajectories in the same mode present similar robustness values, whereas the Crossroad and Navigation case studies present more heterogenous behaviours, where the same mode is associated with different levels of robustness. The Navigation case study presents two modes that are visited less frequently than the others. We use MATLAB Probabilistic Roadmap[3] (PRM) [17] library to generate the synthetic data of each case study.

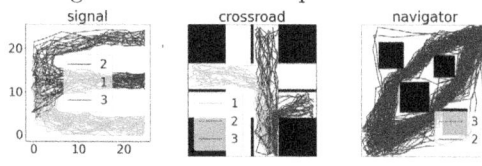

Fig. 5. Mode predictor $\mathcal{M}$ applied to trajectories from Signal, Crossroad and Navigator scenarios.

5.2 Evaluation Metrics

We want our method to be capable of working at runtime in safety-critical applications, which translates into the need for high reliability and high computational efficiency in producing the predictive intervals and calibrating them. We emphasize that the time required to train the generative model does not affect the runtime efficiency, as it is performed in advance (offline) only once. The generation of trajectories evolving from the current state of the system can be easily parallelized on GPU. Such time is constant, i.e., it does not depend on the complexity of the system it approximates but only on the architecture of the generative model, and it is in general, very low. In addition, we do not want an over-conservative predictor as an unnecessarily large interval would reduce the effectiveness of our GenQPM. Keeping that in mind, we introduce some relevant metrics to evaluate the performances of our GenQPM. The generated quantiles are property-specific. However, monitoring a different property requires neither retraining of the generative model nor the generation of novel trajectories. We simply evaluate the quantitative STL semantics for the new property on the already generated trajectories. If a new agent appears in the scene, we generate synthetic trajectories from its current position. The mode-agnostic version of

---
[3] https://www.mathworks.com/help/robotics/ug/probabilistic-roadmaps-prm.html.

Algorithm 1, where all trajectories are assumed to belong to the same mode, acts as a baseline for our experiments.

Coverage and Efficiency. We experimentally check that the guaranteed validity of GenQPM is empirically met in the test evaluation. On the one hand, we compute the empirical coverage as the percentage of test trajectories whose robustness values fall inside the calibrated prediction interval. In particular, we check, for each mode $\in \{1, \ldots, G\}$, whether the empirical coverage of $CPI^{\phi,\texttt{mode}}$ meets the target $1-\alpha$. On the other hand, efficiency represents the average width of the prediction intervals over the test set. For each test input, CPI^{ϕ} contains G prediction intervals. We compute the input-specific efficiency as the width of the disjoint union of such intervals and then average it over the entire test set. In general, the larger the prediction interval the more conservative the GenQPM predictions. If the prediction intervals over the robustness values are always very large we have little information about the satisfaction of property ϕ. However, the predictive efficiency must be compared with the width of the empirical quantile range (EQR), i.e. the interval that contains $(1-\alpha)$ of the simulated robustness values. We can thus measure the conservativeness as the difference in width between the predicted efficiency and the EQR width. Furthermore, we compare the performances under a known exact mode predictor $\mathcal{M}$ with those under an approximate data-driven mode predictor (Table 1). For the experiments, the approximate data-driven mode predictor is a neural network classifier trained over the training set D_t labeled with the exact mode predictor.

5.3 Experiments

The workflow can be divided into steps: (1) collect a pool of trajectories from the stochastic process, define the properties to monitor and evaluate the STL robustness over those trajectories, (2) train the generative model, (3) generate the synthetic trajectories (simulate and compute STL robustness), (4) obtain property-specific quantile intervals, (5) acquire a mode predictor $\mathcal{M}$ (either knowledge-based or data-driven) (6) compute the mode-specific calibration score $\tau^{\phi,\texttt{mode}}$ (obtaining calibrated prediction intervals), (7) evaluate CPI^{ϕ} on a test set.

Experimental Settings. The entire pipeline is implemented in Python. The generative models and the STL semantics are described in PyTorch [24]. The experiments were conducted on a shared virtual machine with a 32-Core Processor, 64 GB of RAM and an NVidia A100 GPU with 20 GB, and 8 VCPU. Our implementation of GenQPM is available at https://github.com/francescacairoli/GenerativeQPM.git.

Datasets. We build training sets with 3000 trajectories, calibration sets with 600 initial states and 300 trajectories per state and test sets with 200 initial states and 300 trajectories per state. States are randomly sampled from a uniform distribution. We validate the $1-\alpha$ coverage guarantees by computing for every initial state the ratio of covered robustness values for the associated 300 trajectories and then average these ratios over the 200 initial states. For each test point, we sample 500 calibration initial states in a bootstrapping manner, allowing calibration sets to vary at each test point.

Training Details and Offline Costs. The diffusion models were trained for 200 epochs with a batch size of 512 and a learning rate of 0.0005. The same architecture and hyper-parameters for all the case studies, leveraging the stability of score-based diffusion models. The training phase takes, on average, 3 min.

Performance Evaluation. For all the experiments we choose a significance level $\alpha = 0.1$ for every mode, so that the expected coverage is 90%. The lower and upper quantiles are computed respectively at $\alpha_{lo} = \alpha/2 = 0.05$ and $\alpha_{hi} = 1 - \alpha/2 = 0.95$.

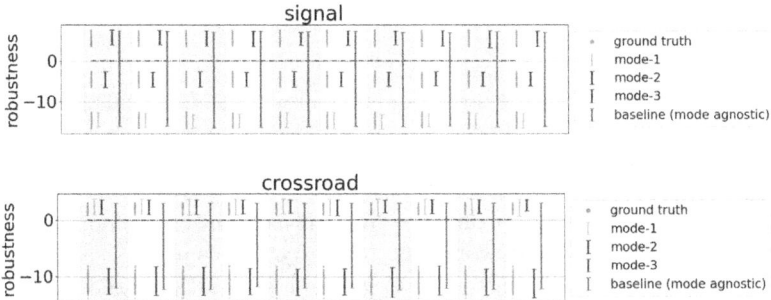

Fig. 6. Mode-specific calibrated prediction interval with mode-specific guarantees for Signal (top) and Crossroad-$\phi_{\texttt{right}}$ (bottom).

5.4 Results

Results are summarized in Fig. 6, 7, and in Table 1. Figure 6, 7 compare the empirical distribution of robustness values (in orange) at 10 different initial states with the predicted CPIs. Initial states vary along the horizontal axis whereas the vertical axis represents the support of the distribution of robustness values. Each CPI comprises G intervals denoted with a mode-specific colour (same colours shown in Fig. 5).

Figure 6 (top) shows the results for the Signal case study. The three modes of the robustness distribution coincide with the dynamical modes of the system. The three modes are well-separated and equally represented. Results show that each mode-specific CPI covers the respective peak of robustness values with the desired 90% coverage. Previous approaches to QPM, as the mode-agnostic version (grey baseline interval), result in a unique interval spanning from -15 to 5, providing no information about which is the safe mode.

Figure 6 (bottom) and Fig. 7 (top) shows the results for the Crossroad case study. Property $\phi_{\texttt{right}}$ is highly bi-modal with two safe modes (going straight

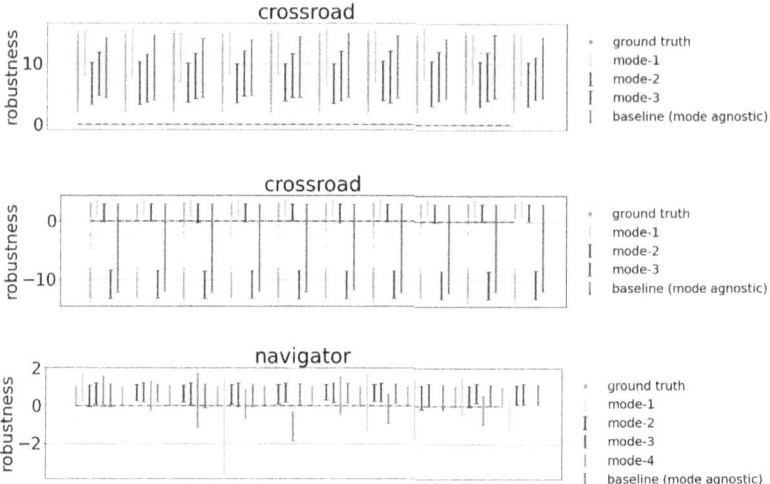

Fig. 7. Mode-specific calibrated prediction interval with mode-specific guarantees for Crossroad-ϕ_{car}, ϕ_{multi} and Navigator.

and turning left) and an unsafe one (the right turns of the ego vehicle). GenQPM always spots the unsafe mode correctly. Property ϕ_{car} is always satisfied in the test set. Despite always being positive, mode 1 shows the highest robustness values, and it would thus be a safer choice compared to modes 2 and 3. In decision making, one could potentially combine the results of GenQPM w.r.t. different STL properties and choose the mode that works better on most of the properties.

Figure 7 (bottom) shows the results for the Navigator case study. Here, mode 1 and mode 4 are under-represented in the dataset as those paths are rarely observed. GenQPM balances the lower representation with higher uncertainty and thus wider prediction intervals.

Figure 7 (middle) shows the results for the Multi-Agent Crossroad case study. The monitored requirement is a combination of ϕ_{right} and ϕ_{car} together with monitoring a safety distance from a stochastically behaving pedestrian that may sometimes cross the street. This stochastic behaviour causes a little shift towards potential violations of the safer mode. The shift is visible in the CPI of mode 2, the mode responsible for scenarios where the ego vehicle decides to go straight. Compared to Fig. 6 (bottom), this interval is indeed shifted towards negative values to account for the uncertainty represented by observing a pedestrian that approaches the crossroad.

Table 1 shows how CPI always meets the mode-wise desired coverage. A comparison of the efficiencies shows how GenQPM is more efficient than the mode-agnostic baseline whose values are always close to the empirical quantile range (EQR). We report the percentage width gain achieved by GenQPM compared to the mode-agnostic baseline. When the robustness distribution is multi-modal,

Table 1. Exact and **Approximate** mode predictor vs mode-agnostic baseline: Efficiency and Coverage results across Case Studies.

Case Study	EQR	Baseline Width	Cov.	Exact Width	Mode-wise Coverage	Approximate Width	Mode-wise Coverage
Signal	22.68	23.20	93.6	10.80 (−53%)	(90.5, 90.4, 89.9)	10.82 (−52%)	(89.9, 90.2, 89.9)
Xroad - $\phi_\texttt{right}$	15.50	15.37	92.6	7.42 (−51%)	(99.7, 95.3, 96.0)	7.66 (−50%)	(98.6, 93.6, 95.6)
Xroad - $\phi_\texttt{car}$	9.74	10.02	90.0	11.86 (+18%)	(93.9 86.6, 89.4)	11.92 (+17%)	(94.2, 87.4, 88.6)
Xroad - $\phi_\texttt{multi}$	15.50	15.03	91.4	8.46 (−43%)	(97.3, 92.6, 95.6)	8.44 (−44%)	(99.4, 93.3 96.0)
Navigation	0.93	1.09	93.5	inf	(86.2, 90.1, 90.3, 88.0)	inf	(100., 90.7, 90.6, 100.)

e.g. in Signal, Crossroad-$\phi_\texttt{right}$ and Multi-Agent Crossroad, the efficiency is around half w.r.t. EQR and the baseline. We qualitatively show how coverage (w.r.t. ground truth modes) and efficiency of CPIs obtained with a properly trained approximate mode predictor do not significantly deviate from the exact results. However, a poorly trained mode predictor may show poor performance. Underrepresented modes, such as those in Navigation, result in more conservative prediction intervals. In states where the predicted interval $CPI^{\phi,\texttt{mode}}$ has infinite width, we can conclude that the generative model is not properly capturing the dynamic in mode, leading to under-represented calibration sets $D_c^{\phi,\texttt{mode}}$ (see Sect. 4.1). Table 1 (*Approximate* column) illustrates how the approximate mode predictor yields prediction intervals of infinite width for these underrepresented modes. This occurs because the classifier struggles to accurately distinguish between classes with limited representation.

6 Related Work

Recent advancements in runtime predictive monitoring (PM) have seen the emergence of various learning-based approaches that employ conformal inference to provide statistical guarantees. Among these, the Neural Predictive Monitoring (NPM) framework [6,7,9,11,12,21] stands out for its application to a range of predictive tasks. Additionally, there has been substantial progress in reachability prediction for stochastic systems, with several methods [5,8,13,15,27,33] leveraging learning techniques to address uncertainties in system behaviours. A comprehensive survey on formal verification and control algorithms for autonomous systems, which uses conformal prediction (CP) to enhance safety guarantees, can be found in [22]. Moreover, recent work has started exploring the use of CP in multimodal and dynamic environments [18,20,31,35], expanding the applicability of these methods. Our contribution builds on these foundations by introducing a quantitative predictive monitoring approach that adapts flexibly to dynamic environments, demonstrates robust scalability, and maintains statistical guarantees. In particular, GenQPM is designed to support complex stochastic systems with expressive STL-based requirements. Utilizing deep generative models, GenQPM also provides interpretable insights, shedding light on potential failure causes.

7 Conclusions

We introduced GenQPM, a learning-based technique for monitoring the behaviour of highly stochastic systems in real-time. GenQPM evaluates the satisfaction of requirements—expressed as Signal Temporal Logic (STL) formulas—by computing a range of STL robustness values. These values are calibrated through principled adjustments, based on conformalized quantile regression, that ensure desired coverage levels, meaning each interval reliably captures STL robustness values with specified confidence. This feature is especially valuable for safety-critical applications, where statistical guarantees are essential. Our method demonstrates effectiveness in complex, multimodal scenarios and provides the flexibility to monitor evolving properties without retraining the underlying generative model or generating new trajectories. This adaptability reduces runtime overhead, as the property-specific calibration score computation introduces minimal additional cost. GenQPM incorporates the uncertainty related to moving hazards, e.g. external agents, by using generative models as surrogates for their dynamics. This approach allows us to estimate the potential impact of such agents on the system's safety, enhancing predictive accuracy in dynamic environments. Thanks to such generative surrogate models, GenQPM provides interpretable insights into the causes of a potential imminent failure. Overall, our experimental results confirm that GenQPM offers an efficient and reliable solution to the quantitative predictive monitoring problem.

Acknowledgments. This work has been partially supported by the "REXASI-PRO" H-EU project, call HORIZON-CL4-2021-HUMAN-01-01, Grant agreement ID: 101070028 and by the PNRR project iNEST (Interconnected North-Est Innovation Ecosystem) funded by the European Union Next-GenerationEU (Piano Nazionale di Ripresa e Resilienza (PNRR) – Missione 4 Componente 2, Investimento 1.5 – D.D. 1058 23/06/2022, ECS 00000043).

References

1. Angelopoulos, A.N., Bates, S.: A gentle introduction to conformal prediction and distribution-free uncertainty quantification. arXiv preprint arXiv:2107.07511 (2021)
2. Baier, C., Katoen, J.P.: Principles of Model Checking. MIT Press (2008)
3. Balasubramanian, V., Ho, S.S., Vovk, V.: Conformal prediction for reliable machine learning: theory, adaptations and applications. Newnes (2014)
4. Bansal, A., et al.: Universal guidance for diffusion models. In: Proceedings of the IEEE/CVF Conference on Computer Vision and Pattern Recognition, pp. 843–852 (2023)
5. Bortolussi, L., Cairoli, F., Carbone, G., Pulcini, P.: Stochastic variational smoothed model checking. arXiv preprint arXiv:2205.05398 (2022)
6. Bortolussi, L., Cairoli, F., Paoletti, N., Smolka, S.A., Stoller, S.D.: Neural predictive monitoring. In: Finkbeiner, B., Mariani, L. (eds.) RV 2019. LNCS, vol. 11757, pp. 129–147. Springer, Cham (2019). https://doi.org/10.1007/978-3-030-32079-9_8

7. Bortolussi, L., Cairoli, F., Paoletti, N., Smolka, S.A., Stoller, S.D.: Neural predictive monitoring and a comparison of frequentist and bayesian approaches. Int. J. Softw. Tools Technol. Transfer **23**(4), 615–640 (2021)
8. Bortolussi, L., Milios, D., Sanguinetti, G.: Smoothed model checking for uncertain continuous-time Markov chains. Inf. Comput. **247**, 235–253 (2016)
9. Cairoli, F., Bortolussi, L., Paoletti, N.: Neural predictive monitoring under partial observability (2021)
10. Cairoli, F., Kuipers, T., Bortolussi, L., Paoletti, N.: Conformal quantitative predictive monitoring of stochastic systems with conditional validity. Nonlinear Anal. Hybrid Syst. **57**, 101606 (2025)
11. Cairoli, F., Paoletti, N., Bortolussi, L.: Neural predictive monitoring for collective adaptive systems. In: ISoLA 2022 Symposium (2022, to appear)
12. Cairoli, F., Paoletti, N., Bortolussi, L.: Conformal quantitative predictive monitoring of STL requirements for stochastic processes. In: Proceedings of the 26th ACM International Conference on Hybrid Systems: Computation and Control, pp. 1–11 (2023)
13. Djeridane, B., Lygeros, J.: Neural approximation of PDE solutions: an application to reachability computations. In: Proceedings of the 45th IEEE Conference on Decision and Control, pp. 3034–3039. IEEE (2006)
14. Donzé, A., Maler, O.: Robust satisfaction of temporal logic over real-valued signals. In: Chatterjee, K., Henzinger, T.A. (eds.) FORMATS 2010. LNCS, vol. 6246, pp. 92–106. Springer, Heidelberg (2010). https://doi.org/10.1007/978-3-642-15297-9_9
15. Granig, W., Jakšić, S., Lewitschnig, H., Mateis, C., Ničković, D.: Weakness monitors for fail-aware systems. In: Bertrand, N., Jansen, N. (eds.) FORMATS 2020. LNCS, vol. 12288, pp. 283–299. Springer, Cham (2020). https://doi.org/10.1007/978-3-030-57628-8_17
16. Ho, J., Jain, A., Abbeel, P.: Denoising diffusion probabilistic models (2020)
17. Kavraki, L.E., Svestka, P., Latombe, J.C., Overmars, M.H.: Probabilistic roadmaps for path planning in high-dimensional configuration spaces. IEEE Trans. Robot. Autom. **12**(4), 566–580 (1996)
18. Kiyani, S., Pappas, G., Hassani, H.: Conformal prediction with learned features. arXiv preprint arXiv:2404.17487 (2024)
19. Leucker, M., Schallhart, C.: A brief account of runtime verification. J. Logic Algebraic Program. **78**(5), 293–303 (2009)
20. Lindemann, L., Cleaveland, M., Shim, G., Pappas, G.J.: Safe planning in dynamic environments using conformal prediction. IEEE Robot. Autom. Lett. (2023)
21. Lindemann, L., Qin, X., Deshmukh, J.V., Pappas, G.J.: Conformal prediction for STL runtime verification. In: Proceedings of the ACM/IEEE 14th International Conference on Cyber-Physical Systems (with CPS-IoT Week 2023), pp. 142–153 (2023)
22. Lindemann, L., Zhao, Y., Yu, X., Pappas, G.J., Deshmukh, J.V.: Formal verification and control with conformal prediction. arXiv preprint arXiv:2409.00536 (2024)
23. Maler, O., Nickovic, D.: Monitoring temporal properties of continuous signals. In: Lakhnech, Y., Yovine, S. (eds.) FORMATS/FTRTFT -2004. LNCS, vol. 3253, pp. 152–166. Springer, Heidelberg (2004). https://doi.org/10.1007/978-3-540-30206-3_12
24. Paszke, A., et al.: PyTorch: an imperative style, high-performance deep learning library. In: Advances in Neural Information Processing Systems, pp. 8024–8035 (2019)

25. Rodionova, A., Lindemann, L., Morari, M., Pappas, G.J.: Time-robust control for STL specifications. In: 2021 60th IEEE Conference on Decision and Control (CDC), pp. 572–579. IEEE (2021)
26. Romano, Y., Patterson, E., Candès, E.J.: Conformalized quantile regression. arXiv preprint arXiv:1905.03222 (2019)
27. Royo, V.R., Fridovich-Keil, D., Herbert, S., Tomlin, C.J.: Classification-based approximate reachability with guarantees applied to safe trajectory tracking. arXiv preprint arXiv:1803.03237 (2018)
28. Scassola, D., Saccani, S., Carbone, G., Bortolussi, L.: Conditioning score-based generative models by neuro-symbolic constraints. arXiv preprint arXiv:2308.16534 (2023)
29. Sohl-Dickstein, J., Weiss, E.A., Maheswaranathan, N., Ganguli, S.: Deep unsupervised learning using nonequilibrium thermodynamics (2015)
30. Tashiro, Y., Song, J., Song, Y., Ermon, S.: CSDI: conditional score-based diffusion models for probabilistic time series imputation (2021)
31. Tumu, R., Cleaveland, M., Mangharam, R., Pappas, G., Lindemann, L.: Multimodal conformal prediction regions by optimizing convex shape templates. In: 6th Annual Learning for Dynamics & Control Conference, pp. 1343–1356. PMLR (2024)
32. Vovk, V., Gammerman, A., Shafer, G.: Algorithmic Learning in a Random World. Springer, Cham (2022)
33. Yel, E., et al.: Assured runtime monitoring and planning: toward verification of neural networks for safe autonomous operations. IEEE Robot. Autom. Mag. **27**(2), 102–116 (2020)
34. Younes, H.L., Simmons, R.G.: Statistical probabilistic model checking with a focus on time-bounded properties. Inf. Comput. **204**(9), 1368–1409 (2006)
35. Zecchin, M., Park, S., Simeone, O.: Forking uncertainties: reliable prediction and model predictive control with sequence models via conformal risk control. IEEE J. Sel. Areas Inf. Theory (2024)
36. Zhao, Y., Hoxha, B., Fainekos, G., Deshmukh, J.V., Lindemann, L.: Robust conformal prediction for STL runtime verification under distribution shift. In: 2024 ACM/IEEE 15th International Conference on Cyber-Physical Systems (ICCPS), pp. 169–179. IEEE (2024)

Runtime Verification for LTL in Stochastic Systems

Javier Esparza[✉] and Vincent Fischer

Technical University of Munich, Munich, Germany
{esparza,fischerv}@in.tum.de

Abstract. Runtime verification encompasses several lightweight techniques for checking whether a system's current execution satisfies a given specification. We focus on runtime verification for Linear Temporal Logic (LTL). Previous work describes monitors which produce, at every time step one of three outputs - true, false, or inconclusive - depending on whether the observed execution prefix definitively determines satisfaction of the formula. However, for many LTL formulas, such as liveness properties, satisfaction cannot be concluded from any finite prefix. For these properties traditional monitors will always output inconclusive. In this work, we propose a novel monitoring approach that replaces hard verdicts with probabilistic predictions and an associated confidence score. Our method guarantees eventual correctness of the prediction and ensures that confidence increases without bound from that point on.

Keywords: Runtime verification · Linear Temporal Logic · Stochastic Systems

1 Introduction

Runtime verification is a lightweight verification technique complementing model checking and testing. It focuses on whether a run of the system under scrutiny satisfies or violates a given property [4,17,25]. In the online setting this is achieved by *monitors* that watch the finite prefixes of an infinite run and emits for each prefix a verdict of the form true, false, or "don't know yet". Intuitively, the monitor has no knowledge of the system, and so its verdict at a given time can only depend on the prefix of the run executed until that time.

In this paper we restrict ourselves to runtime verification of properties specified in Linear Temporal Logic (LTL). This problem was studied by Bauer *et al.* in [5–8] (see also work by Barringer *et al.* [2,3]). Bauer *et al.* show how to construct, given an LTL formula φ, a monitor that for any finite trace π emits the verdict true if π is a *good prefix* [22], meaning that every run extending π satisfies φ; false, if π is a *bad prefix*, meaning that every run extending π violates φ; and inconclusive, otherwise. A property is *monitorizable* if for every finite trace π there exists at least one finite trace v such that πv is a good or bad prefix.

Bauer et al. show that the set of monitorizable properties properly includes all safety and co-safety properties.

There exist many LTL formulas for which the monitor answers inconclusive for any π ([8] reports this to be the case for 43 out of a suite of 97 formulas selected from the software specification pattern collection [13]). Examples include **GF**p, which expresses that p holds infinitely often during the execution, or **G**$(r \rightarrow $**F**$a)$, stating that every request is eventually followed by an answer. On the one hand, this is clearly unavoidable, since liveness properties are informally defined as those for which no finite prefix reveals whether the property holds. However, one of the reasons for the introduction of LTL is precisely to have a unique specification formalism for both safety and liveness properties, which makes the situation unsatisfactory.

We show that when the system under scrutiny is an unknown finite-state Markov chain it is possible to design monitors that always outputs a boolean *verdict* (true or false), together with a quantitative *confidence level* in it.

A natural first idea is to relate the confidence to the probability that a run extending π satisfies the property[1]. However, this probability is only defined under the assumption that the Markov chain has been sampled from some set according to some probability distribution, which is not adequate in applications where systems are not sampled but designed. For this reason, we follow a different approach: our monitor delivers a boolean verdict derived from the chain with the *maximum likelihood* of generating the current trace, and a confidence level derived using a *likelihood ratio* estimate. Verdict and confidence level can be computed by a monitor that only knows a) the current finite trace, meaning the sequence of states of the chain visited so far by the sampled execution, and b) a lower bound on the minimal probability of the transitions of the chain. In particular, the size of the chain is unknown. In the rest of the section we provide some more details.

Our Setting. We assume that the Markov chain $\underline{M}$ under scrutiny belongs to the set of all finite-state Markov chains with states drawn from given countable set S, and where all transitions have probability at least $p_{min} \in (0, 1]$. Further, we assume that the property of interest is given as an LTL formula φ over a finite set of atomic propositions AP. We identify each atomic proposition $P \in$ AP with a set of states of S—intuitively, the set of states satisfying the proposition. So we assume $P \subseteq $ S for every atomic proposition P.

Using well-known theory we can construct a *deterministic* Rabin automaton A recognizing the language $L(\varphi) \subseteq $ S$^\omega$ of infinite traces that satisfy φ, see e.g. [1]. Let Q be the set of states of A. Our task is to design a monitor that observes a finite trace $\pi \in$ (Q $\times$ S)* generated by the product Markov chain M := A $\times$ $\underline{M}$, and emits a *verdict* (true or false) and a quantitative *confidence* in the verdict, expressed as a nonnegative real number[2].

---

[1] For example, Bauer et al. mention "monitors yielding a probability with which a given correctness property is satisfied" ([8], page 294).

[2] Observe that, since A is a deterministic automaton, M is well defined: we have $(q, s) \xrightarrow{p} (q', s')$ iff $s \xrightarrow{p} s'$ and $q \xrightarrow{s} q'$ are transitions of $\underline{M}$ and A.

Verdict. Our approach is based on the well-known maximum likelihood principle. Loosely speaking, the principle states that, when betting on which chain has generated the observed trace π, one should bet on a chain with maximal probability of generating π (more precisely, on one of the chains for which the probability of the runs extending π is maximal). We prove the following simple but powerful zero-one law, which allows our monitor to choose its qualitative verdict:

For every finite trace $\pi \in (\mathsf{Q} \times \mathsf{S})^*$, there exists a unique product Markov chain M_π with maximum likelihood of producing π (up to "irrelevant" states and transitions not reachable from the initial state of π). Moreover, the probability that a run of M_π extending π satisfies φ is either 0 or 1.

The chain M_π is just the one containing the states and transitions of π, and can be easily computed on the fly. Our monitor constructs M_π, determines if the probability is 0 or 1, and outputs false or true accordingly.

Confidence. The maximum likelihood principle does not help to derive a confidence level: intuitively, it determines on which chain to bet, but not with which odds. For this, we use another well established statistical notion: the *likelihood ratio* between two different statistical models (see e.g. [24]). In our setting, this is the ratio between the likelihood of M_π, which is maximal, and the supremum of the likelihoods of all chains that disagree with M_π on the satisfaction of φ (and which hence do not have maximal likelihood). The ratio is akin to the odds of the verdict being correct.

Our monitor uses π and $\mathsf{p}_{\min}$ to compute a lower bound on the likelihood ration, and outputs it as confidence measure. We show that the confidence converges a.s. towards ∞ when π grows. In other words, the monitor becomes increasingly confident in its verdict over time.

Related Work. Runtime verification of LTL properties has been extensively studied in the non-stochastic setting, both for boolean properties where a run satisfies a property or not—see e.g. the surveys [4,17,25]—and for quantitative properties [19,20]. We focus on the stochastic setting.

Our work on runtime enforcement of LTL properties [14,15] (which uses ideas from [12]) is closely related to this paper. The goal of [14,15] is, given a Markov chain M and a property φ, design monitors for restarting M that fulfill the following specification: if the runs of M satisfying φ have positive probability, then with probability 1 the number of restarts is finite, and the infinite run executed after the last restart satisfies φ. However, the restarting monitor does not provide any quantitative measure of the likelihood that the current trace extends to an infinite run satisfying φ.

In [18], Gondi *et al.* study runtime monitoring of ω-regular properties of stochastic systems. They consider monitors that only output a boolean verdict, but with a guaranteed probability of answering true for runs satisfying the property. We follow a different approach: our monitors output a confidence in their verdict for the concrete finite trace that has been observed so far.

In [21,27] Stoller *et al.* also study runtime verification of stochastic systems. They interpret temporal formulas on finite traces, and study the problem of designing monitors that can only observe part of the trace. This is different from our approach, where we are interested in liveness properties of infinite runs.

Our problem is also related to statistical model checking—see e.g. [23] for a recent survey. The focus lies in estimating the probability of the runs satisfying a given property, where we study whether a finite trace will extend to a run satisfying the property.

2 Preliminaries and Setting of the Paper

Directed Graphs. A directed graph is a pair $G = (V, E)$, where V is the set of vertices and $E \subseteq V \times V$ is the set of edges. A path (infinite path) of G is a finite (infinite) sequence $v_0 v_1 \ldots$ of vertices such that $(v_i, v_{i+1}) \in E$ for every $i = 0, 1 \ldots$. A strongly connected component (SCC) of G is a largest set V' of vertices satisfying that for every two vertices $v, v' \in V'$ there is a path in G leading from v to v'. A bottom SCC (BSCC) of G is an SCC V' such that $v \in V'$ and $(v, v') \in E$ implies $v' \in V'$.

Markov Chains. We fix a countable set S, called the *state universe*. A *Markov chain* is a triple $M = (S, \mathbf{P}, \mu)$, where

- $S \subseteq \mathsf{S}$ is a set of *states*,
- $\mathbf{P}: S \times S \to [0,1]$ is the *probability matrix*, satisfying $\sum_{s' \in S} \mathbf{P}(s, s') = 1$ for every $s \in S$, and
- μ is the *initial probability distribution* over S.

A pair $(s, s') \in S \times S$ of states is a *transition* of M if $\mathbf{P}(s, s') > 0$. The *graph of* M is the directed graph (V, E) where $V = S$ and $E = \{(s, s'): \mathbf{P}(s, s') > 0\}$. A *run* of M is an infinite path $\rho = s_0 s_1 \cdots$ of (the graph of) M; we let $\rho[i]$ denote the state s_i. Each path π of M determines the set of runs $\mathsf{Cone}(\pi)$ consisting of all runs that start with π. We assign to M the probability space $(\mathsf{Runs}, \mathcal{F}, \mathbb{P})$, where Runs is the set of all runs of M, $\mathcal{F}$ is the σ-algebra generated by all $\mathsf{Cone}(\pi)$, and $\mathbb{P}$ is the unique probability measure such that $\mathbb{P}[\mathsf{Cone}(s_0 s_1 \cdots s_k)] = \mu(s_0) \cdot \prod_{i=1}^{k} \mathbf{P}(s_{i-1}, s_i)$, with $\mathbb{P}[\mathsf{Cone}(s_0)] = \mu(s_0)$ for $k = 0$. The state s_k is *reachable* from s_0 if $\mathbb{P}[\mathsf{Cone}(s_0 s_1 \cdots s_k)] > 0$ or, equivalently, if (s_i, s_{i+1}) is a transition for every $0 \leq i \leq k_1$.

Linear Temporal Logic. Formulas of Linear Temporal Logic (LTL) over a set AP of atomic propositions are expressions over the following syntax:

$$\varphi ::= P \mid \neg \varphi \mid \varphi \wedge \varphi \mid \varphi \vee \varphi \mid \mathbf{X}\varphi \mid \varphi \mathbf{U} \varphi$$

where $P \in \mathsf{AP}$ and $\mathbf{X}, \mathbf{U}$ are the next and strong until operators, respectively. We assume that each atomic proposition is a subset of the state universe S. Using this, we interpret formulas of LTL on *infinite traces*, defined as infinite words over S, as follows. Given an infinite trace $\pi = s_0 s_1 s_2 \cdots \in \mathsf{S}^\omega$, we let

$\pi^{\geq i} := s_i s_{i+1} s_{i+2} \cdots$ denote its i-th suffix. The satisfaction relation $\pi \models \varphi$ is inductively defined as the smallest relation satisfying

$$\begin{aligned}
\pi &\models P & &\text{iff } s_0 \in P \\
\pi &\models \neg \varphi & &\text{iff } \pi \not\models \varphi \\
\pi &\models \varphi \wedge \psi & &\text{iff } \pi \models \varphi \text{ and } \pi \models \psi \\
\pi &\models \varphi \vee \psi & &\text{iff } \pi \models \varphi \text{ or } \pi \models \psi \\
\pi &\models \mathbf{X}\varphi & &\text{iff } \pi^{\geq 1} \models \varphi \\
\pi &\models \varphi \mathbf{U} \psi & &\text{iff } \exists k.\, \pi^{\geq k} \models \psi \text{ and } \forall j < k.\, \pi^{\geq j} \models \varphi\,.
\end{aligned}$$

We use the abbreviations true $:= P \vee \neg P$, false $:= \neg$true, $\mathbf{F}\varphi := $ true $\mathbf{U}\,\varphi$ (eventually φ) and $\mathbf{G}\varphi := \neg \mathbf{F} \neg \varphi$ (always φ). We let $L(\varphi) := \{\pi \in \mathsf{S}^\omega : \pi \models \varphi\}$ denote the language of infinite traces that satisfy φ. So, for example, $\mathbf{G}P$ denotes the infinite traces all whose states belong to P.

Deterministic Rabin Automata. A *deterministic Rabin automaton* (DRA) is a tuple $A = (Q, \Sigma, \gamma, q_0, Acc)$ consisting of a finite set Q of states, a finite alphabet Σ, a transition function $\gamma \colon Q \times \Sigma \to Q$, an initial state q_0, and an acceptance condition $Acc \subseteq 2^Q \times 2^Q$. A set of pairs of states $(F, G) \in Acc$ is called a *Rabin pair*. An infinite word $w \in \Sigma^\omega$ is accepted by A if there is a Rabin pair $(F, G) \in Acc$ such that the unique run $q_0 q_1 q_2 \cdots$ of A on w visits F infinitely often (i.e., $q_i \in F$ for infinitely many i), and every state of G finitely often.

We are interested in DRAs with $\Sigma = 2^{\mathsf{AP}}$ for some finite set AP. We say that such a DRA accepts an infinite trace $s_0 s_1 \ldots \in \mathsf{S}^\omega$ if it accepts the word $\mathcal{P}_0 \mathcal{P}_1 \cdots \in (2^{\mathsf{AP}})^\omega$ where, for every $i \geq 0$, $\mathcal{P}_i \subseteq \mathsf{AP}$ is the set of atomic propositions that contain s_i. The language $L(A) \subseteq \mathsf{S}^\omega$ of such a DRA is the set of all infinite traces it accepts.

We use the following fundamental result of automata theory (see e.g. [1,16]):

Theorem 1. *For every LTL formula φ of length n over a finite set AP of atomic propositions we can effectively construct a DRA over the alphabet 2^{AP} with $2^{2^{O(n)}}$ states such that $L(A) = L(\varphi)$.*

Product Markov Chain. The product of a DRA $A = (Q, 2^{\mathsf{AP}}, \gamma, q_0, Acc)$ and a Markov chain $M = (S, \mathbf{P}, \mu)$ is the Markov chain $A \otimes M = (Q \times S, \mathbf{P}', \mu')$, where

- $\mathbf{P}'((q,s),(q',s')) = \mathbf{P}(s,s')$ if $q' = \gamma(q, \mathsf{AP}_s)$, where AP_s is the set of atomic propositions containing s, and $\mathbf{P}'((q,s),(q',s')) = 0$ otherwise; and
- $\mu'(q,s) = \mu(s)$ if $q = q_0$ and $\mu'(q,s) = 0$ otherwise.

Note that $A \otimes M$ has the same transition probabilities as M.

A run of $A \otimes M$ is *good* if it satisfies φ, i.e., if it is accepted by A, and *bad* otherwise. An SCC B of $A \otimes M$ is *good* if there exists a Rabin pair $(F, G) \in Acc$ such that $B \cap (S \times F) \neq \emptyset$ and $B \cap (S \times G) = \emptyset$. Otherwise, the SCC is *bad*. Observe that good runs of $A \otimes M$ almost surely reach a good BSCC (i.e., more formally, the probability that a run satisfies φ and does not reach a good BSCC is 0), and bad runs almost surely reach a bad BSCC (i.e., more formally, the probability that a run does not satisfy φ and does not reach a bad BSCC is also 0).

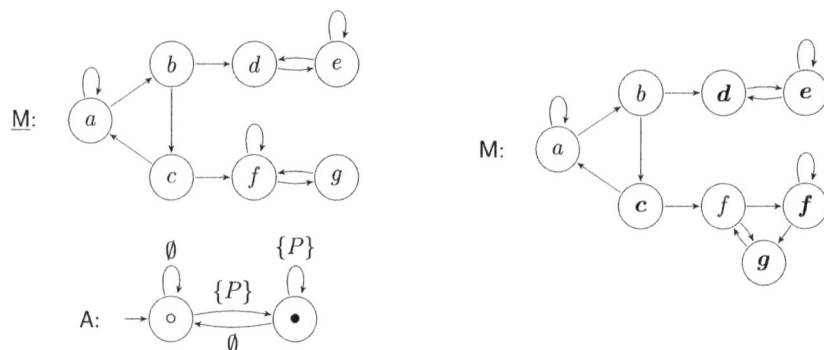

Fig. 1. A Markov chain M under scrutiny (upper left, the transition probabilities and the initial probability distribution are not shown), a DRA A for the property **FG**P, where $P = \{b, d, e, f\}$ (lower left), and their product M = A ⊗ M (right). We have AP = $\{P\}$, and so the alphabet of A is $2^{\text{AP}} = \{\emptyset, \{P\}\}$. The names of the states of M have been abbreviated: $(\circ, x)$ to x and $(\bullet, x)$ to $\boldsymbol{x}$ for $x \in \{a, \ldots, g\}$.

Setting of the Paper. We describe the general setting of the paper. We fix a Markov chain M under scrutiny with states drawn from the state universe S. The to-be-designed monitor only knows that M belongs to the set $\mathcal{M}$ of all finite-state Markov chains with states drawn from S and whose transition probabilities are bounded from below by a constant $\mathsf{p}_{\min} \in (0, 1]$. We fix a property of interest, formalized as an LTL formula φ over a finite set of atomic propositions AP $\subseteq 2^\mathsf{S}$. Finally, we fix a DRA A with set of states Q recognizing the language $L(\varphi) \subseteq \mathsf{S}^\omega$ of infinite traces of M that satisfy φ.

Convention: Underlined symbols like M or $\underline{M}$, possibly with subscripts or superscripts, denote elements of $\mathcal{M}$. Non-underlined symbols like M and M, also possibly with subscripts or superscripts, denote elements of the set $\mathcal{M} = \{\mathsf{A} \otimes \underline{M} : \underline{M} \in \mathcal{M}\}$ of product chains. Notice that states of product chains are drawn from the set Q × S.

Example 1 (Running example). The left diagram of Fig. 1 presents a Markov chain M under scrutiny (unknown to the monitor). Probabilities and initial distribution are omitted. The middle diagram shows a DRA A for the LTL formula $\varphi := \mathbf{FG}P$, where $P = \{b, d, e, f\}$. The runs of M satisfying the formula are those that, from some moment onwards, visit only states of P. For example, $ab(de)^\omega$ and $abcf^\omega$ are accepting, but $abc(fg)^\omega$ is not. The DRA A has one single Rabin pair (F, G), where $F = \{\bullet\}$ and $G = \{\circ\}$; the accepting runs of A eventually stay forever in state $\bullet$. The product chain M := A ⊗ M is shown on the right; states of the form $(\circ, x)$ and $(\bullet, x)$ are abbreviated to x and $\boldsymbol{x}$, respectively. For example, since $b \to d$ is a transition of M, $b \in P$ and $\circ \xrightarrow{\{P\}} \bullet$ is a transition of A, in the product chain M we have $(\circ, b) \to (\bullet, d)$. Observe that M has two BSCCs, namely $\{d, e\}$ and $\{f, \boldsymbol{f}, g\}$. They are good and bad, respectively.

3 Computing the Verdict

We design a monitor that observes a finite trace $\pi \in (Q \times S)^*$ of the product chain $M := A \otimes \underline{M}$ and emits a qualitative *verdict* (true or false) on whether the extension of π to a run of M will satisfy φ. In the next section we show how to add a quantitative confidence to the verdict.

The monitor applies the maximum likelihood principle. Recall the definition of likelihood and maximal likelihood:

Definition 1. *Let $M = (S, \mathbf{P}, \mu)$ be a Markov chain of $\mathcal{M}$. The likelihood that M generates $\pi = r_0 \cdots r_n$ is $\mathcal{L}(M \mid \pi) := \mathbb{P}_M[\mathsf{Cone}(\pi)] = \mu(r_0) \cdot \prod_{i=1}^{n} \mathbf{P}(r_{i-1}, r_i)$. M has* maximal likelihood *of generating π if $\mathcal{L}(M \mid \pi) \geq \mathcal{L}(M' \mid \pi)$ for every $M' \in \mathcal{M}$.*

The monitor constructs the graph of the unique chain $M_\pi \in \mathcal{M}$ with the maximum likelihood of generating π and a smallest number of states. (See e.g. [26], pp. 55–56, for a similar use of maximum likelihood estimation of Markov chains.) Sect. 3.1 defines M_π and shows that it has maximum likelihood, and Sect. 3.2 defines the monitor's verdict.

3.1 The Markov Chain M_π

Fix a finite trace $\pi = r_0 \cdots r_n$, where $r_i \in Q \times S$ for every $0 \leq i \leq n$. Loosely speaking, we define the Markov chain M_π induced by π as the chain whose states and transitions are the ones of π. There is however a minor technical problem. Assume $\pi = r_0 r_1$ with $r_0 \neq r_1$. Then the set of observed states is $\{r_0, r_1\}$ and the only observed transition is $r_0 \to r_1$. This cannot be the graph of a Markov chain because no edges leave state r_1, and so the sum of their probabilities cannot add up to 1. For this reason we assume that the last state r_n occurs at least twice in π.

Definition 2. *A finite trace $\pi = r_0 \cdots r_n$ is* closed *if $r_i = r_n$ for some $0 \leq i < n$, and* open *otherwise.*

For the transition probabilities of M_π, we look at the number of occurrences of each transition in π. Loosely speaking, we let the probabilities of the transitions leaving a given state be proportional to the number of times they occur in π. This gives the following formal definition:

Definition 3. *Let $\pi = r_0 \cdots r_n$ be a closed finite trace, let $T_\pi := \{\!\!\{(r_i, r_{i+1}) : 0 \leq i \leq n-1\}\!\!\}$ be the multiset of transitions that occur in π, and let $T_\pi(t)$ denote the number of occurrences of t in T_π. The Markov chain induced by π is $M_\pi = (S_\pi, \mathbf{P}_\pi, \mu_\pi)$, where*

- $S_\pi = \{r_0, \ldots, r_n\}$,

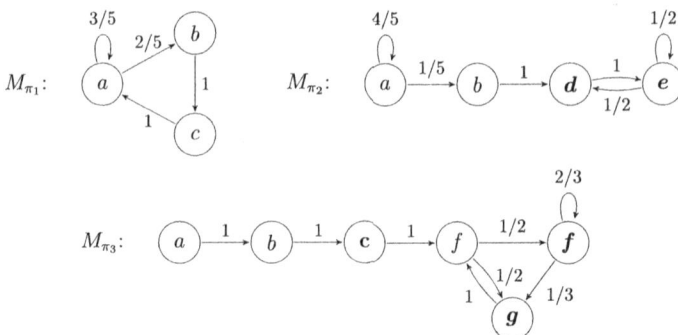

Fig. 2. Markov chains $M_{\pi_1}, M_{\pi_2}, M_{\pi_3}$ for $\pi_1 = a^3bca^2b$, $\pi_2 = a^5b(de^2)^3$ and $\pi_3 = abcff^3(gf)^2$. The initial probability distributions assign probability 1 to the state a and probability 0 to all other states.

- $\mathbf{P}_\pi(r, r') = \dfrac{T_\pi(r, r')}{\sum\limits_{r'' \in Q \times S} T_\pi(r, r'')}$, and
- $\mu_\pi(r) = 1$ if $r = r_0$ and $\mu_\pi(r) = 0$ otherwise.

Observe that M_π is well defined because, since π is closed, for every state $r \in S_\pi$ there is $r' \in S_\pi$ such that $T_\pi(r, r') > 0$.

Example 2. Assume the product chain M generating π is the one on the right of Fig. 1 and let $\pi_1 = a^3bca^2b$. We have $T_{\pi_1}(a, a) = 3$, $T_{\pi_1}(a, b) = 2$, $T_{\pi_1}(b, c) = 1$, $T_{\pi_1}(c, a) = 1$. Figure 2 shows the Markov chain M_{π_1}, as well as the chains M_{π_2} and M_{π_3} for the traces $\pi_2 = a^5b(de^2)^3$ and $\pi_3 = a^2bcf\boldsymbol{f}^3(\boldsymbol{g}f)^2$.

Remark 1. For any trace $\pi = r_0 \cdots r_n$, open or closed, we can define the graph with $r_0, \ldots, r_n$ and vertices and $\{(r_i, r_{i+1}) \mid 0 \leq i \leq n-1\}$ as edges. If π is closed, then this is the graph of M_π. If π is open, then r_n is a sink without outgoing edges.

We show that M_π is the unique Markov chain with maximum likelihood of generating π up to "irrelevant" states and transitions, meaning states and transitions that are not reachable from the initial state of π.

Definition 4. *Let $M = (S, \mathbf{P}, \mu)$ be a Markov chain of $\mathcal{M}$ such that $\mu(r_0) = 1$ for some $r_0 \in S$. The Markov chain $M|_{r_0} = (S|_{r_0}, \mathbf{P}|_{r_0}, \mu|_{r_0})$ is the restriction of M to the states reachable from r_0, that is, $S|_{r_0}$ contains the states of S reachable from r_0, $\mathbf{P}|_{r_0}(r, r') = \mathbf{P}(r, r')$ for every $r, r' \in S|_{r_0}$, and $\mu|_{r_0}(r) = \mu(r)$ for every $r \in S|_{r_0}$.*

Theorem 2. *For every closed finite trace π, a Markov chain $M = (S, \mathbf{P}, \mu)$ has maximum likelihood of generating π iff $\mu(r_0) = 1$ and $M|_{r_0} = M_\pi$, where r_0 is the first state of π.*

Proof. Let $M_m = (S_m, \mathbf{P}_m, \mu_m)$ be a Markov chain of $\mathcal{M}$ with maximal likelihood of generating π, that is $\mathcal{L}(M_m \mid \pi) \geq \mathcal{L}(M \mid \pi)$ for every $M \in \mathcal{M}$. We have $\mu_m(r_0) = 1$, because otherwise the chain $M = (S_m, \mathbf{P}_m, \mu'_m)$ with $\mu'_m(r_0) = 1$ has larger likelihood of generating π than M_m.

We show that $M|_{r_0} = M_\pi$. It suffices to prove $S_m|_{r_0} = S_\pi$, and $\mathbf{P}_m|_{r_0} = \mathbf{P}_\pi$. Indeed, $\mu_m|_{r_0} = \mu_\pi$ follows from $\mu_\pi(r_0) = 1$, $\mu_m(r_0) = 1$ and $S_m|_{r_0} = S_\pi$.

Let T_{r_0} be the set of transitions of $M_m|_{r_0}$, i.e., the set of transitions $(\hat{r}, \hat{r}')$ of M_m such that $\hat{r}$ (and so also $\hat{r}'$) is reachable from r_0. We prove $T_{r_0} = T_\pi$, which implies $S_m|_{r_0} = S_\pi$.

Claim 1. $T_{r_0} \subseteq T_\pi$.

Assume $T_{r_0} \setminus T_\pi$ is nonempty. We derive a contradiction. By the definition of T_{r_0}, some path of M_m starting at r_0 and containing only transitions of T_{r_0} ends with a transition of $T_{r_0} \setminus T_\pi$. Let $(\hat{r}, \hat{r}')$ be the first transition in this path that does not belong to T_π. We have $\hat{r} \in S_\pi$. Since $(\hat{r}, \hat{r}') \notin T_\pi$ and π is closed, we have $(\hat{r}, \hat{r}'') \in T_\pi$ for some $\hat{r}'' \neq \hat{r}'$. Consider the chain $M = (S_m, \mathbf{P}, \mu_m)$ with transition matrix $\mathbf{P}$ given by:

$$\mathbf{P}(r, r') := \begin{cases} 0 & \text{if } r = \hat{r} \text{ and } r' = \hat{r}' \\ \mathbf{P}_m(\hat{r}, \hat{r}'') + \mathbf{P}_m(\hat{r}, \hat{r}') & \text{if } r = \hat{r} \text{ and } r' = \hat{r}'' \\ \mathbf{P}_m(r, r') & \text{otherwise} \end{cases}$$

For every transition t of π we have $\mathbf{P}(t) \geq \mathbf{P}_m(t)$, and further $\mathbf{P}(\hat{r}, \hat{r}'') > \mathbf{P}_m(\hat{r}, \hat{r}'')$. So $\mathcal{L}(M \mid \pi) > \mathcal{L}(M_m \mid \pi)$, contradicting that M_m has maximum likelihood.

Claim 2. $T_\pi \subseteq T_{r_0}$.

Assume there exists $(\hat{r}, \hat{r}') \in T_\pi \setminus T_{r_0}$. Then $\mathbf{P}_m(\hat{r}, \hat{r}') = 0$ and so $\mathcal{L}(M_m \mid \pi) = 0$, which, together with $\mathcal{L}(M \mid \pi) > 0$, contradicts the maximal likelihood of M_m.

It remains to show $\mathbf{P}_m|_{r_0} = \mathbf{P}_\pi$.

Claim 3. $\mathbf{P}_m|_{r_0} = \mathbf{P}_\pi$.

Since $S_m|_{r_0} = S_\pi$, both $\mathbf{P}_m|_{r_0}$ and $\mathbf{P}_\pi$ are mappings $S_\pi \times S_\pi \to [0,1]$. Let $\pi = r_0 r_1 \cdots r_n$. We show $\mathbf{P}_m|_{r_0}(r_i, r_j) = \mathbf{P}_\pi(r_i, r_j)$ for every $0 \leq i, j \leq n$.

For every Markov chain $M = (S_\pi, \mathbf{P}, \mu_\pi)$ and every $r, s \in S_\pi$, let $p_{rs} := \mathbf{P}(r, s)$ and let $c_{rs} := T_\pi(r, s)$, that is, p_{rs} and c_{rs} are abbreviations for the probability of transitioning from r to s (possibly 0) and the number of occurrences of the string rs in π (possibly 0). We have

$$\mathcal{L}(M \mid \pi) = \mu_\pi(r_0) \cdot \prod_{i=0}^{n-1} \mathbf{P}(r_i, r_{i+1}) = \prod_{r \in S_\pi} \prod_{s \in S_\pi} p_{rs}^{c_{rs}}.$$

It follows that $\mathbf{P}_m$ is the solution of the following optimization problem, where the p_{rs} are variables and the c_{rs} are nonnegative constants:

$$\text{maximize} \quad \prod_{r \in S_\pi} \prod_{s \in S_\pi} p_{rs}^{c_{rs}} \quad \text{subject to} \quad \bigwedge_{r \in S_\pi} \left(\sum_{s \in S_\pi} p_{rs} = 1 \right).$$

Since the sets of variables appearing in each conjunct of the constraint are pairwise disjoint, and taking logarithms, the problem splits into independent subproblems:

for every $r \in S_\pi$: maximize $\sum_{s \in S_\pi} c_{rs} \cdot \log p_{rs}$ subject to $\sum_{s \in S_\pi} p_{rs} = 1$.

We solve each subproblem using the standard technique of Lagrange multipliers. (See [26], pp. 55–56 for a similar application of the technique.) The Lagrangian is

$$L(\mathbf{p}_r, \lambda) = \left(\sum_{s \in S_\pi} c_{rs} \cdot \log p_{rs} \right) - \lambda \left(\sum_{s \in S_\pi} p_{rs} - 1 \right) \quad (1)$$

Setting its partial derivatives to 0 and solving for p_{rs} yields

$$\frac{\partial L}{\partial p_{rs}} = \frac{c_{rs}}{p_{rs}} - \lambda = 0 \quad \Rightarrow \quad p_{rs} = \frac{c_{rs}}{\lambda} \quad (2)$$

Substituting into the constraint $\sum_{s \in S_\pi} p_{rs} = 1$ we obtain

$$\sum_{s \in S_\pi} \frac{c_{rs}}{\lambda} = 1 \quad \Rightarrow \quad \lambda = \sum_{s \in S_\pi} c_{rs} \quad (3)$$

Finally, plugging into (2) yields

$$p_{rs} = \frac{c_{rs}}{\sum_{s \in S_\pi} c_{rs}} \quad \text{and so} \quad \mathbf{P}(r, s) = \frac{T_\pi(r, s)}{\sum_{s \in S_\pi} T_\pi(r, s)} = \mathbf{P}_m(r, s). \quad \square$$

3.2 The Verdict

Assume the monitor observes a trace π. For the monitor, the chains with maximum likelihood of generating π are the most likely candidates to be the unknown product chain M. So the monitor must derive its verdict from the conditional probabilities $\mathbb{P}_M(L(\varphi) \mid \mathsf{Cone}(\pi))$—the probabilities that a run extending π satisfies φ—for the chains M with maximum likelihood. We introduce some notation:

Definition 5. *Given a finite trace π and a Markov chain M, we let $\mathbb{P}_M(\varphi \mid \pi) := \mathbb{P}_M(L(\varphi) \mid \mathsf{Cone}(\pi))$.*

In principle, $\mathbb{P}_M(\varphi \mid \pi)$ might depend on M. However, it follows immediately from the definitions that $\mathbb{P}_M(\varphi \mid \pi) = \mathbb{P}_{M|_{r_0}}(\varphi \mid \pi)$ for the initial state r_0 of π. By Theorem 2, we have $\mathbb{P}_M(\varphi \mid \pi) = \mathbb{P}_{M_\pi}(\varphi \mid \pi)$ for every closed trace π, and so we can safely focus on M_π and $\mathbb{P}_{M_\pi}(\varphi \mid \pi)$.

A second problem is how to derive a boolean verdict from the quantitative value $\mathbb{P}_{M_\pi}(\varphi \mid \pi)$. We solve it by proving that $\mathbb{P}_{M_\pi}(\varphi \mid \pi)$ is either 0 or 1. We start the proof with a definition.

Definition 6. *Given two SCCs G_1, G_2 of a directed graph G, we write $G_1 \preceq G_2$ if some path of G leads from a vertex of G_1 to a vertex of G_2.*

By the definition of an SCC, $\preceq$ is a partial order. We have:

Lemma 1. *For every finite trace $\pi = r_0 \cdots r_n$ (open or closed), let $G_\pi = (S_\pi, E_\pi)$ be the graph where $(r, r') \in E_\pi$ if $r = r_i$ and $r' = r_{i+1}$ for some $0 \leq i \leq n - 1$. The relation $\preceq$ on the SCCs of G_π is a total order. In particular, G_π has a unique BSCC.*

Proof. Let $\pi = r_0 r_1 \cdots r_n$ and let G_1, G_2 be two BSCCs of M_π. Let $0 \leq i_1, i_2 \leq n$ be the maximal indices such that $r_{i_1} \in G_1$ and $r_{i_2} \in G_2$. Assume w.l.o.g. that $i_1 \leq i_2$. Then, by the definition of G_π, the subsequence $r_{i_1} \cdots r_{i_2}$ of π is a path leading from G_1 to G_2 and so $G_1 \preceq G_2$. $\square$

Theorem 3. *For every finite closed trace π, the probability $\mathbb{P}_{M_\pi}(\varphi \mid \pi)$ is either 0 or 1. Further, $\mathbb{P}_{M_\pi}(\varphi \mid \pi) = \mathbb{P}_M(\varphi \mid \pi)$ for every Markov chain M with maximum likelihood of generating π.*

Proof. By Lemma 1, the graph of M_π has a unique BSCC B. Recall that the set R of runs of M_π that eventually get trapped in B and visit each state of B infinitely often has probability 1. So it suffices to show that the probability of the runs of R that satisfy φ is either 0 or 1. This result is folklore (see e.g. [1]), but we give a short proof for completeness. Let $B = \{(q_1, s_1), \ldots, (q_n, s_n)\}$. If the DRA A has a Rabin pair (F, G) such that $F \cap \{q_1, \ldots, q_n\} \neq \emptyset$ and $G \cap \{q_1, \ldots, q_n\} = \emptyset$, then the probability of the runs of R that satisfy φ is 1, and we are done. If A has no such Rabin pair, then a run of R either visits F only finitely often or G infinitely often with probability 1. So the probability of the runs of R that satisfy φ is 0.

For the second part, let M be any chain with maximum likelihood of generating π. Be Theorem 2 we have $M|_{r_0} = M_\pi$, which implies $\mathbb{P}_{M_\pi}(\varphi \mid \pi) = \mathbb{P}_M(\varphi \mid \pi)$. $\square$

We are now ready to define the verdict of our monitor on a trace π. It extends the monitor of Bauer et al. in [8], which we now recall, formulated in a slightly different way. We partition the states of A into three classes: empty states, universal states, and the rest. Given a state q, let $L(q)$ denote the language of A with q as initial state. We say that q is *empty* if $L(q) = \emptyset$ and *universal* if $L(q) = S^\omega$. It is easy to see that the partition can be computed in polynomial time.

For a trace π ending in a state $(q, s) \in Q \times S$, the monitor of [8] outputs verdict true if q is universal, false if q is empty, and "?" otherwise. Our monitor is a refinement. If q is neither empty nor universal and π is closed, it picks true or false according to the value of $\mathbb{P}_{M_\pi}(\varphi \mid \pi)$. If π is open, it answers "?".

Definition 7. *Let π be a finite trace ending in a state $(q, s) \in Q \times S$. The verdict $\nu(\pi) \in \{\text{true}, \text{false}, ?\}$ is defined as follows:*

- *If q is an universal state of A, then $\nu(\pi) := \text{true}$.*
- *If q is a empty state of A, then $\nu(\pi) := \text{false}$.*

– Otherwise,

$$\nu(\pi) := \begin{cases} \text{true} & \text{if } \pi \text{ is closed and } \mathbb{P}_{M_\pi}(\varphi \,|\, \pi) = 1 \\ \text{false} & \text{if } \pi \text{ is closed and } \mathbb{P}_{M_\pi}(\varphi \,|\, \pi) = 0 \\ ? & \text{if } \pi \text{ is open} \end{cases}$$

Observe that, by the definition of an open trace, in every run the verdict is "?" for only finitely many prefixes of the run. Indeed, since by assumption the Markov chain under scrutiny is finite, every run has a prefix, say π', that already contains all states visited by the run. So after π' all prefixes of the run are closed traces, and the monitor always delivers true or false as verdict.

Example 3. Consider again the traces $\pi_1 = a^3bca^2b, \pi_2 = a^5b(\boldsymbol{de}^2)^3$ and $\pi_3 = a^2bcf\boldsymbol{f}^3(\boldsymbol{g}f)^2$ of Example 2. Recall that x stands for $(\circ, x)$ and $\boldsymbol{x}$ for $(\bullet, x)$, and that the unique Rabin pair is $(F, G) = (\{\bullet\}, \{\circ\})$. The verdict for a closed trace is true if its unique BSCC intersects $\{\boldsymbol{a}, \cdots, \boldsymbol{g}\}$ and does not intersect $\{a, \ldots, g\}$. So the verdicts $\nu(\pi_1), \nu(\pi_2), \nu(\pi_3)$ are respectively false, true and false.

An example of a open trace is ab. Since state b is neither empty (because of e.g. $ab(\boldsymbol{de})^\omega$) nor universal (because of e.g. $abc(f\boldsymbol{fg})^\omega$), the verdict is "?".

4 Computing the Confidence Score

Let π be a closed finite trace, and assume w.l.o.g. $\nu(\pi) = $ true (otherwise set $\varphi := \neg\varphi$). If the chain M under scrutiny satisfies $\mathbb{P}_\mathsf{M}(\varphi \,|\, \pi) = 1$ then, by definition, a run of M extending π satisfies φ with probability 1, and so the probability that the verdict is correct is also 1. This implies:

Our confidence in the statement "M satisfies $\mathbb{P}_\mathsf{M}(\varphi \,|\, \pi) = 1$" is a lower bound for our confidence in the statement "the verdict true is correct."

For our confidence in $\mathbb{P}_\mathsf{M}(\varphi \,|\, \pi) = 1$ there is a standard statistical confidence measure: the *likelihood ratio* (see e.g. [24]). Given a partition of the set $\mathcal{M}$ of Markov chains into two subsets $\mathcal{M}_0, \mathcal{M}_1$ and an observation π, the *likelihood ratio* that M belongs to $\mathcal{M}_1$ is defined as

$$\frac{\sup\{\mathcal{L}(M \,|\, \pi) : M \in \mathcal{M}_1\}}{\sup\{\mathcal{L}(M \,|\, \pi) : M \in \mathcal{M}_0\}}$$

So we choose:

Definition 8. *We let* $\mathcal{M}_1 := \{M : \mathbb{P}_M(\varphi \,|\, \pi) = 1\}$ *and* $\mathcal{M}_0 := \{M : \mathbb{P}_M(\varphi \,|\, \pi) < 1\}$.

By Theorem 3, all chains with maximal likelihood of generating π belong to $\mathcal{M}_1$, hence $\sup\{\mathcal{L}(M \,|\, \pi) : M \in \mathcal{M}_1\} = \mathcal{L}(M_\pi \,|\, \pi)$. So, intuitively, a likelihood ratio of 10 means that the probability of generating π is at least 10 times higher in M_π, than in any Markov chain where the verdict might be incorrect with non-zero probability.

We can now introduce our confidence score:

Definition 9. Let π be a trace ending in a state $(q, s) \in \mathsf{Q} \times \mathsf{S}$. The confidence score $\Gamma(\pi) \in [1, \infty) \cup \{\infty\}$ is defined as follows:

- If q is an empty or universal state of A, or π is open, then $\Gamma(\pi) := \infty$.
- Otherwise
$$\Gamma(\pi) := \frac{\mathcal{L}(M_\pi \mid \pi)}{\sup\{\mathcal{L}(M \mid \pi) : M \in \mathcal{M}_0\}}$$

Remark 2. Recall that if q is an empty or universal state of A then the verdict is necessarily correct because *every* run extending π satisfies φ. So in this case we have unbounded confidence in the verdict. If q is neither universal nor empty but π is open, then the verdict is "?". The confidence in this verdict can be defined arbitrarily[3].

We use the assumption that transitions of chains in $\mathcal{M}$ have at least probability $\mathsf{p}_{\min} > 0$ to obtain a lower bound on $\Gamma(\pi)$. We start with a definition.

Definition 10. Let $\pi = r_0 \ldots r_n$ be a closed trace and let B be the unique BSCC of the graph of M_π. For every state $r \in B$, we let $\#_\pi(r)$ denote the number of times that r appears in $r_0 \cdots r_{n-1}$, and define $m_\pi := \min_{r \in B}\{\#_\pi(r)\}$.

Loosely speaking, $\#_\pi(r)$ denotes the number of times that π *leaves* the state r, and m_π is the minimum number of times that π leaves any of the states of B.

Definition 11. Let π be a closed trace. We define
$$\gamma(\pi) := \left(\frac{1}{1 - \mathsf{p}_{\min}}\right)^{m_\pi} \tag{4}$$

Theorem 4. *For every closed path π and every Markov chain $M \in \mathcal{M}_0$:*
$$\mathcal{L}(M_\pi \mid \pi) \geq \gamma(\pi) \cdot \mathcal{L}(M \mid \pi).$$
In particular, $\Gamma(\pi) \geq \gamma(\pi)$.

Proof. Let $M = (S, \mathbf{P}, \mu) \in \mathcal{M}_0$. If $\mathcal{L}(M \mid \pi) = 0$ we are done. Assume $\mathcal{L}(M \mid \pi) > 0$. Then the graph G_π containing the states and transitions of π is a subgraph of M. Let B be the unique BSCC of G_π. If B is also a BSCC of M, then $\mathbb{P}_M(\varphi \mid \pi) = 1$, contradicting the assumption $M \in \mathcal{M}_0$. Hence B is not a BSCC of M, and so there exist states $r_B, \bar{r}_B \in S$ such that $r_B \in B$, $\bar{r}_B \notin B$, and $\mathbf{P}(r_B, \bar{r}_B) > 0$. Let $M' := (S, \mathbf{P}', \mu)$ be the Markov chain with

$$\mathbf{P}'(r, r') := \begin{cases} 0 & \text{if } r = r_B \text{ and } r' = \bar{r}_B \\ \frac{\mathbf{P}(r,r')}{1 - \mathbf{P}(r_B, \bar{r}_B)} & \text{if } r = r_B \text{ and } r' \neq \bar{r}_B \\ \mathbf{P}(r, r') & \text{otherwise} \end{cases} \tag{5}$$

---

[3] Our choice corresponds to the monitor declaring "I have unbounded confidence in my ignorance.".

(Loosely speaking, we remove the transition $(r_B, \bar{r}_B)$ from M and distribute its probability among the other output transitions of r_B.)

We compare the likelihoods of M and M'. Recall that $T_\pi(r, r')$ denotes the number of times that $r\,r'$ appears in π. We have:

$$\frac{\mathcal{L}(M_\pi \mid \pi)}{\mathcal{L}(M \mid \pi)} \geq \frac{\mathcal{L}(M' \mid \pi)}{\mathcal{L}(M \mid \pi)} = \prod_{r \in S} \prod_{r' \in S} \left(\frac{\mathbf{P}'(r, r')}{\mathbf{P}(r, r')}\right)^{T_\pi(r, r')}$$

$$\stackrel{(5)}{=} \prod_{r' \in S} \left(\frac{1}{1 - \mathbf{P}(r_B, \bar{r}_B)}\right)^{T_\pi(r_B, r')} \geq \prod_{r' \in S} \left(\frac{1}{1 - \mathsf{p}_{\min}}\right)^{T_\pi(r_B, r')}$$

$$= \left(\frac{1}{1 - \mathsf{p}_{\min}}\right)^{\sum_{r' \in S} T_\pi(r_B, r')} = \left(\frac{1}{1 - \mathsf{p}_{\min}}\right)^{\#_\pi(r_B)} \geq \left(\frac{1}{1 - \mathsf{p}_{\min}}\right)^{m_\pi}$$

which concludes the proof. □

Remark 3. For closed paths not ending in an empty or universal state we can also do a similar construction in reverse, proving that $\gamma(\pi) = \Gamma(\pi)$. Loosely speaking, we start with the Markov chain M_π. There exists a state r in the unique BSCC of M_π, which was visited m_π times. To this state we add a new "escape transition", with transition probability $c \geq \mathsf{p}_{\min}$ leading to a new BSCC where good runs have probability 0. The old transition probabilities get rescaled by a factor $1-c$ to compensate. The resulting Markov chain M_c then has likelihood $\mathcal{L}(M_c \mid \pi) = (1-c)^{m_\pi} \mathcal{L}(M_\pi \mid \pi)$, but runs extending π now satisfy φ with probability 0, so $M_c \in \mathcal{M}_0$. This also illustrates why we require $\mathsf{p}_{\min} > 0$. Without this restriction we could make c arbitrarily small (but still positive to ensure $M_c \in \mathcal{M}_0$). This would result in the vacuous confidence score $\Gamma(\pi) \leq \sup \left\{\frac{\mathcal{L}(M_\pi \mid \pi)}{\mathcal{L}(M_c \mid \pi)} \mid c > 0\right\} = 1$.

Example 4. Consider again the traces $\pi_1 = a^3bca^2b$, $\pi_2 = a^5b(\boldsymbol{de}^2)^3$ and $\pi_3 = a^2bc\boldsymbol{ff}^3(\boldsymbol{gf})^2$ of Example 2. For π_1 the BSCC is $\{a, b, c\}$ and we have $m_{\pi_1} = \#_{\pi_1}(b) = 1$. So $\gamma(\pi_1) = 1/(1 - \mathsf{p}_{\min})$. For π_2 the BSCC is $\{\boldsymbol{d}, \boldsymbol{e}\}$, $m_{\pi_2} = \#_{\pi_2}(d) = 3$, and $\gamma(\pi_2) = (1/(1 - \mathsf{p}_{\min}))^3$. Finally, for π_3 the BSCC is $\{f, \boldsymbol{f}, \boldsymbol{g}\}$, $m_{\pi_3} = \#_{\pi_3}(f) = 2$ and $\gamma(\pi_2) = (1/(1 - \mathsf{p}_{\min}))^2$.

We finish with a proposition stating that the confidence of the monitor tends to infinity almost surely as it observes longer and longer prefixes of a run.

Proposition 1. *Given an infinite trace $\rho = r_0 r_1 \cdots \in S^\omega$ let $\rho^{\geq i} := r_i r_{i+1} \cdots$ for every $i \geq 0$, and let γ_{lim} be the random variable given by $\gamma_{lim}(\rho) := \liminf_{i \to \infty} \gamma(\rho^{\geq i})$. For every Markov chain $M \in \mathcal{M}$, we have $\mathbb{P}_M(\gamma_{\lim} = \infty) = 1$.*

Proof. Follows immediately from the fact that, with probability 1, a run of M eventually enters a BSCC of M and then visits every state of the BSCC infinitely often. So m_π a.s. tends to infinity for longer and longer prefixes π of the run, making $\gamma(\pi)$ also tend to infinity a.s. □

5 Complexity

The monitor has to compute verdict and confidence on the fly, updating it each time the current trace is extended with a new state. In [15], which discussed runtime enforcement of LTL properties, Esparza et al. presented an algorithm for computing the *complete sequence of verdicts* for all the prefixes of a trace π of length n in $O(n \log n)$ time (i.e., in $O(\log n)$ amortized time) and $O(n)$ space. Here we briefly discuss how to trade space for time.

Definition 12. *For every finite trace π, let scc_π denote the sequence of SCCs of G_π sorted according to the total order $\preceq$ (see Definition 6). Further, for every $k \in \mathbb{N}$, let $scc_\pi[k]$ denote the largest suffix of scc_π such that the total number of states in all SCCs of $scc_\pi[k]$, called the size of $scc_\pi[k]$ is at most k.*

The algorithm of [15] maintains variables scc and vi satisfying $\text{scc} = scc_\pi$, and $\text{vi}(r) = \#_\pi(r)$ (the number of times π leaves r) for every state r in scc_π and for every trace π. We define a new algorithm that, on top of scc and vi, maintains an integer bound bd such that $\text{scc} = scc_\pi[\text{bd}]$ and $\text{vi}(r) = \#_\pi(r)$ for every state r of scc.

Intuitively, before adding a new SCC to scc, the new algorithm first checks if the size of scc would then exceed the current value of bd. If so, it deletes the first SCC from scc, adds the new one, and increases bd by 1.

- Initialization: $\text{bd} := 0$, $\text{scc} := \varepsilon$, and vi is the empty table.
- Assume the algorithm has sampled a finite trace π so far, and the current values of scc is $S_1 S_2 \cdots S_\ell$. Assume the next transition sampled from M is (r, r'). The algorithm sets $\text{vi}(r) := \text{vi}(r) + 1$, and then proceeds as follows:
  - If $\text{vi}(r') > 0$ (that is, if r' was already been visited before), then bd does not change and $\text{scc} := S_1 \cdots S_{\ell'-1} \bigcup_{i=\ell'}^{\ell} S_i$, where $S_{\ell'}$ with $\ell' \leq \ell$ is the SCC containing r'.
  - If $\text{vi}(r') = 0$ and $\sum_{i=1}^{\ell} |S_i| < \text{bd}$, then bd does not change and $\text{scc} := S_1 \cdots S_k \{r'\}$.
  - If $\text{vi}(r') = 0$ and $\sum_{i=1}^{\ell} |S_i| = \text{bd}$, then $\text{bd} := \text{bd} + 1$, $\text{scc} := S_2 \cdots S_\ell \{r'\}$, and $\text{vi}(s) := 0$ for every $s \in S_1$.

For every trace π, the algorithm returns a verdict and a confidence level. Let scc_π and vi_π be the values of scc and vi after π. The algorithm computes whether the last SCC of scc_π is accepting or not, and answers **true** or **false** accordingly. The confidence is computed as $(1/(1 - \mathsf{p}_{\min}))^{m_\pi}$, where m_π is computed from vi according to its definition (Definition 10).

Let us call the monitor that uses the new algorithm the *memory-saving* monitor.

Proposition 2. *Let $\gamma'(\pi)$ be the confidence returned by the memory-saving monitor on a trace π. Define $\gamma'_{\lim}$ in the same way as $\gamma_{\lim}$ (see Proposition 1), replacing γ by γ'.*

1. *For every Markov chain $M \in \mathcal{M}$, we have $\mathbb{P}_M(\gamma'_{\lim} = \infty) = 1$.*

2. The size of the variable scc is bounded at all times by the number of states of the largest SCC of M.

Proof. Part (2) follows immediately from the description of the algorithm. For part (1), recall that the set of runs that reach some BSCC of M and then visit all its states infinitely often has probability 1. So it suffices to show that every such run, say ρ, satisfies $\gamma'_{\lim}(\rho) = \infty$.

After ρ reaches a BSCC, say S_ρ, the last SCC of scc is always a subset of S_ρ. Therefore, from some moment on we have $\mathsf{bd} \geq |S_\rho|$, and so, from some moment on, the last SCC of scc is equal to S_ρ. Further, the number of visits to each state of S_ρ tends to ∞. It follows that the $\gamma'_{\lim}$ also tends to ∞. □

6 An Illustrative Experiment

The main interest of our paper is conceptual: it gives a statistically sound answer to the natural question of estimating our confidence that a given finite trace will develop into a run satisfying a given property. In this section we illustrate a possible application to black-box testing of LTL properties in stochastic systems. For safety or co-safety properties one can conduct a number of tests, each of them consisting of sampling the system for a given number of steps, and stopping the test whenever the property is violated. Monitoring the violation can be done using the monitor of Bauer et al. [8]. For liveness properties, however, this monitor always answers "inconclusive". Our monitor allows for a better approach: in each test, sample the system until a given confidence level is reached.

We conduct a little experiment illustrating that our approach is especially suitable for systems where the maximal size of an SCC is small compared to the total number of states.

Consider the family of Markov chains depicted in Fig. 3. We fix the parameters $l = 4, r = 6, m = 4$ as well as $p = 0.5, q = 0.45, r = 0.08$ and vary only the parameter n. Every run will (with probability 1) eventually enter one of two

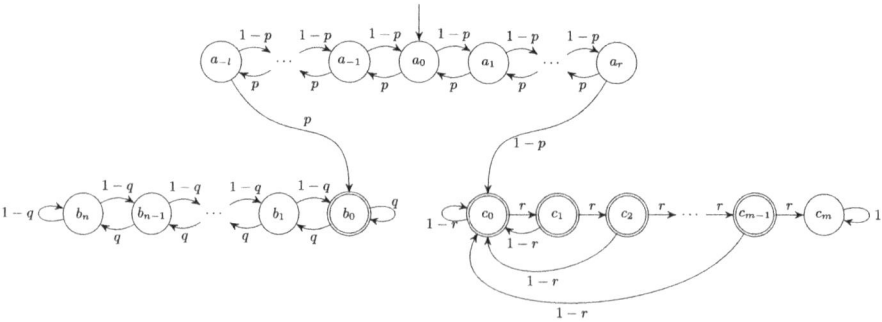

Fig. 3. A family of Markov chains with two bottom strongly connected components. In the left BSCC, accepting states are visited infinitely often with probability 1. In the right BSCC, they are only visited finitely often.

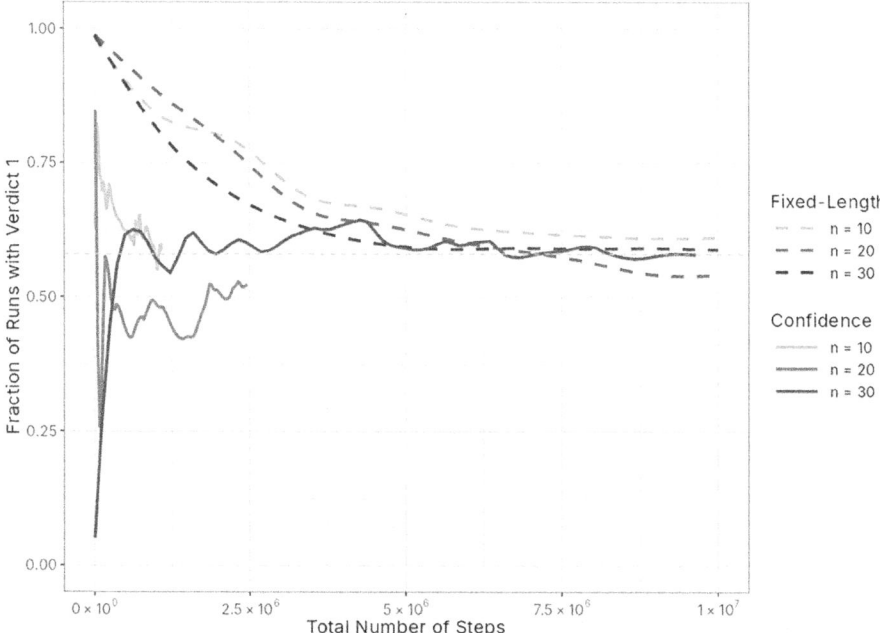

Fig. 4. Estimated probability of accepting runs in the Markov chain depicted in Fig. 3 using the parameters $p = 0.5, q = 0.45, r = 0.08, l = 4, r = 6, m = 4$, and $n \in \{10, 20, 30\}$.

SCCs. Runs entering the left BSCC will visit the accepting state b_0 infinitely often and be accepted. Runs entering the right intermediate SCC will eventually reach the second BSCC consisting only of the non-accepting state c_m and be rejected. Thus the probability p_{acc} of accepting runs corresponds to the probability of reaching state b_0 from the initial state a_0. Using PRISM we determined $p_{acc} \approx 0.58$ for our choice of parameters[4].

We now compare two methods of estimating this probability experimentally using testing. For both methods we first sample a sequence $\mathcal{R}$ of 100 runs and a step quota k. We compare how accurately both methods estimate the probability given the same step quota.

1. **Fixed-Length Estimation:** For every run ρ in $\mathcal{R}$ we take the prefix π of length $\frac{k}{100}$ and determine $\nu(\pi)$ as described in the fraction of runs for which this verdict 3. The estimate is the fraction of runs for which this verdict is 1.
2. **Confidence-based Estimation:** We repeatedly take the shortest prefix π that has a confidence of at least $\gamma(\pi) \geq 100$ from the next run ρ in $\mathcal{R}$. We stop once the total number of steps exceeds our quota and determine the fraction of runs with verdict 1 from that subset. This potentially uses fewer runs, but the likelihood of the verdicts being correct is higher.

---

[4] This obviously only depends on l, r and p.

First of all, observe that the fixed-length estimation has a fundamental problem: Independently of the *accuracy* of the estimate of p_{acc}, the method does not provide any statistical *confidence* in it. On the contrary, the confidence-based estimation allows us to derive a confidence using the standard likelihood ratio statistical test (see e.g. [24]).

Despite this, the comparison of the accuracies of both methods is interesting, as it shows that our method is particularly suitable for systems with small SCCs. Figure 4 plots the estimated probability for both methods and three different values for the parameter n. For small values of n the confidence-based approach has a clear advantage, converging to the correct value much faster. This is to be expected as runs entering the left BSCC can quickly fully explore it and reach a high confidence. This saves step quota, which can then be used in runs entering the right intermediate SCC. While the fixed-length approach is improbable to reach the state rejecting c_m in time given low quota, our confidence-based approach can use this surplus quota to correctly classify these runs as rejecting.

For large values of n, however, our confidence-based approach becomes less efficient. For runs entering the left BSSC, a lot of steps are needed, until a high confidence is reached, which reduces the number of runs that can be inspected. This in turn also lowers the accuracy of the estimate. The fixed-length approach, on the other hand, converges approximately equally fast for all values of n, which is to be expected, as runs entering the left BSCC are likely to be classified correctly, even if the BSCC is not fully explored.

7 Conclusion

We have presented a monitor for arbitrary LTL properties of systems modeled as Markov chains. Given a finite trace, the monitor returns a qualitative verdict on whether the trace will extend to a run satisfying a given property, and a quantitative confidence in the verdict. Our monitor refines the one introduced by Bauer *et al.* in their seminal work on runtime verification of LTL [5–8]. We have shown that verdict and confidence can be canonically derived from the maximum likelihood and likelihood ratio principles.

There are some interesting directions for future work. In our approach the monitor has full information about states. We are planning to investigate the case in which information is only partial, as studied for runtime enforcement in [14]. We also need the assumption that the Markov chain under scrutiny is finite. We would also like to study runtime verification for infinite chains of specific kinds, like probabilistic basic parallel processes, probabilistic programs with an unbounded counter, or probabilistic pushdown systems, [9–11].

Acknowledgments. We thank two anonymous reviewers for their detailed comments. Vincent Fischer is funded by the DFG Research Training Group 2428 "ConVeY".

References

1. Baier, C., Katoen, J.P.: Principles of model checking. MIT Press, Cambridge, Massachusetts (2008)
2. Barringer, H., Goldberg, A., Havelund, K., Sen, K.: Program monitoring with LTL in EAGLE. In: IPDPS. IEEE Computer Society (2004)
3. Barringer, H., Goldberg, A., Havelund, K., Sen, K.: Rule-based runtime verification. In: VMCAI. Lecture Notes in Computer Science, vol. 2937, pp. 44–57. Springer (2004)
4. Bartocci, E., Falcone, Y., Francalanza, A., Reger, G.: Introduction to runtime verification. In: Lectures on Runtime Verification, Lecture Notes in Computer Science, vol. 10457, pp. 1–33. Springer (2018)
5. Bauer, A., Leucker, M., Schallhart, C.: Monitoring of real-time properties. In: FSTTCS. Lecture Notes in Computer Science, vol. 4337, pp. 260–272. Springer (2006)
6. Bauer, A., Leucker, M., Schallhart, C.: The good, the bad, and the ugly, but how ugly is ugly? In: RV. Lecture Notes in Computer Science, vol. 4839, pp. 126–138. Springer (2007)
7. Bauer, A., Leucker, M., Schallhart, C.: Comparing LTL semantics for runtime verification. J. Log. Comput. **20**(3), 651–674 (2010)
8. Bauer, A., Leucker, M., Schallhart, C.: Runtime verification for LTL and TLTL. ACM Trans. Softw. Eng. Methodol. **20**(4), 14:1–14:64 (2011)
9. Bonnet, R., Kiefer, S., Lin, A.W.: Analysis of probabilistic basic parallel processes. In: FoSSaCS. Lecture Notes in Computer Science, vol. 8412, pp. 43–57. Springer (2014)
10. Brázdil, T., Esparza, J., Kiefer, S., Kucera, A.: Analyzing probabilistic pushdown automata. Formal Methods Syst. Des. **43**(2), 124–163 (2013)
11. Brázdil, T., Kiefer, S., Kucera, A.: Efficient analysis of probabilistic programs with an unbounded counter. J. ACM **61**(6), 41:1–41:35 (2014)
12. Daca, P., Henzinger, T.A., Kretínský, J., Petrov, T.: Faster statistical model checking for unbounded temporal properties. ACM Trans. Comput. Log. **18**(2), 12:1–12:25 (2017)
13. Dwyer, M.B., Avrunin, G.S., Corbett, J.C.: Patterns in property specifications for finite-state verification. In: ICSE, pp. 411–420. ACM (1999)
14. Esparza, J., Grande, V.P.: Black-box testing liveness properties of partially observable stochastic systems. In: ICALP. LIPIcs, vol. 261, pp. 126:1–126:17. Schloss Dagstuhl - Leibniz-Zentrum für Informatik (2023)
15. Esparza, J., Kiefer, S., Kretínský, J., Weininger, M.: Enforcing ω-regular properties in markov chains by restarting. In: CONCUR. LIPIcs, vol. 203, pp. 5:1–5:22. Schloss Dagstuhl - Leibniz-Zentrum für Informatik (2021)
16. Esparza, J., Kretínský, J., Sickert, S.: A unified translation of linear temporal logic to ω-automata. J. ACM **67**(6), 33:1–33:61 (2020)
17. Falcone, Y., Havelund, K., Reger, G.: A tutorial on runtime verification. In: Engineering Dependable Software Systems, NATO Science for Peace and Security Series, D: Information and Communication Security, vol. 34, pp. 141–175. IOS Press (2013)
18. Gondi, K., Patel, Y., Sistla, A.P.: Monitoring the full range of omega-regular properties of stochastic systems. In: VMCAI. Lecture Notes in Computer Science, vol. 5403, pp. 105–119. Springer (2009)

19. Henzinger, T.A., Mazzocchi, N., Saraç, N.E.: Abstract monitors for quantitative specifications. In: RV. Lecture Notes in Computer Science, vol. 13498, pp. 200–220. Springer (2022)
20. Henzinger, T.A., Saraç, N.E.: Quantitative and approximate monitoring. In: LICS. pp. 1–14. IEEE (2021)
21. Huang, X., et al.: Software monitoring with controllable overhead. Int. J. Softw. Tools Technol. Transf. **14**(3), 327–347 (2012)
22. Kupferman, O., Vardi, M.Y.: Model checking of safety properties. Formal Methods Syst. Des. **19**(3), 291–314 (2001)
23. Legay, A., Lukina, A., Traonouez, L., Yang, J., Smolka, S.A., Grosu, R.: Statistical model checking. In: Computing and Software Science, Lecture Notes in Computer Science, vol. 10000, pp. 478–504. Springer (2019)
24. Lehmann, E.L., Romano, J.P.: Testing statistical hypotheses. Springer Texts in Statistics, Springer, New York (2005)
25. Leucker, M., Schallhart, C.: A brief account of runtime verification. J. Log. Algebraic Methods Program. **78**(5), 293–303 (2009)
26. Norris, J.R.: Markov Chains. Cambridge University Press (1997)
27. Stoller, S.D., et al.: Runtime verification with state estimation. In: RV. Lecture Notes in Computer Science, vol. 7186, pp. 193–207. Springer (2011)

A Practical Approach to Runtime Verification

Raik Hipler[1](✉)[iD], Hannes Kallwies[1][iD], Martin Leucker[1][iD],
Kevin Gillian van Dommele[2], and Jannis Wien[1]

[1] University of Lübeck, Lübeck, Germany
{hipler,kallwies,leucker}@isp.uni-luebeck.de
[2] Infineon Technologies Austria AG, Villach, Austria
kevingillian.vandommele@infineon.com

Abstract. Runtime Verification (RV) is a formal method used to check whether the execution of a system adheres to a given specification. While extensive research has focused on developing foundational theories and tools—as well as domain-specific applications, such as in the space or automotive industries—the benefits of RV in the context of general-purpose software system development remain relatively underexplored. In this paper, we propose a flexible and generic workflow for integrating RV into the development and verification processes of general-purpose software systems. We designed and implemented a prototypical RV framework based on TeSSLa, a stream-based runtime verification specification language, to monitor elicited requirements. Our approach was applied in a case study on ValiBridge, an internal software tool developed by Infineon Austria to facilitate information exchange among stakeholders involved in post-silicon verification, where it was able to detect a previously unknown bug in the software. We analyze the impact of the RV setup on development efficiency and compare its effectiveness against an existing unit test suite.

Keywords: Runtime Verification · Software Testing · Requirement Syntax · TeSSLa

1 Introduction

Runtime Verification (RV) is a lightweight and dynamic formal method for verifying that individual runs of systems adhere to a given specification, that is, a correctness property [3,25]. This specification emits a monitor which the *run* or *trace* of the *system under scrutiny (SuS)* is fed to in order to check said property. In offline monitoring, the entire run is already available (e.g., as a log file), while in online monitoring the monitor has to produce verdicts regularly while the system is running. Pioneered by Lola [14], *Stream Runtime Verification (SRV)* [32] is concerned about data streams and transforms streams of inputs to streams of outputs; the last of which may cast verdicts wrt. to some correctness property.

Other SRV tools include RTLola [8], Striver [19], and TeSSLa [13] which we use in this paper.

Initially, our goal was to conduct a simple study in which we observe a software using TeSSLa. However, during the study we came across multiple hurdles that we did not forsee in the beginning and that make it inefficient and impractical to try to directly derive a TeSSLa specification. This includes (1) how to bridge the gap between a developer of the observed software who is likely unfamiliar with formal methods, and someone who knows how to use RV but is not part of the core development team; (2) how to generically describe requirements in a way that they can be easily formalized by a developer while still being precise enough to be understandable without a lot of background information about the software; and (3) how to be able to easily extend a specification after the initial implementation to account for software updates as well as changing requirements. While tackling these hurdles, we noticed that our solutions can be generalized for many applications aside from our specific study.

Therefore, in this paper, we propose a practical and generic workflow to conduct Runtime Verification on software systems. First, the software developers extract requirements the system has to adhere to using a semi-formal intermediate language based on the EARS syntax [28]. Then, these semi-formal requirements are translated into a formal RV specification language. For this purpose, we provide a generic framework in TeSSLa that allows to relatively easily specify such requirements. In fact, depending on the complexity of the requirements, this can often be done automatically. Finally, the events have to be fed from the observed system to the runtime monitor which then produces a verdict based on the specification.

We applied our approach to a case study in the important domain of post-silicon *validation and verification (V&V)* and use it as a running example throughout this paper to show the effectiveness of our approach. The V&V process of semiconductor components is done at multiple stages: while designing the system (pre-silicon), during manufactoring, and after production (post-silicon). While one can control and observe the component's internal signals during the design phase rather comfortably, this is not the case after production. This is due to limited access to internal signals, possibly non-deterministic behavior of the components, and higher costs for fixing faults [29]. Therefore, post-silicon verification is a complex and arduous task involving many people as well as a multitude of requirements, and it is important to ensure that it can be carried out reliably.

The study was conducted in cooperation with Infineon Austria[1] on the basis of their company-internal software *ValiBridge* which is used in Infineon's semiconductor validation process. Specifically, we are verifying this V&V software. The purpose of ValiBridge is to fetch requirements concerning microelectronic components from an external requirement management system (RQMS) and redistribute them within the company. It defines a joint data model for all processes and provides the requirements over a structured interface. In particular,

---

[1] https://www.infineon.com/cms/austria/en/.

it allows the different teams at Infineon Austria involved in post-silicon V&V, each with their own data formats and ways of communication, to have access to the same data, thus bridging the validation procedure through different APIs.

Since the entirety of ValiBridge was too extensive for this study, we limited our scope to its subcomponent responsible for synchronizing and storing the requirements from the external requirement management system (RQMS). We call this the SuS. The decision for that particular subcomponent lies in (1) the external system being known to be unreliable and erroneous, thus the need for a reliable procedure for retrieving and updating the requirements including proper error-handling; and (2) the inherent difficulty to provide a test suite able to satisfactorily verify a system that heavily depends on external factors under real world conditions, thus needing a verification procedure observing the system during execution. Using the application of our approach, we were able to find a previously unknown bug.

This study was conducted while ValiBridge was actively being refactored and optimized. Although prior versions were verified using traditional testing methods, such as unit testing, the increasing complexity and reliance on the system made it necessary to implement a second verification method to ensure a more reliable system. Due to the fact that ValiBridge is used in conjunction with many third-party systems, a dynamic solution like RV was deemed suitable to observe not just static tests but actual executions during operation. We will compare our RV approach to the existing testing suite later on.

Related Work and Contributions. The usefulness and effectivness of verifying software systems using Runtime Verification has been shown many times in many different domains. Just in the last couple of years it has been studied how to apply RV in the context of distributed systems [15,18,26], autonomous vehicles [17,36] and ROS-based robotic systems [10,11]. For example, in [1] RV has been used to predict abnormal behavior within Cyber-Physical Systems by learning patterns (as LTL [30] formulas) from one CPS's usual behavior and then observing anomalies through monitoring said property.

Runtime Verification has also been used in many recent concrete case studies. In [35], a robot is monitored to decide when the optimal, but potentially unsafe, neural networks-based controller should be switched to a safe, but less optimal, obstacle avoiding controller to guarantee safe movement; in [38], RV is used to verify functional and safety properties for an implementation of the TPM (Trusted Platform Module) software stack; and the authors of [33] apply RV to verify cryptographic APIs.

While there has been a lot of research about applying RV to specific domains, there is a noticeable lack of a generic procedure of how to apply RV to software in general. Another problem is that many formalisms such as LTL [30] are developed from a theoretical point of view and are, thus, difficult to use in practice. Languages such as SALT [7] try to ease the usage of a formalism by providing a more practical syntax.

To conduct studies like the ones from the aforementioned publications, one needs knowledge in both the software system of interest *and* Runtime Verification. In this paper, we instead propose a procedure that splits this task into semi-formally describing the desired behavior and formally translating such descriptions into the actual RV formalism. In summary, our contributions are (1) said semi-formally intermediate format; (2) a TeSSLa framework for applying the proposed procedure; and (3) the prototypical application and evaluation of the framework on ValiBridge.

This work was mainly developed in the thesis of the last author which also serves as an extended reference [34].

2 Requirement Elicitation and Formalization

In this section, we first introduce the semi-formal format for eliciting requirements from the SuS. In order to gain some language-independent intuition for the concepts, we then discuss step-by-step how such requirements can be formalized.

Semi-formal Intermediary Requirement Format. Since one cannot expect the developers of a software to be familiar with formal methods and verification techniques, the syntax for transcribing the requirements of a software should be easy to use while still being formal enough to allow easy translation into an actual specification language. As running examples, we use the following three verbally formulated requirements from our case study for ValiBridge:

- R1: If an exception is thrown while the synchronization procedure is active, the system must terminate.
- R2: If a request to the RQMS is pending for two minutes while the synchronization procedure is active, the request must fail.
- R3: When the version of an entity gets updated, there must not be an entity with the same ID stored whose version is the same or greater than the new version.

A first observation is that every requirement consists of a *postcondition* that has to hold once a *trigger* has been observed while an optional *precondition* holds. In the first requirement, the precondition would be the active synchronization procedure, the trigger would be the thrown exception and the postcondition would be the termination of the system. Conditions can be seen as part of the program state, e.g., that the current user is authenticated, the synchronization process was started but is not yet finished or that the RQMS did not yet respond. Triggers, while observed similarly to conditions, correspond to momentary events, e.g., that a database entry is updated or created, that a list of requested requirements was retrieved or that an exception was thrown. We call the event where a trigger and the precondition belonging to the same requirement are fulfilled at the same time a *qualifying trigger event*.

A second observation is that there are different categories of requirements. We distinguish between three categories: (a) (pure) pattern requirements describing certain relative patterns or orderings between events or states, (b) time requirements concerned about absolute time intervals, and (c) data requirements reasoning over carried data. A single requirement can fall into multiple categories; in fact, all three example requirements describe patterns but only R1 describes purely a pattern. R2 and R3 are additionally time and data requirements, respectively. One could argue that R2 is also a data requirement, as to check the requirement one would need to store a request identifier to correspond the events belonging to the same request; however, since ValiBridge is known to only maintain one request at a time, we can assume *Requested*, *RequestIdle* and *RequestFail*, as shown below, all belong to the same request.

The challenge of translating natural language requirements into formal notations was already explored in [28]. They identified similar patterns as we did and suggested a semi-formal notation called *EARS* for capturing requirements. We build on this and use a slight modification of the EARS syntax of the form

$$(Pre \land Trigger) \rightarrow Post$$

to semi-formally denote a requirement. For the examples from above we get:

$$(Synced \land Exception) \rightarrow ProgTermination \qquad (1)$$
$$(Synced \land Requested \land RequestIdle \text{ for two minutes}) \rightarrow RequestFail \qquad (2)$$
$$VersionUpdate \text{ for } e \rightarrow \text{No entity with same ID as } e$$
$$\text{has a version equal or greater than that of } e. \qquad (3)$$

Most requirements, like (2) and (3), might be triggered multiple times during a single execution while others, like (1), can only happen at most once per execution. For the ValiBridge case study, we elicited a total of 15 requirements.

Formalizing Requirements in Temporal Logics. While this sytnax is intuitive for developers without a formal background, it does not convey what a requirement written in this format exactly entails. One issue with using an implication $a \rightarrow b$ for describing a software's behavior is that it is often not meant in a strictly logical sense and does not necessarily require a and b to hold at the same time. Rather, it typically means that the occurrence of a should be followed by the occurrence of b within a certain timeframe. In practice, this implies a *minimum reaction time* after which b is expected to hold and a *maximum reaction time* by which b must hold at the latest. For the minimum reaction time, we only require that the postcondition holds *after* the qualifying trigger event and not just at the same time. Depending on the concrete implementation, it could otherwise happen that the events describing the postcondition indicate fulfillment although they were produced before the qualifying trigger event occurred, i.e., false positives due to race conditions may be possible. Using LTL (linear temporal logic) [30] this can be formalized as $\mathcal{G}((Pre \land Trigger) \rightarrow \mathcal{X}\mathcal{F}(Post))$. E.g., for (1) we get $\mathcal{G}((Synced \land Exception) \rightarrow \mathcal{X}\mathcal{F}(ProgTermination))$. LTL is, however, only suited for pure pattern requirements as it is not able to express absolute time or to refer to data.

Time requirements can instead be interpreted as MTL (metric temporal logic) [23] or STL (signal temporal logic) [27] formulas which add time to operators. In MTL requirement (2) could then be understood as $\mathcal{G}((\textit{Synced} \wedge \textit{Requested} \wedge \mathcal{H}_{\leq 120s}(\textit{RequestIdle})) \to \mathcal{X}\,\mathcal{F}\,(\textit{RequestFail}))$. The Next operator ($\mathcal{X}$) indicates that the following event has to occur strictly later than the current time, i.e., there has to be a minimal time unit that passes before the requirement can be fulfilled.

Theoretically, data requirements can also be formalized in MTL by introducing separate atomic propositions for each data object (as long as there are finitely many of them), but more appropriate would be to use a data-carrying logic like the MTL extension MFOTL [4] which uses first-order expressions to reason over objects. Requirement (3) could then be represented as $\mathcal{G}(\forall e \in E\colon \textit{update}(e) \to \mathcal{X}\,\mathcal{F}\,(\neg \exists e' \in E \setminus \{e\}\colon \textit{id}(e) = \textit{id}(e') \wedge \textit{version}(e) \leq \textit{version}(e')))$ with E being the set of all versioned entities.

Liveliness and Reactivity. While the above specifications allow a system to be able to react to a triggered requirement, waiting infinitely long would mean that every postcondition could recover in the future, thus staying "on hold" until the execution's end. Therefore, we also need an appropriate maximum reaction time $t \in \mathbb{N}$, called *reactivity time*, in which the postcondition has to be fulfilled, effectively converting our requirements into real-time properties [2]. Thus, $\textit{time}(\textit{Post}) - t \leq \textit{time}(\textit{Pre} \wedge \textit{Trigger}) < \textit{time}(\textit{Post})$ has to hold, where *time* is the absolute time of an event. The concrete value for t may vary from requirement to requirement. Note that for a time requirement demanding that its postcondition holds within a certain time, t should corespond to exactly that time.

We optionally further relax this condition, such that a requirement can still be fulfilled after its reactivity time has elapsed; namely as long as no subsequent trigger event was observed. This ensures that the program is allowed to idle (e.g. caused by the operating system) without the monitor needlessly claiming that a requirement is violated. In MTL or MFOTL this can be formalized as

$$\mathcal{G}\,((\textit{Pre} \wedge \textit{Trigger}) \to \mathcal{X}(\mathcal{F}_{\leq t}(\textit{Post}) \vee \neg \textit{anotherTrigger}\,\mathcal{U}\,\textit{Post})).$$

To prevent positive verdicts when the system was, in fact, not idling, it may be advisable to define a trigger producing events in regular intervals to be able to distinguish from actual idling.

Impartiality and Anticipation. For online monitoring, RV monitors should ideally be impartial and anticipatory [16,24]. An impartial monitor will only yield a verdict $\top$ (*true*) or $\bot$ (*false*) if there is no continuation of the trace leading to the other verdict; otherwise it should yield a non-final verdict that can change after more events have been observed. An anticipatory monitor, on the other hand, must yield final verdicts as soon as every possible continuation leads to the same verdict. Typical truth domains able to represent not yet final verdicts are $\mathbb{B}_3 = \{\top, ?, \bot\}$ and $\mathbb{B}_4 = \{\top, \top^p, \bot^p, \bot\}$ [6,24] on their intuitive orderings, the last of which we use for our framework. The verdicts $\top^p$ ("presumably true") and $\bot^p$ ("presumably false") represent that the verdict is not yet final but in the case that the trace ends right then, the final verdict would be $\top$ or $\bot$, respectively. Given a trace not yet containing a for the LTL formula $\mathcal{F}a$, e.g., would lead to $\bot^p$ as long as the trace end is not reached as a could hold in a future observation.

Unfortunately, since our requirements have to hold globally, casting $\top$ is – at least in online monitoring – only possible at the end of the trace. Conversely, $\bot^p$ can be finalized to $\bot$ once a requirement can no longer be fulfilled, i.e., because a new trigger event was observed and the reactivity time elapsed. As in our setting we use the RV approach mainly for bug finding purposes, it is most important for us to detect the locations in the trace where the conditions are breached, i.e., where a $\bot$ verdict is cast. For future work, it could be possible to apply predictive semantics [37] in order to improve the anticipation capabilities.

3 TeSSLa

Based on the previously outlined formalization steps, we implemented our monitoring framework in TeSSLa which will be described in the next section. In order to be able to better understand said framework, we will now give a short introduction to TeSSLa.

TeSSLa[2], short for Temporal Stream Specification Language, is an opensource Stream Runtime Verification (SRV) language [13] and toolchain [21]. Similarly to other SRV languages like Lola [14] and Striver [19], a TeSSLa specification describes stream transformations from input to output streams. The inputs are incrementally received from the observed system and passed to the TeSSLa monitor generated from the specification. Boolean output streams can then indicate whether a certain property over the inputs holds, thus enabling Runtime Verification. However, TeSSLa streams are not limited to the Boolean domain and may be of richer data types, e.g., numerical.

See Fig. 1 for an example specification and a possible corresponding trace. This specification observes a temperature input **temp** and alerts the user if it increases above a certain threshold (here 30) and continues to do so. For this, a Boolean stream **risingTemp** indicates whether the current temperature is higher than the previous one and **hotAlert** emits a unit event if this is the case while the temperature is above or at the threshold. Finally, **alertCounter** counts such alerts but resets the counter when the temperature drops below the threshold again. Another output stream holds the temperature corresponding to an alert.

In contrast to other SRV formalisms like Lola, a specialty of TeSSLa lies in its asynchronicity. This means that TeSSLa does not require events to be received for all input streams on a fixed grid of timestamps but instead each input event is associated with a timestamp from a global clock. These timestamps can then be accessed and used in calculations, e.g., to measure latencies. Analogously, output events can be emitted at arbitrary time points as well.

While six core operators of TeSSLa are in theory sufficient for any specification [13], for convenience the users can also define their own operators, so called

---
[2] https://www.tessla.io/.

```
1  in temp: Events[Int]
2  def threshold = 30
3
4  def risingTemp = temp > prev(temp)
5  def hotAlert = unitIf(risingTemp && temp >= threshold)
6  def alertCounter =
7      resetCount(hotAlert, unitIf(temp < threshold))
8
9  out on(hotAlert, temp)
10 out alertCounter
```

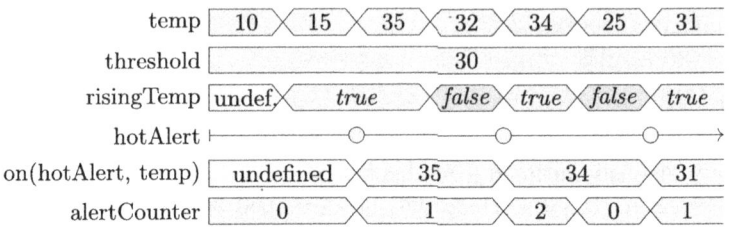

Fig. 1. Example TeSSLa specification and corresponding trace.

macros, on top of these with many useful operators already being part of the standard library. Macros can also be grouped into modules for shareability and reusability. There are, for example, libraries for monitoring AUTOSAR timing contraints [17], Timed Petri Nets [31], Timed Dyadic Deontic Logics [22] and the TeSSLa-ROS-Bridge [10], the last of which allows TeSSLa to interact with robots running the robot operating system ROS. TeSSLa specifications can either be run without compilation via an interpreter on the JVM or by compiling them into software monitors for different target platforms, namely Scala and Rust.

Other SRV tools include hLola [12] and hStriver [20] (Haskell implementations of Lola and Striver) as well as RTLola [9]. We have chosen TeSSLa for its extensive ecosystem, documentation, standard library and application history. Outside of the SRV realm, an alternative would also be the MFOTL implementation MonPoly [5]. Generally, SRV offers a high flexibility by mixing general purpose programming languages and logic-based specification languages.

4 Specification Design

We will now describe step-by-step how the TeSSLa framework for monitoring requirements as outlined in Sect. 2 is designed.

Conditions and Triggers. First of all, for the pre- and postconditions as well as for the triggers, input streams receive the observations from the system. Triggers are unit streams indicating when particular trigger events occur. Conditions are in most cases Boolean streams indicating that a particular condition holds but they

```
1   in exceptionTrigger: Events[Unit]
2   in progTerminationTrigger: Events[Unit]
3   in synced: Events[Bool]
4   in request: Events[Bool]
5   type VersionUpdate =
6     {version: Int, sameIdVersions: List[Int]}
7   in versionedItemUpdate: Events[VersionUpdate]
8   def syncTrigger = rising(default(synced, false))
9   def versionedItemUpdateTrigger =
10        onChange(versionedItemUpdate)
```

Listing 1: Condition and trigger encoding examples.

can also carry events of other types if the information the condition describes cannot be represented by a simple Boolean value.

For example, as can be seen in Listing 1, the triggers `exceptionTrigger` and `progTerminationTrigger` are unit streams to indicate that an exception was observed or the program terminated, respectively, `synced` and `request` are Boolean conditions indicating that the synchronization procedure is active or a request to the RQMS has been made, and `versionedItemUpdate` is a condition associating an updated object with all previously stored versions of that object.

Often, triggers and postconditions can actually be inferred from already defined inputs without the need for additional input streams. E.g., `syncTrigger` to indicate that a synchronization procedure was initiated can be inferred from `synced` by producing a unit event everytime the `synced` condition changes to *true*, or `versionedItemUpdateTrigger` to indicate a new update for an item can be inferred by looking for a change on the `versionedItemUpdate` stream. The helper function `onChange` produces a unit event everytime the agument stream changes its value.

Generic RV Framework. We designed our framework to be generic to allow for easy extendability. We have defined three macros, which can be utilized to easily transduce the general requirement structure – as introduced in Sect. 2 – to a TeSSLa specification. This abstracts away the technical details of the TeSSLa specification, thus increasing readability and easing the specification of the requirements, especially for non-experts. The three macros are discussed in detail in the following:

First, `qualifiedTrigger`, shown in Listing 2, produces an event whenever a trigger and its corresponding precondition are fulfilled at the same time, i.e., when the trigger event is qualified. Secondly, `isRequirementExpired`, shown in Listing 3, checks if a requirement can already be finalized, i.e., whether $\bot$ can be cast instead of $\bot^p$. This is done by checking if the reactivity time has been exceeded and optionally if also a subsequent trigger event has occurred. Thirdly, `isRequirementFulfilled`, shown in Listing 4, checks if the postcondition holds in time. The `trigger` and `isDecided` arguments here are the results of

```
1  def qualifiedTrigger(
2    trigger: Events[Unit],
3    preCondition: Events[Bool]
4  ): Events[Unit] = {
5    unitIf(on(trigger, preCondition))
6  }
```

Listing 2: Function for producing qualifying triggers.

```
1  def isRequirementExpired(
2    qualifiedTrigger: Events[Unit],
3    waitingPeriod: Int,  # in seconds
4    waitUntilNewTrigger: Bool
5  ): Events[Bool] = {
6    def hasSubsequentTrigger =
7      # at least one trigger after this one?
8      resetCount(allTriggers, qualifiedTrigger) >= 1
9    # assuming the global clock measures milliseconds
10   def isExpired =
11     time(allTriggers) - time(qualifiedTrigger)
12     > waitingPeriod * 1000
13   if (waitUntilNewTrigger)
14   then hasSubsequentTrigger && isExpired
15   else isExpired
16 }
```

Listing 3: Function for determining if a decision for a requirement can be made.

qualifiedTrigger and isRequirementExpired, respectively. Since the verdict can only change if either the qualifying trigger event is observed, or the status of the postcondition changes, we relay the fulfillment of the postcondition only when one of these condition changes.

Combining the expiration indicator with the fulfillment check then allows to cast a four-valued verdict via fourValueEval, shown in Listing 5 where the output encodes a verdict from $\mathbb{B}_4$ (represented as a number). If a requirement was triggered but is neither fulfilled nor expired, the output is $\bot^p$ (represented as -1); if it is expired but not fulfilled, the output is $\bot$ (represented as -2); otherwise it is $\top^p$ (represented as 1). A not yet triggered requirement always defaults to $\top^p$. Figure 2 shows two example traces, one fulfilling and one unfulfilling.

Putting it All Together. Now, the input streams for conditions and triggers can be applied to this framework to encode concrete requirements. This is done by first combining the trigger and precondition streams to a qualifying trigger stream and then applying fourValueEval to said qualifying trigger, the postcondition and the desired waiting time. For example, Listing 6 shows the application for

```
1  def isRequirementFulfilled(
2    trigger: Events[Unit],
3    postCondition: Events[Bool],
4    isDecided: Events[Bool]
5  ): Events[Bool] = {
6    def actualPost = default(postCondition, false)
7    def onDecision = unitIf(defined(rising(isDecided)))
8    def onSatisfaction = rising(actualPost)
9    def wasDecidedInThePast = default(
10     && time(onDecision) >= time(onSatisfaction), false
11   )
12   def risingPostAfterTrigger = unitIf(
13     defined(rising(actualPost)) && defined(trigger)
14   )
15   def isPostFulfilled = default(
16     actualPost && (!defined(onDecision) || !isDecided
17     || wasDecidedInThePast), false
18   )
19   on(merge(trigger, risingPostAfterTrigger),
20     isPostFulfilled)
21 }
```

Listing 4: Function for evaluating timely fulfillment of a postcondition.

requirements (1), (2) and (3), each as a function, using the defined conditions and triggers from Listing 1.

Pure pattern requirements like (1) are easy to implement given streams for precondition, trigger and postcondition. Note that in this case the postcondition is derived from a trigger stream. Many requirements can even be automatically generated when pre- and postcondition are directly given as Boolean streams and the trigger as a unit stream. As long as the names of these streams match with the names from the intermediate format, the requirement function can then be derived automatically.

Time and especially data requirements, however, require more individual care. For the time requirement (2) the trigger stream should produce an event when the request has been idling for two minutes. Therefore, we use the Boolean precondition stream request and check whether it has been *true* for at least two minutes. We use a global helper stream periodicalCheck to obtain a reference point to which we can compare the time of the request. In this case, we check every five seconds whether the request stream has been *true* for 120 s already. Similarly to syncedTrigger from Listing 1, the trigger stream can then be constructed.

For data requirement (3) the postcondition indicates that the highest version of all other entities with the same ID is not bigger than the one from the currently updated ID.

```
 1  def fourValueEval(
 2    trigger: Events[Unit],
 3    post: Events[Bool],
 4    waitingPeriod: Int, # in seconds
 5    waitUntilNewTrigger: Bool
 6  ): Events[Int] = {
 7    def decided = default(isRequirementExpired(
 8      trigger, waitingPeriod, waitUntilNewTrigger), false)
 9    def fulfilled = default(
10      isRequirementFulfilled(trigger, post, decided), true)
11
12    default(lift3(
13      constIf(-2, decided && !fulfilled),
14      constIf(-1, !decided && !fulfilled),
15      constIf(1, fulfilled),
16      (a, b, c) =>
17        if isSome(a) then a
18        else if isSome(b) then b
19        else c
20    ), 1)
21  }
```

Listing 5: Core function to cast four-valued verdicts.

Finally, merging the verdicts of every requirement gives a verdict for the entire specification. Since, as mentioned, most requirements are global properties, ⊤ is only possible at the trace end and, therefore, only possible when doing offline monitoring. It would, however, be possible to add a second output verdict stream that represents the verdict in case that the trace ends right there, i.e., outputting ⊤ instead of $\top^p$ and ⊥ instead of $\bot^p$.

The entire TeSSLa specification for the ValiBridge case study for all 15 requirements consists of circa 320 lines of code, about 80 of which make up the framework itself. To specify all conditions and triggers 18 input streams were needed. While most requirements could be denoted very concisely in under ten lines each (including input stream definitions), two requirements were significantly more complex because they reason about state transitions within ValiBridge. Although in pure TeSSLa this is quite arduous, since we only had to consider a relatively small number of states (less than five), it was still manageable. The framework including the ValiBridge case study is publicly available[3].

5 Instrumentation and Evaluation

Since the ValiBridge case study was carried out during a major refactoring of ValiBridge by the main development team, it was important that the specification and implementation were as independent from each other as possible in

---

[3] https://github.com/janniswien/TeSSLa-RV-Framework-Case-Study.

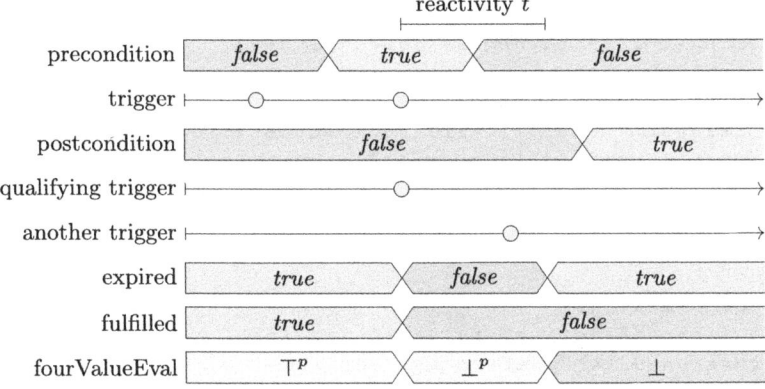

(a) Presumably satisfied property. While the postcondition does not hold within the reactivity time, it does hold before a subsequent trigger is observed.

(b) Unsatisfied property. The postcondition only holds after the reactivity time ends and a subsequent trigger is observed.

Fig. 2. Visualization of the framework on two example traces.

order to maintain flexibility during development. Therefore, we introduced a contract defining the common interface of both which was fulfilled as long as the implementation yields at least the events necessary to verify the requirements and the specification only requires these events as inputs. The SuS simply logged the events (112 logging statements in total) during runtime alongside the usual logs which where then intercepted and filtered by a separate monitoring service that dispatched the events to the synthesized TeSSLa monitor (see Fig. 3). The monitoring setup runs in a Nuxt[4] server providing a frontend user interface for both, offline verification of prerecorded traces as well as online verification (see Fig. 4).

To properly evaluate the specification details, we purposely interfered with the environment while ValiBridge and the monitor were running, such as mutating or truncating the database or disabling the network connection. Since almost

---

[4] https://nuxt.com/.

```
1  def requirement1() = {
2    def pre = sync
3    def trigger = qualifiedTrigger(exceptionTrigger, pre)
4    def post = defined(progTerminationTrigger)
5
6    fourValueEval(trigger, post, 10, true)
7  }
8
9  def periodicalCheck = period(5000)
10
11 def requirement2() = {
12   def isRequestIdle =
13     request && runtime(rising(default(request, false)),
14                       periodicalCheck) > 120000
15   def requestIdleTrigger =
16     rising(default(isRequestIdle, false))
17
18   def pre = sync && request
19   def trigger = qualifiedTrigger(requestIdleTrigger, pre)
20   def post = defined(requestFailTrigger)
21
22   fourValueEval(trigger, post, 10, true)
23 }
24
25 def requirement3() = {
26     def highestExistingVersion = List.fold(
27       versionedItemUpdate.sameIdVersions, 0, max
28     )
29     def post = highestExistingVersion <=
30       versionedItemUpdate.version
31
32   fourValueEval(versionedItemUpdateTrigger,
33               post, 10, true)
34 }
```

Listing 6: Implemented requirements (1), (2) and (3) using our framework.

all real executions of ValiBridge are quite homogeneous, this was necessary to trigger edge cases as well as unusual and erroneous inputs and configurations without the need for an extensive amount of executions. In total, 620 executions were evaluated with 41 trace events per synchronization cycle on average.

We identified three traces where the system did not behave as intended. Namely, entities with one version number were created while entities with the same ID but a higher version number were already existing, leading to requirement (3) being violated. Aside from these three traces the verdicts were as expected, i.e., without interferences the SuS behaved as required and with interferences the specification was always able to detect the issue. This means that the

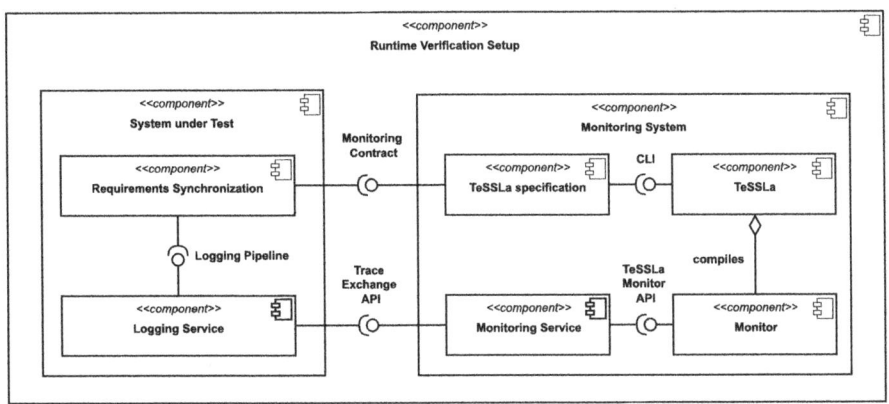

Fig. 3. Component diagram of the RV setup for the SuS.

monitor was always able to cast the ⊥ verdict if the system behaved incorrectly due to a deliberate intrusion.

Logging the additional trace events increased the average runtime of the SuS by 40.4%, from 1734 ms on average per synchronization cycle to 2435 ms. This is for the most part due to the many additional database lookups necessary to supply data-carrying events to the monitor which the SuS would not do outside of the RV setup. When the database is already synchronized, most of the additional lookups get omitted and the average runtime only increased by 13.1%. Neither efficiency loss is really meaningful because the SuS is only running sporadically (at least once per seven days) and does not need to be particularly efficient. For other systems, however, if used during production and not just as an aid during development, it may be advisable to only emit the monitoring events while the system is running in a kind of debug mode.

During the refactoring of ValiBridge and in parallel to this study, also conventional testing was employed to assure quality. This consisted mainly of whitebox unit tests aiming to maximize code coverage. In contrast, our short-term RV setup is more akin to black-box integration testing since the specification is only concerned about input and output behavior for the entire SuS; therefore, complementing the testing suite from a different perspective. While this study was only of prototypical nature, it is feasable to employ this setup or an extension of it long-term to observe a large number of execution samples under real world usage, which the test suite is unable to do. Another advantage is that, due to the independency of SuS and specification, as long as both parties uphold the contract, either can be changed in the future without consideration for the other.

Notable is also that the RV setup is vastly more compact. While each of the 15 requirements needs several hundred lines of C# unit test code, our RV setup only needs around 1100 in total, including specification, monitoring service and logging statements. Note that most of our codebase is generic and each

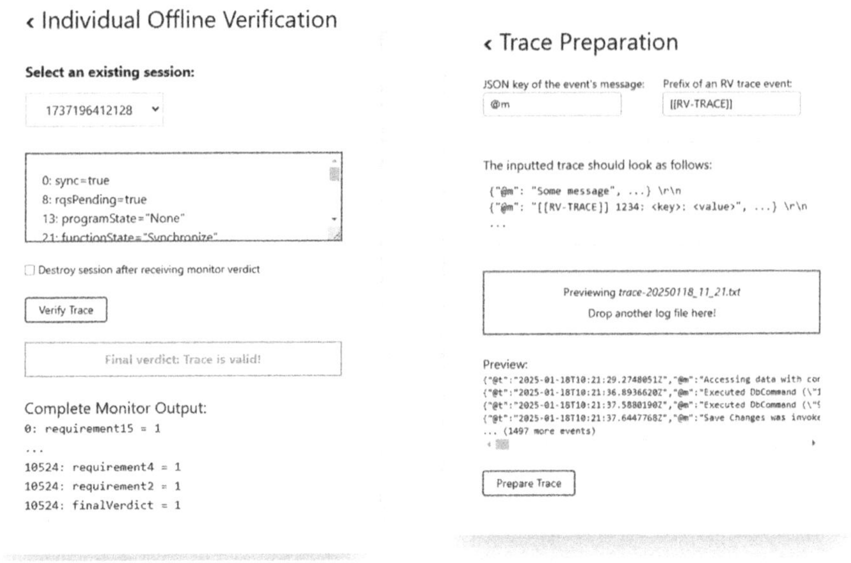

Fig. 4. Screenshots of the monitoring service Web application for single offline verification (left) and trace processing (right).

requirement only needs on average 23.6 lines specific to that particular requirement. This is indeed an indication that the framework is useful for the handy specification of various requirements.

6 Conclusion

In this paper we propose a generic workflow to verify software systems using Runtime Verification with the goal of bridging software development and formal verification. We present a semi-formal specification format based on the EARS syntax that the development team of the considered system can use to denote their system's requirements in a semi-formal notation. Someone not involved in the project but with a background in formal methods can then translate such notation into an actual RV specification. We first describe a general formalization in MFOTL and then a full framework in the stream specification language TeSSLa. Key features of the framework include understanding the requirements as real-time properties and impartial verdict rendering. We show the process of transforming verbally formulated requirements into the semi-formal format and then into TeSSLa specifications on examples from a case study. Specifically, we applied our approach on a subcomponent of the V&V-software ValiBridge by Infineon Austria. We implemented a prototypical Runtime Verification setup to verify that the SuS works reliably. The study consisted of eliciting the requirements for the SuS, formally specifying them, extracting the trace events from

ValiBridge, as well as evaluating the correctness and efficiency. The resulting monitoring setup allows to verify traces from ValiBridge both online and offline. In fact, in the course of our case study we were able to identify a prevously unrecognized error in the tool. Our setup thus successfully complemented the simultaneously employed unit testing by providing the option to continuously monitor the deployed SuS.

Future work includes to generalize the TeSSLa framework to be able to use it as a user library and to explore which critera requirements have to fulfill, such that specifications can be generated automatically.

References

1. Akande, A.J., Hou, Z., Foo, E., Li, Q.: LTL-based runtime verification framework for cyber-attack anomaly prediction in cyber-physical systems. Comput. Secur. **155**, 104455 (2025). https://doi.org/10.1016/J.COSE.2025.104455
2. Anderson, T., Knight, J.C.: A framework for software fault tolerance in real-time systems. IEEE Trans. Softw. Eng. **9**(3), 355–364 (1983). https://doi.org/10.1109/TSE.1983.237017
3. Bartocci, E., Falcone, Y. (eds.): Lectures on Runtime Verification - Introductory and Advanced Topics, Lecture Notes in Computer Science, vol. 10457. Springer (2018). https://doi.org/10.1007/978-3-319-75632-5
4. Basin, D.A., Klaedtke, F., Müller, S., Zalinescu, E.: Monitoring metric first-order temporal properties. J. ACM **62**(2), 15:1–15:45 (2015). https://doi.org/10.1145/2699444
5. Basin, D.A., Klaedtke, F., Zalinescu, E.: The monpoly monitoring tool. In: Reger, G., Havelund, K. (eds.) RV-CuBES 2017. An International Workshop on Competitions, Usability, Benchmarks, Evaluation, and Standardisation for Runtime Verification Tools, September 15, 2017, Seattle, WA, USA. Kalpa Publications in Computing, vol. 3, pp. 19–28. EasyChair (2017). https://doi.org/10.29007/89HS
6. Bauer, A., Leucker, M., Schallhart, C.: The good, the bad, and the ugly, but how ugly is ugly? In: Sokolsky, O., Tasiran, S. (eds.) Runtime Verification, 7th International Workshop, RV 2007, Vancouver, Canada, March 13, 2007, Revised Selected Papers. Lecture Notes in Computer Science, vol. 4839, pp. 126–138. Springer (2007). https://doi.org/10.1007/978-3-540-77395-5_11
7. Bauer, A., Leucker, M., Streit, J.: SALT - structured assertion language for temporal logic. In: Liu, Z., He, J. (eds.) Formal Methods and Software Engineering, 8th International Conference on Formal Engineering Methods, ICFEM 2006, Macao, China, November 1-3, 2006, Proceedings. Lecture Notes in Computer Science, vol. 4260, pp. 757–775. Springer (2006). https://doi.org/10.1007/11901433_41
8. Baumeister, J., Finkbeiner, B., Schirmer, S., Schwenger, M., Torens, C.: RTLola cleared for take-off: monitoring autonomous aircraft. In: Proceedings of 32nd Int'l Conf. on Computer-Aided Verification CAV'20, pp. 28–39. Springer (2020)
9. Baumeister, J., Finkbeiner, B., Schirmer, S., Schwenger, M., Torens, C.: Rtlola cleared for take-off: monitoring autonomous aircraft. In: Lahiri, S.K., Wang, C. (eds.) Computer Aided Verification - 32nd International Conference, CAV 2020, Los Angeles, CA, USA, July 21-24, 2020, Proceedings, Part II. Lecture Notes in Computer Science, vol. 12225, pp. 28–39. Springer (2020). https://doi.org/10.1007/978-3-030-53291-8_3

10. Begemann, M.J., Kallwies, H., Leucker, M., Schmitz, M.: Tessla-ros-bridge - runtime verification of robotic systems. In: Ábrahám, E., Dubslaff, C., Tarifa, S.L.T. (eds.) Theoretical Aspects of Computing - ICTAC 2023 - 20th International Colloquium, Lima, Peru, December 4-8, 2023, Proceedings. Lecture Notes in Computer Science, vol. 14446, pp. 388–398. Springer (2023). https://doi.org/10.1007/978-3-031-47963-2_23
11. Caldas, R., García, J.A.P., Schiopu, M., Pelliccione, P., Rodrigues, G.N., Berger, T.: Runtime verification and field-based testing for ROS-based robotic systems. IEEE Trans. Softw. Eng. **50**(10), 2544–2567 (2024). https://doi.org/10.1109/TSE.2024.3444697
12. Ceresa, M., Gorostiaga, F., Sánchez, C.: Declarative stream runtime verification (hLola). In: d. S. Oliveira, B.C. (ed.) Programming Languages and Systems - 18th Asian Symposium, APLAS 2020, Fukuoka, Japan, November 30 - December 2, 2020, Proceedings. Lecture Notes in Computer Science, vol. 12470, pp. 25–43. Springer (2020). https://doi.org/10.1007/978-3-030-64437-6_2
13. Convent, L., Hungerecker, S., Leucker, M., Scheffel, T., Schmitz, M., Thoma, D.: TeSSLa: Temporal stream-based specification language. In: Proceedings of the 21th Brazilian Symposium on Formal Methods (SBMF'18). LNCS, vol. 11254, pp. 144–162. Springer (2018). https://doi.org/10.1007/978-3-030-03044-5_10
14. D'Angelo, B., et al.: LOLA: runtime monitoring of synchronous systems. In: Proceedings of the 12th International Symposium of Temporal Representation and Reasoning (TIME'05), pp. 166–174. IEEE Computer Society (2005). https://doi.org/10.1109/TIME.2005.26
15. Danielsson, L.M., Sánchez, C.: Decentralized stream runtime verification for timed asynchronous networks. IEEE Access **11**, 84091–84112 (2023). https://doi.org/10.1109/ACCESS.2023.3298329
16. Dong, W., Leucker, M., Schallhart, C.: Impartial anticipation in runtime-verification. In: Cha, S.D., Choi, J., Kim, M., Lee, I., Viswanathan, M. (eds.) Automated Technology for Verification and Analysis, 6th International Symposium, ATVA 2008, Seoul, Korea, October 20-23, 2008. Proceedings. Lecture Notes in Computer Science, vol. 5311, pp. 386–396. Springer (2008). https://doi.org/10.1007/978-3-540-88387-6_33
17. Friese, M.J., Kallwies, H., Leucker, M., Sachenbacher, M., Streichhahn, H., Thoma, D.: Runtime verification of AUTOSAR timing extensions. In: Abdeddaïm, Y., Cucu-Grosjean, L., Nelissen, G., Pautet, L. (eds.) RTNS 2022: The 30th International Conference on Real-Time Networks and Systems, Paris, France, June 7 - 8, 2022, pp. 173–183. ACM (2022). https://doi.org/10.1145/3534879.3534898
18. Ganguly, R., Momtaz, A., Bonakdarpour, B.: Runtime verification of partially-synchronous distributed system. Formal Methods Syst. Des. **64**(1), 146–177 (2024). https://doi.org/10.1007/S10703-024-00450-5
19. Gorostiaga, F., Sánchez, C.: Striver: stream runtime verification for real-time event-streams. In: Proceedings of the 18th International Conference on Runtime Verification (RV'18). LNCS, vol. 11237, pp. 282–298. Springer (2018). https://doi.org/10.1007/978-3-030-03769-7_16
20. Gorostiaga, F., Sánchez, C.: HStriver: a very functional extensible tool for the runtime verification of real-time event streams. In: Huisman, M., Pasareanu, C.S., Zhan, N. (eds.) Formal Methods - 24th International Symposium, FM 2021, Virtual Event, November 20-26, 2021, Proceedings. Lecture Notes in Computer Science, vol. 13047, pp. 563–580. Springer (2021). https://doi.org/10.1007/978-3-030-90870-6_30

21. Kallwies, H., Leucker, M., Schmitz, M., Schulz, A., Thoma, D., Weiss, A.: TeSSLa - an ecosystem for runtime verification. In: Proceedings of the 22nd International Conference on Runtime Verification (RV'22). LNCS, vol. 13498, pp. 314–324. Springer (2022). https://doi.org/10.1007/978-3-031-17196-3_20
22. Kharraz, K.Y., Leucker, M., Schneider, G.: Timed dyadic deontic logic. In: Schweighofer, E. (ed.) Legal Knowledge and Information Systems - JURIX 2021: The Thirty-fourth Annual Conference, Vilnius, Lithuania, 8-10 December 2021. Frontiers in Artificial Intelligence and Applications, vol. 346, pp. 197–204. IOS Press (2021).https://doi.org/10.3233/FAIA210336
23. Koymans, R.: Specifying real-time properties with metric temporal logic. Real Time Syst. **2**(4), 255–299 (1990). https://doi.org/10.1007/BF01995674
24. Leucker, M.: Teaching runtime verification. In: Khurshid, S., Sen, K. (eds.) Runtime Verification - Second International Conference, RV 2011, San Francisco, CA, USA, September 27-30, 2011, Revised Selected Papers. Lecture Notes in Computer Science, vol. 7186, pp. 34–48. Springer (2011). https://doi.org/10.1007/978-3-642-29860-8_4
25. Leucker, M., Schallhart, C.: A brief account of runtime verification. J. Logic Algebr. Progr. **78**(5), 293–303 (2009).
26. Mahe, E., Bannour, B., Gaston, C., Gall, P.L.: Efficient interaction-based offline runtime verification of distributed systems with lifeline removal. Sci. Comput. Program. **241**, 103230 (2025). https://doi.org/10.1016/J.SCICO.2024.103230
27. Maler, O., Nickovic, D.: Monitoring temporal properties of continuous signals. In: Proceedings of the Joint International Conferences on Formal Modelling and Analysis of Timed Systems (FORMATS'04) and Formal Techniques in Real-Time and Fault-Tolerant Systems (FTRTFT'04). LNCS, vol. 3253, pp. 152–166. Springer (2004). https://doi.org/10.1007/978-3-540-30206-3_12
28. Mavin, A., Wilkinson, P., Harwood, A.R.G., Novak, M.: Easy approach to requirements syntax (EARS). In: RE 2009, 17th IEEE International Requirements Engineering Conference, Atlanta, Georgia, USA, August 31 - September 4, 2009, pp. 317–322. IEEE Computer Society (2009). https://doi.org/10.1109/RE.2009.9
29. Mitra, S., Seshia, S.A., Nicolici, N.: Post-silicon validation opportunities, challenges and recent advances. In: Sapatnekar, S.S. (ed.) Proceedings of the 47th Design Automation Conference, DAC 2010, Anaheim, California, USA, July 13-18, 2010, pp. 12–17. ACM (2010). https://doi.org/10.1145/1837274.1837280
30. Pnueli, A.: The temporal logic of programs. In: 18th Annual Symposium on Foundations of Computer Science, Providence, Rhode Island, USA, 31 October - 1 November 1977, pp. 46–57. IEEE Computer Society (1977). https://doi.org/10.1109/SFCS.1977.32
31. Requeno, J.I., et al.: Runtime verification of timed petri nets. In: Köhler-Bussmeier, M., Moldt, D., Rölke, H. (eds.) Proceedings of the International Workshop on Petri Nets and Software Engineering 2024 co-located with the 45th International Conference on Application and Theory of Petri Nets and Concurrency (PETRI NETS 2024), June 24 - 25, 2024, Geneva, Switzerland. CEUR Workshop Proceedings, vol. 3730, pp. 122–131. CEUR-WS.org (2024). https://ceur-ws.org/Vol-3730/paper07.pdf
32. Sánchez, C.: Online and offline stream runtime verification of synchronous systems. In: Proceedings of the 18th International Conference on Runtime Verification (RV'18). LNCS, vol. 11237, pp. 138–163. Springer (2018). https://doi.org/10.1007/978-3-030-03769-7_9

33. Torres, A., et al.: Runtime verification of crypto APIs: an empirical study. IEEE Trans. Softw. Eng. **49**(10), 4510–4525 (2023). https://doi.org/10.1109/TSE.2023.3301660
34. Wien, J.: Runtime Verification for a Semiconductor V&V Software. Master's thesis, University of Lübeck (2025)
35. Yang, F., Zhan, S.S., Wang, Y., Huang, C., Zhu, Q.: Case study: runtime safety verification of neural network controlled system. In: Ábrahám, E., Abbas, H. (eds.) Runtime Verification - 24th International Conference, RV 2024, Istanbul, Turkey, October 15-17, 2024, Proceedings. Lecture Notes in Computer Science, vol. 15191, pp. 205–217. Springer (2024). https://doi.org/10.1007/978-3-031-74234-7_13
36. Yousefinejad, F., Jalili, S.: Runtime verification of electronic stability control system in automated vehicles with stl$_3$ formalism. Computing **107**(1), 33 (2025). https://doi.org/10.1007/S00607-024-01375-X
37. Zhang, X., Leucker, M., Dong, W.: Runtime verification with predictive semantics. In: Goodloe, A., Person, S. (eds.) NASA Formal Methods - 4th International Symposium, NFM 2012, Norfolk, VA, USA, April 3-5, 2012. Proceedings. Lecture Notes in Computer Science, vol. 7226, pp. 418–432. Springer (2012). https://doi.org/10.1007/978-3-642-28891-3_37
38. Ziani, Y., Kosmatov, N., Loulergue, F., Pérez, D.G.: Runtime verification for high-level security properties: case study on the TPM software stack. In: Huisman, M., Howar, F. (eds.) Tests and Proofs - 18th International Conference, TAP 2024, Milan, Italy, September 9-10, 2024, Proceedings. Lecture Notes in Computer Science, vol. 15153, pp. 87–106. Springer (2024). https://doi.org/10.1007/978-3-031-72044-4_5

Hyper Pattern Matching

Masaki Waga[1,2](✉) and Étienne André[3,4]

[1] Graduate School of Informatics, Kyoto University, Kyoto, Japan
[2] National Institute of Informatics, Tokyo, Japan
mwaga@fos.kuis.kyoto-u.ac.jp
[3] Université Sorbonne Paris Nord, CNRS, Laboratoire d'Informatique de Paris Nord, LIPN, 93430 Villetaneuse, France
[4] Institut universitaire de France (IUF), Paris, France

Abstract. In runtime verification, pattern matching, which searches for occurrences of a specific pattern within a word, provides more information than a simple violation detection of the monitored property, by locating concrete evidence of the violation. However, witnessing violations of some properties, particularly *hyperproperties*, requires evidence across multiple input words or different parts of the same word, which goes beyond the scope of conventional pattern matching. We propose here *hyper pattern matching*, a generalization of pattern matching over a set of words. Properties of interest include robustness and (non-)interference. As a formalism for patterns, we use nondeterministic asynchronous finite automata (NAAs). We first provide a naive algorithm for hyper pattern matching and then devise several heuristics for better efficiency. Although we prove the NP-completeness of the problem, our implementation HYPPAU is able to address several case studies scalable in the length, number of words (or logs) and number of dimensions, suggesting the practical relevance of our approach.

Keywords: runtime verification · hyperproperties · pattern matching

1 Introduction

Runtime verification is a lightweight formal method that focuses on monitoring and analyzing system executions (or logs) to ensure they comply with desired specifications. Pattern matching consists of searching for occurrences of a specific *pattern* (such as a sequence of symbols or a regular expression) within a word or log. Many important system requirements, such as noninterference, symmetry, and information flow control, cannot be expressed as trace properties alone: witnessing violations of such requirements requires evidence across *multiple* input words or *different parts* of the same word—which goes beyond the scope of conventional pattern matching. For example, one may want to detect occurrences

---

Due to space limitations, we omit some proofs and concrete examples. See the extended version [38] for details.

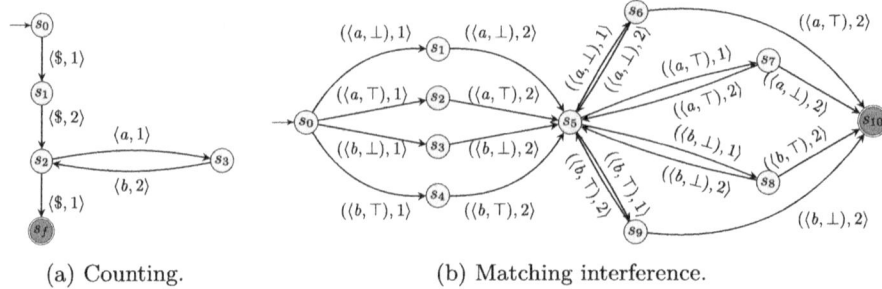

Fig. 1. Examples of NAAs.

of n "a"s in one word *and* the same number n of "b"s in another word. Or, when monitoring certain activities of a network bus, one may detect sequences of packets that are of the same size but serve two different purposes (e.g., requests and responses) and may potentially be interwoven.

To this end, we introduce *hyper pattern matching*, the process of searching for occurrences of patterns involving multiple words (or multiple portions of the same words) within a set of words (or logs). Hyper pattern matching can extract evidence of violation of *hyperproperties* [22], a generalization of trace properties that describe *sets of sets* of execution traces, rather than sets of traces.

To represent patterns in hyper pattern matching, we use nondeterministic asynchronous finite automata (NAAs) [28] as an extension of finite-state automata with "directions", that are assigned words from a set of words. We show that NAAs are rich enough to represent violations of interesting security properties, e.g., noninterference and robustness.

Example 1 (Counting). Consider the NAA in Fig. 1a, with two *directions* 1 and 2; directions are assigned a (sub)word, and can be seen informally as variables "reading" letters in a given subword. This NAA defines pairs of words such that both words start with a "$" (transition from s_0 to s_1 for the first word, and from s_1 to s_2 for the second word), followed by the same number of "a"s in the first word as of "b"s in the second word (loop over s_2 and s_3). Finally, the first word must end with a "$". Let us consider pattern matching, with an input singleton word $\mathbf{w} = \{w\}$, with $w = d\$aa\$bbb\$aaa\$$. The match set $\mathcal{M}(A, \mathbf{w})$ is $\{\langle(w, 2, 5), (w, 5, 7)\rangle, \langle(w, 9, 13), (w, 5, 8)\rangle\}$, i.e., two pairs of two subwords, where $(w, 2, 5)$ denotes the subword made of the 2nd to the 5th letter of w.

Example 2 (Interference). Noninterference [34] is one of the most typical examples of hyperproperties. A program P satisfies noninterference if for any memory states $\mu, \nu \in \mathbb{M}$ that agree on public variables, the memory states after running P from μ and ν with an input sequence $w \in \Sigma_I^*$ also agree on public variables. Hyper pattern matching can extract witnesses of violation of noninterference. For instance, the NAA given in Fig. 1b accepts evidences of interference for input actions $\Sigma_I = \{a, b\}$, and public memory states $\mathbb{M} = \{\bot, \top\}$. Technically, the NAA in Fig. 1b looks for pairs of executions starting from the same value of the variable, following the same sequence of actions, but leading to different values of the variable; for example, the execution going through s_0, s_1, s_5, s_6, s_{10} detects a pair of executions starting with variable value $\bot$, reading two "a"s, but the first execution (encoded by 1) ends with value $\bot$ while the second one ends with value $\top$—which violates noninterference.

We evaluate hyper pattern matching from both theoretical and empirical perspectives. Theoretically, we prove that it is NP-complete to decide the nonemptiness of the match set, which indicates the intractability of hyper pattern matching. Specifically, the time complexity of our algorithm is exponential with respect to the number of directions, polynomial with respect to the maximum length of the monitored words, and quadratic with respect to the size of the NAA. Empirically, we implement a prototype tool HypPAu for hyper pattern matching in the context of monitoring, and evaluate its efficiency via experiments. We propose a naive algorithm and two heuristics to improve its efficiency by 1) skipping unnecessary matching trials inspired by efficient string matching algorithms, and 2) pruning matching candidates by first performing non-hyper pattern matching over automata projected over directions. HypPAu can handle words with thousands of letters within one minute for benchmarks with two directions, including the NAA in Fig. 1b, which suggests the usefulness of hyper pattern matching for analysing a reasonably sized set of logs.

Contributions. Our contributions are summarized as follows:

1. we propose hyper pattern matching, a generalization of pattern matching across multiple words or multiple portions of the same word;
2. we show that nonemptiness checking of the match set in hyper pattern matching is NP-complete;
3. we provide a naive algorithm for hyper pattern matching as well as two heuristics to enhance its efficiency;
4. we implement our algorithms into a tool HypPAu, and demonstrate its capabilities over several benchmarks.

Related Work. NAAs, which is also called multi-tape automata [33], have been studied in various domains with some variations, e.g., [27,33,41]. We mostly follow the formulation and terminologies in [28]. Although the membership problem (i.e., determining if a tuple of words is accepted by an NAA) has been studied well, the pattern matching problem we study (i.e., from a set of words, returning a tuple of words with intervals such that the tuple of words projected to the intervals is accepted by an NAA) has not been studied, to the best of our knowledge.

In [11], two-dimensional pattern matching is considered, i.e., matching a two-dimensional array of symbols in a text itself represented as a two-dimensional array. In [5], two-dimensional pattern matching is extended for a set of patterns, called two-dimensional dictionary matching. Although these problems have been extensively studied [4,20,31,42], to the best of our knowledge, all these works focus on two-dimensional patterns without branching or loops, unlike our hyper pattern matching supporting multi-dimensional "regular" patterns against word sets of an arbitrary size.

Various algorithms have been proposed for monitoring hyperproperties [1–3,10,15–17,19,21–23,29]. Most of these algorithms use HyperLTL [18] to represent the monitored property. Due to the synchronous nature of HyperLTL, these algorithms cannot handle asynchronous hyperproperties, such as stuttering robustness (see Example 6). The same limitation also applies to the algorithms using other related logics, such as Hyper-μHML used in [1,2]. Moreover, when a violation of the monitored property is detected, these algorithms only return a Boolean verdict, a (minimal) subset of complete traces, or relevant prefixes of traces. In contrast, our algorithm identifies the tuples of subwords matching the given property, which are finer-grained witnesses.

Recently, several papers have proposed monitoring algorithms for asynchronous hyperproperties. In [16], an automata-based formalism is introduced for monitoring asynchronous hyperproperties. *Hypernode automata* [7] is another automata-based formalism for asynchronous hyperproperties. Each state of a hypernode automaton is labeled with a relational constraint on words represented by *hypernode logic*. *Extended hypernode logic* [17] is an extension of hypernode logic with regular expressions and the stutter-reduction operation to reason about 1) the structure of the words and 2) the synchronous and asynchronous comparison between the words. In [10], a monitoring algorithm for $\text{Hyper}^2\text{LTL}_f$, a temporal logic representing second-order hyperproperties, is proposed. The witnesses provided by these algorithms are also less informative than ours, analogous to the monitoring algorithms for synchronous hyperproperties. Nevertheless, an extension of our algorithm to a more general class of hyperproperties, such as second-order hyperproperties, is one of the future directions.

In addition to the formalisms above, various logics have been proposed for representing asynchronous hyperproperties, such as A-HyperLTL [8], HyperLTL_S [14], HyperLTL_C [14], GHyperLTL_{S+C} [12], HyperMTL [13], and H_μ [28]. In [28], a construction of alternating asynchronous parity automata from H_μ formulas is shown. A similar construction of NAAs to support these logics in hyper pattern matching is a future work.

2 Preliminaries

We write $\mathbb{N}$ and $\mathbb{N}_+$ for the naturals and positive naturals. For a partial function $f\colon Y \nrightarrow Z$, we denote its domain by $\text{dom}(f)$. For a set Y, we denote by $\mathcal{P}(Y)$ the powerset of Y. For a set Y, we denote its cardinality by $|Y|$.

An *alphabet* is a nonempty finite set Σ of letters. A (finite) *word* over Σ is a finite sequence of letters from Σ. The *empty word* is denoted by ε, and the set of all finite words is denoted by Σ^*. For a word $w = \sigma_1\sigma_2\cdots\sigma_n$, we use $w|_{[i,j]}$ to denote the subword $\sigma_i\sigma_{i+1}\ldots\sigma_j$. We write the i-th letter of a word $w \in \Sigma^*$ as w_i. A *language* is a subset of Σ^*.

Hyper Pattern Matching 401

Definition 3 (NFA). *A* nondeterministic finite-word automaton *(NFA) is a tuple* $\mathcal{A} = \langle \Sigma, S, S_0, \Delta, S_F \rangle$, *where* Σ *is an alphabet, S is a finite set of states,* $S_0 \subseteq S$ *is a set of initial states,* $S_F \subseteq S$ *is a set of accepting states, and* $\Delta \subseteq S \times \Sigma \times S$ *is a transition relation.*

A *deterministic finite-word automaton (DFA)* is an NFA such that S_0 is a singleton and for any $s \in S$ and $\sigma \in \Sigma$, there is exactly one $s' \in S$ satisfying $(s, \sigma, s') \in \Delta$. For DFAs, we regard Δ as a transition *function*. Given a word $w = \sigma_1 \sigma_2 \cdots \sigma_n$ over Σ, a *run* of $\mathcal{A}$ on w is a sequence of states $(s_0, s_1, \cdots, s_n)$ such that $s_0 \in S_0$ and, for every $0 < i \leq n$, it holds that $(s_{i-1}, \sigma_i, s_i) \in \Delta$. The run is *accepting* if $s_n \in S_F$. We say that $\mathcal{A}$ *accepts* w if there exists an accepting run of $\mathcal{A}$ on w. The *language* $\mathcal{L}(\mathcal{A})$ of $\mathcal{A}$ is the set of all words accepted by $\mathcal{A}$.

We use *nondeterministic asynchronous finite automata (NAAs)* [28] to represent asynchronous hyperproperties. Intuitively, an NAA is an NFA equipped with *directions* to asynchronously read multiple words.

Definition 4 (NAA). *A* nondeterministic asynchronous finite automaton *(NAA) is a tuple* $\mathsf{A} = \langle \Sigma, K, S, S_0, \Delta, S_F \rangle$, *where* Σ, *S*, S_0, *and* S_F *are the same as in an NFA, and* $K = \{1, 2, \ldots, k\}$ *is a set of* directions, *and* $\Delta \subseteq S \times \Sigma \times K \times S$ *is a transition relation.*

For an NAA $\mathsf{A} = \langle \Sigma, K, S, S_0, \Delta, S_F \rangle$, we let the underlying NFA as $\overline{\mathsf{A}} = \langle \Sigma \times K, S, S_0, \Delta, S_F \rangle$, i.e., we use $\Sigma \times K$ as the alphabet and deem Δ as a transition relation of an NFA. For a word $\overline{w}$ over $\Sigma \times K$ and $l \in K$, we let $\pi(\overline{w}, l) \in \Sigma^*$ be the word constructed by i) removing the letters $\langle a, l' \rangle$ with $l' \neq l$ and ii) projecting to the first element of each letter. We naturally extend π to languages, i.e., for $\mathcal{L} \subseteq (\Sigma \times K)^*$, $\pi(\mathcal{L}, l) = \{\pi(\overline{w}, l) \mid \overline{w} \in \mathcal{L}\}$. An NAA A accepts k-tuple $\langle w^1, w^2, \ldots, w^k \rangle$ of words if there is $\overline{w} \in \mathcal{L}(\overline{\mathsf{A}})$ satisfying $w^l = \pi(\overline{w}, l)$ for each $l \in K$. We let $\mathfrak{L}(\mathsf{A})$ be the set of k-tuples of words accepted by A.

Example 5. Let us revisit Example 1 in a more formal manner. Consider the NAA $\mathsf{A} = \langle \Sigma, K, S, S_0, \Delta, S_F \rangle$, with directions $K = \{1, 2\}$. Figure 1a illustrates A. Since we have $\mathcal{L}(\overline{\mathcal{A}}) = \langle \$, 1 \rangle \langle \$, 1 \rangle (\langle a, 1 \rangle \langle b, 2 \rangle)^* \langle \$, 1 \rangle$, a 2-tuple $\langle w^1, w^2 \rangle$ of words is accepted by A if and only if we have $w^1 = \$a^n\$$ and $w^2 = \$b^n$ for some $n \in \mathbb{N}$, i.e., A accepts a pair of words with the same number of "a"s (preceded and followed by a "$\$$") and of "b"s (preceded by a "$\$$").

Example 6 (Stuttering Robustness). Robustness is another common hyperproperty. Robustness requires that for two similar inputs, the system's behavior must be the same (or similar). One of its instances is robustness with respect to stuttering, i.e., if two sequences $w, w' \in \Sigma_I^*$ of inputs are identical by reducing stuttering, these sequences accompanied by their corresponding outputs, (i.e., $\tilde{w}, \tilde{w}' \in (\Sigma_I \times \Sigma_O)^*$ whose projections to Σ_I^* are w and w', respectively) must be also the same after removing the stuttering. The NAA $\mathsf{A} = \langle \Sigma, K, S, S_0, \Delta, S_F \rangle$, with directions $K = \{1, 2\}$ in Fig. 2, accepts evidences of non-robust execution. Intuitively, after reading each letter from direction 1, it asserts that the next letter from direction 2 has the same output if its input is the same as direction 1, where the stuttering is reduced by the self-loops, which are omitted in Fig. 2.

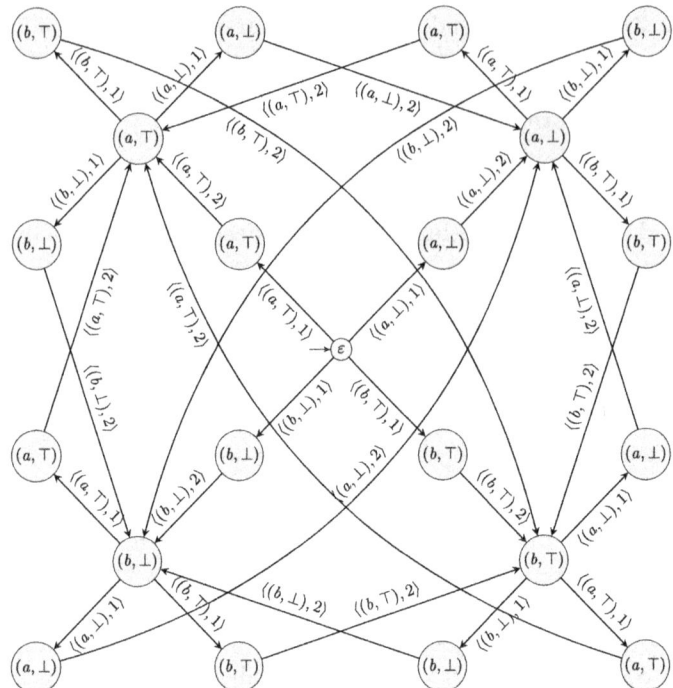

Fig. 2. Example: matching evidences of violations of stuttering robustness, with $\Sigma = \Sigma_I \times \Sigma_O$, $\Sigma_I = \{a, b\}$, and $\Sigma_O = \{\top, \bot\}$. The self-loops, the accepting state, and the transitions to the accepting state are omitted: for each state labeled with $x \in \Sigma$, we have a self-loop labeled with (x, l), where $l \in K$ is the direction of the incoming transition; for each state labeled with (σ, γ), with an outgoing transition labeled with $\langle(\sigma, \gamma), 2\rangle$ and with an incoming transition from a state labeled with ε or (σ', γ), where $\sigma \neq \sigma'$, we have a transition to the accepting state labeled with $\langle(\sigma, \neg\gamma), 2\rangle$, where $\neg\top = \bot$ and $\neg\bot = \top$.

Recall that we also showed in Example 2 that (non-)interference can be encoded using NAAs. In addition, we give in Example 22 in [38] an example of monitoring packets of similar size over a network (typically using a UDP-based protocol, e.g., RTP [26]).

3 Hyper Pattern Matching Problem

> **Hyper pattern matching problem:**
> INPUT: A finite set $\mathbf{w} \in \mathcal{P}(\Sigma^*)$ of words and an NAA $\mathsf{A} = \langle \Sigma, K, S, S_0, \Delta, S_F \rangle$ with $K = \{1, \ldots, k\}$
> OUTPUT: The match set $\mathcal{M}(\mathsf{A}, \mathbf{w}) = \{\langle(w^1, i^1, j^1), \ldots, (w^k, i^k, j^k)\rangle \in (\mathbf{w} \times \mathbb{N} \times \mathbb{N})^k \mid \langle w^1|_{[i^1, j^1]}, w^2|_{[i^2, j^2]}, \ldots, w^k|_{[i^k, j^k]}\rangle \in \mathfrak{L}(\mathsf{A})\}$

Example 7. Consider again the NAA A in Fig. 1a. Let $\mathbf{w} = \{w\}$ be a singleton word set, with $w = d\$aa\$bbb\$aaa\$\$e$. For instance, $\langle(w,2,5),(w,5,7)\rangle \in \mathcal{M}(\mathsf{A},\mathbf{w})$ holds because $\overline{w} = \langle\$,1\rangle\langle\$,2\rangle\langle a,1\rangle\langle b,2\rangle\langle a,1\rangle\langle b,2\rangle\langle\$,1\rangle$ satisfies $\overline{w} \in \mathcal{L}(\overline{\mathsf{A}})$, $\pi(\overline{w},1) = w|_{[2,5]}$, and $\pi(\overline{w},2) = w|_{[5,7]}$. The match set $\mathcal{M}(\mathsf{A},\mathbf{w})$ is

$$\Big\{\langle(w,2,5),(w,5,7)\rangle, \langle(w,9,13),(w,5,8)\rangle\Big\} \cup \Big\{\langle(w,13,14),(w,i,i)\rangle \mid i \in \{2,5,9,13,14\}\Big\}.$$

Deciding the nonemptiness of the match set is NP-complete. This complexity suggests that the exponential blowup in the worst case of the hyper pattern matching algorithms we propose later in Sects. 4 and 5 is inevitable. (The proofs of this result and subsequent results are in the appendix.)

Theorem 8. *The nonemptiness decision problem for the match set $\mathcal{M}(\mathsf{A},\mathbf{w})$ for an NAA A and a finite set $\mathbf{w}$ of words is NP-complete.*

4 A Naive Algorithm for Hyper Pattern Matching

Before presenting a naive algorithm for hyper pattern matching, we define an auxiliary notation. For an NFA $\mathcal{A} = \langle \Sigma \times K, S, S_0, \Delta, S_F \rangle$ with $K = \{1, 2, \ldots, k\}$, we define a relation $\to \subseteq \big((\Sigma^*)^k \times S\big) \times \big((\Sigma^*)^k \times S\big)$ such that $\langle v^1, v^2, \ldots, v^k, s \rangle \to \langle u^1, u^2, \ldots, u^k, s' \rangle$ if and only if there is $l \in \{1, 2, \ldots, k\}$ and $(s, (\sigma, l), s') \in \Delta$ satisfying $v^l = \sigma \cdot u^l$, and for any $m \neq l$, $v^m = u^m$ holds.

Algorithm 1 shows a naive algorithm for hyper pattern matching. In Algorithm 1, we use a priority queue $\mathcal{Q}$ containing the information of the upcoming matching trials. In $\mathcal{Q}$, we use the lexicographic order, assuming that the set $\mathbf{w}$ of the examined words is totally ordered. The exponential blowup with respect to k at line 1 is most likely inevitable because the nonemptiness checking of $\mathcal{M}(\mathsf{A},\mathbf{w})$ is already NP-hard (Theorem 8)[1]. One can easily enforce additional constraints (e.g., one word can be used in one matching only once) to the match set by modifying the definition of $\mathcal{Q}$.

For each $\langle i_1, \ldots, i_k, w^1, \ldots, w^k \rangle \in \mathcal{Q}$, we try to find matching trials starting from $w^1_{i_1}, \ldots w^k_{i_k}$ (lines 7 to 19). In matching trials, we maintain the set $\mathcal{C}$ of configurations. Each configuration $\langle v^1, \ldots, v^k, s \rangle$ consists of a tuple $\langle v^1, \ldots, v^k \rangle$ of words that are read by Algorithm 1 but not yet fed to the NAA A and the current state s. We update $\mathcal{C}$ by appending a new letter (line 10), applying transitions (lines 12 to 15), and removing "non-waiting" configurations, i.e., the configurations $\langle v^1, \ldots, v^k, s \rangle$ with $v^l \neq \varepsilon$ for any $l \in K$ (line 19). These configurations can be removed because no additional transitions are enabled by appending letters.

---

[1] Here, we show an algorithm fully constructing $\mathcal{Q}$ at the beginning, to simplify the explanation of skipping in Sect. 5.1. In our tool HYPPAU, we lazily construct $\mathcal{Q}$ and memorize the skipped indices separately to reduce the memory usage.

Algorithm 1: A naive algorithm $\mathcal{HPM}$ for hyper pattern matching.

Input: A finite set $\mathbf{w} \subseteq \Sigma^*$ of words and an NAA $\mathsf{A} = \langle \Sigma, K, S, S_0, \Delta, S_F \rangle$ with $K = \{1, 2, \ldots, k\}$
Output: The match set $\mathcal{M}(\mathsf{A}, \mathbf{w}) = \big\{ \langle (w^1, i^1, j^1), \ldots, (w^k, i^k, j^k) \rangle \mid \langle w^1|_{[i^1, j^1]}, w^2|_{[i^2, j^2]}, \ldots, w^k|_{[i^k, j^k]} \rangle \in \mathfrak{L}(\mathsf{A}) \big\}$

1 $\mathcal{M} \leftarrow \emptyset$
   // Priority queue of the beginning of the matching trials
2 $\mathcal{Q} \leftarrow \big\{ \langle i_1, \ldots, i_k, w^1, \ldots, w^k \rangle \mid \forall m \in \{1, \ldots, k\}. \, w^m \in \mathbf{w}, 1 \leq i_m \leq |w^m| \big\}$
3 **while** $|\mathcal{Q}| > 0$ **do**
      // Pop the "smallest" element from the priority queue
4   **pop** $\langle i_1, \ldots, i_k, w^1, \ldots, w^k \rangle$ from $\mathcal{Q}$
5     $p_1, p_2, \ldots, p_k \leftarrow i_1, i_2, \ldots, i_k$
6     $\mathcal{C} \leftarrow \big\{ \langle w^1_{i_1}, w^2_{i_2}, \ldots, w^k_{i_k}, s_0 \rangle \mid s_0 \in S_0 \big\}$ // Start new matching trials
7   **while** $\mathcal{C} \neq \emptyset \wedge \exists m \in \{1, 2, \ldots, k\}. \, p_m < |w^m|$ **do**
8   **for** $m \in \{1, 2, \ldots, k\}$ satisfying $p_m < |w^m|$ **do**
9           $p_m \leftarrow p_m + 1$ // Read the $(p_m + 1)$-th letter $w^m_{p_m+1}$ of w^m
10          $\mathcal{C} \leftarrow \big\{ \langle v^1, \ldots, v^k, s \rangle [v^m \leftarrow v^m \cdot w^m_{p_m}] \mid \langle v^1, \ldots, v^k, s \rangle \in \mathcal{C} \big\}$
11          $\mathcal{C}' \leftarrow \mathcal{C}$ // Compute the next configuration
12   **while** $\mathcal{C}' \neq \emptyset$ **do**
13   **pop** $\langle v^1, \ldots, v^k, s \rangle$ from $\mathcal{C}'$
14   **for** $\langle u^1, \ldots, u^k, s' \rangle \notin \mathcal{C}$ s.t. $\langle v^1, \ldots, v^k, s \rangle \rightarrow \langle u^1, \ldots, u^k, s' \rangle$ **do**
                  // Apply transitions
15                $\mathcal{C} \leftarrow \mathcal{C} \cup \{\langle u^1, \ldots, u^k, s' \rangle\}$; $\mathcal{C}' \leftarrow \mathcal{C}' \cup \{\langle u^1, \ldots, u^k, s' \rangle\}$
16   **for** $\langle v^1, \ldots, v^k, s \rangle \in \mathcal{C}$ **do**
17   **if** $s \in S_F$ **then**   // Detect matching and update $\mathcal{M}$
18   add $\langle (w^1, i_1, p_1 - |v_i|), \ldots, (w^k, i_k, p_k - |v_k|) \rangle$ to $\mathcal{M}$
             // Remove the "non-waiting" configurations
19          $\mathcal{C} \leftarrow \big\{ \langle v^1, v^2, \ldots, v^k, s \rangle \in \mathcal{C} \mid \exists m \in \{1, 2, \ldots, k\}. \, v^m = \varepsilon \big\}$
20 **return** $\mathcal{M}$

Example 9. Consider again the NAA A in Example 5. Let $\mathbf{w} = \{w\}$ be a singleton word set, with $w = \$a\$b$. The initial priority queue (with an exponential blowup) at line 2 is

$$\mathcal{Q} = \{ \, \langle 1,1,w,w \rangle, \langle 1,2,w,w \rangle, \langle 1,3,w,w \rangle, \langle 1,4,w,w \rangle, \langle 2,1,w,w \rangle, \langle 2,2,w,w \rangle,$$
$$\langle 2,3,w,w \rangle, \langle 2,4,w,w \rangle, \langle 3,1,w,w \rangle, \langle 3,2,w,w \rangle, \langle 3,3,w,w \rangle, \langle 3,4,w,w \rangle,$$
$$\langle 4,1,w,w \rangle, \langle 4,2,w,w \rangle, \langle 4,3,w,w \rangle, \langle 4,4,w,w \rangle \, \}.$$

Then, at line 4, we pop from $\mathcal{Q}$ the smallest element, i.e., $\langle 1, 1, w, w \rangle$. We let $p_1, p_2 \leftarrow 1, 1$ (line 5). We let $\mathcal{C} \leftarrow \{\langle w_1, w_1, s_0 \rangle\} = \{\langle \$, \$, s_0 \rangle\}$ (line 6). Because $\mathcal{C} \neq \emptyset$ and both $m = 1$ and $m = 2$ satisfy $p_m = 1 < |w| = 4$ (line 7), we enter the **while** loop. We iterate over both values for m (line 8). Let us first consider $m = 1$. We set $p_1 \leftarrow 2$ (line 9). We update $\mathcal{C} \leftarrow \{\langle \$a, \$, s_0 \rangle\}$ (line 10). After applying transitions (line 15) gives $\mathcal{C} \leftarrow \{\langle \$a, \$, s_0 \rangle, \langle a, \$, s_1 \rangle, \langle a, \varepsilon, s_2 \rangle, \langle \varepsilon, \varepsilon, s_3 \rangle\}$, since $\langle \$a, \$, s_0 \rangle \rightarrow \langle a, \$, s_1 \rangle \rightarrow \langle a, \varepsilon, s_2 \rangle \rightarrow \langle \varepsilon, \varepsilon, s_3 \rangle$. No final configuration is reached (line 17), and therefore, no match is detected, and the non-waiting configurations (line 19) are removed, giving $\mathcal{C} \leftarrow \{\langle a, \varepsilon, s_2\rangle, \langle \varepsilon, \varepsilon, s_3\rangle\}$. We then move to $m = 2$ and set $p_2 \leftarrow 2$ (line 9). We update $\mathcal{C} \leftarrow \{\langle a, a, s_2\rangle, \langle \varepsilon, a, s_3\rangle\}$ (line 10). No transition can be taken, and we exit the **for** loop (line 8) with $\mathcal{C} = \{\langle \varepsilon, a, s_3\rangle\}$. In the second iteration of the **while** loop, we set $p_1 \leftarrow 3$ (line 9), giving $\mathcal{C} \leftarrow \{\langle \$, a, s_3\rangle\}$ (line 10). No transition can be applied, and the non-waiting configurations are removed, yielding $\mathcal{C} \leftarrow \emptyset$. This concludes the search for a match starting from $\langle 1, 1, w, w\rangle$ with a failure.

Now, let us pop $\langle 1, 3, w, w\rangle$ from $\mathcal{Q}$; we set $\mathcal{C} \leftarrow \{\langle \$, \$, s_0\rangle\}$. We let $p_1, p_2 \leftarrow 1, 3$ (line 5. In the first iteration of the **while** loop (line 7), we first set $p_1 \leftarrow 2$ (line 9), and we set $\mathcal{C} \leftarrow \{\langle \$a, \$, s_0\rangle\}$. We then apply transitions. After removing non-waiting configurations, we have $\mathcal{C} \leftarrow \{\langle \varepsilon, \varepsilon, s_3\rangle\}$. We then set $p_2 \leftarrow 4$ (line 9), and we set $\mathcal{C} \leftarrow \{\langle \varepsilon, b, s_3\rangle\}$. This time, we can apply transitions, yielding $\mathcal{C} \leftarrow \{\langle \varepsilon, b, s_3\rangle, \langle \varepsilon, \varepsilon, s_2\rangle\}$. In the second iteration of the **while** loop (line 7), we first set $p_1 \leftarrow 3$ (line 9), and we set $\mathcal{C} \leftarrow \{\langle \$, b, s_3\rangle, \langle \$, \varepsilon, s_2\rangle\}$. We then apply transitions, giving $\mathcal{C} \leftarrow \{\langle \$, b, s_3\rangle, \langle \$, \varepsilon, s_2\rangle, \langle \varepsilon, \varepsilon, s_f\rangle\}$. We found an accepting state (line 17), and we update $\mathcal{M} \leftarrow \{\langle (w, 1, 3), (w, 3, 4)\rangle\}$ (line 18). After removing non-waiting configurations, we have $\mathcal{C} \leftarrow \{\langle \$, \varepsilon, s_2\rangle, \langle \varepsilon, \varepsilon, s_f\rangle\}$. We then do not consider p_2, as $p_2 < 4$ does not hold anymore (line 8). In the third iteration of the **while** loop (line 7), we set $p_1 \leftarrow 4$ (line 9), and we set $\mathcal{C} \leftarrow \{\langle \$b, \varepsilon, s_2\rangle, \langle b, \varepsilon, s_f\rangle\}$. We then apply transitions, giving $\mathcal{C} \leftarrow \{\langle \$b, \varepsilon, s_2\rangle, \langle b, \varepsilon, s_f\rangle\}$. We found another match $\{\langle (w, 1, 4-1), (w, 3, 4)\rangle\}$, which does not modify $\mathcal{M}$ as it was found before. Any other starting configuration will result in failure, and the final match set is—as expected—$\mathcal{M}(A, \mathbf{w}) = \{\langle (w, 1, 3), (w, 3, 4)\rangle\}$.

Complexity Analysis. The initial size of the priority queue $\mathcal{Q}$ at line 2 is bounded by $|\mathbf{w}|^k \times (\max_{w \in \mathbf{w}} |w|)^k$. The number of iterations of the **while** loop from line 7 is bounded by $\max_{w \in \mathbf{w}} |w|$. For each such iteration, the number of iterations of the **while** loop from line 12, is bounded by $|S| \times \max_{w \in \mathbf{w}}^k$, and for each iteration, at most $|S|$ configurations are added to $\mathcal{C}$ and $\mathcal{C}'$. Overall, the time complexity of Algorithm 1 is bounded by $\mathcal{O}(|\mathbf{w}|^k \times \max_{w \in \mathbf{w}} |w|^{k+1} \times |S|^2)$.

5 Heuristics for Hyper Pattern Matching

Here, we present two heuristics to improve the efficiency of hyper pattern matching: FJS-style skipping (Sect. 5.1) and projection-based pruning (Sect. 5.2).

5.1 FJS-Style Skipping of Matching Trials

The FJS algorithm [25] is an efficient algorithm for the string matching problem: given a pattern word w_p and a target word w, it finds all occurrences of w_p within w. The idea of the FJS algorithm has been used to improve the efficiency of automata-based pattern matching, e.g., [39,40]. We apply a similar idea to Algorithm 1 to improve its efficiency.

```
         i i+1 i+2 i+3 i+4                            i i+1 i+2 i+3
     ··· $   a   $   a   b ···                    ··· $   a   b   a   ···
                         ↑x                               ─────────────
         $   a   b   $        ⎫                           $  a   b   $
         $   a   b   $        ⎬  aligned   partial matching  $   a   b   $
         $   a   b   $        ⎭               vs.            $   a   b   $
                                         w_p shifted by n ↓  $   a   b $
```

(a) QS-style skipping based on letter alignment. (b) KMP-style skipping utilizing the latest successful partial matching.

Fig. 3. Illustration of skipping in the FJS algorithm for string matching, with the pattern word $w_p = \$ab\$$. The skipped matching trials are shown in grey.

The central idea of FJS-style algorithms is to efficiently identify some matching trials as unnecessary and skip them. FJS-style algorithms combine QS-style skipping and KMP-style skipping, which originate from the Quick Search (QS) algorithm [35] and the Knuth-Morris-Pratt (KMP) algorithm [32], respectively.

Figure 3 illustrates the idea of skipping in the FJS algorithm for string matching. The QS-style skipping moves the pattern word w_p so that the letter in a certain position of the target word w aligns with the same letter in w_p. We first compare the last letter of w_p (\$ in Fig. 3a) with the corresponding letter in w (the $(i+3)$-th letter of w, i.e., a, in Fig. 3a). If they are different, we move w_p so that the letter in the target word immediately after the mismatched letter can have a matching. In this example, we move w_p so that the $(i+4)$-th letter of w, i.e., b, aligns with the next occurrence of b in w_p. One can efficiently perform such skipping by constructing $\Delta_{\mathrm{QS}}\colon \Sigma \to \mathbb{N}$ that maps the aligned letter (b in Fig. 3a) to the length of the skip (2 in Fig. 3a) in advance.

The KMP-style skipping uses the information of the partial matching in the latest matching trial to identify unnecessary matching trials. In the example in Fig. 3b, the latest matching trial was successful for three letters. Based solely on this information, we know that the i-th to $(i+2)$-th letters of w are \$ab. Since the minimum $n \in \mathbb{N}_+$ satisfying $\$ab \cdot \Sigma^* \cap \Sigma^n \cdot w_p \neq \emptyset$ is 3, we can skip the matching trials from the $(i+j)$-th letter of w with $j \in \{1,2\}$. One can efficiently perform such skipping by constructing $\Delta_{\mathrm{KMP}}\colon \{0,1,\ldots,|w_p|\} \to \mathbb{N}$ that maps the length of partial matching (3 in Fig. 3b) to the minimum n above (3 in Fig. 3b) in advance.

In [40], an FJS-style algorithm for NFA pattern matching was proposed. The main ideas of this extension are summarized as follows: 1) The length $\mathcal{SM}$ of the shortest matching is used instead of the length $|w_p|$ of the pattern word; 2) The set Λ_{QS} of letters that can appear as the $\mathcal{SM}$-th letter of a word accepted by the pattern NFA is constructed beforehand; 3) A partial matching is characterized by a state of the pattern NFA instead of its length, i.e., Δ_{KMP} takes a state $s \in S$ instead of $n \in \{0,1,\ldots,|w_p|\}$. Here, we further generalize these ideas for hyper pattern matching by parametrising the above concepts with directions. In this multi-directional extension, we reformulate the notion of "skipping" as "invalidating some positions". Thanks to this formulation, we can skip matching trials focusing on *each word* rather than *each tuple of words*.

Definition 10 (QS-style skip values). *Let $K = \{1, 2, \ldots, k\}$ and $\mathcal{A}$ be an NFA over $\Sigma \times K$. We let $\mathcal{SM}$ be the length of the shortest word accepted by $\mathcal{A}$, i.e., $\mathcal{SM} = \min_{w \in \mathcal{L}(\mathcal{A})} |w|$. For $m \in K$, we let $\mathcal{SM}^m$ be the minimum number of occurrences of m in the first $\mathcal{SM}$ letters of $w \in \mathcal{L}(\mathcal{A})$, i.e., $\mathcal{SM}^m = \min_{w \in \mathcal{L}(\mathcal{A})} |\pi(w|_{[1, \mathcal{SM}]}, m)|$. For $m \in K$, we let $\Lambda_{\mathrm{QS}}^m \subseteq \Sigma$ be the set of $\mathcal{SM}^m$-th letters of $\pi(\mathcal{L}(\mathcal{A}), m)$. For $m \in K$ and $\sigma \in \Sigma$, we let $\Delta_{\mathrm{QS}}^m(\sigma) \in \mathbb{N}$ be $\Delta_{\mathrm{QS}}^m(\sigma) = \min\{\mathcal{SM}^m + 1, \min\{i \in \{1, 2, \ldots, \mathcal{SM}^m\} \mid \exists w \in \mathcal{L}(\mathcal{A}). \text{ the } (\mathcal{SM}^m + 1 - i)\text{-th letter of } \pi(w, m) \text{ is } \sigma\}\}$.*

Theorem 11 (correctness of QS-style skipping). *Let $\mathbf{w}$ be a finite set of words, $K = \{1, 2, \ldots, k\}$, and $\mathsf{A} = \langle \Sigma, K, S, S_0, \Delta, S_F \rangle$ be an NAA. For any $w \in \mathbf{w}$, $m \in \{1, 2, \ldots, k\}$, $i \in \{1, 2, \ldots, |w| - \mathcal{SM}^m\}$, and $\langle (w^1, i^1, j^1), \ldots, (w^k, i^k, j^k) \rangle \in \mathcal{M}(\mathsf{A}, \mathbf{w})$, if $\mathcal{SM}^m > 0$, $w_{i + \mathcal{SM}^m - 1} \notin \Lambda_{\mathrm{QS}}^m$, and $w^m = w$, we have $i^m < i$ or $i^m \geq i + \Delta_{\mathrm{QS}}^m(w_{i + \mathcal{SM}^m})$.*

Definition 12 (KMP-style skip values). *Let $\mathcal{A} = \langle \Sigma \times K, S, S_0, \Delta, S_F \rangle$ be an NFA over $\Sigma \times K$ with $K = \{1, 2, \ldots, k\}$. For any $s \in S$, we let $\mathcal{A}_s$ be $\mathcal{A}$ with accepting states $\{s\}$, i.e., $\mathcal{A}_s = \langle \Sigma \times K, S, S_0, \Delta, \{s\} \rangle$. For any $m \in K$ and $s \in S$, we let $\Delta_{\mathrm{KMP}}^m(s) \in \mathbb{N}_+$ be $\Delta_{\mathrm{KMP}}^m(s) = \min\{n \in \mathbb{N}_+ \mid (\pi(\mathcal{L}(\mathcal{A}_s), m) \cdot \Sigma^*) \cap (\Sigma^n \cdot \pi(\mathcal{L}(\mathcal{A}), m) \cdot \Sigma^*) \neq \emptyset\}$.*

For an NFA $\mathcal{A} = \langle \Sigma \times K, S, S_0, \Delta, S_F \rangle$ with $K = \{1, 2, \ldots, k\}$, $w \in \Sigma^*$, and $m \in K$, we let $S_w^m \subseteq S$ be the set of states reachable by a word $\overline{w} \in (\Sigma \times K)^*$ whose m-projection $\pi(\overline{w}, m)$ is w, i.e., $S_w^m = \{s \in S \mid w \in \pi(\mathcal{L}(\mathcal{A}_s), m)\}$.

Theorem 13 (correctness of the KMP-style skipping). *Let $\mathbf{w}$ be a finite set of words, $K = \{1, 2, \ldots, k\}$, and $\mathsf{A} = \langle \Sigma, K, S, S_0, \Delta, S_F \rangle$ be an NAA. For any $m \in \{1, 2, \ldots, k\}$, $w \in \mathbf{w}$, $i \in \{1, 2, \ldots, |w|\}$, $j \geq i$, and $s \in S_w^m$, there is no $\langle (w^1, i^1, j^1), \ldots, (w^k, i^k, j^k) \rangle \in \mathcal{M}(\mathsf{A}, \mathbf{w})$, with $w^m = w$ and $i^m \in \{i+1, i+2, \ldots, i + \Delta_{\mathrm{KMP}}^m(s) - 1\}$.*

Algorithm 2 outlines our FJS-style algorithm for hyper pattern matching. In Algorithm 2, the QS-style skipping is used so that: i) we first test if the $\mathcal{SM}^m$-th letter of w^m is in Λ_{QS}^m (line 5) and ii) if it is not in Λ_{QS}^m, we remove the skipped starting indices from the waiting queue using Δ_{QS}^m (line 7). The KMP-style skipping is used so that: i) we keep track of the states $\mathcal{R}$ reached during the latest matching trial (line 14) and ii) we remove the unnecessary starting indices from the waiting queue using Δ_{KMP}^m (line 17).

Algorithm 2: An FJS-style algorithm $\mathcal{HPM}^{FJS}$ for hyper pattern matching.

Input: A finite set $\mathbf{w} \subseteq \Sigma^*$ of words and an NAA $\mathsf{A} = \langle \Sigma, K, S, S_0, \Delta, S_F \rangle$ with $K = \{1, 2, \ldots, k\}$
Output: The match set $\mathcal{M}(\mathsf{A}, \mathbf{w}) = \{\langle (w^1, i^1, j^1), \ldots, (w^k, i^k, j^k) \rangle \mid \langle w^1|_{[i^1, j^1]}, w^2|_{[i^2, j^2]}, \ldots, w^k|_{[i^k, j^k]} \rangle \in \mathfrak{L}(\mathsf{A})\}$

1   $\mathcal{M} \leftarrow \emptyset$
2   $\mathcal{Q} \leftarrow \{\langle i_1, \ldots, i_k, w^1, \ldots, w^k \rangle \mid \forall m \in K. w^m \in \mathbf{w}, 1 \leq i_m \leq |w^m| - \mathcal{SM}^m + 1\}$
3   **while** $|\mathcal{Q}| > 0$ **do**
4   pop $\langle i_1, \ldots, i_k, w^1, \ldots, w^k \rangle$ from $\mathcal{Q}$
5   **if** $\exists m \in K. w^m_{i_m + \mathcal{SM}^m - 1} \notin \Lambda^m_{\mathrm{QS}}$ **then**   // QS-style skipping
        // Remove the skipped starting indices
6   **for** $m \in K$ *satisfying* $w^m_{i_m + \mathcal{SM}^m - 1} \notin \Lambda^m_{\mathrm{QS}}$ **do**
7          $\mathcal{Q} \leftarrow \{\langle i'_1, \ldots, i'_k, v^1, \ldots, v^k \rangle \in \mathcal{Q} \mid \forall m \in K. v^m = w^m \implies i'_m < i_m \vee i'_m \geq i_m + \Delta^m_{\mathrm{QS}}(w^m_{i_m + \mathcal{SM}^m})\}$
8   **continue**
9      $p_1, p_2, \ldots, p_k \leftarrow i_1, i_2, \ldots, i_k; \mathcal{C} \leftarrow \{\langle w^1_{i_1}, w^2_{i_2}, \ldots, w^k_{i_k}, s_0 \rangle \mid s_0 \in S_0\}$
10    $\mathcal{R} \leftarrow S_0$ // Reached locations
11   **while** $\mathcal{C} \neq \emptyset \wedge \exists m \in K. p_m < |w^m|$ **do**
12   **for** $m \in \{1, 2, \ldots, k\}$ *satisfying* $p_m < |w^m|$ **do**
13   Update $\mathcal{C}$ and $\mathcal{M}$ // Same as Algorithms 9 to 18 of Algorithm 1
14      $\mathcal{R} \leftarrow \mathcal{R} \cup \{s \mid \langle v^1, v^2, \ldots, v^k, s \rangle \in \mathcal{C}\}$
15      $\mathcal{C} \leftarrow \{\langle v^1, v^2, \ldots, v^k, s \rangle \in \mathcal{C} \mid \exists m \in K. v^m = \varepsilon\}$
16   **for** $s \in \mathcal{R}$ **do**   // KMP-style skipping
17      $\mathcal{Q} \leftarrow \{\langle i'_1, \ldots, i'_k, v^1, \ldots, v^k \rangle \in \mathcal{Q} \mid (\forall m \in K. v^m = w^m) \implies (\forall m \in K. i'_m \leq i_m \vee i'_m \geq i_m + \Delta^m_{\mathrm{KMP}}(s))\}$
18   **return** $\mathcal{M}$

5.2 Pruning of Matching Trials via Projection

We now propose a heuristics reducing the blowup of $\mathcal{Q}$ at line 2 in Algorithm 1.

Example 14. Assume a set $\mathbf{w} = \{w_1, w_2, \ldots, w_k\}$ of words made of n identical letters "a_i" ($1 \leq i \leq k$) followed by a "b", i.e., $w_i = a_i^n b$. Consider a pattern recognizing 3 consecutive occurrences of "a_i" followed by a "b", for each $1 \leq i \leq k$; this pattern can be easily encoded by an NAA over k directions (omitted due to space concern—see Appendix C of [38]). The initial $\mathcal{Q}$ at line 2 in Algorithm 1 contains already $k^k \times (n+1)^k$ tuples; even worse, each of these tuples (but one) will be explored for 3 letters in all k directions until failing (technically, the tuples starting with $n+1$ and n, $n-1$ will explore a little less). But in fact, the only match will be $\mathcal{M}(\mathsf{A}, \{w_1, \ldots, w_k\}) = \{\langle (w_1, n-2, n+1), \ldots, (w_k, n-2, n+1) \rangle\}$.

In Example 14, if we knew before starting Algorithm 1 that the only potential match starts at $n-2$ in each word, we would considerably reduce this initial blowup. This is the heuristics we propose here: instead of starting Algorithm 1

Fig. 4. Projections of A from Fig. 1a.

Algorithm 3: Projection heuristics for hyper pattern matching.

Input: A finite set $\mathbf{w} \subseteq \Sigma^*$ of words and an NAA $\mathsf{A} = \langle \Sigma, K, S, S_0, \Delta, S_F \rangle$ with $K = \{1, 2, \ldots, k\}$
Output: Priority queue of the beginning of the matching trials
1 **for** $m \in \{1, 2, \ldots, k\}$ **do**
2 $\quad \mathcal{M}_m \leftarrow \mathcal{PM}(\mathbf{w}, \pi(\mathsf{A}, m))$ // Compute matches projected on each m
   // Restrict the priority queue to possible matches projected on m
3 $\mathcal{Q} \leftarrow \{\langle i_1, \ldots, i_k, w^1, \ldots, w^k \rangle \mid \forall m \in \{1, \ldots, k\}. \exists j_m. \langle (w^m, i_m, j_m) \rangle \in \mathcal{M}_m \}$

---

with any potential starting position, we first filter out positions in each word by keeping only these matching the pattern projected on the current direction.

Definition 15 (Projection of an NAA). *Given an NAA* $\mathsf{A} = \langle \Sigma, K, S, S_0, \Delta, S_F \rangle$ *and given* $l \in K$, *we let* $\pi(\mathsf{A}, l)$ *be the DFA constructed by i) replacing any transition* $\langle a, l' \rangle$ *with "a" whenever* $l' = l$, *ii) replacing any transition* $\langle a, l' \rangle$ *with "ε" whenever* $l' \neq l$, *and iii) removing in the obtained automaton any transition labeled by* ε, *e.g., using the powerset construction [30].*

Example 16. Consider again A in Fig. 1a. We give $\pi(\mathsf{A}, 1)$ and $\pi(\mathsf{A}, 2)$ in Fig. 4.

We can now define the hyper pattern matching algorithm with projection ($\mathcal{HPM}_P$) as Algorithm 1 in which we replace line 2 with the algorithm fragment in Algorithm 3. The call to $\mathcal{PM}$ at line 2 denotes classical non-hyper pattern matching on a DFA. Even in the worst case, this heuristics only incurs a loss of time consisting of k calls to a non-hyper pattern matching algorithm, while its gain may be an exponential decrease of the computation time in hyper pattern matching.

Example 17. Consider again A in Fig. 1a, and consider again $w = \$a\$b$ from Example 9. We have $\mathcal{M}_1 \leftarrow \mathcal{HPM}(\{w\}, \pi(\mathsf{A}, 1)) = \{\langle (w, 1, 3) \rangle\}$ and $\mathcal{M}_2 \leftarrow \{\langle (w, 3, 3) \rangle, \langle (w, 3, 4) \rangle\}$. Therefore, $\mathcal{Q} \leftarrow \{\langle 1, 3, w, w \rangle\}$—a singleton to be compared to the 16 elements in the initial queue in Example 9.

Although classical pattern matching in Algorithm 3 can be conducted efficiently, the overhead can be further reduced by overapproximating the exact matching. For instance, one can use the set of indices appearing in some matching rather than the matching itself. Algorithm 4 shows an algorithm to identify such a set of indices. More precisely, it maps a word $w \in \Sigma^*$ to another word $w^\perp \in (\Sigma \cup \{\perp\})^*$, where the letters irrelevant to hyper pattern matching according to the projection $\mathcal{A}$ are replaced with $\perp$. In Algorithm 4, for each state $s \in S$

Algorithm 4: Pruning of indices irrelevant to hyper pattern matching.

Input: A word $w \in \Sigma^*$ and a DFA $\pi(\mathsf{A}, l) = \langle \Sigma, S, s_0, \Delta, S_F \rangle$.
Output: A word $w^\perp \in (\Sigma \cup \{\perp\})^*$ such that $w_h^\perp = w_h$ if there are i and j satisfying $i \leq h \leq j$ and $w|_{[i,j]} \in \mathcal{L}(\mathcal{A})$, and $w_h^\perp = \perp$ otherwise.

1   $w^\perp \leftarrow \varepsilon;\ U \leftarrow \emptyset$
    // c maintains the minimum i s.t. we reach $s \in S$ by using $w|_{[i,j]}$
2   let $c\colon S \to \mathbb{N} \cup \{\perp\}$ such that $c(s) = \perp$ for any $s \in S$
3   **for** $j \in \{1, 2, \ldots, |w|\}$ **do**
4   **if** $c(s_0) = \perp$ **then** $c \leftarrow c[s_0 \leftarrow j]$
      // Update c by applying the transition function Δ
5   let $c'\colon S \to \mathbb{N} \cup \{\perp\}$ such that $c'(s) = \perp$ for any $s \in S$
6   **for** $s \in S$ satisfying $c(s) \neq \perp$ **do**
7        $c' \leftarrow c'[\Delta(s, w_j) \leftarrow \min\{c(s), c'(\Delta(s, w_j))\}]$
8      $c \leftarrow c'$
      // Update U using the matching we currently have
9   **for** $s_f \in S_F$ satisfying $c(s_f) \neq \perp$ **do**
10      $U \leftarrow U \cup \{h \mid c(s_f) \leq h \leq j\}$
      // Append the already determined filtering result to $w^\perp$
11   **for** $h \in \{|w^\perp|+1, |w^\perp|+2, \ldots, \min_{s \in S, c(s) \neq \perp} c(s) - 1\}$ **do**
12   **if** $h \in U$ **then** $w_h^\perp \leftarrow w_h$ **else** $w_h^\perp \leftarrow \perp$
13 **for** $h \in \{|w^\perp|+1, |w^\perp|+2, \ldots, |w|\}$ **do**
14   **if** $h \in U$ **then** $w_h^\perp \leftarrow w_h$ **else** $w_h^\perp \leftarrow \perp$
15 **return** $w^\perp$

of the DFA $\mathcal{A}$, we maintain the minimum $i \in \mathbb{N}$ such that we reach s by feeding $w|_{[i,j]}$ to $\mathcal{A}$ as a mapping c, where j is the index of the current letter to be examined. In the loop at lines 6 to 7, we update c using the transition function Δ. In the loop at lines 9 to 10 we update the set U of indices deemed relevant to hyper pattern matching according to the projection $\mathcal{A}$. In the loop at lines 11 to 12, we update the resulting word $w^\perp$ in the range where the result is already determined. Thanks to this incremental construction, we can start using the result of filtering as soon as possible. In the loop from lines 13 to 14, we use the remaining part of U to update $w^\perp$.

The time complexity of Algorithm 4 is linear in the length $|w|$ of the examined word. In contrast, the time complexity of classical pattern matching is linear in the number of matches, which is at most $|w|^2$. Since we run Algorithm 4 for each $(w, l) \in \mathbf{w} \times K$, the overall time complexity of projection-based pruning is in $\mathcal{O}(N \times |\mathbf{w}| \times |K|)$, where N is the maximum length of $w \in \mathbf{w}$. This is more scalable than Algorithm 1.

6 Implementation and Experiments

We implemented our algorithms for hyper pattern matching as a prototype tool HypPAu[2] in Rust. In particular, we implemented the following four algorithms: the naive algorithm in Algorithm 1 ($\mathcal{HPM}$), the algorithm with FJS-style skipping in Algorithm 2 ($\mathcal{HPM}^{FJS}$), the naive algorithm with projection-based pruning with Algorithm 4 ($\mathcal{HPM}_P$), and the algorithm with both FJS-style skipping and projection-based pruning ($\mathcal{HPM}_P^{FJS}$), i.e., the initialization of the priority queue $\mathcal{Q}$ at line 2 in Algorithm 2 is replaced with Algorithm 3. In our implementation HypPAu, the priority queue $\mathcal{Q}$ is constructed in a lazy manner to reduce memory consumption. We conducted experiments to evaluate the efficiency of our algorithms.

6.1 Benchmarks

In our experiments, we used the following four benchmarks: INTERFERENCE, ROBUSTNESS, PACKETPAIRS, and MANYDIRS. All the benchmarks are our original work. The NAAs in INTERFERENCE and ROBUSTNESS are shown in Figs. 1b and 2, respectively. PACKETPAIRS is a benchmark inspired by monitoring of network packets for data streams; see Appendix B.2 of [38] for details. MANYDIRS is an artificial benchmark to evaluate the scalability of HypPAu w.r.t. the number of directions. The NAAs of MANYDIRS are obtained by generalizing the NAA in Fig. 1a. In all the benchmarks, we randomly generated the set of input words.

6.2 Experiments

We used INTERFERENCE, ROBUSTNESS, and PACKETPAIRS to observe the scalability of HypPAu w.r.t. the word length and the number of words, whereas we used MANYDIRS to observe the scalability w.r.t. the number of directions. To observe the scalability w.r.t. the word length, we measured the execution time using words of different lengths. We randomly generated words of length 500–5000, 200–2000, and 1000–10 000 for INTERFERENCE, ROBUSTNESS, and PACKETPAIRS, respectively. To observe the scalability w.r.t. the number of words, we measured the execution time using multiple words of the same length. We randomly generated 2–10 words of length 500, 200, and 1000 for INTERFERENCE, ROBUSTNESS, and PACKETPAIRS, respectively. To observe the scalability w.r.t. the number of directions, we measured the execution time using NAAs of different numbers of directions and words of the same length. We generated NAAs of directions 2–4 and randomly generated words of length 200.

We ran each of the above configurations 10 times. We report the average execution time. We ran all the experiments on a computing server with Intel Xeon w5-3435X 4.5 GHz 63 GiB RAM that runs Ubuntu 24.04.2 LTS. We set the timeout to 1800 seconds.

---

[2] HypPAu is distributed under the GPLv3 license at https://github.com/MasWag/hyppau.

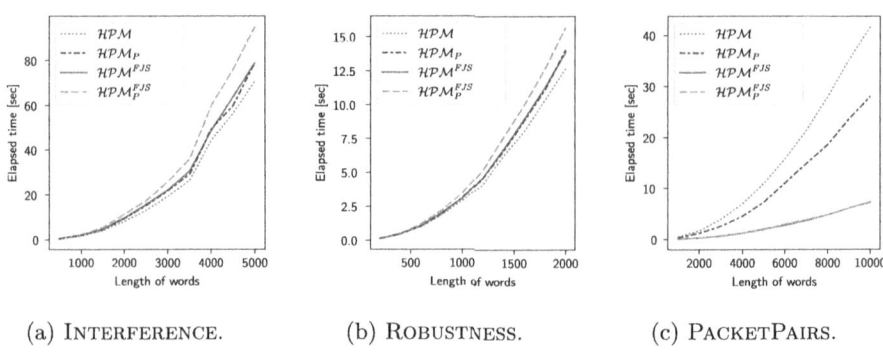

(a) INTERFERENCE. (b) ROBUSTNESS. (c) PACKETPAIRS.

Fig. 5. Elapsed time with respect to the length of the monitored words.

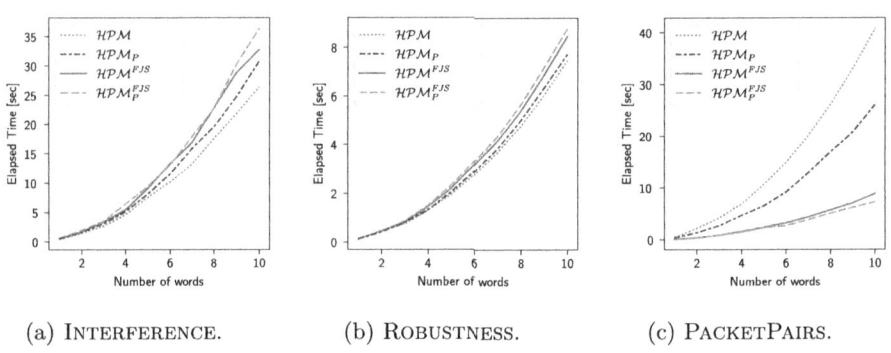

(a) INTERFERENCE. (b) ROBUSTNESS. (c) PACKETPAIRS.

Fig. 6. Elapsed time with respect to the number of words to be monitored.

6.3 Results and Discussions

Figures 5 and 6 show the elapsed time with respect to the length and the number of monitored words, respectively. In Figs. 5 and 6, we observe that for INTERFERENCE and ROBUSTNESS, the execution time of $\mathcal{HPM}^{FJS}$ is slightly longer than that of $\mathcal{HPM}$, while for PACKETPAIRS, the execution time of $\mathcal{HPM}^{FJS}$ is much shorter than that of $\mathcal{HPM}$. This is because for INTERFERENCE and ROBUSTNESS, the skip values Δ_{KMP} and Δ_{QS} are at most 1, and we have no performance gain from skipping. Due to the overhead in the use of skip values, $\mathcal{HPM}^{FJS}$ is slightly slower than $\mathcal{HPM}$. It is also possible to minimize this overhead by switching from $\mathcal{HPM}^{FJS}$ to $\mathcal{HPM}$ when Δ_{KMP} and Δ_{QS} are 1 since we compute them beforehand. In contrast, for PACKETPAIRS, the skip values Δ_{KMP} and Δ_{QS} are 2 for many inputs and states, and $\mathcal{HPM}^{FJS}$ is much more efficient than $\mathcal{HPM}$ by skipping unnecessary matching trials.

In Figs. 5 and 6, we also observe a similar trend for $\mathcal{HPM}$ and $\mathcal{HPM}_P$. This is because, for INTERFERENCE and ROBUSTNESS, no letters in monitored words can be filtered out solely based on the projection, due to the comparison of letters observed in one word with another. In contrast, for PACKETPAIRS, some letters can be filtered out because each matching for 1 (resp. 2) must start and end with s^Q and e^Q (resp. s^P and e^P), and the letters outside these ranges can be filtered out. In Fig. 6c, we also observe performance gain by using both FJS-style skipping and projection-based pruning, i.e., $\mathcal{HPM}_P^{FJS}$, compared to $\mathcal{HPM}^{FJS}$ and $\mathcal{HPM}_P$.

Table 1. Elapsed time (in seconds) with respect to the number of directions for MANY-DIRS. T/O denotes an execution exceeding the timeout of 1800 seconds.

	$\mathcal{HPM}$	$\mathcal{HPM}^{FJS}$	$\mathcal{HPM}_P$	$\mathcal{HPM}_P^{FJS}$
$|K|=2$	0.03	0.01	0.02	0.02
$|K|=3$	4.65	0.95	1.34	1.12
$|K|=4$	T/O	95.48	140.42	130.05

Table 1 shows the elapsed time with respect to the number of directions. We observe that the performance gain from our heuristics is much more evident when the number of directions is large. This is because filtering out one letter for one direction allows us to skip all the matching trials that include that letter for the direction, which also has a combinatorial explosion with respect to the number of directions. Therefore, we conclude that our heuristics in Theorem 5 can improve the efficiency of hyper pattern matching, particularly when the number of directions is large.

Overall, although the scalability with respect to the number of directions is not good as suggested by Theorem 8, one can conduct hyper pattern matching for words with thousands of letters within one minute when the number of directions is two. Moreover, even when there are four directions, hyper pattern matching can be conducted within a few minutes for words of length 200. Although these results may look restrictive, we believe that this is sufficient for most of the realistic use cases. For instance, all the hyperproperties in [9,24] bind at most two words, i.e., can be encoded using at most two directions.

7 Conclusions and Future Perspectives

Toward more informative monitoring of hyperproperties, we introduced hyper pattern matching with nondeterministic asynchronous finite automata (NAAs) for representing hyperlanguages. In addition to a naive algorithm, we developed two heuristics, FJS-style skipping and projection-based pruning, to improve its efficiency. We evaluated the problem from both theoretical and empirical perspectives: theoretically, we proved it is NP-complete to decide the nonemptiness of the match set $\mathcal{M}(\mathsf{A}, \mathbf{w})$; empirically, our experimental results demonstrate that the match set can be computed for words with thousands of letters within one minute, which is likely useful for monitoring of reasonable size of data.

One future direction is to generalize the problem, e.g., to handle properties with timing constraints as in the context of *timed pattern matching* [6,36,37,39,40]. Another future direction is to investigate approximate algorithms, i.e., identifying matches within a certain threshold of errors [20], e.g., measured using edit distance or Hamming distance, with better complexity.

Acknowledgements. This work is partially supported by JST PRESTO (JPMJPR22CA), JST BOOST (JPMJBY24H8), JSPS KAKENHI (22K17873), ANR BisoUS (ANR-22-CE48-0012) and ANR TAPAS (PRC ANR-24-CE25-5742).

References

1. Aceto, L., Achilleos, A., Anastasiadi, E., Francalanza, A.: Monitoring hyperproperties with circuits. In: Mousavi, M.R., Philippou, A. (eds.) FORTE. LNCS, vol. 13273, pp. 1–10. Springer (2022). https://doi.org/10.1007/978-3-031-08679-3_1
2. Aceto, L., Achilleos, A., Anastasiadi, E., Francalanza, A., Gorla, D., Wagemaker, J.: Centralized vs decentralized monitors for hyperproperties. In: Majumdar, R., Silva, A. (eds.) CONCUR. LIPIcs, vol. 311, pp. 4:1–4:19. Schloss Dagstuhl - Leibniz-Zentrum für Informatik (2024). https://doi.org/10.4230/LIPICS.CONCUR.2024.4, https://doi.org/10.4230/LIPIcs.CONCUR.2024.4
3. Agrawal, S., Bonakdarpour, B.: Runtime verification of k-safety hyperproperties in HyperLTL. In: CSF, pp. 239–252. IEEE Computer Society (2016). https://doi.org/10.1109/CSF.2016.24
4. Amir, A., Benson, G., Farach, M.: An alphabet independent approach to two-dimensional pattern matching. SIAM J. Comput. **23**(2), 313–323 (1994). https://doi.org/10.1137/S0097539792226321
5. Amir, A., Farach, M.: Two-dimensional dictionary matching. IPL **44**(5), 233–239 (1992). https://doi.org/10.1016/0020-0190(92)90206-B
6. Bakhirkin, A., Ferrère, T., Nickovic, D., Maler, O., Asarin, E.: Online timed pattern matching using automata. In: Jansen, D.N., Prabhakar, P. (eds.) FORMATS 2018. LNCS, vol. 11022, pp. 215–232. Springer, Cham (2018). https://doi.org/10.1007/978-3-030-00151-3_13
7. Bartocci, E., Henzinger, T.A., Nickovic, D., da Costa, A.O.: Hypernode automata. In: Pérez, G.A., Raskin, J.F. (eds.) CONCUR. LIPIcs, vol. 279, pp. 21:1–21:16. Schloss Dagstuhl - Leibniz-Zentrum für Informatik (2023). https://doi.org/10.4230/LIPICS.CONCUR.2023.21
8. Baumeister, J., Coenen, N., Bonakdarpour, B., Finkbeiner, B., Sánchez, C.: A temporal logic for asynchronous hyperproperties. In: Silva, A., Leino, K.R.M. (eds.) CAV 2021. LNCS, vol. 12759, pp. 694–717. Springer, Cham (2021). https://doi.org/10.1007/978-3-030-81685-8_33
9. Beutner, R., Finkbeiner, B.: AutoHyper: Explicit-state model checking for HyperLTL. In: Sankaranarayanan, S., Sharygina, N. (eds.) TACAS, Part I. LNCS, vol. 13993, pp. 145–163. Springer (2023). https://doi.org/10.1007/978-3-031-30823-9_8
10. Beutner, R., Finkbeiner, B., Frenkel, H., Metzger, N.: Monitoring second-order hyperproperties. In: Dastani, M., Sichman, J.S., Alechina, N., Dignum, V. (eds.) AAMAS. pp. 180–188. International Foundation for Autonomous Agents and Multiagent Systems/ACM (2024). https://doi.org/10.5555/3635637.3662865

11. Bird, R.S.: Two dimensional pattern matching. IPL **6**(5), 168–170 (1977). https://doi.org/10.1016/0020-0190(77)90017-5
12. Bombardelli, A., Bozzelli, L., Sánchez, C., Tonetta, S.: Unifying asynchronous logics for hyperproperties. In: Barman, S., Lasota, S. (eds.) FSTTCS. LIPIcs, vol. 323, pp. 14:1–14:18. Schloss Dagstuhl - Leibniz-Zentrum für Informatik (2024). https://doi.org/10.4230/LIPICS.FSTTCS.2024.14
13. Bonakdarpour, B., Prabhakar, P., Sánchez, C.: Model checking timed hyperproperties in discrete-time systems. In: Lee, R., Jha, S., Mavridou, A., Giannakopoulou, D. (eds.) NFM 2020. LNCS, vol. 12229, pp. 311–328. Springer, Cham (2020). https://doi.org/10.1007/978-3-030-55754-6_18
14. Bozzelli, L., Peron, A., Sánchez, C.: Asynchronous extensions of HyperLTL. In: LiCS, pp. 1–13. IEEE (2021). https://doi.org/10.1109/LICS52264.2021.9470583
15. Brett, N., Siddique, U., Bonakdarpour, B.: Rewriting-based runtime verification for alternation-free HyperLTL. In: Legay, A., Margaria, T. (eds.) TACAS 2017. LNCS, vol. 10206, pp. 77–93. Springer, Heidelberg (2017). https://doi.org/10.1007/978-3-662-54580-5_5
16. Chalupa, M., Henzinger, T.A.: Monitoring hyperproperties with prefix transducers. In: Katsaros, P., Nenzi, L. (eds.) RV. LNCS, vol. 14245, pp. 168–190. Springer (2023). https://doi.org/10.1007/978-3-031-44267-4_9
17. Chalupa, M., Henzinger, T.A., da Costa, A.O.: Monitoring extended hypernode logic. In: Kosmatov, N., Kovács, L. (eds.) iFM. LNCS, vol. 15234, pp. 151–171. Springer (2024). https://doi.org/10.1007/978-3-031-76554-4_9
18. Clarkson, M.R., Finkbeiner, B., Koleini, M., Micinski, K.K., Rabe, M.N., Sánchez, C.: Temporal logics for hyperproperties. In: Abadi, M., Kremer, S. (eds.) POST 2014. LNCS, vol. 8414, pp. 265–284. Springer, Heidelberg (2014). https://doi.org/10.1007/978-3-642-54792-8_15
19. Dimitrova, R., Finkbeiner, B., Rabe, M.N.: Monitoring temporal information flow. In: Margaria, T., Steffen, B. (eds.) ISoLA 2012. LNCS, vol. 7609, pp. 342–357. Springer, Heidelberg (2012). https://doi.org/10.1007/978-3-642-34026-0_26
20. Ellert, J., Gawrychowski, P., Górkiewicz, A., Starikovskaya, T.: Faster two-dimensional pattern matching with k mismatches. In: Azar, Y., Panigrahi, D. (eds.) SODA, pp. 4031–4060. SIAM (2025). https://doi.org/10.1137/1.9781611978322.138
21. Finkbeiner, B., Hahn, C., Stenger, M., Tentrup, L.: RVHyper: a runtime verification tool for temporal hyperproperties. In: Beyer, D., Huisman, M. (eds.) TACAS 2018. LNCS, vol. 10806, pp. 194–200. Springer, Cham (2018). https://doi.org/10.1007/978-3-319-89963-3_11
22. Finkbeiner, B., Hahn, C., Stenger, M., Tentrup, L.: Monitoring hyperproperties. FMSD **54**(3), 336–363 (2019). https://doi.org/10.1007/S10703-019-00334-Z
23. Finkbeiner, B., Hahn, C., Stenger, M., Tentrup, L.: Efficient monitoring of hyperproperties using prefix trees. STTT **22**(6), 729–740 (2020). https://doi.org/10.1007/S10009-020-00552-5
24. Finkbeiner, B., Rabe, M.N., Sánchez, C.: Algorithms for model checking HyperLTL and HyperCTL*. In: Kroening, D., Păsăreanu, C.S. (eds.) CAV 2015. LNCS, vol. 9206, pp. 30–48. Springer, Cham (2015). https://doi.org/10.1007/978-3-319-21690-4_3
25. Franek, F., Jennings, C.G., Smyth, W.F.: A simple fast hybrid pattern-matching algorithm. J. Discrete Algor. **5**(4), 682–695 (2007). https://doi.org/10.1016/j.jda.2006.11.004

26. Frederick, R., Casner, S.L., Jacobson, V., Schulzrinne, H.: RTP: A transport protocol for real-time applications. RFC 1889 (Jan 1996). https://doi.org/10.17487/RFC1889, https://www.rfc-editor.org/info/rfc1889
27. Furia, C.A.: A survey of multi-tape automata (2012)
28. Gutsfeld, J.O., Müller-Olm, M., Ohrem, C.: Automata and fixpoints for asynchronous hyperproperties. Proc. ACM Programming Lang. 5(POPL), 1–29 (2021). https://doi.org/10.1145/3434319
29. Hahn, C.: Algorithms for monitoring hyperproperties. In: Finkbeiner, B., Mariani, L. (eds.) RV 2019. LNCS, vol. 11757, pp. 70–90. Springer, Cham (2019). https://doi.org/10.1007/978-3-030-32079-9_5
30. Hopcroft, J.E., Motwani, R., Ullman, J.D.: Introduction to automata theory, languages, and computation, 3rd edn. Addison-Wesley, Pearson international edition (2007)
31. Karhumäki, J., Plandowski, W., Rytter, W.: Pattern-matching problems for two-dimensional images described by finite automata. Nordic J. Comput. **7**(1), 1–13 (2000)
32. Knuth, D.E., Morris, J.H., Jr., Pratt, V.R.: Fast pattern matching in strings. SIAM J. Comput. **6**(2), 323–350 (1977). https://doi.org/10.1137/0206024
33. Rabin, M.O., Scott, D.S.: Finite automata and their decision problems. IBM J. Res. Dev. **3**(2), 114–125 (1959). https://doi.org/10.1147/RD.32.0114
34. Smith, G.: Principles of secure information flow analysis. In: Christodorescu, M., Jha, S., Maughan, D., Song, D., Wang, C. (eds.) Malware Detection, Advances in Information Security, vol. 27, pp. 291–307. Springer (2007). https://doi.org/10.1007/978-0-387-44599-1_13
35. Sunday, D.: A very fast substring search algorithm. Commun. ACM **33**(8), 132–142 (1990). https://doi.org/10.1145/79173.79184
36. Ulus, D., Ferrère, T., Asarin, E., Maler, O.: Timed pattern matching. In: Legay, A., Bozga, M. (eds.) FORMATS 2014. LNCS, vol. 8711, pp. 222–236. Springer, Cham (2014). https://doi.org/10.1007/978-3-319-10512-3_16
37. Waga, M.: Online quantitative timed pattern matching with semiring-valued weighted automata. In: André, É., Stoelinga, M. (eds.) FORMATS 2019. LNCS, vol. 11750, pp. 3–22. Springer, Cham (2019). https://doi.org/10.1007/978-3-030-29662-9_1
38. Waga, M., André, É.: Hyper pattern matching (2025). https://doi.org/10.48550/arXiv.2507.12102
39. Waga, M., André, É., Hasuo, I.: Parametric timed pattern matching. ACM Trans Softw. Eng. Methodol. **32**(1), 10:1–10:35 (2023). https://doi.org/10.1145/3517194
40. Waga, M., Hasuo, I., Suenaga, K.: Efficient online timed pattern matching by automata-based skipping. In: Abate, A., Geeraerts, G. (eds.) FORMATS 2017. LNCS, vol. 10419, pp. 224–243. Springer, Cham (2017). https://doi.org/10.1007/978-3-319-65765-3_13
41. Worrell, J.: Revisiting the equivalence problem for finite multitape automata. In: Fomin, F.V., Freivalds, R., Kwiatkowska, M., Peleg, D. (eds.) ICALP 2013. LNCS, vol. 7966, pp. 422–433. Springer, Heidelberg (2013). https://doi.org/10.1007/978-3-642-39212-2_38
42. Žd'árek, J., Melichar, B.: On Two-dimensional pattern matching by finite automata. In: Farré, J., Litovsky, I., Schmitz, S. (eds.) CIAA 2005. LNCS, vol. 3845, pp. 329–340. Springer, Heidelberg (2006). https://doi.org/10.1007/11605157_28

Monitoring Hypernode Logic Over Infinite Domains

Marek Chalupa(✉), Thomas A. Henzinger, and Ana Oliveira da Costa

Institute of Science and Technology Austria (ISTA), Klosterneuburg, Austria
{mchalupa,tah,ana.costa}@ist.ac.at

Abstract. We propose a monitoring approach for hyperproperties where the system's observations range over infinite domains. The specifications are given as formulas of *symbolic hypernode logic*, an extension of earlier versions of hypernode logic that supports events with data. We demonstrate how to translate terms of symbolic hypernode logic into *multi-tape symbolic transducers* and we present a monitoring algorithm for universally quantified formulas that is based on this translation. We evaluate our approach against the previous approach for monitoring hypernode logic, and we also compare it to other monitors for hyperproperties.

Keywords: symbolic automata · symbolic transducers · hyperproperties · runtime verification · monitoring · k-safety

1 Introduction

Hyperproperties express system requirements by defining relationships between multiple executions [16]. Unlike trace properties, which specify requirements on isolated executions, hyperproperties can express specifications such as confidentiality of sensitive data or consistency guarantees in concurrent and distributed systems [16,30]. In recent years, numerous formalisms and techniques have been developed to support the verification of hyperproperties. We focus on the problem of *runtime verification (monitoring)*: verifying whether the observed runtime behavior of a system satisfies a given hyperproperty.

Early approaches for monitoring hyperproperties were limited to specifications where executions are compared in lock-step. More recently, researchers introduced techniques for monitoring *asynchronous hyperproperties* that are suitable for systems where observations may not be aligned with one another [7,12,13]. All existing approaches for monitoring, however, remain constrained to settings where one can observe only a finite number of different events, limiting their applicability to real-world applications.

In this work, we introduce *symbolic hypernode logic (sHL)*, which enables the specification of asynchronous hyperproperties over infinite domains. At its core, hypernode logic compares different executions using string-based operators and

---

This work was supported in part by the ERC-2020-AdG 101020093 and in part by the FWF-2022-SFB F8502 (SPyCoDe).

© The Author(s), under exclusive license to Springer Nature Switzerland AG 2026
B. Königshofer and H. Torfah (Eds.): RV 2025, LNCS 16087, pp. 417–437, 2026.
https://doi.org/10.1007/978-3-032-05435-7_23

relations. It was initially limited to prefix comparisons modulo stuttering [3] but has since been extended to support synchronous (i.e., not ignoring stuttering) prefix comparisons and operators for specifying regular trace patterns [13]. In sHL, we removed the need for finite alphabets and we added the possibility to define explicit slices of observed traces. These extensions enable runtime verification of realistic systems, as supported by the examples below.

For our first example, we consider *atomicity in smart contracts*. In Solidity contracts, every executed operation costs *gas*, which is paid upfront by the user. Normally, if a transaction (i.e., contract's execution) runs out of gas at any point, an exception is raised and all changes made by the transaction are reverted. However, there are cases when function calls may fail due to insufficient gas without raising the exception. This can happen, for example, when the contract puts a limit on the amount of gas that a particular call may consume. Instead of rising an exception, the failure is reflected in the return value of the call in this case. If a programmer does not check for this failure and the transaction still has enough gas to complete, the system may enter an inconsistent *global state*.

Atomicity is the property which states that the effect of executing a contract is independent on the amount of available gas, unless the execution failed, in which case it has no effect on the global state at all [25]. In Fig. 1, we depict a Solidity contract that does not satisfy atomicity. The contract maintains user balances and allows to transfer the funds using the *send* operation (lines 5–6) which can fail depending on the amount of gas it needs. The contract zeroes the user's balance regardless of whether sending the funds succeeded (line 8). In Fig. 2, we depict balances of an address addr for two executions τ_1 and τ_2 starting from the same initial global state. In τ_1, gas was sufficient for the execution to complete successfully, while in τ_2, *send* runs out of gas, rolling back the update of the user's balance but not the updates on line 8.

```
1   contract SimpleBank{
2     mapping(address => uint) balances;
3
4     function withdraw(){
5       msg.sender.call{gas: 2000}
6       ("send(uint)", balances[msg.sender]);
7
8       balances[msg.sender] = 0;
9     }
10  }
```

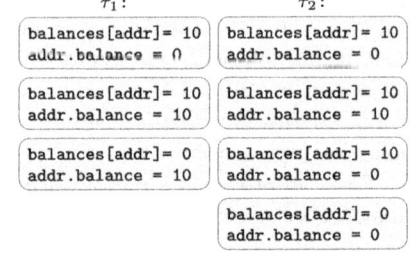

Fig. 1. A contract that violates atomicity. The code is a modification of the example in [25].

Fig. 2. Two possible runs (for the address addr) with different gas but the same initial state.

Following the formalization proposed in [25,32], we specify atomicity as follows:

$$\forall \pi \forall \pi' \; (\textbf{state}(\pi)[0] = \textbf{state}(\pi')[0] \rightarrow (\textbf{state}(\pi)[-1] = \textbf{state}(\pi')[-1] \vee$$
$$\textbf{state}(\pi)[0] = \textbf{state}(\pi)[-1] \vee \textbf{state}(\pi')[0] = \textbf{state}(\pi')[-1])). \quad (1)$$

In the formula above, $\textbf{state}(\pi)$ is a *data projection* that maps the trace π to a sequence of values that represent states (while elements in the trace can contain more information, e.g., the value of gas or timestamps). The projected sequences of values can be *sliced* using the operator [·]. In particular, [0] refers to the first element of a sequence and [-1] to the last element. In summary, the formula requires that for all pairs of executions π and π' starting from the same initial global state ($\mathbf{state}(\pi)[0] = \mathbf{state}(\pi')[0]$), then either their final state is the same ($\mathbf{state}(\pi)[-1] = \mathbf{state}(\pi')[-1]$) or at least one of the traces must have rolled back to its initial state ($\mathbf{state}(\pi)[0] = \mathbf{state}(\pi)[-1] \vee \mathbf{state}(\pi')[0] = \mathbf{state}(\pi')[-1]$).

Symbolic hypernode logic formulas allow us to also express regular patterns involving multiple observations of the system. In this next example, we look into voting protocols and their requirement to preserve *vote privacy* [19]. Concretely, for all two honest voters A and B, an external observer should not be able to distinguish between runs of the protocol where the voters flipped their vote. Assuming we record the runs of the protocol step-by-step (i.e., the set of observed traces is prefix-closed), we can specify vote privacy as:

$$\forall \pi \forall \pi' \forall \pi_{AB} \forall \pi_{BA} \big((\mathbf{vote}(\pi_{AB}) = \mathbf{vote}(\pi).(A,0).\mathbf{vote}(\pi').(B,1) \wedge \quad (2)$$
$$\mathbf{vote}(\pi_{BA}) = \mathbf{vote}(\pi).(B,0).\mathbf{vote}(\pi').(A,1))$$
$$\rightarrow \mathbf{out}(\pi_{AB})[-1] = \mathbf{out}(\pi_{BA})[-1] \big)$$

In the formula above, the **vote** projection maps each event into a pair where the first element is the voter's identification and the second element is the vote itself (e.g., $\mathbf{vote}(e) = (A,0)$ means that in the event e the voter A votes 0). The projection **out** maps an event to the output of the protocol run at the moment of the event. To identify runs π_{AB} and π_{BA} of the protocol that are the same except for A's and B's votes, we concatenate (partial) observations of the protocol run π and π' with events $(A, \cdot)$ and $(B, \cdot)$ for specific votes of A and B. We then check whether the current observed outcome is the same in these runs.

Data projections in sHL are not merely a way how to get a value contained in an event. For example, we can use them to transform and filter the values. Assume that in the voting example, the protocol implements majority voting. We can define two projections **ones** and **zeroes** as:

$$\mathbf{ones}(e) = \begin{cases} 1 & \text{if } \mathbf{vote}(e) = (\cdot, 1) \\ \epsilon & \text{otherwise} \end{cases} \qquad \mathbf{zeroes}(e) = \begin{cases} 1 & \text{if } \mathbf{vote}(e) = (\cdot, 0) \\ \epsilon & \text{otherwise} \end{cases}$$

With these projections, we can check that the output of the protocol implements majority voting by monitoring the formula:

$$\forall \pi \; \mathbf{ones}(\pi) \preceq \mathbf{zeroes}(\pi) \iff \mathbf{out}(\pi)[-1] = 0 \quad (3)$$

The core of the monitoring algorithm for sHL is a translation of terms of sHL (e.g., $\mathbf{state}(\pi)[-1]$) and their comparisons (e.g., $\mathbf{state}(\pi)[0] = \mathbf{state}(\pi)[-1]$) to *multi-tape symbolic transducers (MST)*. These transducers are the backbone of the monitoring algorithm proposed in this work. In Fig. 3, we depict the MST used for evaluating the formula $\mathbf{state}(\pi)[0] = \mathbf{state}(\pi)[-1]$. This transducer is in fact an automaton as it does not output anything. At each step, it can read input from two tapes, t_1 and t_2. For example, in the first step, the transducer

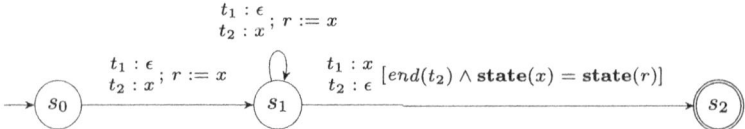

Fig. 3. Multi-trace symbolic automaton (transducer with no outputs) for the formula $\text{state}(t_1)[0] = \text{state}(t_2)[-1]$. Given that the trace variable π is assigned a trace τ, we can evaluate $\text{state}(\pi)[0] = \text{state}(\pi)[-1]$ (part of formula (1)), by evaluating this MST with τ assigned to both t_1 and t_2.

reads value x from t_2 while it does not read anything from t_1. The automaton can also store values in registers for later use; storing the value x in r is written as $r := x$. Finally, transitions can be conditioned by formulas describing relations between values read at the current step or stored in registers, and by a special predicate that checks for the end of a trace. For instance, the transition from s_1 to s_2 is enabled only if tape t_2 has reached its end, and the value stored in register r (which is the last value read from t_2) matches the (only) value read from t_1. The automaton accepts once it reaches the accepting state, without the need to entirely read all input traces.

Contributions. In this work, we make the following contributions:

- We introduce sHL, an extension of hypernode logic that adds support for data, trace slicing, and values filtering. These additions significantly expand its expressive power, enabling the specification of a wide range of asynchronous hyperproperties over infinite domains.
- We define a translation of terms and comparison formulas of sHL into multi-tape symbolic transducers. This translation is used to develop a monitoring algorithm for universally quantified formulas of sHL.
- We implement the translation and the monitoring algorithm for universally quantified sHL formulas, and evaluate it on several use cases, showcasing the effectiveness of our approach.

2 Symbolic Hypernode Logic

In this section, we present *symbolic hypernode logic* (sHL), an extension of hypernode logic [3,13] for infinite alphabets.

Preliminaries and Notation. Given a set of *symbols* D, a *word* over D is a finite sequence of symbols from D, and D^* is the set of all words over D. The empty word is denoted ϵ. The set D^* forms a monoid w.r.t. the concatenation of words. Given two alphabets and a function $f : D_1^* \to D_2^*$, f is a *homomorphism* iff $f(\epsilon) = \epsilon$ and $f(u.v) = f(u).f(v)$ for any $u, v \in D_1^*$. For a function $f : A \to B$, we denote $Dom(f)$ its domain A and $Img(f)$ its codomain B. We denote $f[x \leftarrow a]$ the function that is the same as f except it maps x to a. Whenever convenient, we treat functions as relations. The restriction $f_{\downarrow C}$ of a function f to $C \subseteq Dom(f)$ is defined as $f_{\downarrow C} = f \cap (C \times Img(f))$.

For a word w, we denote its length as $|w|$ and its i-th symbol as w_i, for $0 \leq i < |w|$ (i.e., indices start from 0). The *subword* $w_i w_{i+1}...w_k$ of w is denoted $w_{i..k}$ for $k \geq i \geq 0$ and $k < |w|$. If $w = uv$, we say that u is a *prefix* of w.

A *data domain* is a finite or infinite set $\mathbb{D}$ together with a list of *projection functions* $\mathbf{proj}_1, ..., \mathbf{proj}_n$, and a list of *value predicates* $\mathbf{e}_1, ..., \mathbf{e}_k$. We refer to the elements of $\mathbb{D}$ as *events*, while a finite sequence of events (a word over $\mathbb{D}$) is a *trace*. For $1 \leq i \leq n$, each projection function $\mathbf{proj}_i : \mathbb{D}^* \to \mathbb{V}_i^*$ defines a monoid homomorphism of traces to words over a set $\mathbb{V}_i^*$. We call sets $\mathbb{V}_i$ *value domains* and a word over a value domain is a *value trace*. We require that elements of every value domain can be compared for equality. Every value predicate $\mathbf{e}_j : \mathbb{V}_i \to \mathbf{2}$ maps elements of some value domain $\mathbb{V}_i$ to *true* or *false*. If a value predicate $\mathbf{e}_i$ is true for a single value v only, it represents a constant and we may write v instead of $\mathbf{e}_i$.

Example 1. Consider the voting privacy property in Sect. 1. Let $\mathbb{D} = \mathcal{A} \times \mathbf{2} \times \mathbf{2}$, where $\mathcal{A} = \{A, B, ...\}$ is a set of voters (agents) and the other two elements in events are the vote and the current output of the run (for majority voting, for example, the output would be a boolean saying if the run has seen more 1's than 0's). The projections $\mathbf{vote} : \mathbb{D}^* \to (\mathcal{A} \times \mathbf{2})^*$ and $\mathbf{out} : \mathbb{D}^* \to \mathbf{2}^*$ from the example are fully defined by acting on words of length 1 as $\mathbf{vote}((a, v, o)) = (a, v)$ and $\mathbf{out}((a, v, o)) = o$. The other two projections defined in the example have the signature $\mathbf{zeroes}, \mathbf{ones} : \mathbb{D}^* \to \{1\}^*$. Thus, we have three value domains: $\mathbb{V}_1 = \mathcal{A} \times \mathbf{2}$, $\mathbb{V}_2 = \mathbf{2}$, and $\mathbb{V}_3 = \{1\}$.

Value predicates "match" sets of values. For example, we can define $\mathbf{e_A} : \mathbb{V}_1 \to \mathbf{2}$ as $\mathbf{e_A}((a, v)) = 1$ iff $a = A$ matching all votes with agent A (which we can equivalently represent by the set $\{(A, v) \in \mathbb{V}_1\}$). Next, we can define $\mathbf{e_1} = \{(e, 1) \in \mathbb{V}_1\}$ matching votes with the vote 1, or $\mathbf{e_{(A,1)}} = \mathbf{e_A} \cap \mathbf{e_1}$ where agent A voted 1.

Note that the domain and projections of the voting example are not given uniquely, it is rather based on a concrete situation. Alternatively, we could have, for example, $\mathbb{D} = (\mathcal{A} \times \mathbf{2}) \cup \mathbf{2}$ where the votes and outputs in traces come separately. The projection $\mathbf{vote}$ then would have to be defined by cases, filtering out the output events ($\mathbf{vote}(b) = \epsilon$ for $b \in \mathbf{2}$) and analogously for the other projections.

Syntax. The syntax of sHL is given by the following grammar:

$$\psi ::= \epsilon \mid \mathbf{e} \mid \mathbf{proj}(\pi) \mid \psi.\psi \mid \psi + \psi \mid \psi^* \mid \lfloor \psi \rfloor \mid \psi[z_1 : z_2]$$
$$\varphi ::= \exists \pi \, \varphi \mid \neg \varphi \mid \varphi \wedge \varphi \mid \psi \preceq \psi \mid \psi \simeq \psi$$

where π is a trace variable from a set of trace variables $\mathcal{V}$, $\mathbf{e}$ is a value predicate, $\mathbf{proj}$ is a projection function, $\lfloor \cdot \rfloor$ is the stutter-reduction operator (removing repetitions), and $\psi[z_1 : z_2]$ with $z_1, z_2 \in \mathbb{Z}$ is the *slicing* operator that returns sub-words between given indices. The relations $\preceq$ and $\simeq$ check for prefixing and equality, resp., of words in the sets of words defined by the left- and right-side operands. The rest of the constructs are classical logical quantifiers and connectives, and operations on regular expressions.

We call the formulas defined by ψ in the grammar *trace formulas*, while the formulas of the form $\psi \bowtie \psi$, for $\bowtie \in \{\preceq, \simeq\}$ are referred to as *atomic comparisons*. A trace formula is *well-formed* for a given data domain if all its elements range over the same values. This we ensure by requiring that the formula is typable with following typing rules:

$$\frac{Img(\mathbf{proj}) = D}{\mathbf{proj}: D} \qquad \frac{Dom(\mathbf{e}) = D}{\mathbf{e}: D} \qquad \frac{\psi_1: D \quad \psi_2: D \quad \bowtie \in \{., +, \simeq, \preceq\}}{\psi_1 \bowtie \psi_2 : D}$$

$$\frac{\text{for any } D}{\epsilon: D} \qquad \frac{\psi \text{ is one of } {\psi'}^* \text{ or } \lfloor \psi' \rfloor \text{ or } \psi'[i:i] \quad \psi': D}{\psi: D}$$

In a nutshell, we require that if, in a trace formula, we have a projection that maps to a value domain D, then any other projection in this formula must also map into the same value domain D and it can use only value predicates that have D as their domain.

Semantics. We interpret sHL over finite traces with events from $\mathbb{D}$. Trace formulas are interpreted w.r.t. a trace assignment $\Pi: \mathcal{V} \to \mathbb{D}^*$ as follows:

$$[\![\epsilon]\!]_\Pi = \{\epsilon\}$$
$$[\![\mathbf{e}]\!]_\Pi = \{c \in Dom(\mathbf{e}) \mid \mathbf{e}(c)\}$$
$$[\![\mathbf{proj}(\pi)]\!]_\Pi = \{\mathbf{proj}(\Pi(\pi))\}$$

$$[\![\psi.\psi']\!]_\Pi = [\![\psi]\!]_\Pi . [\![\psi']\!]_\Pi$$
$$[\![\psi + \psi']\!]_\Pi = [\![\psi]\!]_\Pi \cup [\![\psi']\!]_\Pi$$
$$[\![\psi^*]\!]_\Pi = \bigcup_{n \in \mathbb{N}} ([\![\psi]\!]_\Pi)^n$$

$$[\![\lfloor \psi \rfloor]\!]_\Pi = \{<_1 \cdots <_k \mid <_1^+ \cdots <_k^+ \in [\![\psi]\!]_\Pi, <_i \neq <_{i+1}, i < k\}$$
$$[\![\psi[i:j]]\!]_\Pi = \{\|\tau[i:j]\| \mid \tau \in [\![\psi]\!]_\Pi\}$$

$\|\tau[i:j]\| = \tau_{i_\tau..j_\tau}$ with $i_\tau = \max(0, |\tau|+i)$ if $i < 0$ else $i_\tau = \min(i, |\tau|-1|)$, and the same for j_τ. We additionally define that $\tau_{i_\tau..j_\tau} = \epsilon$ if $i_\tau > j_\tau$.

Operators related to *regular expressions*, i.e., concatenation ($\psi.\psi$), union ($\psi + \psi$) and Kleene star (ψ^*), have the usual interpretation. When clear, we write $\psi\psi$ instead of $\psi.\psi$. The semantics of a value predicate is the set of elements from its domain that map to *true*, and the semantics of a projection just applies the projection to the trace specified by the trace assignment Π. The slicing operator $\psi[i:j]$ is defined over integers, allowing indices to be specified relative to the end of the trace. The operator $\|\tau[i:j]\|$ turns slicing using possibly negative numbers to slicing over natural numbers. We also use the abbreviation $\tau[i] = \tau[i:i]$. For example, for a value trace $\tau = w_0 w_1 w_2$, $\|\tau[-2]\| = \|\tau[-2:-2]\| = \tau_{1..1} = w_1$.

The comparison predicates $\preceq$ and $\simeq$ generalize the prefixing and equality of single words to sets of words[1]. For them, we define the denotation function as:

$$[\![\psi_1 \preceq \psi_2]\!]_\Pi = \exists w_1 \in [\![\psi_1]\!]_\Pi \text{ and } \exists w_2 \in [\![\psi_2]\!]_\Pi \text{ s.t. } w_1 \leq w_2$$
$$[\![\psi_1 \simeq \psi_2]\!]_\Pi = \exists w_1 \in [\![\psi_1]\!]_\Pi \text{ and } \exists w_2 \in [\![\psi_2]\!]_\Pi \text{ s.t. } w_1 = w_2$$

---

[1] In previous work [13], we used $\leq$ to stand for what is $\preceq$ in this paper. We decided to change this so that it is clear that the comparison is not the classical prefixing relation. The relation $\simeq$ had no counterpart in previous works.

The semantics of $\psi_1 \simeq \psi_2$ is equivalent to $[\![\psi_1]\!]_\Pi \cap [\![\psi_2]\!]_\Pi \neq \emptyset$. Note that, unlike for $\leq$ and $=$ on words, it does not hold that $\varphi_1 \simeq \varphi_2$ iff $\varphi_1 \preceq \varphi_2 \wedge \varphi_1 \preceq \varphi_2$. To see a counterexample, assume that the models of φ_1 and φ_2 are $\{a, bb\}$ and $\{b, aa\}$. Then, they satisfy the formula $\varphi_1 \preceq \varphi_2 \wedge \varphi_2 \preceq \varphi_1$ but not $\varphi_1 \simeq \varphi_2$.

Example 2. We continue with the voting example from Seciton 1. For the formula $\mathbf{e_A}^*$, we have $[\![\mathbf{e_A}^*]\!]_\Pi = \{(A, v_0)(A, v_1)...(A, v_k)) \mid k \in \mathbb{N}, v_i \in \mathbf{2}\}$ (for any Π). Similarly, $[\![\mathbf{e_A}.\mathbf{e_1}]\!]_\Pi = \{(A, v_0)(a, 1)) \mid v_0 \in \mathbf{2}, a \in \mathcal{A}\}$. If, for example, $\Pi(\pi) = (A, 1, 1)(B, 1, 1)$, then we have $[\![\mathbf{vote}(\pi)]\!]_\Pi = \{(A, 1).(B, 1)\}$ and

$[\![\mathbf{vote}(\pi) \preceq \mathbf{e_A}^*]\!]_\Pi = \mathit{false}$ $[\![\mathbf{e_{(A,1)}} \preceq \mathbf{vote}(\pi)]\!]_\Pi = \mathit{true}$

$[\![\mathbf{vote}(\pi) \preceq \mathbf{e_1}^*]\!]_\Pi = \mathit{true}$ $[\![\mathbf{vote}(\pi)[0] \simeq \mathbf{e_{(A,1)}}]\!]_\Pi = \mathit{true}$

$[\![\mathbf{vote}(\pi) \simeq \mathbf{e_A}.\mathbf{e_1}]\!]_\Pi = \mathit{true}$ $[\![\mathbf{vote}(\pi) \simeq \mathbf{e_A}.(\mathbf{e_A} + \mathbf{e_1})^*]\!]_\Pi = \mathit{true}$

Also, $[\![\mathbf{zeroes}(\pi)]\!]_\Pi = \{\epsilon\}$ and $[\![\mathbf{ones}(\pi)]\!]_\Pi = \{11\}$ and therefore we have $[\![\mathbf{zeroes}(\pi) \preceq \mathbf{ones}(\pi)]\!]_\Pi = \mathit{true}$. Finally, note that, e.g., $\mathbf{ones}(\pi).\mathbf{e_A}$ or $\mathbf{e_1} \preceq (1 \cdot 1 + \mathbf{e_1})$ (where 1 is the constant value predicate matching $1 \in \mathbb{V}_3$) are not well-formed formulas as they do not type according to our rules above.

The satisfaction relation of sHL is defined w.r.t. a trace assignment Π and a set of traces $T \subseteq \mathbb{D}^*$ as:

$T, \Pi \models \exists \pi \; \varphi$ iff $\exists t \in T$ s.t. $T, \Pi[\pi \mapsto t] \models \varphi$

$T, \Pi \models \varphi_1 \wedge \varphi_2$ iff $T, \Pi \models \varphi_1$ and $T, \Pi \models \varphi_2$

$T, \Pi \models \neg \varphi$ iff $T, \Pi \not\models \varphi$

$T, \Pi \models \psi_1 \bowtie \psi_2$ iff $[\![\psi_1 \bowtie \psi_2]\!]_\Pi$ for $\bowtie \in \{\preceq, \simeq\}$

3 Multi-tape Symbolic Transducers

In this section, we recall *symbolic transducers* [34] and extend them to *multi-tape symbolic transducers (MST)*. We use this computational model to evaluate atomic comparisons of sHL. More concretely, we encode trace formulas as MSTs and then, to evaluate atomic comparisons, we compare the output of the transducers with a *multi-tape symbolic register automaton*, which is a multi-tape MST with no output. This section is concerned with the definitions, examples of MSTs can be found in the next section.

A *symbolic transducer (ST)* [34], also called *symbolic finite-state transducer with registers* [34] is a finite-state automaton whose transitions are labeled with predicates that form an effective boolean algebra. Each predicate matches a potentially infinite set of concrete symbols, and therefore symbolic transducers are suitable for working with infinite or large alphabets.

In the defining work, symbolic automata and transducers are defined over *some* theory [17,34]. We present transducers instantiated with predicates corresponding with the semantics of sHL. Let Q be a finite set of states, $\mathcal{R}$ a finite set of registers and $\mathcal{X}$ a countable set of *symbol variables* (with $\mathcal{R} \cap \mathcal{X} = \emptyset$). A (1-tape) symbolic transducer has transitions of the form

	Assignments
$\nu ::= r \mid x$	$U ::= r := \nu \mid r := \mathbf{proj}(\nu) \mid r := d$
Constraints	*Outputs*
$\gamma ::= \mathbf{e} \mid \nu \mid \mathbf{proj}(\nu)$	$o ::= \epsilon \mid \mathbf{e} \mid \nu \mid \mathbf{proj}(\nu)$
$C ::= C \wedge C \mid \neg C \mid \gamma = \gamma \mid end(t) \mid \mathbf{proj}(\nu) = \epsilon$	

Fig. 4. Syntax of constraints of a transition in a transducer is given by the non-terminal C and the syntax of the output by the non-terminal o. Register updates is a list of terms generated by the non-terminal u. In the productions, t is a trace variable, $x \in \mathcal{X}$ is a symbol variable, $r \in \mathcal{R}$ is a register, and $d \in \mathcal{D}_{in}$ (ν is a register or a symbol variable).

$$q \xrightarrow{x[C];U/o} q' \quad \text{or} \quad q \xrightarrow{\epsilon[C];U/o} q'$$

where

- q and q' are states from Q,
- $x \in \mathcal{X}$ is a *symbol variable*[2] with its value in the *input domain* $\mathcal{D}_{in}$ of the transducer. If ϵ is used instead of x (the transition pattern on the right), it means no symbol is read from the input word and we call this transition *input-ϵ* transition.
- C is a *constraint* which is a boolean combination of terms $\gamma_1 = \gamma_2$ and $end(t)$ where t is a trace variable and γ can be a register or a symbol variable, a projection of a register or a symbol variable, or a value predicate with domain $\mathcal{D}_{in}$. Additionally, we allow checking if projection erased a symbol (its output is ϵ for a given element).
- U is a list of register updates where each update is of the form $r := \nu$ or $r := \mathbf{proj}(\nu)$ or $r := d$ where $r \in \mathcal{R}$ is a register, ν is a register or a symbol variable, and $d \in \mathcal{D}_{in}$.
- o is the output symbol which is either ϵ, a value predicate symbol with the domain $\mathcal{D}_{out}$ – the *output domain* of the transducer – or ν or $\mathbf{proj}(\nu)$ where ν is a symbol variable or a register.

Syntax of components of transitions is summarized in Fig. 4. We call the part $x[C]$ (or $\epsilon[C]$) the *guard* of the transition, and U is the *update* of the transition. If the space allows, we may break the line in the label instead of using the semi-colon, and we leave out U and/or $[C]$ if they are empty (*true*, resp.).

A multi-tape symbolic transducer can read multiple traces at each transition, which we achieve by replacing the symbol variable read by a transition (if any)

---

[2] Because we will have multiple input traces to a transducer, we have to be explicit about the symbol variable so that we are able to differentiate between symbols from different input words. This is in contrast to the standard presentation of symbolic transducers, where the name of the variable is irrelevant and often kept implicit [17].

with a partial mapping σ from trace variables $\mathcal{V}$ to symbol variables $\mathcal{X}$. For example $\sigma = \{t_1 \mapsto x_1, t_2 \mapsto x_2\}$. The mapping σ tells us what traces should we proceed on and how to refer to their events. Non-terminals C, U, and o are as in the 1-tape case. For example, we can have the following transition in an MST:

$$q \xrightarrow{\begin{subarray}{c} t_1\,:\,x_1 \\ t_2\,:\,x_2 \end{subarray} [x_1 = r \wedge x_1 \neq x_2]; r := x_2 \,/\, \mathbf{val}(x_2)} q'$$

In the graphical form, we write $\begin{subarray}{c} t_1\,:\,x_1 \\ t_2\,:\,x_2 \end{subarray}$ instead of $\{t_1 \mapsto x_1, t_2 \mapsto x_2\}$. The transition above reads a symbol from trace t_1 and refers to it through the variable x_1; it also reads a symbol from t_2 and refers to it through x_2. This happens only if the symbols are different ($x_1 \neq x_2$) and the symbol from trace t_1 agrees with the symbol stored in the register r ($x_1 = r$). If the transition is taken, the symbol x_2 is stored into the register r, and the projection of x_2 to $\mathbf{val}$ is put to the output.

We denote the set of all transitions with states from Q, trace variables $\mathcal{V}$, data domains $\mathcal{D}_{in}$ and $\mathcal{D}_{out}$, and registers $\mathcal{R}$ as $\mathcal{T}(Q, \mathcal{V}, \mathcal{D}_{in}, \mathcal{D}_{out}, \mathcal{R})$. An MST is a finite register automaton with transitions as defined above.

Definition 1 (Multi-tape symbolic transducer). A *multi-tape symbolic transducer (MST)* is a tuple $(Q, q_0, q_f, \mathcal{V}, \mathcal{D}_{in}, \mathcal{D}_{out}, \Delta, \mathcal{R})$ where Q is a finite set of states with $q_0 \in Q$ being the initial state. The state $q_f \in Q$ is the unique final state with no outgoing transitions. Sets $\mathcal{D}_{in}$ and $\mathcal{D}_{out}$ are the input and output domains (alphabets) of the transducer, $\mathcal{V}$ are trace variables, and $\mathcal{R}$ is a finite set of registers. Finally, $\Delta \subseteq \mathcal{T}(Q, \mathcal{V}, \mathcal{D}_{in}, \mathcal{D}_{out}, \mathcal{R})$ is the transition relation.

Having a unique final state with no successors will be important for the composition of MSTs. Note that because we allow epsilon steps and predicates that check for the end of traces, having a unique final state with no successors does not change the expressivity of MSTs:

For the rest of the paper, we assume that every MST is well-formed, which encompasses these conditions. First, any register is assigned before its use (this can be checked by a simple traversal of the transducer). Second, for every transition $t \in \Delta$:

- if $t = q \xrightarrow{\sigma[C]; U/o} q'$, then C, U, and o use no other symbol variables than those in $Img(\sigma)$, and
- if $t = q \xrightarrow{\epsilon[C]; U/o} q'$, then C, U, o do not use any symbol variable.

We evaluate MSTs over multiple input words that we represent as a *multi-word*, a mapping from trace variables to words. Formally, for a set of variables $\mathcal{V}$, a multi-word over domain $\mathcal{D}_{in}$ is a mapping $\omega : \mathcal{V} \to \mathcal{D}_{in}^*$. To define a run of a symbolic transducer, we first must define how to interpret conditions on labels of transitions. Given an MST with trace variables $\mathcal{V}$ and the input domain $\mathcal{D}_{in}$, the semantics of the conditions is given relative to a multi-word ω, a mapping $\eta : \mathcal{V} \to \mathbb{N}$ that keeps track of the position for each input word, symbol variables valuation $V : \mathcal{X} \to \mathcal{D}_{in}$, and register valuation $R : \mathcal{R} \to \mathcal{D}_{in}$:

$[\![x]\!] = V(x) \quad [\![r]\!] = R(r) \quad [\![\mathbf{proj}(\nu)]\!] = \mathbf{proj}([\![\nu]\!]) \quad [\![end(t)]\!] = \eta(t) \geq |\omega(t)|$

$[\![\mathbf{e}_1 = \mathbf{e}_2]\!] = \exists c \in \mathcal{D}_{in} : \mathbf{e}_1(c) \wedge \mathbf{e}_2(c) \qquad [\![\mathbf{e} = \mathbf{proj}(\nu)]\!] = \mathbf{e}([\![\mathbf{proj}(\nu)]\!])$

$[\![\mathbf{e} = \nu]\!] = \mathbf{e}([\![\nu]\!]) \qquad\qquad\qquad\qquad\quad [\![\mathbf{proj}(\nu) = \epsilon]\!] = \mathbf{proj}([\![\nu]\!]) = \epsilon$

Analogously for symmetric terms. The interpretation of conjunction and negation in constraints is as usual. We write $\omega, \eta, V, R \models c$ iff $[\![c]\!] = true$.

Given an MST $T = (Q, q_0, q_f, \mathcal{V}, \mathcal{D}_{in}, \mathcal{D}_{out}, \Delta, \mathcal{R})$, an *evaluation state* is a tuple (q, R, η) where q is a state, $R : \mathcal{R} \to \mathcal{D}_{in}$ is a register valuation, and $\eta : \mathcal{V} \to \mathbb{N}$ is the position mapping. Evaluation of T on a multi-word ω induces a transition system $TS(T, \omega)$ defined by these rules:

$$\dfrac{\forall t \in \mathcal{V} : \eta(t) = 0}{(q_0, \emptyset, \eta)} \qquad \dfrac{q \xrightarrow{\epsilon[C];U/o} q' \quad \omega, \eta, \emptyset, R \models C \quad R' = update(R, U, \emptyset)}{(q, R, \eta) \xrightarrow{o} (q', R', \eta)}$$

$$\dfrac{\begin{array}{c} q \xrightarrow{\sigma[C];U/o} q' \\ \forall t \in Dom(\sigma) : \eta(t) < |\omega(t)| \quad V = \{\sigma(t) \mapsto \omega(t)_{\eta(t)} \mid t \in Dom(\sigma)\} \\ \omega, \eta, V, R \models C \quad R' = update(R, U, V) \quad \eta'(t) = move(\eta, \sigma) \end{array}}{(q, R, \eta) \xrightarrow{o} (q', R', \eta')}$$

where the auxiliary function *update* applies the assignments of registers in the list U and the function *move* increases the positions on words that were read by the transition. These functions can be defined as $update(R, \epsilon, V) = R$ and $update(R, (r := v).U', V) = update(R[r \leftarrow V(v)], U', V)$, and $move(\eta, \sigma) = \eta(t)$ if $t \notin Dom(\sigma)$ and $\eta(t) + 1$ if $t \in Dom(\sigma)$.

The only complicated terms in the definition of $TS(T, \omega)$ are concerned with mapping between symbol variables and symbols in words. In particular, the expression $V = \{\sigma(t) \mapsto \omega(t)_{\eta(t)} \mid t \in Dom(\sigma)\}$ takes every trace variable t read by the transition ($t \in Dom(\sigma)$), and maps its associated symbol variable $\sigma(t)$ to the symbol in its word that should be read next ($\omega(t)_{\eta(t)}$). This rule is taken only under the condition that there are symbols to be read on each of the affected words ($\forall t \in Dom(\sigma) : \eta(t) < |\omega(t)|$).

A *run* of T on w is a *finite path*[3] $s_0 \xrightarrow{o_0} \ldots \xrightarrow{o_k} s_{k+1}$ in $TS(T, \omega)$, and it is *accepting* if $s_{k+1} = (q_f, R, \eta)$ with q_f being the accepting state. The sequence $o_0...o_k$ is the output of the run.

Notice that we do not require the input words to be read entirely. This is particularly useful with transducers that check for prefixing or that output a

---

[3] $TS(T, \omega)$ can contain also infinite paths in the form of input-ϵ cycles and, in general, we cannot eliminate them as it is the case in finite-state automata. Some of our constructions may temporarily contain such cycles, but they will not be present in the final monitors.

slice of an input word because there, reading the traces to their very end may not be necessary. Nevertheless, a transducer can enforce reading a word entirely by checking if the predicate end holds for the word.

If an MST T has an accepting run on a multi-word ω while outputting a word y, we say that T *transduces* ω to y and we write $T(\omega, y)$. We also say that T *accepts* ω if $T(\omega, y)$ for some y and y is not important to us.

Classical 1-tape symbolic transducers are closed under concatenation and union, and algorithms for these constructions are analogous to those for finite state automata [8,17,34]. This is true also for MSTs, provided they use different trace variables. MSTs are closed also under sequential composition, which is an important operation that we discuss next.

Sequential Composition of MSTs. Given two 1-tape transducers T_1 and T_2, we can compose them together to obtain the transducer $T_2(T_1)$ that recognizes the composition of relations recognized by T_1 and T_2. That is, $T_2(T_1)(x,y)$ iff $\exists z : T_1(x,z)$ and $T_2(z,y)$. In the multi-trace setting, we can define an analogous composition but if the "outer" transducer reads multiple input words, we must specify to which of the input words we feed the output of the "inner" transducer. That is, given MSTs T_1 and T_2 with input trace variables $\mathcal{V}_{T_1}$ and $\mathcal{V}_{T_2}$, resp., such that $\mathcal{V}_{T_1} \cap \mathcal{V}_{T_2} = \emptyset$, and a trace $t \in \mathcal{V}_{T_2}$, we can compute the MST $(T_1 \gg_t T_2)$ with trace variables $\mathcal{V} = \mathcal{V}_{T_1} \cup (\mathcal{V}_{T_2} \setminus \{t\})$ such that if $T_1(\omega_1, y)$ and $T_2(\omega_2, z)$, where $\omega_2(t) = y$, then $(T_1 \gg_t T_2)((\omega_1 \cup \omega_2)_{\downarrow \mathcal{V}}, z)$. In words, $(T \gg_t T')$ transduces words from ω_1 and ω_2 (without the word $\omega_2(t)$) to the word z.

Sequential compositions for MSTs is formally defined as follows. Let $T_1 = (Q_1, q_1^i, q_1^f, \mathcal{V}_{T_1}, \mathcal{D}_{in}, \mathcal{D}_{out_1}, \Delta_1, R_1)$ and let $T_2 = (Q_2, q_2^i, q_2^f, \mathcal{V}_{T_2}, \mathcal{D}_{out_1}, \mathcal{D}_{out}, \Delta_2, R_2)$ be two MSTs with no epsilon transitions (i.e., transitions that have ϵ as both input and output and empty constraint and updates – we can pre-process MSTs to eliminate such transitions [34]). Further, w.l.o.g. assume that $R_1 \cap R_2 = \emptyset$ and $\mathcal{V}_1 \cap \mathcal{V}_2 = \emptyset$. Given $t \in \mathcal{V}_2$, the composition $(T_1 \gg_t T_2)$ is the MST $(Q_1 \times Q_2, (q_1^i, q_2^i), (q_1^f, q_2^f), \mathcal{V}_1 \cup \mathcal{V}_2 \setminus \{t\}, \mathcal{D}_{in}, \mathcal{D}_{out}, \Delta, R_1 \cup R_2)$ with the transition relation Δ defined by the following rules:

$$\frac{q_1 \xrightarrow{\sigma_1[C_1];U_1 \ / \ o_1} q_1' \in \Delta_1 \quad q_2 \xrightarrow{\sigma_2[C_2];U_2 \ / \ o_2} q_2' \in \Delta_2 \quad o_1 \neq \epsilon}{(q_1, q_2) \xrightarrow{s[C_1 \wedge C_2 \theta];U_1.U_2\theta \ / \ o_2\theta} (q_1', q_2')}$$

$$\frac{q_1 \xrightarrow{\sigma_1[C_1];U_1 \ / \ \epsilon} q_1'}{(q_1, q_2) \xrightarrow{\sigma_1[C_1];U_1 \ / \ \epsilon} (q_1', q_2)} \qquad \frac{q_2 \xrightarrow{\epsilon[C_2];U_2 \ / \ o_2} q_2'}{(q_1, q_2) \xrightarrow{\epsilon[C_2];U_2 \ / \ o_2} (q_1, q_2')}$$

where w.l.o.g $Img(\sigma_1) \cap Img(\sigma_2) = \emptyset$ (we rename symbol variables if necessary), and $t\theta$ is a term t after applying the substitution $\theta = \{\sigma_2(t) \leftarrow o_1, end(t) \leftarrow q_1' = q_1^f\}$. This substitution replaces the symbol variable associated to the trace t with the output of the "inner" MST and also assigns *true* or *false* to the condition

$end(t)$ – this we can do because the "inner" MST has a unique final state with no successors and therefore it accepts and produces no more output iff it is in this final state. Finally, we require the constraints of the composed transitions to be satisfiable.

4 Translating sHL to Symbolic Register Automata

In this section, we show how to translate atomic comparisons of sHL to MSTs. This translation is defined recursively by giving MSTs for basic constructs like projection of a trace variable or "constants" in the form of value predicates. These basic MSTs are then composed into MSTs for trace formulas using concatenation, union, and sequential composition. When we have two MSTs for trace formulas ψ_1 and ψ_2, we then define a *multi-tape symbolic register automaton (MSRA)* that compares the outputs of the MSTs, computing $\psi_1 \preceq \psi_2$ or $\psi_1 \simeq \psi_2$. An MSRA is simply an MST with no outputs.

The translation has a restriction: we cannot handle formulas where a trace variable is inside Kleene iteration. Henceforth, we assume that formulas comply with this restriction. Also, sequential composition and concatenation of projections require that transducers have different trace variables, and therefore before the translating an atomic comparison into the automaton, we rename variables in the formula to have unique names. We do that by numbering the occurences of trace variables. For example, we turn the formula $\mathbf{x}(\pi) \cdot \mathbf{y}(\pi) + \mathbf{y}(\pi') \preceq \mathbf{y}(\pi')$ into $\mathbf{x}(\pi^1) \cdot \mathbf{y}(\pi^2) + \mathbf{y}(\pi'^1) \preceq \mathbf{y}(\pi'^2)$. Later, when evaluating the transducer on input traces, different versions of a trace variable get assigned the same trace. For example, if π should be assigned τ, we assign τ to both π^1 and π^2.

4.1 Transducers for Trace Formulas

MSTs for trace formulas are built up recursively by this procedure.

- For a value predicate **e**, we construct this two-state MST

$$T_\mathbf{e}: \quad \to \bigcirc \xrightarrow{\epsilon \,/\, \mathbf{e}} \bigcirc$$

- For a projection $\mathbf{proj}(t)$, we create the MST $T_{\mathbf{proj}(t)}$ that reads events from t, and for each event d it outputs either $\mathbf{proj}(d)$ or ϵ depending on whether $\mathbf{proj}(d) = \epsilon$. This MST is shown in Fig. 5 on the left.
- For a formula $\psi_1.\psi_2$, we construct the transducer $T_{\psi_1}.T_{\psi_2}$ using the classical construction for concatenation of transducers.
- For a formula $\psi_1 + \psi_2$ we create the union $T_{\psi_1} \cup T_{\psi_2}$ of transducers using the classical construction. Then, we create a unique final state to which the transducer transitions with ϵ steps from the original finial states of T_{ψ_1} and T_{ψ_2} (which are made non-final).
- For the stutter reduction $\lfloor \psi \rfloor$ of formula ψ, we build the composed transducer $T_{\lfloor \psi \rfloor} = T_{\lfloor \cdot \rfloor}(T_\psi)$ with $T_{\lfloor \cdot \rfloor}$ as defined in Fig. 5 on the right.

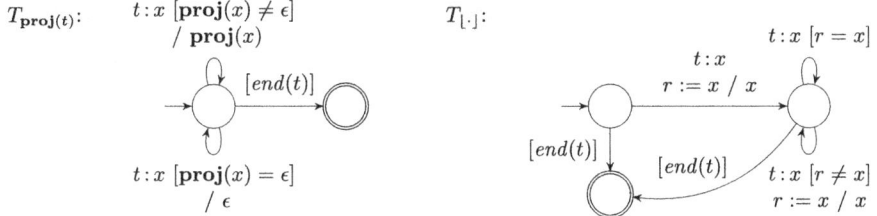

Fig. 5. Transducers $T_{\mathbf{proj}(\cdot)}$ for projecting a trace (left) and $T_{\lfloor \cdot \rfloor}$ for doing stutter reduction (right).

- For a formula $\psi[i:j]$, we build the composed transducer $T_{[i:j]}(T_\psi)$ with $T_{[i:j]}$ being an MST that outputs the slice $[i:j]$ of its input. The definition of this transducer depends on values of i and j. For cases $0 \leq i \leq j$ and $j \leq i < 0$, we show these MSTs in Fig. 6. For the other two cases (i and j with different signs), we can define MSTs analogously, but we have omitted them here because of the space restrictions.

We remark that the definition of $T_{\mathbf{proj}(t)}$ is the place where we need projections to be homomorphisms, so that it is guaranteed that projecting each event separately is the same as projecting the whole trace. Note that we could remove this restriction of projections to homomorphisms if we are given (or we know how to generate) the projection directly as an MST. Then we could just use this MST in place of $T_{\mathbf{proj}(t)}$.

4.2 Automata for Comparisons

When we have an MST for each side of an atomic comparison, we compose these MSTs into a single multi-tape symbolic register automaton (MSRA). Let $T_l = (Q_l, q_l^i, q_l^f, \mathcal{V}_l, \mathcal{D}_{in_l}, \mathcal{D}_{out}, \Delta_l, R_l)$ and let $T_r = (Q_r, q_r^i, q_r^f, \mathcal{V}_r, \mathcal{D}_{in_r}, \mathcal{D}_{out}, \Delta_r, R_r)$ be two MSTs that share the output domain. We assume that these MSTs have no epsilon steps and that $R_l \cap R_r = \mathcal{V}_l \cap \mathcal{V}_r = \emptyset$. The automaton $A_{T \bowtie T'}$ for $\bowtie \in \{\preceq, \simeq\}$ is the MSRA $((Q_l \times Q_r) \cup \{q_f\}, (q_l^i, q_r^i), q_f, \mathcal{V}_l \cup \mathcal{V}_r, \mathcal{D}_{in_l} \cup \mathcal{D}_{in_r}, \Delta, R_l \cup R_r)$ with the transition relation Δ defined by the following rules:

$$\frac{q_l \xrightarrow{\sigma_l[C_l];U_l \ / \ o_l} q_l' \quad q_r \xrightarrow{\sigma_r[C_r];U_r \ / \ o_r} q_r' \quad o_l \neq \epsilon \quad o_r \neq \epsilon}{(q_l, q_r) \xrightarrow{\sigma_l \cup \sigma_r \ [o_l = o_r \wedge C_l \wedge C_r]\ ;\ U_l.U_r} (q_l', q_r')}$$

$$\frac{q_l \xrightarrow{\sigma_l[C_l];U_l \ / \ \epsilon} q_l'}{(q_l, q_r) \xrightarrow{\sigma_l \ [C_l]\ ;\ U_l} (q_l', q_r)} \qquad \frac{q_r \xrightarrow{\sigma_r[C_r];U_r \ / \ \epsilon} q_r' \quad \bowtie\ =\ \preceq\ \implies\ q_l \neq q_l^f}{(q_l, q_r) \xrightarrow{\sigma_r \ [C_r]\ ;\ U_r} (q_l, q_r')}$$

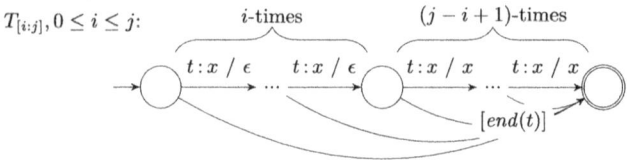

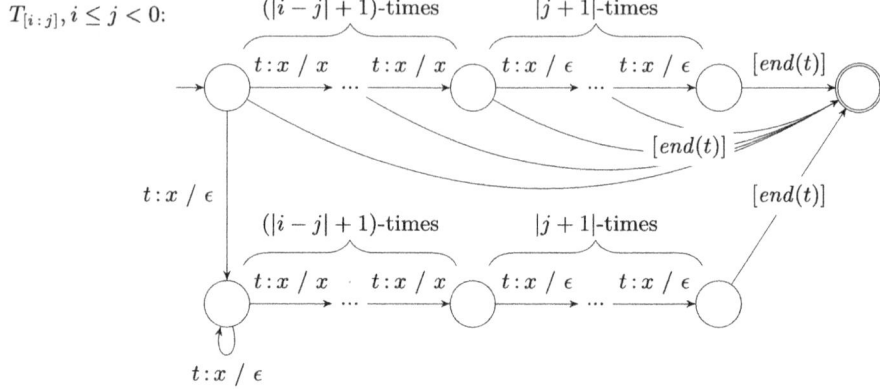

Fig. 6. MSTs for taking the slice $[i:j]$ in cases when either $0 \le i \le j$ or $i \le j < 0$.

$$\frac{\bowtie\; =\; \preceq}{(q_l^f, q_r) \xrightarrow{\epsilon} q_f} \qquad \frac{\bowtie\; =\; \simeq}{(q_l^f, q_r^f) \xrightarrow{\epsilon} q_f}$$

where we rename symbol variables in σ_l and σ_r if necessary (i.e., so that $Img(\sigma_l) \cap Img(\sigma_r) = \emptyset$). Again, we require the constraints of the composed transitions to be satisfiable. Notice that in the case of $\bowtie\; =\; \simeq$, the new final state is redundant and we could also use (q_l^f, q_r^f) instead.

5 Monitoring sHL

The monitoring algorithm for sHL is the same as for *extended hypernode logic (eHL)* [13] with only minor modifications. We briefly introduce eHL and its monitoring algorithm here.

Extended Hypernode Logic and Its Monitoring Algorithm. We can obtain eHL by restricting sHL to domains of the form Σ^X where Σ is a *finite* alphabet and X is a finite set of variables (and thus the domain is finite). Projection functions are fixed to be $\mathbf{x} : (\Sigma^X)^* \to \Sigma^*$ for each $x \in X$, where $\mathbf{x}$ returns the projection of a trace to the sequence of values of variable x. Instead of value predicates, eHL has a finite set of constants. Finally, eHL does not have the slicing operator and the $\simeq$ predicate.

The algorithm for monitoring eHL [13] translates atomic comparisons of eHL into *finite 2-track automata with priorities* and use these automata to evaluate instances of the formula over all possible tuples of input traces.

More concretely, assume a universally quantified formula $\psi = \forall \pi_1...\pi_k : \psi_{qf}$ where ψ_{qf} is quantifier-free. The algorithm instantiates quantifiers $\pi_1...\pi_k$ with every k-tuple of input traces and then evaluates ψ_{qf} on these trace tuples. Formula ψ_{qf} is a boolean combination of atomic comparisons and its evaluation on a k-tuple of traces proceeds by evaluating the comparisons in the order given by a binary decision diagram (BDD) that captures the boolean structure of ψ_{qf}: The nodes of the BDD represent the results of evaluating the atomic comparisons and the BDD evaluates to *true* iff the whole formula evaluates to *true* given the results of comparisons. Every comparison is evaluated on input traces by running its corresponding automaton on the traces. The whole algorithm works incrementally, driven by new events on traces and new traces. For more details, we refer the reader to [13].

The Monitoring Algorithm for sHL. The monitoring algorithm for sHL is identical to the one for eHL, only instead of using the automata generated for eHL comparisons, we use MSRAs generated for sHL comparisons. We also make sure that trace variables are assigned the right traces: recall that before translating comparisons formulas to automata, we assign versions to trace variables. Now, when instantiating the automata, we assign the same trace to all the versions of a variable, as discussed in Sect. 4. Note that for eHL this step was not necessary as the monitoring algorithm for eHL is restricted only to formulas that have a single trace variable in every trace formula [13].

6 Evaluation

We implemented monitoring sHL by extending the implementation for monitoring eHL [13], re-using the common parts. Parsing of formulas and manipulation with transducers is implemented in Python; the final monitoring system is then generated as C++ code that is compiled to an executable binary. We evaluated sHL monitors against eHL monitors, but also against monitors based on *multi-trace prefix transducers (MPTs)* [12] and the tool *RVHyper* [22].

The experiments were run on a laptop with the *11th Gen Intel(R) i7 @ 2.8 Ghz* processor and 16 GB of RAM. Timeout per run of a monitor was 120 s if not stated otherwise. The experiments are available in an online artifact [14].

Optimizations. In our implementation, we avoid generating some redundant configurations when evaluating automata, in the style of *partial-order reduction* [15]: if a monitor can take two transitions that read different traces and do not update registers, then we take them at once instead of taking first one and later the other (avoiding the well-known dimond shape in the searched space of configurations).

6.1 Monitoring Observational Determinism

A classical benchmark for monitoring hyperproperties is to evaluate on *observational determinism (OD)* [35]. This hyperproperty states that if two traces have the same observable inputs, they must have the same observable outputs (regardless of unobservable – i.e., secret – inputs). One way to specify *synchronous OD (Sync-OD)* is with this sHL formula:

$$\forall \pi \forall \pi'. \ (\mathbf{in}(\pi) \simeq \mathbf{in}(\pi')) \rightarrow (\mathbf{out}(\pi) \simeq \mathbf{out}(\pi')) \tag{4}$$

Comparison on Sync-OD. We compared sHL monitors to eHL monitors, MPTs and RVHyper on monitoring Sync-OD. All monitors were setup to use the reflexivity and symmetry reductions of instances of the formula [23]. RVHyper was set up to use the sequential input mode as otherwise it crashes after reading approx. 1000 traces. Because eHL does not support equality, the equality in formula (4) was broken down using $\leq$ and $\geq$. sHL monitor used this formula as well. For the lack of better benchmarks, we used randomly generated traces with n-bit integers as inputs and one n-bit integer as the output (n is a parameter). In experiments with RVHyper, the integers were broken down to bits (*bit-blasted*) because RVHyper requires this format.

Figure 7 on the top shows the result of monitoring 8-bit integers on these traces. sHL monitors performed slightly worse than eHL. For small alphabets, evaluating eHL monitors is faster – the guards on conditions are simpler and even though eHL monitors can have considerably more transitions, their simplicity gives them advantage if the number of bits is small enough. The MPT monitors performed the best, which we can attribute to their optimized implementation and the fact that this task suits them well.

On the bottom of Fig. 7, we show the comparison of eHL and sHL monitors on monitoring Sync-OD on traces with n-bit integers with no bit-blasting. The plot shows that it is indeed the size of alphabet that makes a difference for eHL monitors. As the number of bits grows, eHL monitors loose their performance and for 12 bits they are only able to analyze at most 1000 traces in the given time limit of 120 s. For sHL monitors, we see almost constant performance irregardless of the number of bits, depending only on the number of traces.

Monitor Generation Time. Not only that eHL monitors do not scale with the size of the alphabet, but it is even infeasible to generate them for larger alphabets. Figure 8 shows the time it takes to generate monitors (including also compilation to a binary) for Sync-OD. Monitors with the $_{sr}$ subscript are for the Sync-OD formula where every trace sub-formula has been stutter reduced (*Async-OD*). Monitors with the ^{LTO} superscript are compiled with *link-time optimizations (LTO)* which greatly improve their performance, but also slows down the compilation. We see that for Sync-OD, for 15-bits alphabet the monitor generation takes already around 5 min and for more bits the generation hits the timeout of 400 s. With LTO, this limit is 13 bits. For Async-OD, we cannot generate monitors for more than 7-bit alphabet in the time limit, as stutter reduction

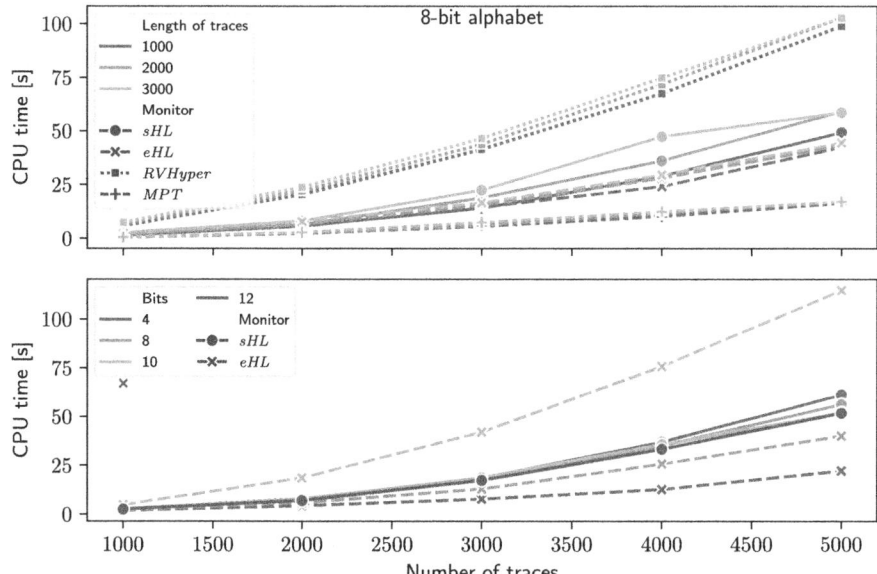

Fig. 7. Time of monitoring Sync-OD for traces with 8-bit bit-blasted integers (top), and monitoring the same formula on traces with n-bit integers without bit-blasting (bottom).

introduces a lot of non-determinism into the automata. With LTO, only 6-bit alphabet is feasible. In contrary, generating sHL monitors takes around $9\,s$ for both formulas with or without LTO.

Monitoring OpenSSL. Because sHL does not have a limit on the size of the alphabet, we can monitor traces from practical projects. For example, we used fuzzing to generate traces from *OpenSSL* library in the scenario where a client connects to a server. The traces contained sequences of 64-bit integers encoding observable inputs and outputs. The results of checking these for Sync-OD are shown in Table 1. Our monitors were able to analyze 20000 traces taking roughly $1\,ms$ per trace, which should be good enough for online monitoring.

7 Related Work

Agrawal and Bonakdarpour were the first to address hyperproperty monitoring [2]. They presented an algorithm for a restricted class of k-safety properties expressed in HyperLTL built from monitors for 3-value LTL. Later, Brett et al. introduced a monitor for HyperLTL formulas based on formula rewriting [11]. For deterministic programs, Pinisetty et al. [31] showed how to monitor for a restricted class of HyperLTL formulas expressing k-safety by monitoring instead for an equivalent trace property. Automata-based monitoring algorithms for HyperLTL were introduced by Finkbeiner et al. [21,23] and implemented in

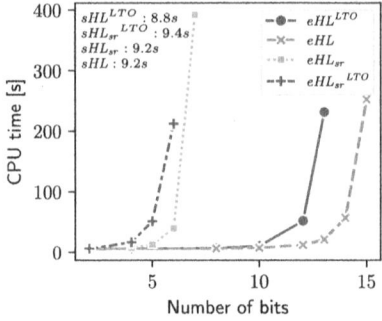

Fig. 8. Time of generating eHL and sHL monitors.

Table 1. Time of monitoring Sync-OD for traces from OpenSSL.

# traces	time [s]
1000	0.4
5000	6.7
10000	39.3
15000	111.1
20000	229.1

the tool *RVHyper* [22]. Hahn et al. [27,28] presented constraint-based monitors for HyperLTL formulas. Aceto et al. introduce an extension of the safety fragment of Hennessy-Milner Logic (μHML) with trace quantifiers and define monitor synthesis for this logic [1]. All of these address synchronous hyperproperties.

Asynchronous hyperproperties have attracted attention recently, with various formalisms proposed in the literature [4–6,9,10,26]. For the runtime verification of asynchronous hyperproperties, Chalupa and Henzinger introduced transducers for RV of hyperproperties [12], which can be used to monitor universally quantified asynchronous hyperproperties. A different approach was presented by Beutner et al. [7], who introduced finite trace semantics for second-order HyperLTL along its monitoring algorithm. In [13], Chalupa et al. introduced extended hypernode logic (eHL), which includes both synchronous and asynchronous comparison of traces for prefixing, as well as the possibility to define regular patterns. All the aforementioned approaches are limited to finite domains.

In stream runtime verification (SRV) [33], monitors are specified as a transformation of input streams to output streams. This resembles our use of transducers; however, in our approach, the output stream is used only as an intermediate step in determining whether a given hyperproperty is satisfied or violated. Other techniques proposed in the literature to monitor for trace properties over events carrying data [29] have used different flavors of symbolic automata [18,20] and register automata [24]. To the best of our knowledge, none of these approaches have been extended to support runtime verification of hyperproperties.

8 Conclusion

We introduced sHL, an extension of prior work on hypernode logic, to specify asynchronous hyperproperties of traces with data. We present a monitoring algorithm based on a translation of formulas expressing comparison of sets of traces to multi-tape symbolic transducers. We implemented our approach and compared it to other available monitors for hyperproperties. For future work, we plan to explore further how to leverage the power of symbolic transducers to monitor infinite-domain hyperproperties more efficiently. We also intend to explore new techniques for verifying hyperproperties that involve quantifier-alternation.

References

1. Aceto, L., Achilleos, A., Anastasiadi, E., Francalanza, A.: Monitoring hyperproperties with circuits. In: Proceedings of Formal Techniques for Distributed Objects, Components, and Systems (FORTE 2022). LNCS, vol. 13273, pp. 1–10. Springer (2022). https://doi.org/10.1007/978-3-031-08679-3_1
2. Agrawal, S., Bonakdarpour, B.: Runtime verification of k-safety hyperproperties in HyperLTL. In: IEEE 29th Computer Security Foundations Symposium (CSF 2016), pp. 239–252 (2016). https://doi.org/10.1109/CSF.2016.24
3. Bartocci, E., Henzinger, T.A., Nickovic, D., da Costa, A.O.: Hypernode automata. In: 34th International Conference on Concurrency Theory, (CONCUR 2023). LIPIcs, vol. 279, pp. 21:1–21:16. Schloss Dagstuhl - Leibniz-Zentrum für Informatik (2023). https://doi.org/10.4230/LIPICS.CONCUR.2023.21
4. Baumeister, J., Coenen, N., Bonakdarpour, B., Finkbeiner, B., Sánchez, C.: A temporal logic for asynchronous hyperproperties. In: Silva, A., Leino, K.R.M. (eds.) CAV 2021. LNCS, vol. 12759, pp. 694–717. Springer, Cham (2021). https://doi.org/10.1007/978-3-030-81685-8_33
5. Beutner, R., Finkbeiner, B.: A temporal logic for strategic hyperproperties. In: 32nd International Conference on Concurrency Theory, (CONCUR 2021). LIPIcs, vol. 203, pp. 24:1–24:19. Schloss Dagstuhl - Leibniz-Zentrum für Informatik (2021). https://doi.org/10.4230/LIPICS.CONCUR.2021.24
6. Beutner, R., Finkbeiner, B., Frenkel, H., Metzger, N.: Second-order hyperproperties. In: Computer Aided Verification (CAV 2023). LNCS, vol. 13965, pp. 309–332. Springer (2023). https://doi.org/10.1007/978-3-031-37703-7_15
7. Beutner, R., Finkbeiner, B., Frenkel, H., Metzger, N.: Monitoring second-order hyperproperties. In: 23rd International Conference on Autonomous Agents and Multiagent Systems (AAMAS 2024), pp. 180–188 (2024). https://dl.acm.org/doi/10.5555/3635637.3662865
8. Bjørner, N., Veanes, M.: Symbolic transducers. Tech. Rep. MSR-TR-2011-3, Microsoft Research, Redmond (2011), https://www.microsoft.com/en-us/research/wp-content/uploads/2016/02/MSR-TR-2011-3.pdf
9. Bozzelli, L., Peron, A., Sánchez, C.: Asynchronous extensions of HyperLTL. In: 36th Annual ACM/IEEE Symposium on Logic in Computer Science (LICS 2021), pp. 1–13. IEEE (2021). https://doi.org/10.1109/LICS52264.2021.9470583
10. Bozzelli, L., Peron, A., Sánchez, C.: Expressiveness and decidability of temporal logics for asynchronous hyperproperties. In: 33rd International Conference on Concurrency Theory, (CONCUR 2022). LIPIcs, vol. 243, pp. 27:1–27:16. Schloss Dagstuhl - Leibniz-Zentrum für Informatik (2022). https://doi.org/10.4230/LIPICS.CONCUR.2022.27
11. Brett, N., Siddique, U., Bonakdarpour, B.: Rewriting-based runtime verification for alternation-free HyperLTL. In: Legay, A., Margaria, T. (eds.) TACAS 2017. LNCS, vol. 10206, pp. 77–93. Springer, Heidelberg (2017). https://doi.org/10.1007/978-3-662-54580-5_5

12. Chalupa, M., Henzinger, T.A.: Monitoring hyperproperties with prefix transducers. In: Runtime Verification - 23rd International Conference (RV 2023). LNCS, vol. 14245, pp. 168–190. Springer (2023). https://doi.org/10.1007/978-3-031-44267-4_9
13. Chalupa, M., Henzinger, T.A., da Costa, A.O.: Monitoring extended hypernode logic. In: Integrated Formal Methods - 19th International Conference (iFM 2024). LNCS, vol. 15234, pp. 151–171. Springer (2024). https://doi.org/10.1007/978-3-031-76554-4_9
14. Chalupa, M., Henzinger, T.A., da Costa, A.O.: Monitoring hypernode logic over infinite domains (artifact) (2025). https://doi.org/10.5281/zenodo.16357544
15. Clarke, E.M., Grumberg, O., Peled, D.A.: Model checking, 1st Edition. MIT Press (2001). http://books.google.de/books?id=Nmc4wEaLXFEC, ISBN: 978-0-262-03270-4
16. Clarkson, M.R., Schneider, F.B.: Hyperproperties. J. Comput. Secur. **18**(6), 1157–1210 (2010). https://doi.org/10.3233/JCS-2009-0393
17. D'Antoni, L., Veanes, M.: The power of symbolic automata and transducers. In: Majumdar, R., Kunčak, V. (eds.) CAV 2017. LNCS, vol. 10426, pp. 47–67. Springer, Cham (2017). https://doi.org/10.1007/978-3-319-63387-9_3
18. Decker, N., Leucker, M., Thoma, D.: Monitoring modulo theories. Int. J. Softw. Tools Technol. Transf. (STTT) **18**(2), 205–225 (2016). https://doi.org/10.1007/S10009-015-0380-3
19. Delaune, S., Kremer, S., Ryan, M.: Verifying privacy-type properties of electronic voting protocols. J. Comput. Secur. **17**(4), 435–487 (2009). https://doi.org/10.3233/JCS-2009-0340
20. Faella, M., Parlato, G.: A unified automata-theoretic approach to LTL_f modulo theories. In: 27th European Conference on Artificial Intelligence (ECAI 2024), Frontiers in Artificial Intelligence and Applications, vol. 392, pp. 1254–1261. IOS Press (2024). https://doi.org/10.3233/FAIA240622
21. Finkbeiner, B., Hahn, C., Stenger, M., Tentrup, L.: Monitoring hyperproperties. In: Lahiri, S., Reger, G. (eds.) RV 2017. LNCS, vol. 10548, pp. 190–207. Springer, Cham (2017). https://doi.org/10.1007/978-3-319-67531-2_12
22. Finkbeiner, B., Hahn, C., Stenger, M., Tentrup, L.: RVHyper: a runtime verification tool for temporal hyperproperties. In: Beyer, D., Huisman, M. (eds.) TACAS 2018. LNCS, vol. 10806, pp. 194–200. Springer, Cham (2018). https://doi.org/10.1007/978-3-319-89963-3_11
23. Finkbeiner, B., Hahn, C., Stenger, M., Tentrup, L.: Monitoring hyperproperties. Formal Methods Syst. Design **54**(3), 336–363 (2019). https://doi.org/10.1007/s10703-019-00334-z
24. Grigore, R., Distefano, D., Petersen, R.L., Tzevelekos, N.: Runtime verification based on register automata. In: Piterman, N., Smolka, S.A. (eds.) TACAS 2013. LNCS, vol. 7795, pp. 260–276. Springer, Heidelberg (2013). https://doi.org/10.1007/978-3-642-36742-7_19
25. Grishchenko, I., Maffei, M., Schneidewind, C.: A semantic framework for the security analysis of ethereum smart contracts. In: Bauer, L., Küsters, R. (eds.) POST 2018. LNCS, vol. 10804, pp. 243–269. Springer, Cham (2018). https://doi.org/10.1007/978-3-319-89722-6_10
26. Gutsfeld, J.O., Müller-Olm, M., Ohrem, C.: Automata and fixpoints for asynchronous hyperproperties. Proc. ACM Program. Lang. **5**(POPL), 1–29 (2021). https://doi.org/10.1145/3434319

27. Hahn, C.: Algorithms for monitoring hyperproperties. In: Finkbeiner, B., Mariani, L. (eds.) RV 2019. LNCS, vol. 11757, pp. 70–90. Springer, Cham (2019). https://doi.org/10.1007/978-3-030-32079-9_5
28. Hahn, C., Stenger, M., Tentrup, L.: Constraint-based monitoring of hyperproperties. In: Vojnar, T., Zhang, L. (eds.) TACAS 2019. LNCS, vol. 11428, pp. 115–131. Springer, Cham (2019). https://doi.org/10.1007/978-3-030-17465-1_7
29. Havelund, K., Reger, G., Thoma, D., Zălinescu, E.: Monitoring events that carry data. In: Bartocci, E., Falcone, Y. (eds.) Lectures on Runtime Verification. LNCS, vol. 10457, pp. 61–102. Springer, Cham (2018). https://doi.org/10.1007/978-3-319-75632-5_3
30. Hsu, T.-H., Sánchez, C., Bonakdarpour, B.: Bounded model checking for hyperproperties. In: TACAS 2021. LNCS, vol. 12651, pp. 94–112. Springer, Cham (2021). https://doi.org/10.1007/978-3-030-72016-2_6
31. Pinisetty, S., Schneider, G., Sands, D.: Runtime verification of hyperproperties for deterministic programs. In: Proceedings of the 6th Conference on Formal Methods in Software Engineering (FormaliSE 2018), pp. 20–29. ACM (2018).https://doi.org/10.1145/3193992.3193995
32. Rakotonirina, I., Barthe, G., Schneidewind, C.: Decision and complexity of dolev-yao hyperproperties. Proc. ACM Program. Lang. 8(POPL), 1913–1944 (2024). https://doi.org/10.1145/3632906
33. Sánchez, C.: Synchronous and asynchronous stream runtime verification. In: 5th ACM International Workshop on Verification and mOnitoring at Runtime EXecution (VORTEX 2021), pp. 5–7. ACM (2021). https://doi.org/10.1145/3464974.3468453
34. Veanes, M., Hooimeijer, P., Livshits, B., Molnar, D., Bjørner, N.S.: Symbolic finite state transducers: algorithms and applications. In: Proceedings of the 39th ACM SIGPLAN-SIGACT Symposium on Principles of Programming Languages (POPL 2012), pp. 137–150. ACM (2012). https://doi.org/10.1145/2103656.2103674
35. Zdancewic, S., Myers, A.: Observational determinism for concurrent program security. In: 16th IEEE Computer Security Foundations Workshop (CSF 2003), pp. 29–43 (2003). https://doi.org/10.1109/CSFW.2003.1212703

A Compositional Approach to Diagnosing Faults in Cyber-Physical Systems

Josefine B. Graebener[1](✉)[iD], Inigo Incer[2](✉)[iD], and Richard M. Murray[1][iD]

[1] California Institute of Technology, Pasadena, CA 91125, USA
jgraeben@caltech.edu, murray@cds.caltech.edu
[2] University of Michigan, Ann Arbor, MI 48109, USA
iir@umich.edu

Abstract. Identifying the cause of a system-level failure in a cyber-physical system (CPS) can be like tracing a needle in a haystack. This paper approaches the problem by assuming that the CPS has been designed compositionally and that each component in the system is associated with an assume-guarantee contract. We exploit recent advances in contract-based design that show how to compute the contract for the entire system using the component-level contracts. When presented with a system-level failure, our approach is able to efficiently identify the components that are responsible for the system-level failure together with the specific predicates in those components' specifications that are involved in the fault. We implemented this approach using Pacti and demonstrate it through illustrative examples inspired by an autonomous vehicle in the DARPA urban challenge.

Keywords: assume-guarantee contracts · diagnostics

1 Introduction

Any safety-critical system requires efficient detection of system abnormalities and faults to avoid dangerous situations and safety hazards. The rising adoption of autonomy has only increased the need for such diagnostics [5]. Faults are defined as deviations from the correct, expected system behavior, observable in at least one system property or parameter [27]. Diagnostics refers to the process of identifying, analyzing, and resolving problems that become apparent during the operation of a system, product, or process. Diagnosing the cause of a system-level failure in a complex CPS can be a difficult process.

Fault diagnosis consists of three areas: detection, isolation, and identification [12]. Detection refers to identifying when and where a fault occurs from the observable system output. Isolation considers the location of the fault, and identification refers to finding the type, shape, and size of the fault. There are five main fault diagnosis methods: model-based, signal-based, knowledge-based, hybrid, and active. In 1971, Beard introduced model-based fault diagnosis with the intent to replace hardware redundancy by analytical redundancy [1]. Model-based fault diagnosis uses different techniques to monitor the actual system outputs and compare them to the predicted values. Signal-based fault diagnosis uses measured signals instead of input-output models, and extracts features (or patterns) from a signal to make a diagnostic decision [12]. Knowledge-based fault diagnosis consists of a knowledge base and an inference engine [6]. Hybrid approaches are a combination of the above-mentioned methods [12]. Active fault detection is concerned with designing auxiliary input vectors to reveal faults [22].

Diagnostics has been studied extensively in computer science and engineering. Some early and influential works include [10] and [25]. In [10], a model-based approach to diagnose faults in complex systems by observing symptoms and using reasoning techniques was introduced in 1987 by De Kleer and Williams. In 1987, Reiter developed a formal logical framework to diagnose faults consisting of three main components: a knowledge base, an observation base, and a set of inference rules [25]. In formal methods, the problem of explaining why for certain robot specifications no implementing control strategy exists has been studied in [24], while 'repairing' specifications has been studied in [3]. In [20], assume-guarantee contract operators have been used for specification repair. Recently, TRACE, a tool for requirements analysis was introduced in [28], which uses SMT solvers to analyze system guarantees.

This paper presents a diagnostics approach that utilizes assume-guarantee reasoning and leverages the syntax of specifications to facilitate tracing the causes of violated system-level guarantees to potential subsystems. The use of contracts in diagnostics simplifies the attribution of blame. For example, suppose that we have a trace for a component. If this trace violates the assumption of the component, the component cannot be blamed for any undesired behavior. On the other hand, under satisfied assumptions, the behavior has to satisfy the promised guarantees. If the component does not deliver its guarantees in this case, then it did not satisfy its specification. Now we can further analyze the component and determine whether the implementation was faulty or if anything was missed when defining the specification.

Problem Definition. Suppose we implement a system with n interconnected components having contracts $\mathcal{C}_i = (\bigwedge_j a^i_j, \bigwedge_j g^i_j)$ for $i \in \{1, \ldots, n\}$, where a^i_j and g^i_j represent the j-th assumption and guarantee, respectively, of component i. Suppose that the specification of the entire system is given by $\mathcal{C}_S = (\bigwedge_j a_j, \bigwedge_j g_j)$ and that we have access to a log file Log containing values for a subset of system variables such that the assumptions of $\mathcal{C}_S$ are satisfied, but there is at least one guarantee of $\mathcal{C}_S$ that is violated. This paper introduces a technique to identify both the contract $\mathcal{C}_k$ and its specific assumptions and guarantees that were responsible for the system-level fault. The technique can indicate exactly the predicates that need to be evaluated to diagnose the failure, as opposed to checking every single assumption and guarantee of all components in the system. While the application of contracts in runtime verification and diagnostics has been pursued—see, e.g., [7–9,13,15]—our work is the first to exploit the explicit computation of the contract operation of composition in order to determine not only what component in the system is the likely cause of the system-level fault, but also the specific predicates in the component's contract that are responsible for the fault.

Our problem setup assumes that we have a log file witnessing a system-level failure and contracts for each component. We may ask, why should not we simply check every assumption and guarantee of all components? We believe that the targeted approach discussed in this paper is preferable for various reasons. First, the log file can contain several errors that are not related to the system-level issue we are interested in debugging. Lacking the means to pinpoint exactly the predicates that are involved in the system-level failure can lead designers to long debugging campaigns of unrelated, but tempting, issues, resulting in distractions and loss of time, which may be costly in time-sensitive projects or when deadlines approach. Second, suppose there is a specific system-level guarantee we want to monitor. The methods discussed in this paper can locate exactly which predicates should be monitored in the system to ascribe blame to a component for the violation of the property we are tracking. Knowledge of these internal predicates can be used to instrument the system to monitor the desired predicates when running a second test, i.e., this methodology can be used in designing test campaigns.

Contributions. We propose a diagnostics methodology based on contracts that enables a systematic search over system variables to trace violated system guarantees back to the responsible component. Our approach reduces the number of predicates and components that need to be evaluated during fault localization by exploiting the explicit computation of the composition operation of contracts. We implement this methodology using Pacti [18], a tool for compositional reasoning over assume-guarantee contracts. Finally, we demonstrate the effectiveness of our approach through illustrative examples and case studies inspired by autonomous vehicle behavior in the DARPA Urban Challenge [4]. A preliminary version of this work appeared in Chap. 5 of [14]. The presentation has been expanded and the current case study has not appeared before.

2 Background

The framework presented in this paper is based on contract-based design, first introduced as a design methodology for modular software systems [11,19,21] and later extended to cyber-physical systems [23,26].

Definition 1 (Assume-Guarantee Contract [2,16]). Let T be the language used to express specifications in our system. We assume this language has Boolean semantics. A *contract* is a pair $C = (a, g) \in T^2$, where a are the assumptions, and g the guarantees. A model $E \models a$ is said to be an *environment* of the contract C. A model $M \models a \to g$ is said to be an *implementation* of the contract C, meaning that M provides the specified guarantees when it operates in an environment that satisfies the contract's assumptions. There exists a preorder of contracts: we say $\mathcal{C}_1$ is a refinement of $\mathcal{C}_2$, denoted $\mathcal{C}_1 \leq \mathcal{C}_2$, if $(a_2 \leq a_1)$ and $(a_1 \to g_1 \leq a_2 \to g_2)$, where the preorder $\phi \leq \phi'$ on formulas ϕ and ϕ' means that $\phi \to \phi'$ is a tautology. Contracts $\mathcal{C}_1$ and $\mathcal{C}_2$ are said to be equivalent if $\mathcal{C}_1 \leq \mathcal{C}_2$ and $\mathcal{C}_2 \leq \mathcal{C}_1$.

As shown in [17], the contract algebra is a Stone algebra, but not a Boolean algebra. A contract has three possible evaluations—not two—as requirements normally do (i.e., a requirement is either SAT or UNSAT). A contract can evaluate to either FAIL, ACTIVE, or IDLE. It evaluates to FAIL when the assumptions are satisfied but the guarantees are not. It evaluates to ACTIVE when both the assumptions and guarantees are satisfied. A contract evaluates to IDLE when the assumptions are not satisfied. Given a system-level failure, the diagnostics process corresponds to identifying the component contract that evaluates to FAIL. It is key to our diagnostics process to compute the composition operation of contracts. A recent breakthrough in contract-based design showed how to compute this operation efficiently—see [18].

The results of this paper are implemented in Pacti, an open-source Python package for compositional system analysis and design. Components are defined using assume-guarantee contracts, and contract operations can be performed, such as composition, merging, and quotient. Contracts in Pacti are defined over a term algebra T with Boolean semantics. Pacti's basic data structure is the IO contract.

Definition 2 (IO Contract[18]). Let V be a set of variables. An *IO contract* is the tuple $(I, O, \mathfrak{a}, \mathfrak{g})$, where $I, O \in V$ are disjoint sets of input and output variables respectively, $\mathfrak{a} \in T$ a set of assumptions, and $\mathfrak{g} \in T$ a set of guarantees. The terms in the assumptions only refer to input variables, and the terms in the guarantees only refer to input and output variables.

The key contract operation for system-level design is composition, which yields the contract of a system obtained by interconnecting components represented using contracts. The composition of contract $\mathcal{C} = (a, g)$ and contract $\mathcal{C}' = (a', g')$ can be directly computed as

$$\mathcal{C}_c = \mathcal{C} \parallel \mathcal{C}' = ((a \wedge a') \vee (a \wedge \neg g) \vee (a' \wedge \neg g'), (g \vee \neg a) \wedge (g' \vee \neg a')). \quad (1)$$

This yields the most refined contract that a system comprising two components, M and M', will satisfy, provided that M and M' were implemented such that they satisfy their corresponding contracts $\mathcal{C}$, and $\mathcal{C}'$, respectively. Whereas this operation satisfies optimality criteria, the authors of [18] observe that the output of composition should be a contract expressed using only the variables that lie at the interface of the resulting system, which equation (1) does not provide.

To express contract composition using only interface variables, equation (1) can be relaxed by either refining the assumptions, relaxing the guarantees, or both. For two assumptions a and a', we say that a' refines a, denoted $a \geq a'$, if the denotation set corresponding to a' is a subset of the set corresponding to a. Similarly, for guarantees g and g', we say that g' is a relaxation of g, $g \leq g'$, if the denotation set corresponding to g is a subset of the set corresponding to g'. When thinking about assumptions and guarantees each as conjunctions of terms (or constraints), refining a contract informally corresponds to either assuming *less*, guaranteeing *more*, or both. Pacti makes use of this contract relaxation to eliminate internal variables so that the returned composition is expressed only using the interface variables of the system. Any relaxed contract that is computed in this way will be satisfied by a correct implementation of the system. Nevertheless, for a contract to be useful, we need to compute the relaxation systematically, as in the extreme case a contract that guarantees every possible behavior is a valid, yet pointless refinement in the context of capturing the system's behavior.

When computing a composition of contracts $\mathcal{C}$ and $\mathcal{C}'$, the assumptions of the composed contract are given as follows:

$$a_c = \overbrace{(a \wedge a')}^{\text{stem}} \vee \overbrace{(a \wedge \neg g') \vee (a' \wedge \neg g)}^{\text{failure terms}}. \qquad (2)$$

We refer to the first term as the *stem*, as this is where the composed system should operate—where the assumptions of both components are satisfied. The second and third terms are referred to as *failure terms*, where each term refers to one of the components having its assumptions satisfied but not delivering their guarantees. As we want the composition to operate in the stem, Pacti uses the failure terms to eliminate from the stem the variables that are not part of the interface of the resulting system. These failure terms serve as the context for the elimination of variables in the stem—the details about this are contained in [18]. Once the failure terms are no longer needed to eliminate variables in the stem they are discarded, and we define the assumption of the relaxed contract as the transformed stem by refinement. The transformation of the guarantees follows a similar argument, but ensures that the variables are eliminated by relaxing the guarantees. The guarantees of a composition are given as follows:

$$g_c = (g \vee \neg a) \wedge (g' \vee \neg a') = \underbrace{(g \wedge g')}_{\text{stem}} \vee (\neg a \wedge g') \vee (\neg a' \wedge g) \vee (\neg a \wedge \neg a'),$$

where the *stem* again refers to the desired area of operation, when both components satisfy their guarantees. The stem may contain variables that should be eliminated. We can use the remaining terms as a *context* to transform the stem to eliminate these variables. The transformation of either assumptions or guarantees is carried out in Pacti by functions that take as arguments the term to be transformed, the variables that need to be eliminated, and the context that can be used to carry out such elimination. Pacti currently supports linear inequalities and propositional logic as the term algebras for expressing assumptions and guarantees. However, the framework is extensible to other formalisms by implementing the variable elimination routines discussed in [18].

3 Tracing System Guarantees

This section presents a methodological approach to modeling the system and its constituent components to support an effective fault diagnosis mechanism. Our approach is based on the computation of contract operations in Pacti. We extended this tool to support diagnostics.

To begin, we assume that each component in the system is modeled as an IO contract. For example, for a component M, we can define the corresponding IO contract $\mathcal{C} = (I, O, \mathfrak{a}, \mathfrak{g})$, where the set $\mathfrak{a}$ contains the term $i \leq 2$ and the guarantee set $\mathfrak{g}$ contains the term $o \leq 2i + 1$, where $I = \{i\}$, and $O = \{o\}$ are the singleton sets of the input and output variables.

Definition 3 (Faulty component). Given a component M and the corresponding contract $\mathcal{C} = (I, O, \mathfrak{a}, \mathfrak{g})$, M is *faulty* if it contains a behavior that does not satisfy the guarantees $\mathfrak{g}$, but the assumptions $\mathfrak{a}$ are satisfied.

As discussed in the background section, Pacti uses a filtering procedure to determine the relevant context terms when computing the assumptions and guarantees of the composed contract. These context terms come from the assumptions and guarantees of the contracts being composed. We extended Pacti with an ID system to keep track of which context terms were used to generate a resulting term for the assumptions and guarantees of the composed contract. For each composition operation, we can thus define a composition graph that allows us to map the composed assumption and guarantee terms to the terms that were used in their transformation. A composition graph consists of a set of vertices, where each vertex corresponds to a term in the assumptions or guarantees of the individual contracts, and the composed contract. The edges in the composition graph connect vertices if the corresponding individual contract term was used to generate the composed contract term, shown as the edges from left to right in Fig. 1b

Definition 4 (Composition Graph). Let components M_1 and M_2 have corresponding IO contracts $\mathcal{C}_1 = (I_1, O_1, \mathfrak{a}_1, \mathfrak{g}_1)$ and $\mathcal{C}_2 = (I_2, O_2, \mathfrak{a}_2, \mathfrak{g}_2)$, with their composition given by $\mathcal{C} = (I, O, \mathfrak{a}, \mathfrak{g})$. A *composition graph* is a directed graph $G = (V, E)$, where each vertex in V corresponds to a term from the assumptions or guarantees of $\mathcal{C}_1$, $\mathcal{C}_2$, or $\mathcal{C}$. Specifically, $V_{i,a} \subseteq V$ and $V_{i,g} \subseteq V$ represent the assumptions $\mathfrak{a}_i$ and guarantees $\mathfrak{g}_i$ of component i, while $V_a \subseteq V$ and $V_g \subseteq V$ represent the composed assumptions and guarantees. For simplicity, we use the same symbol s to refer to both a term and its corresponding vertex $s \in V$. An edge $(u, v) \in E$ exists if the term u was used to generate term v. A path from vertex s to t in G, denoted $\text{path}(G, s, t)$, exists if there is a sequence of edges connecting the vertices.

Example 1. Given two components M_1 and M_2 and their inputs and outputs as illustrated in Fig. 1a and their IO contracts as $\mathcal{C}_1 = (\{i\}, \{o\}, \mathfrak{a}_1, \mathfrak{g}_1)$, where $\mathfrak{a}_1 = \{i \geq 0, i \leq 2\}$, and $\mathfrak{g}_1 = \{o + i \leq 3\}$ and $\mathcal{C}_2 = (\{o\}, \{o'\}, \mathfrak{a}_2, \mathfrak{g}_2)$, where $\mathfrak{a}_2 = \{o \leq 5\}$, and $\mathfrak{g}_2 = \{o + 2o' \geq 6\}$. The composition results in the contract

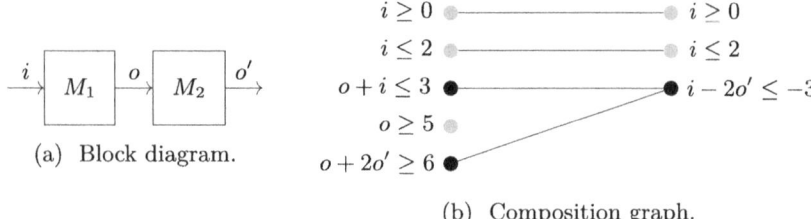

Fig. 1. Block diagram and composition graph for Example 1. The yellow vertices correspond to assumption terms and the blue vertices correspond to guarantee terms.

$\mathcal{C} = (\{i\}, \{o'\}, \mathfrak{a}, \mathfrak{g})$, where $\mathfrak{a} = \{i \geq 0, i \leq 2\}$, and $\mathfrak{g} = \{i - 2o' \leq -3\}$. The composition graph corresponding to the composition $\mathcal{C}_1 \parallel \mathcal{C}_2$ is shown in Fig. 1b

From our experience, the transformation of an assumption or guarantee usually involves few context terms. This means that the resulting composition graph is very sparse. This allows us to trace a composition-level guarantee back to a small set of terms on the component level.

All operations in Pacti are computed under the assumption that the components operate correctly as specified by their contracts. The entire premise of testing lies in the difference between a 'perfectly' specified system and its real-world implementation. In a real-world system, specifications might be incomplete, or implementations might be faulty. A single component failure might present itself in multiple ways; it might result in a system-level guarantee violation, or it might not. If a component failure is latent, meaning it does not show itself in the system-level guarantee violation, our proposed framework cannot detect it. If the fault does show itself in a system-level guarantee violation, we can trace it to the responsible component(s) by tracking which relevant component's guarantees were violated under satisfied assumptions.

At this point, we can create a composition graph for the composition of two components and their corresponding IO contracts. To build the overall system, we need to compose multiple components. Contract composition is a binary operation. Therefore, to compose the entire system, we need to compose two components at a time, and then compose their composition with the next component. There are many ways of composing the same system, and the resulting contract for the composition is dependent on the order of composition. As Pacti hides internal variables, the composition has to be chosen carefully such that the variables necessary for future compositions are kept. Another important aspect that can guide the composition order is the availability of component data. When there is a lack of available information from inside a block of components it might be beneficial to compose these components first and treat them as a meta-component—a grouping of multiple components. If the analysis ends up pointing to this meta-component as the possible cause, a more detailed analysis can still be set up focusing on these components. For this framework, we assume that a composition order has been chosen. This order will be maintained for the remainder of the diagnostics process.

Definition 5 (Composition Order). The component contracts are given as a *composition order* CompOrd $= [\mathcal{C}_1, \ldots, \mathcal{C}_N]$, where N is the number of components. CompOrd specifies the order in which contracts are composed to compute the system specification. The composition up to the kth contract is denoted $\mathcal{C}_{\text{comp},k} := \mathcal{C}_1 \parallel \ldots \parallel \mathcal{C}_k$, where the composition operator $\parallel$ binds left-associatively.

This composition order requires composing the system starting from a single component and building the system up from there. If it is desired to start by composing certain regions of the system first, this framework can easily be extended to include this approach. Otherwise, the component contracts in the composition order need to be provided at the level of granularity such that they can be composed according to a composition order defined in Definition 5. We will now define the diagnostics graph that corresponds to the composition of multiple components and outline how it is constructed. The union of two graphs G_1 and G_2 is defined as $G = (V_1 \cup V_2, E_1 \cup E_2)$, and we will denote it by $G = G_1 \cup G_2$. Simply stated, the diagnostics graph consists of multiple composition graphs. The system is composed step-by-step according to the composition order, and for every composition, the diagnostics graph is extended by the composition graph for this composition. An example is shown in Fig. 2b, where we can see the union of two composition graphs. Each 'column' of vertices corresponds to the individual contract terms in a composition, where the top nodes correspond to the already composed system (or the first component for the first composition), and the bottom vertices correspond to the next contract in the composition order.

Definition 6 (Diagnostics Graph). Given component contracts in a composition order CompOrd $= [\mathcal{C}_1, \ldots, \mathcal{C}_N]$, the *diagnostics graph* $G = (V, E)$ is constructed as follows. For each i, $2 \leq i \leq N$, we compute the composition $\mathcal{C}_{\text{comp},i-1} \parallel \mathcal{C}_i$ and the corresponding graph G_i. Then the diagnostics graph G is defined as $G = \bigcup_{i=2}^{N} G_i$.

Definition 7 (Diagnostics Map). Let CompOrd be the composition order for N components and their contracts. Let $\mathcal{C} = \parallel_{i=1}^{N} \mathcal{C}_i = (\mathfrak{a}, \mathfrak{g})$ be the system-level composition according to the composition order, and let the corresponding diagnostics graph be G. Then, we can define the *diagnostics map* $\text{CM}: \mathfrak{g} \to 2^{(\bigcup_{i=1}^{N}(\mathfrak{a}_i \cup \mathfrak{g}_i)) \times \{\mathcal{C}_i\}_{i=1}^{N}}$, that maps each composed assumption and guarantee term to a set of component level assumption or guarantee terms through the diagnostics graph. That is, for system-level term s and the corresponding vertex $s \in V$, we have

$$\begin{aligned} \text{CM}(s) = \{&(t, \mathcal{C}_i) \,|\, \forall \mathcal{C}_i \in \text{CompOrd},\ t \in \mathfrak{g}_i \cup \mathfrak{a}_i,\ \text{if} \\ &\exists \text{path}(G, t, s) \text{ and } \forall u \in V, u \neq t \implies \nexists (u, t) \in E\}, \end{aligned} \quad (3)$$

where $t \in V$ corresponds to a component-level term used to generate s, and i is the index of the component the term belongs to.

The diagnostics map finds the leaf nodes in the diagnostics graph that have a path to the vertex corresponding to the violated guarantee. For each leaf node, it returns the term corresponding to the leaf node and the contract that this term belongs to in the form of a tuple. With this information, we can now focus our attention on these terms first and start the diagnostics process by evaluating these terms using the available test data.

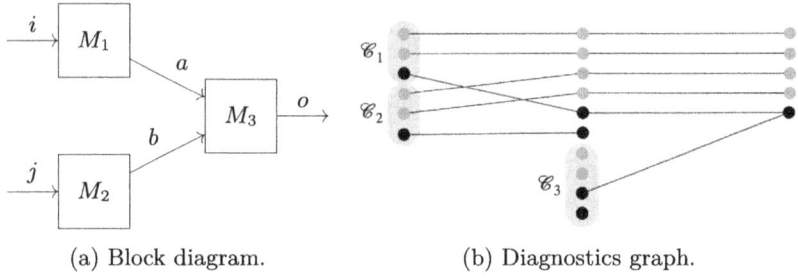

Fig. 2. Block diagram and diagnostics graph for composition in Example 2.

Using the diagnostics graph and the system block diagram, we can identify the component assumptions and guarantees that were relevant to the generation of the top-level system guarantee that was violated. We can then focus on the relevant components of the system block diagram and analyze whether the guarantee was satisfied or violated. Once we find a component where the guarantee was violated we can shift our focus to the assumptions of this term. From then on two different scenarios can occur: i) the assumptions are satisfied, or ii) the assumptions are violated.

Case i) When a contract's assumptions are satisfied, but the component does not deliver the contract's guarantees, it either means that the component failed or that the contract did not adequately characterize the context of operation of the component. The analysis at this level terminates, and the component designer needs to analyze the behavior of this component.

Case ii) In the case of violated assumptions, the component is likely not the cause of the failure, as another component's behavior resulted in the violation of the assumptions. To diagnose this fault, we need to trace the violated assumption back to the guarantees of one or more components. We do this by searching over the composition order for the instance of a composition of the component whose assumptions were violated. As this component's contract was composed with another contract, we identify the guarantees of this second contract that are relevant for the satisfaction of the violated assumption. The function ELIM-VARSBYREFINEMENT in Pacti identifies a subset of terms that participate in the satisfaction of formulas—see [18] for details about this function. After we identify the assumptions and guarantees of the second contract, we refer to the diagnostics graph again to trace these newly identified guarantees back.

It is important to note that this process of tracking assumptions only applies to components whose assumptions are not solely dependent on the overall system input variables. A system-level failure is defined as having satisfied the system-level assumptions, but failing to satisfy the guarantees of the system. Thus, the system-level assumptions are satisfied—this will ensure that component-level assumptions that are only dependent on the system-level input variables are also satisfied.

Identifying Causes for Violated Assumptions. Assume we are given the component M, its corresponding contract $\mathcal{C} = (I, O, \mathfrak{a}, \mathfrak{g})$, the component M_{other} in the composition order that is composed with component M, and the contract $\mathcal{C}_{\text{other}} = (I_{\text{other}}, O_{\text{other}}, \mathfrak{a}_{\text{other}}, \mathfrak{g}_{\text{other}})$ corresponding to M_{other}. The component assumption that was violated is denoted $a_v \in \mathfrak{a}$. We will use Pacti to find the relevant context used to refine this assumption, referred to as the function FINDCAUSEFORASSUMPTION($a_v, \mathfrak{a}_{\text{other}} \cup \mathfrak{g}_{\text{other}}$).

This function exploits the function call ELIMVARSBYREFINEMENT in Pacti, which transforms the assumption a_v with the use of $\mathfrak{a}_{\text{other}} \cup \mathfrak{g}_{\text{other}}$ as the context to eliminate any unwanted variables. We can make use of the same function augmentation that we created to compute the diagnostics graph to analyze the transformation at this level. The instrumentation of the filtering step will return the relevant context terms $\mathfrak{c}_r \subseteq \mathfrak{a}_{\text{other}} \cup \mathfrak{g}_{\text{other}}$ in the assumptions and guarantees of $\mathcal{C}_{\text{other}}$. Once we have determined $\mathfrak{c}_r$, the diagnostics map allows us to trace back the terms in CM(c) for each $c \in \mathfrak{c}_r$ to the responsible component level terms. The entire diagnostics procedure is outlined in Algorithm 1.

This approach can identify multiple component faults under certain conditions. As discussed above, we can only find the faulty component if a system-level guarantee is violated. If two component faults end up cancelling each other out (i.e., are not observable at the system level), then this approach cannot identify them as no system-level guarantee was violated. If a faulty component results in violated assumptions for another component, we cannot determine whether the component with the violated assumption also failed. This is due to the fact that for a contract with violated assumptions, any behavior is allowed. Under the condition that all faulty components are independent (i.e., a faulty component does not lead to violated assumptions of another faulty component), this procedure is able to identify all faulty components.

Example 2. Let there be a system consisting of three component contracts in the composition order CompOrd = $[\mathcal{C}_1, \mathcal{C}_2, \mathcal{C}_3]$ with their inputs and outputs as illustrated in Fig. 2a. The IO contracts are given as $\mathcal{C}_1 = (\{i\}, \{a\}, \mathfrak{a}_1, \mathfrak{g}_1)$, where $\mathfrak{a}_1 = \{i \leq 2, i \geq 0\}$, and $\mathfrak{g}_1 = \{a \leq 2\}$ and $\mathcal{C}_2 = (\{j\}, \{b\}, \mathfrak{a}_2, \mathfrak{g}_2)$, where $\mathfrak{a}_2 = \{j \leq 2, j \geq 0\}$, and $\mathfrak{g}_2 = \{b \leq 3\}$ and $\mathcal{C}_3 = (\{a,b\}, \{o\}, \mathfrak{a}_3, \mathfrak{g}_3)$, where $\mathfrak{a}_3 = \{a \leq 5, b \leq 5\}$, and $\mathfrak{g}_3 = \{o \leq a, o \leq b\}$. The system-level contract is computed as $\mathcal{C} = (\{i,j\}, \{o\}, \mathfrak{a}, \mathfrak{g})$, where $\mathfrak{a} = \{i \leq 2, i \geq 0, j \leq 2, j \geq 0\}$, and $\mathfrak{g} = \{o \leq 2\}$. Suppose the following trace is observed during execution:

Algorithm 1. Diagnosing Violated Guarantee g_v

1: **procedure** DIAGNOSE(g_v, CompOrd, Log)
   Input: failed guarantee g_v, composition order CompOrd $= [\mathcal{C}_1, \ldots, \mathcal{C}_N]$, log data Log
   Output: set of failed components C_f
2: $\quad$ G $\leftarrow (\emptyset, \emptyset)$ $\qquad\qquad\qquad\qquad\qquad$ ▷ Initialize empty diagnostics graph
3: $\quad$ **for** $\mathcal{C}_i \in$ CompOrd **do**
4: $\quad\quad$ $\mathcal{C}_{\text{comp},i-1} \leftarrow \mathcal{C}_1 \| \ldots \| \mathcal{C}_{i-1}$
5: $\quad\quad$ $G_i \leftarrow$ COMPOSITIONGRAPH($\mathcal{C}_{\text{comp},i-1}, \mathcal{C}_i$)
6: $\quad\quad$ $G \leftarrow G \cup G_i$ $\qquad\qquad$ ▷ Add composition graph to diagnostics graph
7: $\quad\quad$ CM $\leftarrow$ define diagnostics map according to equation (3)
8: $\quad\quad$ $C_f \leftarrow$ TRACE(g_v, CompOrd, CM, Log) $\qquad$ ▷ Find set of failed components
9: $\quad$ **return** C_f
10:
11: **procedure** TRACE(g_v, CompOrd, CM, Log)
    Input: guarantee to trace g_v, composition order CompOrd $= [\mathcal{C}_1, \ldots, \mathcal{C}_N]$, diagnostics map CM, log data Log, components $M_1, \ldots, M_N$
    Output: set of failed components C_f
12: $\quad$ $C_f \leftarrow \emptyset$ $\qquad\qquad\qquad\qquad$ ▷ Initialize empty set of failed components
13: $\quad$ **for** $(t, \mathcal{C}_i) \in$ CM(g_v) **do** $\qquad$ ▷ Component-level term t, component index i
14: $\quad\quad$ **if** $t \in \mathfrak{g}_i$ **then** $\qquad\qquad\qquad\qquad$ ▷ $\mathfrak{g}_i$ are the guarantees of $\mathcal{C}_i$
15: $\quad\quad\quad$ **if** NOTSATISFIED(t, Log) **then** $\qquad$ ▷ Check if t is satisfied in log data
16: $\quad\quad\quad\quad$ AssumptionsSatisfied $\leftarrow$ True $\qquad$ ▷ Initialize flag as True
17: $\quad\quad\quad\quad$ **for** $a_i \in \mathfrak{a}_i$ **do**
18: $\quad\quad\quad\quad\quad$ **if** NOTSATISFIED(a_i, Log) **then** $\qquad$ ▷ Check a_i in log data
19: $\quad\quad\quad\quad\quad\quad$ AssumptionsSatisfied $\leftarrow$ False
20: $\quad\quad\quad\quad\quad\quad$ $\mathcal{C}_{\text{other}} \leftarrow \mathcal{C}_1 \| \ldots \| \mathcal{C}_{i-1}$
21: $\quad\quad\quad\quad\quad\quad$ $\mathfrak{c} \leftarrow$ FINDCAUSEFORASSUMPTION(a_i, $\mathfrak{a}_{\text{other}} \cup \mathfrak{g}_{\text{other}}$)
22: $\quad\quad\quad\quad\quad\quad$ **for** $c_k \in \mathfrak{c}$ **do**
23: $\quad\quad\quad\quad\quad\quad\quad$ $C_f \leftarrow C_f \cup$ TRACE(c_k, CompOrd, CM)
24: $\quad\quad\quad\quad$ **if** AssumptionsSatisfied **then**
25: $\quad\quad\quad\quad\quad$ $C_f \leftarrow C_f \cup M_i$ $\qquad\qquad\qquad$ ▷ Add component i to the list
26: $\quad$ **return** C_f
27:
28: **procedure** FINDCAUSEFORASSUMPTION(a_i, $\mathfrak{a}_{\text{other}} \cup \mathfrak{g}_{\text{other}}$)
    Input: assumption to trace a_i, context terms $\mathfrak{a}_{\text{other}} \cup \mathfrak{g}_{\text{other}}$
    Output: list of relevant context terms $\mathfrak{c}$
29: $\quad$ $\_, \mathfrak{c} \leftarrow$ ELIMVARSBYREFINEMENT(a_i, $\mathfrak{a}_{\text{other}} \cup \mathfrak{g}_{\text{other}}$) $\quad$ ▷ Refine the assumption a_i using the context terms $\mathfrak{a}_{\text{other}} \cup \mathfrak{g}_{\text{other}}$ and return the relevant context terms
30: $\quad$ **return** $\mathfrak{c}$
31:

$i = 1$, $j = 1$, $a = 2$, $b = 7$, $o = 3$. The system-level guarantee $g_v := o \leq 2$ is violated while the assumptions are satisfied. The diagnostics map is given by CM(g_v) $= \{(a \leq 2, \mathcal{C}_1), (o \leq a, \mathcal{C}_3)\}$. Applying Algorithm 1, we check the guarantee of component M_1 first and see that $a \leq 2$ is satisfied. Next, we check $o \leq a$, which is not satisfied, as $3 \nleq 2$. This narrows our analysis on component M_3. Evaluating the assumptions of contract C_3, we find that $a \leq 5$ is satisfied, but $b \leq 5$ is not. Therefore, M_3 is not responsible for the violation. We can now trace which terms were used to transform $b \leq 5$ to find which terms to evaluate next in our search for the failed component. For this, we compute $C_{\text{other}} = C_1 \parallel C_2$ from the composition order and evaluate FINDCAUSEFORASSUMPTION($b \leq 5, \mathfrak{a}_{\text{other}} \cup \mathfrak{g}_{\text{other}}$), which returns the relevant context term as the following guarantee from component contract C_2, $b \leq 3$. This guarantee is not satisfied, as $7 \not\leq 3$. Subsequently, we check the assumptions for C_2, $0 \leq j \leq 2$, which are satisfied, leading to the identification of M_2 as the component responsible for the violation. In this example, only 6 terms were checked instead of all 10, showing that tracing the cause of a violated assumption can require fewer checks than evaluating all component-level terms from the log.

Theorem 1. *Suppose we have a list of components $M_1, \ldots, M_N$, their contracts in a composition order* CompOrd $= [C_1, \ldots C_N]$, *a violated system-level guarantee g_v, and the complete log data of a failing trace* Log. *If g_v is a guarantee of the composed system, we can identify the faulty component(s) using Algorithm 1.*

Proof. Let us denote the composed contract as $C = (I, O, \mathfrak{a}, \mathfrak{g})$. For a given composition and the corresponding contract C, under satisfied system-level assumptions $\mathfrak{a}$ and a violated system-level guarantee $g_v \in \mathfrak{g}$, by construction of the composition, there exists at least one faulty component. From CompOrd, we can construct a diagnostics map CM. If $g_v \in \mathfrak{g}$, CM(g_v) is guaranteed to contain at least one component-level guarantee $g_k \in \mathfrak{g}_k$, a guarantee of contract C_k, where $1 \leq k \leq N$. For each $g \in$ CM(g_v), we evaluate from the trace Log whether it is satisfied or violated. If g_k is violated, we have two different cases: i) if the assumptions $\mathfrak{a}_k$ of contract C_k, are satisfied, then M_k is added to the list of responsible components; in case ii), if the assumptions of C_k are violated, from the composition operation in Pacti, we can identify which component-level terms were used to refine this assumption and identify which terms to evaluate next. By definition of assume-guarantee contracts, an implementation of a contract where the assumptions are satisfied and whose guarantees are violated is faulty. Any component in the analysis that violated its guarantees under satisfied assumptions is faulty.

4 Examples

The following example was inspired by Alice, Caltech's entry in the 2007 DARPA Urban Challenge. While conducting the pre-challenge testing campaign, Alice faced scenarios where it failed to accomplish its objective because of an unforeseen behavior arising from the interaction of various subsystems in that particular situation. In this section, we will illustrate a scenario that is loosely based on the real-world scenarios that Alice faced in the DARPA Urban Challenge, which are described in detail in [4].

Alice at Intersection using Propositional Logic. In this example, the test was set up such that Alice was approaching an intersection with multiple cars already waiting at the intersection as shown in Fig. 3a. While Alice was approaching, its sensors detected the other cars in the intersection and commanded Alice to stop and give way to the other cars. The unforeseen circumstance was that the deceleration tilted the LIDARs forward and towards the ground such that Alice lost sight of the other cars momentarily. Once Alice came to a full stop, the line of sight of the LIDARs tilted back up and detected the cars again, but now Alice was under the impression that the cars just arrived, leading to the control system commanding Alice to drive into the intersection and resulting in unsafe behavior.

We model the components in Alice's control architecture as shown in Fig. 3bAlice's system consists of three components, the *Perception*, the *Planner* and the *Tracker* (highlighted in the red dashed box). For each component in Alice's system, we can define an IO contract that describes the correct component behavior. The perception component is modeled as follows

$$\mathcal{C}_{\text{perception}} = \{I_P, O_P, \mathfrak{a}_{\text{perception}}, \mathfrak{g}_{\text{perception}}\},$$

with the input variables $I_{\text{perception}} = \{c^i_{T_1}, c^i_{T_2}, c^i_{T_3}, \text{poor\_visibility}\}$, the output variables are $O_{\text{perception}} = \{c^i_{P_1}, c^i_{P_2}, c^i_{P_3}\}$, the assumptions $\mathfrak{a}_{\text{perception}} = \{\neg\text{poor\_visibility}\}$, and guarantees $\mathfrak{g}_{\text{perception}} = \{c^i_{T_1} \Leftrightarrow c^i_{P_1}, c^i_{T_2} \Leftrightarrow c^i_{P_2}, c^i_{T_3} \Leftrightarrow c^i_{P_3}\}$. The variables $c^i_{T_1}, c^i_{T_2}, c^i_{T_3}$ correspond to whether there is a car in the 1st, 2nd, and 3rd position in the intersection, and $c^i_{P_1}, c^i_{P_2}, c^i_{P_3}$ corresponds to the perceived state of the cars in the intersection; the variable poor_visibility represents to the visibility conditions. This contract describes that the perception component guarantees that the cars in the intersection will be detected correctly if there is no poor visibility.

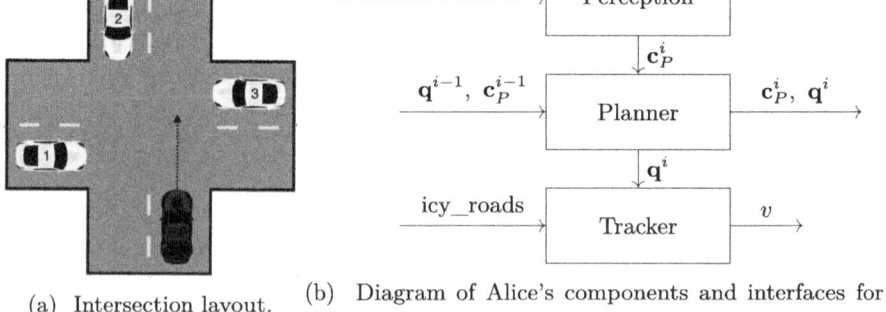

(a) Intersection layout. (b) Diagram of Alice's components and interfaces for timestep i.

Fig. 3. Layout of the intersection and Alice's component block diagram.

The planner component is tasked with determining Alice's spot in the queue of arriving cars to determine whether Alice has the right of way or needs to stop for other cars to take their turn first. For this, the Planner needs to keep track of the arrival order of the cars at the intersection. The planner inputs are

$$I_{\text{planner}} = \{c_{P_1}^i, c_{P_2}^i, c_{P_3}^i, c_{P_1}^{i-1}, c_{P_2}^{i-1}, c_{P_3}^{i-1}, q_1^{i-1}, q_2^{i-1}, q_3^{i-1}, q_4^{i-1}\},$$

where $c_{P_1}^i, c_{P_2}^i, c_{P_3}^i$ are the detected cars at the intersection at the current timestep i, $c_{P_1}^{i-1}, c_{P_2}^{i-1}, c_{P_3}^{i-1}$ are the detected cars in the previous timestep $i-1$, and $q_1^{i-1}, q_2^{i-1}, q_3^{i-1}, q_4^{i-1}$ corresponds to Alice's position in the queue from the previous timestep. The planner output is given as $O_{\text{Planner}} = \{q_1^i, q_2^i, q_3^i, q_4^i\}$, which corresponds to Alice's updated position in the queue for this timestep. The Planner contract is given as

$$C_{\text{planner}} = \{I_{\text{planner}}, O_{\text{planner}}, \mathfrak{a}_{\text{planner}}, \mathfrak{g}_{\text{planner}}\},$$

where the assumptions are $\mathfrak{a}_{\text{planner}} = \{(q_1^{i-1} \land \neg q_2^{i-1} \land \neg q_3^{i-1} \land \neg q_4^{i-1}) \lor (\neg q_1^{i-1} \land q_2^{i-1} \land \neg q_3^{i-1} \land \neg q_4^{i-1}) \lor (\neg q_1^{i-1} \land \neg q_2^{i-1} \land q_3^{i-1} \land \neg q_4^{i-1}) \lor (\neg q_1^{i-1} \land \neg q_2^{i-1} \land \neg q_3^{i-1} \land q_4^{i-1})\}$, which ensures that Alice can only be in one position in the queue in the previous timestep. The guarantees $\mathfrak{g}_{\text{planner}}$ describe how Alice's updated position in the queue will be determined. If none of the other cars leave the intersection, Alice will stay in the same position in the queue,

$$\mathfrak{g}_0 = \{(c_{P_1}^i \Leftrightarrow c_{P_1}^{i-1}) \land (c_{P_2}^i \Leftrightarrow c_{P_2}^{i-1}) \land (c_{P_3}^i \Leftrightarrow c_{P_3}^{i-1}) \land q_4^{i-1} \Rightarrow q_4^i,$$
$$(c_{P_1}^i \Leftrightarrow c_{P_1}^{i-1}) \land (c_{P_2}^i \Leftrightarrow c_{P_2}^{i-1}) \land (c_{P_3}^i \Leftrightarrow c_{P_3}^{i-1}) \land q_3^{i-1} \Rightarrow q_3^i,$$
$$(c_{P_1}^i \Leftrightarrow c_{P_1}^{i-1}) \land (c_{P_2}^i \Leftrightarrow c_{P_2}^{i-1}) \land (c_{P_3}^i \Leftrightarrow c_{P_3}^{i-1}) \land q_2^{i-1} \Rightarrow q_2^i,$$
$$(c_{P_1}^i \Leftrightarrow c_{P_1}^{i-1}) \land (c_{P_2}^i \Leftrightarrow c_{P_2}^{i-1}) \land (c_{P_3}^i \Leftrightarrow c_{P_3}^{i-1}) \land q_1^{i-1} \Rightarrow q_1^i\}.$$

In the case of a single car leaving the intersection, Alice would advance by one in the queue, described as follows

$$\mathfrak{g}_1 = \{(c_{P_1}^i \Leftrightarrow c_{P_1}^{i-1}) \land (\neg c_{P_2}^i \land c_{P_2}^{i-1}) \land (\neg c_{P_3}^i \land c_{P_3}^{i-1}) \land q_4^{i-1} \Rightarrow q_3,$$
$$(c_{P_1}^i \Leftrightarrow c_{P_1}^{i-1}) \land (\neg c_{P_2}^i \land c_{P_2}^{i-1}) \land (\neg c_{P_3}^i \land c_{P_3}^{i-1}) \land q_3^{i-1} \Rightarrow q_2,$$
$$(c_{P_1}^i \Leftrightarrow c_{P_1}^{i-1}) \land (\neg c_{P_2}^i \land c_{P_2}^{i-1}) \land (\neg c_{P_3}^i \land c_{P_3}^{i-1}) \land q_2^{i-1} \Rightarrow q_1,$$
$$(\neg c_{P_1}^i \land c_{P_1}^{i-1}) \land (c_{P_2}^i \Leftrightarrow c_{P_2}^{i-1}) \land (\neg c_{P_3}^i \land c_{P_3}^{i-1}) \land q_4^{i-1} \Rightarrow q_3,$$
$$(\neg c_{P_1}^i \land c_{P_1}^{i-1}) \land (c_{P_2}^i \Leftrightarrow c_{P_2}^{i-1}) \land (\neg c_{P_3}^i \land c_{P_3}^{i-1}) \land q_3^{i-1} \Rightarrow q_2,$$
$$(\neg c_{P_1}^i \land c_{P_1}^{i-1}) \land (c_{P_2}^i \Leftrightarrow c_{P_2}^{i-1}) \land (\neg c_{P_3}^i \land c_{P_3}^{i-1}) \land q_2^{i-1} \Rightarrow q_1,$$
$$(\neg c_{P_1}^i \land c_{P_1}^{i-1}) \land (\neg c_{P_2}^i \land c_{P_2}^{i-1}) \land (c_{P_3}^i \Leftrightarrow c_{P_3}^{i-1}) \land q_4^{i-1} \Rightarrow q_3,$$
$$(\neg c_{P_1}^i \land c_{P_1}^{i-1}) \land (\neg c_{P_2}^i \land c_{P_2}^{i-1}) \land (c_{P_3}^i \Leftrightarrow c_{P_3}^{i-1}) \land q_3^{i-1} \Rightarrow q_2,$$
$$(\neg c_{P_1}^i \land c_{P_1}^{i-1}) \land (\neg c_{P_2}^i \land c_{P_2}^{i-1}) \land (c_{P_3}^i \Leftrightarrow c_{P_3}^{i-1}) \land q_2^{i-1} \Rightarrow q_1\}.$$

If any two cars leave the intersection, Alice would advance in the queue by two steps, given by the following

$$\begin{aligned}
\mathfrak{g}_2 = \{&(c^i_{P_1} \Leftrightarrow c^{i-1}_{P_1}) \wedge (\neg c^i_{P_2} \wedge c^{i-1}_{P_2}) \wedge (\neg c^i_{P_3} \wedge c^{i-1}_{P_3}) \wedge q^{i-1}_4 \Rightarrow q_3, \\
&(c^i_{P_1} \Leftrightarrow c^{i-1}_{P_1}) \wedge (\neg c^i_{P_2} \wedge c^{i-1}_{P_2}) \wedge (\neg c^i_{P_3} \wedge c^{i-1}_{P_3}) \wedge q^{i-1}_3 \Rightarrow q_1, \\
&(\neg c^i_{P_1} \wedge c^{i-1}_{P_1}) \wedge (c^i_{P_2} \Leftrightarrow c^{i-1}_{P_2}) \wedge (\neg c^i_{P_3} \wedge c^{i-1}_{P_3}) \wedge q^{i-1}_4 \Rightarrow q_3, \\
&(\neg c^i_{P_1} \wedge c^{i-1}_{P_1}) \wedge (c^i_{P_2} \Leftrightarrow c^{i-1}_{P_2}) \wedge (\neg c^i_{P_3} \wedge c^{i-1}_{P_3}) \wedge q^{i-1}_3 \Rightarrow q_1, \\
&(\neg c^i_{P_1} \wedge c^{i-1}_{P_1}) \wedge (\neg c^i_{P_2} \wedge c^{i-1}_{P_2}) \wedge (c^i_{P_3} \Leftrightarrow c^{i-1}_{P_3}) \wedge q^{i-1}_4 \Rightarrow q_3, \\
&(\neg c^i_{P_1} \wedge c^{i-1}_{P_1}) \wedge (\neg c^i_{P_2} \wedge c^{i-1}_{P_2}) \wedge (c^i_{P_3} \Leftrightarrow c^{i-1}_{P_3}) \wedge q^{i-1}_3 \Rightarrow q_1\}.
\end{aligned}$$

If all three cars left the intersection in this timestep, Alice would move from 4th position to the 1st position in the queue, this is given by

$$\mathfrak{g}_3 = \{((\neg c^i_{P_1} \wedge c^{i-1}_{P_1}) \wedge (\neg c^i_{P_2} \wedge c^{i-1}_{P_2}) \wedge (\neg c^i_{P_3} \wedge c^{i-1}_{P_3}) \wedge q^{i-1}_4 \Rightarrow q_1)\}.$$

Additionally, if Alice is in the first spot, it will stay in this spot until it takes its turn, $\mathfrak{g}_4 = \{q^{i-1}_1 \Rightarrow q_1\}$. The Planner guarantees are thus given as

$$\mathfrak{g}_{\text{planner}} = \mathfrak{g}_0 \cup \mathfrak{g}_1 \cup \mathfrak{g}_2 \cup \mathfrak{g}_3 \cup \mathfrak{g}_4.$$

The Tracker component ensures that Alice will only move into the intersection if it has the right of way. The contract is given as

$$\mathcal{C}_{\text{tracker}} = \{\{q^i_1, \text{icy\_roads}\}, \{v^i\}, \mathfrak{a}_{\text{tracker}}, \mathfrak{g}_{\text{tracker}}\},$$

with the input variables whether it is Alice's turn (q^i_1 provided by the Planner, and the output variable being Alice's speed v^i (where v evaluating to True corresponds to a positive speed). The assumptions are $\mathfrak{a}_{Tracker} = \{\neg\text{icy\_roads}\}$, and the guarantees are $\mathfrak{g} = \{q^i_1 \Leftrightarrow v^i\}$. This ensures that only when q^i_1 is True, Alice will move into the intersection with a positive speed. In addition to the above explained component assumptions and guarantees, the three components also contain additional assumptions and guarantees that are unrelated to the process of determining whether it is Alice's turn. These other guarantees represent different viewpoints of the components, and we will show that our framework accurately pinpoints the potential causes within the relevant terms outlined above. For each component, we added 100 input and output variables, and 100 component guarantees each, which result in 100 system observations per timestep (tracker output variables), as shown in gray in Fig. 4. These variables and their interactions correspond to other component functionalities of Alice's system.

Next, we compose Alice's system for one timestep by composing the contracts in their provided composition order $\texttt{CompOrd} = [\mathcal{C}_{\text{perception}}, \mathcal{C}_{\text{planner}}, \mathcal{C}_{\text{tracker}}]$. We can then compose the system for a sequence of time steps, which allows us to evaluate the system behavior using the system-level variables. This composition is shown in Fig. 4. The resulting system contract comprises 212 guarantee terms, each involving a logical statement with some being lengthy and complex. We are given the test trace as valuations of the variables for a series of time steps shown in Table 1. The trace contains the observations of the other cars in the intersection, and the visibility and road conditions. Alice's system-level output is its speed v^i and the additional tracker output variables (not shown in the table). The internal variables are not accessible from the system level, except for the initial timestep as we require an initial condition as input for our contracts.

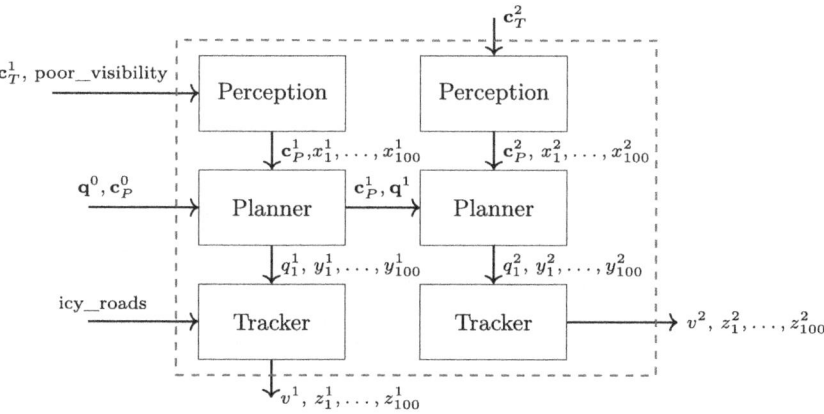

Fig. 4. Two-step execution of a perception–planner–tracker pipeline with intermediate signals. The bold variables denote vectors of the indicator variables.

Table 1. System-level violating trace (relevant variables)

Time step i	poor_visibility	icy_roads	$c^i_{T_1}$	$c^i_{T_2}$	$c^i_{T_3}$	$c^i_{P_1}$	$c^i_{P_2}$	$c^i_{P_3}$	q^i_1	q^i_2	q^i_3	q^i_4	v^i
0	0	0	1	1	1	1	1	1	0	0	0	1	0
1	0	0	1	1	1	–	–	–	–	–	–	–	1
2	0	0	1	1	1	–	–	–	–	–	–	–	1

We can now analyze the given trace and we notice that five of the 212 system-level guarantees are violated. We use the diagnostics process to track these guarantees to the possible component causes, which requires us to check 50 component-level statements (out of 656 total). Using this framework, we only have to check 7.6% of the component level terms. This now guides the debugging process to access the relevant internal variables to evaluate the component-level statements and we will identify that the perception component did not provide its guarantees and did not detect the cars in time step 1. For implementation details, please refer to the notebook in this repository[1].

---

[1] https://github.com/pacti-org/cs-selfdriving-diagnostics.

5 Conclusion and Future Work

In this paper, we proposed a diagnostics methodology based on assume-guarantee contracts using Pacti, a tool for compositional system analysis and design. We formally characterized when a system-level guarantee failure can be traced to a component, defined the required structure for contract composition, and identified the information that must be stored to enable diagnostics.

The diagnostics framework involves composing the system, generating a diagnostics map, and systematically checking component-level guarantees and assumptions using log data. We show that if the log contains valuations of the full system state, the method reliably identifies the responsible component. By focusing on the most relevant contract terms first, the approach often reduces the number of evaluated statements. In the worst case, all component-level contracts must be checked—but the framework prioritizes likely culprits and can significantly reduce effort in practice.

We demonstrated the methodology on abstract examples and two simplified scenarios inspired by real-world autonomous system tests. As future work, we plan to explore connections to behavior explainability in robotics. While our current method uses the contract composition operator, a similar approach could be developed using the contract quotient to identify missing components and trace the origin of contract terms, offering additional insight into system behavior.

Acknowledgments. This work was funded by the Air Force Office of Scientific Research (grant number FA9550-22-1-0333).

References

1. Beard, R.V.: Failure accomodation in linear systems through self-reorganization. Ph.D. thesis, Massachusetts Institute of Technology (1971)
2. Benveniste, A., Caillaud, B., Ferrari, A., Mangeruca, L., Passerone, R., Sofronis, C.: Multiple viewpoint contract-based specification and design. In: de Boer, F.S., Bonsangue, M.M., Graf, S., de Roever, W.-P. (eds.) FMCO 2007. LNCS, vol. 5382, pp. 200–225. Springer, Heidelberg (2008). https://doi.org/10.1007/978-3-540-92188-2_9
3. Boteanu, A., Arkin, J., Patki, S., Howard, T., Kress-Gazit, H.: Robot-initiated specification repair through grounded language interaction. arXiv preprint arXiv:1710.01417 (2017)
4. Burdick, J.W., DuToit, N., Howard, A., Looman, C., Ma, J., Murray, R.M., Wongpiromsarn, T.: Sensing, navigation and reasoning technologies for the DARPA urban challenge. Tech. Rep, DARPA Urban Challenge Final Report (2007)
5. Chen, J., Patton, R.J.: Robust model-based fault diagnosis for dynamic systems, vol. 3. Springer Science & Business Media (2012)
6. Chi, Y., Dong, Y., Wang, Z.J., Yu, F.R., Leung, V.C.: Knowledge-based fault diagnosis in industrial internet of things: a survey. IEEE Internet Things J. **9**(15), 12886–12900 (2022)

7. Cimatti, A., Grosen, T.M., Larsen, K.G., Tonetta, S., Zimmermann, M.: Exploiting assumptions for effective monitoring of real-time properties under partial observability. In: Madeira, A., Knapp, A. (eds.) Software Engineering and Formal Methods, pp. 70–88. Springer Nature Switzerland, Cham (2025). https://doi.org/10.1007/978-3-031-77382-2_5
8. Cimatti, A., Tian, C., Tonetta, S.: Assumption-based runtime verification with partial observability and resets. In: Finkbeiner, B., Mariani, L. (eds.) RV 2019. LNCS, vol. 11757, pp. 165–184. Springer, Cham (2019). https://doi.org/10.1007/978-3-030-32079-9_10
9. Cobleigh, J.M., Giannakopoulou, D., PǎsǎReanu, C.S.: Learning assumptions for compositional verification. In: Garavel, H., Hatcliff, J. (eds.) TACAS 2003. LNCS, vol. 2619, pp. 331–346. Springer, Heidelberg (2003). https://doi.org/10.1007/3-540-36577-X_24
10. De Kleer, J., Williams, B.C.: Diagnosing multiple faults. Artifi. Intell. **32**(1), 97–130 (1987)
11. Dijkstra, E.W.: Guarded commands, nondeterminacy and formal derivation of programs. Commun. ACM **18**(8), 453–457 (1975)
12. Gao, Z., Cecati, C., Ding, S.X.: A survey of fault diagnosis and fault-tolerant techniques–part i: fault diagnosis with model-based and signal-based approaches. IEEE Trans. Industr. Electron. **62**(6), 3757–3767 (2015)
13. Goyal, S., Griggio, A., Tonetta, S.: Leveraging contracts for failure monitoring and identification in automated driving systems. In: Madeira, A., Knapp, A. (eds.) Software Engineering and Formal Methods, pp. 441–460. Springer Nature Switzerland, Cham (2025)
14. Graebener, J.B.M.: Formal Methods for Test and Evaluation: Reasoning over Tests, Automated Test Synthesis, and System Diagnostics. Ph.D. thesis, California Institute of Technology (2024)
15. Henzinger, T.A., Saraç, N.E.: Monitorability under assumptions. In: Deshmukh, J., Ničković, D. (eds.) RV 2020. LNCS, vol. 12399, pp. 3–18. Springer, Cham (2020). https://doi.org/10.1007/978-3-030-60508-7_1
16. Incer, I.: The Algebra of Contracts. Ph.D. thesis, EECS Department, University of California, Berkeley (2022)
17. Incer, I.: An adjunction between Boolean algebras and a subcategory of stone algebras. Theory Appl. Categ. **41**, Paper No. 57, 2041–2057 (2024)
18. Incer, I., et al.: Pacti: assume-guarantee contracts for efficient compositional analysis and design. ACM Trans. Cyber-Phys. Syst. **9**(1), 1–35 (2025)
19. Lamport, L.: win and sin: predicate transformers for concurrency. ACM Trans. Programming Lang. Syst. (TOPLAS) **12**(3), 396–428 (1990)
20. Mallozzi, P., Incer, I., Nuzzo, P., Sangiovanni-Vincentelli, A.: Contract-based specification refinement and repair for mission planning. In: 2023 IEEE/ACM 11th International Conference on Formal Methods in Software Engineering (FormaliSE), pp. 29–38. IEEE (2023)
21. Meyer, B.: Applying 'design by contract'. Computer **25**(10), 40–51 (1992)
22. Niemann, H.: A setup for active fault diagnosis. IEEE Trans. Autom. Control **51**(9), 1572–1578 (2006)
23. Nuzzo, P., Sangiovanni-Vincentelli, A.L., Bresolin, D., Geretti, L., Villa, T.: A platform-based design methodology with contracts and related tools for the design of cyber-physical systems. Proc. IEEE **103**(11), 2104–2132 (2015)
24. Raman, V., Kress-Gazit, H.: Explaining impossible high-level robot behaviors. IEEE Trans. Rob. **29**(1), 94–104 (2012)

25. Reiter, R.: A theory of diagnosis from first principles. Artif. Intell. **32**(1), 57–95 (1987)
26. Sangiovanni-Vincentelli, A.L., Damm, W., Passerone, R.: Taming Dr. Frankenstein: contract-based design for cyber-physical systems. Eur. J. Control **18**(3), 217–238 (2012). https://doi.org/10.3166/ejc.18.217-238
27. van Schrick, D.: Remarks on terminology in the field of supervision, fault detection and diagnosis. IFAC Proceedings Volumes **30**(18), 959–964 (1997)
28. Varanasi, S.C., et al.: Trace: toolkit for requirements analysis, capture, and elicitation. In: Dutle, A., Humphrey, L., Titolo, L. (eds.) NASA Formal Methods, pp. 380–399. Springer Nature Switzerland, Cham (2025). https://doi.org/10.1007/978-3-031-93706-4_22

Statistical Runtime Verification for LLMs via Robustness Estimation

Natan Levy, Adiel Ashrov[(✉)], and Guy Katz

The Hebrew University of Jerusalem, Jerusalem, Israel
{natan.levy1,adiel.ashrov,g.katz}@mail.huji.ac.il

Abstract. Adversarial robustness verification is essential for ensuring the safe deployment of Large Language Models (LLMs) in runtime-critical applications. However, formal verification techniques remain computationally infeasible for modern LLMs due to their exponential runtime and white-box access requirements. This paper presents a case study adapting and extending the RoMA statistical verification framework to assess its feasibility as an online runtime robustness monitor for LLMs in black-box deployment settings. Our adaptation of RoMA analyzes confidence score distributions under semantic perturbations to provide quantitative robustness assessments with statistically validated bounds. Our empirical validation against formal verification baselines demonstrates that RoMA achieves comparable accuracy (within 1% deviation), and reduces verification times from hours to minutes. We evaluate this framework across semantic, categorial, and orthographic perturbation domains. Our results demonstrate RoMA's effectiveness for robustness monitoring in operational LLM deployments. These findings point to RoMA as a potentially scalable alternative when formal methods are infeasible, with promising implications for runtime verification in LLM-based systems.

Keywords: LLM safety · Neural Network Verification · LLM verification · Robustness

1 Introduction

Large Language Models (LLMs) such as GPT, BERT, and LLaMA [9,43,49] operate over sequences of embedded tokens and obtain state-of-the-art results across diverse domains, demonstrating unprecedented capabilities in natural language understanding, reasoning, and generation tasks [35,41,49]. This success has driven their rapid deployment across virtually every sector, from medicine [14] and education [31] to scientific research [11] and creative industries [57]. LLMs are increasingly being integrated into safety-critical domains such as autonomous systems [18], legal decision-making [7], and healthcare [14], where their deployment will only continue to expand. However, as LLMs become widespread in

---

N. Levy and A. Ashrov—Equal contribution.

© The Author(s), under exclusive license to Springer Nature Switzerland AG 2026
B. Könighofer and H. Torfah (Eds.): RV 2025, LNCS 16087, pp. 457–476, 2026.
https://doi.org/10.1007/978-3-032-05435-7_25

applications where failures can lead to severe consequences, ensuring these powerful models are safe becomes crucial.

LLMs, like their Deep Neural Network (DNN) predecessors, are highly vulnerable to *adversarial perturbations*: subtle modifications to input data that can cause incorrect outputs [3,47]. In contrast to adversarial attacks in computer vision, these perturbations in natural language are often coherent and contextually meaningful [39], making them particularly challenging to detect using traditional validation methods [34]. This fragility poses significant risks in safety-critical systems, highlighting the need for runtime verification tools capable of monitoring LLM behavior during real-world deployment.

Formal verification methods [5,23] provide strong theoretical guarantees but scale poorly with large models, making them impractical for billion-parameter LLMs [24,52]. Statistical methods [8,17,54] offer better scalability but often rely on assumptions like Lipschitz continuity or Gaussian distributions, which are frequently violated in transformer-based models [26]. While several runtime verification techniques have been developed for neural networks, they are unsuitable for LLMs: Activation-based monitors [15,16] require white-box access to model internals, and dynamic reachability methods like POLAR-Express [55] assume explicit system dynamics incompatible with natural language. These limitations highlight the critical gap in runtime verification capabilities for modern language models.

To address the gap in runtime verification for LLMs, we propose adapting the *Robustness Measurement and Assessment (RoMA)* method [29] as a statistical framework for real-time robustness monitoring in operational environments. RoMA operates as a black-box framework, requiring no access to model internals, and efficiently handles high-dimensional inputs while empirically validating its statistical assumptions. These properties make RoMA particularly well-suited to overcome the limitations of existing verification approaches that fail to scale to modern LLMs. While RoMA has been used in the original study for vision classification tasks on small-scale networks, it has not previously been tested or adapted for LLMs, which is a novel contribution of this work.

This work presents a case study demonstrating the adaptation and extension of RoMA from offline image verification to online runtime monitoring for LLMs in operational environments. We perform an empirical evaluation of BERT-based [9] sentiment classifiers on the SST-2 dataset [46], examining three core robustness dimensions: (i) *embedding robustness*, which measures how sensitive the model is to semantic perturbations in the Word2Vec [33] embedding space; (ii) *categorial robustness*, measuring systematic performance differences across sentiment classes; and (iii) *orthographic robustness*, measuring model tolerance to typographical errors in real-world text. Our experimental results demonstrate that our adapted RoMA framework achieves computational efficiency suitable for runtime deployment: with 50% of SST-2 sentences were processed within 15 min, with full evaluation completed in under 36 min. Our robustness assessment reveals that optimally trained models maintain 97.18% robustness under semantic perturbations. Categorial analysis indicates systematic robustness differences of up to 1.5% across sentiment classes. Additionally, orthographic analysis shows 94.44% robustness under typographical errors. Taken together, these findings suggest that our adapted RoMA framework offers a scalable approach for runtime verification in LLMs.

An important consideration for statistical verification frameworks is whether they can deliver sufficiently accurate robustness estimates for practical deployment. To address this question, we empirically validate RoMA's accuracy against the *Exact Count* formal verification algorithm [32], which provides precise robustness measurements. We conduct systematic experiments across synthetic neural network models and the ACAS Xu safety-critical aviation benchmark [21,22] that appeared in the original Exact Count study. Our evaluation demonstrates that RoMA estimates robustness within 1% deviation from Exact Count's results while reducing verification time from hours to minutes. This efficiency suggests that statistical frameworks like RoMA could be suitable for runtime monitoring, potentially helping to narrow the gap between theoretical robustness guarantees and practical operational constraints, though broader validation is needed to fully assess their applicability.

To summarize, our contributions include: (i) adapting and extending RoMA from offline CNN verification to an online black-box runtime monitor for LLMs, (ii) empirically validating its accuracy against formal verification baselines, showing comparable accuracy with reduced computational requirements, and (iii) demonstrating its application across embedding, categorial, and orthographic perturbation domains relevant to NLP deployments.

The rest of the paper is organized as follows. In Sect. 2, we provide the necessary background to contextualize our work. In Sect. 3 we review the related work to this paper. Building on this foundation, Sect. 4 introduces our proposed framework, detailing the methodology for assessing LLM robustness. In Sect. 5, we present our experimental setup, evaluation metrics, and empirical findings, offering insights into the robustness profiles of widely-used LLMs. Finally, in Sect. 6, we summarize our contributions and outline future research aimed at enhancing the reliability and trustworthiness of language models in real-world applications.

2 Background

DNNs, Adversarial Perturbations, and Robustness. A DNN N is defined as a function $N : \mathbb{R}^n \to \mathbb{R}^m$ that maps an input vector $\boldsymbol{x} \in \mathbb{R}^n$ to an output vector $\boldsymbol{y} \in \mathbb{R}^m$. In this work, we focus on classification networks, where an input $\boldsymbol{x}$ is classified as label l when $\arg\max(N(\boldsymbol{x})) = l$. In such networks, the final layer is usually a *softmax layer*, whose outputs are commonly interpreted as *confidence scores*.

In real-world settings, models are often exposed to *adversarial perturbations*: input modifications that cause misclassification yet remain imperceptible to human operators [6,12]. This vulnerability is particularly problematic for runtime-critical systems, which require mechanisms to monitor model behavior during operation and detect such adversarial perturbations.

Local robustness quantifies a network's resilience within some input bounds [24]:

Definition 1. *A DNN N is ϵ-locally-robust at input point x_0 if and only if*

$$\forall x. \|x - x_0\|_\infty \leq \epsilon \Rightarrow \arg\max(N(x)) = \arg\max(N(x_0))$$

Intuitively, Definition 1 specifies that a DNN is locally robust if, for all input vectors x within an ϵ-ball centered at a fixed input vector x_0, the network assigns the same label to x as it does to x_0. Verifying local robustness is computationally intractable for large networks due to its NP-complete nature [23]. As a result, runtime verification must often rely on *probabilistic* estimates of robustness.

Definition 2. *The probabilistic-local-robustness (plr) score of a DNN N at input point x_0, abbreviated $plr_\epsilon(N, x_0)$, is defined as:*

$$plr_\epsilon(N, x_0) \triangleq P_{x:\|x-x_0\|_\infty \leq \epsilon}(\arg\max(N(x)) = \arg\max(N(x_0)))$$

The plr score quantifies the likelihood that predictions remain unchanged within an ϵ-ball and is particularly suitable for runtime certification under uncertainty [27]. Approximating plr efficiently enables real-time assessment of robustness in black-box settings [8,17,54]. This probabilistic measure aligns with certification standards requiring quantitative failure probability assessments, such as ARP 4754 guidelines [27], while remaining computationally feasible for runtime evaluation.

Statistical Verification Under Runtime Constraints. Statistical verification methods hold significant potential for addressing the scalability challenges that limit formal verification approaches. Here, we set out to examine this possibility by systematically evaluating statistical verification for LLM runtime monitoring.

The first approach involves methods that rely on *Gaussian distributional assumptions*, such as randomized smoothing techniques [8]. However, these assumptions are frequently violated in transformer-based models [13]. The second approach is *importance sampling* techniques such as [54], but these can exhibit sensitivity to outlier samples, resulting in erratic monitoring behavior. Several approaches, such as Lipschitz-margin training [50] and spectral norm regularization [56], assume *Lipschitz-continuity*, but these constants may not be well-defined for contemporary transformer architectures [26]. Finally, we select RoMA [29] as our statistical verification framework for LLM runtime monitoring because it addresses these limitations through several distinguishing characteristics.

RoMA [29] and gRoMA [30] are black-box robustness estimation frameworks designed to evaluate the robustness of DNNs. These methods analyze confidence scores from thousands of uniformly-sampled perturbations around an input point, employing Anderson-Darling goodness-of-fit [1] testing to validate normal distribution assumptions. When necessary, they apply the Box-Cox power transformation [4] to achieve normality, enabling reliable probabilistic analysis. Specifically, RoMA focuses on the second-highest confidence score across all classes (the runner-up class), which reflects the margin between the predicted label and the nearest alternative. By analyzing the distribution of these scores across perturbations, RoMA quantifies how close the model is to misclassification, providing a sensitive measure of local robustness tied to Definition 2. This approach enables probabilistic assessment of model reliability under the input variations encountered during operational deployment.

RoMA's key runtime advantages include no white-box access requirements, making it compatible with proprietary model deployments, empirically validated statistical assumptions that ensure distributional validity, and consistent computational overhead with linear scaling that enables predictable runtime resource consumption. Although RoMA was originally evaluated on vision tasks (CIFAR-10), it has not yet been extended to the unique challenges of high-dimensional NLP tasks. This gap is addressed in our work, where we apply the RoMA framework to LLMs, demonstrating its effectiveness in this new domain.

3 Related Work

Robustness to Text Perturbations in Language Models. The robustness of language models to text perturbations is a vital research area, particularly as LLMs are increasingly deployed in real-world applications. Jin et al. [19] explored BERT's vulnerability to adversarial attacks with *TextFooler*, a method that generates adversarial examples through synonym replacement, revealing that even advanced models can be misled by subtle changes. In addition, Singh et al. [45] conducted a comprehensive analysis of LLM robustness to systematic text perturbations across different architectures and tasks, demonstrating that model behavior can be highly sensitive to small input changes. Finally, Romero-Alvarado et al. [42] investigated language models' resilience to various perturbation types, revealing systematic brittleness patterns across different input categories. While these studies provide valuable insights into LLM vulnerabilities through offline analysis, RoMA differentiates itself by enabling black-box statistical verification with quantitative robustness bounds designed for continuous monitoring during operational deployment.

DNN Enable Monitor (DEM). A closely related approach is *DNN Enable Monitor (DEM)* [25], which provides output-centric, black-box certification for DNNs in safety-critical aerospace settings. While both DEM and our method rely on perturbation-based analysis without requiring model internals, they differ in scope and methodology. DEM applies hypothesis testing to detect adversarial inputs in image classifiers based on label consistency, producing binary accept/reject outcomes. Additionally, DEM requires a lengthy and sensitive calibration process before deployment, whereas our RoMA framework operates without any calibration requirements. Our RoMA-based framework targets LLMs and computes continuous robustness scores via distributional analysis of runner-up confidence margins under semantic, categorial, and orthographic perturbations. This enables more expressive and fine-grained monitoring suited to natural language domains.

Runtime Monitoring for Neural Networks. Runtime monitoring techniques for neural networks follow several paradigms. *POLAR-Express* [55] performs online reachability analysis in NN-controlled systems, enabling dynamic controller switching upon detecting unsafe states. The combined *Gaussian and Outside-the-Box monitor* [15] detects *out-of-distribution (OOD)* inputs via activation-based analysis, blending neuron-wise Gaussian modeling with clustering. Similarly, the *box-based monitor for YOLO* [16] constructs hyper-rectangular activation zones to identify OOD behavior at runtime. While effective, these approaches rely on binary decisions and require access to internal activations [15,16] or explicit dynamics [55]. In contrast, RoMA's black-box methodology supports scalable, model-agnostic monitoring for LLMs, providing probabilistic robustness estimates that capture nuanced behavior under realistic input shifts.

4 Method: Statistical Distribution Analysis for LLM Classification Resilience

The RoMA framework is a statistical verification technique originally developed to assess the robustness of image classifiers. RoMA operates as a black-box method, meaning it requires no access to internal model weights or gradients. Instead, it evaluates robustness by sampling perturbations around a given input and analyzing their effect on the model's confidence scores. A key innovation of RoMA is its focus on the *runner-up confidence score*—the second-highest class probability—across perturbed inputs. This score serves as a proxy for how close the model is to changing its prediction. For example, consider a classifier that assigns cat to an image with 92% confidence and dog with 8%. If slight perturbations cause the runner-up score (dog) to rise significantly, this indicates an unstable prediction. RoMA collects thousands of such perturbed inputs, tests whether the runner-up scores follow a normal distribution using the Anderson-Darling test [1], and applies the Box-Cox transformation [4] if needed to enforce normality. This enables robust estimation of the probability that random perturbations will flip the classification, providing a quantitative measure of local robustness (plr).

While RoMA was originally designed for image classifiers, extending it to LLMs introduces several significant challenges. First, unlike images, where perturbations involve continuous pixel value changes, language inputs consist of discrete tokens embedded in high-dimensional semantic spaces. Text perturbations must preserve syntactic validity and semantic meaning, and arbitrary token replacements can easily produce nonsensical inputs. Second, in practical deployment settings, LLMs are typically accessed as black-box services via APIs, providing only output probabilities without access to internal embeddings or model parameters. Third, the distributional assumptions underpinning RoMA, particularly the normality of runner-up confidence scores, are not guaranteed to hold for natural language data, which exhibits complex statistical patterns distinct from image data. These challenges necessitate fundamental adaptations in how perturbations are generated, how model responses are analyzed, and how statistical validity is ensured for NLP applications.

Word embeddings play a central role in natural language processing by mapping discrete words to continuous high-dimensional vectors that capture semantic similarity. In this space, words with related meanings are located near one another, enabling quantitative reasoning over language. Embedding models such as Word2Vec [33], GloVe [38], and contextualized embeddings from transformers like BERT [9] allow us to compare words using cosine similarity, facilitating controlled semantic perturbations without compromising linguistic validity. In our adaptation, we use pre-trained Word2Vec embeddings as a lightweight and interpretable basis for generating meaning-preserving input variations. While Word2Vec was chosen for its simplicity and transparency, our framework is general and can accommodate other perturbation techniques, such as paraphrasing or syntactic restructuring, which may further enhance robustness evaluation.

Building on this embedding-based representation of semantic similarity, we adapt RoMA's perturbation strategy to the linguistic domain. Instead of injecting pixel-level noise as in vision tasks, we introduce semantically meaningful perturbations by replacing words with similar alternatives in the embedding space. Specifically, we use Word2Vec embeddings to identify replacement candidates whose cosine similarity to the original word exceeds a threshold of $1 - \epsilon$, where ϵ is derived from the original RoMA framework and controls the magnitude of allowed semantic drift. This constraint ensures that perturbed sentences remain semantically coherent while still exploring the model's decision boundaries. For example, with $\epsilon = 0.35$ (as used in our experiments), when perturbing the word "good" in the sentence "This movie is really good", we might select "great" (word similarity to "good": 0.68) or "excellent" (word similarity to "good": 0.73), yielding variants such as "This movie is really great" and "This movie is really excellent". By generating hundreds of such semantically constrained perturbations and analyzing the resulting confidence distributions, our adaptation enables RoMA's statistical framework to operate on LLMs while preserving the black-box deployment setting required for runtime verification.

Several perturbation strategies have been explored for evaluating LLM robustness, each with trade-offs that limit their applicability for runtime verification. One approach perturbs internal model embeddings directly by modifying hidden layer activations [44], but this requires white-box access incompatible with most deployed systems. Another common strategy is character-level noise injection, simulating typographical errors by inserting or substituting letters [45]. While such perturbations may not always preserve full semantic coherence, they offer a lightweight and realistic proxy for input noise encountered in real-world deployments, and can still yield meaningful robustness estimates, as demonstrated in our orthographic robustness evaluation (See Sect. 5.4). Finally, semantic substitution, replacing words with meaning-preserving alternatives, offers the most promise for black-box runtime verification as it maintains linguistic validity while testing model stability. This approach, which we implement through controlled word embedding similarities, forms the foundation of our adaptation.

Our perturbation generation process systematically explores the semantic neighborhood around each input while maintaining linguistic validity. Given an input sentence, we first tokenize it and randomly select multiple word positions for perturbation, ensuring coverage across the entire sentence rather than concentrating changes in a single region. For each selected word, we query the Word2Vec [33] embedding space to retrieve semantically similar candidates whose cosine similarity exceeds a threshold of $(1-\epsilon)$. To preserve sentence quality, we filter out stopwords, proper nouns, and out-of-vocabulary terms that could compromise coherence. By sampling different combinations of word replacements across multiple positions, we generate up to 1,000 unique variants per sentence, sufficient for RoMA's statistical analysis while ensuring comprehensive exploration of the local semantic space. This structured approach balances semantic coverage with computational efficiency, enabling robust statistical estimation within runtime constraints.

For each perturbed variant generated from a given input sentence, we query the LLM sentiment classifier to obtain confidence scores for the positive and negative sentiment classes. Following the RoMA framework, we focus on the runner-up confidence score, which in binary sentiment analysis corresponds to the confidence score of the non-predicted class. For example, if the model predicts "positive" sentiment with 85% confidence, the runner-up score is 15% for "negative". A high runner-up score signals uncertainty and indicates that the model's prediction could easily flip under slight perturbations. By aggregating runner-up scores across all perturbations (up to 1,000 per sentence), we construct an empirical distribution that captures classification stability in the local semantic neighborhood. To validate this distribution for statistical analysis, we apply the Anderson-Darling goodness-of-fit test [1] to assess normality. When this assumption is violated, we apply the Box-Cox power transformation [4] to approximate normality and enable reliable probabilistic inference. This allows us to estimate the probability that a random semantic perturbation will cause the model to misclassify the sentiment, yielding a quantitative robustness score aligned with the probabilistic-local-robustness (plr) metric defined in Sect. 2.

While RoMA was originally designed as an offline evaluation tool for image classifiers, extending it to online runtime LLM verification required significant methodological modifications. These adjustments include developing semantically-constrained text perturbations (replacing pixel noise), validating statistical assumptions for transformer confidence distributions, and addressing the strict computational constraints of continuous monitoring. Our framework operates entirely through black-box API queries, making it suitable for proprietary LLM deployments where internal model access is unavailable. Perturbation analysis is performed during inference gaps or alongside batched requests, allowing for continuous robustness monitoring without disrupting service. The linear scalability of perturbation generation and consistent processing times support predictable resource allocation, which is critical for deployment scenarios where latency must remain bounded. In summary, our work transforms an offline framework into an online runtime verification system, demonstrating the potential of statistical verification for practical LLM monitoring in operational environments.

5 Evaluation

Our experimental evaluation comprises two complementary phases designed to establish both the empirical validity and practical applicability of our runtime verification framework. We first conduct an empirical validation of RoMA's statistical methodology against Exact Count, a formal verification baseline, to demonstrate precision and reliability on established benchmarks where ground truth verification is computationally feasible. This validates RoMA's statistical approach and quantifies its accuracy relative to exhaustive formal methods.

Subsequently, we demonstrate the framework's significance by applying it to contemporary LLM verification scenarios that exceed the computational scope of formal methods. Our evaluation addresses three dimensions of LLM verification: (i) embedding space robustness under semantic perturbations, (ii) categorial performance consistency across classification boundaries, and (iii) orthographic resilience to typographical variations commonly encountered in operational deployments. These evaluations collectively establish RoMA's capability to provide quantitative robustness guarantees for large-scale neural architectures while maintaining computational efficiency suitable for runtime monitoring.

All experiments were conducted on dedicated research infrastructure to ensure reproducible and controlled evaluation conditions. The baseline validation experiments (Sect. 5.1) utilized an AMD EPYC 7313 CPU with 128GB RAM and NVIDIA A10 GPU acceleration. The LLM verification experiments (Sects. 5.2, 5.3, and 5.4) were performed using equivalent computational resources with NVIDIA A5000 GPU acceleration to accommodate the increased memory requirements of transformer-based architectures. Complete implementation details, experimental configurations, and reproducibility materials are publicly available through our research repository [28], enabling independent validation and extension of our findings.

5.1 Validating RoMA Against Formal Verification

Formal verification methods provide mathematical guarantees by proving the absence of adversarial perturbations within specified input regions. If adversarial perturbations exist, a formal verifier will usually return a concrete example that demonstrates this. These techniques rely on SMT solving, abstract interpretation, or reachability analysis [5,23], and are implemented in tools such as Marabou [24], Beta-CROWN [52], and PyRAT [48]. However, to the best of our knowledge, such methods do not scale to the architectural complexity and size of modern LLMs, which include components like multi-head attention and large embedding layers. This motivates our use of smaller models, where exact robustness bounds remain tractable and can serve as a reliable reference.

Formal verification's primary strength is *soundness*: once verified, a property holds universally. However, their practical use in runtime scenarios is limited due to the following reasons: (i) the verification problem is NP complete [23], making it challenging for verifiers to scale to modern LLMs; (ii) verification techniques typically require white-box access to a model's parameters, which is often impossible; and (iii) the high latency of these approaches typically renders them unsuitable for deployment-time constraints.

The *Exact Count* algorithm [32] constitutes a formal methodology for the precise quantification of DNN safety violations through exhaustive domain analysis. This approach implements a systematic recursive partitioning strategy of the input space, decomposing it into regions that can be definitively classified according to their adherence to specified safety properties.

Exact Count computes the violation rate with mathematical precision, defined formally as the ratio of unsafe regions to the total input space volume. This metric provides an exact measure of the *probability of encountering adversarial perturbations*, which is $1 - \text{plr}$ as defined in Definition 2. This establishes a connection between formal verification and probabilistic robustness assessment.

However, the computational complexity of Exact Count, which increases exponentially with input dimensionality and network size, fundamentally constrains its practical application. Even for relatively small networks like those in the ACAS Xu collision avoidance systems [37] (approximately 300 neurons), Exact Count becomes computationally intractable within practical time limits. Our experimental evaluation shows that Exact Count consistently timed out after 24 h (See Table 1). This highlights the need for more scalable alternatives, such as RoMA, which was able to produce reliable estimates for the same models in under 16 min.

CountingProVe [32] offers a scalable, randomized alternative by sampling subregions and bounding the violation rate statistically. While more tractable, it sacrifices precision and requires repeated solver queries that limit its applicability in real-time systems.

We acknowledge that the feedforward networks and ACAS Xu models used in our formal validation differ from transformer-based LLMs in architectural complexity, including the presence of multi-head attention, positional encodings, and high-dimensional embeddings. While this validation demonstrates the statistical reliability of RoMA's methodology, it does not capture these LLM-specific characteristics. The LLM experiments in subsequent sections provide complementary evidence of RoMA's effectiveness on transformer architectures, although direct comparison with formal verification remains infeasible for such large-scale models.

Experimental Design. To establish the accuracy and reliability of our statistical verification framework, we conduct a comprehensive empirical validation against the Exact Count algorithm [32], a formal verification method that computes mathematically precise probabilistic robustness (plr) scores. While Exact

Table 1. RoMA vs. Exact Count—Robustness Measurement

Model	Exact Count			RoMA	
	Violation Rate	PLR	Run time	PLR	Run time
Model_2_20	20.88%	79.12%	794 s	79.24%	487 s
Model_2_56	55.44%	44.56%	374 s	45.56%	458 s
Model_2_68	68.20%	31.80%	211 s	32.06%	466 s
Model_5_09	10.60%	89.40%	2,636 s	90.36%	467 s
Model_5_50	50.33%	49.67%	3,696 s	49.52%	486 s
Model_5_95	95.35%	4.65%	3,561 s	4.59%	444 s
Model_10_76	—	—	24 h	22.78%	465 sec
ϕ_2 ACAS Xu_2.1	—	—	24 h	99.18%	775 s
ϕ_2 ACAS Xu_2.3	—	—	24 h	98.24%	638 s
ϕ_2 ACAS Xu_2.4	—	—	24 h	98.96%	915 s
ϕ_2 ACAS Xu_2.5	—	—	24 h	98.09%	679 s
ϕ_2 ACAS Xu_2.7	—	—	24 h	97.21%	616 s

Count provides definitive ground truth robustness measurements for small-scale neural networks, its exponential computational complexity fundamentally limits applicability to contemporary large-scale architectures. Nevertheless, it serves as an authoritative benchmark for evaluating the precision of RoMA's probabilistic approximations under rigorously controlled experimental conditions.

We implemented a complete reproduction of the Exact Count algorithm and conducted systematic experiments across two established benchmark suites from the original paper: (i) synthetic neural network models with varying architectural complexities, and (ii) the ACAS Xu safety-critical aviation collision avoidance benchmark [23], representing real-world verification challenges in autonomous systems. This benchmark selection ensures comprehensive evaluation across both controlled synthetic scenarios and practical safety-critical applications, providing robust validation of RoMA's statistical methodology across diverse verification contexts.

Results. The scalability advantages of RoMA become particularly pronounced for larger networks, including ACAS Xu benchmarks with property ϕ_2, where Exact Count consistently terminates with a timeout after 24 h of computation. In contrast, RoMA provides reliable and accurate robustness measurements in under 16 min for these identical verification challenges, demonstrating applicability to complex models that fundamentally exceed the computational reach of formal verification methods. These results, summarized in Table 1 and illustrated in Figs. 1 and 2, establish RoMA's capability to address the computational intractability barrier that prevents formal verification deployment in runtime scenarios.

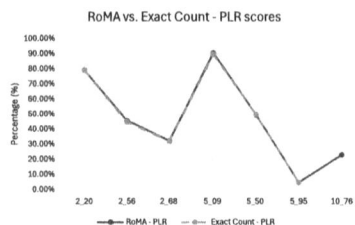
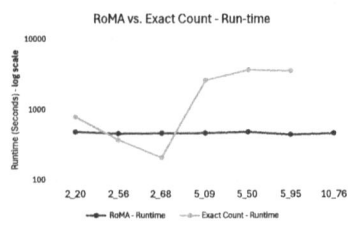
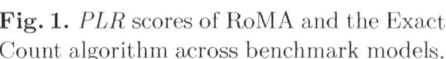

Fig. 1. *PLR* scores of RoMA and the Exact Count algorithm across benchmark models.

Fig. 2. Runtime comparison between RoMA and the Exact Count algorithm.

Implications for Runtime Verification. The experimental validation demonstrates that RoMA can bridge the gap between theoretical verification guarantees and practical runtime applicability. The consistent sub-1% accuracy achieved across diverse benchmark scenarios, combined with predictable computational overhead independent of model scale, establishes RoMA as a statistically accurate and operationally viable alternative to formal verification for large-scale neural network verification. While these empirical results cannot provide universal mathematical guarantees across all possible network architectures, they offer compelling evidence of RoMA's precision and computational efficiency across representative verification scenarios. This validation extends statistical verification to contemporary LLM architectures. The demonstrated reliability of RoMA's statistical methodology against formal verification baselines provides the necessary confidence to proceed with LLM verification applications, where ground truth formal verification is computationally infeasible but statistical reliability assessment remains critical for operational deployment.

5.2 Statistical Verification of LLM Embedding Robustness

Experimental Design. To demonstrate the practical applicability of our statistical verification framework for contemporary language models, we conducted a comprehensive robustness assessment on fine-tuned BERT architectures [9] using the SST-2 classification task from the GLUE benchmark [51]. This evaluation employs two distinct BERT-base-uncased variants [2] (110M parameters) to examine how training optimization affects distributional robustness under semantic perturbations. The GLUE dataset and BERT model have been widely used to evaluate generalization and robustness in NLP models, and have become the de-facto standard frameworks for such assessments. Our experimental design utilizes two model configurations representing different training strategies: M_{best}, corresponding to the optimal performance checkpoint during training, and M_{final}, representing the final training iteration.

For each of the 1,821 test sentences in the SST-2 evaluation set, we applied our semantic perturbation methodology to generate up to 1,000 variations per input, subsequently analyzing the distributional properties of runner-up confidence scores to assess classification stability. The statistical validation process revealed that confidence score distributions satisfied normality assumptions in 81.60% of cases for M_{best} and 75.07% for M_{final}, demonstrating the reliability of our distributional approach for the majority of inputs. This high rate of distributional normality validates the fundamental statistical assumptions underlying our verification framework, providing confidence in the reliability of probabilistic robustness estimates for operational LLM deployment scenarios.

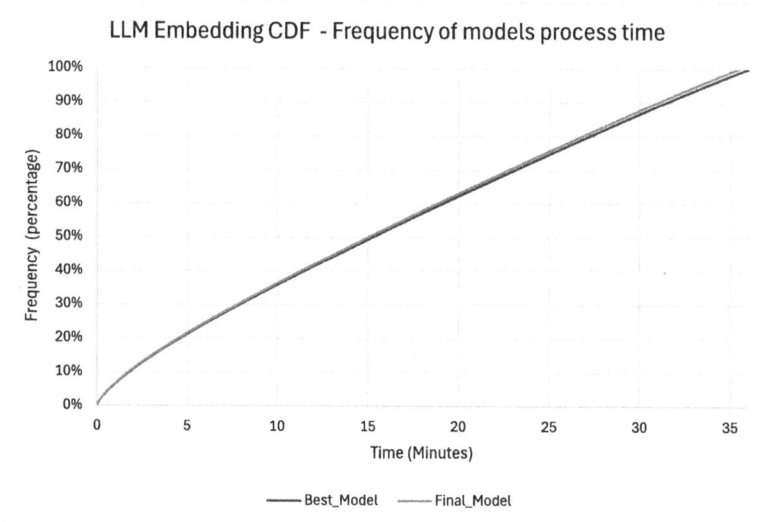

Fig. 3. Cumulative distribution function (CDF) showing the percentage of SST-2 dataset instances processed over time by RoMA in the LLM embedding case study for the two models.

Results. We quantified embedding robustness as the percentage of semantically perturbed inputs maintaining classification confidence scores above the 0.50 threshold for correct sentiment classification. Lower confidence scores indicate reduced classification certainty and potential vulnerability to distributional shifts encountered during runtime operation.

The robustness performance results show 97.18% robustness score for M_{best}, and 96.60% robustness score for M_{final}. The superior robustness exhibited by M_{best} supports the hypothesis that optimization for classification performance may simultaneously enhance resilience to semantic perturbations, a finding which is consistent with previous work on neural network robustness [29]. This correlation suggests that performance-driven training optimization can contribute to improved distributional stability, with important implications for model selection in runtime-critical applications.

Beyond robustness quantification, we evaluated the computational efficiency of our statistical verification approach to determine its viability for large-scale LLM assessment in production environments. Figure 3 presents the *Cumulative Distribution Function (CDF)* of RoMA processing times across the complete evaluation dataset. We observe that 50% of the instances were processed within 15 min, and the entire dataset was evaluated in under 36 min.

Implications for Runtime Verification. These results suggest that our statistical framework meets the performance demands of runtime monitoring in deployed LLM systems. By delivering timely robustness estimates based on semantically meaningful perturbations, our adaptation and extension of RoMA enables continuous assessment of classification stability during operation. This capability is essential for runtime verification pipelines that must monitor model behavior under distributional drift, without relying on white-box access or introducing latency that disrupts real-time service.

5.3 Categorial Robustness

Prior work in computer vision has established that neural network robustness exhibits significant variation across distinct input categories [29]. To examine whether this categorial heterogeneity extends to natural language processing architectures, we conducted a systematic analysis of distributional robustness patterns across sentiment classification categories using our statistical verification framework.

We define *categorial robustness* as the statistical measure of model resilience computed independently for each classification category, enabling identification of systematic vulnerabilities that may not be apparent in aggregate robustness assessments. For our binary sentiment analysis evaluation, we partitioned the SST-2 test dataset according to ground truth labels (positive and negative sentiment) and calculated category-specific robustness scores through our semantic perturbation methodology.

Experimental Design. Categorial Analysis Protocol: (i) Partition inputs by true classification labels to isolate category-specific behavior (ii) Apply the semantic perturbation framework independently within each category (iii) Compute distributional statistics for runner-up confidence scores per category (iv) Calculate category-specific robustness metrics using the 0.50 confidence threshold (v) Analyze asymmetric patterns across classification boundaries

Results. Our analysis reveals systematic variation in distributional robustness across categories, consistent with prior observations in computer vision architectures [29]. This suggests that asymmetries in categorial robustness may be an inherent property of neural networks. Figure 4 illustrates the categorial robustness across sentiment classes for both M_{best} and M_{final}.

Implications for Runtime Verification. These findings have important implications for runtime verification, as they highlight that model resilience is not uniformly distributed across classes. Runtime monitors must therefore account for

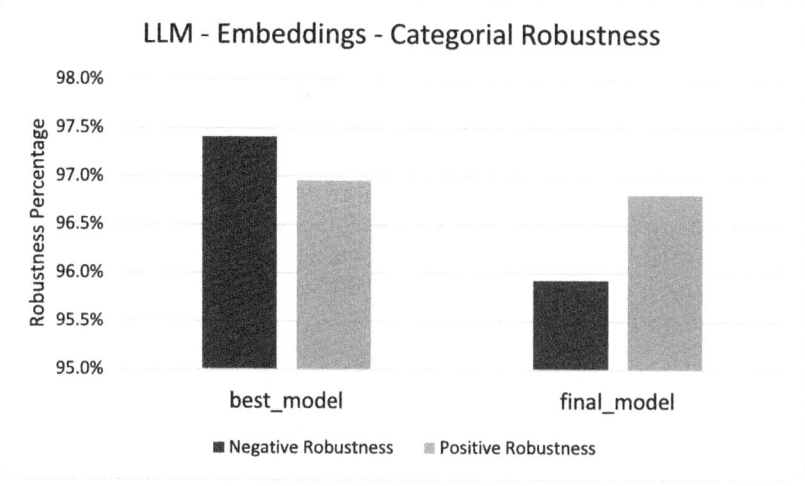

Fig. 4. A comparison of categorial robustness between M_{best} and M_{final}.

class-conditional robustness profiles to ensure reliable behavior across all inputs. Integrating category-aware metrics into verification pipelines can enable early detection of systematic vulnerabilities and support targeted mitigation strategies in safety-critical NLP applications.

5.4 Orthographic Perturbation Analysis for Runtime Input Validation

Experimental Design. To evaluate LLM resilience to typographical errors in operational environments, we implemented systematic character-level perturbations simulating common human typing mistakes. Specifically, each character in every word was systematically replaced with all possible alphabetic alternatives, generating a broad set of single-character substitution variants. While this method is simple by design, it provides comprehensive coverage of potential character-level noise in user input, such as accidental character substitutions (e.g., "great" → "grebt"). We limited perturbations to alphabetic characters, avoiding modifications to whitespace and punctuation. We acknowledge that this process does not replicate empirical human error distributions, but rather serves as a lightweight proxy for orthographic noise. Incorporating more realistic perturbation models, such as those based on keyboard adjacency or observed typo patterns, remains a promising direction for future work.

Results. Analysis of 500 SST-2 sentences with 500 character-level perturbations each revealed that runner-up confidence scores failed Anderson-Darling goodness-of-fit normality tests even after Box-Cox transformation. Despite non-normal distributions, our framework produced robustness estimates of 94.44% for M_{best} and 93.94% for M_{final}. To validate these estimates, we conducted an exhaustive evaluation across all 1,821 test sentences, yielding ground truth scores of 94.61% and 93.84% respectively.

Implications for Runtime Verification. This agreement between estimated and ground truth robustness scores (within 0.17%), provides preliminary evidence that RoMA may remain effective even when distributional assumptions such as normality are violated. This potential resilience is relevant for runtime verification, where inputs are often subject to noise, typographical errors, or other irregularities. While further validation is needed, these results suggest that statistically grounded robustness assessments could remain informative under realistic deployment conditions.

6 Conclusion and Future Work

This paper presented a case study on adapting and extending the RoMA framework for runtime robustness assessment of LLM systems. We examine the feasibility of applying statistical verification techniques for continuous reliability monitoring in black-box settings, where white-box access is not available. The case study illustrates how RoMA could potentially support LLM robustness auditing under practical deployment constraints. Preliminary empirical comparisons with the Exact Count formal verification baseline indicate that RoMA can approximate robustness within sub-1% error margins, while reducing computation time significantly. While these results are encouraging, they represent an initial step toward evaluating the role of statistical methods in runtime verification for large-scale models.

Technical Contributions. This study presents an initial exploration into adapting and extending RoMA for runtime robustness assessment of LLMs. The proposed methodology incorporates the following components: (i) an adaptation of RoMA from offline evaluation to online monitoring for language models in black-box settings, (ii) a semantic perturbation strategy based on word embedding transformations to examine distributional sensitivity, (iii) a categorial robustness analysis aimed at identifying potential variation in resilience across sentiment classes, and (iv) an orthographic perturbation evaluation designed to assess model behavior under character-level input noise. These contributions form the basis for assessing runtime behavior under realistic perturbation domains, though further validation is needed to generalize beyond the specific case study explored here.

Operational Impact. Our analysis suggests that robustness characteristics may vary across models and input categories, highlighting the potential value of adaptive monitoring strategies in practice. The statistical nature of the proposed methodology, which does not rely on internal model access, indicates that it may be applicable to a range of LLM deployments, including settings where models are accessed through black-box APIs. Initial findings on computational efficiency point toward the feasibility of integrating such methods into runtime environments, where verification must be performed under time and resource constraints. Further investigation is needed to confirm these observations across a broader range of applications and model types.

Future Directions. Several directions remain for further exploration. One avenue is to extend the framework to additional supervised learning domains, such as speech recognition, to examine its applicability beyond text-based tasks. Another is to adapt the approach for reinforcement learning, which poses unique challenges for runtime verification. In addition, incorporating more diverse semantic perturbation techniques, such as paraphrasing, sentence restructuring, or syntactic transformations, could further enrich the robustness evaluation beyond simple synonym substitution with Word2Vec. Another promising direction is to perform empirical comparisons with established robustness benchmarks and attack frameworks, such as TextFooler, Adversarial GLUE, and other recent evaluations [10,20,53], which would provide valuable insights into the scalability and competitiveness of our approach. Lastly, while this study focused on encoder-only architectures (specifically BERT), future work should evaluate the applicability of the proposed framework to decoder-only models [36] and encoder-decoder architectures [40]. These directions may help assess the generalizability of the framework and identify domain-specific considerations for broader deployment.

Runtime Verification Contribution. This study explores the use of a statistical methodology for monitoring learning-enabled components in operational settings where formal verification techniques may be impractical. The proposed framework offers an initial step toward enabling continuous reliability assessment in large-scale neural architectures, particularly in scenarios where white-box access is unavailable. While preliminary, the ability to estimate classification resilience under perturbations may contribute to the development of runtime assurance strategies for safety-critical applications that rely on LLMs.

Acknowledgments. We would like to thank Davide Corsi for his assistance in this project and his insightful comments. This work was partially funded by the European Union (RobustifAI project, ID 101212818). Views and opinions expressed are however those of the author(s) only and do not necessarily reflect those of the European Union or the European Health and Digital Executive Agency (HADEA). Neither the European Union nor the granting authority can be held responsible for them. Additionally, this work was partially supported by the Israeli Smart Transportation Research Center (ISTRC).

References

1. Anderson, T.: Anderson–Darling tests of goodness-of-fit. Int. Encyclopedia Stat. Sci. **1**, 52–54 (2011)
2. BERT-Base-Uncased (2023). https://huggingface.co/google-bert/bert-base-uncased
3. Bērziņš, J., Kalniņa, E.: Robustness of pre-trained language models against adversarial attacks. MZ Comput. J. **5**(2) (2024)

4. Box, G., Cox, D.: An analysis of transformations revisited, rebutted. J. Am. Stat. Assoc. **77**(377), 209–210 (1982)
5. Brix, C., Bak, S., Liu, C., Johnson, T.: The Fourth Int. Verification of Neural Networks Competition (VNN-COMP): Summary and Results. Technical report (2023). https://arxiv.org/abs/2312.16760
6. Carlini, N., Katz, G., Barrett, C., Dill, D.: Provably Minimally-Distorted Adversarial Examples. Technical report (2017). https://arxiv.org/abs/1709.10207
7. Cheong, I., Xia, K., Feng, K.K., Chen, Q.Z., Zhang, A.X.: (A) i am not a lawyer, but...: engaging legal experts towards responsible LLM policies for legal advice. In: Proceedings of the ACM Conference on Fairness, Accountability, and Transparency (FACCT), pp. 2454–2469 (2024)
8. Cohen, J., Rosenfeld, E., Kolter, Z.: Certified adversarial robustness via randomized smoothing. In: Proceedings of the 36th International Conference on Machine Learning (ICML), pp. 1310–1320 (2019)
9. Devlin, J., Chang, M., Lee, K., Toutanova, K.: BERT: Pre-Training of Deep Bidirectional Transformers for Language Understanding, Technical report (2018). http://arxiv.org/abs/1810.04805
10. Dong, X., Luu, A.T., Ji, R., Liu, H.: Towards Robustness Against Natural Language Word Substitutions, Technical report (2021). https://arxiv.org/abs/2107.13541
11. Elbadawi, M., Li, H., Basit, A.W., Gaisford, S.: The role of artificial intelligence in generating original scientific research. Int. J. Pharmaceut. **652**, 123741 (2024)
12. Goodfellow, I., Shlens, J., Szegedy, C.: Explaining and Harnessing Adversarial Examples, Technical report (2014). http://arxiv.org/abs/1412.6572
13. Guo, C., Pleiss, G., Sun, Y., Weinberger, Q.: On calibration of modern neural networks. In: Proceedings of the 34th International Conference on Machine Learning, pp. 1321–1330 (2017)
14. Hadar, A., Levy, N., Winokur, M.: Management and Detection System for Medical Surgical Equipment, Technical report (2022). http://arxiv.org/abs/2211.02351
15. Hashemi, V., Křetínský, J., Rieder, S., Schön, T., Vorhoff, J.: Gaussian-based and outside-the-box runtime monitoring join forces. In: Proceedings of the 24th International Conference on Runtime Verification, pp. 218–228 (2024)
16. He, W., Wu, C., Bensalem, S.: Box-based monitor approach for out-of-distribution detection in YOLO: an exploratory study. In: Proceedings of the 24th International Conference on Runtime Verification (RV), pp. 229–239 (2024)
17. Huang, C., Hu, Z., Huang, X., Pei, K.: Statistical certification of acceptable robustness for neural networks. In: Farkaš, I., Masulli, P., Otte, S., Wermter, S. (eds.) ICANN 2021. LNCS, vol. 12891, pp. 79–90. Springer, Cham (2021). https://doi.org/10.1007/978-3-030-86362-3_7
18. Huang, Y., Sansom, J., Ma, Z., Gervits, F., Chai, J.: Drivlme: enhancing LLM-based autonomous driving agents with embodied and social experiences. In: IEEE/RSJ International Conference on Intelligent Robots and Systems (IROS), pp. 3153–3160. IEEE (2024)
19. Jin, D., Jin, Z., Zhou, J.T., Szolovits, P.: Is Bert really robust? A strong baseline for natural language attack on text classification and entailment. In: Proceedings 34th of the AAAI Conference on Artificial Intelligence, pp. 8018–8025 (2020)
20. Jones, E., Jia, R., Raghunathan, A., Liang, P.: Robust Encodings: A Framework for Combating Adversarial Typos, Technical report (2020). https://arxiv.org/abs/2005.01229
21. Julian, D., Kochenderfer, J., Owen, P.: Deep neural network compression for aircraft collision avoidance systems. J. Guid. Control. Dyn. **42**(3), 598–608 (2019)

22. Katz, G., Barrett, C., Dill, D.L., Julian, K., Kochenderfer, M.J.: Reluplex: an efficient SMT solver for verifying deep neural networks. In: Majumdar, R., Kunčak, V. (eds.) CAV 2017. LNCS, vol. 10426, pp. 97–117. Springer, Cham (2017). https://doi.org/10.1007/978-3-319-63387-9_5
23. Katz, G., Barrett, C., Dill, D., Julian, K., Kochenderfer, M.: Reluplex: a calculus for reasoning about deep neural networks. Formal Methods in System Design (FMSD) (2021)
24. Katz, G., et al.: The marabou framework for verification and analysis of deep neural networks. In: Dillig, I., Tasiran, S. (eds.) CAV 2019. LNCS, vol. 11561, pp. 443–452. Springer, Cham (2019). https://doi.org/10.1007/978-3-030-25540-4_26
25. Katz, G., Levy, N., Refaeli, I., Yerushalmi, R.: DEM: a method for certifying deep neural network classifier outputs in aerospace. In: Proceedings of the 43rd Digital Avionics Systems Conference (DASC) (2024)
26. Kim, H., Papamakarios, G., Mnih, A.: The lipschitz constant of self-attention. In: Proceedings of the 38th International Conference on Machine Learning (ICML), pp. 5562–5571 (2021)
27. Landi, A., Nicholson, M.: ARP4754A/ED-79A-guidelines for development of civil aircraft and systems-enhancements, novelties and key topics. SAE Int. J. Aerospace **4**, 871–879 (2011)
28. Levy, N., Ashrov, A., Katz, G.: Towards Robust LLMs: an adversarial robustness measurement framework — code (2024). https://github.com/adielashrov/trust-ai-roma-for-llm
29. Levy, N., Katz, G.: RoMA: a method for neural network robustness measurement and assessment. In: Proceedings of the 29th International Conference on Neural Information Processing (ICONIP) (2021)
30. Levy, N., Yerushalmi, R., Katz, G.: gRoMA: a tool for measuring the global robustness of deep neural networks. In: Proceedings o the 12th International Symposium on Leveraging Applications of Formal Methods, Verification and Validation (ISoLA), pp. 160–170 (2023)
31. Levy, O., Dikman, I., Levy, N., Winokur, M.: Work in progress: AI-powered engineering-bridging theory and practice. In: Proceedings of the 9th IEEE World Engineering Education Conference (EDUNINE) (2025)
32. Marzari, L., Corsi, D., Cicalese, F., Farinelli, A.: The #Dnn-Verification Problem: Counting Unsafe Inputs for Deep Neural Networks, Technical report (2023). https://arxiv.org/abs/2301.07068
33. Mikolov, T., Chen, K., Corrado, G., Dean, J.: Efficient Estimation of Word Representations in Vector Space, Technical report (2013). https://arxiv.org/abs/1301.3781
34. Morris, J.X., Lifland, E., Yoo, J.Y., Grigsby, J., Jin, D., Qi, Y.: Textattack: A Framework for Adversarial Attacks, Data Augmentation, and Adversarial Training in NLP, Technical report (2020). https://arxiv.org/abs/2005.05909
35. OpenAI: GPT-4 Technical Report, Technical report (2024). https://arxiv.org/abs/2303.08774
36. OpenAI: Chatgpt (july 2025 version) (2025). https://chat.openai.com. Accessed Jul 2025
37. Owen, M., Panken, A., Moss, R., Alvarez, L., Leeper, C.: ACAS Xu: integrated collision avoidance and detect and avoid capability for UAS. In: Proceedings of the 38th IEEE/AIAA Digital Avionics Systems Conference (DASC), pp. 1–10 (2019)
38. Pennington, J., Socher, R., Manning, C.: Glove: global vectors for word representation. In: Proceedings of the International Conference on Empirical Methods in Natural Language Processing (EMNLP), pp. 1532–1543 (2014)

39. Qiu, S., et al.: Hard label adversarial attack with high query efficiency against NLP models. Sci. Rep. **15**(1), 9378 (2025)
40. Raffel, C., et al.: Exploring the Limits of Transfer Learning with a Unified Text-to-Text Transformer, Technical report (2023). https://arxiv.org/abs/1910.10683
41. Rohan, A., et al.: PaLM 2 Technical Report, Technical report (2023). https://arxiv.org/abs/2305.10403
42. Romero-Alvarado, D., Hernández-Orallo, J., Martínez-Plumed, F.: How resilient are language models to text perturbations? In: Proceedings of the 25th International Conference on Intelligent Data Engineering and Automated Learning (IDEAL), pp. 85–96 (2024)
43. Roumeliotis, K., Tselikas, N.: ChatGPT and open-AI models: a preliminary review. Future Internet **15**(6), 192 (2023)
44. Sato, M., Suzuki, J., Shindo, H., Matsumoto, Y.: Interpretable Adversarial Perturbation in Input Embedding Space for Text, Technical report (2018). https://arxiv.org/abs/1805.02917
45. Singh, A., Singh, N., Vatsal, S.: Robustness of LLMs to Perturbations in Text, Technical report (2024). https://arxiv.org/abs/2407.08989
46. Socher, R., et al.: Recursive deep models for semantic compositionality over a sentiment treebank. In: Proceedings of the 2013 Conference on Empirical Methods in Natural Language Processing (EMNLP), pp. 1631–1642 (2013)
47. Subramanian, V., Benetos, E., Xu, N., McDonald, S., Sandler, M.: Adversarial Attacks in Sound Event Classification, Technical report (2019). https://arxiv.org/abs/1907.02477
48. Temple, B., Buescher, K., Armstrong, J.: PyRAT-Python Radiography Analysis Tool (u), Los Alamos National Laboratory (LANL) (2011)
49. Touvron, H., et al.: LLaMA: Open and Efficient Foundation Language Models, Technical report (2023). https://arxiv.org/abs/2302.13971
50. Tsuzuku, Y., Sato, I., Sugiyama, M.: Lipschitz-margin training: scalable certification of perturbation invariance for deep neural networks. In: Proceedings of the 32nd Advances in Neural Information Processing Systems (NeurIPS), pp. 6541–6550 (2018)
51. Wang, B., et al.: Adversarial GLUE: A Multi-Task Benchmark for Robustness Evaluation of Language Models, Technical report (2021). https://arxiv.org/abs/2111.02840
52. Wang, S., et al.: Beta-CROWN: efficient bound propagation with per-neuron split constraints for complete and incomplete neural network verification. In: Proceedings 35th Conference on Neural Information Processing Systems (NeurIPS) (2021)
53. Wang, Y., Zhao, Y.: Rupbench: benchmarking reasoning under perturbations for robustness evaluation in large language models, Technical report (2024). https://arxiv.org/abs/2406.11020
54. Webb, S., Rainforth, T., Teh, Y.W., Kumar, P.: A statistical approach to assessing neural network robustness. In: Proceedings of the 7th International Conference on Learning Representations (ICLR) (2019)
55. Yang, F., Zhan, S.S., Wang, Y., Huang, C., Zhu, Q.: Case study: runtime safety verification of neural network controlled system. In: Proceedings of the 24th International Conference on Runtime Verification (RV), pp. 205–217 (2024)
56. Yoshida, Y., Miyato, T.: Spectral Norm Regularization for Improving the Generalizability of Deep Learning, Technical report (2017). https://arxiv.org/abs/1705.10941
57. Zhao, W.X., et al.: A Survey of Large Language Models, Technical report (2025). https://arxiv.org/abs/2303.18223

ISL: Monitoring Image Segmentation Logic in Medical Imaging Analysis

Ziyan An, Daniel Moyer, Ipek Oguz, Taylor T. Johnson, and Meiyi Ma(✉)

Vanderbilt University, Nashville, TN, USA
{ziyan.an,daniel.moyer,ipek.oguz,taylor.johnson,meiyi.ma}@vanderbilt.edu

Abstract. Medical image segmentation plays a critical role in both image interpretation and disease diagnosis. Data-driven approaches such as U-Net have significantly advanced the field by enabling pixel-level classification of anatomical structures. However, the resulting segmentation masks often fail to comply with spatial anatomical constraints. Although properties such as organ connectedness and relative position are well understood by experts, current segmentation practices lack a systematic and explicit means to express, incorporate, or monitor this domain knowledge. In this work, we conduct a systematic study of formal specification rules across diverse medical imaging tasks with domain experts. Based on our analysis, we introduce Image Segmentation Logic (ISL), a novel spatial formalism designed to bridge the gap between expert knowledge and automated analysis. This logic provides an expressive and interpretable framework to specify critical domain knowledge and spatial constraints, and to automatically monitor their satisfaction with segmentation outputs. It integrates variables such as intensity, predicted class labels, confidence scores, and directional relationships, enabling both pixel-level and region-level specification checking. To support practical adoption, we develop an efficient monitoring tool for evaluating segmentation outputs against ISL specifications and formally prove the soundness and correctness of ISL's semantics. We demonstrate the expressiveness and utility of ISL through two case studies on established medical image segmentation datasets. Our results show that ISL enables precise detection of segmentation violations and provides more fine-grained validation than traditional metrics.

Keywords: Specification Language · Medical Image Segmentation · Monitoring Techniques

1 Introduction

Medical image segmentation plays a vital role in facilitating clinical applications such as disease assessment and diagnosis. Data-driven algorithms, particularly convolutional neural networks such as the U-Net [38] architecture, have significantly advanced segmentation performance and are widely adopted as effective tools in medical imaging [39]. At a micro level, segmentation models generate

© The Author(s), under exclusive license to Springer Nature Switzerland AG 2026
B. Könighofer and H. Torfah (Eds.): RV 2025, LNCS 16087, pp. 477–496, 2026.
https://doi.org/10.1007/978-3-032-05435-7_26

classification results, also known as masks, for an input image by assigning each pixel to a class such as an organ, lesion, or background. Connected pixels in the segmentation mask form regions, and a well-performing model is expected to comply with spatial rules or constraints defined by biological plausibility, diagnostic accuracy, and model interpretability. As a simple example, for healthy patients, each anatomical structure, such as a lung lobe or an organ, should form a single connected component across the entire image. Additionally, specific positional or directional relationships must hold between segmented regions. For instance, the liver lies below the right lung, and the heart is located between the lungs. Within a region, certain properties must also hold. For example, every boundary pixel of a tumor region should be adjacent to pixels belonging to a specific organ class. Concrete examples of segmentation failures that violate such anatomical and spatial constraints are shown in Fig. 1.

Developing a formal framework to specify and evaluate aforementioned region-level and pixel-level properties and specifications offers several key benefits. First, given the severity and safety-critical nature of data-driven algorithms used for medical imaging segmentation, the European Union's Artificial Intelligence (AI) Act [13] stipulates that high-risk AI systems must ensure robustness, which may involve backup or fail-safe measures. In line with this requirement, a formal framework for medical image segmentation provides an interpretable mechanism to verify and potentially enforce spatial and semantic consistency in model outputs. Second, such a formal framework can serve as an evaluation tool for quantitatively assessing segmentation models beyond standard metrics like IoU, Dice score [11], and Jaccard index [24]. Third, the formal framework can function as a runtime monitor and post-processing tool within clinical pipelines to timely detect violations or anomalies in the outputs of data-driven algorithms. Fourth, for segmentation datasets with existing labels, the formal framework can be used to verify and reassess label quality by identifying potential human errors or inaccuracies caused by automated labeling tools.

However, despite advances in bounding-box-based specification frameworks for image data [12,22], no existing formal logic framework offers built-in operators that support both pixel-level and region-level reasoning for medical image segmentation, while also integrating learned model attributes (e.g., model confidence, segmentation mask) and directional spatial relations. Therefore, in this paper, we propose a spatial formalism dubbed Image Segmentation Logic (IsL) to specify and evaluate the compliance of medical imaging segmentation algorithms. The design of IsL is motivated by real-world needs in the medical domain, informed by our study of specification requirements across diverse imaging tasks with domain experts, and by the observation that current models lack the means to formally encode or verify such recurring domain knowledge. IsL enables specifications over both pixel-level and region-level properties, defined in terms of image-derived variables such as intensity, anatomical class labels from segmentation, and algorithmic confidence scores, etc. The logic covers key criteria for assessing the usability of medical image segmentation, including specifications about the resulting segmented image, such as the connectivity of a single anatom-

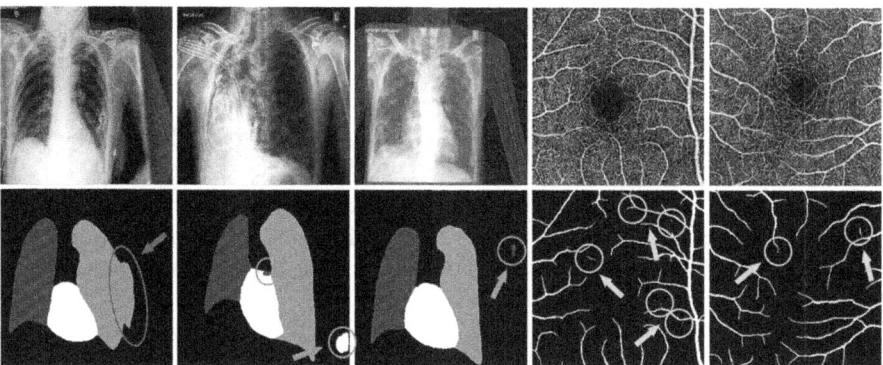

Fig. 1. The first row shows the input image; the second row shows the corresponding predicted segmentation. Violations include incorrect anatomical structure (col. 1), lack of organ coherence (col. 2 and col. 3), and disconnected regions (col. 4 and col. 5). Circled areas and arrows highlight the specific locations where violations occur. Since these constraints are **not** explicitly enforced by standard data-driven models, ISL provides a formal mechanism to monitor such violations.

ical region (e.g., the segmented cochlea must be a single connected component), directional distance between multiple regions (e.g., the left lung is to the left of the heart), as well as specifications about the algorithm itself, such as requiring the model to be at least 95% certain about its output.

To facilitate practical use, we develop both qualitative (Boolean) and quantitative semantics for ISL, and implement an efficient monitoring tool that supports checking segmentation outputs under both semantics. We also provide formal proofs of the logic's soundness and correctness, and derive the computational complexity of the monitoring algorithm. We demonstrate the practicality and comprehensiveness of ISL through two case studies using well-established medical imaging datasets: OCTA-500 [28], which contains retinal images with micron-level resolution, and CheXpert [23], a large-scale, annotated, multi-class segmentation dataset of chest X-rays. The code implementation of ISL is available at https://github.com/AICPS-Lab/isl.git.

Contribution. The key contributions of this paper are summarized as follows. First, we provide an overview of the need for spatial reasoning in medical image segmentation and identify challenges in developing formal specification frameworks. Second, we introduce ISL, a new specification language designed to express and evaluate both pixel-level and region-level properties in image segmentation outputs. The language supports capabilities including connectivity constraints, confidence-based conditions, and relative spatial positioning. Third, we define both qualitative and quantitative semantics for ISL, and develop a monitoring algorithm that implements these semantics to evaluate segmentation outputs. Fourth, we empirically evaluate the ISL monitor on two medical imaging datasets to demonstrate its effectiveness in detecting specification violations and supporting downstream analysis.

2 Segmentation Tasks and Specification Challenges

In this section, we provide background on medical image segmentation tasks, define key data structures associated with them, including the input image and output segmentation mask, and present a comprehensive list of relevant segmentation specifications collected from related literature.

2.1 Medical Image Segmentation Tasks

The use case we consider focuses on the segmentation of anatomical regions such as the brain, left and right lungs, and the heart. Given an input image $\mathbf{I}$, the goal of the segmentation model is to generate a corresponding segmentation mask $\mathcal{S}$ that accurately identifies the targeted semantic label for each pixel.

We consider two-dimensional input images. Each image provided to the segmentation model is represented as $\mathbf{I} \in \mathbb{R}^{H \times W}$, where H and W denote the height and width of the image, respectively. We use f_θ to denote a parameterized segmentation model with learnable parameters θ. Given an input image $\mathbf{I}$, the model outputs a segmentation mask $\hat{y} = f_\theta(\mathbf{I})$, where $\hat{y} \in \mathcal{S}^{H \times W}$. The predicted class label for each pixel $p_{row,col}$ is given by $\text{class}_{row,col} = \arg\max f_\theta(\mathbf{I})_{row,col}$.

The segmentation model is trained using supervised learning methods, where ground-truth annotations $y \in \mathcal{S}^{H \times W}$ are provided either by domain experts or automated labeling tools. The learning objective is to minimize a pixel-wise loss function $\mathcal{L}(\hat{y}, y)$. Two common choices of the loss function are cross-entropy and Dice loss [11]. To optimize the model parameters θ, we adopt a gradient-based optimization algorithm, specifically Adam [26], which iteratively update the parameters until convergence is achieved [45].

2.2 Pixels of Segmented Images

In our formal logic framework, each image is modeled as a structured collection of pixels, where each pixel is augmented with information derived from both the original input image and the corresponding segmentation mask. We refer to this augmented image as $\mathcal{X}$. Let p denote a pixel in $\mathcal{X}$, and let $p_{row,col}$ represent the specific pixel located at the row and column numbers. We define each pixel in $\mathcal{X}$ to follow the structured format: $p_{row,col} = (\text{row}, \text{col}, \mathcal{I}, \text{class}, \text{prob}, \text{id})$.

Here, $\text{class} \in \{\text{Lung}, \text{Heart}, \text{Background}, \ldots\}$ denotes the predicted semantic label, $\text{id} \in \mathbb{N}$ represents the region identifier to which the pixel belongs, and $\text{prob} \in [0, 1]$ is the associated probability score for that prediction. In this work, we use the maximum softmax probability [16] as a proxy for model confidence in the predicted class. Alternative approaches for estimating or interpreting pixel-level confidence include entropy-based uncertainty [25] and Bayesian sampling methods such as Monte Carlo dropout [35]. For grayscale images considered in

ISL: Monitoring Image Segmentation Logic in Medical Imaging Analysis   481

this paper, $\mathcal{I}$ refers to the intensity value of each pixel. In the case of RGB images, however, $\mathcal{I}$ can be replaced by a three-dimensional color vector.

In addition to local attributes, each pixel is aware of its four immediate neighbors in the cardinal directions left $(row, col-1)$, right $(row, col+1)$, up $(row-1, col)$, and down $(row+1, col)$. Therefore, let $p_{row,col}$ and $p'_{row',col'}$, we have $(p, p') \in \mathsf{Adj}_B$ iff p' is the immediate neighbor of p in direction B, that is:

- $B \in \{\uparrow, \downarrow\}$: $col' = col$, $row' = row-1$ if B is $\uparrow$; $row' = row+1$ if B is $\downarrow$
- $B \in \{\leftarrow, \rightarrow\}$: $row' = row$, $col' = col-1$ if B is $\leftarrow$; $col' = col+1$ if B is $\rightarrow$

2.3 Regions of Segmented Images

Since the image $\mathcal{X}$ includes predicted semantic labels for each pixel, we partition the image into distinct regions, denoted by $\mathcal{R} = \{\tau_1, \tau_2, \ldots, \tau_n\}$, where each region $\tau_i \subseteq \mathcal{X}$ consists of a connected set of pixels sharing the same predicted class label. In practice, each region corresponds to an anatomical or pathological structure, as defined by its semantic class. To distinguish between spatially disjoint regions of the same class, each region is assigned a unique identifier.

We implement a region identifier assignment function to assign unique region IDs to connected regions. Starting from an unvisited pixel, the function performs connected component labeling to grow a region by assigning the same ID to all connected pixels sharing the same class label. This process is repeated across the entire image grid until all class-labeled pixels have been assigned region IDs. As a result, multiple spatially disconnected regions with the same class label are assigned distinct region identifiers.

For any region τ, we define its extremal points as the leftmost and rightmost columns, and the topmost and bottommost rows, that contain pixels belonging to τ. Based on this representation, we define positional relations in the four cardinal directions, above, below, left of, and right of, to characterize spatial relationships within the image space.

2.4 Analysis of Medical Image Segmentation Requirements

To motivate our specification language and identify the requirements of medical image segmentation, we compile and detail specification rules across segmentation tasks involving various anatomical regions, such as the chest and brain.

In Table 1, we list a few key examples of segmentation specifications across different anatomical regions. As shown, the specifications can be categorized into different types. First, for single-class segmentations, properties can be enforced within the target region itself. For example, one can define constraints on the intensity distribution of pixels, such as specifying minimum or maximum allowable intensity values. Second, specifications of the type spatial distance express that a region with certain properties is expected to exist within a specific distance and direction relative to a target region. These constraints define the spatial relationship between two anatomical regions within the segmentation mask, describing both directional position and proximity. Such specifications are common in

Table 1. Example segmentation specifications for various anatomical regions.

Region	Type	Textual Description	Ref.
Chest	Spatial distance	For segmented heart region, there exists a left lung to the left and a right lung to the right within a fixed distance.	[9]
Lung	Spatial distance	For segmented left lung region, there exists a right lung region to the right that does not overlap with it.	[17]
Lung	Region class label	For all pixels segmented as trachea, they do not belong to either left or right lung regions.	[40]
Brain	Spatial symmetry	For segmented left hemisphere region, there exists a corresponding right hemisphere to the right such that the class labels are the same.	[49]
Retinal	Region class label	For segmented FAZ region, all pixels within it are not labeled as vessel, and for segmented artery region, no pixel within it is labeled as vein.	[20]
Cochlea	Spatial distance	For segmented cochlea region, there exists a vestibule region posterior to it within some pixels.	[36]
Cochlea	Region intensity	For segmented cochlea region, at least a certain percentage of pixels have intensity between a specified range.	[30]
Tumor	Region intensity	For segmented tumor region, no pixel within it has intensity within the typical cerebrospinal fluid (CSF) range.	[34]

anatomical areas like the chest, lungs, and eyes, where the relative arrangement of structures is clinically well-defined. The type spatial symmetry, also describing the relation between two regions, can be viewed as a special case of spatial distance, where there exists a corresponding region at a fixed mirrored distance along a defined axis. These observations inform the design of ISL, which lead to a specification language that encompasses the diverse constraints observed in medical segmentation tasks. This includes intra-region properties such as "region intensity" and inter-region relationships such as "spatial distance" and "spatial symmetry." The examples also highlight the need for a unified formalism capable of expressing a broad range of clinically meaningful properties, both within individual regions and between multiple anatomical structures.

3 Image Segmentation Logic (ISL)

Targeting the above-mentioned unique challenge, we propose a new specification language dubbed Image Segmentation Logic (ISL) to reason about medical image segmentation tasks. Figure 2 illustrates the overall ISL framework. In this section, we first present the syntax and the semantics of the ISL specification language.

Building on the data structures defined for pixels and regions in the augmented image $\mathcal{X}$, we now formally define the spatial model over which the ISL logic is interpreted. The image model is denoted as $\mathcal{M} = ((\mathcal{X}, \mathcal{R}), \mathcal{V})$, where $\mathcal{V}$ is a valuation function that maps each pixel p to a tuple of attributes: $\mathcal{V}(p) = (\mathcal{I}(p), \texttt{class}(p), \texttt{prob}(p), \texttt{id}(p), \texttt{row}(p), \texttt{col}(p))$. In addition, we define pixel objects and region objects as two types of input objects of ISL. Specifically, a pixel object is defined by its coordinate position $p := (\texttt{row}, \texttt{col}) \in \mathcal{X}$. A region object $\tau := (p_{\text{tl}}, p_{\text{tr}}, p_{\text{bl}}, p_{\text{br}}) \in \mathcal{R}$ is represented by the coordinates of its four corners: top-left, top-right, bottom-left, and bottom-right.

ISL: Monitoring Image Segmentation Logic in Medical Imaging Analysis   483

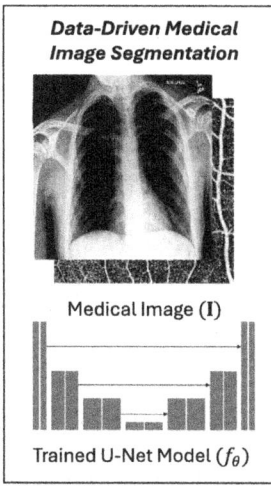 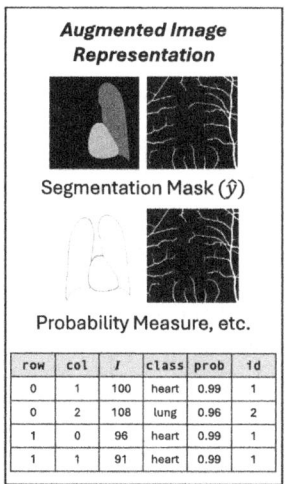 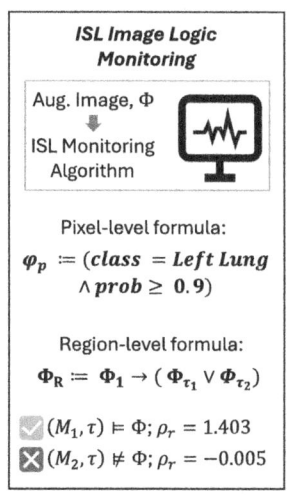

Fig. 2. Overview of the ISL framework for specification monitoring in medical image segmentation. Framework begins with images segmented into class-labeled regions by a model. Each output is augmented with pixel-level attributes. ISL then evaluates logic specifications encoding anatomical priors and spatial rules, producing Boolean and robustness scores to detect structural violations.

3.1 Syntax

To support both intra-region and inter-region reasoning over medical image segmentations, we define the syntax of ISL in a hierarchical manner, with separate formulas for pixel-level and region-level specifications. Pixel-level formulas enable reasoning about local attributes such as intensity and class labels, while region-level formulas support spatial reasoning across different segmented regions. These two levels are connected using quantifiers and spatial operators, which aggregate pixel-level predicates into region-level statements.

Definition 1 (Syntax of ISL). *The pixel-level and region-level formulas of* ISL *are defined as:*

$$\varphi ::= \top \mid \pi \sim d \mid \neg \varphi \mid \varphi \wedge \varphi \mid \varphi \vee \varphi \mid \bigcirc_B \varphi$$
$$\Phi ::= \boxed{\exists}\,\varphi \mid \boxed{\forall}\,\varphi \mid \neg \Phi \mid \Phi \wedge \Phi \mid \Phi \vee \Phi \mid \blacktriangleright_s \Phi \mid \triangleright_s \Phi$$

In this definition, φ denotes a pixel-level formula, and Φ denotes a region-level formula. The constant $\top$ is the Boolean value *True*, $\sim\, \in \{=, \geq, \leq\}$, $s \in \mathbb{R}_{\geq 0}$, and $B \in \{\uparrow, \downarrow, \leftarrow, \rightarrow\}, B \neq \emptyset$. The operators $\neg, \wedge, \vee$ follow the standard first-order semantics. The implication operator $\varphi \rightarrow \varphi$ is equivalent to $\neg \varphi \vee \varphi$.

Atomic predicates of a pixel-level formula φ take the form $\pi \sim d$, where d is a numeric or symbolic constant, and π is a pixel-level attribute defined as:

$$\pi ::= \mathtt{id} \mid \mathtt{class} \mid \mathtt{prob} \mid \mathcal{I} \mid \mathtt{row} \mid \mathtt{col}$$

The predicate $\text{id} = d$ specifies that pixel p is assigned the region identifier d, while $\text{class} = d$ indicates that p is labeled with the semantic class $d \in \mathcal{C}$. The predicate $\text{prob} \sim d$ compares the predicted confidence score of p to a threshold d using a relational operator. The term $\mathcal{I} \sim d$ constrains the pixel's intensity value, while $\text{row} \sim d$ and $\text{col} \sim d$ impose spatial constraints on the pixel's vertical and horizontal coordinates, respectively. In addition, the operator $\bigcirc_B \varphi$ is a directional pixel-level operator that evaluates whether the formula φ holds at the neighboring pixel of a given pixel p in the directions specified by B. Intuitively, $\bigcirc_B$ moves to the next pixel from the current pixel in direction B and checks whether φ is satisfied there.

Region-level formulas Φ allow reasoning over segmented regions through quantification and directional operators. The boxed quantifiers $\boxed{\forall}\varphi$ and $\boxed{\exists}\varphi$ enable the assertion of the existence or universality of the pixel-level property φ. Region formulas also support logical negation, conjunction, and disjunction with $\neg$, $\wedge$, and $\vee$ operators, respectively. Directional spatial relations between regions are expressed using a family of direction-specific operators, each annotated with a subscript s that specifies the distance threshold. The operator $\blacktriangleright_s \Phi$ evaluates whether there exists a region located strictly to the right, at a directional Manhattan distance of at least s, in which the spatial property Φ holds. Similarly, $\blacktriangleleft_s$, $\blacktriangle_s$, and $\blacktriangledown_s$ correspond to left, up, and down each directional relations, respectively. Two variants of each directional operator are supported. Specifically, ISL includes a strict version (i.e., $\blacktriangleright_s$), which requires the entirety of the target region to lie in the specified direction, and a weak version (i.e., $\triangleright_s$), which allows partial overlap as long as some part of the region lies in the given direction.

Running Example. We illustrate how ISL can express local connectivity and directional constraints. Consider the specification: "a segmented class (e.g., left lung) must appear as a single connected region." This requires that the segmentation does not contain multiple high-confidence, spatially disconnected components with the same class label. We define a pixel-level formula as $\varphi_1 := (\text{class} = \text{LeftLung}) \wedge (\text{prob} \geq 0.9) \wedge (\text{id} = \text{id1})$, asserting that a pixel belongs to a confident left lung region id1. The region-level formula $\Phi_1 := \boxed{\forall}\varphi_1$ ensures all pixels in region id1 satisfy these conditions. To enforce uniqueness, we require that no other region satisfies the same predicate. For each region $\tau \neq \text{id1}$, let $\varphi_\tau := (\text{class} = \text{LeftLung}) \wedge (\text{prob} \geq 0.9) \wedge (\text{id} = \tau)$ and $\Phi_\tau := \boxed{\forall}\varphi_\tau$. The uniqueness constraint is then $\Phi_{\text{uniqueness}} := \neg (\Phi_1 \wedge (\vee_{\tau \neq \text{id1}} \Phi_\tau))$.

As a second example, we can specify a directional constraint between two anatomical structures as follows: $\Phi_{\text{direction}} := \neg(\Phi_{\text{LeftLung}}) \vee \blacktriangleright_{20} \Phi_{\text{RightLung}}$, where $\varphi_{\text{LeftLung}} := (\text{class} = \text{LeftLung})$, $\varphi_{\text{RightLung}} := (\text{class} = \text{RightLung})$, and $\Phi_{\text{LeftLung}} := \boxed{\forall}\varphi_{\text{LeftLung}}$, $\Phi_{\text{RightLung}} := \boxed{\forall}\varphi_{\text{RightLung}}$. This formula asserts that if a region exists in which every pixel is labeled as LeftLung, then there must also exist a region labeled as RightLung that lies strictly to its right, with a minimum directional Manhattan distance of 20 pixels between them.

3.2 Qualitative Semantics

In the following sections, we present the qualitative and quantitative semantics of IsL. The qualitative semantics returns a Boolean truth value, while the quantitative semantics returns a real number that measures the degree of satisfaction for a given image model. In Definition 2, we first present the Boolean, or qualitative, semantics of IsL. Given an image model $\mathcal{M}$ and either a pixel object p or a region object τ, the truth relation is defined as follows:

Definition 2 (Qualitative Semantics of IsL)

$$(\mathcal{M}, \tau) \models \boxed{\exists} \varphi \Leftrightarrow \exists p \in \tau : (\mathcal{M}, \tau, p) \models \varphi$$
$$(\mathcal{M}, \tau) \models \boxed{\forall} \varphi \Leftrightarrow \forall p \in \tau : (\mathcal{M}, \tau, p) \models \varphi$$
$$(\mathcal{M}, \tau) \models \neg \Phi \Leftrightarrow (\mathcal{M}, \tau) \not\models \Phi$$
$$(\mathcal{M}, \tau) \models \Phi_1 \wedge \Phi_2 \Leftrightarrow (\mathcal{M}, \tau) \models \Phi_1 \text{ and } (\mathcal{M}, \tau) \models \Phi_2$$
$$(\mathcal{M}, \tau) \models \Phi_1 \vee \Phi_2 \Leftrightarrow (\mathcal{M}, \tau) \models \Phi_1 \text{ or } (\mathcal{M}, \tau) \models \Phi_2$$
$$(\mathcal{M}, \tau) \models \blacktriangleright_s \Phi \Leftrightarrow \exists \tau' \in \mathsf{AlignedRegions}(\tau, s) : (\mathcal{M}, \tau') \models \Phi$$
$$(\mathcal{M}, \tau) \models \triangleright_s \Phi \Leftrightarrow \exists \tau' \in \mathsf{AlignedRegionsWeak}(\tau, s) : (\mathcal{M}, \tau') \models \Phi$$
$$(\mathcal{M}, \tau, p) \models \top \Leftrightarrow True$$
$$(\mathcal{M}, \tau, p) \models \pi \sim d \Leftrightarrow \delta_{bool}(\pi, \sim, d, p)$$
$$(\mathcal{M}, \tau, p) \models \neg \varphi \Leftrightarrow (\mathcal{M}, \tau, p) \not\models \varphi$$
$$(\mathcal{M}, \tau, p) \models \varphi_1 \wedge \varphi_2 \Leftrightarrow (\mathcal{M}, \tau, p) \models \varphi_1 \text{ and } (\mathcal{M}, \tau, p) \models \varphi_2$$
$$(\mathcal{M}, \tau, p) \models \varphi_1 \vee \varphi_2 \Leftrightarrow (\mathcal{M}, \tau, p) \models \varphi_1 \text{ or } (\mathcal{M}, \tau, p) \models \varphi_2$$
$$(\mathcal{M}, \tau, p) \models \bigcirc_B \varphi \Leftrightarrow \exists p' : (p, p') \in \mathsf{Adj}_B \text{ and } (\mathcal{M}, \tau, p') \models \varphi$$

In this definition, the satisfaction of atomic predicates $\pi \sim d$ at pixel p is determined by a Boolean evaluation function δ_{bool}, defined as follows:

$$\delta_{\text{bool}}(\pi, \sim, d, p) = \begin{cases} [\pi](p) = d & \text{if } \pi \in \{\text{id}, \text{class}\} \\ [\pi](p) \sim d & \text{if } \pi \in \{\text{prob}, \mathcal{I}, \text{row}, \text{col}\} \end{cases}$$

To define directional spatial relationships between regions, we introduce the concept of aligned regions. Given a prototype region specified by four labeled corner points (top-left, top-right, bottom-left, bottom-right), we construct a sequence of translated regions by shifting this prototype away from a reference region in a specified cardinal direction by a minimum step size s.

We denote the set of aligned regions at distance s as $\mathsf{AlignedRegions}(\tau, s)$, where each candidate region is obtained by incrementally translating the prototype region's corner points in the chosen direction. The translation continues as long as the resulting region remains within the image bounds. For each translated region, we check whether there exists a segmented component in the image whose corner points are fully enclosed within the translated rectangle. These enclosed components are collected as the valid aligned regions. The directional satisfaction operator $\blacktriangleright_s \Phi$ then evaluates whether the region-level formula Φ holds on at least one such aligned region. In addition, to support more flexible specifications, we define a relaxed variant $\mathsf{AlignedRegionsWeak}(\tau, s)$, which includes all segmented components that intersect the translated prototype region.

3.3 Quantitative Semantics

In Definition 3, we present the quantitative semantics of IsL, where ρ_p denotes the satisfaction degree for pixel-level formulas and ρ_r denotes the satisfaction degree for region-level formulas. Intuitively, the quantitative semantics reflect how strongly the image components satisfy or violate a given formula.

Definition 3 (Quantitative Semantics of IsL)

$$\rho_r(\boxed{\exists}\varphi, \tau) = \max_{p \in \tau} \rho_p(\varphi, p)$$
$$\rho_r(\boxed{\forall}\varphi, \tau) = \min_{p \in \tau} \rho_p(\varphi, p)$$
$$\rho_r(\neg \Phi, \tau) = -\rho_r(\Phi, \tau)$$
$$\rho_r(\Phi_1 \wedge \Phi_2, \tau) = \min(\rho_r(\Phi_1, \tau), \rho_r(\Phi_2, \tau))$$
$$\rho_r(\Phi_1 \vee \Phi_2, \tau) = \max(\rho_r(\Phi_1, \tau), \rho_r(\Phi_2, \tau))$$
$$\rho_r(\blacktriangleright_s \Phi, \tau) = \max_{\tau' \in \mathsf{AlignedRegions}(\tau, s)} \rho_r(\Phi, \tau')$$
$$\rho_r(\triangleright_s \Phi, \tau) = \max_{\tau' \in \mathsf{AlignedRegionsWeak}(\tau, s)} \rho_r(\Phi, \tau')$$
$$\rho_p(\top, p) = +\infty$$
$$\rho_p(\pi \sim d, p) = \delta_{quant}(\pi, \sim, d, p)$$
$$\rho_p(\neg \varphi, p) = -\rho_p(\varphi, p)$$
$$\rho_p(\varphi_1 \wedge \varphi_2, p) = \min(\rho_p(\varphi_1, p), \rho_p(\varphi_2, p))$$
$$\rho_p(\varphi_1 \vee \varphi_2, p) = \max(\rho_p(\varphi_1, p), \rho_p(\varphi_2, p))$$
$$\rho_p(\bigcirc_B \varphi, p) = \begin{cases} \rho_p(\varphi, p') & \text{if } (p, p') \in \mathsf{Adj}_B \text{ and } p' \in \mathcal{X} \\ -\infty & \text{otherwise} \end{cases}$$

In the quantitative semantics, atomic predicates are evaluated using a scoring function δ_{quant}, which measures the degree to which a pixel satisfies the specified condition and is defined as follows:

$$\delta_{\text{quant}}(\pi, \sim, d, p) = \begin{cases} 1 & \text{if } \pi \in \{\texttt{id}, \texttt{class}\} \text{ and } [\pi](p) = d \\ -1 & \text{if } \pi \in \{\texttt{id}, \texttt{class}\} \text{ and } [\pi](p) \neq d \\ [\pi](p) - d & \text{if } \sim \text{ is } \geq \text{ and } \pi \in \{\texttt{prob}, \mathcal{I}, \texttt{row}, \texttt{col}\} \\ d - [\pi](p) & \text{if } \sim \text{ is } \leq \text{ and } \pi \in \{\texttt{prob}, \mathcal{I}, \texttt{row}, \texttt{col}\} \end{cases}$$

Running Example. Using the examples above, we illustrate how IsL semantics are applied. For Φ_1, the Boolean semantics evaluate to true if every pixel in region id1 satisfies the class, confidence, and region identifier conditions. The quantitative semantics compute a robustness score by measuring values such as the margin between each pixel's confidence and the threshold of 0.9, with the overall region score given by the minimum margin across all pixels. For the uniqueness constraint $\Phi_{\text{uniqueness}}$, Boolean satisfaction holds if no other region besides id1 satisfies the same conjunction. Quantitatively, violation can be measured by the maximum robustness score among all conflicting regions $\tau \neq$ id1. For the directional constraint $\Phi_{\text{direction}}$, the semantics check whether there exists a region satisfying $\Phi_{\text{RightLung}}$ that lies at least 20 pixels to the right of a region satisfying Φ_{LeftLung}. We first construct a set of aligned regions translated in the specified direction by the required distance. For each aligned region, we evaluate whether it satisfies $\Phi_{\text{RightLung}}$, and if so, compute its robustness score. The final quantitative score is the maximum robustness value among all candidate regions.

3.4 Semantic Properties of ISL

We define two key properties of the quantitative semantics of ISL, namely soundness and correctness. Intuitively, the soundness property states that the sign of the quantitative semantics corresponds to the Boolean truth value. Specifically, a positive quantitative measure ρ indicates satisfaction, while a negative value indicates violation. The correctness property states that if two images differ by a bounded distance, and one of them satisfies a given property, then the other image also satisfies the same property, if the distance between them is less than the robustness value of the satisfying image.

Theorem 1 (Soundness). *We define the soundness property of* ISL *as follows. Let Φ be an* ISL *region-level formula and τ be a region in image model $\mathcal{M}$. Then:*

$$(\mathcal{M}, \tau) \models \Phi \Rightarrow \rho_r(\Phi, \tau) > 0 \quad \text{and} \quad (\mathcal{M}, \tau) \not\models \Phi \Rightarrow \rho_r(\Phi, \tau) < 0.$$

Let $\mathcal{M}^{(1)}$ and $\mathcal{M}^{(2)}$ be two image models defined over the same spatial domain $\mathcal{X}$: $\mathcal{M}^{(1)} = ((\mathcal{X}, \mathcal{R}), \mathcal{V}^{(1)})$, $\mathcal{M}^{(2)} = ((\mathcal{X}, \mathcal{R}), \mathcal{V}^{(2)})$. Let $\tau \in \mathcal{R}$ be a region object common to both models. Define the per-pixel attribute distance as $\delta(\mathcal{V}^{(1)}(p), \mathcal{V}^{(2)}(p)) = \max_i d_i \left(v_i^{(1)}(p), v_i^{(2)}(p)\right)$, where $v_i(p)$ denotes the i-th attribute in $\mathcal{V}(p)$, and d_i is either an absolute difference or an indicator function. Let the model-wise distance be: $d_\infty(\mathcal{V}^{(1)}, \mathcal{V}^{(2)}) := \sup_{p \in \mathcal{X}} \delta(\mathcal{V}^{(1)}(p), \mathcal{V}^{(2)}(p))$.

Theorem 2 (Correctness). *We define the correctness property of* ISL *region-level formulas as follows. If the following conditions hold:*

$$(\mathcal{M}^{(1)}, \tau) \models \Phi, \rho_r(\Phi, \tau; \mathcal{M}^{(1)}) > 0, d_\infty(\mathcal{V}^{(1)}, \mathcal{V}^{(2)}) < \rho_r(\Phi, \tau; \mathcal{M}^{(1)})$$

Then, $(\mathcal{M}^{(2)}, \tau) \models \Phi$.

4 Monitoring Algorithm for ISL

4.1 Monitoring of Segmented Images

Algorithm 1 presents the pseudocode for the quantitative monitoring algorithm of ISL, implemented based on the logic's recursive quantitative semantics. A corresponding qualitative monitoring algorithm, which returns a Boolean satisfaction value based on the qualitative semantics, is also developed but omitted here for brevity. Below, we describe the quantitative monitoring algorithm and its key components. The monitoring algorithm begins by parsing the logical formula and recursively computing the quantitative scores of its subformulas, aggregating the results using the corresponding semantic operators. For spatial operators, the algorithm updates the evaluation context by traversing aligned or adjacent structures within the image.

Algorithm 1. ISL Quantitative Scoring Function

Require: Φ: ISL formula, object: pixel or region, image: augmented image
1: **function** SCORE(Φ, object, image)
2:    **if** Φ is PixelAtomic **then**
3:       **return** EVALPIXELATOMS(Φ, object, image)
4:    **else if** Φ is Next **then**
5:       $p \leftarrow$ object
6:       $p' \leftarrow$ NEIGHBORBYDIRECTION(p, Φ.direction)
7:       **return** SCORE(Φ, p', image)
8:    **else if** Φ is Exists or Forall **then**
9:       $\tau \leftarrow$ object
10:      $pixels \leftarrow$ ENUMERATEPIXELSINREGION(τ)
11:      **if** Φ is Exists **then**
12:         **return** $\sup_{p \in pixels}$ SCORE(Φ, p, image)
13:      **else if** Φ is Forall **then**
14:         **return** $\inf_{p \in pixels}$ SCORE(Φ, p, image)
15:      **end if**
16:    **else if** Φ is StrongDistance or WeakDistance **then**
17:      $\tau \leftarrow$ object
18:      **if** Φ is StrongDistance **then**
19:         $regions \leftarrow$ ALIGNEDREGIONS(τ, Φ.direction, $\Phi.s$)
20:      **else**
21:         $regions \leftarrow$ ALIGNEDREGIONSWEAK(τ, Φ.direction, $\Phi.s$)
22:      **end if**
23:      **return** $\sup_{\tau' \in regions}$ SCORE(Φ, τ', image)
24:    **else if** Φ is Negation **then**
25:      **return** $-$SCORE($\neg\Phi$, object, image)
26:    **else if** Φ is And **then**
27:      **return** min(SCORE(Φ_1, object, image), SCORE(Φ_2, object, image))
28:    **else if** Φ is Or **then**
29:      **return** max(SCORE(Φ_1, object, image), SCORE(Φ_2, object, image))
30:    **end if**
31: **end function**

In Algorithm 1, the EvalPixelAtoms function evaluates pixel-level atomic predicates at a given pixel location by querying the valuation function according to the predicate type specified in the formula. The NeighborByDirection function returns the adjacent pixel of the current pixel in the direction specified by B. The EnumeratePixelsInRegion function enumerates all pixels enclosed within the queried region τ. Finally, the AlignedRegions function returns all region candidates that are spatially aligned with the queried region τ in the direction and at the distance specified by the operator and parameter s.

4.2 Complexity Analysis

The overall time complexity of the ISL monitoring algorithm depends on the image size, the structure of the logic formula, and the number of segmented regions. We define $R = |\mathcal{R}|$ as the total number of regions identified by the segmentation algorithm, m as the maximum number of pixels in any region, s as the maximum number of aligned regions reachable from a given region, and S_φ as the total number of nodes in the syntax tree of the monitored formula.

By the semantics definition, the time complexity for evaluating operators $\pi \sim d$, $\neg$, $\wedge$, and $\vee$ is $O(1)$, as they only require constant-time operations. The pixel-level operator $\bigcirc_B$ also incurs constant time $O(1)$, as it accesses a neighboring pixel based on a fixed direction. For the quantifiers $\boxed{\exists}$ and $\boxed{\forall}$, the worst-case complexity is $O(m)$. For spatial reachability operators $\blacktriangleright_s$, the worst-case complexity is $O(s)$. Therefore, for one ISL formula monitoring a single object in the image, the time complexity is bounded by $O(S_\varphi \times \max\{m, s\})$. For an ISL formula monitoring every region across the entire image, the overall worst-case time complexity is $O(R \times S_\varphi \times \max\{m, s\})$.

5 Case Studies

To evaluate the usefulness and efficiency of ISL and its monitoring algorithm, we conduct two case studies using state-of-the-art medical image segmentation datasets. The objectives of the case studies are twofold: (1) to demonstrate whether monitoring image segmentation properties in multi-class segmentations provides additional safety-relevant information beyond traditional metrics for state-of-the-art segmentation models; (2) to investigate whether the properties specified by ISL accurately capture the spatial requirements of the segmentation mask, and whether the monitor can faithfully identify violations.

To assess the overhead of our monitoring approach, we conduct a runtime evaluation of the ISL monitoring algorithm across a range of formula types. We implemented both the quantitative and qualitative versions of Algorithm 1 for use in our case studies. We tested the monitoring algorithm on a MacOS Sequoia system equipped with an Apple M2 chip. All deep learning models for medical image segmentation were trained and evaluated on a Linux PC running Ubuntu 18.04, equipped with an Intel Core i9-10850K CPU and an NVIDIA GeForce RTX 3070 GPU. Results show that even the most complex multi-region quantitative specifications average under 280 milliseconds per image, while simpler pixel-level formulas execute in under 10 microseconds.

5.1 Case 1: Single Class Segmentation Connectivity

In the first case study, we examine the OCTA-500 dataset [27] and evaluate the connectivity of large retinal vessels, which is considered one of the most difficult spatial requirements in medical image segmentation [6,41]. We evaluate four U-Net models. Two of them are trained using pixel-wise binary cross-entropy loss, and the other two are trained with an additional Betti matching loss that encourages topological consistency between predictions and ground truth.

To formalize vessel connectivity, we define an ISL specification that enforces border contact for each predicted vessel region. Anatomically, large vessels enter the retina through the image boundary. There should be no standalone vessel segments entirely within the center of the image. We define the pixel-level formula as $\varphi_r = (\texttt{class} = \texttt{vessel})$ and the corresponding region-level formula as $\Phi_r = \boxed{\forall}\varphi_r$. The border contact requirement is expressed as $\Phi_r^{\text{border}} = \boxed{\exists}(\texttt{row} = 0) \vee \boxed{\exists}(\texttt{col} = 0) \vee \boxed{\exists}(\texttt{row} = 303) \vee \boxed{\exists}(\texttt{col} = 303)$. The complete specification is written as $\Phi_r^{\text{connect}} = \Phi_r \rightarrow \Phi_r^{\text{border}}$, which ensures that any segmented vessel region with high confidence must intersect the image border.

Table 2. Performance comparison of segmentation models for OCTA-500.

Seg. Model	Vio. Rate (%)	Vio. Count	Dice↑	mIoU↑
U-Net-m1	33.71	238	0.92	0.85
U-Net-m2	30.63	208	0.92	0.85
U-Net-Betti-m1	24.34	148	0.91	0.84
U-Net-Betti-m2	32.23	223	0.92	0.85
Ground Truth	5.84	29	1.00	1.00

In Table 2, we present the results of evaluating the specification Φ_r^{connect} on the test set of 20 images from the OCTA dataset. Specifically, the violation rate refers to the percentage of regions that violate the border connectivity specification among all identified regions in the segmentation mask, while the violation count is the total number of such violations across the entire test set. The Dice score and mIoU represent the mean pixel-level performance metrics computed over the test set. In addition, we assess the structural quality of the provided ground truth annotations using the same connectivity specification.

While all U-Net variants achieve similar pixel-level performance in terms of Dice and mIoU scores, their violation rates differ substantially. Notably, U-Net-Betti-m1 achieves the lowest violation count (148), suggesting some benefit from topological supervision through Betti matching loss. However, the inconsistency across models indicates that Betti loss alone is insufficient to ensure structural correctness. These results also highlight that structural validation metrics, such as region-level violation rate, offer complementary insights beyond traditional pixel-wise metrics. Despite consistently high Dice and mIoU scores, violation counts vary by up to 90 regions across models, demonstrating that standard metrics do not reliably enforce topological fidelity. Interestingly, the ground truth exhibits a violation count of 29, highlighting that structural imperfections exist in manual annotation errors. Overall, this case study indicates that the integration of logic-based constraints using ISL provides more targeted and anatomically meaningful supervision.

5.2 Case 2: Multi-class Segmentation Spatial Alignment

In the second case study, we evaluate multi-class chest organ segmentation using the CheXmask dataset [14], which provides pixel-level anatomical segmentation masks for chest X-ray images. These masks were generated by the HybridGNet model and refined using the Reverse Classification Accuracy (RCA) technique for quality control [15]. This combination ensures consistent and high-quality segmentations across multiple public datasets, including CheXpert [23]. In our study, we used the CheXmask-provided segmentations as ground truth and trained a U-Net model using a combination of Dice loss and cross-entropy loss. Model performance was evaluated using the Dice Similarity Coefficient (DSC) for both lung and heart structures. The test set contains 159 images in total.

Table 3. Evaluation of ISL specifications on CheXmask multi-class dataset.

ISL Formula	Target Variable	Semantics	Results
Region distance $\blacktriangleright_s$	L. lung, R. lung	Quanlitative	99%
Weak distance $\triangleright_s$	R. lung, Heart	Quanlitative	99%
Universality $\boxed{\forall}$	Heart, Max Intensity	Quantitative	1.403
Universality $\boxed{\forall}$	Heart, Min Intensity	Quantitative	9.996

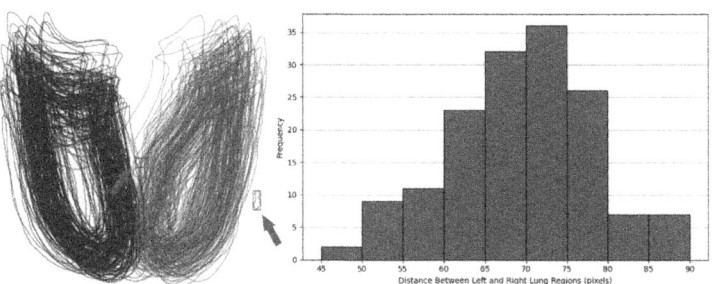

Fig. 3. Evaluation of directional spatial separation between left and right lungs.

We evaluate spatial logic specifications that capture left–right anatomical relationships. We define an ISL specification that enforces the expected spatial arrangement in which the right lung lies to the right of the left lung. More specifically, if a region is classified as the right lung, there must exist another region classified as the left lung that lies a sufficient distance to its left to ensure spatial separation. In addition to lung positioning, we also define a spatial relationship between the heart and the right lung using a weak directional distance constraint. Moreover, we include two specifications that assess pixel intensity distributions within the segmented heart. Specifically, we use universal quantification to verify that the maximum and minimum intensity values within the heart fall within expected bounds, where the expected values are derived from the actual intensity distribution of the heart region in the ground truth mask.

Table 3 shows the evaluation outcomes for four ISL specifications. The first two specifications, based on directional distance operators, are satisfied with 99% accuracy. The violated test images are marked by red arrows and boxes in the left subfigure of Fig. 3, where the visualization confirms that the ISL monitor correctly identifies the violating cases. The remaining two specifications assess pixel intensity properties within the heart using universal quantification. The average quantitative satisfaction scores for maximum and minimum intensity bounds are 1.403 and 9.996, respectively. These values indicate that the model preserves reasonable intensity consistency, which supports anatomical plausibility, as different organs exhibit distinct radiodensity characteristics.

To assess whether model predictions reflect anatomically plausible spatial separation between the lungs, we defined a region-level ISL specification requiring

Table 4. Average monitoring time per image for different ISL formula types.

Formula Type	Image Size	R Count	Semantics	Avg. Time (s)
Nested Pixel	320×320	N/A	Qualitative	2e-5 ± 7e-6
Nested Pixel	320×320	N/A	Quantitative	2e-5 ± 4e-6
Single Region	320×320	4	Qualitative	0.04 ± 0.00
Single Region	320×320	4	Quantitative	0.07 ± 0.01
Distance	320×320	4	Qualitative	0.18 ± 0.04
Distance	320×320	4	Quantitative	0.24 ± 0.05
Nested Pixel	304×304	N/A	Qualitative	7e-6 ± 0e-6
Nested Pixel	304×304	N/A	Quantitative	8e-6 ± 1e-6
Single Region	304×304	30	Qualitative	0.05 ± 0.00
Single Region	304×304	30	Quantitative	0.05 ± 0.00
Multi-Region	304×304	30	Qualitative	0.15 ± 0.02
Multi-Region	304×304	30	Quantitative	0.28 ± 0.01

the right lung to lie to the right of the left lung by at least d pixels. For each image, we computed the minimum value of d for which the specification was satisfied. The results shown in the right subfigure of Fig. 3 indicate that most segmentations satisfy the constraint at relatively low distance thresholds, which is consistent with the visualizations in the left subfigure.

5.3 Runtime Evaluation

We assess the computational efficiency of the ISL monitoring framework by measuring the average runtime per image for different formula types and semantics. Table 4 summarizes the results across both chest X-ray images (320 × 320) and retinal OCTA images (304 × 304). These results demonstrates that both formula structure and semantic type affect monitoring time. Pixel-level formulas, whether evaluated qualitatively or quantitatively, exhibit negligible runtime due to their simplicity and localized computation. In contrast, region-based specifications incur higher runtime costs due to component extraction and region-wise logical evaluation. Specifically, single-region formulas take 40–70 milliseconds per image, while directional distance constraints, which require spatial reasoning across regions, are the most expensive, averaging up to 240 milliseconds for quantitative semantics. For OCTA data with higher region counts (up to 30 per image), multi-region implications further increase runtime, especially under quantitative evaluation. These results demonstrate that while ISL enables expressive specification of spatial constraints, the associated computational overhead remains acceptable for both online and offline use cases.

6 Related Work

Two major lines of work have shaped formal reasoning for image data. The first focuses on topological properties such as connectedness and concavity [4,29,37], while the second addresses geometric relations like position and orientation [7,19,22]. RCC-8 [37] and $S4_u$ [4] form the foundation of topological reasoning, with extensions adding Boolean combinations [46] and temporal support [5]. On the geometric side, DAC [7] and SpaTeL [19] enable reasoning over directional or rectangular regions, while logics such as STPL [22] and STSL [29] adapt to grid-based visual domains. SaSTL [31] extends these frameworks with spatial aggregation and counting, and builds on STL [33]. These logics have been applied to structured reasoning over pixel-wise and region-wise properties in image segmentation and layout validation [18]. More recently, formal specification frameworks that leverage scene graphs to monitor semantic-level properties have emerged to bridge the gap between visual data and logical reasoning [42,47,48].

Formal logic has also been applied to monitor and guide learning-enabled systems in recent literature [2,10]. STLnet [32] and FedSTL [1] monitor RNN and federated models via STL-based runtime checks. TQTL [12] targets safety-critical perception in autonomous driving, while An et al. [3] apply logic to multi-level driving video monitoring. Related works use logic supervision to improve verification [8,21,43] and ensure safety in RL-based medical devices [44]. ISL advances the state of the art by introducing the first image segmentation logic for medical image analysis that unifies pixel and region-level reasoning, supports directional and spatial constraints, and incorporates model-derived attributes like confidence, with potential to improve both validation and learning.

7 Conclusion

In this paper, we present ISL, a novel specification language for expressing specifications in image segmentation. ISL supports qualitative and quantitative semantics, and we develop a monitoring algorithm to enable its practical application. Inspired by real-world medical image segmentation anatomical plausibility requirements, we evaluate the effectiveness of ISL on two medical imaging datasets. Results show that, even for well-performing models, ISL can accurately identify rare but critical segmentation failures. For more challenging segmentation tasks, the semantic insights provided by ISL offer an additional layer of safety and diagnostic value beyond traditional image segmentation metrics. Future work includes extending ISL to spatiotemporal settings, integrating it into learning frameworks for segmentation, and applying it to safety-critical domains like autonomous driving.

Acknowledgement. This material is based upon work supported by the National Science Foundation (NSF) under Award Numbers 2220401 and CNS-2443803. The paper reflects only the authors' view and does not necessarily reflect the views of the sponsoring agencies.

References

1. An, Z., Johnson, T.T., Ma, M.: Formal logic enabled personalized federated learning through property inference. In: Proceedings of the AAAI Conference on Artificial Intelligence. vol. 38, pp. 10882–10890 (2024)
2. An, Z., et al.: Combining LLMs with a logic-based framework to explain MCTS. In: Proceedings of the 24th International Conference on Autonomous Agents and Multiagent Systems, pp. 2405–2407. AAMAS '25, International Foundation for Autonomous Agents and Multiagent Systems, Richland, SC (2025)
3. An, Z., Wang, X., T. Johnson, T., Sprinkle, J., Ma, M.: Runtime monitoring of accidents in driving recordings with multi-type logic in empirical models. In: International Conference on Runtime Verification, pp. 376–388. Springer (2023)
4. Bennett, B.: Spatial reasoning with propositional logics. In: Principles of Knowledge Representation and Reasoning, pp. 51–62. Elsevier (1994)
5. Bennett, B., Cohn, A.G., Wolter, F., Zakharyaschev, M.: Multi-dimensional modal logic as a framework for Spatio-temporal reasoning. Appl. Intell. **17**, 239–251 (2002)
6. Berger, A.H., et al.: Topologically faithful multi-class segmentation in medical images. In: International Conference on Medical Image Computing and Computer-Assisted Intervention, pp. 721–731. Springer (2024)
7. Bresolin, D., Sala, P., Della Monica, D., Montanari, A., Sciavicco, G.: A decidable spatial generalization of metric interval temporal logic. In: 2010 17th International Symposium on Temporal Representation and Reasoning, pp. 95–102. IEEE (2010)
8. Chang, K.K.C., Xu, K., Kim, E., Sangiovanni-Vincentelli, A., Seshia, S.A.: Dynamic, multi-objective specification and falsification of autonomous CPS. In: International Conference on Runtime Verification, pp. 40–58. Springer (2024)
9. Chaudhry, R., Omole, A.E., Bordoni, B.: Anatomy, thorax, lungs. In: StatPearls [Internet]. StatPearls Publishing (2024)
10. Chen, Z., An, Z., Reynolds, J., Mullen, K., Martini, S., Ma, M.: LogiDebrief: a signal-temporal logic based automated debriefing approach with large language models integration. arXiv preprint arXiv:2505.03985 (2025)
11. Dice, L.R.: Measures of the amount of ecologic association between species. Ecology **26**(3), 297–302 (1945). https://doi.org/10.2307/1932409
12. Dokhanchi, A., Amor, H.B., Deshmukh, J.V., Fainekos, G.: Evaluating perception systems for autonomous vehicles using quality temporal logic. In: Runtime Verification: 18th International Conference, RV 2018, Limassol, Cyprus, November 10–13, 2018, Proceedings 18, pp. 409–416. Springer (2018)
13. European Union: Artificial intelligence act – article 15: Accuracy, robustness and cybersecurity. https://artificialintelligenceact.eu/article/15/ (2024). Accessed 05 May 2025
14. Gaggion, N., et al.: CheXmask: a large-scale dataset of anatomical segmentation masks for multi-center chest X-ray images. Sci. Data **11**(1), 511 (2024)
15. Gaggion, N., Mansilla, L., Mosquera, C., Milone, D.H., Ferrante, E.: Improving anatomical plausibility in medical image segmentation via hybrid graph neural networks: Applications to chest x-ray analysis. IEEE Transactions on Medical Imaging (2022)
16. Gal, Y., Ghahramani, Z.: Dropout as a Bayesian approximation: Representing model uncertainty in deep learning. International Conference on Machine Learning (ICML) (2016)

17. Gill, G., Bauer, C., Beichel, R.R.: A method for avoiding overlap of left and right lungs in shape model guided segmentation of lungs in CT volumes. Med. Phys. **41**(10), 101908 (2014)
18. Gol, E.A., Bartocci, E., Belta, C.: A formal methods approach to pattern synthesis in reaction diffusion systems. In: 53rd IEEE Conference on Decision and Control, pp. 108–113. IEEE (2014)
19. Haghighi, I., Jones, A., Kong, Z., Bartocci, E., Gros, R., Belta, C.: Spatel: a novel spatial-temporal logic and its applications to networked systems. In: Proceedings of the 18th International Conference on Hybrid Systems: Computation and Control, pp. 189–198 (2015)
20. Hao, J., et al.: Retinal structure detection in octa image via voting-based multitask learning. IEEE Trans. Med. Imaging **41**(12), 3969–3980 (2022)
21. He, W., Wu, C., Bensalem, S.: Box-based monitor approach for out-of-distribution detection in YOLO: an exploratory study. In: International Conference on Runtime Verification, pp. 229–239. Springer (2024)
22. Hekmatnejad, M., Hoxha, B., Deshmukh, J.V., Yang, Y., Fainekos, G.: Formalizing and evaluating requirements of perception systems for automated vehicles using spatio-temporal perception logic. Int. J. Robot. Res. **43**(2), 203–238 (2024)
23. Irvin, J., et al.: CheXpert: a large chest radiograph dataset with uncertainty labels and expert comparison. In: Proceedings of the AAAI Conference on Artificial Intelligence. vol. 33, pp. 590–597 (2019)
24. Jaccard, P.: Étude comparative de la distribution florale dans une portion des alpes et des jura. Bull Soc Vaudoise Sci Nat **37**, 547–579 (1901)
25. Kendall, A., Gal, Y.: What uncertainties do we need in Bayesian deep learning for computer vision? Adv. Neural Inf. Process. Syst. (NeurIPS) **30** (2017)
26. Kingma, D.P.: Adam: A method for stochastic optimization. arXiv preprint arXiv:1412.6980 (2014)
27. Li, M., et al.: OCTA-500: a retinal dataset for optical coherence tomography angiography study. Med. Image Anal. **93**, 103092 (2024)
28. Li, M., Huang, K., Xu, Q., Yang, J., Zhang, Y., Yang, J.: OCTA-500: a novel dataset for retinal optical coherence tomography angiography analysis. Med. Image Anal. **91**, 103092 (2024). https://doi.org/10.1016/j.media.2024.103092, https://www.sciencedirect.com/science/article/pii/S1361841524000173
29. Li, T., et al.: STSL: a novel spatio-temporal specification language for cyber-physical systems. In: 2020 IEEE 20th International Conference on Software Quality, Reliability and Security (QRS), pp. 309–319. IEEE (2020)
30. Lim, J., Abily, A., Ben Salem, D., Gaillandre, L., Attye, A., Ognard, J.: Training and validation of a deep learning u-net architecture general model for automated segmentation of inner ear from ct. Eur. Radiol. Exp. **8**(1), 104 (2024)
31. Ma, M., Bartocci, E., Lifland, E., Stankovic, J., Feng, L.: SaSTL: spatial aggregation signal temporal logic for runtime monitoring in smart cities. In: 2020 ACM/IEEE 11th International Conference on Cyber-Physical Systems (ICCPS), pp. 51–62. IEEE (2020)
32. Ma, M., Gao, J., Feng, L., Stankovic, J.: STLnet: signal temporal logic enforced multivariate recurrent neural networks. Adv. Neural. Inf. Process. Syst. **33**, 14604–14614 (2020)
33. Maler, O., Nickovic, D.: Monitoring temporal properties of continuous signals. In: International Symposium on Formal Techniques in Real-Time and Fault-Tolerant Systems, pp. 152–166. Springer (2004)

34. Moon, N., Bullitt, E., Van Leemput, K., Gerig, G.: Automatic brain and tumor segmentation. In: Medical Image Computing and Computer-Assisted Intervention—MICCAI 2002: 5th International Conference Tokyo, Japan, September 25–28, 2002 Proceedings, Part I 5, pp. 372–379. Springer (2002)
35. Nair, T., Precup, D., Arbel, T.: Exploring uncertainty measures in deep networks for multiple sclerosis lesion detection and segmentation. Med. Image Anal. **59**, 101557 (2020)
36. Panara, K., Hoffer, M.: Anatomy, head and neck, ear internal auditory canal (internal auditory meatus, internal acoustic canal) (2019)
37. Randell, D.A., Cui, Z., Cohn, A.G.: A spatial logic based on regions and connection. KR **92**, 165–176 (1992)
38. Ronneberger, O., Fischer, P., Brox, T.: U-Net: convolutional networks for biomedical image segmentation. In: MICCAI 2015: 18th International Conference, Munich, Germany, October 5-9, 2015, proceedings, part III 18, pp. 234–241. Springer (2015)
39. Siddique, N., Paheding, S., Elkin, C.P., Devabhaktuni, V.: U-net and its variants for medical image segmentation: a review of theory and applications. IEEE Access **9**, 82031–82057 (2021)
40. Sousa, A.M., et al.: ALTIS: a fast and automatic lung and trachea CT-image segmentation method. Med. Phys. **46**(11), 4970–4982 (2019)
41. Stucki, N., Paetzold, J.C., Shit, S., Menze, B., Bauer, U.: Topologically faithful image segmentation via induced matching of persistence barcodes. In: International Conference on Machine Learning, pp. 32698–32727. PMLR (2023)
42. Toledo, F., Woodlief, T., Elbaum, S., Dwyer, M.B.: Specifying and monitoring safe driving properties with scene graphs. In: 2024 IEEE International Conference on Robotics and Automation (ICRA), pp. 15577–15584. IEEE (2024)
43. Tran, H.D., et al.: NNV: the neural network verification tool for deep neural networks and learning-enabled cyber-physical systems. In: International Conference on Computer Aided Verification, pp. 3–17. Springer (2020)
44. Vuppala, S.R.H., Allen, N., Pinisetty, S., Roop, P.: A formal approach for safe reinforcement learning: a rate-adaptive pacemaker case study. In: International Conference on Runtime Verification, pp. 3–21. Springer (2024)
45. Wang, R., et al.: Medical image segmentation using deep learning: a survey. IET Image Proc. **16**(5), 1243–1267 (2022)
46. Wolter, F., Zakharyaschev, M.: Spatial representation and reasoning in RCC-8 with Boolean region terms. In: Proceedings of the 14th European Conference on Artificial Intelligence, pp. 244–248. Citeseer (2000)
47. Woodlief, T., Toledo, F., Elbaum, S., Dwyer, M.B.: S3c: spatial semantic scene coverage for autonomous vehicles. In: Proceedings of the IEEE/ACM 46th International Conference on Software Engineering, pp. 1–13 (2024)
48. Woodlief, T., Toledo, F., Elbaum, S., Dwyer, M.B.: The SGSM framework: enabling the specification and monitor synthesis of safe driving properties through scene graphs. Sci. Comput. Program. **242**, 103252 (2025)
49. Zhao, L., Tohka, J., Ruotsalainen, U.: Accurate 3D left-right brain hemisphere segmentation in MR images based on shape bottlenecks and partial volume estimation. In: Image Analysis: 15th Scandinavian Conference, SCIA 2007, Aalborg, Denmark, June 10-14, 2007 15, pp. 581–590. Springer (2007)

Runtime Consultants

Dana Fisman[(✉)] and Elina Sudit

Ben-Gurion University, Beer-Sheva, Israel
dana@bgu.ac.il , elinasu@post.bgu.ac.il

Abstract. In this paper we introduce the notion of a *runtime consultant*. A runtime consultant is defined with respect to some value function on infinite words. Similar to a runtime monitor, it runs in parallel to an execution of the system and provides inputs at every step of the run. While a runtime monitor alerts when a violation occurs, the idea behind a consultant is to be *pro-active* and provide recommendations for which action to take next in order to avoid violation (or obtain a maximal value for quantitative objectives). It is assumed that a *runtime-controller* can take these recommendations into consideration. The runtime consultant does not assume that its recommendations are always followed. Instead, it adjusts to the actions actually taken (similar to a vehicle navigation system). We show how to compute a runtime consultant for common value functions used in verification, and that almost all have a runtime consultant that works in constant time. We also develop consultants for ω-regular properties, under both their classical Boolean semantics and their recently proposed quantitative interpretation.

1 Introduction

In *runtime verification* [1,2,9,13,17,19] the system under test is monitored against its formal specification, so that if and when it can be deduced that the current execution of the system violates the specification, an alert can be issued and measures to prevent further escalation can be taken. In many cases, feedback that the specification has been violated might be too late in the sense that preventing further escalation is meaningless as the bad thing has already happened. For this reason, a recent thread of research in runtime verification concerns predictive analysis, where one tries to provide indication for possible failures as early as possible [24,32,33]. Taking this a step forward, in this work we introduce the notion of a *runtime consultant*.

The idea of a *runtime consultant* is to generalize the notion of a runtime monitor so that instead of alerting when a problem occurred, it provides a recommendation of which actions are preferable to take next in order to satisfy the property (and so avoid violation before it occurs). In this setting it is assumed that a *runtime controller* has some control over the next action and can take the

---

E. Sudit—Supported by ISF grant 2507/21 and Frankel Center for Computer Science, BGU.

consultant's recommendation into account. The consultant, like a GPS navigation system, does not assume its recommendations are always followed. Instead, it adjusts along the way and simply recommends the best actions from the current point of the run.

One motivation for a runtime consultant (RC) is to have an entity that can assist in systems involving human decision-making by offering proactive, realtime recommendations toward achieving qualitative or quantitative goals. In clinical settings, for instance during surgery or emergency care, an RC might suggest immediate actions such as adjusting drug dosage, initiating a procedure, or switching protocols in response to changes in vital signs—helping ensure guideline adherence, patient stability, and risk minimization. In pilot-assistance systems or semi-autonomous vehicles, the RC can recommend maneuvers like decelerating, changing lanes, or rerouting, guided by qualitative goals (e.g., avoiding collisions, complying with airspace rules) and quantitative ones (e.g., minimizing fuel use or turbulence). In all cases, the RC continuously adapts to the operator's actual decisions, much like a navigation system recalibrates after a missed turn. This paper lays the theoretical foundations for a runtime consultant, considering common value functions used in formal verification.

The definition of a runtime consultant assumes some value function by which some runs are determined better than others. The value function can be qualitative (Boolean) or quantitative (with many and even infinitely many values). Based on the value function and the current state of the execution, the runtime consultant gives recommendation on which action to take next in order to achieve the best value in the long run (given the history of the execution so far).

In this work we formally define the notion of a runtime consultant for a given value function. We assume higher values are preferable. Two types of runtime consultants are proposed: the $\leadsto$-RC that gives recommendations for obtaining the highest achievable value in the overall system and the $\circlearrowright$-RC that gives recommendations for obtaining the highest value achievable on an execution that loops back to the current state. We say that a runtime consultant is *strong* if it makes no arbitrary choices in its recommendation; that is, it recommends *all* actions from the current state that can ultimately result in the highest achievable value. Otherwise we term it *weak*.

We prove some general properties on arbitrary RCs as well as Boolean RCs (i.e. RCs for a Boolean value function). We examine the widely used limit operators Sup, Inf, LimSup, LimInf and LimAvg as value functions; and show how to calculate runtime consultants for them. With regard to $\circlearrowright$-RC we show that for Sup and LimSup it is impossible to construct a strong $\circlearrowright$-RC in the general case, but for all other limit operators it is possible. With regard to $\leadsto$-RC only for Inf it is possible to construct a strong RC. The construction of these RCs can be done in polynomial time for all operators except for LimAvg in the case of $\circlearrowright$-RC, for which we show the problem is coNP-complete.

The construction of the RC is done at the preprocessing step. The interesting parameter is the runtime of the constructed RC. To keep up with the monitored run, it is desirable that the running time would be constant. Regarding the runtime of the RCs for the above operators, the picture is as follows. They are constant in all cases but the ones for Sup and Inf in which they are logarithmic in the size of the maximal weight in the graph, which is also quite reasonable.

We then turn to discuss RCs for ω-regular properties, given by some parity automaton. We show that in the qualitative setting strong RCs may not exist in the general case; the preprocessing time is polynomial; and the running time is constant as desired.

However, strong runtime consultants can be obtained for ω-regular properties if we adopt a quantitative rather than qualitative value function. The quantitative interpretation of ω-regular properties introduced in [11] defines a value function, Rbst_L, which assigns each lasso word w a robustness score $\mathsf{Rbst}_L(w)$, reflecting how robust w is with respect to the property L. The range of $\mathsf{Rbst}_L(w)$ is infinite, distinguishing accepted words from rejected ones, while also capturing nuances based on both the periodic and transient parts of the word (with greater weight on the periodic part). We show that strong RCs can be constructed for this quantitative robustness function, with a coNP-complete preprocessing step. Once constructed, the RC operates in constant time, as required.

Related Work. The concept of a runtime consultant bears some resemblance to runtime enforcement mechanisms such as *enforcement monitors* (EMs) [7, 27–29, 31], but introduces several key differences. An EM is designed to handle untrusted programs by actively modifying their outputs—through suppression, termination, or insertion—to ensure compliance with a specification. In contrast, an RC acts passively: it does not interfere with the system's actions but issues recommendations for the next step, which the system may or may not follow.

Technically, an EM observes a sequence of outputs $\sigma_1, ..., \sigma_i$ produced by the system and eventually emits a modified sequence $\sigma'_1, ..., \sigma'_j$ that satisfies the specification while minimally deviating from the original sequence. An RC, by contrast, on observing the same prefix $\sigma_1, ..., \sigma_i$ outputs a set of recommended next actions Σ_{next}, from which it is recommended to choose the next action σ_{i+1} in order to achieve correct or optimal behavior.

While EMs were originally conceived for enforcing security properties in sequential programs, they are less suitable for reactive systems, where interventions like buffering, suppression, or delaying actions are often infeasible. Shield synthesis was introduced to address this gap by adapting enforcement to reactive settings, enforcing safety properties without delays or skipped steps [26].

However, both EMs and shield synthesis are fundamentally limited to safety properties [6,8,18]. While predictive EM can handle some liveness properties [28], it requires partial knowledge of the system's language—effectively treating the system as a gray-box. In contrast, runtime consultants are applicable to both safety and liveness properties, and operate in a fully black-box setting: they make no assumptions about the system's structure or behavior. Moreover, RCs naturally generalize beyond Boolean specifications, supporting quantitative value functions—a capability that, to our knowledge, has not been addressed by prior runtime enforcement approaches.

Complete proofs are available in the full version of the paper [12].

2 Preliminaries

The set of all infinite words over Σ is denoted Σ^ω. A word $w \in \Sigma^\omega$ of the form $w = u(v)^\omega$ for some $u \in \Sigma^*$ and $v \in \Sigma^+$ is termed a *lasso word*. We say that u is the *spoke* of the lasso word and v is its *period*. For the lasso word $u(v)^\omega$ we denote the pair (u,v) for $u \in \Sigma^*$ and $v \in \Sigma^+$ as the *representation* of the lasso word.

$\mathbb{B}$ abbreviates $\{\text{T}, \text{F}\}$. For $i \leq j$, we write $[i..j]$ for the set $\{i, i+1, ..., j\}$. For a word $v = \sigma_1 \sigma_2 ... \sigma_m$, the infix of v that starts at σ_i and ends at σ_j inclusive is termed $v[i..j]$. Similarly, the prefix (resp. suffix) of v that ends (resp. starts) in σ_i inclusive is termed $v[..i]$ (resp. $v[i..]$). The notation $x \preceq y$ (resp. $x \prec y$) denotes that x is a prefix (resp. proper prefix) of y.

Since we are interested in both quantitative and qualitative (Boolean) value functions we introduce a computational model that generalizes both. A *quantitative automaton* (abbr. *quatomaton*) $\mathcal{A}$ is a tuple $(\Sigma, Q, q_0, \delta, \kappa, \alpha)$ where Σ is an alphabet, Q a finite set of states, $q_0 \in Q$ the initial state, and $\alpha : (\mathbb{T}_\delta \times \mathbb{T}_\kappa)^\omega \to \mathbb{T}$ is the objective. A run of $\mathcal{A}$ on a word $w = \sigma_1 \sigma_2 ... \in \Sigma^\omega$ is a sequence $\rho = q_0 \xrightarrow[t_1, d_1]{\sigma_1} q_1 \xrightarrow[t_2, d_2]{\sigma_2} q_2 \cdots$ such that $\delta(q_{i-1}, \sigma_i) = (q_i, t_i)$ and $\kappa(q_i) = d_i$. The value of the run ρ is $\alpha((t_1, d_1)(t_2, d_2) \cdots)$. The value that $\mathcal{A}$ gives w, denoted $[\![\mathcal{A}]\!](w)$, is the value of the unique run of $\mathcal{A}$ on w. We say that $\mathcal{A}$ *implements* Val : $\Sigma^\omega \to \mathbb{T}$ if for every $w \in \Sigma^\omega$ we have $[\![\mathcal{A}]\!](w) = \text{Val}(w)$. For a finite word $u \in \Sigma^*$ we use $\mathcal{A}(u)$ to denote the state that $\mathcal{A}$ arrives at on reading u.

A *labeled weighted graph* is a quantitative automaton where $\mathbb{T}_\kappa$ is a singleton and thus plays no role. A *parity automaton* is a quantitative automaton where $\mathbb{T}_\kappa$ is a finite set of integers, $\mathbb{T}_\delta$ is a singleton (hence plays no role), $\mathbb{T} = \mathbb{B}$ and $\alpha((-,d_1),(-,d_2),...)$ is T iff min $\text{inft}(d_1, d_2, ...)$ is even, where $\text{inft}(d_1, d_2, ...)$ is the set of items occurring infinitely often in the sequence, namely $\{d \in \mathbb{T}_\kappa \mid \forall i \in \mathbb{N}. \exists j > i. d_j = d\}$. We use DPA for deterministic parity automata. Note that DPA can express all ω-regular languages [25].

We associate with $\mathcal{A}$ its automaton graph $G=(V,E)$ where $V=Q$ and $E = \{(v,v') \mid \delta(v,\sigma)=(v',t) \text{ for some } \sigma \in \Sigma, t \in \mathbb{T}_\delta\}$. A subset C of vertices (i.e., states) is a *strongly connected component* (SCC) if there exists a non empty path between any two vertices in C. An SCC is a *maximal strongly connected component* (MSCC) if there is no SCC C' such that $C \subsetneq C'$. Every run of an automaton $\mathcal{A}$ on a word w eventually stays within a single MSCC (i.e. visits no state outside of this MSCC). We term this MSCC the *final* MSCC of w wrt L. A (possibly non-simple) path (resp. cycle) $\rho = e_1 e_2 ... e_m$ for edges $e_i \in E$ is termed a *trail* (resp. *cyclic trail*) if no edge occurs more than once (i.e., $e_i \neq e_j$ for $i, j \in [1..m]$, $i \neq j$).

The following value functions on infinite words are defined wrt a weighted labeled graph. The *supremum* (resp. *infimum*), abbreviated Sup (resp. Inf), value of an infinite word w is Sup : $\Sigma^\omega \to \mathbb{R}$ for $\sup_{i \in \mathbb{N}} \{\theta(w,i)\}$ (resp. Inf : $\Sigma^\omega \to \mathbb{R}$ for $\inf_{i \in \mathbb{N}} \{\theta(w,i)\}$) where $\theta(w,i)$ is the weight of the corresponding graph edge that the run visits by reading the i-th letter of w. The *limit supremum* (resp. *limit infimum*), abbreviated LimSup (resp. LimInf), value of an infinite word w is defined as $\lim_{n \to \infty} \sup_{i \geq n} \{\theta(w,i)\}$ (resp. $\lim_{n \to \infty} \inf_{i \geq n} \{\theta(w,i)\}$). Limit average value functions on infinite words, LimInfAvg and LimSupAvg for short, are defined as $\mathsf{LimSup}_{n\to\infty} \frac{1}{n}\sum_{i=1}^{n} \theta(w,i)$ and $\mathsf{LimInf}_{n\to\infty} \frac{1}{n}\sum_{i=1}^{n} \theta(w,i)$. Since we consider lasso words and on lasso words LimInfAvg and LimSupAvg coincide, we do not distinguish between them and simply use LimAvg.

3 Definition of a Consultant

As mentioned in the introduction, a runtime consultant can be thought of as extending the idea of a runtime monitor—instead of alerting when something bad has happened which might be too late, a runtime consultant should be proactive and recommend what action to take next, in order to avoid violation, and in the long run satisfy the property. Similar to a runtime monitor for a given property L, a runtime consultant bases its decision taking into account the history of the run so far. Clearly, a runtime consultant should recommend taking actions that avoid violating the property, but given a value function on L, it can do more than that and try to direct the run towards not only satisfying L, but doing it better, where *better* means obtaining a larger value according to a given value function μ. In the next sections we discuss runtime consultants for value functions for common limit operators. We further discuss the runtime consultant for a new value function that captures the notion of *robustness* [11], so larger will coincide with being more robust. Since we would like to apply the notion of a runtime consultant to both quantitative and qualitative properties, we define them wrt a quantitative automaton that generalizes both notions.

Since modeling all system detail is often infeasible, we assume the runtime consultant has only a partial view of the system's behavior. Formally, we assume the alphabet of the property or value function is Σ, the alphabet of the system is $\widehat{\Sigma}$ and there exists a mapping $h : \widehat{\Sigma}^* \to \Sigma^*$ translating system executions into traces relevant to the property. E.g. it could be that $\widehat{\Sigma} = \Sigma \cup \Sigma'$ (or $\widehat{\Sigma} = \Sigma \times \Sigma'$) and h projects onto letters in Σ (or to the Σ component of the letter, resp.).

Let $\mathcal{A}$ be a quatomaton implementing a value function $\mu_\mathcal{A} : \Sigma^\omega \to \mathbb{T}$ where $\mathbb{T}$ is some totally ordered domain. While μ assigns values to infinite words, at runtime only finite words are observed. We thus need to derive from $\mathcal{A}$ a value to associate with a finite word, a prefix of an infinite word. We provide two value functions for finite words, denoted $\mu_\mathcal{A}^\rightarrow(u)$ and $\mu_\mathcal{A}^\circlearrowleft(u)$. Intuitively, for a finite word u the value function $\mu_\mathcal{A}^\rightarrow(u)$ returns the maximal value any infinite extension w of u can take. The value function $\mu_\mathcal{A}^\circlearrowleft(u)$ restricts attention to infinite words obtained by looping on the state $\mathcal{A}$ arrives at when reading u, namely $\mathcal{A}(u)$.

Definition 3.1 ($\mu_\mathcal{A}^\rightarrow, \mu_\mathcal{A}^\circlearrowleft$). Let $u \in \Sigma^*$ and $\mathcal{A}$ a quatomaton for $\mu_\mathcal{A} : \Sigma^\omega \to \mathbb{T}$.

- $\mu_\mathcal{A}^\rightarrow(u) = \sup \{\mu_\mathcal{A}(uw) \mid w \in \Sigma^\omega\}$ is the *any-extension value* of u.
- $\mu_\mathcal{A}^\circlearrowleft(u) = \sup \{\mu_\mathcal{A}(uv^\omega) \mid v \in \Sigma^+, \mathcal{A}(uv)=\mathcal{A}(u)\}$ is the *cyclic-extension value*.

Example 3.1. Consider the quatomaton $\mathcal{A}$ in Fig. 1(left) whose objective we call LimAvg *with the shortest path to period*—formally, $\mathcal{A}$ gives a lasso word $u(v)^\omega$ the

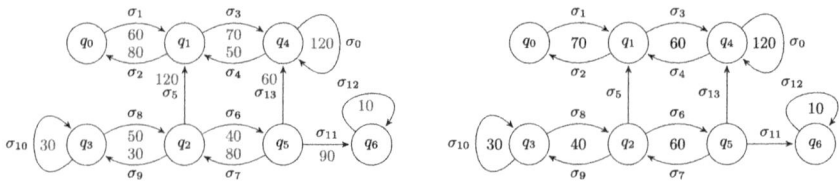

Fig. 1. The quautomaton for Example 3.1 and its simple-loops view.

value corresponding to the average of the edges' weights on the (not necessary simple) loop v, minus the length of u. For example, the values of the words $\sigma_8\sigma_5(\sigma_3\sigma_4)^\omega$ and $\sigma_4(\sigma_2\sigma_1)^\omega$ are $60-2$ and $70-1$ resp., while the value of the word $\sigma_8\sigma_5(\sigma_3\sigma_4\sigma_2\sigma_1)^\omega$ is $65-2$. It is thus convenient to consider the graph on the right which simply visualizes the values of simple loops.

Let us see what do $\mu_{\mathcal{A}}^{\rightarrow}(\cdot)$ and $\mu_{\mathcal{A}}^{\circlearrowleft}(\cdot)$ return for some prefixes u. Note first that $\mu_{\mathcal{A}}^{\rightarrow}(u)=120-x$ for any u that does not have σ_{11} or σ_{12} as an infix, where x is the length of the shortest path to q_4. Otherwise, $\mu_{\mathcal{A}}^{\rightarrow}(u)=10-y$ where y is the length of the shortest path to q_6 since a word that traversed σ_{11} or σ_{12} can only reach the final cycle σ_{12}. Considering $\mu_{\mathcal{A}}^{\circlearrowleft}(\cdot)$, we observe that for any u that reaches vertex q_4, we have $\mu_{\mathcal{A}}^{\circlearrowleft}(u)=120-x$ as 120 is the highest value for a cycle from q_4. For words u ending in vertex q_1 we get $\mu_{\mathcal{A}}^{\circlearrowleft}(u)=80-z$ since the highest-value cycle starting at vertex q_1 is $(\sigma_3\sigma_0\sigma_4)$ and its averaged value is 80.

It is not hard to see that as we read a prefix of an infinite word, with every step the value $\mu_{\mathcal{A}}^{\rightarrow}$ can either remain unchanged or decrease (but it may not increase). The situation is different for cyclic-extensions. Here the value can increase along a prefix of an infinite word.

Remark 3.1 (Monotonicity of $\mu_{\mathcal{A}}^{\rightarrow}$). Let $\mu_{\mathcal{A}}$ be as above, and $u, u' \in \Sigma^*$.

1. $\mu_{\mathcal{A}}^{\rightarrow}$ is monotonically non-increasing: If $u \preceq u'$ then $\mu_{\mathcal{A}}^{\rightarrow}(u) \geq \mu_{\mathcal{A}}^{\rightarrow}(u')$.
2. $\mu_{\mathcal{A}}^{\circlearrowleft}$ is <u>not</u> monotonic: Given $u \prec u'$, both $\mu_{\mathcal{A}}^{\circlearrowleft}(u) < \mu_{\mathcal{A}}^{\circlearrowleft}(u')$ and $\mu_{\mathcal{A}}^{\circlearrowleft}(u) \geq \mu_{\mathcal{A}}^{\circlearrowleft}(u')$ are possible.
3. $\mu_{\mathcal{A}}^{\rightarrow}(u) \geq \mu_{\mathcal{A}}^{\circlearrowleft}(u)$ for all $u \in \Sigma^*$.

The runtime consultant should recommend which letters it is preferable to take next. We thus provide the following definitions.

Definition 3.2 ($\Sigma_{\mathcal{A}}^{\rightarrow}(u)$). *Let $\mu_{\mathcal{A}}$ and u be as above. For $t \in \mathbb{T}$, a word $w \in \Sigma^\omega$ is a t-any-extension of u if $\mu_{\mathcal{A}}(uw) = t$. If, in addition, $t = \mu_{\mathcal{A}}^{\rightarrow}(u)$ we say that w is a preferred any-extension of u and the set of first letters of such extension is $\Sigma_{\mathcal{A}}^{\rightarrow}(u) = \{\sigma \in \Sigma \mid \exists w \in \Sigma^\omega \text{ s.t. } \sigma w \text{ is a preferred any-extension of } u\}$.*

Definition 3.3 ($\Sigma_{\mathcal{A}}^{\circlearrowleft}(u)$). *We say that $v \in \Sigma^+$ is a cycle on u if $\mathcal{A}(uv) = \mathcal{A}(u)$. If v is a cycle on u and $\mu_{\mathcal{A}}(u(v)^\omega) = t$ we say that v is a t-cyclic-extension of u. If for every cycle v' of u such that $v' \prec v$ we* have that v' is a t'-cyclic-extension for $t' \geq t$ we say that v is a t-preferred cyclic-extension.[1] If, in addition, $t = \mu_{\mathcal{A}}^{\circlearrowleft}(u)$ we say that v is a preferred cyclic-extension and the set of first letters of such extension is $\Sigma_{\mathcal{A}}^{\circlearrowleft}(u) = \{\sigma \in \Sigma \mid \exists v \in \Sigma^* \text{ s.t. } \sigma v \text{ is a preferred cyclic extension of } u\}$.

In Example 3.1 the preferred any-extension of σ_7 is any word that starts with σ_5 or σ_6 and has suffix $(\sigma_0)^\omega$ since a word with such suffix has the highest achievable value. Thus $\Sigma_{\mathcal{A}}^{\rightsquigarrow}(\sigma_7) = \{\sigma_5, \sigma_6\}$ as otherwise the letter σ_9 is chosen, and the path to the best loop (namely, σ_0) becomes longer. The preferred cyclic-extension of σ_7 is $(\sigma_6\sigma_7)$, thus, $\Sigma_{\mathcal{A}}^{\circlearrowleft}(\sigma_7) = \{\sigma_6\}$. This is since the only cycles that include the vertex q_2 are $(\sigma_6\sigma_7)$, $(\sigma_8\sigma_9)$, $(\sigma_8\sigma_9\sigma_{10})$ and their combinations, and among them the cycle $(\sigma_6\sigma_7)$ has the highest value. Note that the edge σ_5 is not considered for $\Sigma_{\mathcal{A}}^{\circlearrowleft}(\sigma_7)$ since it takes the run to another MSCC from which vertex q_2 is unreachable, so no cycle can be closed.

Definition 3.4 (A runtime consultant (RC)). Let $\mathcal{A}$ be quatomaton, and $\hookrightarrow \in \{\rightsquigarrow, \circlearrowleft\}$. A $\hookrightarrow$-runtime consultant for $\mathcal{A}$ is a procedure that given $u \in \Sigma^*$ returns a set $\Sigma' \subseteq \Sigma_{\mathcal{A}}^{\hookrightarrow}(u)$, such that Σ' can be empty only if $\Sigma_{\mathcal{A}}^{\hookrightarrow}(u)$ is. If, also, $\Sigma' = \Sigma_{\mathcal{A}}^{\hookrightarrow}(u)$ we say that the consultant is strong. Otherwise we say it is weak. We refer to $\Sigma_{\mathcal{A}}^{\rightsquigarrow}(u)$ and $\Sigma_{\mathcal{A}}^{\circlearrowleft}(u)$ as the $\rightsquigarrow$- and $\circlearrowleft$-recommendations, resp.

Ideally, an RC should work in constant time in order to keep up with the observed run and provide recommendations that can be taken in a timely manner.

Example 3.2 ($\rightsquigarrow$- and $\circlearrowleft$-recommendations). Let μ be the value function discussed in Example 3.1 and implemented by the quatomaton in Fig. 1. Recall that the values μ assigns a lasso word depends mainly on the average weight of the loop, and the values of simple loops are given in Fig. 1 on the right.

Figure 2 represents the runtime recommendations given by the RC. In the left figure we annotate in blue the $\rightsquigarrow$-recommendations from each state. In the middle the $\circlearrowleft$-recommendations from each state are annotated orange. The rightmost figure shows the paths obtained by following the $\rightsquigarrow$- and $\circlearrowleft$-recommendations from the initial state, in blue and orange, respectively.

The quatomaton has three MSCCs. The $\rightsquigarrow$-recommendations suggest reaching as fastest as possible the best loop (σ_0) from each state of the automaton that σ_0 is reachable from. These are all states except the one that is reached by σ_{11}. From the latter state the best reachable cycle is σ_{12}. The $\circlearrowleft$-RC never recommends moving to another MSCC, because its definition requires returning to the state the run is currently at. Accordingly, an edge that is not a part of any MSCC will not be recommended. Therefore, the loop (σ_0) cannot be reached by these recommendations as long as the run is in a bottom MSCC.

Considering the initial state, the runs obtained by following $\rightsquigarrow$-recommendation are different from the run obtained following the $\circlearrowleft$-recommendation. The $\rightsquigarrow$-recommendation reaches the MSCC with the highest-value loop and the

---

[1] That is, if v starts with a cycle v' then v' cannot have a value t' lower than t.

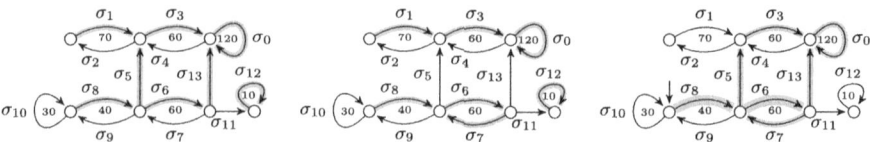

Fig. 2. The $\rightsquigarrow$- and $\circlearrowright$-recommendations (in blue and orange resp.) for μ of Example 3.2. (Color figure online)

resulting word is either $\sigma_8\sigma_5\sigma_3(\sigma_0)^\omega$ or $\sigma_8\sigma_6\sigma_{13}(\sigma_0)^\omega$. Note that there are two edges by which the run can move from the bottom MSCC to the top one and both have same path length to the best loop, so both edges are recommended by the $\rightsquigarrow$-RC. The $\circlearrowright$-recommendation stays in the initial MSCC and in every step compares the cycles that include the current state. The resulting word is $\sigma_8(\sigma_6\sigma_7)^\omega$.

4 Properties of Runtime Consultants

Recall that an RC does not assume its recommendations are always followed. Below we articulate the guarantees that can be provided on *partially* obeying the $\rightsquigarrow$- and $\circlearrowright$-recommendations. We discuss first the qualitative case, namely when the value function is Boolean, and then turn to the quantitative case.

4.1 Properties of RCs for Boolean Value Function

Before providing a proposition we exemplify what happens in the Boolean case when the $\rightsquigarrow$- and $\circlearrowright$-recommendations are followed.

Example 4.1 (A qualitative value function). Consider an automatic call distributor (ACD) in a business' phone system that routes calls to support staff consisting of two employees, whose functionality is implemented in Fig. 3 by the DPA $\mathcal{A}$. Recall that a DPA accepts if the minimal rank visited infinitely often is even, thus accepting words are those that loop on the state ranked 0 (henceforth, the 0-state).

The $\rightsquigarrow$-recommendation for a prefix u that is ε (the empty word), INIT_SYS or INIT_SYS·INIT_DB, is {INIT_SYS}, {INIT_DB} and {CNCT} resp. (since otherwise the sink state is reached, meaning a violation occurred and the word is rejected). The $\circlearrowright$-recommendation is $\emptyset$ (since there is no option to close a cycle in the automaton on the state reached by reading this prefix).

For prefix that has not reached the sink state, $\Sigma_{\mathcal{A}}^{\rightsquigarrow}(u) = \Sigma$ (since an accepted word can be obtained regardless of the next read letter). For u that reaches the 0-state we have $\Sigma_{\mathcal{A}}^{\circlearrowright}(u) = \Sigma$ as well (since any cycle starting there is accepted). For prefix u ending with CALL we get $\Sigma_{\mathcal{A}}^{\circlearrowright}(u) = \{\texttt{QUE1}, \texttt{QUE2}\}$ as these letters are part of cycles that include the 0-state. For prefix u ending with QUE1 (resp. QUE2) the $\circlearrowright$-recommendation is {ANS1} ({ANS2} resp.) as this letter must be taken in order to obtain a cycle including the 0-state, as per Definition 3.3.

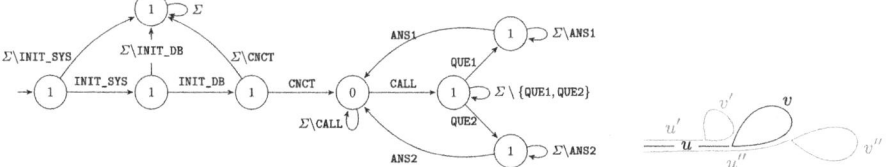

Fig. 3. The DPA for the ACD from Example 4.1.

Fig. 4. Following $\circlearrowright$-RC as discussed in Sect. 4.2.

Proposition 4.1 (RC compliance guarantees: qualitative case). *Let $\mathcal{A}_L$ an automaton recognizing a non-empty ω-regular language L. Let $w \in \Sigma^\omega$.*

1. *If $w[i+1] \notin \Sigma_{\mathcal{A}_L}^{\leadsto}(w[..i])$ for some $i \in \mathbb{N}$ then $w \notin L$.*
2. *If for some $i \in \mathbb{N}$ and for all $j > i$ we have $w[j+1] \notin \Sigma_{\mathcal{A}_L}^{\circlearrowright}(w[..j])$ then $w \notin L$.*
3. *If for all $i \in \mathbb{N}$ we have that $w[i+1] \in \Sigma_{\mathcal{A}_L}^{\leadsto}(w[..i])$ and for some $j \in \mathbb{N}$ we have that $w[k+1] \in \Sigma_{\mathcal{A}_L}^{\circlearrowright}(w[..k])$ for all $k \geq j$ then $w \in L$.*

Proof. 1. There are only two options for values for a word wrt the language in this setting: T and F. If there exists an $i \in \mathbb{N}$ such that $w[i+1] \notin \Sigma_{\mathcal{A}_L}^{\leadsto}(w[..i])$ then none of the actions that can achieve T are chosen. Then only value F can be achieved from now on. The $\mu_{\mathcal{A}}^{\leadsto}$ values are non-increasing, so once the maximum value is F it will remain F all along, implying the obtained property is not in L.

2. If there exists an $i \in \mathbb{N}$ such that for all $j > i$ we have that $w[j+1] \notin \Sigma_{\mathcal{A}_L}^{\circlearrowright}(w[..j])$ then for each step starting from i, the next letter is not on a path to close a cycle with value T. Therefore, a cycle with value T is never achieved, implying the cycles that will be closed have value F and the word is rejected.[2]

3. If for every $i \in \mathbb{N}$ the next letter $w[i+1]$ is a letter from $\Sigma_{\mathcal{A}_L}^{\leadsto}(w[..i])$ then value T can be achieved. If in addition, from some $j \in \mathbb{N}$ onward the next letter is a letter from $\Sigma_{\mathcal{A}_L}^{\circlearrowright}(w[..j])$ then a cycle of value T can be achieved and only such cycles are closed from now on. Hence, a word of value T is achieved and such words are accepted. □

We exemplify Proposition 4.1 on Example 4.1. Note first that deviation from $\Sigma_{\mathcal{A}}^{\leadsto}(\cdot)$ is possible only in the first three steps, since after reading CNCT, for any letter read there exists a continuation that leads to an accepted word. If such a deviation occurs, the sink-state is reached and the property is violated, as per item 1.

With regard to item 2, consider the state reached by reading CALL. If $\Sigma_{\mathcal{A}}^{\circlearrowright}(\cdot)$ is ignored indefinitely, that is, neither QUE1 nor QUE2 are read, then the run will be stuck at a state ranked 1 and the word will be rejected.

Last, if $\Sigma_{\mathcal{A}}^{\leadsto}(\cdot)$ is always followed then the execution does not reach the sink and the word can be accepted. If from some point onward $\Sigma_{\mathcal{A}}^{\circlearrowright}(\cdot)$ is followed then

---

[2] From some point the word has to close cycles, since the automaton for L has a finite number of states.

as per Example 4.1 ANS1 or ANS2 will be taken, hence the 0-state will be visited infinitely often and the word is accepted, as per item 3.

Remark 4.1 (Generalizing a runtime monitor). Note that Proposition 4.1, item 1 essentially says that the runtime consultant generalizes a runtime monitor: if a letter that is not a ⤳-recommendation of the runtime-consultant is taken, we can report violation occurred, as a traditional monitor would do.

Remark 4.2 (Converting an RC to an EM). An RC can be turned into an enforcement monitor as follows: as long as the action is in both the ⤳- and ↻- recommendations, it is passed as is. If it is not in the ⤳-recommendation it is corrected to an action in the ⤳-recommendation. At some point it should be decided that from now on all actions follow also the ↻-recommendation and turned into such if they are not.

Remark 4.3 (Limitation of RC for qualitative value function). Note that in the qualitative case the RC does not recommend what might intuitively be a better word, since it has a binary classification of words. A word is either accepted or rejected, and there is no distinction between accepted words. Consider a scenario similar to what happens in the ACD (Example 4.1), only that for some reason answers from the first employee are only possible after another round of waiting. The RC will still recommend either QUE1 or QUE2 since both lead to accepting cycle, even though recommending QUE2 is likely faster. For this reason we define RC not only on qualitative value functions, but also on quantitative ones. In particular, in Sect. 6.2 we discuss a quantitative interpretation of ω-regular properties following [11].

4.2 Properties of RCs for a General Value Function

Consider now an RC for a general value function μ. As we assert next, if from some point onward all choices follow both ⤳- and ↻-recommendations, then a best word from that point is obtained. Furthermore, a run that follows the ⤳-recommendation all along and from some point follows the ↻-recommendation, creates an ω-word with the best possible value of μ overall.

To understand the idea of the ↻-recommendation note that if starting the periodic part after the next letter is better than starting after the current letter, the value will improve. This way for a run following the ↻-recommendations the value will never decrease and may improve until settling on a sufficiently good word. Put otherwise, if starting from some point i onward the ↻-recommendation is always followed and the word that is formed is $w = u(v)^\omega$, then for any prefix u' of w of length at least i there is no lasso word $u'(v')^\omega$ that obtains a better value than $u(v)^\omega$. This is true regardless if u' is a prefix or an extension of u, as exemplified in Fig. 4.

Proposition 4.2 (RC compliance guarantees: quantitative case). *Let μ be a value function and $\mathcal{A}$ be a quatomaton implementing μ. Let $w \in \Sigma^\omega$.*

1. Let i,l such that $l \geq i$, $w[j+1] \in \Sigma_{\mathcal{A}}^{\leadsto}(w[..j])$ for all $j \geq i$, and $w[k+1] \in \Sigma_{\mathcal{A}}^{\circlearrowright}(w[..k])$ for all $k \geq l$. Then $\mu(w) \geq \mu(w[..i]w')$ for all $w' \in \Sigma^\omega$.
2. Let i be such that $w[j+1] \in \Sigma_{\mathcal{A}}^{\circlearrowright}(w[..j])$ for all $j \geq i$. Let $u \prec w$ s.t. $|u| \geq i$ and let $v \in \Sigma^+$ close a cycle on u. Then $\mu(w) \geq \mu(u(v)^\omega)$.

Proof. 1. Given $w[..i]$, the highest value that can be achieved is $\mu(w[..i]w')$ for some $w' \in \Sigma^\omega$. If $w[j+1] \in \Sigma_{\mathcal{A}}^{\leadsto}(w[..j])$ for every j starting from index i onward, then for every step $j \geq i$ it holds that $\mu_{\mathcal{A}}^{\leadsto}(w[..j]) = \mu_{\mathcal{A}}^{\leadsto}(w[..j-1])$. By Remark 3.1, $\mu_{\mathcal{A}}^{\leadsto}$ is non-increasing so the highest achievable value for each step is the same. Moreover, there exists $l \geq i$ such that the word w reaches its highest-value achievable period on the l-th letter of w. If $w[k+1] \in \Sigma_{\mathcal{A}}^{\circlearrowright}(w[..k])$ for every k starting from index l onward, then by choosing a letter from $\Sigma_{\mathcal{A}}^{\leadsto}(w[..k])$ the highest value is achievable and, according to item 2, by choosing a letter from $\Sigma_{\mathcal{A}}^{\circlearrowright}(w[..k])$ for each step the maximal value is achieved and $\mu(w) \geq \mu(w[..i]w')$ for all $w' \in \Sigma^\omega$.

2. If $w[j+1] \in \Sigma_{\mathcal{A}}^{\circlearrowright}(w[..j])$ from index i onward then for every $j \geq i$ it holds that $\mu_{\mathcal{A}}^{\circlearrowright}(w[..j]) \geq \mu_{\mathcal{A}}^{\circlearrowright}(w[..j-1])$ because $\mathcal{A}(w[..j])$ and $\mathcal{A}(w[..j-1])$ have a common cycle. That is, by reading a letter $w[j] \in \Sigma_{\mathcal{A}}^{\circlearrowright}(w[..j-1])$, the value for this cycle is still an option for $w[..j]$. But $\mathcal{A}(w[..j])$ can be a part of a better cycle so the possible value for $w[..j]$ can be higher than for $w[..j-1]$. That is, at each step the chosen letter is the first letter of a highest-value cycle that could be read starting from current prefix. Since the number of simple cycles and trails is finite, eventually the non-decreasing sequence of values $\mu_{\mathcal{A}}^{\circlearrowright}(w[..j])$ reaches its maximum for a prefix of w and then continues to go over this cycle. Then, each cycle that is closed before reaching the cycle described above is at most as good as the chosen one. Also, every cycle that is closed after reaching the cycle described above is at most as good as this cycle, according to the maximality of its cyclic-value. Therefore, for all prefixes $u \preceq w$ such that $u > |i|$ and for all v s.t. $\mathcal{A}(uv) = \mathcal{A}(u)$ we have $\mu(w) \geq \mu(u(v)^\omega)$. □

4.3 A Strong RC is not Always Possible

Recall that the definition of a runtime consultant includes a weak and a strong version. The strong version returns the set of all letters that following them can lead to a best value for the infinite word, whereas the weak version settles with a subset of these. The motivation for the strong version is that we do not want the RC to make arbitrary choices, rather we would like it to provide the runtime controller with all the options that are equally best, and let it decide. As we show next, there are cases where it is *impossible* to construct a strong RC.

Proposition 4.3. *There exist instances of the reachability problem for which there is no strong $\leadsto$-RC.*[3]

---

[3] A reachability objective aims to reach some target to satisfy the property.

Proof. Assume towards contradiction that there exists a strong $\leadsto$-RC for any reachability problem, call it **R**. Consider a graph with two reachability targets r_1 and r_2. Assume current vertex v has a path of length k_1 that starts with edge e_1 to r_1. Also, v has a path of length k_2 that starts from edge e_2 to r_2. Edge e_1 (resp. e_2) connects v to v_1 (resp. v_2) and v_1 (resp. v_2) has an edge back to v. Since both e_1 and e_2 lead to a reachability target, **R** has to recommend both letters corresponding to e_1 and e_2. Assume wlog e_1 is chosen and the run moves to v_1. Then, v_1 has a path of length k_1-1 to r_1 and a path of length k_2+1 to r_2. Then, the recommendation of **R** from v_1 consists of both letters corresponding to the first edges of the paths described above, as they both lead to a reachability target. Thus, an edge that returns to v can be chosen. Note that neither v and v_1, nor one of the edges between them is a reachability target. Thus, if the run continues indefinitely by cycling between v and v_1, without ever reaching r_1 or r_2—the resulting word violates the reachability objective—contradicting the claim that following **R**'s recommendations ensures maximal value. □

Intuitively, the absence of a strong $\leadsto$-RC for reachability stems from the Boolean nature of the reachability value function, that ignores how far a target is. As a result, the recommendations need not guide the system toward a closer target. In fact, suggesting all actions that might eventually lead to a target can result in cycles where the run loops indefinitely without ever reaching the target.

In cases where no strong RC is possible, we thus suffice with a weak RC. A weak RC for reachability targets can be implemented by recommending actions that lead to vertices whose distance from the reachability targets is smaller. In other words, replacing the Boolean reachability value function, with a quantitative value function of getting closer to a reachability target.

As we shall see in the next section, this impossibility implies various common quantitative operators do not have a strong $\leadsto$-RC.

For $\circlearrowleft$-RC we shall see that various value functions reduce to the problem we term the *cycle-reachability* problem. This is the problem of reaching from a current vertex v one of the reachability targets t from which v is reachable. This problem has no strong $\circlearrowleft$-RC.

Proposition 4.4. *There exist instances of the cycle-reachability problem for which there is no strong $\circlearrowleft$-RC.*

The proof follows the same idea as in the proof of Proposition 4.3.

5 Runtime Consultants for Widely Used Operators

We turn to discuss RCs for limit operators. These operators are often used in verification to model parameters of the examined system. For example, given a weighted labeled graph that represents power usage, the *supremum* models peak power consumption. In a system that receives requests and generates responses, the *limit average* value function models the average response time [4]. Recall that our aim is to maximize the value wrt the examined value function.

Throughout this section we assume $\mathcal{A}$ is a weighed labeled graph $(\Sigma, Q, q_0, \delta,$ Val) where Val is the considered operator, and θ_{max} is the largest weight on the graph. We give here proof sketches, the complete proofs are in the full version.

LimSup and Sup We start with the LimSup and Sup operators.

Proposition 5.1 (RC for LimSup). *Let* $\hookrightarrow \in \{\rightsquigarrow, \circlearrowright\}$.

1. *A strong $\hookrightarrow$-RC for LimSup does not always exist.*
2. *A weak $\hookrightarrow$-RC for LimSup can be constructed in polynomial time, such that the running time of the constructed weak $\hookrightarrow$-RC is constant.*

Proof sketch. The question of constructing a $\rightsquigarrow$-RC and a $\circlearrowright$-RC for LimSup reduces to reachability and cycle-reachability resp. where the reachability targets are cycles with an edge of the highest weight. It follows from Proposition 4.3 and Proposition 4.4 that LimSup has no strong RCs in the general case. To obtain constant running time, during preprocessing we associate with each vertex the set of letters on its outgoing edges that can lead to the highest weight from that point. □

Proposition 5.2 (RC for Sup). *Let* $\hookrightarrow \in \{\rightsquigarrow, \circlearrowright\}$.

1. *A strong $\hookrightarrow$-RC for Sup does not always exist.*
2. *A weak $\hookrightarrow$-RC for Sup can be constructed in polynomial time, such that the running time of the constructed weak $\hookrightarrow$-RC is $\log(\theta_{max})$.*

Proof Sketch. The $\rightsquigarrow$-RC problem for Sup reduces to reachability problem where the reachability targets are the edges with maximal weight that are greater than the maximal weight seen so far. Accordingly, a strong RC does not always exist. Given the maximal weight in the graph is θ_{max}, the maximal weight seen so far, call it θ_{cur}, can be saved in $\log(\theta_{max})$ bits. To obtain $\log(\theta_{max})$ running time, during preprocessing we associate with each vertex and each weight corresponding to θ_{cur}, the set of letters on outgoing edges that can lead to the highest weight above θ_{cur} from that point. If this set is empty the RC recommends Σ. The $\circlearrowright$-RC for Sup question reduces to the above reachability problem restricted to the current MSCC. □

LimInf and Inf

Proposition 5.3 (RC for LimInf)

1. *A strong $\rightsquigarrow$-RC for LimInf does not always exist.*
2. *A weak $\rightsquigarrow$-RC and a strong $\circlearrowright$-RC for LimInf can be constructed in polynomial time, such that the running time of the constructed RC is constant.*

Proof Sketch. The $\rightsquigarrow$-RC problem for LimInf reduces to a reachability problem where the reachability targets are the edges of a cycle with maximal minimum-weight. Accordingly, a strong RC does not always exist. To obtain constant running time for the weak $\rightsquigarrow$-RC, during preprocessing we associate with each vertex the set of letters on outgoing edges that lead to a cycle with highest minimum-weight from that point. For the strong ↻-RC the set of letters corresponds to outgoing edges that lead to a cycle with highest minimum-weight that includes the current vertex. □

Proposition 5.4 (RC for Inf). *Let* $\hookrightarrow \in \{\rightsquigarrow, \circlearrowright\}$.

A strong $\hookrightarrow$-RC for Inf can be constructed in polynomial time, such that the running time of the constructed strong $\hookrightarrow$-RC is $\log(\theta_{max})$.

Proof sketch. Given the maximal weight in the graph is θ_{max}, the minimal value seen so far, call it θ_{cur}, can be saved in $\log(\theta_{max})$ bits. For the $\rightsquigarrow$-RC, to obtain $\log(\theta_{max})$ running time, during preprocessing we associate with each vertex the maximal minimum-value that can be obtained, based on θ_{cur}. Similarly for ↻-RC, but there we compute the maximal minimum-value that can be obtained by a cycle that includes the current vertex. □

LimAvg. So far, RC construction for all operators was feasible in polynomial time. For LimAvg this is not the case. That is, the $\rightsquigarrow$-RC construction can be done in polynomial time, but the construction for ↻-RC is more challenging. Here the problem reduces to the problem of finding a cyclic-trail, where a path is a *trail* if no edge in it appears twice. Note that vertices can appear more than once in a trail. For instance, recall the quatomaton for a value function similar to LimAvg given in Fig. 1. As discussed in Example 3.1, when in state q_1 the best cyclic-extension is the non-simple loop, i.e. trail, $\sigma_3\sigma_0\sigma_4$. The following proposition states this reduction.

Proposition 5.5. *Finding ↻-recommendations for LimAvg reduces to finding cyclic trails of maximal mean-weight involving the current vertex.*

Intuitively, the reason is that the ↻-RC looks for the maximal mean-weight cycle that includes the current vertex, and if there is no maximal mean-weight simple cycle reachable from the current vertex it has to be extended to a trail that contains the path from the current vertex to the cycle and from there back to the current vertex. See the proof in the full version. This maximization problem can be turned into a minimization problem by multiplying the weights by -1. We show that the respective decision problem is coNP-complete. We define

$$L_{trail} = \left\{ (G, k, v) \;\middle|\; \begin{array}{l} G = (V, E, \theta) \text{ is a weighted graph, } v \in V, \\ k \in \mathbb{Q} \text{ and } \textbf{every cyclic trail } c \text{ going} \\ \text{through } v \text{ has mean weight} \geq k \end{array} \right\}.$$

Proposition 5.6. L_{trail} *is coNP-complete.*

This can be proven by a reduction from 3SAT, see in the full version. The following propostition summarizes the results for LimAvg.

Proposition 5.7 (RC for LimAvg).

1. A strong $\rightsquigarrow$-RC for LimAvg does not always exist.
2. A weak $\rightsquigarrow$-RC for LimAvg can be constructed in polynomial time, such that the running time of the constructed weak $\rightsquigarrow$-RC is constant.
3. A strong $\circlearrowleft$-RC for LimAvg can be constructed in exponential time, such that the running time of the constructed strong $\circlearrowleft$-RC is constant.
4. Computing the strong $\circlearrowleft$-RC for LimAvg value function is coNP-complete.

Proof sketch. $\rightsquigarrow$-RC reduces to reachability of cycles with maximal mean-weight. Thus the impossibility result for strong $\rightsquigarrow$-RC.

A weak $\rightsquigarrow$-RC can be constructed by associating with each vertex v the set of letters Σ_v that are on a shortest path to a cycle with the maximal mean-weight that is reachable from v. This association can be done in polynomial time by first finding the maximal mean-weight cycles using Karp's algorithm [16], and then propagating this information backwards.

For $\circlearrowleft$-RC the problem reduces to finding the maximal mean-weight trails that include the current vertex (Proposition 5.5) and is coNP-complete by Proposition 5.6. We can construct a $\circlearrowleft$-RC in exponential time by considering all paths of length bounded by $|E|$ as candidates for trails. □

6 Runtime Consultants for ω-Regular Properties

We turn to discuss ω-regular properties, i.e. properties expressible using an ω-automaton such as a deterministic parity automaton.

6.1 RCs for the Qualitative Case

Consider an ω-regular property given by a DPA $\mathcal{A}$. It induces a Boolean value function: T for accepted words and F otherwise. Recall that a word is accepted iff the minimal rank visited infinitely often is even—implying the existence of a cycle with minimal even rank, called an accepting cycle. It follows that the problem of constructing $\rightsquigarrow$- and $\circlearrowleft$-RCs in this setting reduces to reachability and cycle-reachability, respectively, where the reachability targets are accepting cycles. Thus, by Proposition 4.3 and Proposition 4.4, we have to suffice with weak $\rightsquigarrow$- and $\circlearrowleft$-RCs. These can be constructed in polynomial time. The running time is constant as desired. The proposition, proven in the full version, follows.

Proposition 6.1 (RC for an ω-regular property – qualitative case). *Let $\mathcal{A}$ be a DPA inducing $\chi_\mathcal{A} : \Sigma^\omega \to \{\text{T}, \text{F}\}$. Let $\hookrightarrow \in \{\rightsquigarrow, \circlearrowleft\}$.*

1. A strong $\hookrightarrow$-RC for $\chi_\mathcal{A}$ does not always exist.
2. A weak $\hookrightarrow$-RC for $\chi_\mathcal{A}$ can be constructed in polynomial time, such that the running time of the constructed weak $\hookrightarrow$-RC is constant.

6.2 From Qualitative to Quantitative: ω-Regular Robustness

To obtain strong RCs for ω-regular properties, we can try strengthening the value function and turning it from qualitative into quantitative. Such a transformation was recently proposed in [11]. The idea there is to *distill* from an ω-regular language L, a value function $\mathsf{Rbst}_L : \Sigma^\omega \to \mathbb{T}$ that given a lasso word w, returns a value quantifying the *robustness* of w wrt L.[4] The set $\mathbb{T}$ is a totally ordered set from which one can infer the robustness preference relation, denoted $\triangleright_L$. That is, $w_1 \triangleright_L w_2$ if $\mathsf{Rbst}_L(w_1) > \mathsf{Rbst}_L(w_2)$. For example, wrt the property "a should occur infinitely often", and $i<j$, the robustness value function determines $b^i(a)^\omega \triangleright_L b^j(a)^\omega$, $(b^i a)^\omega \triangleright_L (b^j a)^\omega$ and $(ba^j)^\omega \triangleright_L (ba^i)^\omega$. That is, it prefers words with a higher frequency of a's in the period. Further, for words with the same a's frequency in the period, it prefers words with more a's in the transient part.

For lack of space we do not provide further intuitions regarding the generalization of this idea to arbitrary ω-regular properties and refer the reader to [11]. We continue with providing the necessary building blocks of the definition in order to discuss later RCs for the Rbst value function. While Rbst_L is a semantic notion that is agonistic to a particular representation of L, it is easier to explain it on the *robustness automaton* developed in [11].

The robustness automaton is a canonical parity automaton for an ω-regular property.[5] It can be used to compute the robustness value of a lasso word, which is a tuple of three components: an acceptance bit, a period value and a spoke value. The period and spoke values are pairs corresponding to a value computed from the respective edges of the period and the spoke, formally defined as follows.

The Robustness Value Function. Given the robustness DPA, we color its edges using the ranks of the states the edge connects. Given an edge $e = (v, v')$ where v and v' have ranks d and d', resp., the color of e is defined as follows:

white if $d' = -2$ green if d' is even and $d \geq d'$ yellow if $d < d'$
black if $d' = -1$ red   if d' is odd and $d \geq d'$.

We use $\mathsf{color}_w(i)$ to denote the color of the edge e the robustness DPA goes through when reading the i-the letter of w. Let $w \in \Sigma^\omega$ and consider its infix $w[j..k]$. For $i \in [j..k]$ let $c_i = \mathsf{color}_w(i)$. Let $\mathrm{W} = |\{i \in [j..k] : c_i = \text{white}\}|$. The values $\mathrm{G}, \mathrm{Y}, \mathrm{R}, \mathrm{B}$ are defined similarly, wrt colors green, yellow, red, black, resp.

We use $\mathsf{colors}_w(j, k)$, for the tuple $(\mathrm{W}, \mathrm{G}, \mathrm{Y}, \mathrm{R}, \mathrm{B})$ providing the number of letters of each color in the infix $w[j..k]$. The *score of the infix* $w[j..k]$ wrt L,

---

[4] The question of robustness of a system has been studied a lot in formal verification [3, 5,10,14,15,20]. Most works assume weights are part of the input. In contrast, [21–23,30] suggest to enhance two-valued semantics of temporal logic into a five-valued semantics, where the values reflect the robustness of a word wrt a temporal logic formula. The work [11] generalizes this idea by providing infinitely many values, and providing a semantic notion agnostic to a particular representation.

[5] More precisely, the robustness automaton is a dual DPA, as introduced in [11].

denoted $\text{score}_w(j,k)$, is the tuple (WB, GR) where WB = W−B, GR = G−R. Its averaged score, denoted $\text{avgscore}_w(j,k)$ is $(\frac{\text{WB}}{l}, \frac{\text{GR}}{l})$ where $l = |w[j..k]|$.

Finally, let w be a lasso word, and assume $w = uv^\omega$ where u is the shortest prefix of w on which the robustness automaton loops at, and v is the corresponding loop. Let $|u| = k$ and $|v| = l$, $\tau_u = \text{avgscore}_w(1,k)$, $\tau_v = \text{avgscore}_w(k+1, k+l)$, and a_w is the acceptance bit (i.e. $a_w = \text{T}$ iff $w \in L$). The robustness value of w wrt L, denoted $\text{Rbst}_L(w)$ is the tuple $(a_w, \tau_v, k(\tau_u - \tau_v))$. The significance of the components is from left (most-significant) to right.

6.3 RCs for the Quantitative Case

We turn to discuss the construction of RCs for ω-regular robustness, namely for the value function Rbst_L induced from an ω-regular property L.

We use $\mathcal{P}_L^+$ for the robustness automaton of an ω-regular language L. We can assign weights to its edges based on their color, allowing us to derive back the number of edges of each color from the total path weight. Specifically, edge e gets weight C^2, C, 0, $-C$, $-C^2$, resp. if it is colored *white, green, yellow, red, black*, resp. where C is the number of edges in $\mathcal{P}_L^+$ plus one.

$\leadsto$-*RC for* Rbst_L. Note that $\leadsto$-RC for Rbst_L looks for the most robust word. Such a word is one that is accepted and has the most robust period and spoke. Since the value of the period is more significant, we first look for accepting cycles with best period. Then we look for the most robust spoke reaching such period.

Proposition 6.2. *The problem of finding the most robust accepting cycle in a parity automaton reduces to the question of finding the cycle with maximal mean-weight in a weighted graph that passes via a certain state.*

The proposition is proven in the full version.

Recall that computing the weak $\leadsto$-RC for LimAvg can be done in polynomial time (Proposition 5.7). However, for the robustness value function we show that computing the strong $\leadsto$-RC is coNP-complete. Loosely, this is since for the robustness value we need not only maximal mean-weight cycle but also verifying that the cycle's minimal rank is even. The weights described above for the maximum problem can be multiplied by -1 to make it a minimum problem. The decision version of the minimum problem can be stated as

$$L_{simple} = \left\{ (G, k, v) \;\middle|\; \begin{array}{l} G = (V, E, \theta) \text{ is a weighted graph, } v \in V, k \in \mathbb{Q} \\ \text{and } \textbf{every simple cycle } c \text{ going through } v \\ \text{has mean weight} \geq k \end{array} \right\}$$

Proposition 6.3. L_{simple} *is coNP-complete*

The proof, in full version, is by reduction from the Hamiltonian cycle problem.

$\circlearrowright$ *-RC for* Rbst_L

Next we turn to the problem of computing $\circlearrowright$-RC. Here, the problem of finding $\circlearrowright$-recommendation reduces to finding accepting cyclic trails of maximal mean

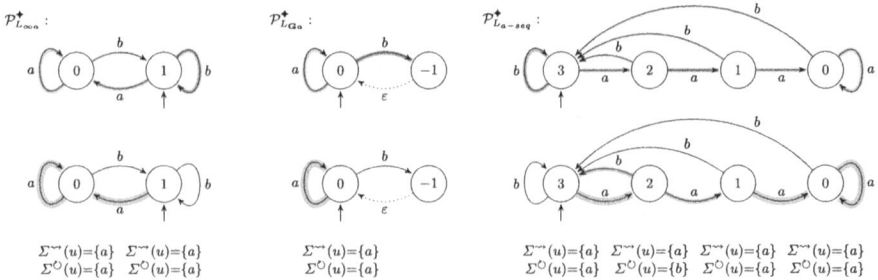

Fig. 5. Runtime recommendations for $L_{\infty a}$, $L_{\mathbf{G}a}$, L_{a-seq}, resp. from Example 6.1.

weight involving the current state q_u and some state from a set of interest U. We show that this problem as well is coNP-complete, by a simple reduction from the respective problem of LimAvg. See propositions and proofs in the full version. The following proposition summarizes the results for the robustness value function.

Proposition 6.4 (RC for an ω-regular property – quantitative case). Let $\mathcal{A}$ be the robustness DPA for language L and $\mathsf{Rbst}_L : \Sigma^\omega \to \mathbb{T}$ the respective robustness value function. Let $\hookrightarrow \in \{\leadsto, \circlearrowright\}$.

A strong $\hookrightarrow$-RC for Rbst_L can be constructed in exponential time, such that the running time of the constructed strong $\hookrightarrow$-RC is constant.

Using exponential time we can go over all simple cycles in the case of $\leadsto$-RC and all cyclic trails in the case of $\circlearrowright$-RC to find the best ones, and propagate the information backwards through the edges and states, so that we can associate with each state the set of letters corresponding to the $\leadsto$- and $\circlearrowright$-recommendations. See the proof in the full version.

RC for Robustness – Example
We provide an example illustrating the robustness DPA for three properties and the resulting $\leadsto$- and $\circlearrowright$-recommendations of the respective strong RCs.

Example 6.1. Consider the following languages (i) $L_{\infty a}$ that accepts words where there are infinitely many a's, (ii) $L_{\mathbf{G}a}$ that accepts words consisting of the letter a only and (iii) $L_{a-seq} = \infty a \wedge (\infty aa \to \infty aaa)$ that accepts words with infinitely many a's but if there are infinitely many occurrences of aa then there have to be also infinitely many occurrences of aaa in the word. The top three automata in Fig. 5 are the robustness automata for these languages. The bottom three automata are the same, annotated with $\Sigma^{\leadsto}(u)$ and $\Sigma^{\circlearrowright}(u)$ for each state. Note that in $\mathcal{P}^+_{L_{a-seq}}$ the $\leadsto$-recommendation for every state q (i.e. for every finite word u reaching q) is to read a since the best period a word in L_{a-seq} can have is a^ω, so the $\leadsto$-recommendation is to reach the self-loop on the state ranked 0. However, the $\circlearrowright$-recommendation is not the same for all prefixes. If the word $u \in \Sigma^*$ read so far is a or has a suffix ba, that is, the automaton is currently in the state ranked 2, then the best trail this state is part of is the simple cycle including it and the state ranked 3. Note that other accepting trails from this state exist but all of them have a lower percentage of green edges and accordingly a lower value. Therefore, the ○-recommendation is to read b from this state.

7 Conclusions

We have introduced the notion of runtime consultant (RC) that generalizes the notion of a runtime monitor. We distinguish between *weak* and *strong* runtime consultants, where the latter is guaranteed to make no arbitrary choices in its recommendations. We have shown that some value functions cannot have strong RC in the general case. We have provided the strongest RCs possible for the widely used operators Sup, Inf, LimSup, LimInf and LimAvg.

In the qualitative case we considered ω-regular properties. We have shown that in general they do not have strong RCs. However, taking the recently proposed robustness value function Rbst_L, that distills from a qualitative ω-regular property L a quantitative value function, it is possible to construct strong RCs.

The construction of most of the RCs is polynomial, except for LimAvg, and Rbst_L, for which we show the problem is coNP-complete. Since the construction of RC is done at preprocessing this is not that bad. The important measure is the running time of the RC. We show that for all cases but Sup and Inf the running time is constant. For these two it is logarithmic in the size of the heaviest weight which may also be acceptable in many settings.

References

1. Barringer, H., Goldberg, A., Havelund, K., Sen, K.: Rule-based runtime verification. In: Steffen, B., Levi, G. (eds.) VMCAI 2004. LNCS, vol. 2937, pp. 44–57. Springer, Heidelberg (2004). https://doi.org/10.1007/978-3-540-24622-0_5
2. Bartocci, E., et al.: Specification-based monitoring of cyber-physical systems: a survey on theory, tools and applications. In: Bartocci, E., Falcone, Y. (eds.) Lectures on Runtime Verification. LNCS, vol. 10457, pp. 135–175. Springer, Cham (2018). https://doi.org/10.1007/978-3-319-75632-5_5
3. Bouyer, P., Markey, N., Sankur, O.: Robust reachability in timed automata and games: a game-based approach. Theor. Comput. Sci. **563**, 43–74 (2015)
4. Chatterjee, K., Doyen, L., Henzinger, T.A.: Quantitative languages. ACM Trans. Comput. Log. **11**(4), 23:1-23:38 (2010)
5. De Wulf, M., Doyen, L., Markey, N., Raskin, J.-F.: Robust safety of timed automata. Formal Methods Syst. Des. **33**(1), 45–84 (2008)
6. Dolzhenko, E., Ligatti, J., Reddy, S.: Modeling runtime enforcement with mandatory results automata. Int. J. Inf. Secur. **14**(1), 47–60 (2014). https://doi.org/10.1007/s10207-014-0239-8
7. Basin, D., Hublet, F., Lima, L., Krstić, S., Traytel, D.: Proactive real-time first-order enforcement. In: Gurfinkel, A., Ganesh, V. (eds.) CAV 2024. LNCS, vol. 14682, pp. 156–181. Springer, Cham (2024). https://doi.org/10.1007/978-3-031-65630-9_8

8. Falcone, Y., Fernandez, J.-C., Mounier, L.: Synthesizing enforcement monitors wrt. The safety-progress classification of properties. In: Sekar, R., Pujari, A.K. (eds.) ICISS 2008. LNCS, vol. 5352, pp. 41–55. Springer, Heidelberg (2008). https://doi.org/10.1007/978-3-540-89862-7_3
9. Falcone, Y., Havelund, K., Reger, G.: A tutorial on runtime verification. In: Broy, M., Peled, D.A., Kalus, G. (eds.) Engineering Dependable Software Systems. NATO Science for Peace and Security Series, D: Information and Communication Security, vol. 34, pp. 141–175. IOS Press (2013)
10. Filiot, E., Mazzocchi, N., Raskin, J.-F., Sankaranarayanan, S., Trivedi, A.: Weighted transducers for robustness verification. In: 31st International Conference on Concurrency Theory, CONCUR 2020, September 1-4, 2020, Vienna, Austria (Virtual Conference), pp. 17:1–17:21 (2020)
11. Fisman, D., Sudit, E.: Omega-regular robustness (2025). https://arxiv.org/abs/2503.12631
12. Fisman, D., Sudit, E.: Runtime Consultants. arXiv 2508.01821 (2025). https://arxiv.org/abs/2508.01821
13. Havelund, K., Peled, D.: Monitorability for runtime verification. In: Runtime Verification - 23rd International Conference, RV 2023, Thessaloniki, Greece, October 3-6, 2023, Proceedings, pp. 447–460 (2023)
14. Henzinger, T.A., Raskin, J.-F.: Robust undecidability of timed and hybrid systems. In: Lynch, N., Krogh, B.H. (eds.) HSCC 2000. LNCS, vol. 1790, pp. 145–159. Springer, Heidelberg (2000). https://doi.org/10.1007/3-540-46430-1_15
15. Jaubert, R., Reynier, P.-A.: Quantitative robustness analysis of flat timed automata. In: Hofmann, M. (ed.) FoSSaCS 2011. LNCS, vol. 6604, pp. 229–244. Springer, Heidelberg (2011). https://doi.org/10.1007/978-3-642-19805-2_16
16. Karp, R.M.: A characterization of the minimum cycle mean in a digraph. Discret. Math. **23**(3), 309–311 (1978)
17. Lee, I., Kannan, S., Kim, M., Sokolsky, O., Viswanathan, M.: Runtime assurance based on formal specifications. In: International Conference on Parallel and Distributed Processing Techniques and Applications, pp. 279–287. PDPTA (1999)
18. Ligatti, J., Reddy, S.: A theory of runtime enforcement, with results. In: Gritzalis, D., Preneel, B., Theoharidou, M. (eds.) ESORICS 2010. LNCS, vol. 6345, pp. 87–100. Springer, Heidelberg (2010). https://doi.org/10.1007/978-3-642-15497-3_6
19. Maler, O.: Some thoughts on runtime verification. In: Falcone, Y., Sánchez, C. (eds.) RV 2016. LNCS, vol. 10012, pp. 3–14. Springer, Cham (2016). https://doi.org/10.1007/978-3-319-46982-9_1
20. Mascle, C., Neider, D., Schwenger, M., Tabuada, P., Weinert, A., Zimmermann, M.: From LTL to rLTL monitoring: improved monitorability through robust semantics. Formal Methods Syst. Des. **59**(1), 170–204 (2021)
21. Murano, A., Neider, D., Zimmermann, M.: Robust alternating-time temporal logic. In: Logics in Artificial Intelligence - 18th European Conference, JELIA 2023, Dresden, Germany, September 20-22, 2023, Proceedings, pp. 796–813 (2023)
22. Nayak, S.P., Neider, D., Zimmermann, M.: Robustness-by-construction synthesis: adapting to the environment at runtime. In: Leveraging Applications of Formal Methods, Verification and Validation. Verification Principles - 11th International Symposium, ISoLA 2022, Rhodes, Greece, October 22-30, 2022, Proceedings, Part I, pp. 149–173 (2022)
23. Neider, D., Weinert, A., Zimmermann, M.: Robust, expressive, and quantitative linear temporal logics: pick any two for free. Inf. Comput. **285**(Part), 104810 (2022)

24. Omer, M., Peled, D.: Runtime verification prediction for traces with data. In: Katsaros, P., Nenzi, L. (eds.) RV 2023. LNCS, vol. 14245, pp. 148–167. Springer, Cham (2023). https://doi.org/10.1007/978-3-031-44267-4_8
25. Perrin, D., Pin, J.-E.: Infinite Words: Automata, Semigroups, Logic and Games. Elsevier (2004)
26. Bloem, R., Könighofer, B., Könighofer, R., Wang, C.: Shield synthesis: runtime enforcement for reactive systems. In: Baier, C., Tinelli, C. (eds.) TACAS 2015. LNCS, vol. 9035, pp. 533–548. Springer, Heidelberg (2015). https://doi.org/10.1007/978-3-662-46681-0_51
27. Merro, M., Lanotte, R., Munteanu, A.: Runtime enforcement for control system security. In: 2020 IEEE 33rd Computer Security Foundations Symposium (CSF), pp. 246–261 (2020). https://doi.org/10.1109/CSF49147.2020.00025
28. Tripakis, S., Pinisetty, S., Preoteasa, V., Jéron, T., Falcone, Y., Marchand, H.: Predictive runtime enforcement. In: SAC '16, page 1628–1633, New York, NY, USA. Association for Computing Machinery (2016). https://doi.org/10.1145/2851613.2851827
29. Schneider, F.B.: Enforceable security policies. ACM Trans. Inf. Syst. Secur. 3(1), 30–50 (2000). https://doi.org/10.1145/353323.353382
30. Tabuada, P., Neider, D.: Robust linear temporal logic. In: 25th EACSL Annual Conference on Computer Science Logic, CSL 2016, August 29 - September 1, 2016, Marseille, France, pp. 10:1–10:21 (2016)
31. Fernandez, J.C., Falcone, Y., Mounier, L., Richier, J.L.: Runtime enforcement monitors: composition, synthesis, and enforcement abilities. Formal Methods in System Design 38 (2011). https://doi.org/10.1007/s10703-011-0114-4
32. Zhang, P., Muccini, H., Polini, A., Li, X.: Run-time systems failure prediction via proactive monitoring, pp. 484–487 (2011). https://doi.org/10.1109/ASE.2011.6100105
33. Zhao, Y., Hoxha, B., Fainekos, G., Deshmukh, J.V., Lindemann, L.: Robust conformal prediction for STL runtime verification under distribution shift. In: 15th ACM/IEEE International Conference on Cyber-Physical Systems, ICCPS 2024, Hong Kong, May 13-16, 2024, pp. 169–179. IEEE (2024)

Author Index

A
An, Ziyan 477
André, Étienne 397
Ashrov, Adiel 457

B
Basin, David 160
Baumeister, Jan 92, 181
Bensalem, Saddek 73
Bortolussi, Luca 296, 336

C
Cairoli, Francesca 296, 336
Calinescu, Radu 213
Cano, Filip 1
Chalupa, Marek 417
Cheng, Chih-Hong 73
Cohen, Itay 202

D
Deshmukh, Jyotirmoy V. 336
Di Stefano, Luca 44

E
Esparza, Javier 357
Esterle, Lukas 101

F
Fatehi, Kavan 213
Finkbeiner, Bernd 92, 181
Fischer, Vincent 357
Fisman, Dana 497

G
Garg, Vijay K. 252
Goldberg, Yoav 202
Gomes, Cláudio 101
Graebener, Josefine B. 438

H
Havelund, Klaus 22, 202
Henzinger, Thomas A. 1, 54, 140, 417
Hipler, Raik 377
Hu, Linda 160
Hublet, François 160

I
Imrie, Calum 213
Incer, Inigo 438

J
Johnson, Taylor T. 477
Jünger, Franz 92

K
Kallwies, Hannes 377
Katz, Guy 457
Kohn, Florian 92
Křetínský, Jan 274
Kristensen, Morten Haahr 101
Krstić, Srđan 160
Kueffner, Konstantin 1, 54, 140

L
Larsen, Kim G. 233
Larsen, Peter Gorm 101
Leucker, Martin 377
Levy, Natan 457
Lindemann, Lars 336
Loreti, Michele 120

M
Ma, Meiyi 477
Mangal, Ravi 213
Mikučionis, Marius 233
Moyer, Daniel 477
Muñiz, Marco 233
Murray, Richard M. 438

N
Nenchev, Vladislav 317
Nenzi, Laura 120

O
Oguz, Ipek 477
Oliveira da Costa, Ana 417
Omer, Moran 22, 252

P
Paoletti, Nicola 336
Păsăreanu, Corina 213
Pearson, Nicholas Andrea 296
Peled, Doron 22, 202, 252
Porat, Ely 252

R
Reese, Lennard 160
Rieder, Sabine 274
Ruess, Harald 73
Russo, Davide 296

S
Scarbro, William 213
Scheerer, Frederik 181
Schirmer, Sebastian 92
Schwalbe, Gesina 274

Shoeb, Youssef 274
Silvetti, Simone 120
Singh, Vasu 140
Sotiriadis, Prodromos 317
Sudit, Elina 497
Sun, I. 140

T
Torens, Christoph 92

V
van Dommele, Kevin Gillian 377

W
Waga, Masaki 397
Wien, Jannis 377
Wright, Thomas 101
Wu, Changshun 73

Y
Yaman, Sinem Getir 213
Yu, Emily 54

Z
Zanello, Francesca 296
Zhao, Xingyu 73

Made in the USA
Monee, IL
03 May 2026

49438646R00295